Advance Praise for *Head First S*

"*Head First Software Development* is a whimsical but very thoughtfully designed series of diagrams and clever illustrations meant to accurately and clearly convey informatioı brain. It's a whole new kind of book."

— **Scott Hanselman**
Software Developer, Speaker, Author
Scott Hanselman's Computer Zen

"This is one of those books experienced developers wish they'd had back when they got started. I know, I'm one of them."

— **Burk Hufnagel, Senior Software Architect**

"I could have avoided a whole world of pain if I had read this book before my last project!"

— **This developer asked to remain anonymous, so her last project's manager wouldn't be upset!**

"*Head First Software Development* teaches many valuable lessons that will help anyone deliver quality software on time and on budget. Following the core principles taught in this book will help keep your project on track from start to finish. No matter how long you've been developing software, *Head First Software Development* will give you essential tools for developing successful projects from start to finish."

— **Adam Z. Szymanski, Software Project Manager, Naval Research Laboratory**

"The ideas in this book can be used by new and experienced managers to immediately improve their overall software development process."

— **Dan Francis, Software Engineering Manager, Fortune 50 company**

"A fresh new perspective on the software development process. A great introduction to managing a development team from requirements through delivery."

— **McClellan Francis, Software Engineer**

Praise for *Head First Object-Oriented Analysis and Design*

"*Head First Object-Oriented Analysis and Design* is a refreshing look at the subject of OOA&D. What sets this book apart is its focus on learning. There are too many books on the market that spend a lot of time telling you why, but do not actually enable the practitioner to start work on a project. Those books are very interesting, but not very practical. I strongly believe that the future of software development practice will focus on the practitioner. The authors have made the content of OOA&D accessible and usable for the practitioner "

— Ivar Jacobson, Ivar Jacobson Consulting

"I just finished reading *HF OOA&D*, and I loved it! The book manages to get across the essentials of object-oriented analysis and design with UML and use cases, and even several lectures on good software design, all in a fast-paced, easy to understand way. The thing I liked most about this book was its focus on why we do OOA&D—to write great software! By defining what great software is and showing how each step in the OOA&D process leads you towards that goal, it can teach even the most jaded Java programmer why OOA&D matters. This is a great 'first book' on design for anyone who is new to Java, or even for those who have been Java programmers for a while but have been scared off by the massive tomes on OO Analysis and Design."

— Kyle Brown, Distinguished Engineer, IBM

"Finally a book on OOA&D that recognizes that the UML is just a notation and that what matters when developing software is taking the time to think the issues through."

— Pete McBreen, Author, *Software Craftsmanship*

"The book does a good job of capturing that entertaining, visually oriented, 'Head First' writing style. But hidden behind the funny pictures and crazy fonts is a serious, intelligent, extremely well-crafted presentation of OO Analysis and Design. This book has a strong opinion of how to design programs, and communicates it effectively. I love the way it uses running examples to lead the reader through the various stages of the design process. As I read the book, I felt like I was looking over the shoulder of an expert designer who was explaining to me what issues were important at each step, and why."

— Edward Sciore, Associate Professor, Computer Science Department
Boston College

"This is a well-designed book that delivers what it promises to its readers: how to analyze, design, and write serious object-oriented software. Its contents flow effortlessly from using use cases for capturing requirements to analysis, design, implementation, testing, and iteration. Every step in the development of object-oriented software is presented in light of sound software engineering principles. The examples are clear and illustrative. This is a solid and refreshing book on object-oriented software development."

— Dung Zung Nguyen, Lecturer
Rice University

Praise for *Head First Design Patterns*

"I received the book yesterday and started to read it on the way home... and I couldn't stop. I took it to the gym and I expect people saw me smiling a lot while I was exercising and reading. This is tres 'cool'. It is fun but they cover a lot of ground and they are right to the point. I'm really impressed."

—Erich Gamma, IBM Distinguished Engineer, and co-author of Design Patterns

"'Head First Design Patterns' manages to mix fun, belly-laughs, insight, technical depth and great practical advice in one entertaining and thought provoking read. Whether you are new to design patterns, or have been using them for years, you are sure to get something from visiting Objectville."

—Richard Helm, coauthor of "Design Patterns" with rest of the Gang of Four—Erich Gamma, Ralph Johnson, and John Vlissides

"I feel like a thousand pounds of books have just been lifted off of my head."

—Ward Cunningham, inventor of the Wiki and founder of the Hillside Group

"This book is close to perfect, because of the way it combines expertise and readability. It speaks with authority and it reads beautifully. It's one of the very few software books I've ever read that strikes me as indispensable. (I'd put maybe 10 books in this category, at the outside.)"

—David Gelernter, Professor of Computer Science, Yale University and author of "Mirror Worlds" and "Machine Beauty"

"A Nose Dive into the realm of patterns, a land where complex things become simple, but where simple things can also become complex. I can think of no better tour guides than the Freemans."

—Miko Matsumura, Industry Analyst, The Middleware Company Former Chief Java Evangelist, Sun Microsystems

"I laughed, I cried, it moved me."

—Daniel Steinberg, Editor-in-Chief, java.net

"My first reaction was to roll on the floor laughing. After I picked myself up, I realized that not only is the book technically accurate, it is the easiest to understand introduction to design patterns that I have seen."

—Dr. Timothy A. Budd, Associate Professor of Computer Science at Oregon State University and author of more than a dozen books, including *C++ for Java Programmers*

"Jerry Rice runs patterns better than any receiver in the NFL, but the Freemans have out run him. Seriously...this is one of the funniest and smartest books on software design I've ever read."

—Aaron LaBerge, VP Technology, ESPN.com

Other related books from O'Reilly

Making Things Happen

Applied Software Project Management

Beautiful Code

Prefactoring

The Art of Agile Development

UML 2.0 In a Nutshell

Learning UML 2.0

Other books in O'Reilly's *Head First* series

Head First Java

Head First Object-Oriented Analysis and Design (OOA&D)

Head Rush Ajax

Head First HTML with CSS and XHTML

Head First Design Patterns

Head First Servlets and JSP

Head First EJB

Head First PMP

Head First SQL

Head First JavaScript

Head First Software Development

Dan Pilone
Russ Miles

O'REILLY®

Beijing • Cambridge • Köln • Paris • Sebastopol • Taipei • Tokyo

SHROFF PUBLISHERS & DISTRIBUTORS PVT. LTD.
Mumbai Bangalore Chennai Kolkata New Delhi

Head First Software Development

by Dan Pilone and Russ Miles

 ISBN-10: 0-596-52735-7, ISBN-13: 978-0-596-52735-8
Originally printed in the United States of America.

Published by O'Reilly Media, Inc., 1005 Gravenstein Highway North, Sebastopol, CA 95472.

O'Reilly books may be purchased for educational, business, or sales promotional use. Online editions are also available for most titles *(safari.oreilly.com)*. For more information, contact our corporate/institutional sales department: (800)998-9938 or *corporate@oreilly.com*.

Series Creators: Kathy Sierra, Bert Bates
Series Editor: Brett D. McLaughlin
Design Editor: Louise Barr
Cover Designers: Louise Barr, Steve Fehler
Production Editor: Sanders Kleinfeld
Indexer: Julie Hawks
Page Viewers: Vinny, Nick, Tracey, and Corinne

Printing History:
December 2007: First Edition.

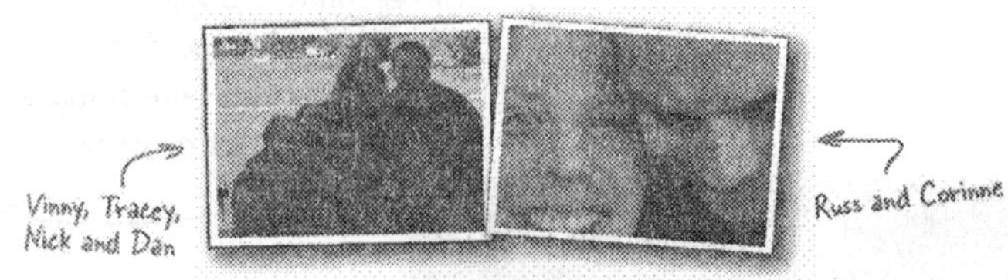

Third Indian Reprint: November 2010

ISBN 13: 978-81-8404-450-8

No sleepovers were conducted in the writing of this book, although one author did purportedly get engaged using his prototype of the iSwoon application. And one pig apparently lost its nose, but we're confident that had nothing to do with the software development techniques espoused by this text.

Published by **Shroff Publishers and Distributors Pvt. Ltd.** C-103, MIDC, TTC Industrial Area, Pawane, Navi Mumbai 400 705, Tel: (91 22) 4158 4158, Fax: (91 22) 4158 4141, e-mail: spdorders@shroffpublishers.com. Printed at Decora Book Prints Pvt. Ltd., Mumbai.

To everyone who's worked on a project with us and told us where we've gone wrong, where we've gone right, and what books to read...here's our contribution back.

Author(s) of Head First Software Development

Russ Miles

Dan Pilone

Russ is totally indebted to his fiancée, Corinne, for her complete love and support while writing this book. Oh, and he still can't believe she said yes to getting married next year, but I guess some guys have all the luck!

Russ has been writing for a long time and gets a huge kick out of demystifying technologies, tools, and techniques that shouldn't have been so mystified in the first place. After being a developer at various ranks for many years, Russ now keeps his days (and sometimes nights) busy by heading up a team of software developers working on super secret services for the music industry. He's also just finished up his Oxford Masters degree that only took him five years. He's looking forward to a bit of rest...but not for too long.

Russ is an avid guitar player and is relishing the spare time to get back to his guitars. The only thing he's missing is **Head First Guitar**...c'mon Brett, you know you want that one!

Dan is eternally grateful to his wife Tracey for letting him finish this book. Dan is a software architect for Vangent, Inc., and has led teams for the Naval Research Laboratory and NASA, building enterprise software. He's taught graduate and undergraduate Software Engineering at Catholic University in Washington, D.C. Some of his classes were interesting.

Dan started writing for O'Reilly by submitting a proposal for this book a little over five years ago. Three UML books, some quality time in Boulder, Colorado, with the O'Reilly Head First team, and a co-author later, he finally got a chance to put this book together.

While leading a team of software developers can be challenging, Dan is waiting patiently for someone to write **Head First Parenting** to help sort out seriously complex management problems.

Table of Contents (Summary)

Table of Contents (the real thing)

Intro

Your brain on Software Development. You're sitting around trying to *learn* something, but your *brain* keeps telling you all that learning *isn't important*. Your brain's saying, "Better leave room for more important things, like which wild animals to avoid and whether naked rock-climbing is a bad idea." So how *do* you trick your brain into thinking that your life really depends on learning how to develop great software?

1 great software development

Pleasing your customer

If the customer's unhappy, *everyone's* unhappy!

Every great piece of software starts with a customer's big idea. It's your job as a professional software developer to **bring those ideas to life**. But taking a vague idea and turning it into working code—code that **satisfies your customer**—isn't so easy. In this chapter you'll learn how to avoid being a software development casualty by delivering software that is **needed, on-time,** and **on-budget**. Grab your laptop and let's set out on the road to shipping great software.

The Goal

gathering requirements

Knowing what the customer wants

2

You can't always get what you want...but the customer better!

Great software development delivers **what the customer wants.** This chapter is all about **talking to the customer** to figure out what their **requirements** are for your software. You'll learn how **user stories**, **brainstorming**, and the **estimation game** help you get inside your customer's head. That way, by the time you finish your project, you'll be confident you've built what your customer wants... and not just a poor imitation.

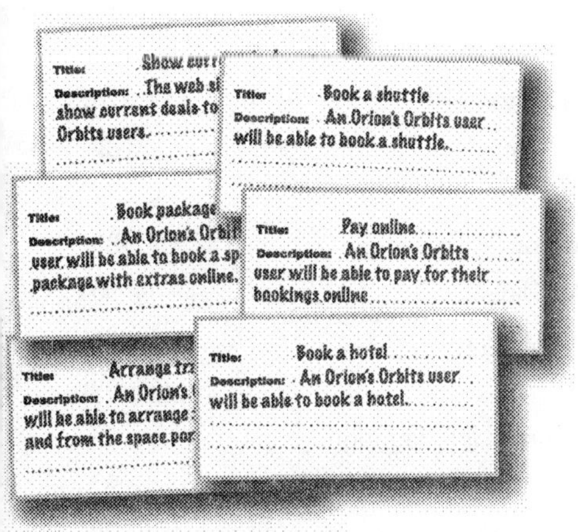

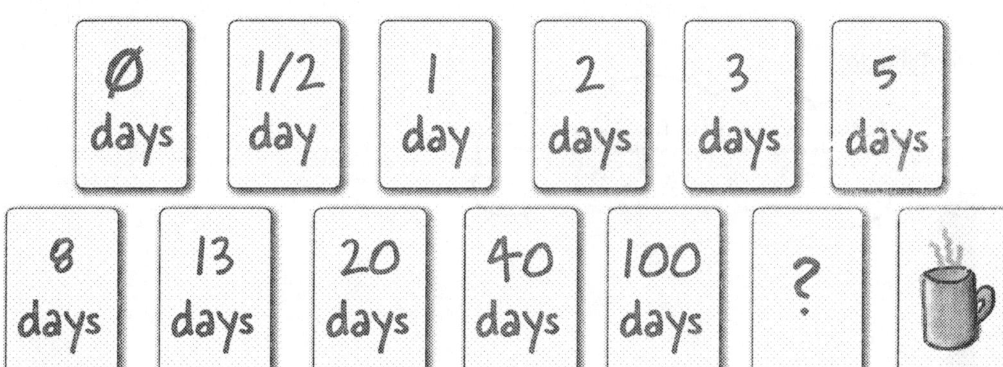

project planning

3 Planning for success

Every great piece of software starts with a great plan.

In this chapter you're going to learn how to create that plan. You're going to learn how to work with the customer to **prioritize their requirements**. You'll **define iterations** that you and your team can then work towards. Finally you'll create an achievable **development plan** that you and your team can confidently **execute** and **monitor.** By the time you're done, you'll know exactly how to get from requirements to milestone 1.0.

Here's what a programmer SAYS...

...but here's what he's really THINKING

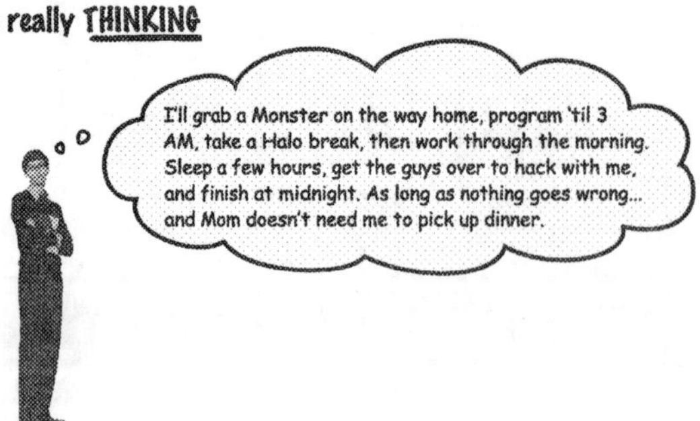

4 user stories and tasks

Getting to the real work

It's time to go to work. User stories captured what you need to develop, but now it's time to knuckle down and **dish out the work that needs to be done** so that you can bring those user stories to life. In this chapter you'll learn how to **break your user stories into tasks,** and how your **task estimates** help you track your project from inception to completion. You'll learn how to update your board, moving tasks from in-progress, to complete, to finally **completing an entire user story**. Along the way, you'll handle and prioritize the inevitable **unexpected work** your customer will add to your plate.

Your first standup meeting...

5

good-enough design

Getting it done with great design

Good design helps you deliver. In the last chapter things were looking pretty dire. A **bad design** was making life **hard for everyone** and, to make matters worse, an unplanned task cropped up. In this chapter you'll see how to **refactor** your design so that you and your team can be **more productive**. You'll apply **principles of good design**, while at the same time being wary of striving for the promise of the ***'perfect design'***. Finally you'll **handle unplanned tasks** in exactly the same way you handle all the other work on your project using the big project board on your wall.

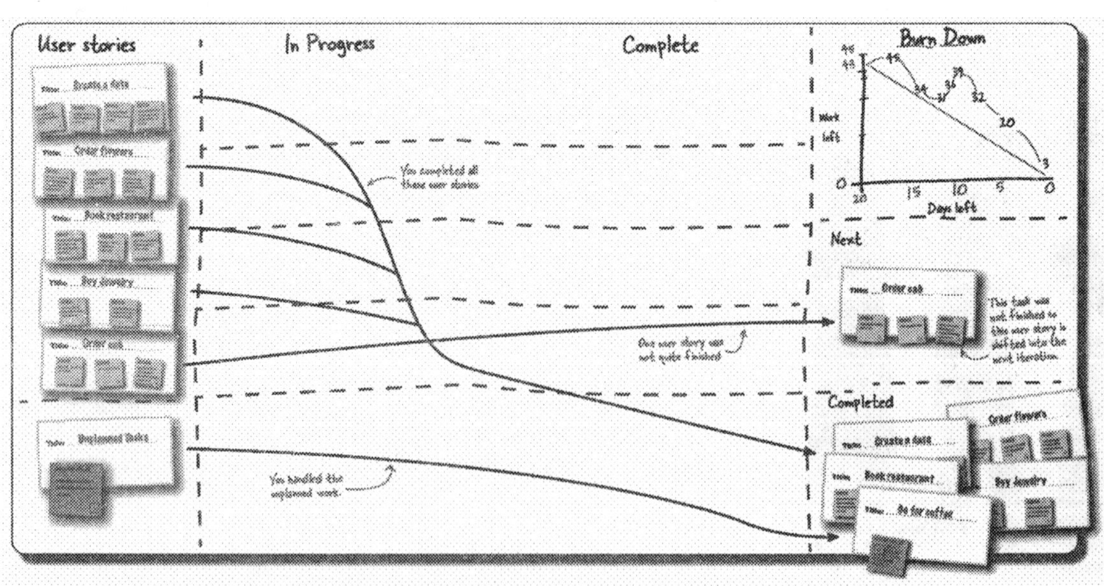

version control

6 Defensive development

When it comes to writing great software, *Safety First!*

Writing great software isn't easy... especially when you've got to make sure your code works, and **make sure it keeps working**. All it takes is one typo, one bad decision from a co-worker, one crashed hard drive, and suddenly all your work goes down the drain. But with **version control**, you can make sure your **code is always safe** in a code repository, you can **undo mistakes**, and you can make **bug fixes**—to new and old versions of your software.

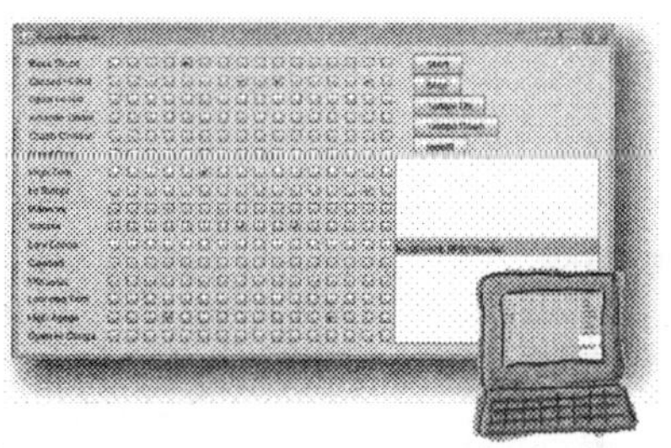

BeatBox Pro 1.0

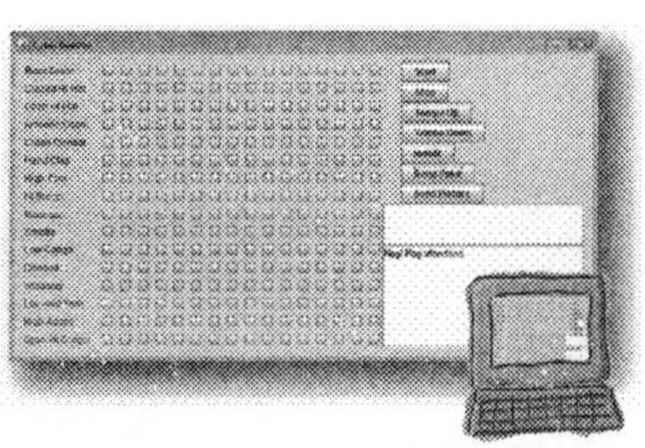

BeatBox Pro 1.x

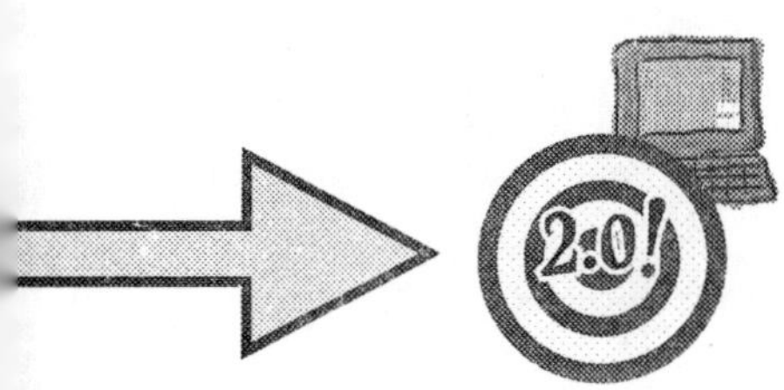

6½ building your code

Insert tab a into slot b...

It pays to follow the instructions...

...especially when you write them yourself.

It's not enough to use configuration management to ensure your code stays safe. You've also got to worry about **compiling your code** and packaging it into a deployable unit. On top of all that, which class should be the main class of your application? How should that class be run? In this chapter, you'll learn how a **build tool** allows you to **write your own instructions** for dealing with your source code.

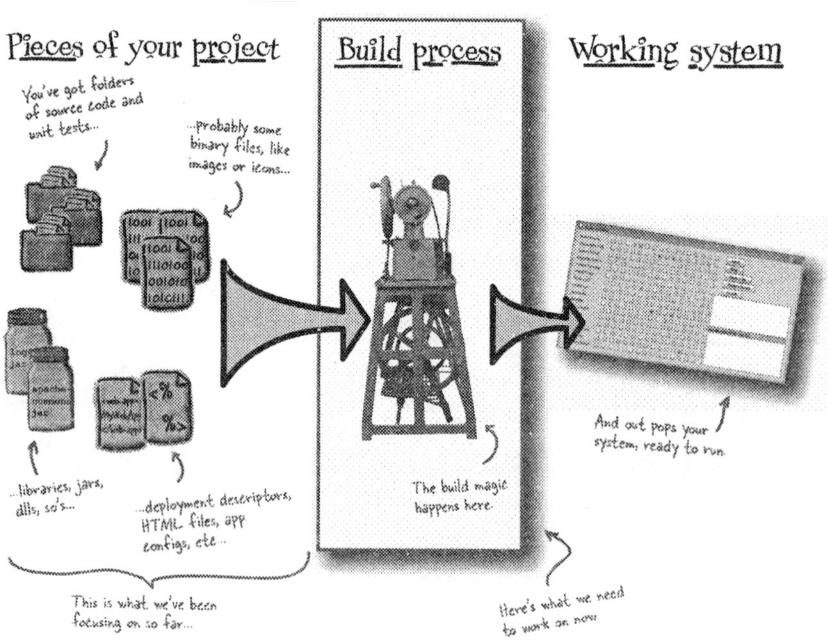

7 testing and continuous integration

Things fall apart

Sometimes even the best developer breaks the build.

Everyone's done it at least once. You're sure **your code compiles**, you've tested it over and over again on your machine and committed it into the repository. But somewhere between your machine and that black box they call a server *someone* must have changed your code. The unlucky soul who does the next checkout is about to have a bad morning sorting out **what used to be working code**. In this chapter we'll talk about how to put together a **safety net** to keep the build in working order and you **productive**.

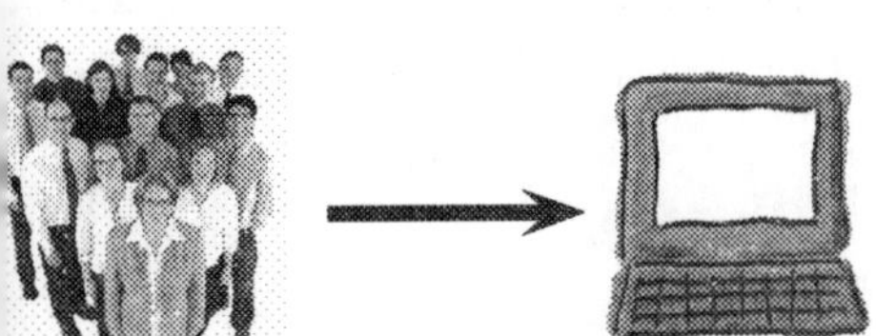

Black-box testing

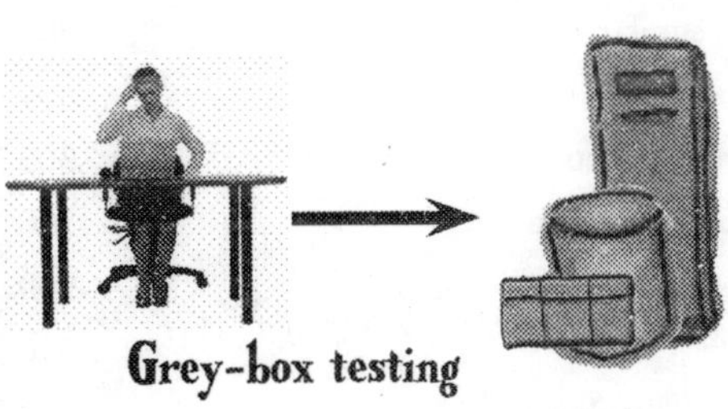

Grey-box testing

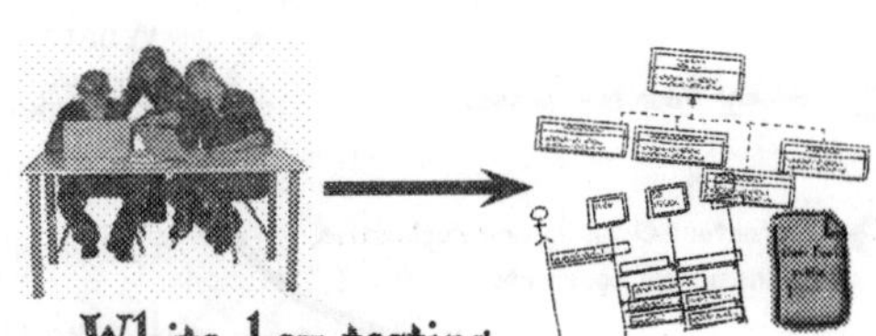

White-box testing

8 test-driven development

Holding your code accountable

Sometimes it's all about setting expectations. Good code needs to work, everyone knows that. But how do **you know your code works**? Even with unit testing, there are still parts of most code that goes untested. But what if testing was a **fundamental part of software development**? What if you did ***everything*** with testing in mind? In this chapter, you'll take what you know about version control, CI, and automated testing and tie it all together into an environment where you can feel **confident** about **fixing bugs, refactoring**, and even **reimplementing** parts of your system.

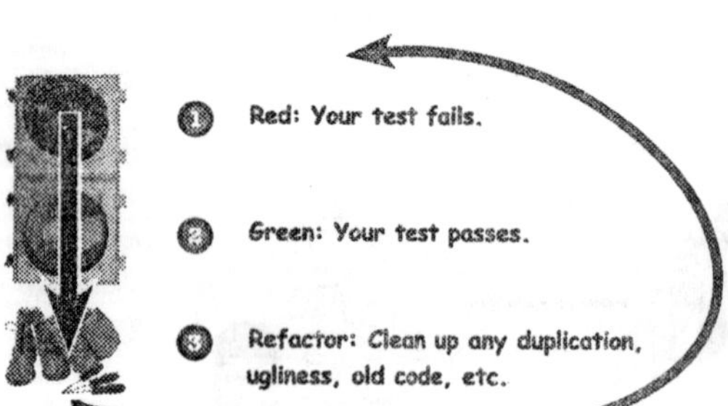

9 ending an iteration

It's all coming together...

You're almost finished! The team's been working hard and things are wrapping up. Your tasks and user stories are **complete**, but what's the best way to spend that extra day you ended up with? Where does **user testing** fit in? Can you squeeze in one more round of **refactoring** and **redesign**? And there sure are a lot of lingering **bugs**... when do those get fixed? It's all part of **the end of an iteration**... so let's get started on getting finished.

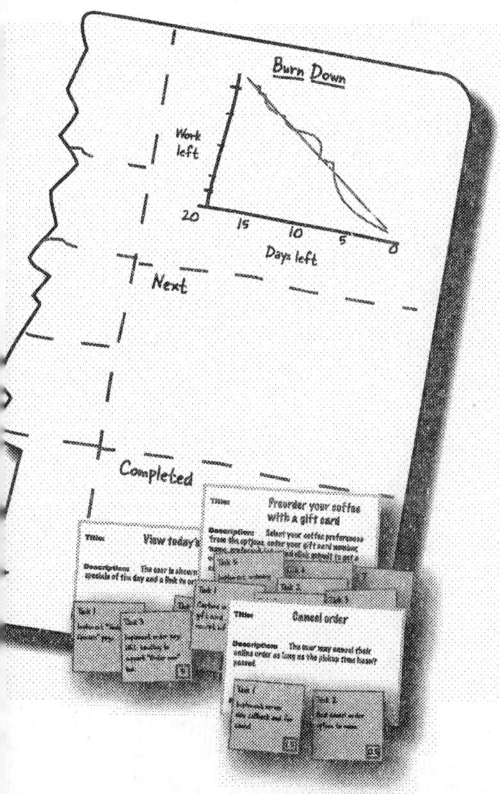

10 the next iteration

If it ain't broke...you still better fix it

Think things are going well?

Hold on, that just might change...

Your iteration went great, and you're delivering working software on-time. Time for the next iteration? No problem, right? Unfortunately, not right at all. Software development is all about **change,** and **moving to your next iteration** is no exception. In this chapter you'll learn how to prepare for the ***next*** iteration. You've got to **rebuild your board** and **adjust your stories** and expecations based on what the customer wants ***NOW***, not a month ago.

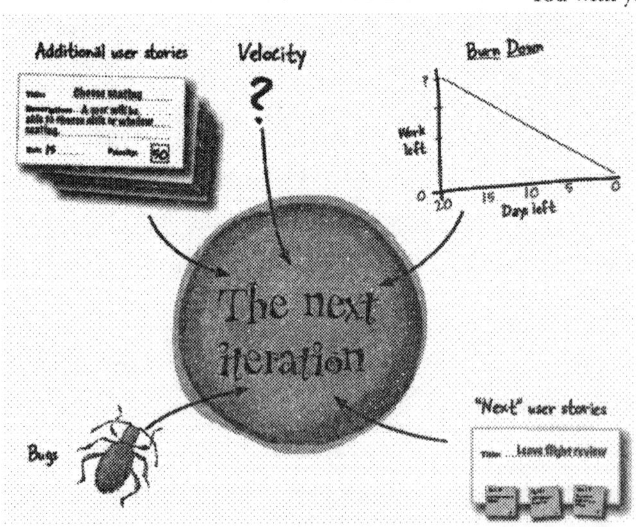

11 bugs

Squashing bugs like a pro

Your code, your responsibility...your bug, your reputation!

When things get tough, it's **up to you** to bring them back from the brink. **Bugs**, whether they're in your code or just in code that your software uses, are a **fact of life** in software development. And, like everything else, the way you handle bugs should fit into the rest of your process. You'll need to **prepare your board**, **keep your customer in the loop**, **confidently estimate** the work it will take to fix your bugs, and apply **refactoring** and **prefactoring** to fix and avoid bugs in the future.

12 the real world

Having a process in life

You've learned a lot about Software Development. But before you go pinning burn down graphs in everyone's office, there's just a little more you need to know about dealing with each project... on its own terms. There are a lot of **similarities** and **best practices** you should carry from project to project, but there are **unique** things everywhere you go, and you need to be ready for them. It's time to look at how to apply what you've learned to **your particular project**, and where to go next for **more learning**.

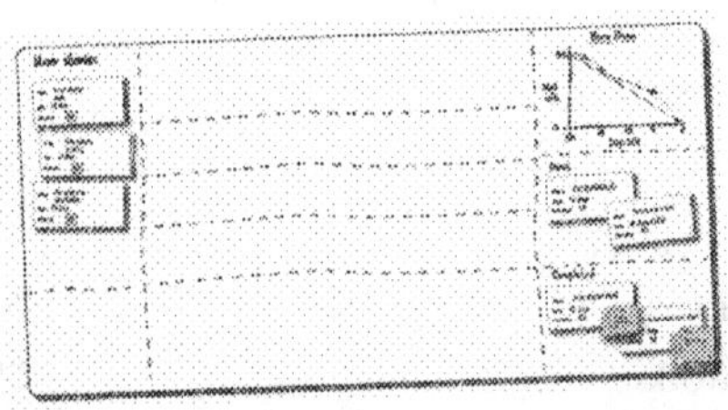

Story and Burn Down board

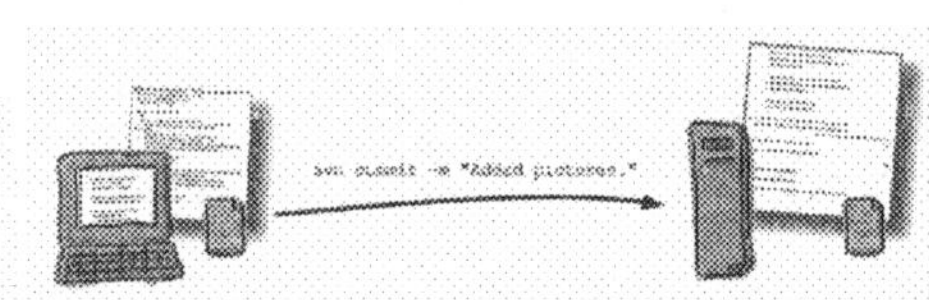

Configuration Management (CM)

User Stories

Continuous Integration (CI)

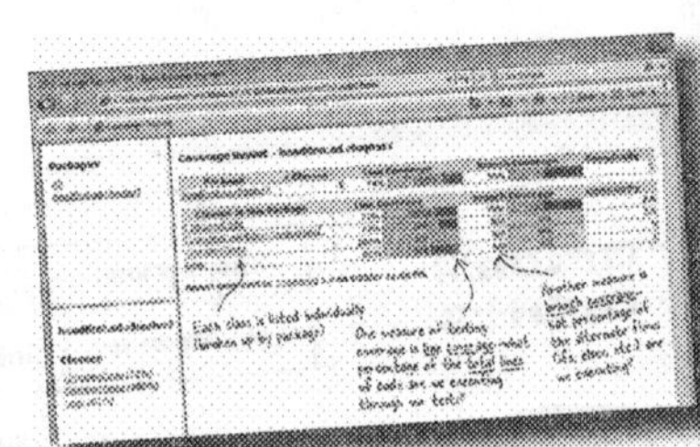

Test Coverage

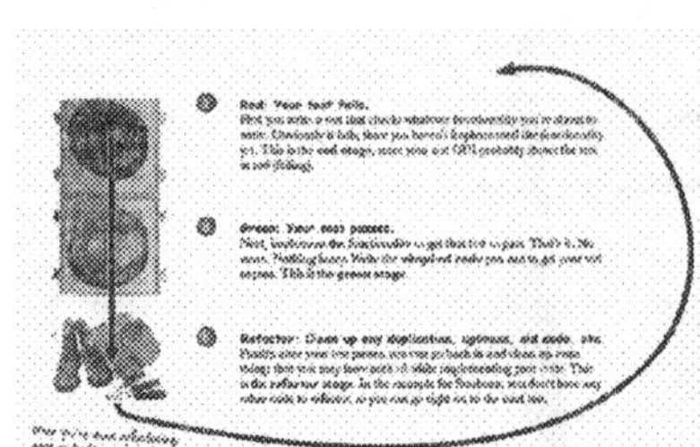

Test Driven Development (TDD)

appendix i: leftovers

The top 5 things (we didn't cover)

Ever feel like something's missing? We know what you mean...

Just when you thought you were done... there's more. We couldn't leave you without a few extra things, things we just couldn't fit into the rest of the book. At least, not if you want to be able to carry this book around without a metallic case and castor wheels on the bottom. So take a peek and see what you (still) might be missing out on.

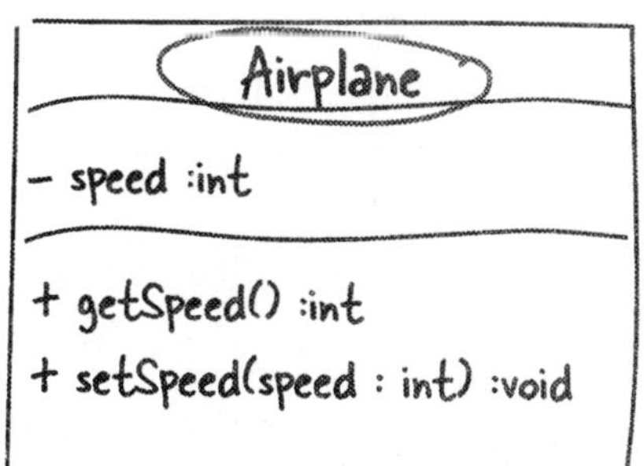

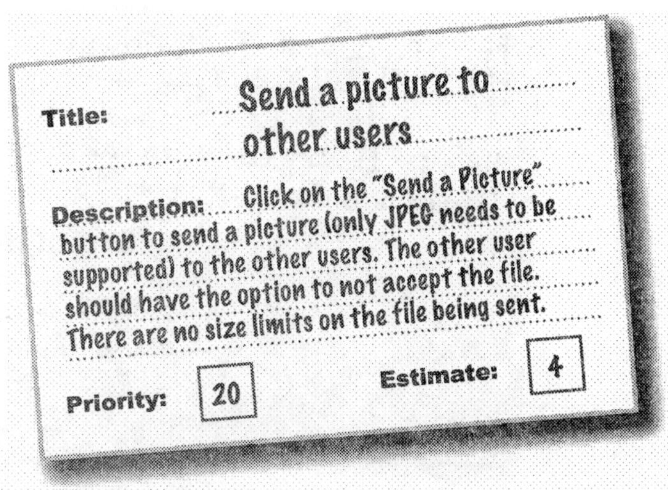

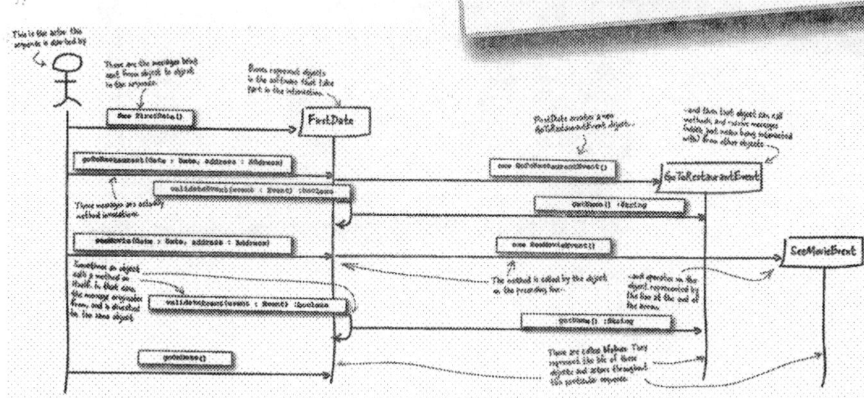

appendix 2: techniques and principles

ii

Tools for the experienced software developer

Ever wished all those great tools and techniques were in one place? This is a roundup of all the software development **techniques** and **principles** we've covered. Take a look over them all, and see if you can **remember what each one means**. You might even want to **cut these pages out** and tape them to the bottom of your **big board**, for everyone to see in your daily standup meetings.

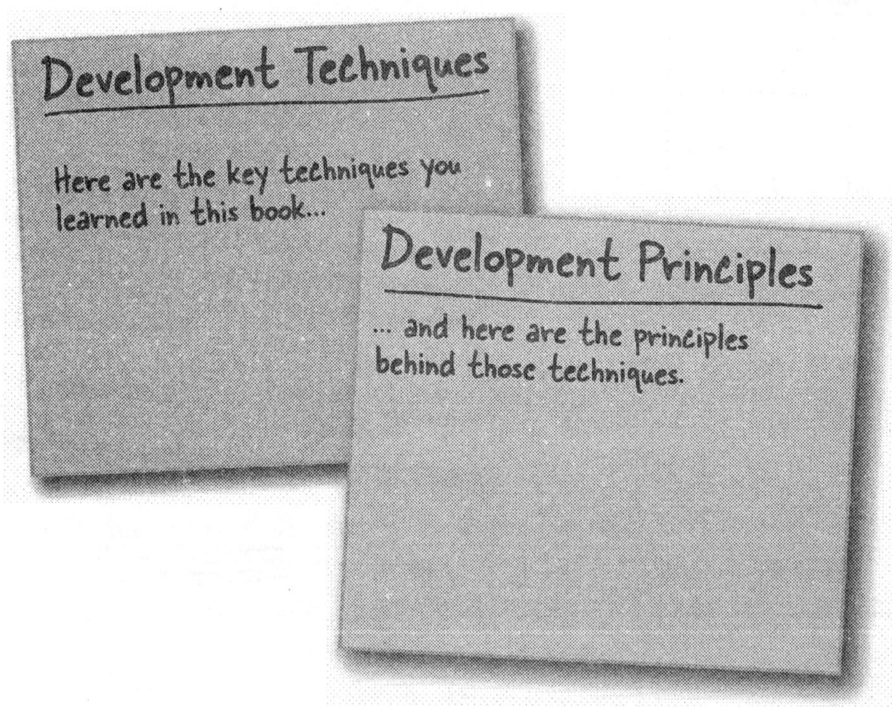

how to use this book

Intro

In this section we answer the burning question: "So why DID they put that in a software development book?"

Who is this book for?

If you can answer "yes" to all of these:

1. Do you have access to a computer and **some background in programming**?

2. Do you want to **learn techniques for building and delivering great software?** Do you want to **understand** the principles behind iterations and test-driven development?

3. Do you prefer **stimulating dinner party conversation** to **dry, dull, academic lectures**?

We use Java in the book, but you can squint and pretend it's C#. No amount of squinting will make you think it's Perl, though.

this book is for you.

Who should probably back away from this book?

If you can answer "yes" to any of these:

1. **Are you completely new to Java?**

   (You don't need to be advanced, and if you know C++ or C# you'll understand the code examples just fine.)

2. Are you a kick-butt development manager looking for a ***reference*** book?

3. Are you **afraid to try something different**? Would you rather have a root canal than mix stripes with plaid? Do you believe that a technical book can't be serious if iterations are anthropomorphized?

this book is not for you.

[Note from marketing: this book is for anyone with a credit card.]

We know what you're thinking

"How can *this* be a serious software development book?"

"What's with all the graphics?"

"Can I actually *learn* it this way?"

We know what your *brain* is thinking

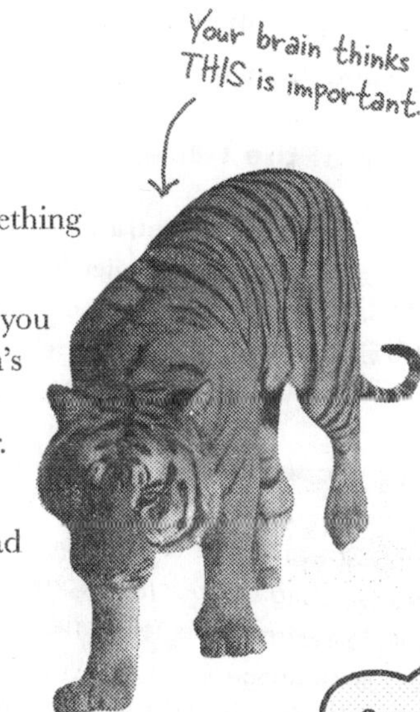

Your brain craves novelty. It's always searching, scanning, *waiting* for something unusual. It was built that way, and it helps you stay alive.

So what does your brain do with all the routine, ordinary, normal things you encounter? Everything it *can* to stop them from interfering with the brain's *real* job—recording things that *matter*. It doesn't bother saving the boring things; they never make it past the "this is obviously not important" filter.

How does your brain *know* what's important? Suppose you're out for a day hike and a tiger jumps in front of you, what happens inside your head and body?

Neurons fire. Emotions crank up. *Chemicals surge.*

And that's how your brain knows...

This must be important! Don't forget it!

But imagine you're at home, or in a library. It's a safe, warm, tiger-free zone. You're studying. Getting ready for an exam. Or trying to learn some tough technical topic your boss thinks will take a week, ten days at the most.

Just one problem. Your brain's trying to do you a big favor. It's trying to make sure that this *obviously* non-important content doesn't clutter up scarce resources. Resources that are better spent storing the really *big* things. Like tigers. Like the danger of fire. Like the guy with the handle "BigDaddy" on MySpace probably isn't someone to meet with after 6 PM.

And there's no simple way to tell your brain, "Hey brain, thank you very much, but no matter how dull this book is, and how little I'm registering on the emotional Richter scale right now, I really *do* want you to keep this stuff around."

We think of a "Head First" reader as a learner.

So what does it take to *learn* something? First, you have to *get* it, then make sure you don't *forget* it. It's not about pushing facts into your head. Based on the latest research in cognitive science, neurobiology, and educational psychology, *learning* takes a lot more than text on a page. We know what turns your brain on.

Some of the Head First learning principles:

Make it visual. Images are far more memorable than words alone, and make learning much more effective (up to 89% improvement in recall and transfer studies). It also makes things more understandable. **Put the words within or near the graphics** they relate to, rather than on the bottom or on another page, and learners will be up to *twice* as likely to solve problems related to the content.

Use a conversational and personalized style. In recent studies, students performed up to 40% better on post-learning tests if the content spoke directly to the reader, using a first-person, conversational style rather than taking a formal tone. Tell stories instead of lecturing. Use casual language. Don't take yourself too seriously. Which would *you* pay more attention to: a stimulating dinner party companion, or a lecture?

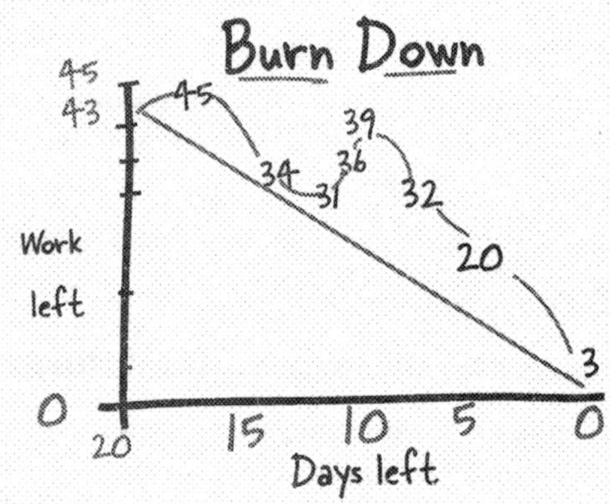

Get the learner to think more deeply. In other words, unless you actively flex your neurons, nothing much happens in your head. A reader has to be motivated, engaged, curious, and inspired to solve problems, draw conclusions, and generate new knowledge. And for that, you need challenges, exercises, and thought-provoking questions, and activities that involve both sides of the brain and multiple senses.

Get—and keep—the reader's attention. We've all had the "I really want to learn this but I can't stay awake past page one" experience. Your brain pays attention to things that are out of the ordinary, interesting, strange, eye-catching, unexpected. Learning a new, tough, technical topic doesn't have to be boring. Your brain will learn much more quickly if it's not.

Touch their emotions. We now know that your ability to remember something is largely dependent on its emotional content. You remember what you care about. You remember when you *feel* something. No, we're not talking heart-wrenching stories about a boy and his dog. We're talking emotions like surprise, curiosity, fun, "what the...?", and the feeling of "I Rule!" that comes when you solve a puzzle, learn something everybody else thinks is hard, or realize you know something that "I'm more technical than thou" Bob from engineering *doesn't*.

Metacognition: thinking about thinking

If you really want to learn, and you want to learn more quickly and more deeply, pay attention to how you pay attention. Think about how you think. Learn how you learn.

Most of us did not take courses on metacognition or learning theory when we were growing up. We were *expected* to learn, but rarely *taught* to learn.

But we assume that if you're holding this book, you really want to learn how to really develop great software. And you probably don't want to spend a lot of time. If you want to use what you read in this book, you need to *remember* what you read. And for that, you've got to *understand* it. To get the most from this book, or *any* book or learning experience, take responsibility for your brain. Your brain on *this* content.

The trick is to get your brain to see the new material you're learning as Really Important. Crucial to your well-being. As important as a tiger. Otherwise, you're in for a constant battle, with your brain doing its best to keep the new content from sticking.

So just how *DO* you get your brain to treat software development like it was a hungry tiger?

There's the slow, tedious way, or the faster, more effective way. The slow way is about sheer repetition. You obviously know that you *are* able to learn and remember even the dullest of topics if you keep pounding the same thing into your brain. With enough repetition, your brain says, "This doesn't *feel* important to him, but he keeps looking at the same thing *over* and *over* and *over*, so I suppose it must be."

The faster way is to do ***anything that increases brain activity,*** especially different *types* of brain activity. The things on the previous page are a big part of the solution, and they're all things that have been proven to help your brain work in your favor. For example, studies show that putting words *within* the pictures they describe (as opposed to somewhere else in the page, like a caption or in the body text) causes your brain to try to makes sense of how the words and picture relate, and this causes more neurons to fire. More neurons firing = more chances for your brain to *get* that this is something worth paying attention to, and possibly recording.

A conversational style helps because people tend to pay more attention when they perceive that they're in a conversation, since they're expected to follow along and hold up their end. The amazing thing is, your brain doesn't necessarily *care* that the "conversation" is between you and a book! On the other hand, if the writing style is formal and dry, your brain perceives it the same way you experience being lectured to while sitting in a roomful of passive attendees. No need to stay awake.

But pictures and conversational style are just the beginning...

Here's what WE did:

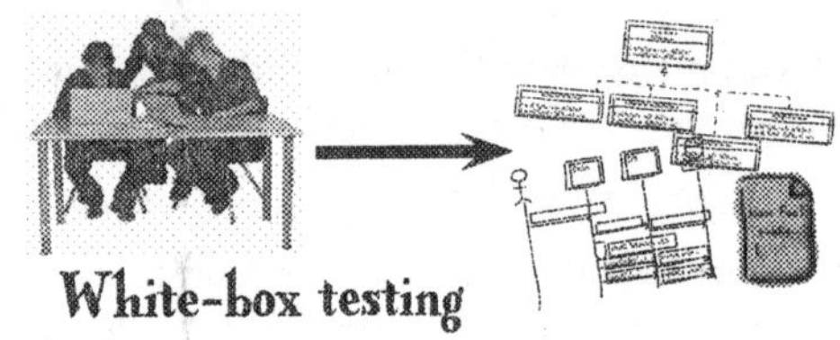

We used ***pictures***, because your brain is tuned for visuals, not text. As far as your brain's concerned, a picture really *is* worth a thousand words. And when text and pictures work together, we embedded the text *in* the pictures because your brain works more effectively when the text is *within* the thing the text refers to, as opposed to in a caption or buried in the text somewhere.

We used ***redundancy***, saying the same thing in *different* ways and with different media types, and *multiple senses*, to increase the chance that the content gets coded into more than one area of your brain.

We used concepts and pictures in ***unexpected*** ways because your brain is tuned for novelty, and we used pictures and ideas with at least *some* ***emotional*** *content*, because your brain is tuned to pay attention to the biochemistry of emotions. That which causes you to *feel* something is more likely to be remembered, even if that feeling is nothing more than a little ***humor***, ***surprise***, or ***interest.***

We used a personalized, ***conversational style***, because your brain is tuned to pay more attention when it believes you're in a conversation than if it thinks you're passively listening to a presentation. Your brain does this even when you're *reading*.

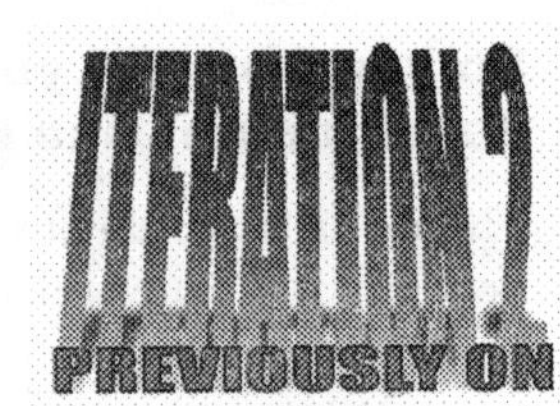

We included more than 80 ***activities***, because your brain is tuned to learn and remember more when you ***do*** things than when you *read* about things. And we made the exercises challenging-yet-do-able, because that's what most people prefer.

We used ***multiple learning styles***, because *you* might prefer step-by-step procedures, while someone else wants to understand the big picture first, and someone else just wants to see an example. But regardless of your own learning preference, *everyone* benefits from seeing the same content represented in multiple ways.

We include content for ***both sides of your brain***, because the more of your brain you engage, the more likely you are to learn and remember, and the longer you can stay focused. Since working one side of the brain often means giving the other side a chance to rest, you can be more productive at learning for a longer period of time.

And we included ***stories*** and exercises that present ***more than one point of view,*** because your brain is tuned to learn more deeply when it's forced to make evaluations and judgments.

We included ***challenges***, with exercises, and by asking ***questions*** that don't always have a straight answer, because your brain is tuned to learn and remember when it has to *work* at something. Think about it—you can't get your *body* in shape just by *watching* people at the gym. But we did our best to make sure that when you're working hard, it's on the *right* things. That ***you're not spending one extra dendrite*** processing a hard-to-understand example, or parsing difficult, jargon-laden, or overly terse text.

We used ***people***. In stories, examples, pictures, etc., because, well, because *you're* a person. And your brain pays more attention to *people* than it does to *things*.

Here's what YOU can do to bend your brain into submission

So, we did our part. The rest is up to you. These tips are a starting point; listen to your brain and figure out what works for you and what doesn't. Try new things.

1. **Slow down. The more you understand, the less you have to memorize.**

   Don't just *read*. Stop and think. When the book asks you a question, don't just skip to the answer. Imagine that someone really *is* asking the question. The more deeply you force your brain to think, the better chance you have of learning and remembering.

2. **Do the exercises. Write your own notes.**

   We put them in, but if we did them for you, that would be like having someone else do your workouts for you. And don't just *look* at the exercises. **Use a pencil.** There's plenty of evidence that physical activity *while* learning can increase the learning.

3. **Read the "There are No Dumb Questions"**

   That means all of them. They're not optional sidebars—***they're part of the core content!*** Don't skip them.

4. **Make this the last thing you read before bed. Or at least the last challenging thing.**

   Part of the learning (especially the transfer to long-term memory) happens *after* you put the book down. Your brain needs time on its own, to do more processing. If you put in something new during that processing time, some of what you just learned will be lost.

5. **Drink water. Lots of it.**

   Your brain works best in a nice bath of fluid. Dehydration (which can happen before you ever feel thirsty) decreases cognitive function.

6. **Talk about it. Out loud.**

   Speaking activates a different part of the brain. If you're trying to understand something, or increase your chance of remembering it later, say it out loud. Better still, try to explain it out loud to someone else. You'll learn more quickly, and you might uncover ideas you hadn't known were there when you were reading about it.

7. **Listen to your brain.**

   Pay attention to whether your brain is getting overloaded. If you find yourself starting to skim the surface or forget what you just read, it's time for a break. Once you go past a certain point, you won't learn faster by trying to shove more in, and you might even hurt the process.

8. **Feel something.**

   Your brain needs to know that this *matters*. Get involved with the stories. Make up your own captions for the photos. Groaning over a bad joke is *still* better than feeling nothing at all.

9. **Write a lot of software!**

   There's only one way to learn to develop software: you have to **actually develop software**. And that's what you're going to do throughout this book. We're going to give you lots of requirements to capture, techniques to evaluate, and code to test and improve: every chapter has exercises that pose a problem for you to solve. Don't just skip over them—a lot of the learning happens when you solve the exercises. We included a solution to each exercise—don't be afraid to **peek at the solution** if you get stuck! (It's easy to get snagged on something small.) But try to solve the problem before you look at the solution.

Read Me

This is a learning experience, not a reference book. We deliberately stripped out everything that might get in the way of learning whatever it is we're working on at that point in the book. And the first time through, you need to begin at the beginning, because the book makes assumptions about what you've already seen and learned.

We assume you are familiar with object-oriented programming.

It would take an entire book to teach you object-oriented programming (like, say, **Head First OOA&D**). We chose to focus this book on software development principles rather than design or language basics. We picked Java for our examples because it's fairly common, and pretty self-documenting; but everything we talk about should apply whether you're using Java, C#, C++, or Visual Basic (or Ruby, or...) However, if you've never programmed using an object-oriented language, you may have some trouble following some of the code. In that case we'd strongly recommend you get familiar with one of those languages before attacking some of the later chapters in the book.

We don't cover every software development process out there.

There are tomes of information about different ways to write software. We don't try to cover every possible approach to developing code. Instead, we focus on techniques that we know work and fit well together to produce great software. Chapter 12 specifically talks about ways to tweak your process to account for unique things on your project.

The activities are NOT optional.

The exercises and activities are not add-ons; they're part of the core content of the book. Some of them are to help with memory, some are for understanding, and some will help you apply what you've learned. Some exercises are there just to make you think about **how** you would solve the problem. ***Don't skip the exercises.*** The crossword puzzles are the only thing you don't *have* to do, but they're good for giving your brain a chance to think about the words and terms you've been learning in a different context.

The redundancy is intentional and important.

One distinct difference in a Head First book is that we want you to *really* get it. And we want you to finish the book remembering what you've learned. Most reference books don't have retention and recall as a goal, but this book is about *learning*, so you'll see some of the same concepts come up more than once.

The examples are as lean as possible.

Our readers tell us that it's frustrating to wade through 200 lines of an example looking for the two lines they need to understand. Most examples in this book are shown within the smallest possible context, so that the part you're trying to learn is clear and simple. Don't expect all of the examples to be robust, or even complete—they are written specifically for learning, and aren't always fully functional.

We've placed the full code for the projects on the Web so you can copy and paste them into your text editor. You'll find them at:

http://www.headfirstlabs.com/books/hfsd/

The Brain Power exercises don't have answers.

For some of them, there is no right answer, and for others, part of the learning experience of the Brain Power activities is for you to decide if and when your answers are right. In some of the Brain Power exercises, you will find hints to point you in the right direction.

The technical review team

Dan Francis

McClellan Francis

Faisal Jawad

Burk Hufnagel

Lisa Kellner

Kristin Stromberg

Adam Szymanski

Technical Reviewers:

This book wouldn't be anything like it is without our technical reviewers. They called us out when they disagreed with something, gave us "hurrah"s when something went right, and sent back lots of great commentary on things that worked and didn't work for them in the real world. Each of them brought a different perspective to the book, and we really appreciate that. For instance, **Dan Francis** and **McClellan Francis** made sure this book didn't turn into *Software Development for Java.*

We'd particularly like to call out **Faisal Jawad** for his thorough and supportive feedback (he started the "hurrahs"). **Burk Hufnagel** provided great suggestions on other approaches he'd used on projects and made one author's late night of updates a lot more fun with his suggestion to include, "Bad dev team. No biscuit."

Finally, we'd like to thank **Lisa Kellner** and **Kristin Stromberg** for their great work on readability and pacing. This book wouldn't be what it is without all of your input.

Acknowledgments

Our editor:

Don't let the picture fool you. **Brett** is one of the sharpest and most professional people we've ever worked with, and his contributions are on every page. Brett supported this book through every positive and negative review and spent quality time with us in Washington, D.C. to make this a success. More than once, he baited us into a good argument and then took notes while we went at it. This book is a result of his hard work and support and we really appreciate it.

Brett McLaughlin

The O'Reilly team:

Lou Barr

Lou's favorite American-ism...

Lou Barr is the reason these pages look so "awesome." She's responsible for turning our vaguely worded "something that conveys this idea and looks cool" comments into pages that teach the material like no other book around.

We'd also like to thank **Laurie Petrycki** for giving us the opportunity and making the tough decisions to get this book to where it is. We'd also like to thank **Catherine Nolan** and **Mary Treseler** for getting this book kicked off. Finally we'd like to thank **Caitrin McCullough**, **Sanders Kleinfeld**, **Keith McNamara**, and the rest of the O'Reilly production team for taking this book from the rough pages we sent in to a printed, high-class book with flawless grammar.

Scrum and XP from the Trenches:

We want to extend a special thanks to Henrik Kniberg for his book **Scrum and XP from the Trenches**. This book had significant influence on how we develop software and is the basis for some of the techniques we describe in this book. We're very grateful for the excellent work he's done.

Good book... highly recommended!

Our families:

No acknowledgments page would be complete without recognizing the contributions and sacrifices our families made for this book. Vinny, Nick, and Tracey have picked up the slack in the Pilone house for almost two years while this book came together. I can't convey how much I appreciate that and how your support and encouragement while "Daddy worked on his book" made this possible. Thank you.

A massive thank you also goes out to the Miles household, that's Corinne (the boss) and Frizbee, Fudge, Snuff, Scrappy, and Stripe (those are the pigs). At every step you guys have kept me going and I really can't tell you how much that means to me. Thanks!

Safari® Books Online

When you see a Safari® icon on the cover of your favorite technology book that means the book is available online through the O'Reilly Network Safari Bookshelf.

Safari offers a solution that's better than e-books. It's a virtual library that lets you easily search thousands of top tech books, cut and paste code samples, download chapters, and find quick answers when you need the most accurate, current information. Try it for free at `http://safari.oreilly.com`.

1 great software development

Pleasing your customer

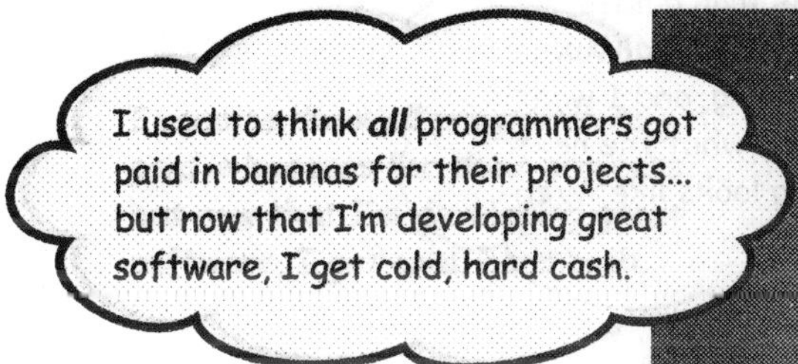

If your customer's unhappy, *everyone's* unhappy!

Every great piece of software starts with a customer's big idea. It's your job as a professional software developer to **bring that idea to life**. But taking a vague idea and turning it into working code—code that **satisfies your customer**—isn't so easy. In this chapter you'll learn how to avoid being a software development casualty by delivering software that is **needed, on time,** and **on budget**. Grab your laptop, and let's set out on the road to shipping great software.

Tom's Trails is going online

Trekkin' Tom has been providing world-famous trail guides and equipment from his shack in the Rockies for years. Now, he wants to ramp up his sales using a bit of the latest technology.

Tom wants to take his business to the Internet.

Tom's vision of Tom's Trails Online

Most projects have two major concerns

Talk to most customers and, besides their big idea, they've probably got two basic concerns:

How much will it cost?

No surprise here. Most customers want to figure out how much cash they'll have to spend. In this case, though, Tom has a pile of money, so that's not much of a concern for him.

Usually, cash is a limitation. In this case, Tom's got money to spare, and figures what he spends will turn into an even bigger pile.

How long will it take?

The other big constraint is time. Almost no customer ever says, "Take as long as you want!" And lots of the time, you have a specific event or date the customer wants their software ready for.

In Tom's case, he wants his website available in three months' time, ready for the big TrailMix Conference coming up.

This is your payday, too...if you get finished on time.

The Big Bang approach to development

With only a month to get finished, there's no time to waste. The lead developer Tom hired gets right to work.

Flash forward: two weeks later

Tom's lead developer has pulled out all the stops to build Tom's Trails Online, putting all her finest coding skills into play and producing what she thinks Tom wants her to build.

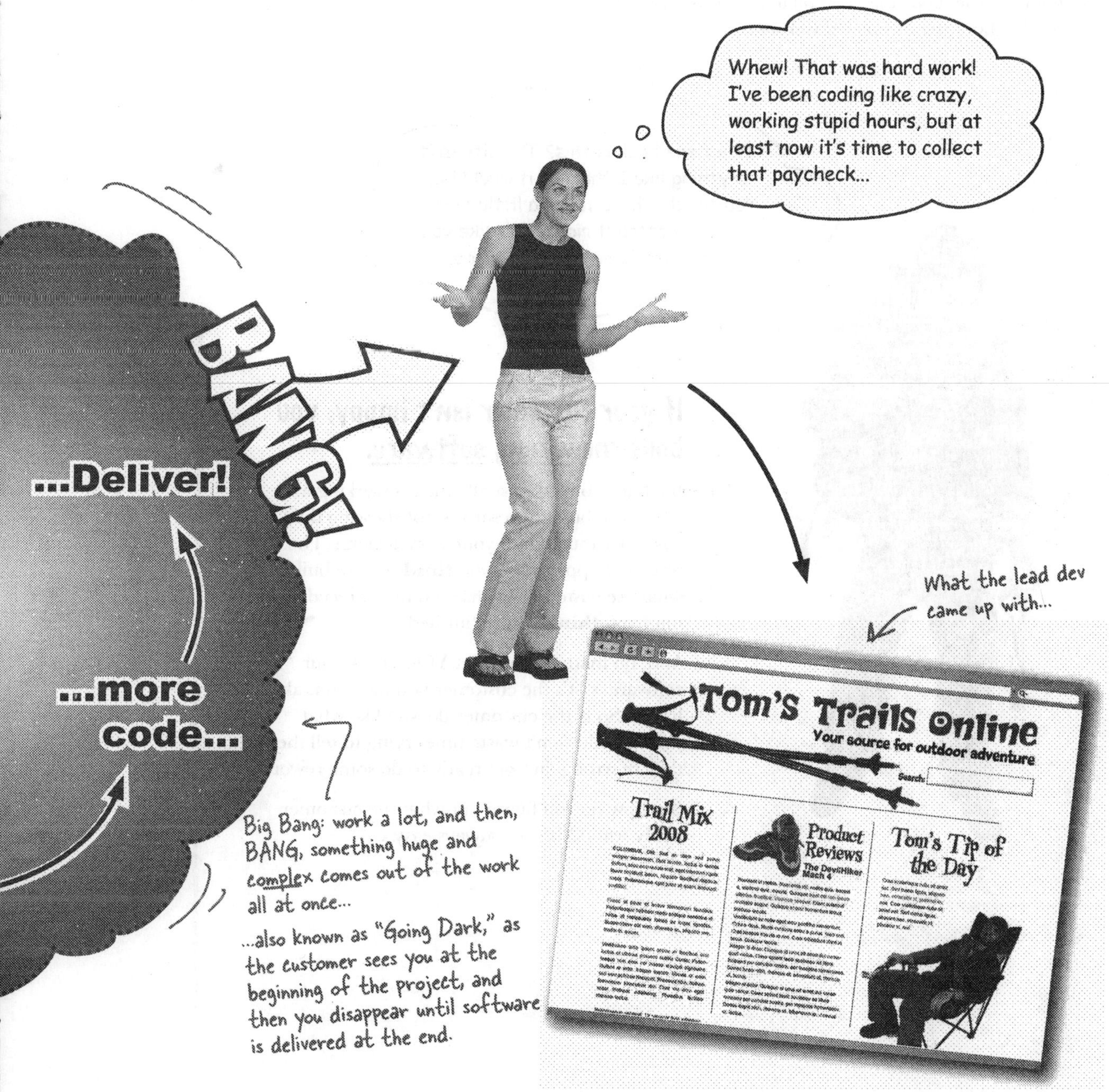

Big bang development usually ends up in a BIG MESS

Even though a lot of work went into the project, Tom hasn't seen any of the (hopefully) completed work yet. Let's see what he thinks about the completed website.

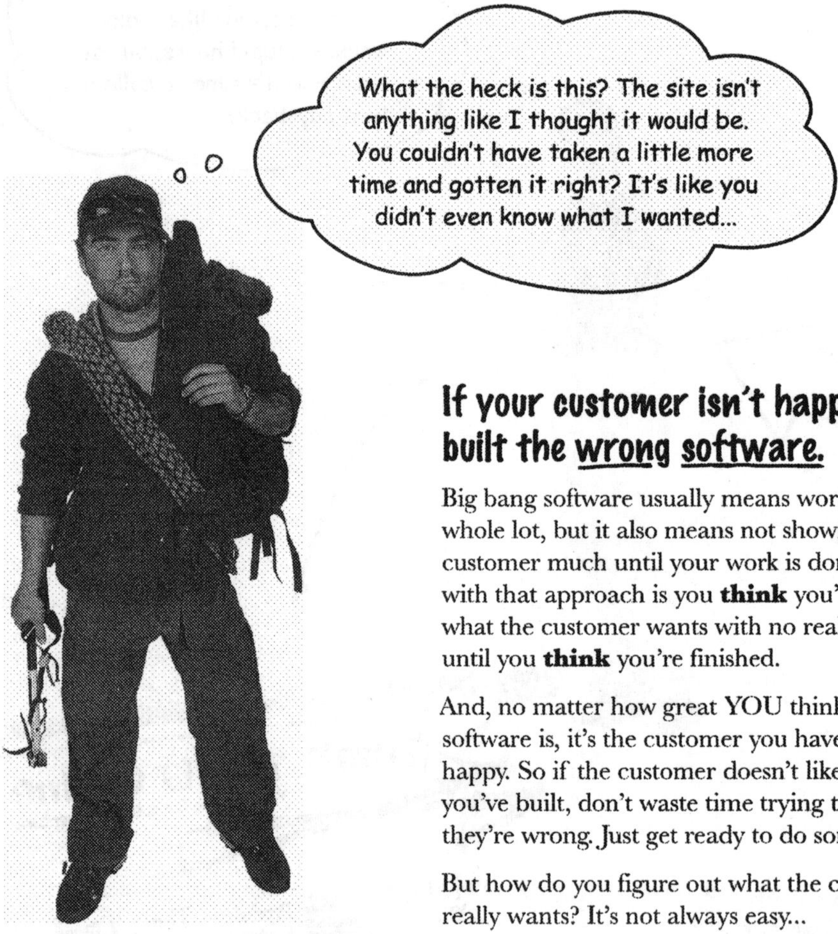

If your customer isn't happy, you built the wrong software.

Big bang software usually means working a whole lot, but it also means not showing the customer much until your work is done. The risk with that approach is you **think** you're building what the customer wants with no real feedback until you **think** you're finished.

The emphasis here is that you think you're finished... but you may not be.

And, no matter how great YOU think your software is, it's the customer you have to make happy. So if the customer doesn't like what you've built, don't waste time trying to tell them they're wrong. Just get ready to do some rework.

But how do you figure out what the customer really wants? It's not always easy...

Sharpen your pencil

Can you figure out where things went wrong? Below are three things Tom said he wanted his site to allow for. Your job is to choose the option underneath each item that most closely matches what Tom means. And for the third one, you've got to figure out what he means on your own. Good luck!

1 **Tom says, "The customer should be able to search for trails."**

- ☐ The customer should see a map of the world and then enter an address to search for trails near a particular location.
- ☐ The customer should be able to scroll through a list of tourist spots and find trails that lead to and from those spots.
- ☐ The customer should be able to enter a zip code and a level of difficulty and find all trails that match that difficulty and are near that zip code.

2 **Tom says, "The customer should be able to order equipment."**

- ☐ The customer should be able to view what equipmentTom has and then create an order for items that are in stock.
- ☐ The customer should be able to order any equipment they need, but depending on stock levels the order may take longer if some of the items are back-ordered.

3 **Tom says, "The customer should be able to book a trip."**

Write what YOU think the software should do here.

....

....

....

Relax

Confused about what Tom really meant? It's okay... just do your best.

If you're having a hard time figuring out which option to choose, that's perfectly normal. Do your best, and we'll spend a lot more time in this chapter talking about how to figure out what the customer means.

Sharpen your pencil Solution

Can you figure out where things went wrong? Your job was to choose the option underneath each item that most closely matches what Tom means. And for the third one, you had to figure out what he means on your own.

?

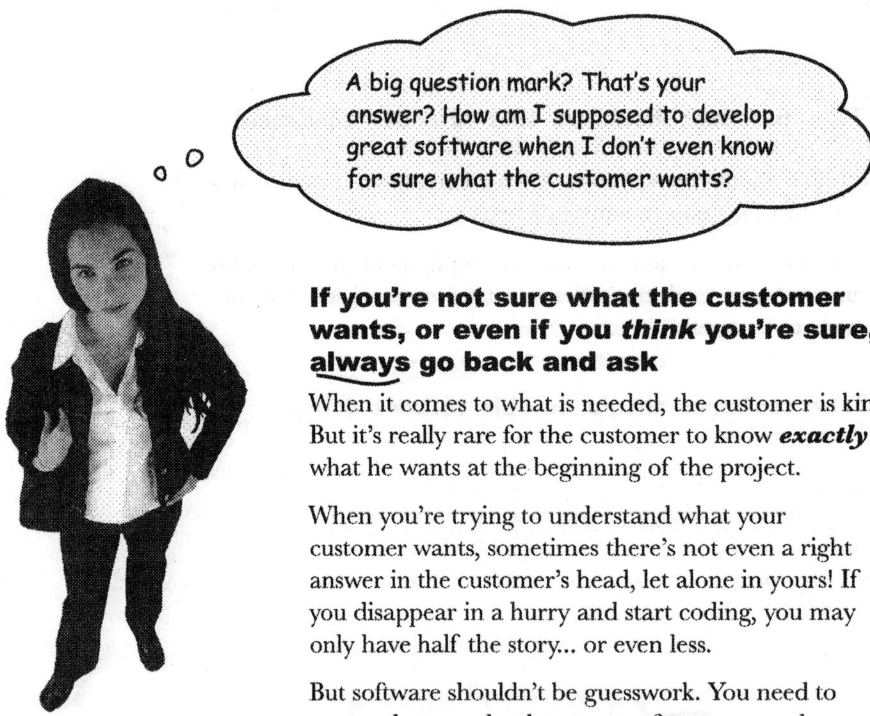

If you're not sure what the customer wants, or even if you *think* you're sure, always go back and ask

When it comes to what is needed, the customer is king. But it's really rare for the customer to know ***exactly*** what he wants at the beginning of the project.

When you're trying to understand what your customer wants, sometimes there's not even a right answer in the customer's head, let alone in yours! If you disappear in a hurry and start coding, you may only have half the story... or even less.

But software shouldn't be guesswork. You need to ensure that you develop great software even when what's needed is not clear up front. So go ***ask*** the customer what they mean. ***Ask*** them for more detail. ***Ask*** them for options about how you might implement about their big ideas.

Software development is NOT guesswork. You need to keep the customer in the loop to make sure you're on the right path.

Great software development is...

We've talked about several things that you'll need for successful software. You've got the customer's big ideas to deal with, their money you're spending, and a schedule you've got to worry about. You've got to get all of those things right if you're going to build consistently great software.

Great software development delivers...

What the customer needs, otherwise called the software requirements. We'll talk more about requirements in the next chapter...

What is needed,

When we agreed with the customer that the software would be finished.

On Time,

and

On Budget

Not billing the customer for more money than was agreed upon.

BRAIN POWER

Can you think of three examples of software you've been involved with where at least one of these rules was broken?

Getting to the goal with ITERATION

The secret to great software development is **iteration**. You've already seen that you can't simply ignore the customer during development. But iteration provides you a way to actually ask the question, at each step of development, "How am I doing?" Here are two projects: one without iteration, and one with.

Without iteration...

Suppose you take the Big Bang approach to development—or any other approach where you're not constantly checking in with the customer. The likely outcome? Missing what the customer wanted, and by a lot, not just a little.

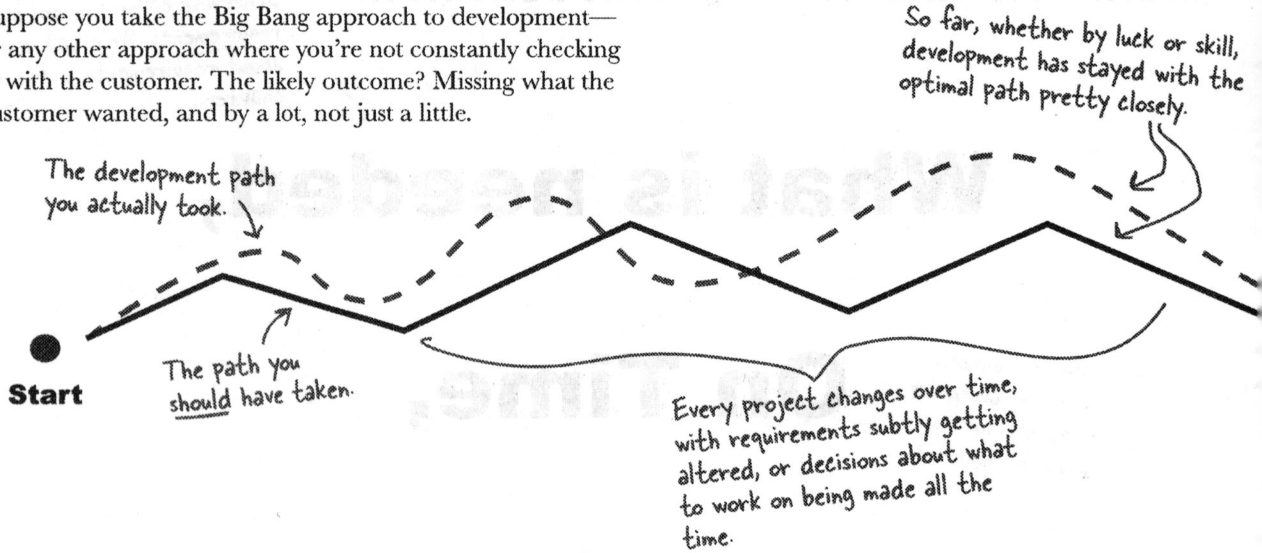

With iteration...

This time, you decide that every time you make significant progress you'll check with the customer and refine what you're working on. You also don't make any major decisions without incorporating customer feedback.

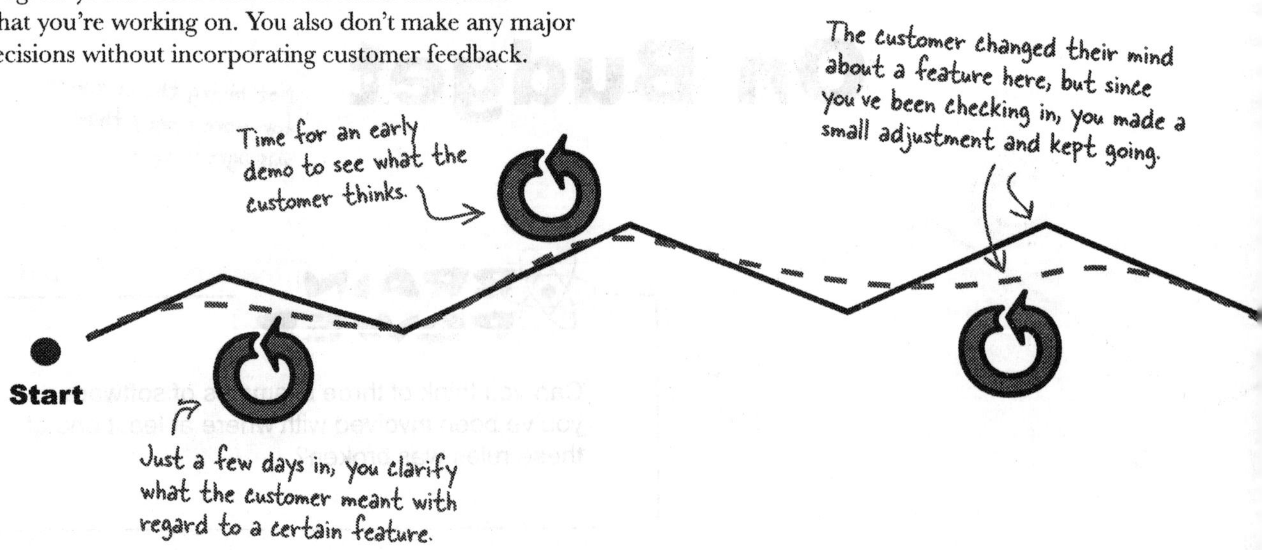

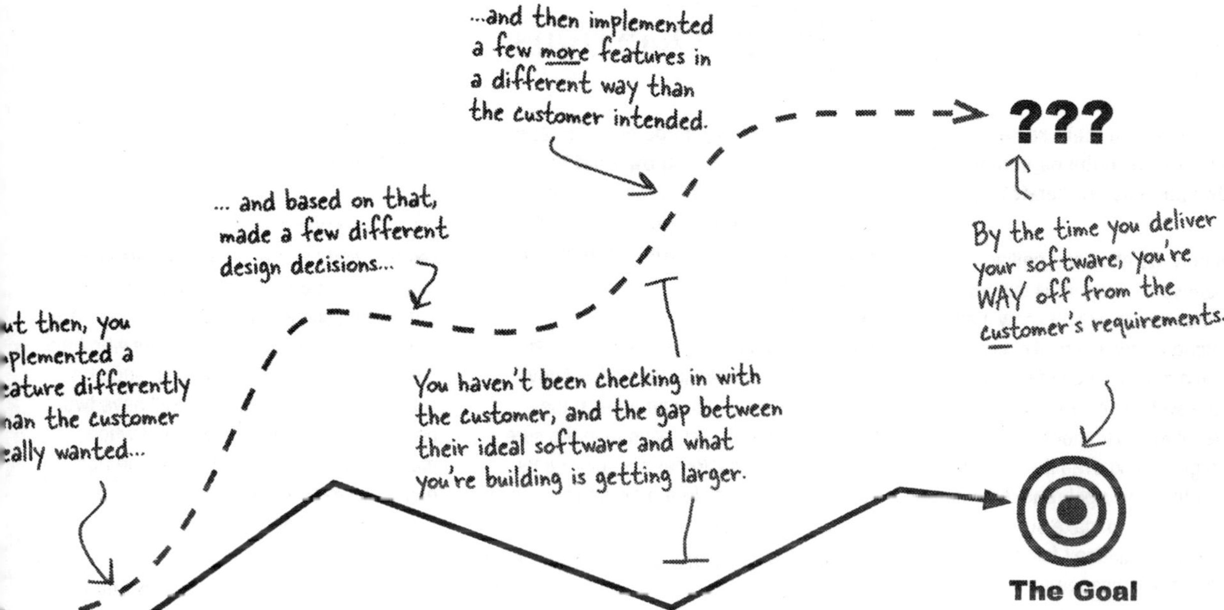

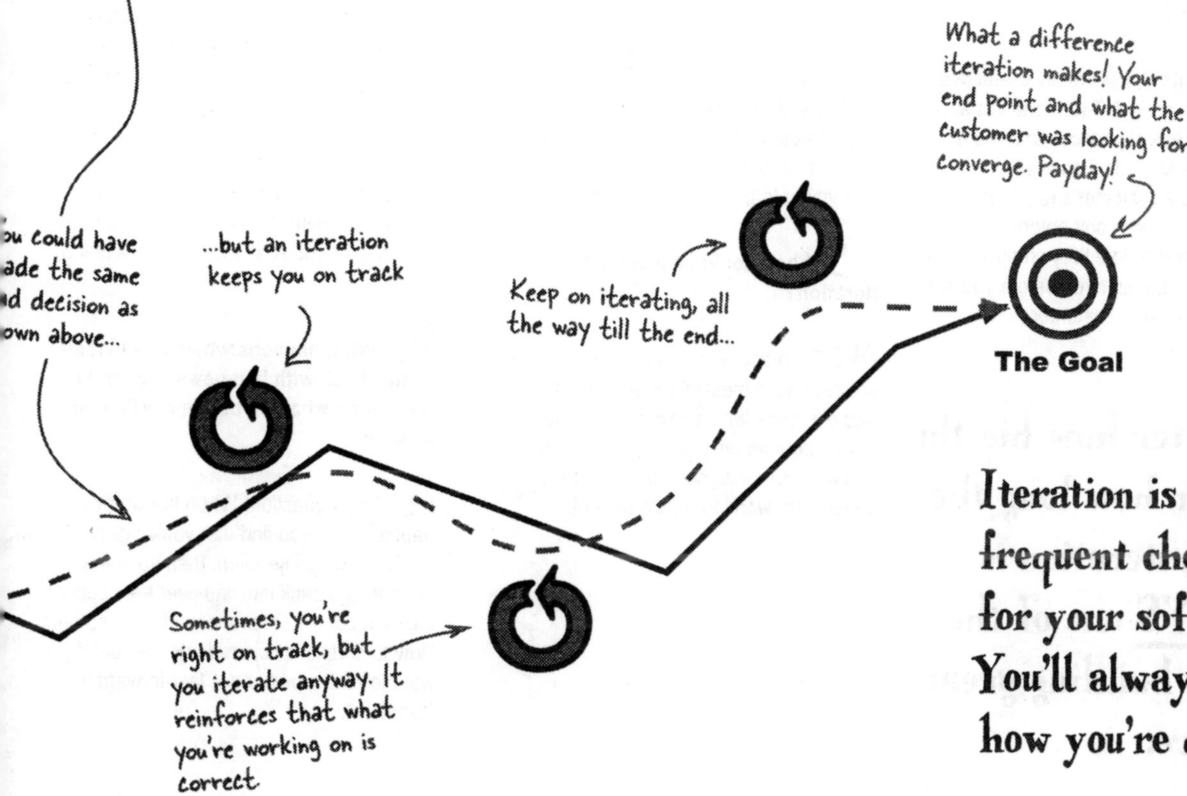

Iteration is like a frequent checkup for your software. You'll always know how you're doing.

there are no Dumb Questions

Q: What if I'm sure that I know what the customer wants at the beginning of a project? Do I still need to iterate?

A: Absolutely. Iteration and getting feedback from your customer is important *especially* when you think you know it all up front. Sometimes it can seem like a complete no-brainer on a simple piece of software, but checking back with the customer is ALWAYS worth it. Even if the customer just tells you you're doing great, and even if you actually do start out with all the right requirements, iteration is still a way to make sure you're on the right track. And, don't forget, the customer can always change their mind.

Q: My entire project is only two months long. Is it worth iterating for such a short project?

A: Yep, iteration is still really useful even on a very short project. Two months is a whopping 60 days of chances to deviate from the customer's ideal software, or misunderstand a customer's requirement. Iteration lets you catch any potential problems like this before they creep into your project. And, better yet, before you look foolish in front of your customer.

No matter how big the team, or how long the project, iteration is ALWAYS one of the keys to building great software.

Q: Wouldn't it just be better to spend more time getting to know what the customer really wants, really getting the requirements down tight, than always letting the customer change their mind midstream?

A: You'd think so, but actually this is a recipe for disaster. In the bad old days, developers used to spend ages at the beginning of a project trying to make sure they got all the customer's requirements down completely before a single line of code or design decision was made.

Unfortunately, this approach still failed. Even if you think that you completely understand what the customer needs at the beginning, the ***customer*** often doesn't understand. So they're figuring out what they want as much as you are.

You need a way of helping your team and your customer grow their understanding of their software as you build it, and you can't do that with a Big Bang, up-front requirements approach that expects everything to be cast in stone from day one.

Q: Who should be involved in an iteration?

A: Everyone who has a say in whether your software meets its requirements, and everyone who is involved in meeting those requirements. At a minimum, that's usually your customer, you, and any other developers working on the project.

Q: But I'm only a team of one, do I still need to iterate?

A: Good question, and the answer is yes (starting to detect a theme here?). You might only be a development team of one, but when it comes to your project there are always, at a minimum, two people who have a stake in your software being a success: your customer and you. You still have two perspectives to take into account when making sure your software is on the right path, so iteration is still really helpful even in the smallest of teams.

Q: How early in a project should I start iterating?

A: As early as you have a piece of software running that you can discuss with your customer. We normally recommend around 20 work days—1 calendar month, per iteration as a rule of thumb—but you could certainly iterate earlier. One- or two-week iterations are not unheard of. If you aren't sure about what a customer means on Day 2, call them. No sense waiting around, guessing about what you should be doing, right?

Q: What happens when my customer comes back with bad news, saying I'm way off on what I'm building. What do I do then?

A: Great question! When the worst happens and you find that you've deviated badly during an iteration, then you need to bring things back into line over the course of the next couple of iterations of development. How to do this is covered later on, but if you want to take a peek now, fast-forward to Chapter 4.

OK, I get it, iteration is important. But you said I should iterate every time I have working software, around every 30 calendar days, or 20 work days. What if I don't have anything that can run after a month? What can I show the customer?

20 working days is only a guideline. You might choose to have longer or shorter iterations for your project.

An iteration produces working software

With the old Big Bang approach to developing software, you probably wouldn't have any software ready until the end of the project, which is the worst time to realize that you've gone wrong!

With iteration, you check every step of the way that you're going in the right direction. That means making sure your software builds from almost day one (and more like hour one if you can manage it). You shouldn't have long periods where code doesn't work or compile, even if it's just small bits of functionality.

Then you show your customer those little pieces of functionality. It's not much, sometimes, but you can still get an OK from the customer.

Continuous building and testing is covered in Chapters 6 and 7.

A working build also makes a big difference to your team's productivity because you don't have to spend time fixing someone else's code before you can get on with your own tasks

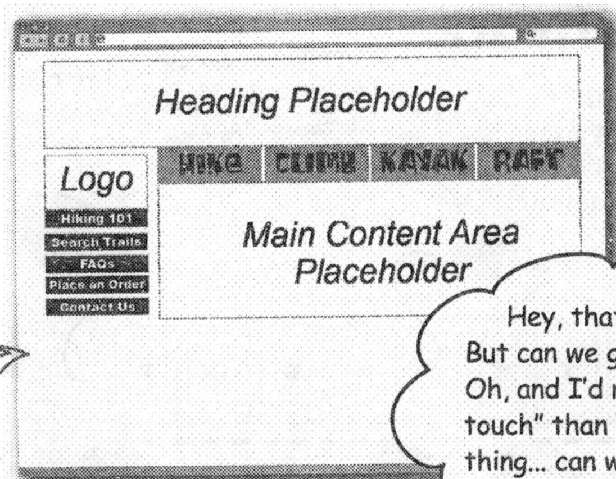

Tom got to see working software, and made some important comments you could address right away.

Hey, that's looking good. But can we go with rounded tabs? Oh, and I'd rather call it "Get in touch" than "Contact Us." Last thing... can we add an option for "Order Status?"

Here's a very simple portion of the Tom's Trails website. It only has the navigation, but it's still worth seeing what Tom thinks.

Instead of building the entire site at once, we broke the problem up into smaller chunks of functionality. Each chunk can then be demonstrated to the customer separately.

Each iteration is a mini-project

With iteration, you take the steps you'd follow to build the entire project, and put those steps into **each iteration**. In fact, each iteration is a mini-project, with its own requirements, design, coding, testing, etc., built right in. So you're not showing your customer junk... you're showing them well-developed bits of the final software.

Think about how most software is developed: You gather requirements (what your customer wants), build a design for the entire project, code for a long time, and then test everything. It looks a bit like this:

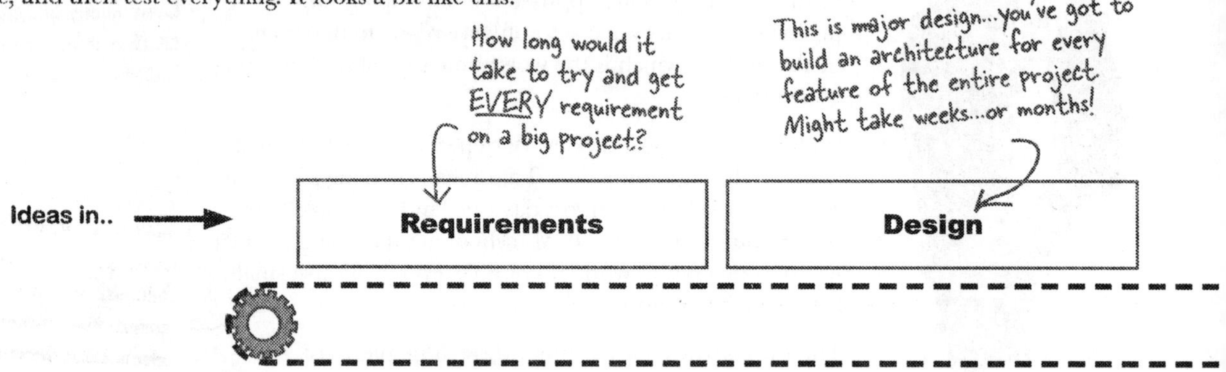

Each iteration is QUALITY software

But suppose you didn't look at iteration as just a way to write big software. Think of iteration as little cycles, where you're gathering requirements, designing, writing code, and testing. Each cycle produces working, quality software:

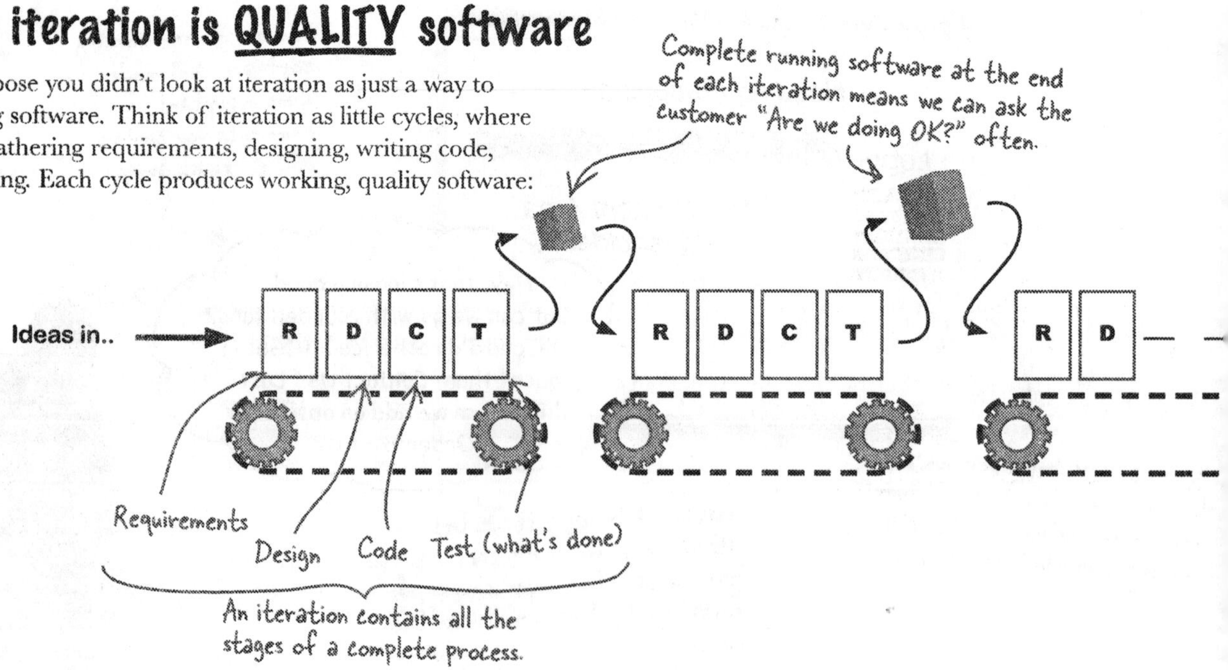

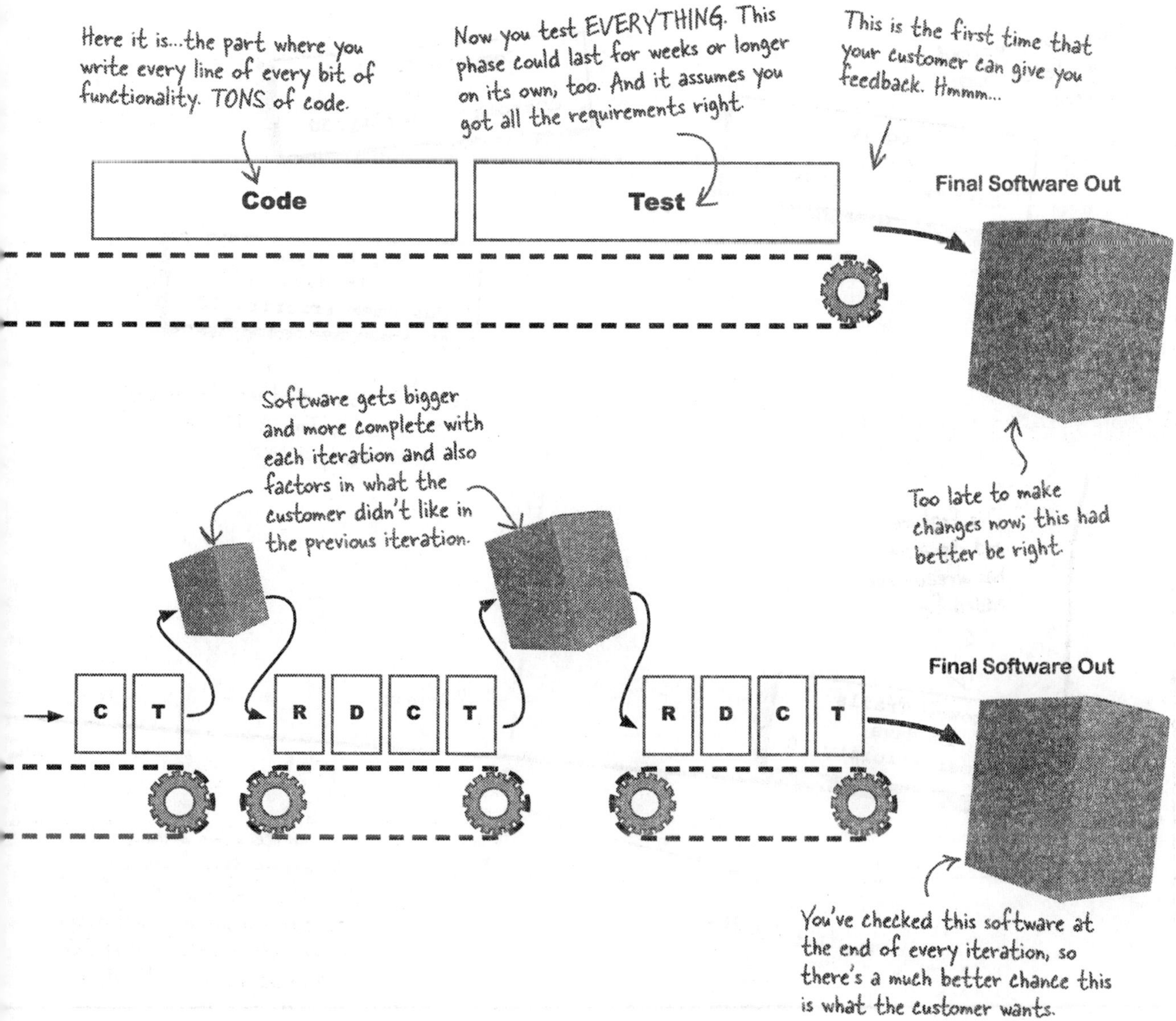
Here it is...the part where you write every line of every bit of functionality. TONS of code.
Now you test EVERYTHING. This phase could last for weeks or longer on its own, too. And it assumes you got all the requirements right.
This is the first time that your customer can give you feedback. Hmmm...
Code
Test
Final Software Out
Too late to make changes now; this had better be right.
Software gets bigger and more complete with each iteration and also factors in what the customer didn't like in the previous iteration.
C
T
R
D
C
T
R
D
C
T
Final Software Out
You've checked this software at the end of every iteration, so there's a much better chance this is what the customer wants.

Exercise

It's time to bring iterations into play on Tom's Trails. Each of the features that Tom wants for Trails Online has had estimates added to specify how long it will take to actually develop. Then we figured out how important each is to Tom and then assigned a priority to each of them (10 being the highest priority, 50 being the lowest). Take each feature and position them along the project's timeline, adding an iteration when you think it might be useful.

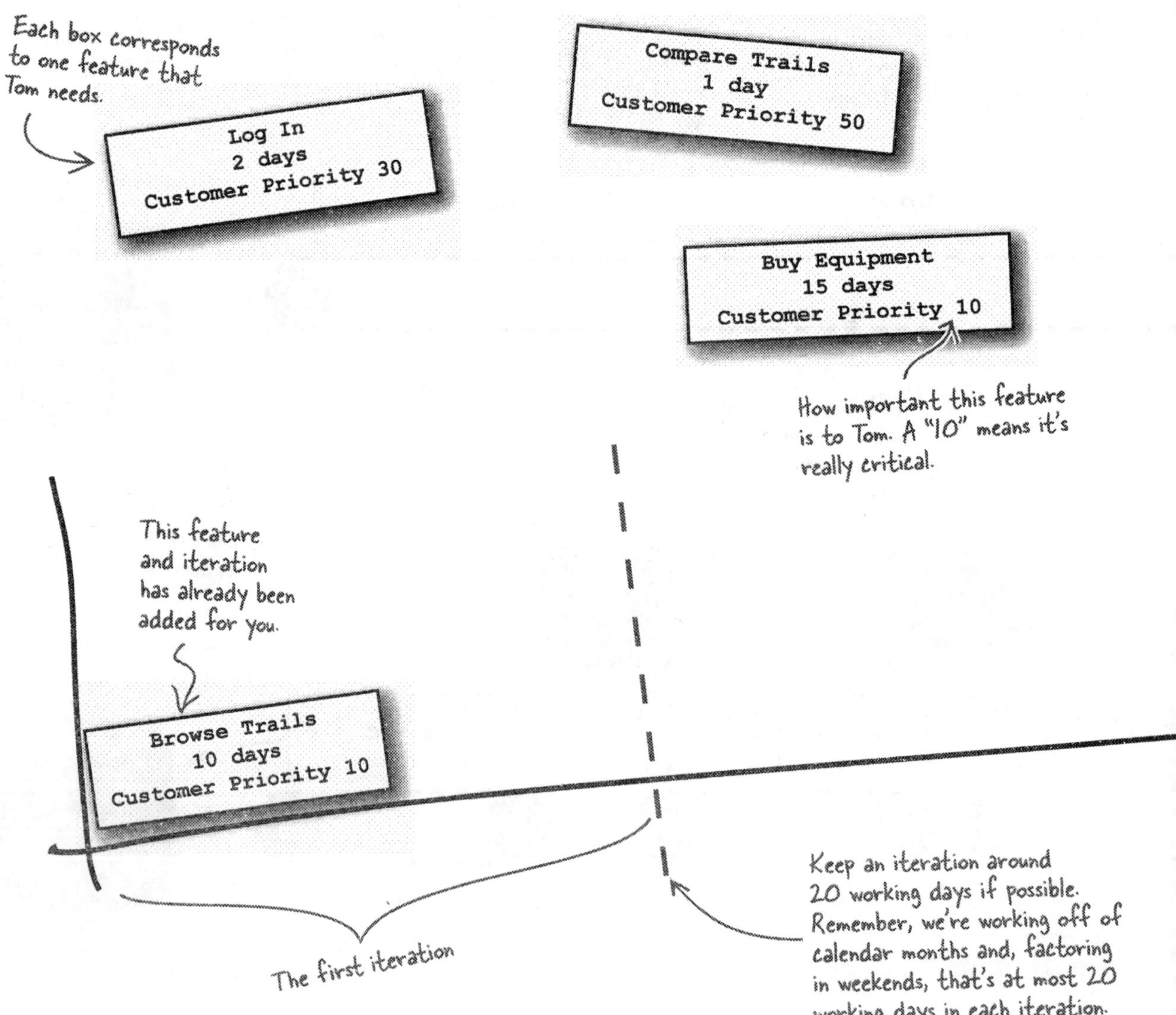

Oh, one other thing. Tom doesn't want customers to be able to buy equipment unless they've logged in to the web site. Be sure and take that into account in your plan.

Each feature has an estimate to show how long it should take to develop that feature (in actual working days).

```
List Equipment
7 days
Customer Priority 10
```

```
Add a Review
2 days
Customer Priority 20
```

```
View Reviews
3 days
Customer Priority 20
```

```
Search Trails
3 days
Customer Priority 20
```

10 is high priority, 50 is low. We'll look at why these priorities are in increments of 10 in Chapter 3.

Don't forget to add as many iterations as you think will be useful.

Exercise Solution

Your job was to build an iteration plan for Tom's Trails. You should have come up with something like we did, below:

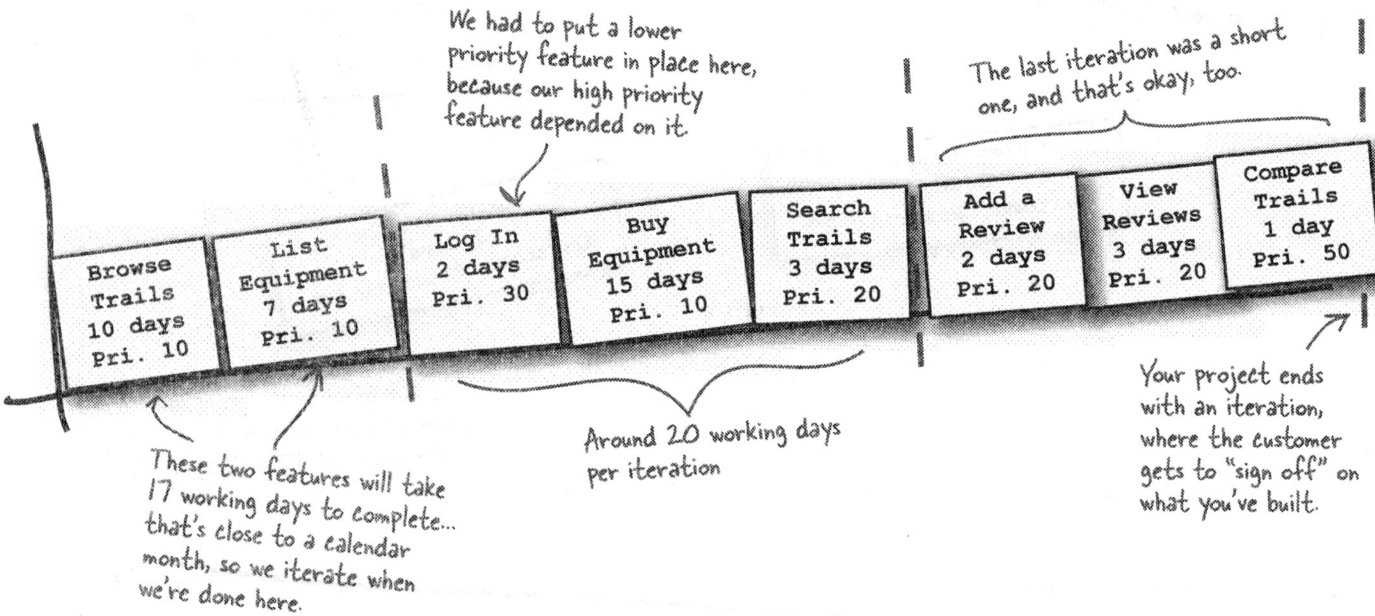

This is probably the only plan that serves the customer's priorities, keeps iterations at a manageable length, and gets the job done. If you came up with something different, take a hard look at why you made different choices than we did.

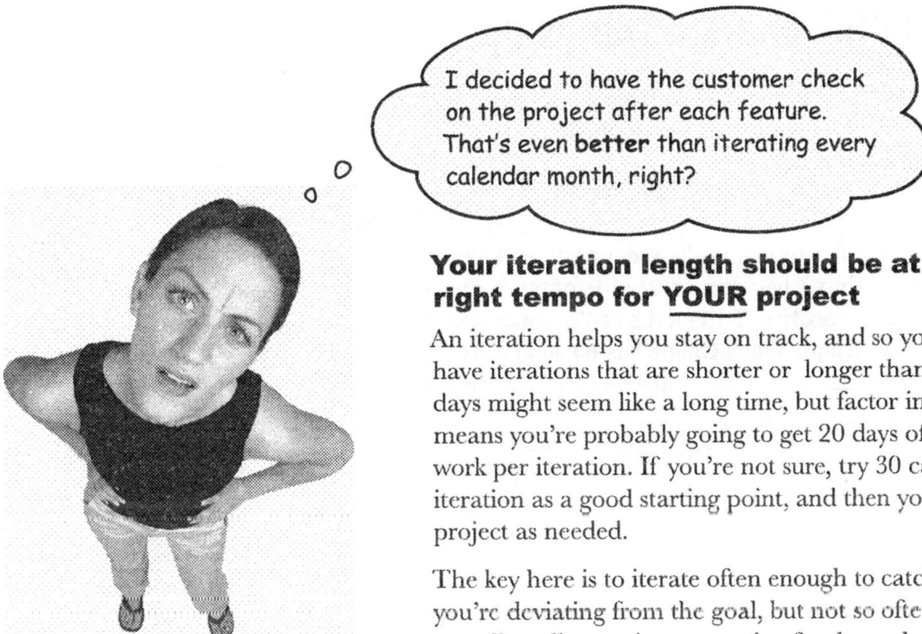

Your iteration length should be at the right tempo for YOUR project

An iteration helps you stay on track, and so you might decide to have iterations that are shorter or longer than 30 days. Thirty days might seem like a long time, but factor in weekends, and that means you're probably going to get 20 days of actual productive work per iteration. If you're not sure, try 30 calendar days per iteration as a good starting point, and then you can tweak for your project as needed.

The key here is to iterate often enough to catch youself when you're deviating from the goal, but not so often that you're spending all your time preparing for the end of an iteration. It takes time to show the customer what you've done and then make course corrections, so make sure to factor this work in when you are deciding how long your iterations should be.

there are no Dumb Questions

Q: The last feature scheduled for my iteration will push the time needed to way over a month. What should I do?

A: Consider shifting that feature into the next iteration. Your features can be shuffled around within the boundaries of a 20-day iteration until you are confident that you can successfully build an iteration within the time allocated. Going longer runs the risk of getting off course.

Q: Ordering things by customer priority is all fine and good, but what happens when I have features that need to be completed before other features?

A: When a feature is dependent on another feature, try to group those features together, and make sure they are placed within the same iteration. You can do this even if it means doing a lower-priority feature before a high-priority one, if it makes the high-priority feature possible.

This occurred in the previous exercise where the "Log In" feature was actually a low customer priority, but needed to be in place before the "Buy Equipment" feature could be implemented.

Q: If I add more people to the project, couldn't I do more in each of my iterations?

A: Yes, but be very careful. Adding another person to a project doesn't halve the time it takes to complete a feature. We'll talk more about how to factor in the overhead of multiple people in Chapter 2, when we talk about velocity.

Q: What happens when a change occurs and my plan needs to change?

A: Change is unfortunately a constant in software development, and any process needs to handle it. Luckily, an iterative process has change baked right in...turn the page and see what we mean.

The customer WILL change things up

Tom signed off on your plan, and Iteraton 1 has been completed. You're now well into your second iteration of development and things are going great. Then Tom calls...

Remember, if your software doesn't do what the customer wants, you're not going to go very far in software development.

It's up to you to make adjustments

Tom's new idea means three new features, all high-priority. And we don't even know how long they'll take, either. But you've got to figure out a way to work these into your projects.

```
Join Mailing List
Customer Priority 20
```

```
Post to Mailing List
Customer Priority 20
```

```
Organize a Trekking Google Group
Customer Priority 20
```

Here are three new features. Tom's given them all a priority of "20", also. Pretty important.

But there are some BIG problems...

You're already a long way into development...

... and you've still got other features to build...

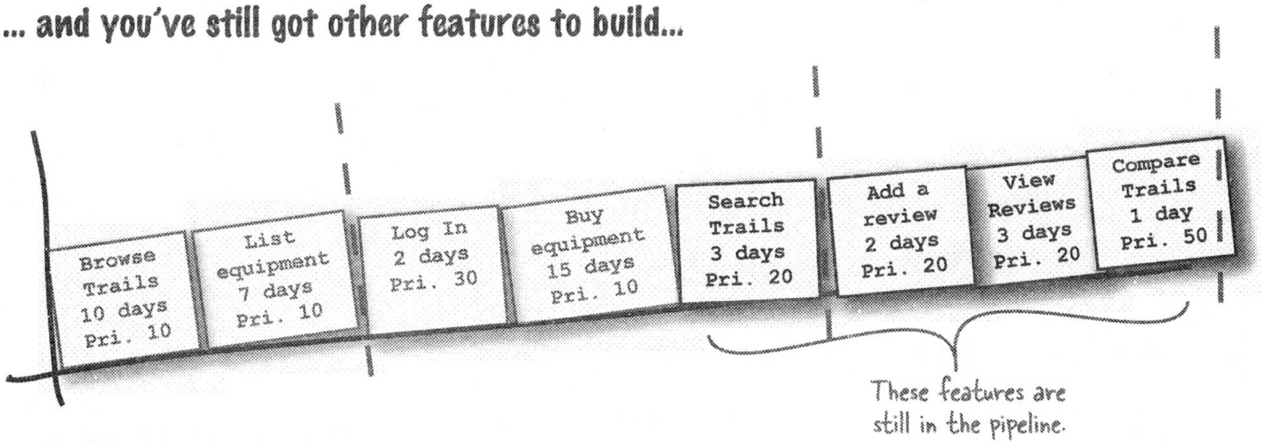

... and the deadline hasn't changed.

Iteration handles change automatically (well, sort of)

Your iteration plan is already structured around short cycles, and is built to handle lots of individual features. Here's what you need to do:

1. **Estimate the new features**
   First, you need to estimate how long each of the new features is going to take. We'll talk a lot more about estimation in a few chapters, but for now, let's say we came up with these estimates for the three new features:

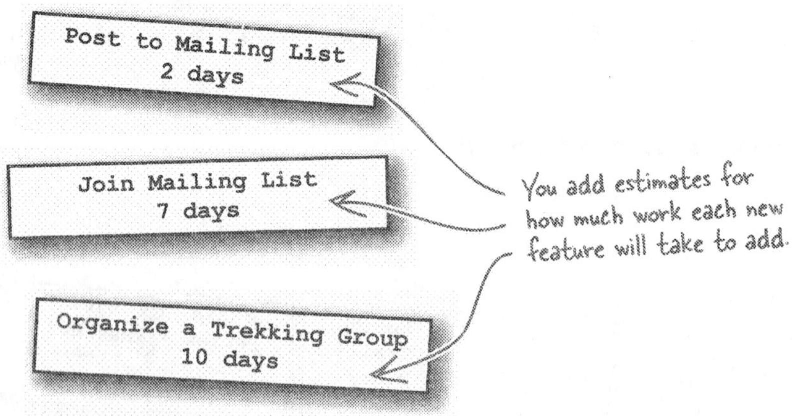

2. **Have your customer prioritize the new features**
   Tom already gave everything a priority of "20," right? But you really need him to look at the other features left to implement as well, and prioritize in relation to those.

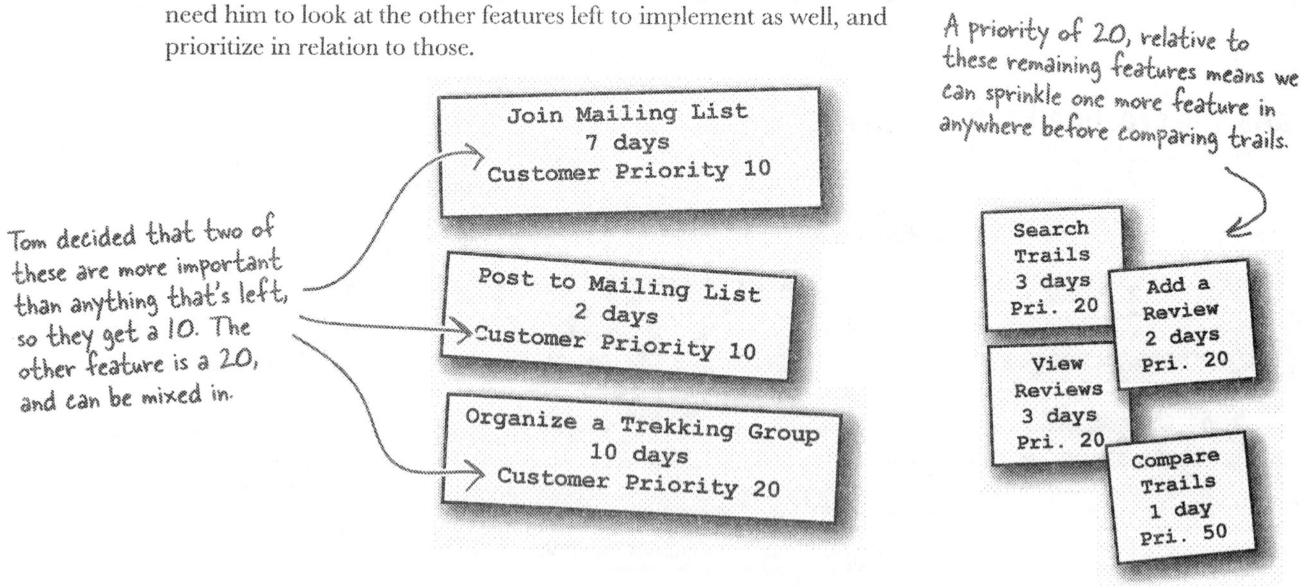

3 **Rework your iteration plan**

The ordering is set based on prioritization, and there aren't any dependencies. So now you change your plan, keeping your iteration length and the overall schedule in mind.

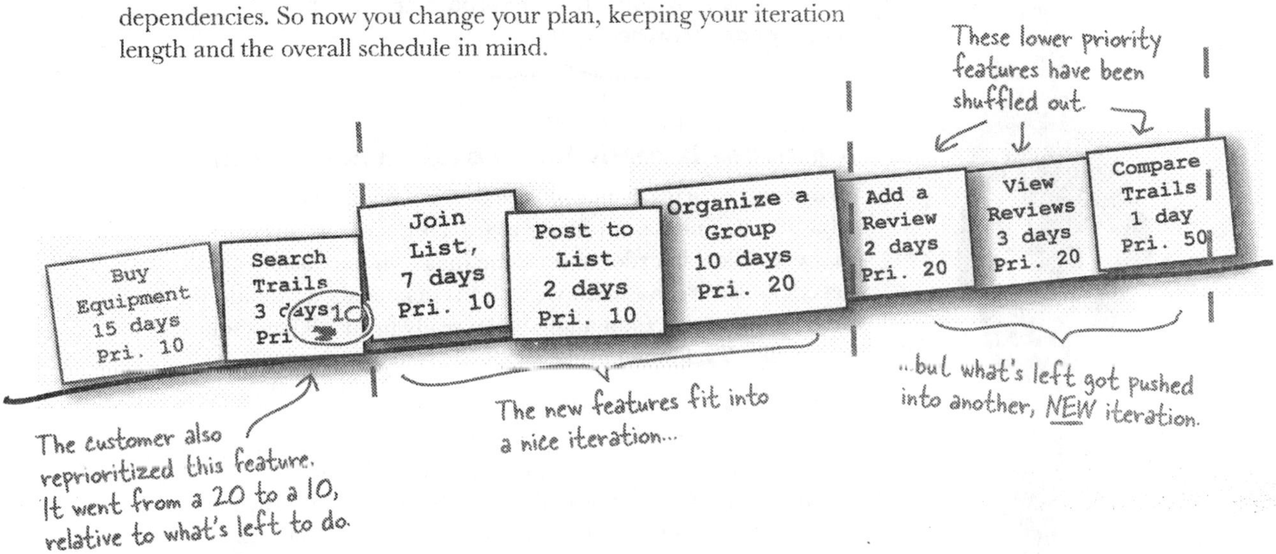

4 **Check your project deadline**

Remember the TrailMix Conference? You need to see if the work you've got left, including the new features, still can get done in time. Otherwise, Tom's got to make some hard choices.

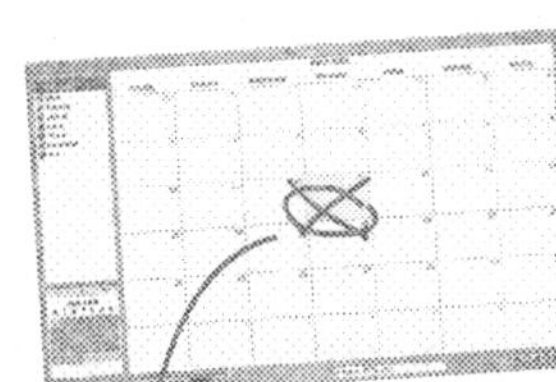

Work left to do

(Days of work left)

–

(Days left before deadline)

Days before TrailMix Con

= Can you do it?

If this number is negative, you're in good shape.

A process is really just a sequence of steps

Process, particularly in software development, has gotten a bit of a bad name. A process is just a sequence of steps that you follow in order to do something—in our case, develop software. So when we've been talking about iteration, prioritization, and estimation, we've really been talking about a software development process.

Rather than being any formal set of rules about what diagrams, documentation, or even testing you should be doing (although testing is something we'd definitely recommend!), a process is really just what to do, and when to do it. And it doesn't need an acronym...it just has to work.

We don't really care what process you use, as long as it has the components that ensure you get great, quality software at the end of your development cycle.

The right software development process for YOU is one that helps YOU develop and deliver great software, on time and on budget.

Iteration is more than a process

Regardless of the actual steps involved in the process you choose, iteration is a best practice. It's an approach that can be applied to ***any*** process, and it gives you a better chance of delivering what is needed, on time and on budget. Whatever process you end up using, iteration should be a major part.

Your software isn't complete until it's been RELEASED

You added the new features, and now you and your team have finished the project on time and on schedule. At every step of the way, you've been getting feedback from the customer at the end of each iteration, incorporating that feedback, and new features, into the next iteration. Now you can deliver your software, and ***then*** you get paid.

Tom isn't talking about your software running on your machine... he cares about the software running in the real world.

Iteration helped you reach an achievable goal that captured what your customer needed.

there are no Dumb Questions

Q: What happens when the customer comes up with new requirements and you can't fit all the extra work into your current iteration?

A: This is when customer priority comes into play. Your customer needs to make a call as to what really needs to be done for this iteration of development. The work that cannot be done then needs to be postponed until the next iteration. We'll talk a lot more about iteration in the next several chapters.

Q: What if you don't *have* a next iteration? What if you're already on the last iteration, and then a top priority feature comes in from the customer?

A: If a crucial feature comes in late to your project and you can't fit it into the last iteration, then the first thing to do is explain to the customer why the feature won't fit. Be honest and show them your iteration plan and explain why, with the resources you have, the work threatens your ability to deliver what they need by the due date.

The best option, if your customer agrees to it, is to factor the new requirement into another iteration on the end of your project, extending the due date. You could also add more developers, or make everyone work longer hours, but be wary of trying to shoehorn the work in like this. Adding more developers or getting everyone to work longer hours will often blow your budget and rarely if ever results in the performance gains you might expect (see Chapter 3).

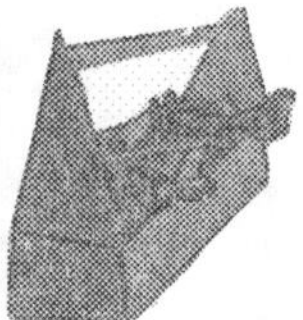

CHAPTER 1

Tools for your Software Development Toolbox

Software Development is all about developing and delivering great software. In this chapter, you learned about several techniques to keep you on track. For a complete list of tools in the book, see Appendix ii.

Development Techniques

Iteration helps you stay on course

Plan out and balance your iterations when (not if) change occurs

Every iteration results in working software and gathers feedback from your customer every step of the way

Here are some of the key techniques you learned in this chapter...

...and some of the principles behind those techniques.

Development Principles

Deliver software that's needed

Deliver software on time

Deliver software on budget

BULLET POINTS

- The **feedback** that comes out of each **iteration** is the best tool for ensuring that your software meets the needs of your customers.
- An iteration is a complete project in **miniature**.
- Successful software is not developed in a vacuum. It needs **constant feedback** from your customer using iterations.
- Good software development delivers great software, **on time** and **on budget**.
- It's always better to deliver **some** of the features **working perfectly** than all of the features that don't work properly.
- Good developers develop software; **great developers** ship software!

Software Development Cross

Let's put what you've learned to use and stretch out your left brain a bit. All of the words below are somewhere in this chapter. Good luck!

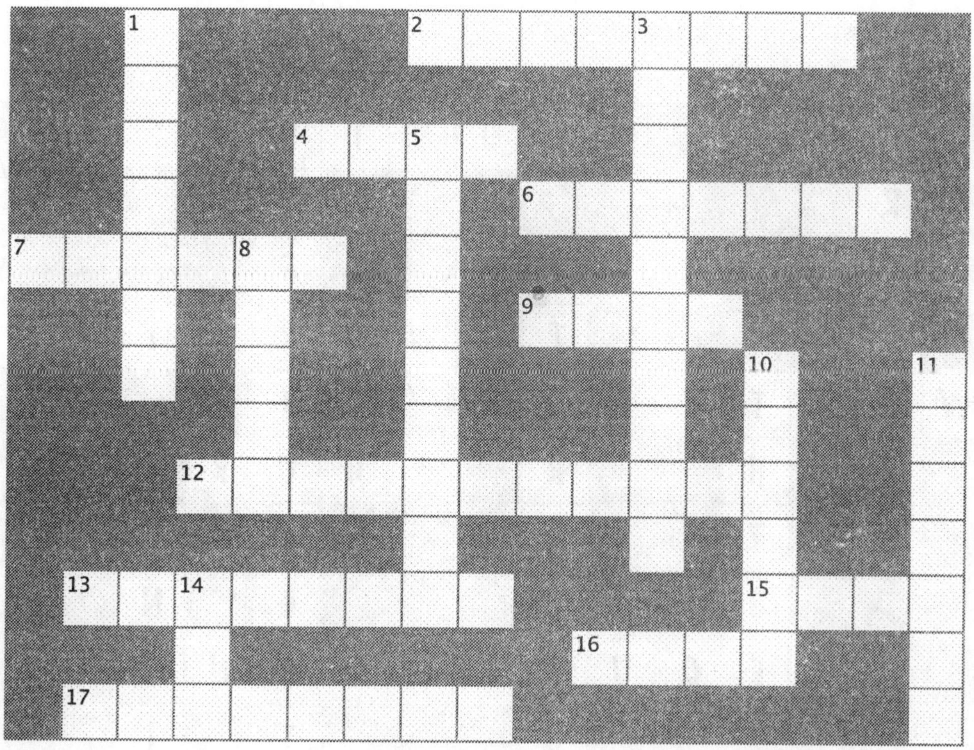

Across

2. I'm the person or company who ultimately decides if your software is worth paying for.
4. Good Developers develop, great developers ....
6. An iteration produces software that is ....
7. Aim for .... working days per iteration.
9. The number of development stages that are executed within an iteration.
12. I am one thing that your software needs to do.
13. The date that you need to deliver your final software on.
15. Iteration is .... than a process.
16. The single most important output from your development process.
17. Software isn't complete until it has been ....

Down

1. A .... is really just a sequence of steps.
3. When a project fails because it costs too much, it is ....
5. I contain every step of the software development process in micro and I result in runnable software.
8. The minimum number of iterations in a 3 month project.
10. Software that arrives when the customer needs it is ....
11. An iteration is a complete mini-.........
14. The types of software development projects where you should use iteration.

Software Development Cross Solution

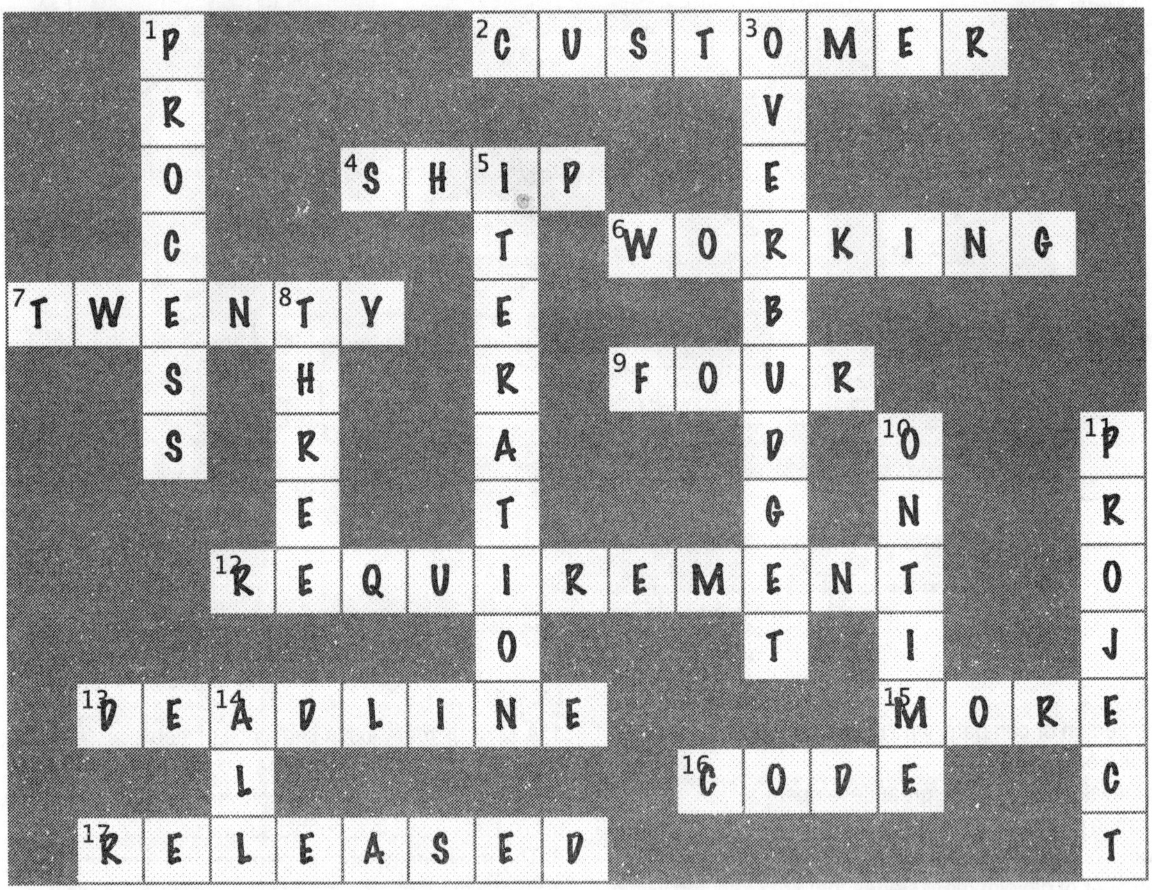

2 gathering requirements

Knowing what the customer wants

You can't always get what you want...but the customer should!

Great software development delivers **what the customer wants**. This chapter is all about **talking to the customer** to figure out what their **requirements** are for your software. You'll learn how **user stories, brainstorming**, and the **estimation game** help you get inside your customer's head. That way, by the time you finish your project, you'll be confident you've built what your customer wants...and not just a poor imitation.

Orion's Orbits is modernizing

Orion's Orbits provides quality space shuttle services to discerning clients, but their reservation system is a little behind the times, and they're ready to take the leap into the 21st century. With the next solar eclipse just four weeks away, they've laid out some serious cash to make sure their big project is done right, and finished on time.

Orion's doesn't have an experienced team of programmers on staff, though, so they've hired you and your team of software experts to handle developing their reservation system. It's up to you to get it right and deliver on time.

BRAIN POWER

How close do you think your final software will be to what the CEO of Orion Orbits wants?

Sharpen your pencil

Your job is to analyze the Orion's CEO's statement, and build some initial requirements. A requirement is a single thing that the software has to do. Write down the things you think you need to build for Orion's Orbits on the cards below.

...ne to ... started.

Title: Show current deals

Description: The web site will show current deals to Orion's Orbits users.

Title:

Description:

Title:

Description:

Title:

Description:

Title:

Description:

Title:

Description:

Remember, each requirement should be a single thing the system has to do.

If you've got index cards, they're perfect for writing requirements down.

Sharpen your pencil Solution

Let's start by breaking out the requirements from what the Orion's Orbits CEO is asking for. Take his loose ideas and turn them into snippets, with each snippet capturing one thing that you think the software will need to do...

Title: Show current deals
Description: The web site will show current deals to Orion's Orbits users.

Title: Book a shuttle
Description: An Orion's Orbits user will be able to book a shuttle.

Each card captures one thing that the software will need to provide.

Title: Book package
Description: An Orion's Orbits user will be able to book a special package with extras online.

Title: Pay online
Description: An Orion's Orbits user will be able to pay for their bookings online

Title: Arrange travel
Description: An Orion's Orbits user will be able to arrange travel to and from the spaceport.

Title: Book a hotel
Description: An Orion's Orbits user will be able to book a hotel.

there are no Dumb Questions

Q: Should we be using a specific format for writing these down?

A: No. Right now you're just grabbing and sorting out the ideas that your customer has and trying to get those ideas into some sort of manageable order.

Q: Aren't these requirements just user stories?

A: You're not far off, but at the moment they are just ideas. In just a few more pages we'll be developing them further into full-fledged user stories. At the moment it's just useful to write these ideas down somewhere.

Q: These descriptions all seem really blurry right now. Don't we need a bit more information before we can call them requirements?

A: Absolutely. There are lots of gaps in understanding in these descriptions. To fill in those gaps, we need to go back and talk to the customer some more...

'alk to your customer to get MORE information

'here are always gaps in your understanding of what your software is supposed to do, specially early in your project. Each time you have more questions, or start to make ssumptions, you need to go back and **talk with the customer** to get answers to our questions.

Iere are a few questions you might have after your first meeting with the CEO:

1. How many different types of shuttles does the software have to support?
2. Should the software print out receipts or monthly reports (and what should be on the reports)?
3. Should the software allow reservations to be canceled or changed?
4. Does the software have an administrator interface for adding new types of shuttles, and/or new packages and deals?
5. Are there any other systems that your software is going to have to talk to, like credit card authorization systems or Air/Space Traffic Control?
6. ....
....

Can you come up with another question you might want to ask the CEO?

Try to gather additional requirements.

Talking to the customer doesn't just give you a chance to get more details about *existing* requirements. You also want to find out about **additional requirements** the customer didn't think to tell you about earlier. There's nothing worse than finishing a project and the customer saying they forgot some important detail.

So how do you get the customer to think of everything you need to know, ***before*** you start building their software?

Bluesky with your customer

When you iterate with the customer on their requirements, **THINK BIG**. Brainstorm with other people; two heads are better than one, and ten heads are better than two, as long as everyone feels they can contribute without criticism. Don't rule out any ideas in the beginning—just capture *everything*. It's OK if you come up with some wild ideas, as long as you're all still focusing on the core needs that the software is trying to meet. This is called ***blueskying*** for requirements.

We call this blue skying because th sky's the limit.

The developer

The customer's team

You can include the users themselves.

Your development team

Never forget to include the customer in these sessions.

Watch it!

Avoid office politics.

Nothing will stifle creative bluesky thinking like a boss that won't let people speak up. Try as much as possible to leave job descriptions and other baggage at the door when blueskying requirements. Everyone should get an equal say to ensure you get the most out of each brainstorming session.

Sharpen your pencil

Take four of the ideas from the bluesky brainstorm and create a new card for each potential requirement. Also, see if you can come up with two additional requirements of your own.

We can refer to each requirement easily by using its title.

Title: Pay with Visa/MC/PayPal

Description: Users will be able to pay for their bookings by credit card.

Title: ....

Description: ....

Title: ....

Description: ....

Title: ....

Description: ....

Make these two your own.

Title: ....

Description: ....

Title: ....

Description: ....

→ Answers on page 38.

Sometimes your bluesky session looks like this...

Sometimes, no matter how hard you try, your bluesky sessions can be as muffled as a foggy day in winter. Often the people that know what the software should really do are just not used to coming out of their shell in a brainstorming environment, and you end up with a long, silent afternoon.

The zen of good requirements

The key to capturing good requirements is to get as many of the stakeholders involved as possible. If getting everyone in the same room is just not working, have people brainstorm individually and then come together and put all their ideas on the board and brainstorm a bit more. Go away and think about what happened and come back together for a second meeting.

There are LOTS of ways to gather good requirements. If one approach doesn't work, simply TRY ANOTHER.

Find out what people REALLY do

Everything (that's ethical and legal) is pretty much fair game when you're trying to get into your customer's head to understand their requirements. Two particularly useful techniques that help you understand the customer are **role playing** and **observation**.

Role playing

If your customer is finding it hard to visualize how they need their software to work, act it out. You pretend to be the software and your customer attempts to instruct you in what they would like you to do. Then write down each thing the software needs to do on one of your requirement cards.

Observation

Sometimes the best way to understand how people will work with your software is to watch them, and figure out where your software will fit in. Nothing beats firsthand evidence, and observation can really help to bring out constraints and details that might have been missed in bluesky brainstorming or even in role playing. Also, try to observe the same interactions more than once with multiple observers so you don't just gain one person's impression of an event.

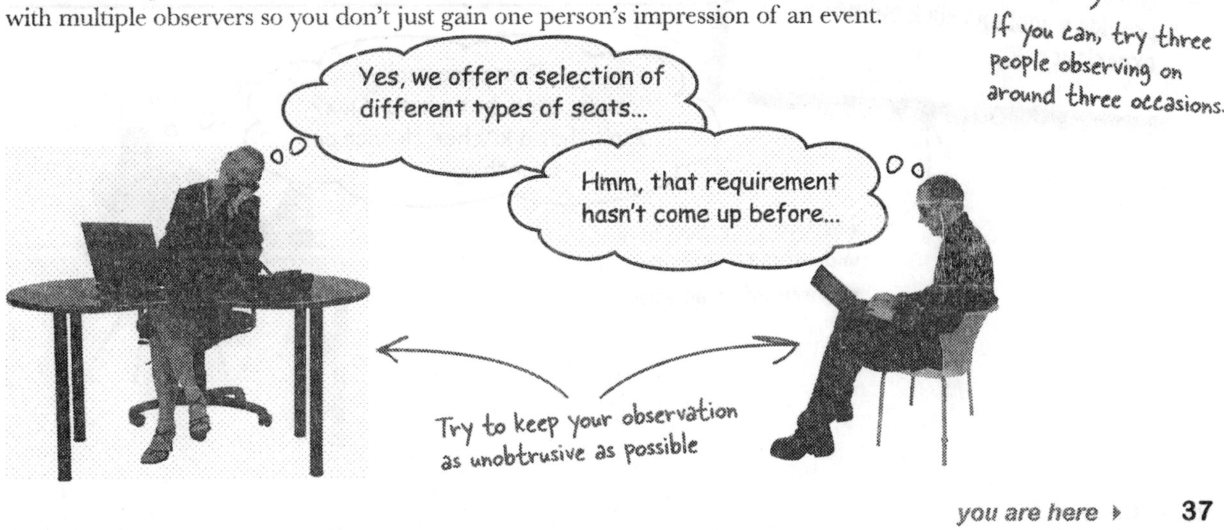

Our Sharpen your pencil Solution

Your job was to take each of the ideas from the bluesky session on page 35 and create a new card for each potential requirement.

You should also role play and observe.

A nonfunctional constraint, but it is still captured as a user story

Title: Support 3000 concurrent users
Description: The traffic for Orion's Orbits is expected to reach 3000 users, all using the site at the same time.

Title: Pay with Visa/MC/PayPal
Description: Users will be able to pay for their bookings by credit card or PayPal.

Title: Review flight
Description: A user will be able to leave a review for a shuttle flight they have been on.

We've added to our cards from page 32 after the brainstorming with the customer.

Title: Order Flight DVD
Description: A user will be able to order a DVD of a flight they have been on.

Title: Order in-flight meals
Description: A user will be able to specify the meals and drinks they want during a flight.

Title: Book a shuttle
Description: A user will be able to book a shuttle specifying the date and time of the flight.

These were the requirements we came up with; yours could have been different.

Title: Choose seating
Description: A user will be able to choose aisle or window seating.

Title: Use Ajax for the UI
Description: The user interface will use Ajax technologies to provide a cool and slick online experience.

And we've added more detail where it was uncovered through brainstorming, role playing, or observation.

These are really looking good, but what's Ajax? Isn't that a kitchen cleaner or something?

The boss isn't sure he understands what this requirement is all about.

Your requirements must be CUSTOMER-oriented

A great requirement is actually written **from your customer's perspective** describing what the software is going to do **for the customer**. Any requirements that your customer doesn't understand are an immediate red flag, since they're not things that the customer could have possibly asked for.

A requirement should be written in the customer's language and read like a **user story**: a story about how their users interact with the software you're building. When deciding if you have good requirements or not, judge each one against the following criteria:

User stories SHOULD...

- ☐ ... describe **one thing** that the software needs to do for the customer.
- ☐ ... be written using language that **the customer understands**.
- ☐ ... be **written by the customer**.
- ☐ ... be **short**. Aim for no more than three sentences.

User stories SHOULD NOT...

- ☐ ... be a long essay.
- ☐ ... use technical terms that are unfamiliar to the customer.
- ☐ ... mention specific technologies.

Think "by the customer, for the customer"

This means the customer drives each one, no matter who scribbles on a notecard.

You should be able to check each box for each of your user stories.

If a user story is long, you should try and break it up into multiple smaller user stories (see page 54 for tips).

This card is not a user story at all; it's really a design decision. Save it for later, when you start implementing the software.

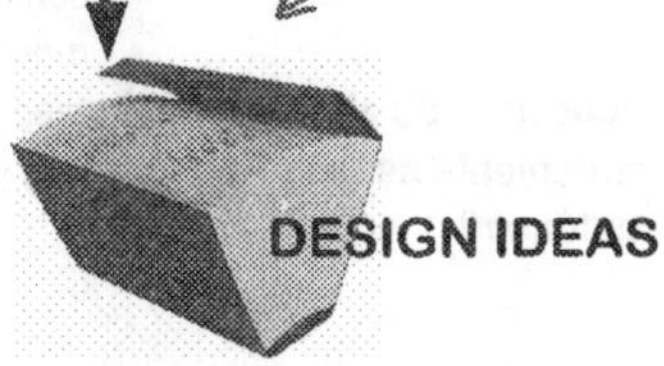

A user story is written from the CUSTOMER'S PERSPECTIVE. Both you AND your customer should understand what a user story means.

Great, so now you've created more user stories, and gotten a bunch more questions. What do you do with all these things you're still unclear about?

Ask the customer (yes, again).

The great thing about user stories is that it's easy for both you and the customer to read them and figure out what might be missing.

When you're writing the stories with the customer, you'll often find that they say things like "Oh, we also do this...", or "Actually, we do that a bit differently..." Those are great opportunities to refine your requirements, and make them more accurate.

If you find that you are unclear about **anything**, then it's time to have another discussion with your customer. Go back and ask them another set of questions. You're only ready to move on to the next stage when you have ***no more questions*** and your customer is also happy that all the user stories capture **everything** they need the software to do—for now.

there are no Dumb Questions

Q: What's the "Title" field on my user stories for? Doesn't my description field have all the information I need?

A: The title field is just a handy way to refer to a user story. It also gives everyone on the team the *same* handy way to refer to a story, so you don't have one developer talking about "Pay by PayPal," another saying, "Pay with credit card," and find out they mean the same thing later on (after they've both done needless work).

Q: Won't adding technical terms and some of my ideas on possible technologies to my user stories make them more useful to me and my team?

A: No, avoid tech terms or technologies at this point. Keep things in the language of the customer, and just describe what the software needs to do. Remember, the user stories are written from the customer's perspective. The customer has to tell you whether you've gotten the story right, so a bunch of tech terms will just confuse them (and possibly obscure whether your requirements are accurate or not).

If you do find that there are some possible technical decisions that you can start to add when writing your user stories, note those ideas down on another set of cards (cross referencing by title). When you get to coding, you can bring those ideas back up to help you at that point, when it's more appropriate.

Q: And I'm supposed to do all this refining of the requirements as user stories with the customer?

A: Yes, absolutely. After all, you're only ready for the next step when both you **and** the customer finally decide that you completely understand the software requirements. You can't make that decision on your own, so keeping your customer in the loop is essential.

Q: This seems like a lot of requirements work up front at the beginning of the project. What about when things change?

A: The work you've done so far is just your first attempt at gathering requirements at the beginning of your prject. You'll continue to refine and capture new requirements throughout your project, feeding those requirements where necessary into your project's iterations.

Develop your requirements with customer feedback

The steps we've followed so far have been all about coming to grips with the customer's ideas and refining those ideas into user stories. You execute these steps, in one form or another, at the beginning of each iteration to make sure that you always have the right set of features going into the next iteration. Let's see how that process currently looks...

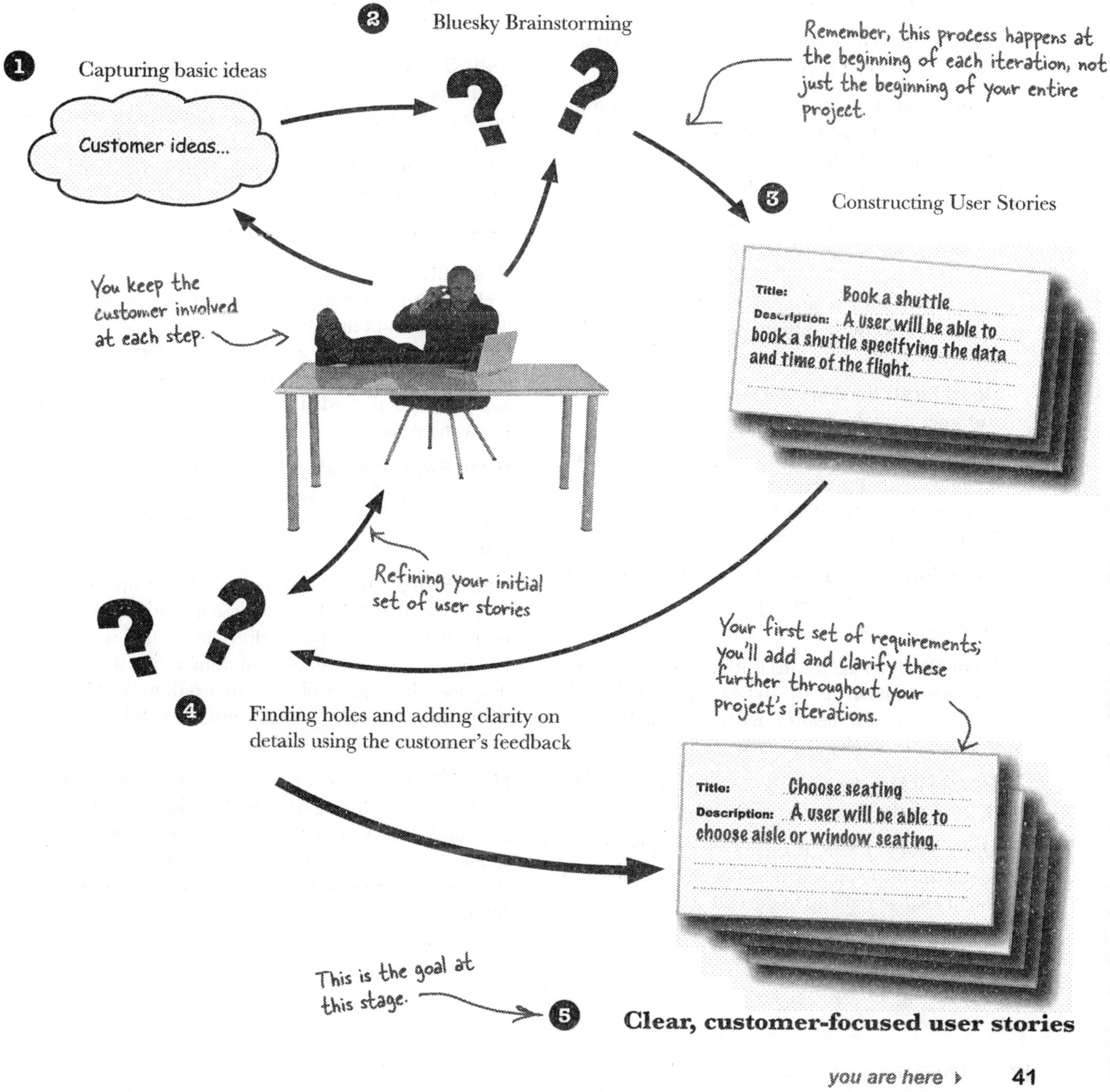

User Story Exposed

This week's interview:
The many faces of a User Story

Head First: Hello there, User Story.

User Story: Hi! Sorry it's taken so long to get an interview, I'm a bit busy at the moment...

Head First: I can imagine, what with you and your friends capturing and updating the requirements for the software at the beginning of each iteration, you must have your hands pretty full.

User Story: Actually, I'm a lot busier than that. I not only describe the requirements, but I'm also the main technique for bridging the gap between what a customer wants in his head and what he receives in delivered software. I pretty much drive everything from here on in.

Head First: But don't you just record what the customer wants?

User Story: Man, I really wish that were the case. As it turns out, I'm pretty much at the heart of an entire project. Every bit of software a team develops has to implement a user story.

Head First: So that means you're the benchmark against which every piece of software that is developed is tested?

User Story: That means if it's not in a user story somewhere, it ain't in the software, period. As you can imagine, that means I'm kept busy all the way through the development cycle.

Head First: Okay, sure, but your job is essentially done after the requirements are set, right?

User Story: I wish. If there's anything I've learned, requirements never stay the same in the real world. I might change right up to the end of a project.

Head First: So how do you handle all this pressure and still keep it together?

User Story: Well, I focus on one single thing: describing what the software needs to do from the customer's perspective. I don't get distracted by the rest of the noise buzzing around the project, I just keep that one mantra in my head. Then everything else tends to fall into place.

Head First: Sounds like a big job, still.

User Story: Ah, it's not too bad. I'm not very sophisticated, you know? Just three lines or so of description and I'm done. The customers like me because I'm simple and in their language, and the developers like me because I'm just a neat description of what their software has to do. Everyone wins.

Head First: What about when things get a bit more formal, like with use cases, main and alternate flows, that sort of thing? You're not really used then, are you?

User Story: Heck, I can smarten myself up with some more details to be a use case if that's what you need, and lots of people do dress me up that way for their bosses. The important thing is that we all describe what a piece of software needs to do, no matter how we look. Use cases are more or less user stories in a tuxedo.

Head First: Well, you heard it here first folks. Next week we'll be catching up with Test to see how he guarantees that software does what a user story requires. Until then, take care and remember, always do only what your user story says, and not an ounce more!

User stories define the WHAT of your project... estimates define the WHEN

After your initial requirement-capture stage you will have a set of clear, customer-focused user stories that you and the customer believe capture **WHAT** it is you're trying to build, at least for the first iteration or so. But don't get too comfortable, because the customer will want to know **WHEN** all those stories will be built.

This is the part where the customer asks the big question: **How long will it all take?**

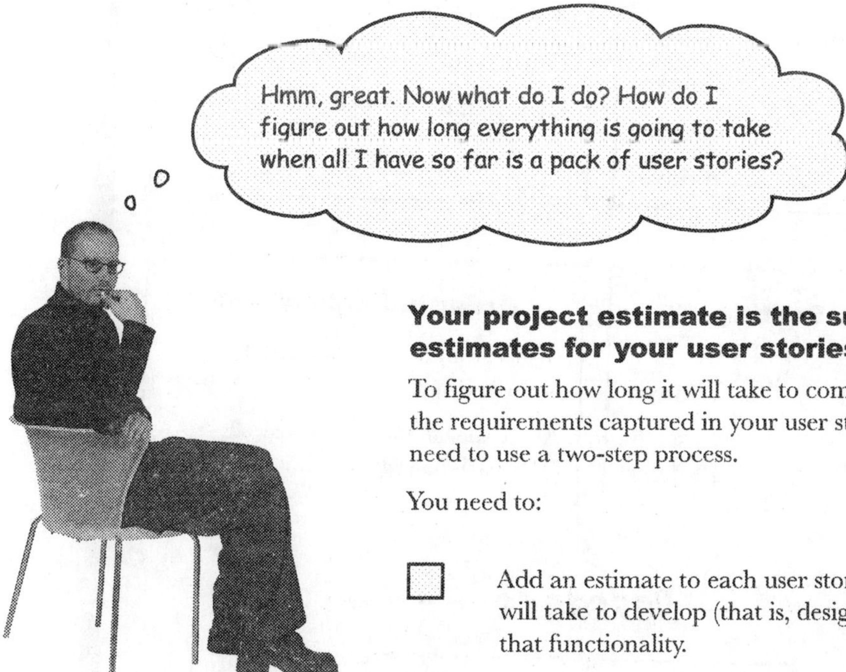

Your project estimate is the sum of the estimates for your user stories

To figure out how long it will take to complete all of the requirements captured in your user stories, you need to use a two-step process.

You need to:

If you can get this figured out...

- [ ] Add an estimate to each user story for how long you think it will take to develop (that is, design, code, test, and deliver) that functionality.
- [ ] Add up all the estimates to get a total estimate for how long your project will take to deliver the required software.

...then this will be a piece of cake.

Exercise

Welcome to the Orion's Orbits Development Diner. Below is the menu...your job is to choose your options for each dish, and come up with an estimate for that dish—ahem—user story. You'll also want to note down any assumptions you made in your calculations.

Entrées

Pay Credit Card or Paypal

- Visa .... **2 days**
- Mastercard .... **2 days**
- PayPal .... **2 days**
- American Express .... **5 days**
- Discover .... **4 days**

Order Flight DVD

- Stock titles with standard definition video .... **2 days**
- Provide custom titles .... **5 days**
- High Definition video .... **5 days**

Choose Seating

- Choose aisle or window seat .... **2 days**
- Choose actual seat on shuttle .... **10 days**

Order In-Flight Meals

- Select from list of three meals & three drinks .... **5 days**
- Allow special dietary needs (Vegetarian, Vegan) .... **2 days**

Desserts

Create Flight Review

- Create a review online .... **3 days**
- Submit a review by email ..... **5 days**

	Estimate for each user story in days	Assumptions?
Title: Pay with Visa/MC/PayPal **Description:** Users will be able to pay for their bookings by credit card or PayPal.		
Title: Order Flight DVD **Description:** A user will be able to order a DVD of a flight they have been on.		
Title: Choose seating **Description:** A user will be able to choose aisle or window seating.		
Title: Order in-flight meals **Description:** A user will be able to specify the meals and drinks they want during a flight.		
Title: Review flight **Description:** A user will be able to leave a review for a shuttle flight they have been on.		

Write your estimate for the user story here.

Jot down any assumptions you think you're making in your estimate.

Exercise Solution

What did you come up with? Rewrite your estimates here. Bob and Laura also did estimates...how did yours compare to theirs?

Put your estimates here.

Title	Your estimates	Bob's estimates	Laura's estimates
Pay with Visa/MC/PayPal		15	10
Order Flight DVD		20	2
Choose seating		12	2
Order in-flight meals		2	7
Review flight		3	3

Well, at least we seem to agree here...

Brain Power

It looks like everyone has a different idea for how long each user story is going to take. Which estimates do you think are **RIGHT?**

Cubicle conversation

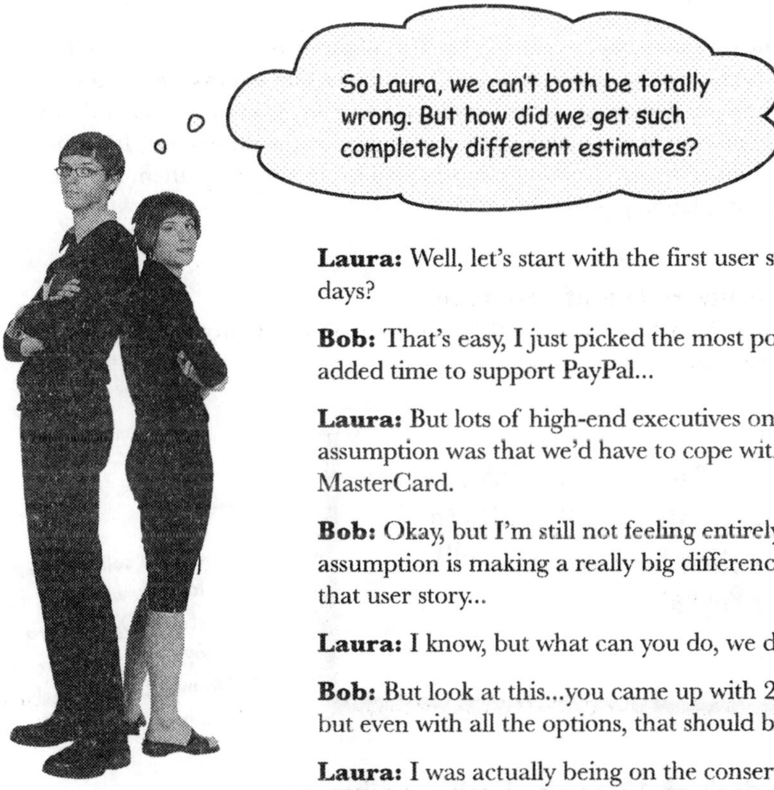

Laura: Well, let's start with the first user story. How did you come up with 10 days?

Bob: That's easy, I just picked the most popular credit cards I could think of, and added time to support PayPal...

Laura: But lots of high-end executives only use American Express, so my assumption was that we'd have to cope with that card, too, not just Visa and MasterCard.

Bob: Okay, but I'm still not feeling entirely happy with that. Just that one assumption is making a really big difference on how long it will take to develop that user story...

Laura: I know, but what can you do, we don't know what the customer expects...

Bob: But look at this...you came up with 20 days for "Ordering a Flight DVD," but even with all the options, that should be 14 days, max!

Laura: I was actually being on the conservative side. The problem is that creating a DVD is a completely new feature, something I haven't done before. I was factoring in overhead for researching how to create DVDs, installing software, and getting everything tested. Everything I thought I'd need to do to get that software written. So it came out a lot higher.

Bob: Wow, I hadn't even thought of those things. I just assumed that they'd been thought of and included. I wonder if the rest of the estimates included tasks like research and software installation?

Laura: In my experience, probably not. That's why I cover my back.

Bob: But then ***all*** of our estimates could be off...

Laura: Well, at least we agree on the "Create a Flight Review" story. That's something.

Bob: Yeah, but I even had assumptions I made there, and that still doesn't take into account some of that overhead you were talking about.

Laura: So all we have are a bunch of estimates we don't feel that confident about. How are we going to come up with a number for the project that we believe when we don't even know what everyone's assumptions are?

Getting rid of assumptions is the most important activity for coming up with estimates you believe in.

Playing planning poker

To come up with accurate estimates, you need to get rid of all those assumptions that put your estimates at risk of being wrong. You want a set of estimates that **everyone believes in** and are confident that they can deliver, or at the very least you want a set of estimates that let you know what assumptions everyone is making before you sign on the dotted line. It's time to grab everyone that's going to be involved in estimating your user stories, sit them around a table, and get ready to play "planning poker."

1 Place a user story in the middle of the table

This focuses everyone on a specific user story so they can get their heads around what their estimates and assumptions might be.

Title: Pay with Visa/MC/PayPal

Description: Users will be able to pay for their bookings by credit card or PayPal.

We want a solid estimate for how long it will take to develop this story. Don't forget that development should include designing, coding, testing, and delivering the user story.

2 Everyone is given a deck of 13 cards. Each card has an estimate written on one side.

You only need a small deck, just enough to give people several options:

All of these estimates are developer-days (f instance, two man-days split betwee two workers is sti two days).

This card means "It's already done."

Everyone has each of these cards.

Hmmm...any thoughts on what it means if someone plays one of these cards for their estimate?

Don't have enough info to estimate? You might consider using this card.

If any player uses this card, you need to take a break from estimating for a bit.

3 **Everyone picks an estimate for the user story and places the corresponding card face down on the table.**
You pick the card that you think is a reasonable estimate for the user story. Don't discuss that estimate with anyone else, though.

Make sure your estimate is for the whole user story, not just a part of it.

4 **Everyone then turns over their cards at exactly the same time.**
Each player at the table shows their hand, which gives their honest estimate for the user story.

5 **The dealer marks down the spread across each of the estimates.**
Whoever is running the game notes the spread across each of the estimates that are on the cards. Then you do a little analysis:

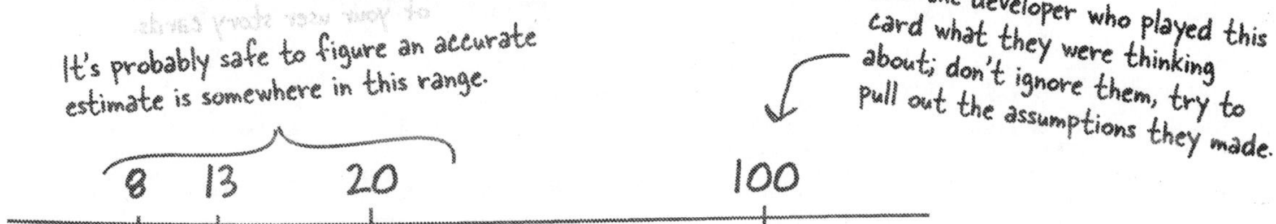

The larger the difference between the estimates, the less confident you are in the estimate, and the more assumptions you need to root out.

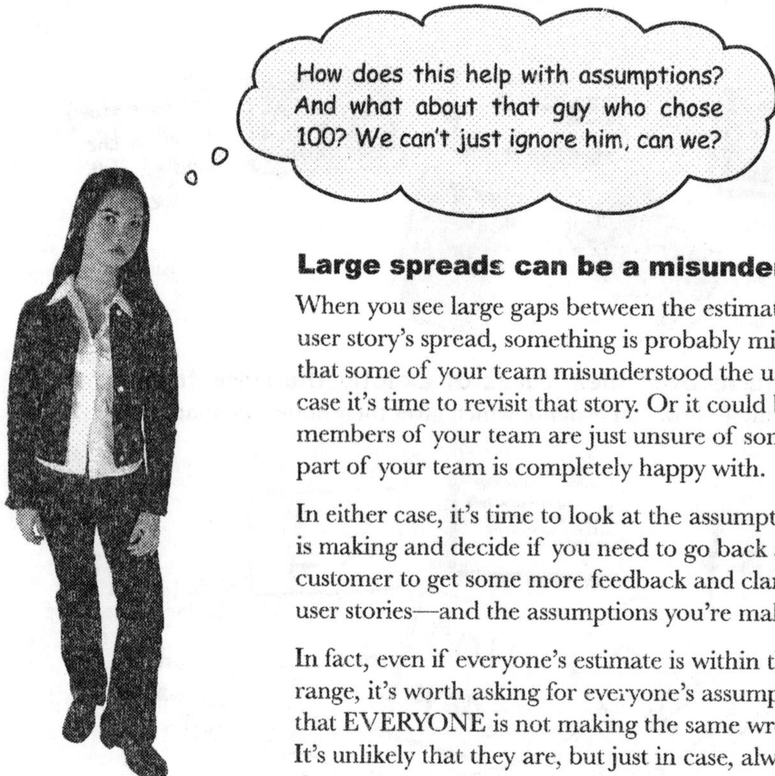

Large spreads can be a misunderstanding

When you see large gaps between the estimates on a particular user story's spread, something is probably missing. It could be that some of your team misunderstood the user story, in which case it's time to revisit that story. Or it could be that some members of your team are just unsure of something that another part of your team is completely happy with.

In either case, it's time to look at the assumptions that your team is making and decide if you need to go back and speak to the customer to get some more feedback and clarification on your user stories—and the assumptions you're making about them.

In fact, even if everyone's estimate is within the same narrow range, it's worth asking for everyone's assumptions to make sure that EVERYONE is not making the same wrong assumption. It's unlikely that they are, but just in case, always discuss and document your assumptions after every round of planning poker.

Try writing your assumptions on the back of your user story cards.

Put assumptions on trial for their lives

When it comes to requirements, ***no assumption is a good assumption***. So whenever planing poker turns up your team's assumptions, don't let that assumption into your project without first doing everything you can to ***beat it out*** of your project...

Put every assumption on trial

*You're aiming for as few assumptions as possible when making your estimates. When an assumption rears its head in planning poker, even if your entire team shares the assumption, expect that assumption to be wrong **until it is clarified by the customer**.*

As opposed to not knowing what you don't know...

At least you know what you don't know

No matter how hard you try, some assumptions really will survive clarification with the customer. That's OK. Sometimes the customer doesn't have a great answer to a particular assumption at the beginning of a project, and in those cases you need to live with the assumption. The important thing is that you know that there is an assumption being made, and you can write it down as a risk for that user story (like on the back of your user story card). This helps you keep an eye on and track your risks, knocking them out at a later stage in your project.

Depending on customer priority, you might even decide to delay the development of a user story that has a number of surviving assumptions until they can be clarified.

While you can't always get rid of all assumptions, the goal during estimation is to <u>eliminate</u> as many assumptions as possible by <u>clarifying</u> those assumptions with the customer. Any surviving assumptions then become <u>risks.</u>

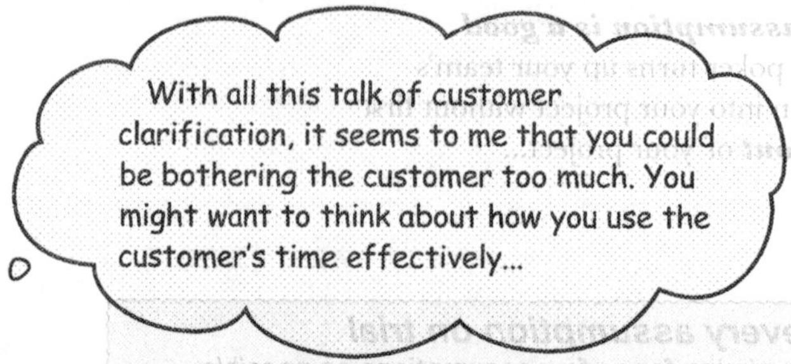

Value your customer's time.

Putting all your asssumptions on trial for their life and seeking clarification from the customer can become a lot of work. You can easily spend a lot, if not all, of your time with your customer. That might be OK with some customers, but what about the ones that are too busy to talk with you every 15 minutes?

In those cases you need to use your customer's time carefully. Even though you're trying to make sure you've gotten things right on their project, you don't want to come across as being not up to the job. So when you do spend time with your customer, make sure that time is organized, efficient, and well-spent.

Try gathering a collection of assumptions together and then clarifying those all at once with the customer. Rather than bothering the customer at the end of every round of planing poker, schedule an **assumption-busting session** where you take in the collected assumptions and try to blast as many of them away as possible.

Once you have your answers, head back for a final round of planning poker.

Once you've gotten a significant number of your assumptions beaten out in your assumption-busting session with the customer, it's time to head back and play a final round of planning poker so that you and your team can come up with estimates that factor in the new clarifications.

there are no Dumb Questions

Q: Why is there a gap between 40 and 100 days on the planning poker cards?

A: Well, the fact is that 40 is a pretty large estimate, so whether you feel that the estimate should be 41 or even 30 days is not really important at this point. 40 just says that you think there's a lot to do in this user story, and you're just on the boundary of not being able to estimate this user story at all...

Q: 100 days seems *really* long; that's around half a year in work time! Why have 100 days on the cards at all?

A: Absolutely, 100 days is a **very** long time. If someone turns up a 100-days card then there's something seriously misunderstood or wrong with the user story. If you find that it's the user story that's simply too long, then it's time to break that user story up into smaller, more easily estimatable stories.

Q: What about the question-mark card? What does that mean?

A: That you simply don't feel that you have enough information to estimate this user story. Either you've misunderstood something, or your assumptions are so big that you don't have any confidence that *any* estimate you place down on the table could be right.

Q: Some people are just bound to pick nutty numbers. What do I do about them?

A: Good question. First, look at the trends in that individual's estimates to see if they really are being "nutty," or whether they in fact tend to be right! However, some people really are inclined to just pick extremely high or very low numbers most of the time and get caught up in the game. However, every estimate, particularly ones that are out of whack with the rest of the player's estimates, should come under scrutiny after every round to highlight the assumptions that are driving those estimates.

After a few rounds where you start to realize that those wacky estimates are not really backed up by good assumptions, you can either think about removing those people from the table, or just having a quiet word with them about why they always insist on being off in left field.

Q: Should we be thinking about who implements a user story when coming up with our estimates?

A: No, every player estimates how long they think it will take for them to develop and deliver the software that implements the user story. At estimation time you can't be sure who is going to actually implement a particular user story, so you're trying to get a feel for the capability of anyone on your team to deliver that user story.

Of course, if one particular user story is perfect for one particular person's skills, then they are likely to estimate it quite low. But this low estimate is balanced by the rest of your team, who should each assume that they are individually going to implement that user story.

In the end, the goal is to come up with an estimate that states "We as a team are all confident that this is how long it will take any one of us to develop this user story."

Q: Each estimate is considering more than just implementation time though, right?

A: Yes. Each player should factor in how much time it will take them to develop and deliver the software including any other deliverables that they think might be needed. This could include documentation, testing, packaging, deployment—basically everything that needs to be done to develop and deliver the software that meets the user story.

If you're not sure what other deliverables might be needed, then that's an assumption, and might be a question for the customer.

Q: What if my team all agree on exactly the same estimate when the cards are turned over. Do I need to worry about assumptions?

A: Yes, for sure. Even if everyone agrees, it's possible that everyone is making the same wrong assumptions. A large spread of different estimates indicates that there is more work to be done and that your team is making different and possibly large assumptions in their estimates. A tiny spread says that your team might be making the same assumptions in error, so examining assumptions is critical regardless of the output from planning poker.

It's important to get any and all assumptions out in the open ***regardless*** of what the spread says, so that you can clarify those assumptions right up front and keep your confidence in your estimates as high as possible.

Don't make assumptions about your assumptions... talk about EVERYTHING.

A BIG user story estimate is a BAD user story estimate

Your user story is too big.

40 days is a long time, and lots can change. Remember, 40 days is ***2 months*** of work time.

Remember this from Chapter 1?

An ***entire iteration*** should ideally be around **1 calendar month** in duration. Take out weekends and holidays, and that's about 20 working days. If your estimate is 40 days for just *one* user story, then it won't even fit in one iteration of development unless you have two people working on it!

If you have to have long estimates like this, then you need to be talking as a team as often as possible. We'll get to that in a few pages.

As a rule of thumb, estimates that are longer than 15 days are *much less likely* to be accurate than estimates below 15 days.

In fact, some people believe that estimates longer than seven days should be double-checked.

When a user story's estimate breaks the 15-day rule you can either:

1. **Break your stories into smaller, more easily estimated stories**
   Apply the AND rule. Any user story that has an "and" in its title or description can probably be split into two or more smaller user stories.

2. **Talk to your customer...again.**
   Maybe there are some assumptions that are pushing your estimate out. If the customer could clarify things, those assumptions might go away, and cut down your estimates significantly.

Starting to sense a pattern?

Estimates greater than 15 days per user story allow too much room for error.

When an estimate is too long, apply the AND rule to break the user story into smaller pieces.

Exercise

The two user stories below resulted in estimates that broke the 15-day rule. Take the two user stories and apply the AND rule to them to break them into smaller, more accurately estimatable stories.

Title: Choose seating

Description: A user will choose aisle or window seating, be able to select the seat they want, and change that seat up to 24 hours before the flight.

Title: Order in-flight meals

Description: A user will choose which meal option they want, from a choice of three, and be able to indicate if they are vegetarian or vegan.

Title: ....

Description: ....

Title: ....

Description: ....

Title: ....

Description: ....

Title: ....

Description: ....

Title: ....

Description: ....

Title: ....

Description: ....

Exercise Solution

Your job was to take the longer user stories at the top of each column and turn them into smaller, easily estimatable user stories.

Title: Choose seating

Description: A user will choose aisle or window seating, be able to select the seat they want, and change that seat up to 24 hours before the flight.

Title: Choose aisle/window seat

Description: A user can choose either aisle or window seating.

Title: Choose specific seat

Description: A user can choose the actual seat that they want for a shuttle flight.

Title: Change seating

Description: A user can change their seat up to 24 hours before launch, provided other seat options are available.

Title: Order in-flight meals

Description: A user will choose which meal option they want, from a choice of three, and be able to indicate if they are vegetarian or vegan.

Title: Select from meal options

Description: A user can choose the meal they want from a set of three meal options.

Title: Specify vegetarian meal

Description: A user will be able to indicate that they are vegetarian when selecting their meal options.

Title: Specify vegan meal

Description: A user will be able to indicate that they are vegan when selecting their meal options.

The goal is convergence

After a solid round of planning poker, you should not only have estimates for each user story but be *confident* in those estimates. The goal now is to get rid of as many assumptions as possible, and to **converge** all of the points on each user story's spread of estimates.

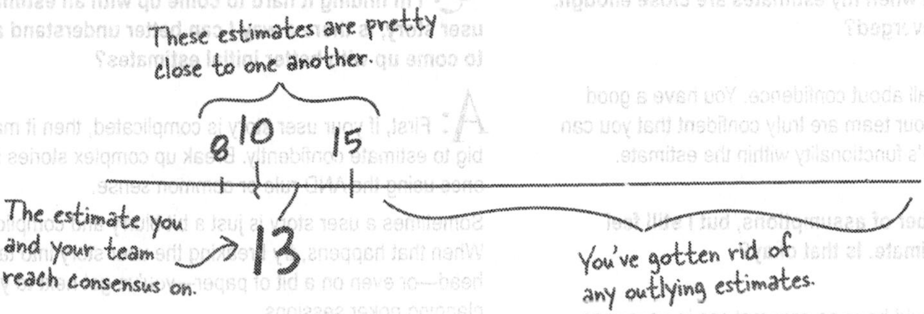

Run through this cycle of steps till you reach a consensus:

1. **Talk to the customer**
   First and foremost, get as much information and remove as many assumptions and misunderstandings as possible by talking to your customer.

2. **Play planning poker**
   Play planning poker with each of your user stories to uproot any hidden assumptions. You'll quickly learn how confident you are that you can estimate the work that needs to be done.

3. **Clarify your assumptions**
   Using the results of planning poker, you'll be able to see where your team may have misunderstood the user stories, and where additional clarification is needed.

   Head back to Step 1 if you find assumptions that only the customer can answer.

4. **Come to a consensus**
   Once everyone's estimates are close, agree on a figure for the user story's estimate.

   It can also be useful to note the low, converged, and high estimates to give you an idea of the best and worst case scenarios.

How close is "close enough"?

Deciding when your estimates are close enough for consensus is really up to you. When you feel **confident in an estimate**, and you're **comfortable with the assumptions** that have been made, then it's time to write that estimate down on your user story card and move on.

there are no Dumb Questions

Q: How can I tell when my estimates are close enough, and have really converged?

A: Estimates are all about confidence. You have a good estimate if you and your team are truly confident that you can deliver the user story's functionality within the estimate.

Q: I have a number of assumptions, but I still feel confident in my estimate. Is that okay?

A: Really, you should have no assumptions in your user stories or in you and your team's understanding of the customer's requirements.

Every assumption is an opportunity to hit unexpected problems as you develop your software. Worse than that, every assumption increases the chances that your software development work will be delayed and might not even deliver what was required.

Even if you're feeling relatively confident, knock out as many of those assumptions as you possibly can by speaking to your team and, most importantly, speaking to your customer.

With a ***zero-tolerance attitude to assumptions***, you'll be on a much more secure path to delivering your customer the software that's needed, on time and on budget. However, you will probably always have some assumptions that survive the estimation process. This is OK, as assumptions are then turned into risks that are noted and tracked, and at least you are aware of those risks.

Your estimates are your PROMISE to your customer about how long it will take you and your team to DELIVER.

Q: I'm finding it hard to come up with an estimate for my user story, is there a way I can better understand a user story to come up with better initial estimates?

A: First, if your user story is complicated, then it may be too big to estimate confidently. Break up complex stories into simpler ones using the AND rule or common sense.

Sometimes a user story is just a bit blurry and complicated. When that happens, try breaking the user story into tasks in your head—or even on a bit of paper—you've got next to you at your planning poker sessions.

Think about the jobs that will be needed to be done to build that piece of software. Imagine you are doing those jobs, figure out how long you would take to do each one, and then add them all up to give you an estimate for that user story.

Q: How much of this process should my customer actually see?

A: Your customer should only see and hear your questions, and then of course your user stories as they develop. In particular, your customer is ***not*** involved in the planning poker game. Customers will want lower-than-reasonable estimates, and can pressure you and your team to get overly aggressive.

When there is a question about what a piece of the software is supposed to do in a given situation, or when an assumption is found, then involving the customer is absolutely critical. When you find a technical assumption being made by your team that you can clarify without the customer, then you don't have to go back and bother them with details they probably won't understand anyway.

But when you're playing planning poker, you are coming up with estimates of how long ***you*** believe that ***your team*** will take to develop and deliver the software. So it's ***your*** neck on the line, and ***your*** promise. So the customer shouldn't be coming up with those for you.

Who am I?

A bunch of techniques for working with requirements, in full costume, are playing a party game, "Who am I?" They'll give you a clue and then you try to guess who they are based on what they say. Assume they always tell the truth about themselves. Fill in the blanks next to each statement with the name (or names) of each attendee that the statement is true for. Attendees may be used in more than one answer

Tonight's attendees:

Blueskying – Role playing – Observation
User story – Estimate – Planning poker

You can dress me up as a use case for a formal occasion.	....
The more of me there are, the clearer things become.	....
I help you capture EVERYTHING.	....
I help you get more from the customer.	....
In court, I'd be admissible as firsthand evidence.	....
Some people say I'm arrogant, but really I'm just about confidence.	....
Everyone's involved when it comes to me.	....

Answers on page 62.

The requirement to estimate iteration cycle

We've now added some new steps in our iterative approach to requirements development. Let's look at how estimation fits into our process...

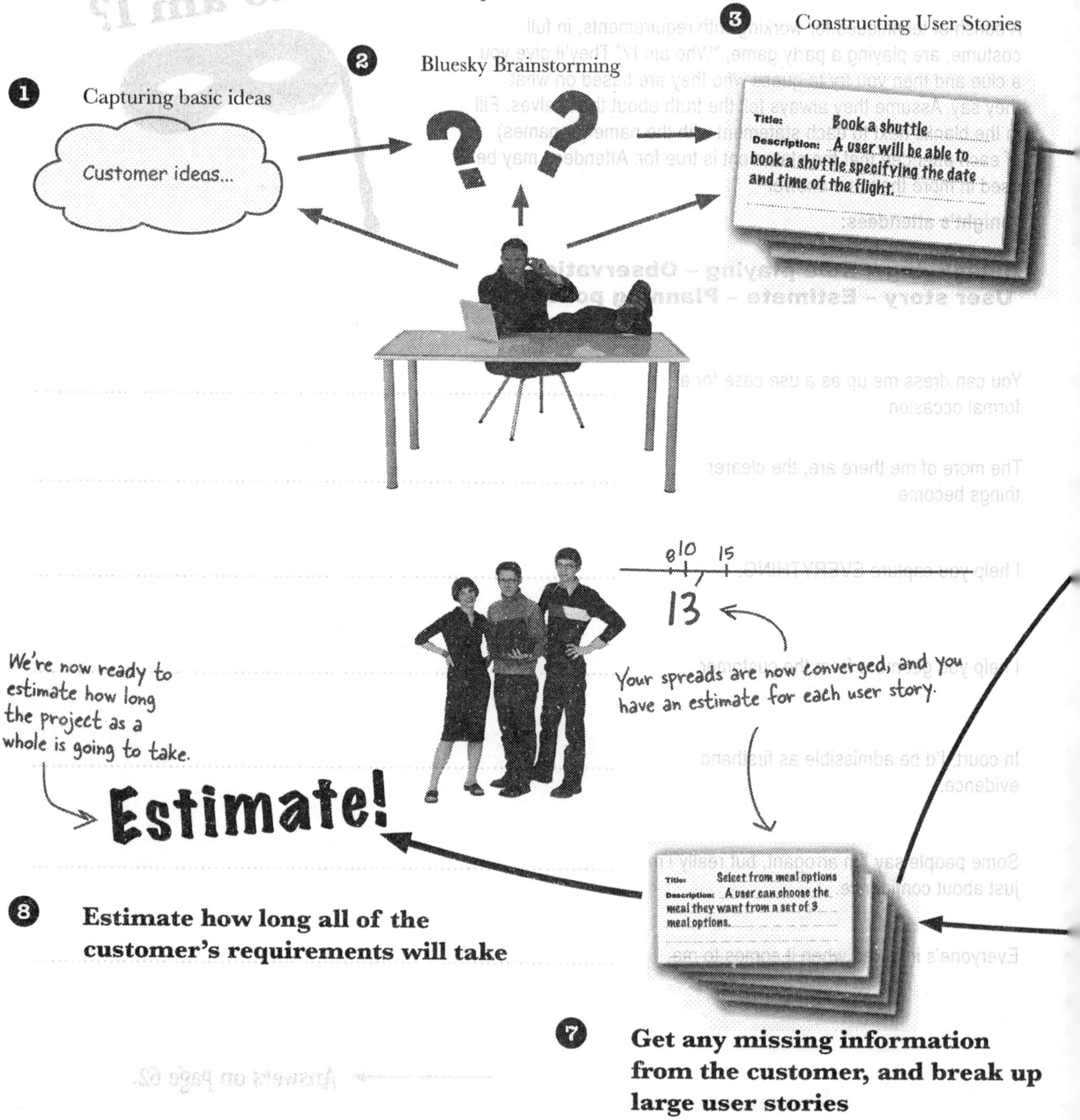

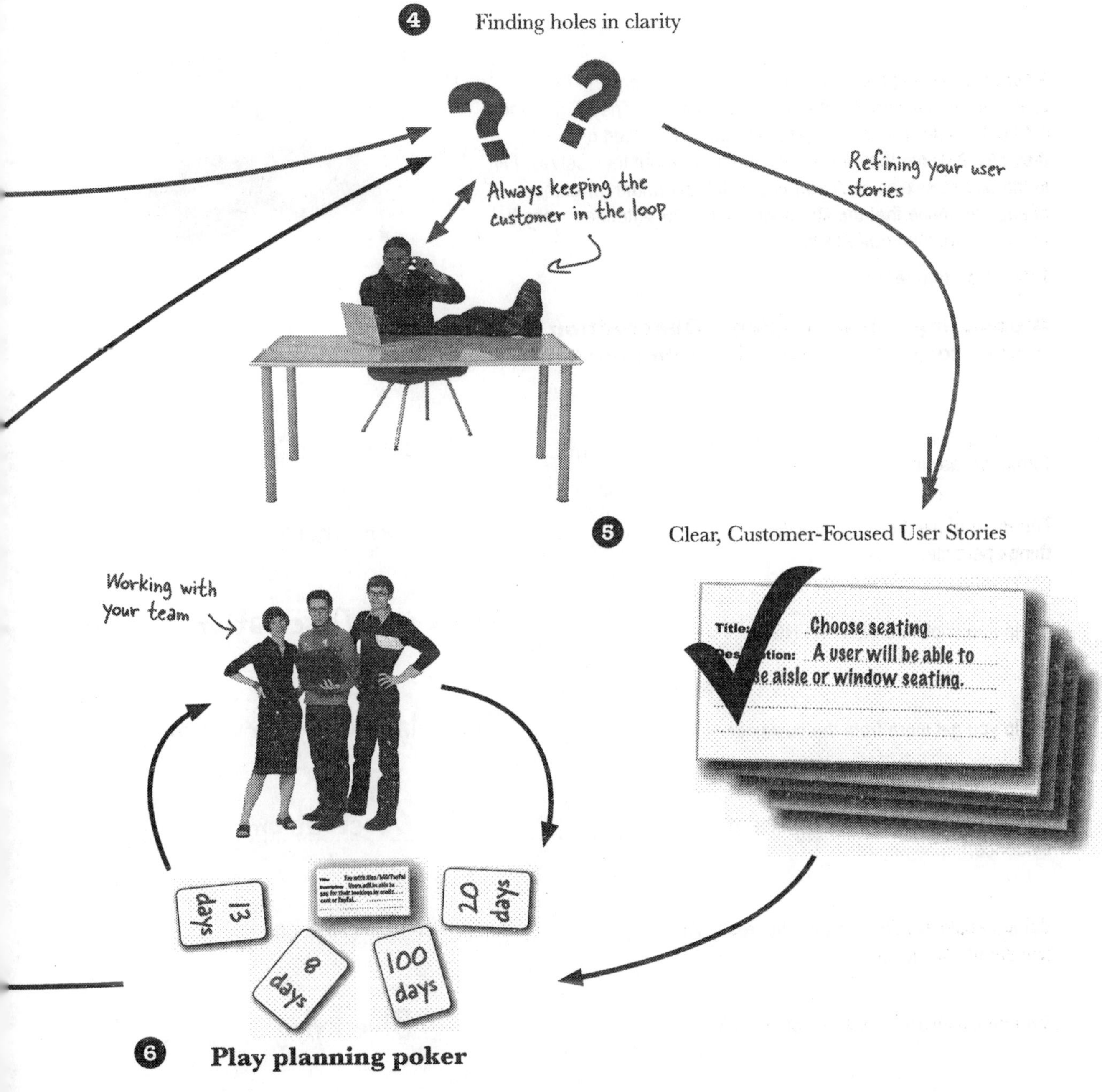
4 Finding holes in clarity
Always keeping the customer in the loop
Refining your user stories
5 Clear, Customer-Focused User Stories
Title: Choose seating
A user will be able to
se aisle or window seating.
Working with your team
13 days
20 days
8 days
100 days
6 Play planning poker

Who am I? Solutions

A bunch of techniques for working with requirements, in full costume, are playing a party game, "Who am I?" They'll give you a clue and then you try to guess who they are based on what they say. Assume they always tell the truth about themselves. Fill in the blanks next to each statement with the name (or names) of each attendee that the statement is true for. Attendees may be used in more than one answer

Tonight's attendees:

Blueskying – Role playing – Observation
User story – Estimate – Planning poker

You can dress me up as a use case for a formal occasion.	User Story
The more of me there are, the clearer things become.	User Story
I help you capture EVERYTHING.	Blueskying, Observation
I help you get more from the customer.	Role playing, Observation
In court, I'd be admissible as firsthand evidence.	Observation
Some people say I'm arrogant, but really I'm just about confidence.	Estimate
Everyone's involved when it comes to me.	Blueskying

Did you say planning poker? Customers aren't involved in that activity.

Finally, you're ready to estimate the whole project...

You've got short, focused user stories, and you've played planning poker on each story. You've dealt with all the assumptions that you and your team were making in your estimates, and now you have a set of estimates that you all believe in. It's time to get back to the customer with your total project estimate...

You've got an estimate for each story now.

- [x] Add an estimate to each user story for how long you think it will take to develop that functionality.
- [ ] Add up all the estimates to get a **total estimate** for how long your project will take to deliver the required software.

Now you can get a total estimate.

And the total project estimate is...

Add up the each of the converged estimates for your user stories, and you will find the total duration for your project, if you were to develop everything the customer wants.

15 16

20 19

12 15

Sum of user story estimates

= 489 days!

What do you do when your estimates are WAY too long?

You've finally got an estimate you believe in, and that takes into account all the requirements that the customer wants. But you've ended up with a monster project that is just going to take too long.

Is it time to go back to the drawing board? Do you admit defeat and hand the work over to someone else? Or do you just ask the customer how long he thinks would work, forgetting about all your hard work to come up with you estimates in the first place?

You'll have to solve a crossword puzzle and work your way to Chapter 3 to find out how to get Orion's Orbits back on track.

Requirements and Estimation Cross

Let's put what you've learned to use and stretch out your left brain a bit. All of the words below are somewhere in this chapter: Good luck!

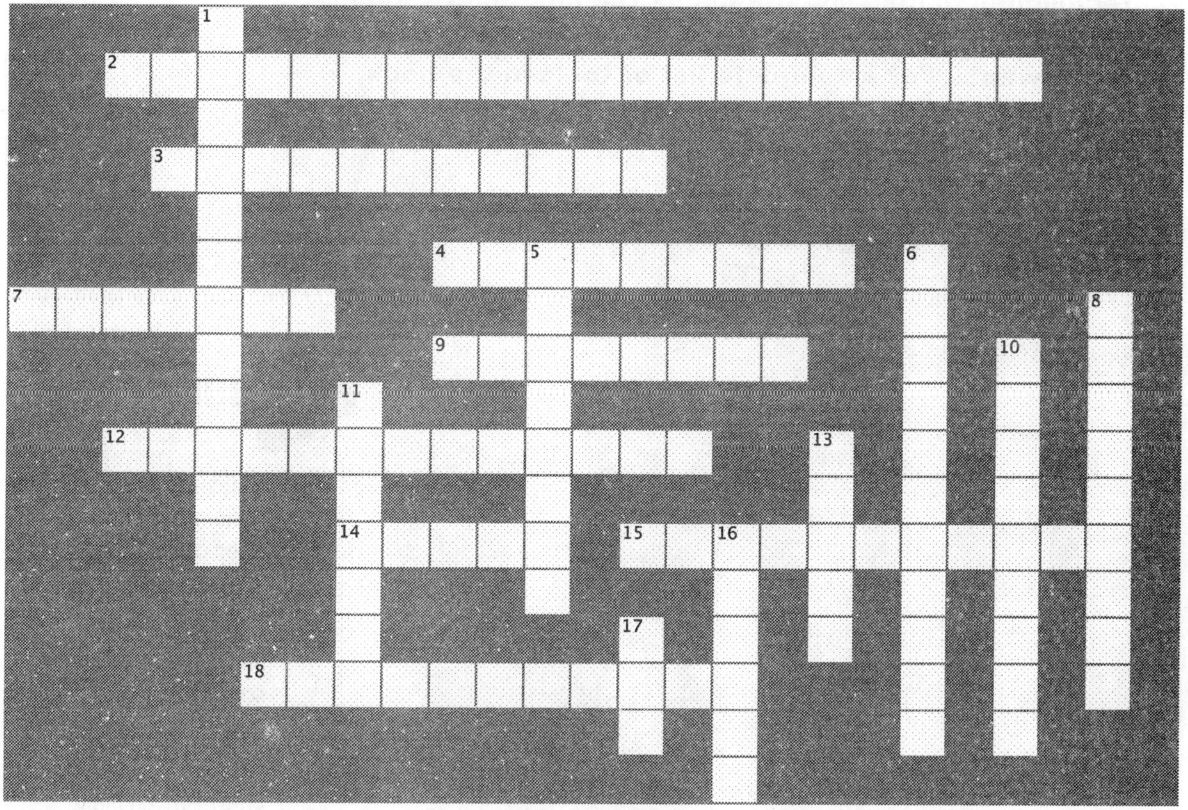

Across

2. When you and the customer are really letting your ideas run wild you are ....
3. When coming up with estimates, you are trying to get rid of as many .... as possible.
4. None of this language is allowed in a user story.
7. If a requirement is the what, an estimate is the ....
9. Requirements are oriented towards the ....
12. The best way to get honest estimates and highlight assumptions.
14. A User Story is made up of a .... and a description.
15. .... is a great way of getting first hand evidence of exactly how your customer works at the moment.
18. The goal of estimation is ....

Down

1. When you just have no idea how to estimate a user story, use a card with this on it.
5. User stories are written from the perspective of the ....
6. When you and the customer act out a particular user story, you are ....
8. When everyone agrees on an estimate, it is called a ....
10. An estimate is good when eveyone on your team is feeling ....
11. The maximum number of days that a good estimate should be for one user story.
13. A great user story is about .... lines long.
16. After a round of planning poker, you plot all of the estimates on a ....
17. You can use the .... rule for breaking up large user stories.

Tools for your Software Development Toolbox

Software Development is all about developing and delivering the software that the customer actually wants. In this chapter, you learned about several techniques to help you get inside the customer's head and capture the requirements that represent what they really want... For a complete list of tools in the book, see Appendix ii.

Development Techniques

Bluesky, Observation and Roleplay

User Stories

Planning poker for estimation

Development Principles

The customer knows what they want, but sometimes you need to help them nail it down

Keep requirements customer-oriented

Develop and refine your requirements iteratively with the customer

BULLET POINTS

- **Blueskying** gets your customer to **think big** when coming up with their requirements.
- A **user story** captures one interaction with the software from the customer's perspective.
- User stories should be **short**, around three sentences in length.
- A short user story is an **estimatable user story**.
- A user story should not take one developer more than 15 days to deliver.
- **Iteratively develop** your requirements with your customer to keep them in the loop at every step of the process.

Requirements and Estimation Cross Solution

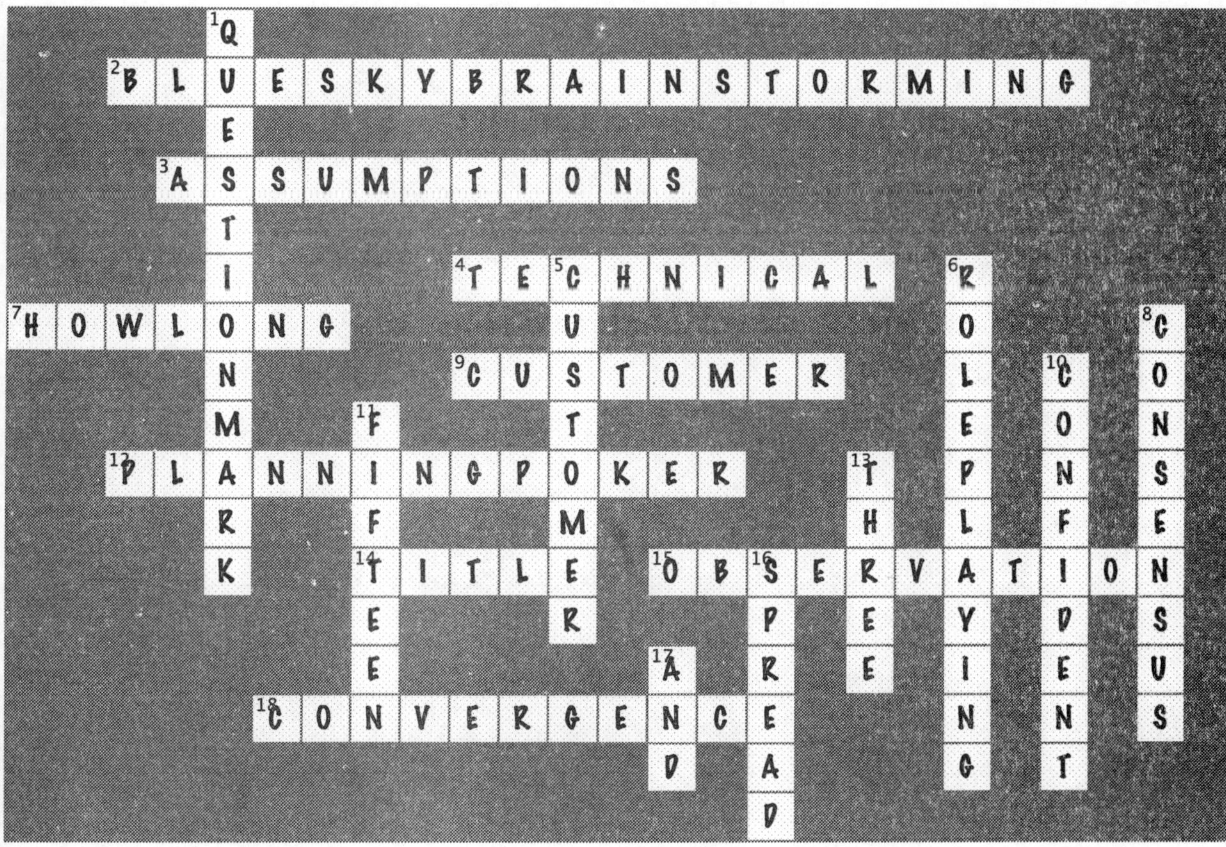

3 project planning

Planning for success

Every great piece of software starts with a great plan.

In this chapter you're going to learn how to create that plan. You're going to learn how to work with the customer to **prioritize their requirements**. You'll **define iterations** that you and your team can then work toward. Finally you'll create an achievable **development plan** that you and your team can confidently **execute** and **monitor.** By the time you're done, you'll know exactly how to get from requirements to your first deliverable.

Customers want their software NOW!

Customers want their software **when they need it**, and not a moment later. You've come to grips with the customer's ideas using brainstorming, you've got a set of user stories that describe everything the customer might need the software to do, and you've even added an estimate to each user story that helped you figure out how long it will take to deliver everything the customer wants. The problem is, developing **everything** the customer said they needed will take **too long**...

Our Estimate	**What the customer wants**
489 days	90 days!

The total after summing up all the estimates for your user stories

Exercise

Orion's Orbits still wants to modernize their booking system; they just can't wait almost two years for the software to get finished. Take the following snippets from the Orion's Orbits user stories, along with their estimates, and circle the ones you think you should develop to come up with a chunk of work that will take **no longer than 90 days**.

Title: Book a shuttle
Estimate: 15 days

Title: Pay with Visa/MC/PayPal
Estimate: 15 days

Title: Review flight
Estimate: 13 days

Title: Order in-flight meals
Estimate: 13 days

Title: Order Flight DVD
Estimate: 12 days

Title: Book Segway in spaceport transport
Estimate: 15 days

Title: View Space Miles Account
Estimate: 14 days

Title: Choose seating
Estimate: 12 days

Title: Apply for "frequent astronaut" card
Estimate: 14 days

Title: Take pet reservation
Estimate: 12 days

Title: Manage special offers
Estimate: 13 days

Total Estimate: ______

Total estimate for all of the user stories you've circled

Problems? ....

....

....

....

See any problems with this approach? Write them down here.

Assumptions? ....

....

....

....

Note down any assumptions you think you are making here.

Our Exercise Solution

Orion's Orbits still wants to modernize their booking system; they just can't wait for a year and a half for the software to turn up. Your job was to take the snippets on page 71 and keep the ones you think you should develop. Here are the stories we kept:

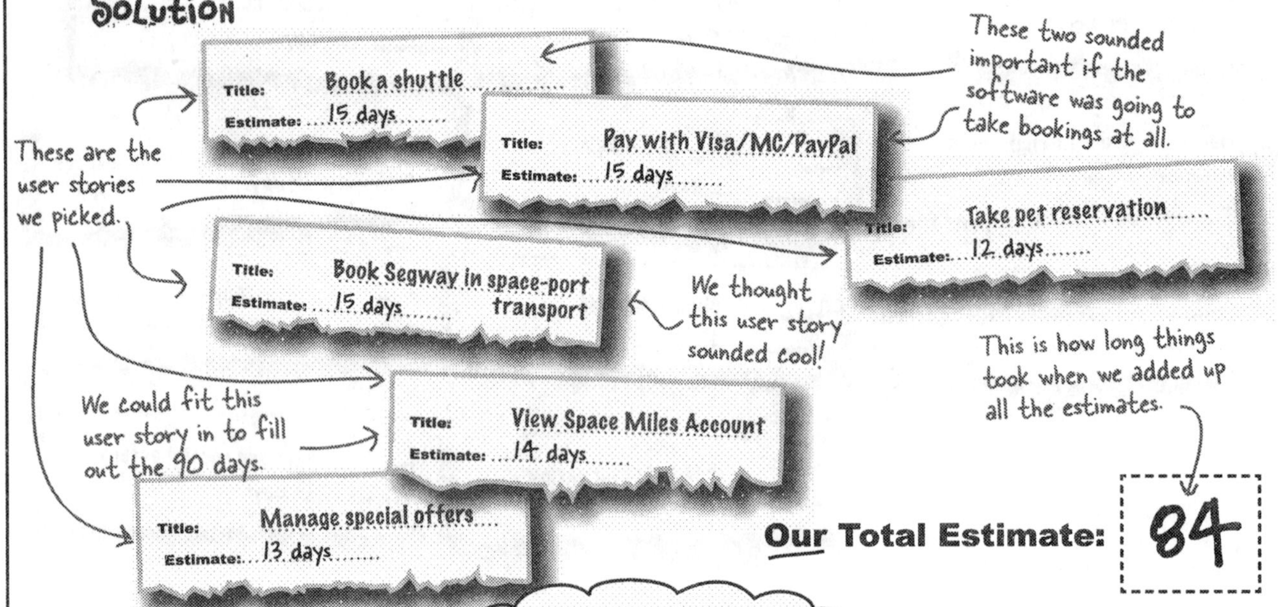

The customer sets the priorities

Seems like the CEO of Orion's Orbits is not happy, and can you blame him? After all that hard work to figure out what he needs, we've ignored him completely when deciding which user stories take priority for the project.

When user stories are being prioritized, you need to **stay customer-focused**. Only the customer knows what is really needed. So when it comes to **deciding what's in and what's out,** you might be able to provide some expert help, but **ultimately it's a choice that the customer has to make**.

Prioritize with the customer

It's your **customer's call** as to what user stories take priority. To help the customer make that decision, shuffle and lay out all your user story cards on the table. Ask your customer to order the user stories by priority (the story most important to them first) and then to select the set of features that need to be delivered in Milestone 1.0 of their software.

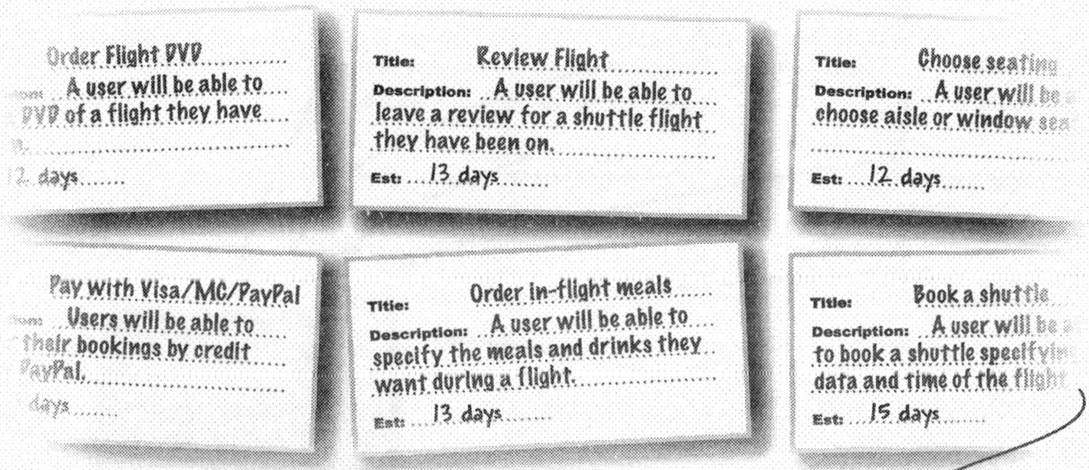

Lay out all your user stories and ask the customer to order them by priority.

What is "Milestone 1.0"?

Milestone 1.0 is your **first major release** of the software to the customer. Unlike smaller iterations where you'll show the customer your software for feedback, this will be the first time you actually **deliver your software** (and expect to get paid for the delivery). Some Do's and Don'ts when planning Milestone 1.0:

Do... balance functionality with customer impatience

Help the customer to understand **what can be done in the time available.** Any user stories that don't make it into Milestone 1.0 are not ignored, just postponed until Milestone 2, or 3...

Don't... get caught planning nice-to-haves

Milestone 1.0 is about **delivering what's needed**, and that means a set of functionality that meets the most important needs of the customer.

Don't... worry about length (yet)

At this point you're just asking your customer which are the most important user stories. **Don't get caught up on how long** those user stories will take to develop. You're just trying to understand the customer's priorities.

Don't worry, we're not ignoring estimation. We'll come right back to this.

We know what's in Milestone 1.0 (well, maybe)

From all of the user stories developed from the customer's ideas, organized into prority order, the customer then selects the user stories that they would like to be a part of Milestone 1.0 of the software...

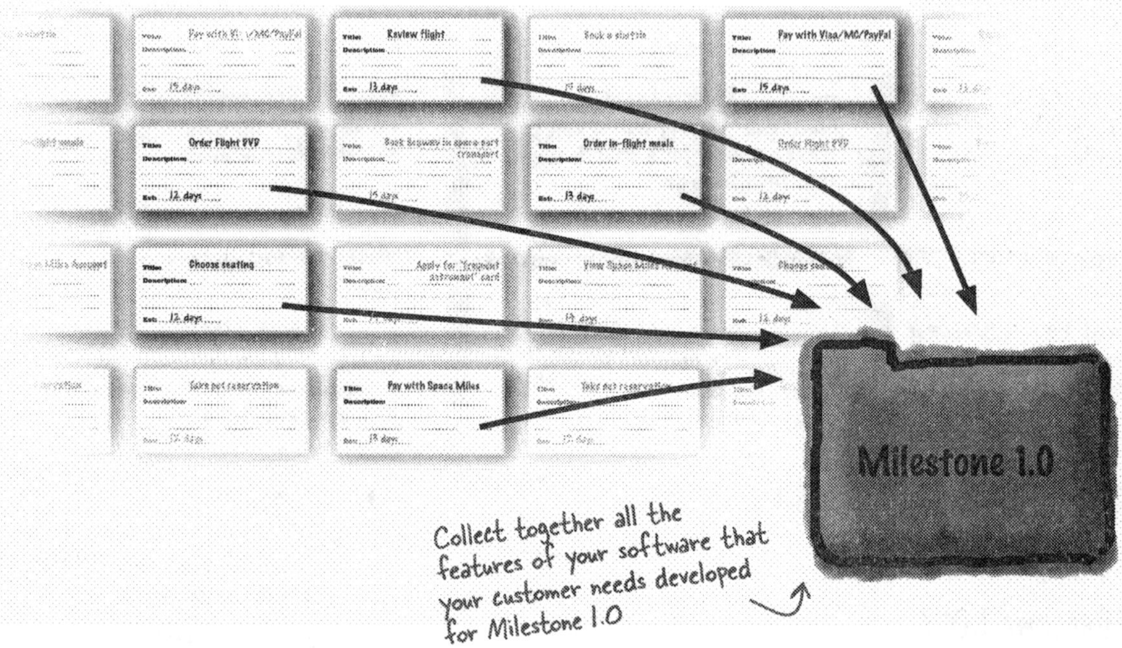

Sanity-check your Milestone 1.0 estimate

Now that you know what features the customer wants in Milestone 1.0, it's time to find out if you now have a reasonable length of project if you develop and deliver all of those most important features...

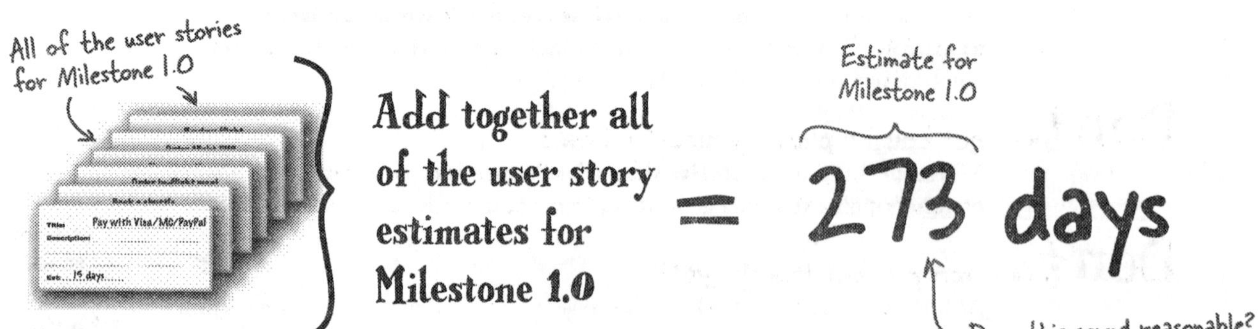

If the features don't fit, reprioritize

You've got 273 days of work for Milestone 1.0, and Orion's Orbits want delivery in **90 days**. Don't worry, this is pretty common. Customers usually want more than you can deliver, and it's your job to go back to them and reprioritize until you come up with a workable feature set.

To reprioritize your user stories for Milestone 1.0 with the customer...

1. **Cut out more FUNCTIONALITY**
   The very first thing you can look at doing to shorten the time to delivering Milestone 1.0 is to cut out some functionality by removing user stories that are not ***absolutely crucial*** to the software working.

   Once you explain the schedule, most customers will admit they don't really need everything they originally said they did.

2. **Ship a milestone build as early as possible**
   Aim to deliver a significant milestone build of your software as early as possible. This keeps your development momentum up by allowing you and your team to focus on a deadline that's not too far off.

   Don't let customers talk you into longer development cycles than you're comfortable with. The sooner your deadline, the more focused you and your team can be on it.

3. **Focus on the BASELINE functionality**
   Milestone 1.0 is all about delivering ***just*** the functionality that is needed for a working version of the software. Any features beyond that can be scheduled for later milestones.

there are no Dumb Questions

Q: What's the difference between a milestone and a version?

A: Not much. In fact you could call your first milestone "Version 1" if you like. The big difference between a milestone and a version is that a milestone marks a point at which you deliver signficant software and get paid by your customer, whereas a version is more of a simple descriptive term that is used to identify a particular release of your software.

The difference is really quite subtle, but the simple way to understand it is that "Version" is a label and doesn't mean anything more, whereas "Milestone" means you deliver signficant functionality and you get paid. It could be that Version 1.0 coincides with Milestone 1.0, but equally Milestone 1.0 could be Version 0.1, 0.2 or any other label you pick.

Q: So what exactly is my software's baseline functionality?

A: The **baseline functionality** of your software is the smallest set of features that it needs to have in order for it to be at all useful to your customer and their users.

Think about a word processing application. Its core functionality is to let you load, edit, and save text to a file. Anything else is beyond core functionality, no matter how useful those features are. Without the ability to load, edit, and save a document with text in it, a word processor simply ***is not useful***.

That's the rule of thumb: If you can get by without a feature, then it isn't really baseline functionality, and it's probably a good candidate for pushing out to a later milestone than Milestone 1.0 if you don't have time to get everything done.

Q: I've done the math and no matter how I cut the user stories up, I just can't deliver what my customer wants when they want me to. What can I do?

A: It's time to confess, unfortunately. If you really can't build the software that is required in the time that it's needed by, and your customer simply won't budge when it comes to removing some user stories from the mix, then you might need to walk away from the project and know that at least you were honest with the customer.

Another option is to try to beef up your team with new people to try and get more work done quicker. However, adding new people to the team will up the costs considerably, and won't necessarily get you all the advantages that you'd think it might.

If it takes you 273 days, with 2 more people like you, that would reduce the overall development time by a factor of 3, right?

It's about more than just development time

While adding more people can look really attractive at first, it's really not as simple as "double the people, halve the estimate."

Every new team member needs to **get up to speed on the project**; they need to **understand the software**, the **technical decisions**, and **how everything fits together**, and while they're doing that ***they can't be 100% productive***.

Then you need to get that new person set up with the right tools and equipment to work with the team. This could mean buying new licenses and purchasing new equipment, but even if it just means downloading some free or open source software, ***it all takes time*** and that time needs to be factored in as you reassess your estimates.

Finally, every person you add to your team makes the job of keeping everyone focused and knowing what they are doing harder. Keeping everyone moving in the same direction and on the same page can become a full-time job, and as your team gets larger you will find that this complex communication can start to hit your team's overall ability to be productive and develop great software.

In fact, there is a maximum number of people that your team can contain and still be productive, but it will depend very much on your project, your team, and who you're adding. The best approach is to monitor your team, and if you start to see your team actually get ***less productive***, even though you have ***more people***, then it's time to re-evaluate the amount of work you have to do or the amount of time in which you have to do it.

Later on in this chapter you'll be introduced to the burn-down rate graph. This is a great tool for monitoring the performance of your team.

More people sometimes means diminishing returns

Adding more people to your team doesn't always work as you'd expect. If 1 person takes 273 days to complete Milestone 1.0, then 3 people ***won't*** necessarily take 91. In fact they could actually take much longer! Take a look...performance doesn't always increase with the size of your team:

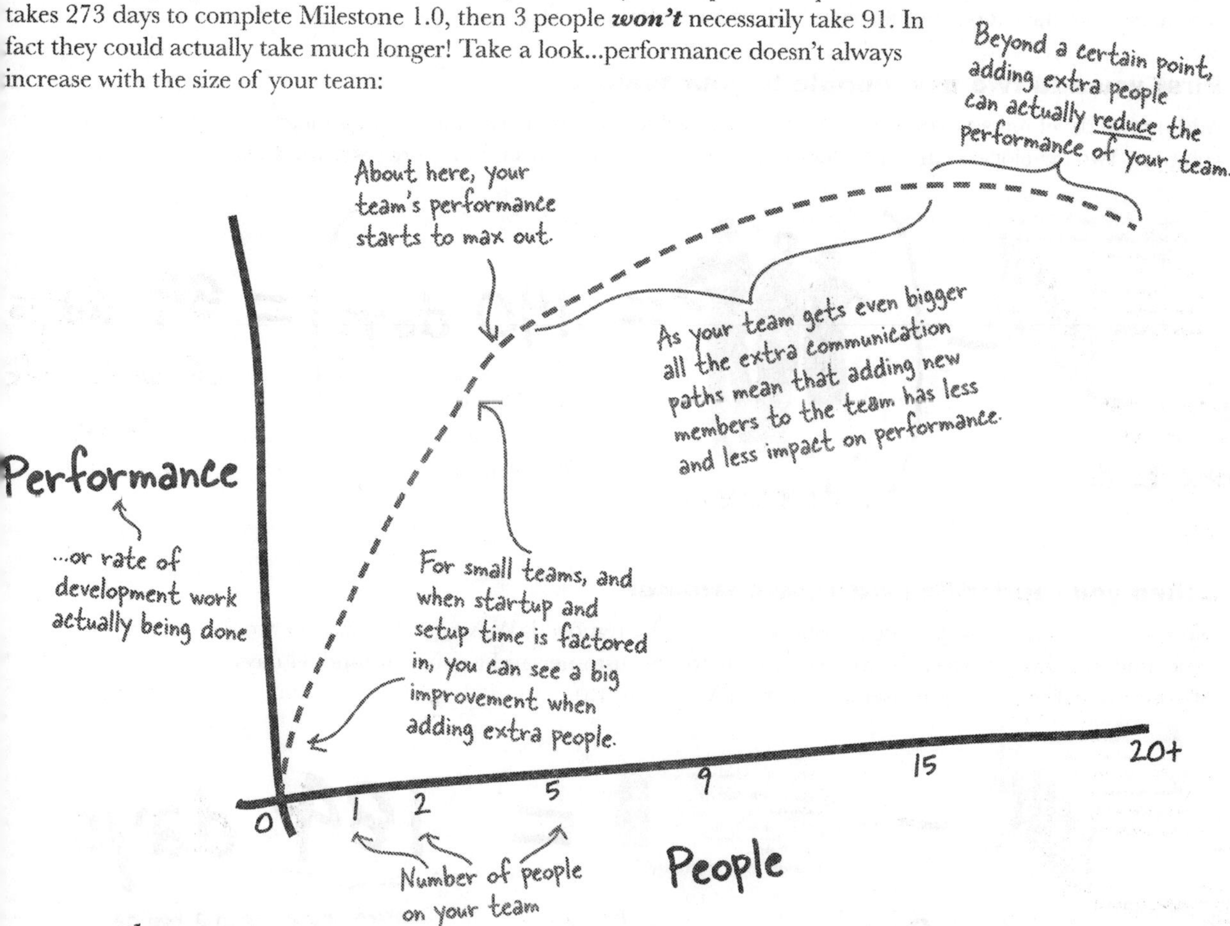

there are no Dumb Questions

Q: Is there a maximum team size that I should ever go over?

A: Not really. Depending on your experience you may find that you can happily handle a 20-person team, but that things become impossible when you hit 21. Alternatively you might find that any more than three developers, and you start to see a dip in productivity. The best approach is to monitor performance closely and make amendments based on your observations.

BRAIN POWER

Do you think the size of your project affects this graph? What about if you broke your project up into smaller sub-projects?

Work your way to a reasonable Milestone 1.0

With Orion's Orbits, going from one person to three—by adding two more developers—can have a positive impact. So let's see how that works out:

First you add two new people to your team...

Adding two developers to your team (that's three including you) helps, but it's not a magical solution. Two developers can add a lot of work time to your project, but there's still work left:

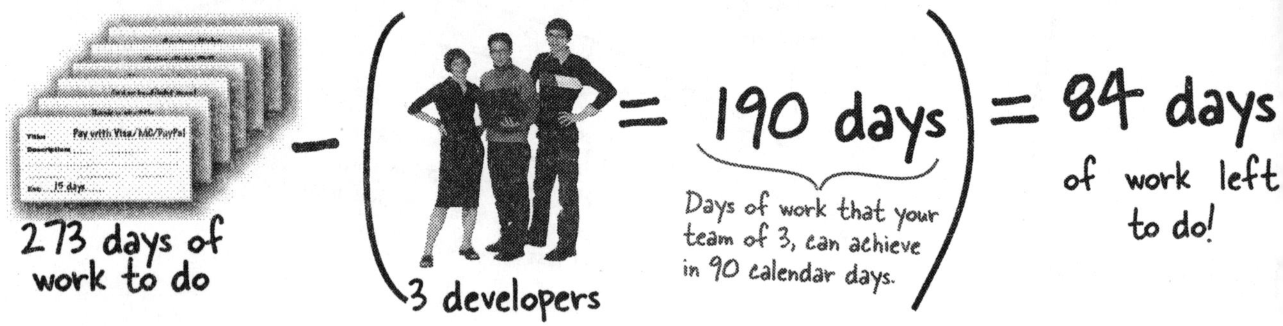

...then you reprioritize with the customer

Now you've got a nice way to figure out what has to be removed. We've got 189 days of work time, and 273 days of work. So we need to talk to the customer and remove around 84 days of work by shifting out some user stories from Milestone 1.0.

there are no Dumb Questions

Q: But 190 days of work is less than the 190 days that our three-developer team can produce, shouldn't we add some more features with the customer?

A: The overall estimate doesn't actually have to be exactly 189 days. Given that we're dealing with estimates anyway, which are rarely 100% accurate, and that we tend to be slightly optimistic in our estimates then 165 days is close enough to the 189-day mark to be reasonably confident of delivering in that time.

Q: How did you come up with 190 days when you added two new developers?

A: At this point this number is a guesstimate. We've guessed that adding two people to build a team of three will mean we can do around 190 days of work in 90 calendar days. There are ways to back up this guess with some evidence using something called "team velocity," but we'll get back to that later on in this chapter.

BE the Customer

Think about baseline functionality. If a feature isn't essential, it's probably not a 10.

Now it's your chance to be the customer. You need to build a plan for when you are going to develop each of the user stories for Milestone 1.0, and to do that you need to ask the customer what features are most important so that you can develop those first. Your job is to play the customer by assigning a priority to the Milestone 1.0 user stories. For each user story, assign it a ranking in the square provided, depending on how important you think that feature is using the key at the bottom of the page.

Title: Pay using "Space Miles"
Est: 15 days
Priority: ☐

Title: Order In-flight meals
Est: 13 days
Priority: ☐

Title: Login to "Frequent Astronaut" account
Est: 15 days
Priority: ☐

Title: Review flight
Est: 13 days
Priority: ☐

Title: Manage special offers
Est: 13 days
Priority: ☐

Title: Book a shuttle
Est: 15 days
Priority: ☐

Title: Pay with Visa/MC/PayPal
Est: 15 days
Priority: ☐

Title: View "Space Miles" account
Est: 14 days
Priority: ☐

Title: View flight reviews
Est: 12 days
Priority: ☐

Title: Choose seating
Est: 12 days
Priority: ☐

Title: Apply for "frequent astronaut" card
Est: 14 days
Priority: ☐

Title: View shuttle deals
Est: 12 days
Priority: ☐

For each user story, specify what priority it is in the box provided.

Priorities Key

10 - **Most Important**
20
30
40
50 - **Least Important**

Our BE the Customer Solution

Your job was to play the customer and prioritize the Milestone 1.0 user stories. Here are the priorities that we assigned to each of the user stories. We also laid out the user stories in order of

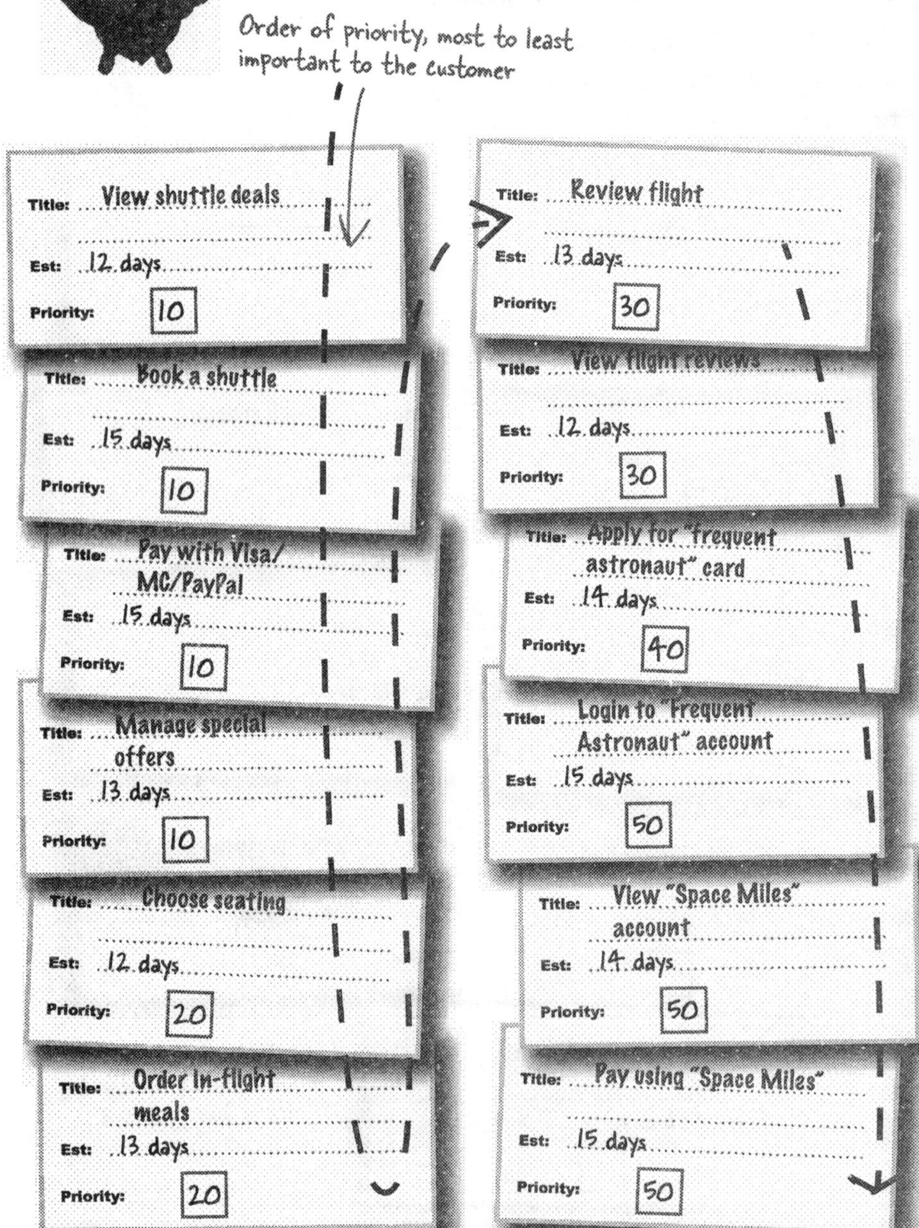

there are no Dumb Questions

Q: Why are the priorities 10, 20, 30, 40, and 50?

A: Powers of ten get the brain thinking about groupings of features, instead of ordering each and every feature separately with numbers like 8 or 26 or 42. You're trying to get the customer to decide what is most important, but not get too hung up on the exact numbers themselves. Also, powers of ten allow you to occasionally specify, say, a 25 for a particular feature when you add something in later, and need to squeeze it between existing features.

Q: If it's a 50, then maybe we can leave it out, right?

A: No, 50 doesn't mean that a user story is a candidate for leaving out. At this point, we're working on the user stories for Milestone 1.0, and so these user stories have ***already*** been filtered down to the customer's most important features. The goal here is to prioritize, not figure out if any of these features aren't important. So a 50 just says it can come later, not that it's not important to the customer

Q: What if I have some non–Milestone 1.0 user story cards?

A: Assign a priority of 60 to those cards for now, so they don't get mixed in with your Milestone 1.0 features.

Q: And the customer does all this work?

A: You can help out and advise, maybe mentioning dependencies between some of the user stories. But the final decision on priorities is ***always*** the customer's to make.

Exercise

Now that you have your user stories for Milestone 1.0 in priority order, it's time to build some iterations. Lay out the user stories so they make iterations that make sense to you. Be sure and write down the total days of work, and how long that will take for your team of three developers.

First one added for you

Iteration 1

Title:	View shuttle deals
Est:	12 days
Priority:	10

Total Days: ______ Divide by 3 developers: ______

Iteration 2

Total Days: ______ Divide by 3 developers: ______

Iteration 3

Total Days: ______ Divide by 3 developers: ______

Bonus question

What do you think you should do at the end of an iteration?

....

....

Answers on page 84.

Fireside Chats

Tonight's talk: **A sit-down discussion between an iteration and a milestone.**

Milestone:

Hello there, iteration, seems like it's only been a month since I saw you last.

Iteration:

Almost exactly a month. And you'll see me again next month, I can guarantee it. About three times, and we're ready for you, Milestone 1.0.

Milestone:

So how are things going on the project? It seems like you're always showing up, and I just arrive for the big finish. Actually, what's your purpose?

Iteration:

To make sure things go great, of course. That's my job really, to make sure that every step of the way from day 1 to day 90, the project stays on track. What, you thought you could just show up three months into the project and everything would be ju like the customer wants it? A bit naive, aren't you?

Milestone:

Naive? Look, just because I've had a few customer run-ins before doesn't mean I'm not important. I mean, without me, you wouldn't have software at all ,let alone get paid! Besides, just because I've shown up and surprised the occasional customer from time to time...

Iteration:

Oh, I really sympathize with you there. I hate it when the customer isn't happy with me. But then again, there's a lot more time to fix things. I mean, we get together, you know, me and the customer, at least once a month. And, if things are bad, I just le the customer know it'll be better next time.

Milestone:

I used to try that, too. I'd try and soften the blow by explaining to the customer that all of their problems would be fixed in the next version of the software, but that wasn't what they wanted to hear. Lots of yelling, and I'd slink off, ready to go back to work for a year or so, and see if the customer liked me better next time.

Iteration:

But you're shorter than a year now, right?

Milestone:

Well, I try to be, but sometimes that's just how long it takes, although I just love seeing the customer more often. At least once a quarter seems to line up with their billing cycles. And not so long that I get forgotten about; there's nothing worse than that.

Iteration:

Yeah, nobody forgets about me. Around every month, there I am, showing up, putting on a song and dance, pleasing the customer. Really, I can't imagine how you ever got by without me.

Milestone:

Are you kidding? You're not even an alpha or a beta....just some code glued together, probably an excuse for everyone to wear jeans to work and drink beer on Friday afternoon.

Iteration:

Oh, it's a little more than that, don't you think? Where would you be without me paving the way, making sure we're on track, handling changes and new features, and even removing existing features that aren't needed any more.

Milestone:

Ha! Where would I be? Same place I am right now, getting ready to show the customer some real...

Iteration:

...***hopefully*** working?

Milestone:

...software. Hey, wait. Hopefully? I've got a few hopes for you, you little...

Iteration:

Well, you got the little part right. Why don't you just shuffle off for another 30 days or so, we'll call you when all the work's done. Then we'll see who Friday beers are on, OK?

Milestone:

Ungrateful little punk...release this!

Iteration:

Sure thing, and since I do my job, I'm sure you'll work just fine. I'm outta here, plenty of work left to be done...

Your job was to lay out the user stories so they make iterations that make sense. Here's what we came up with... note that all our iterations are within one calendar month, about 20 working days (or less).

Your answers could be different, but make sure you went in order of priority.

Title	Est	Priority
Manage special offers	13 days	10
Book a shuttle	15 days	10
Pay with Visa/MC/PayPal	15 days	10
View Shuttle deals	12 days	10

Iteration 1

...and make sure you kept your iterations short.

Total Days: 57 Divide by 3 developers: 19

Title	Est	Priority
Choose seating	12 days	20
Order In-flight meals	13 days	20
Review flight	13 days	30
View flight reviews	12 days	30

Iteration 2

Total Days: 50 Divide by 3 developers: 17

Title	Est	Priority
Apply for "frequent astronaut" card	14 days	40
Login to "Frequent Astronaut" account	15 days	50
View "Space Miles" account	14 days	50
Pay using "Space Miles"	15 days	50

Iteration 3

Total Days: 58 Divide by 3 developers: 20

What do you think you should do at the end of an iteration? Show the customer and get their feedback

there are no Dumb Questions

Q: What if I get to the end of an iteration, and I don't have anything to show my customer?

A: The only way you should end up at the end of an iteration and not have something to show the customer is if no user stories were completed during the iteration. If you've managed to do this, then your project is out of control and you need to get things back on track as quickly as possible.

Keep your software <u>continuously building</u> and your software <u>always runnable</u> so you can always get feedback from the customer at the end of an iteration.

Iterations should be short and sweet

So far Orion's Orbits has focussed on ***30-day iterations***, with 3 iterations in a 90-day project. You can use different size iterations, but make sure you keep these basic principles in mind:

Keep iterations short

The shorter your iterations are, the more chances you get to find and deal with change and unexpected details ***as they arise***. A short iteration will get you feedback earlier and bring changes and extra details to the surface sooner, so you can adjust your plans, and even change what you're doing in the next iteration, before you release a faulty Milestone 1.0.

Keep iterations balanced

Each iteration should be a balance between dealing with change, adding new features, beating out bugs, and accounting for real people working. If you have iterations every month, that's not really 30 days of work time. People take weekends off (at least once in a while), and you have to account for vacation, bugs, and things that come up along the way. A 20-work-day iteration is a safe bet of work time you can handle in an actual 30-day, calendar-month iteration.

30-day iterations are basically 30 CALENDAR days...

...which you can assume turn into about 20 WORKING days of productive development.

SHORT iterations help you deal with change and keep you and your team motivated and focused.

Who Does What?

Below is a particular aspect of a user story, iteration, milestone...or perhaps two, or even all three! Your job is to check off the boxes for the different things that each aspect applies to.

	User story	Iteration	Milestone
I result in a buildable and runnable bit of software.	☐	☐	☐
I'm the smallest buildable piece of software.	☐	☐	☐
In a full year, you should deliver me a maximum of four times.	☐	☐	☐
I contain an estimate set by your team.	☐	☐	☐
I contain a priority set by the customer.	☐	☐	☐
When I'm done, you deliver software to the customer and get paid.	☐	☐	☐
I should be done and dusted in 30 days.	☐	☐	☐

Answers on page 88.

Comparing your plan to reality

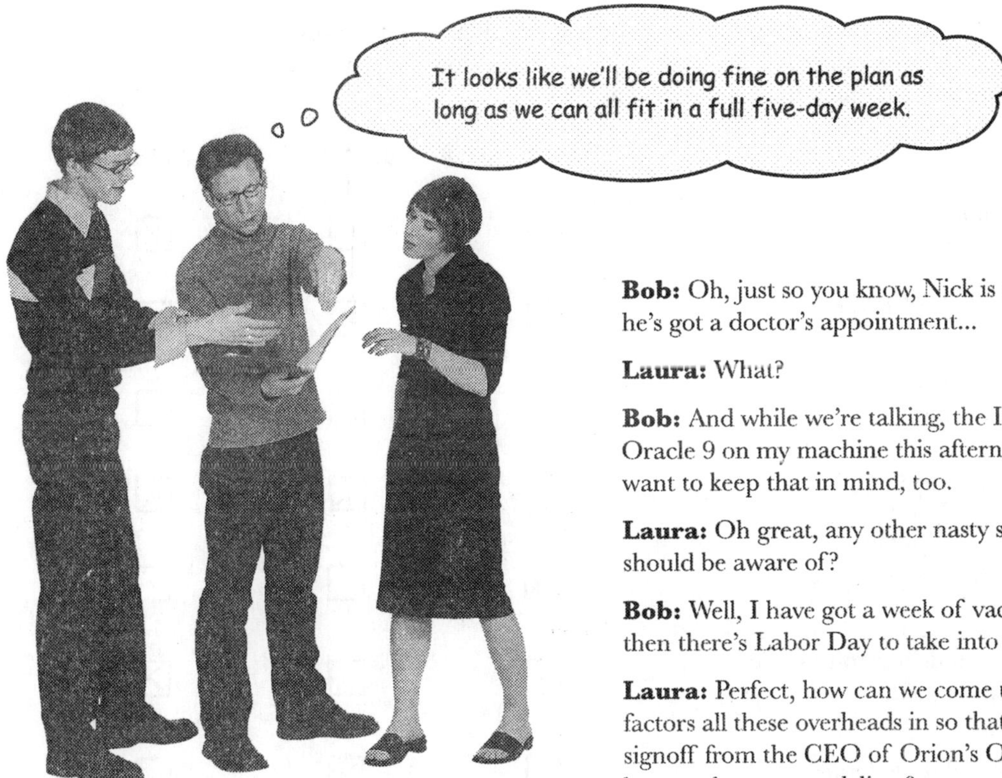

Bob: Oh, just so you know, Nick is coming in at 11 today, he's got a doctor's appointment...

Laura: What?

Bob: And while we're talking, the IT guys are installing Oracle 9 on my machine this afternoon, so you might want to keep that in mind, too.

Laura: Oh great, any other nasty surprises in there that I should be aware of?

Bob: Well, I have got a week of vacation this month, and then there's Labor Day to take into account...

Laura: Perfect, how can we come up with a plan that factors all these overheads in so that when we go get signoff from the CEO of Orion's Orbits we know we have a plan we can deliver?

Do you think our current 20-work-day iterations take these sorts of issues into account?

Sharpen your pencil

See if you can help Bob out. Check all the things that you need to account for when planning your iterations.

- [ ] Paperwork
- [ ] Equipment failure
- [ ] Holidays
- [ ] Sickness
- [ ] Software upgrades
- [ ] Frank winning the lottery

Exercise Solution

WHO DOES WHAT?

Below is a particular aspect of a user story, iteration, milestone...or perhaps two, or even all three! Your job is to check off the boxes for the different things that each aspect applies to.

	User Story	Iteration	Milestone
I result in a buildable and runnable bit of software.	☐	☒	☒
I'm the smallest buildable piece of software.	☐	☒	☐
In a full year, you should deliver me a maximum of four times.	☐	☐	☒
I contain an estimate set by your team.	☒	☒	☒
I contain a priority set by the customer.	☒	☐	☐
When I'm done, you deliver software to the customer and get paid.	☐	☐	☒
I should be done and dusted in 30 days.	☐	☒	☐

Sharpen your pencil

See if you can help Bob out. Check all the things that you need to account for when planning your iterations.

☒ Paperwork ☐ Equipment failure ☒ Holidays

☒ Sickness ☒ Software upgrades ☐ Frank winning the lottery

Things like this always occur... so we have to plan for them.

You really can't factor in complete surprises

Velocity accounts for overhead in your estimates

It's time to add a little reality to your plan. You need to factor in all those annoying bits of overhead by looking at how fast you and your team actually develop software. And that's where **velocity** comes in. Velocity is a percentage: given X number of days, how much of that time is productive work?

But how can I know how fast my team performs? We've only just gotten started!

Start with a velocity of 0.7.

On the first iteration with a new team it's fair to assume that your team's working time will be about 70% of their available time. This means your team has a velocity value of 0.7. In other words, for every 10 days of work time, about 3 of those days will be taken up by holidays, software installation, paperwork, phone calls, and other nondevelopment tasks.

That's a conservative estimate, and you may find that over time, your team's actual velocity is higher. If that's the case, then, at the end of your current iteration, you'll adjust your velocity and use that new figure to determine how many days of work can go into the next iteration.

Yet another reason to have short iterations: you can adjust velocity frequently.

Best of all, though, you can apply velocity to your amount of work, and get a **realistic estimate** of how long that work will actually take.

Take the days of work it will take you to develop a user story, or an iteration, or even an entire milestone...

The result should always be BIGGER than the original days of work, to account for days of administration, holidays, etc.

$$\frac{\text{days of work}}{\text{velocity}} = \text{days required to get work done}$$

...and DIVIDE that number by your velocity, which should be between 0 and 1.0. Start with 0.7 on a new project as a good conservative estimate.

Seeing a trend? 30 days of a calendar month was really 20 days of work, and 20 days of work is really only about 15 days of productive time.

Programmers think in UTOPIAN days...

Ask a programmer how long it takes to get something done, like writing a PHP interface to a MySQL database, or maybe screen-scraping World Series scores from *espn.com*. They're going to give you a ***better-than-best-case estimate***.

Here's what a programmer SAYS...

...but here's what he's really THINKING

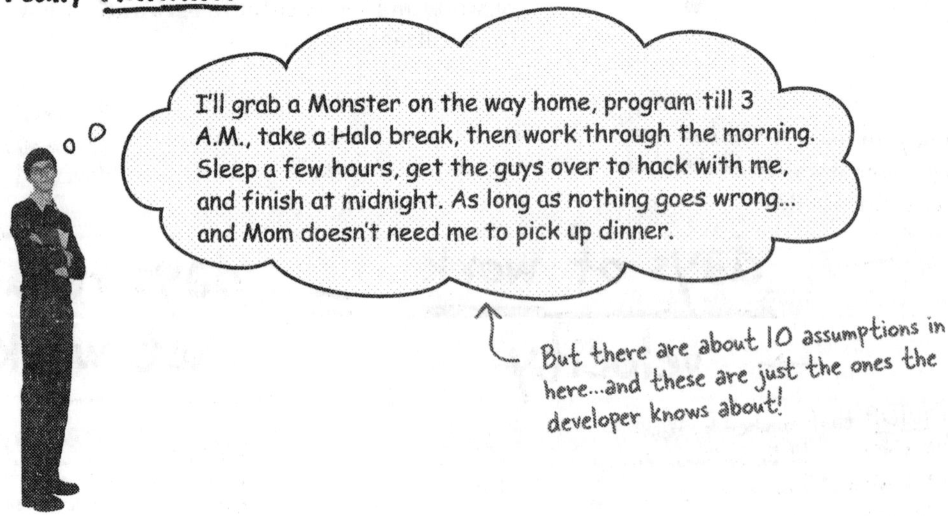

Developers think in REAL-WORLD days...

To be a software developer, though, you have to deal with reality. You've probably got a team of programmers, and you've got a customer who won't pay you if you're late. On top of that, you may even have other people depending on you—so your estimates are more conservative, and take into account real life:

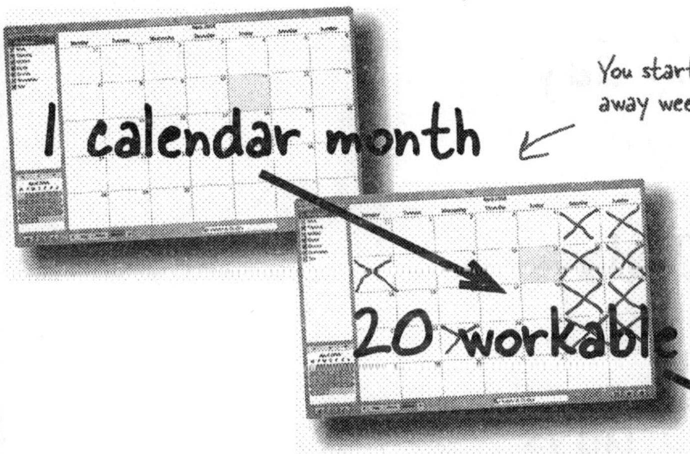

You start with a month, but take away weekends and holidays.

Then, apply velocity to account for time in the office that isn't focused on actual development.

velocity

14 days of REAL work

This is a lot lower number of days, but you can be more CONFIDENT in this number.

Sharpen your pencil

Take your original estimates for each iteration from the solution on page 84 and apply a 70% velocity so that you can come up with a more confident estimate for all the work in Milestone 1.0.

Iteration 1
57 days of work / 0.7 = ...

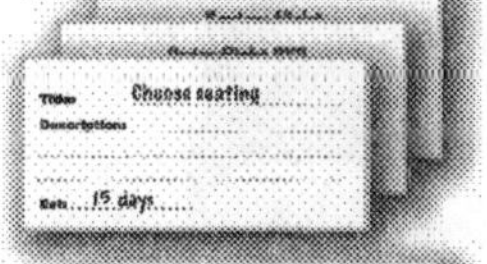

Iteration 2
50 days of work / 0.7 = ...

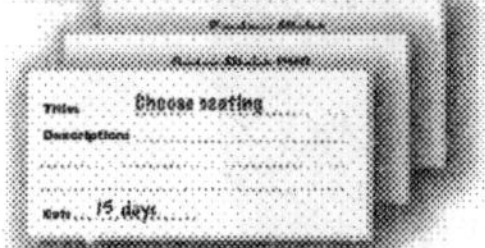

Iteration 3
58 days of work / 0.7 = ...

Milestone 1.0 = ...

When is your iteration too long?

Suppose you have three developers on your team who are working at a velocity of 0.7. This means that to calculate **how long an iteration will really take *your team***, you need to apply your velocity to the iteration's estimate:

Iteration 1
57 days / 0.7 = **82 days**

Yes, these estimates are getting longer...but you're building confidence in your estimate along the way.

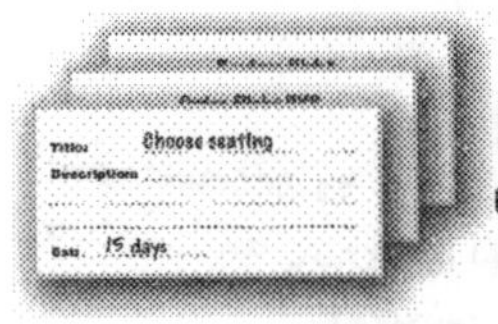

Iteration 2
50 days / 0.7 = **72 days**

All three iterations break the 20 work-day target.

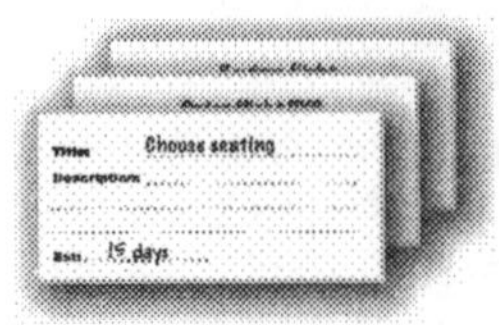

Iteration 3
58 days / 0.7 = **83 days**

= 237 days of work

So if you have 3 developers, each of them has to work 79 days in 3 months... but there are only 60 working days.

Even with three people, we still can't deliver Milestone 1.0 in time!

BRAIN POWER

How would you bring your estimates back to 20 work-day cycles so you can deliver Milestone 1.0 on time, without working weekends?

Deal with velocity BEFORE you break into iterations

A lot of this pain could actually have been avoided if you'd applied velocity at the ***beginning*** of your project. By applying velocity up front, you can calculate how many days of work you and your team can produce in each iteration. Then you'll know exactly what you can ***really*** deliver in Milestone 1.0.

First, apply your team velocity to each iteration

By taking the number of people in your team, multiplied by the number of actual working days in your iteration, multiplied finally by your team's velocity, you can calculate how many **days of actual work** your team can produce in one iteration:

$$3 \times 20 \times 0.7 = 42$$

The number of people on your team.

20 working days in your iteration

Your team's first pass velocity.

The amount of work, in person-days, that your team can handle in one iteration.

Add your iterations up to get a total milestone estimate

Now you should estimate the number of iterations you need for your milestone. Just multiply your days of work per iteration by the number of iterations, and you've got the number of working days you can devote to user stories for your milestone:

$$42 \times 3 = 126$$

Number of iterations in Milestone 1.0.

Amount of work in days that you and your team can do before Milestone 1.0 needs to be shipped.

there are no Dumb Questions

Q: That sucks! So I only have 14 days of actual productive work per iteration if my velocity is 0.7?

A: 0.7 is a conservative estimate for when you have new members of your team coming up to speed and other overheads. As you and your team complete your iterations, you'll keep coming back to that velocity value and updating it to reflect how productive you really are.

Q: With velocity, my Milestone 1.0 is now going to take 79 working days, which means 114 calendar days. That's much more than the 90-day/3-month deadline that Orion's Orbits set, isn't that too long?

A: Yes! Orion's Orbits need Milestone 1.0 in 90 calendar days, so by applying velocity, you've now got too much work to do to meet that deadline. You need to reassess your plan to see what you really can do with the time and team that you have.

Long Exercise

When your iterations contain too much work for your team, there's nothing else to do but reshuffle work until your iterations are manageable. Take the Orion's Orbits Milestone 1.0 user stories and organize them into iterations that each contain no more than 42 days of work.

The maximum amount of work *your* team can do in a 20-day iteration, factoring in your velocity this time.

Title:	Est:	Priority:
View shuttle deals	12 days	10
Book a shuttle	15 days	10
Pay with Visa/MC/PayPal	15 days	10
Manage special offers	13 days	10

Remember to respect the customer's original order of priority in your iterations.

Title:	Est:	Priority:
Choose seating	12 days	20
Order In-flight meals	13 days	20
Review flight	13 days	30
View flight reviews	12 days	30

Title:	Est:	Priority:
Apply for "frequent astronaut" card	14 days	40
Login to "Frequent Astronaut" account	15 days	50
View "Space Miles" account	14 days	50
Pay using "Space Miles"	15 days	50

Plan out each iteration by adding user stories that come out to around 42 days of work.

Iteration 1

Total Days of work:

Iteration 2

Total Days of work:

Iteration 3

Total Days of work:

Put any user stories that won't fit in the three iterations for Milestone 1.0 here

User stories that won't fit

Long Exercise Solution

Your job was to to take the Orion's Orbits user stories and aim for iterations that contain no more than 42 days of work each.

Iteration 1 — Total Days of work: 42

Title	Est	Priority
View shuttle deals	12 days	10
Book a shuttle	15 days	10
Pay with Visa/MC/PayPal	15 days	10

Iteration 2 — Total Days of work: 38

Title	Est	Priority
Manage special offers	13 days	10
Choose seating	12 days	20
Order In-flight meals	13 days	20

Iteration 3 — Total Days of work: 39

Title	Est	Priority
Review flight	13 days	30
View flight reviews	12 days	30
Apply for Space Miles Loyalty Card	14 days	40

These user stories dropped off of the plan...

User stories that won't fit

Title	Est	Priority
Login to "Frequent Astronaut" account	15 days	50
View "Space Miles" account	14 days	50
Pay using "Space Miles"	15 days	50

ime to make an evaluation

o what's left? You've probably got a lot of user stories that still fit nto Milestone 1.0...and maybe a few that don't. That's because we idn't figure out our velocity before our iteration planning.

Estimates without velocity can get you into real trouble with your customer.

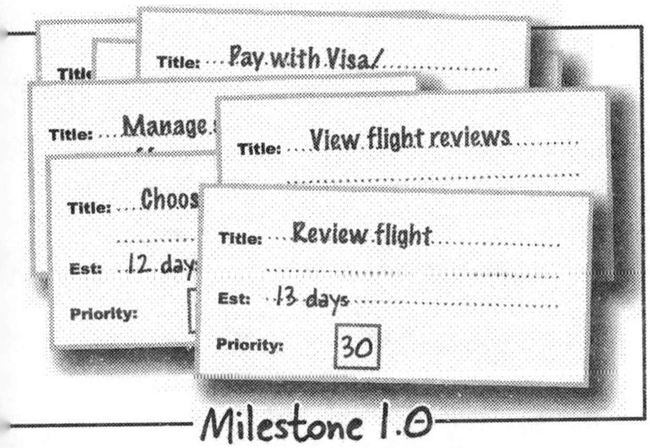

ll the work that an be done for Milestone 1.0

The user stories that fell out of Milestone 1.0

eliver the bad news to the customer

t's the time that every software developer dreads. You've lanned out your iterations, factored in the velocity of your eam, but you still can't get everything your customer wants one in time for their deadline. There's nothing else to do ut come clean...

There's no magic trick here...you have to tell the customer and see what they want to do.

[Note from human resources: we prefer the term unsympathetic customers.]

Managing ~~pissed-off~~ customers

Customers usually aren't happy when you tell them you can't get everything done in the time they want. Be honest, though; you want to come up with a plan for Milestone 1.0 that you can achieve, not a plan that just says what the customer wants it to say.

...and has you on a fast track to failure!

So what do you do when this happens?

It's almost inevitable that you're not going to be able to do everything, so it helps to be prepared with some options when you have to tell the customer the bad news...

1. **Add an iteration to Milestone 1.0**
   Explain that the extra work can be done if an additional iteration is added to the plan. That means a longer development schedule, but the customer will get what they want in Milestone 1.0.

   42 x ~~3~~ 4 = ~~126~~ 168

   Another iteration gives your team plenty of time to develop all the customer's stories—but that pushes out the release date of Milestone 1.0, too.

2. **Explain that the overflow work is not lost, just postponed**
   Sometimes it helps to point out that the user stories that can't make it into Milestone 1.0 are not lost; they are just put on the back burner until the next milestone.

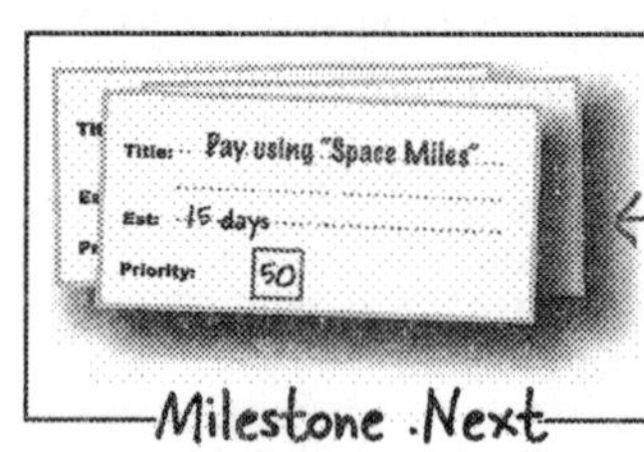

These extra stories a… trashed—they just f… Milestone 2.0. Are s… so important that t… worth starting over… new development te…

3. **Be transparent about how you came up with your figures**
   It sounds strange, but your customer only has your word that you can't deliver everything they want within the deadline they've given you, so it sometimes helps to explain where you're coming from. If you can, show them the calculations that back up your velocity and how this equates to their needs. And tell your customer you ***want*** to deliver them successful software, and that's why you've had to sacrifice some features to give yourself a plan that you are confident that you can deliver on.

there are no Dumb Questions

Q: If I'm close on my estimates, can I fudge a little and squeeze something in?

A: We REALLY wouldn't recommend this. Remember, your estimates are only educated guesses at this point, and they are actually more likely to take slightly longer than originally thought than shorter.

It's a much better idea to leave some breathing room around your estimates to really be confident that you've planned a successful set of iterations.

Q: I have a few days left over in my Milestone 1.0. Can't I add in a user story that breaks my day limit just a little bit?

A: Again, probably not a good idea. If your stories add up to leave you one or two days at the end of the iteration, that's OK. (In Chapter 9 we'll talk about what you can do to round those out.)

Q: OK, without squeezing my last user story in I end up coming under my work-day limit by a LONG way. I have 15 days free at the end of Milestone 1.0! Is there anything I can do about that?

A: To fit a story into that space, try and come up with two simpler stories and fit one of those into Milestone 1.0 instead.

Q: 0.7 seems to add up to a LOT of lost time. What sorts of activities could take up that sort of time?

A: 0.7 is a safe first guess at a team's velocity. One example is where you are installing a new piece of software, like an IDE or a database (naming no specific manufacturers here, of course). In cases like these two hours of interrupted work can actually mean FOUR hours of lost time when you factor in how long it can take a developer to get back in "the zone" and developing productively.

It's also worth bearing in mind that velocity is recalculated at the end of every iteration. So even if 0.7 seems low for your team right now, you'll be able to correct as soon as you have some hard data. In Chapter 9 we'll be refining your velocity based on your team's performance during Iteration 1.

Stay confident that you can achieve the work you sign up for. You should promise and deliver rather than overpromise and fail.

The Big Board on your wall

Once you know exactly what you're building, it's time to set up your **software development dashboard** for Iteration 1 of development. Your dashboard is actually just a **big board** on the wall of your office that you can use to keep tabs on **what work is in the pipeline**, **what's in progress,** and **what's done**.

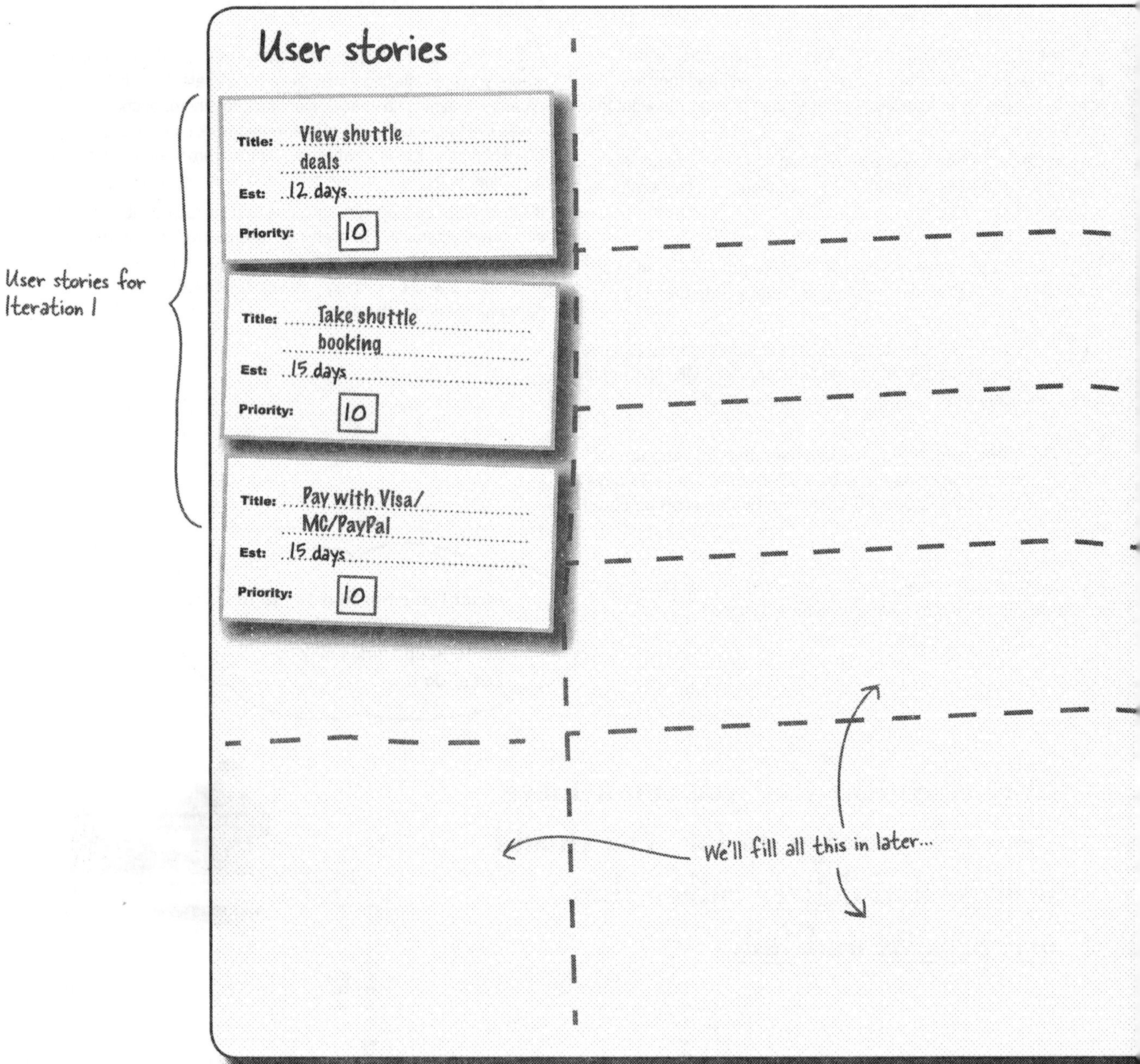

Usually your project board is a whiteboard, so you can use it again and again between iterations and projects.

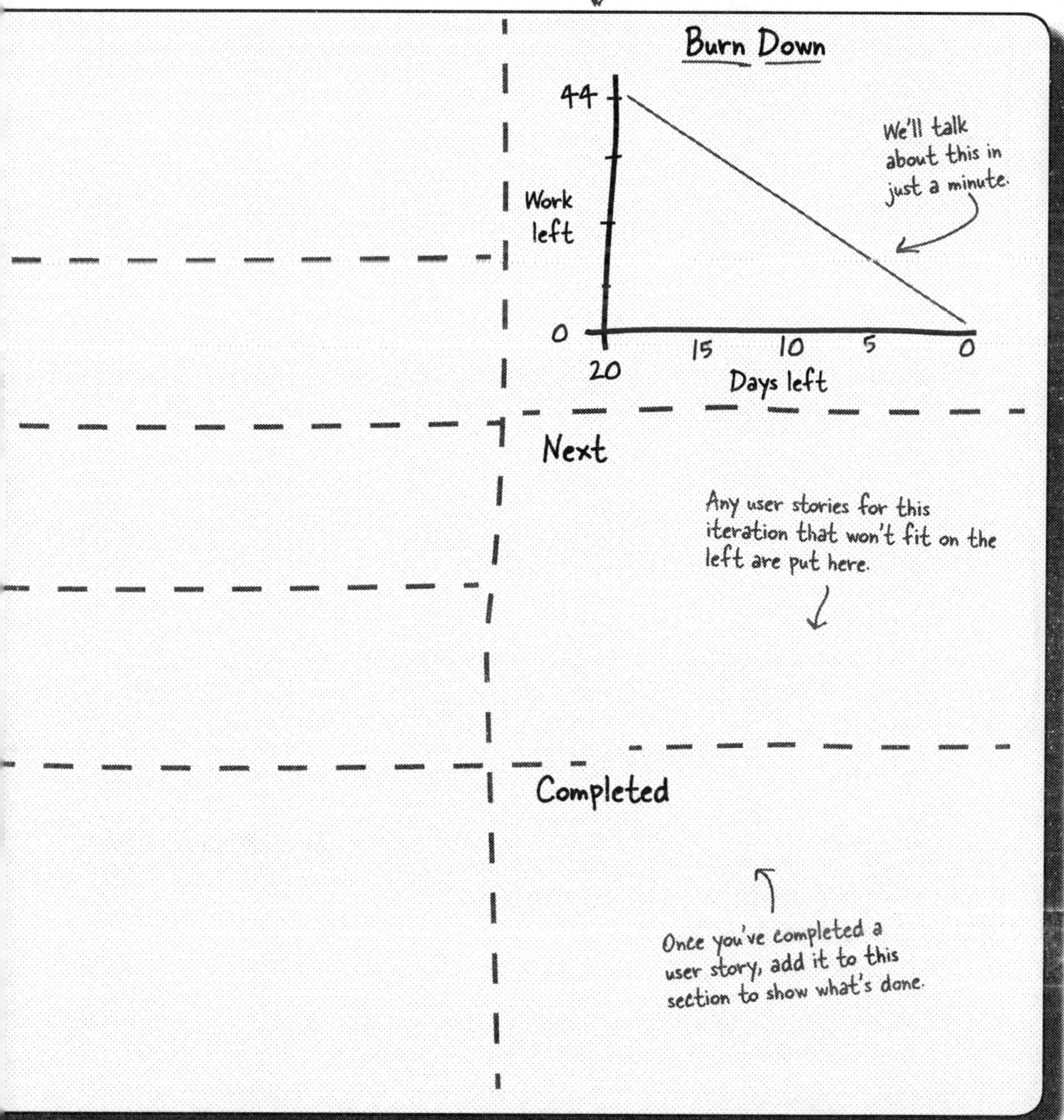

You may have noticed a graph at the top right of your development dashboard, but what is it for? Take a few minutes to glance over the burn-down graph below and write on it what you think the different parts of the graph are for and how it is one of the key tools for monitoring your software development progress and ensuring that you deliver on time.

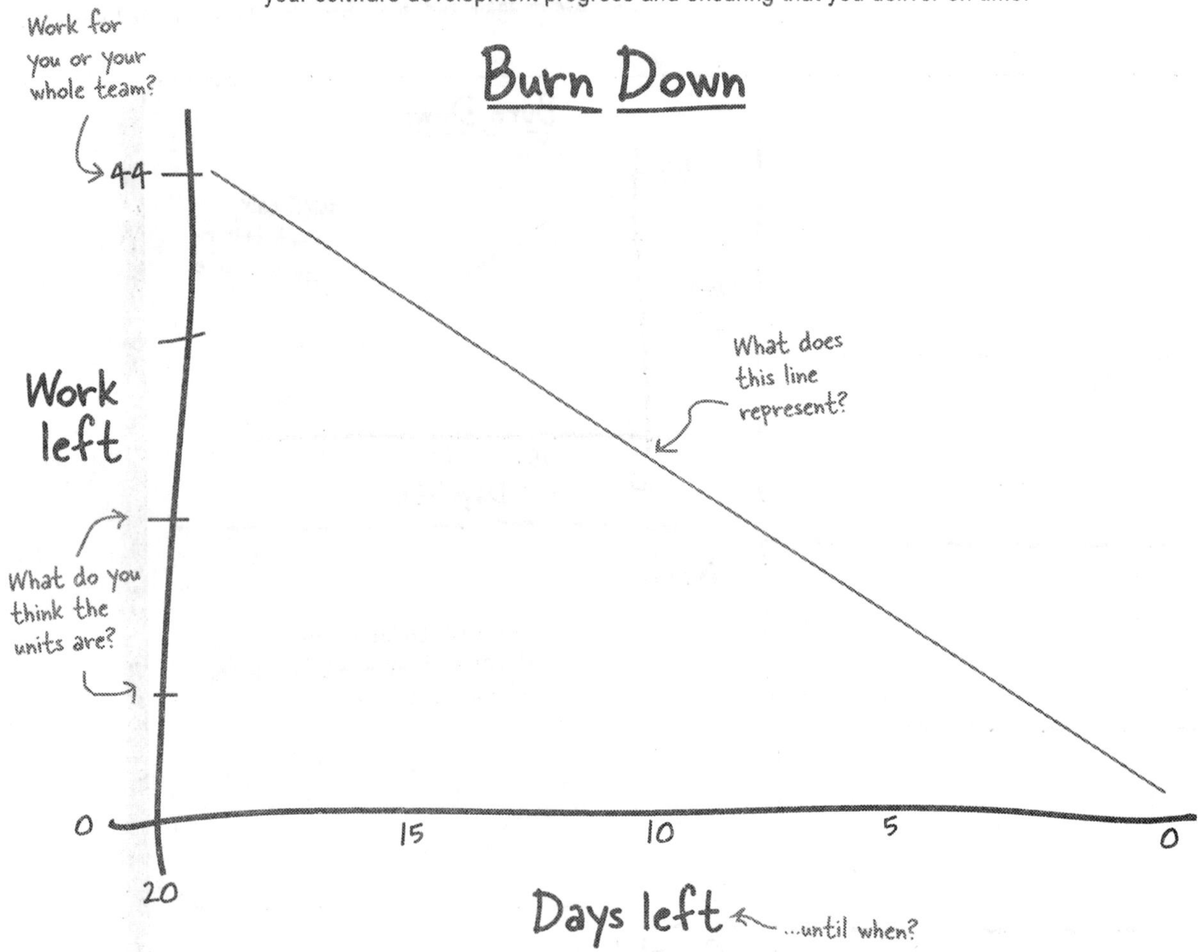

Answers on page 104.

What do you think would be measured on this graph, and how?

....

....

....

....

How to ruin your team's lives

It's easy to look at those long schedules, growing estimates, and diminishing iteration cycles, and start to think, "**My team can work longer weeks!**" If you got your team to agree to that, then you're probably setting yourself up for some trouble down the line.

Personal lives matter

Long hours are eventually going to affect your personal life and the personal lives of the developers on your team. That might seem trite, but a happier team is a more productive team.

Fatigue affects productivity

Tired developers aren't productive. Lots of studies suggest that developers are really only incredibly productive for about three hours a day. The rest of the day isn't a loss, but the more tired your developers are, the less likely they'll even get to that three hours of really productive time.

Be confident in your plans by applying velocity and not overworking yourself and your team.

BULLET POINTS

- The first step to planning what you are going to develop is to ask the customer to **prioritize their requirements**.
- **Milestone 1.0** should be delivered as **early** as you can.
- During Milestone 1.0 try to **iterate around once a month** to keep your development work on track.
- When you don't have enough time to build everything, ask the **customer** to **reprioritize**.
- Plan your iterations by factoring in your team's **velocity** from the **start**.
- If you really can't do what's needed in the time allowed, **be honest** and **explain why** to the customer.
- Once you have an agreed-upon and achievable set of user stories for Milestone 1.0, it's time to set up your **development dashboard** and get developing!

Exercise Solution

You were asked to take a few minutes to glance over the burn-down graph below and describe what you think the different parts of the graph are for and how it is one of the key tools for monitoring your software development progress and ensuring that you deliver on time.

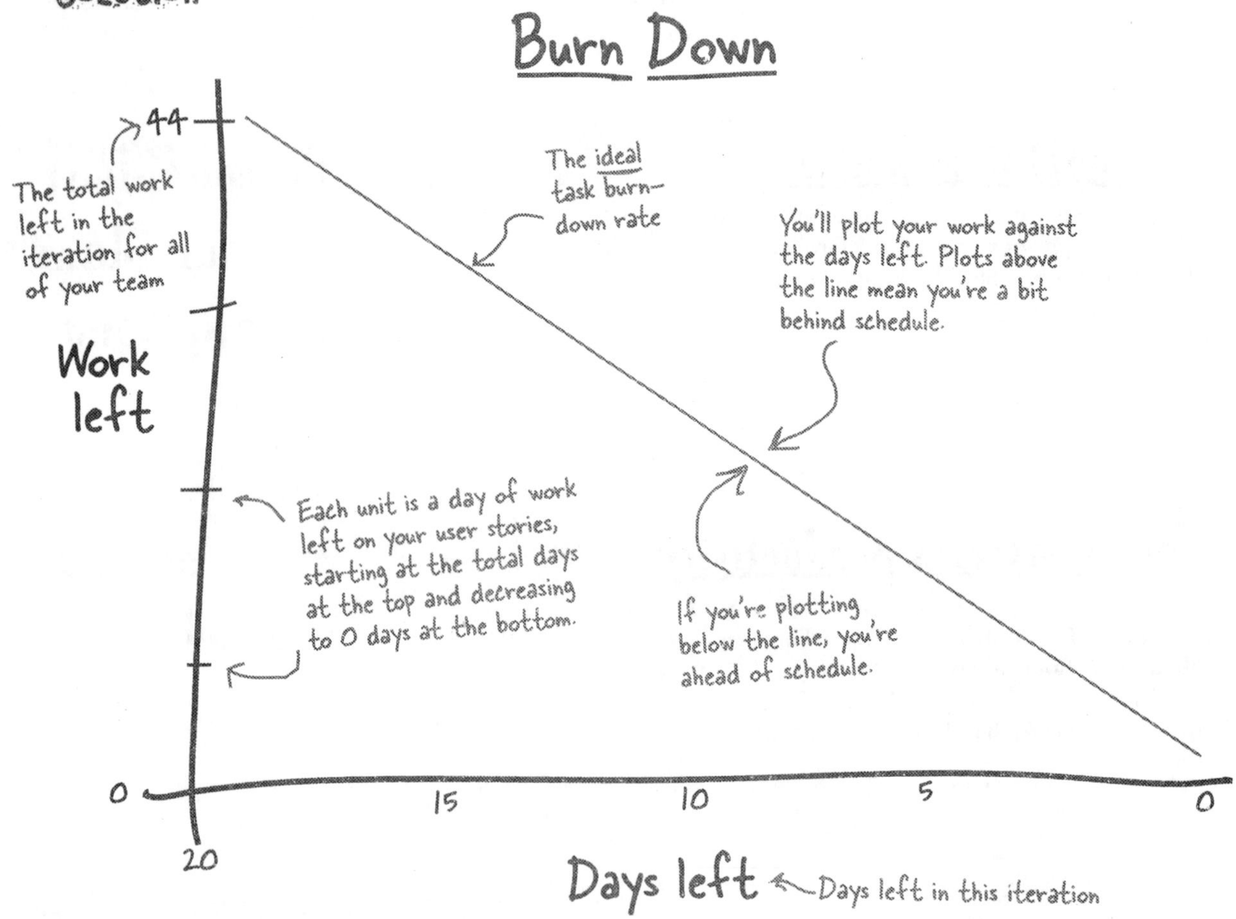

What do you think would be measured on this graph, and how?

This graph monitors how quickly you and your team are completing your work, measured in days on the vertical axis. This chart then plots how quickly you tick off your work remaining against the number of days left in your iteration.

Relax

We'll talk a lot more about burn-down in the next few chapters.

Don't worry if you're still a little fuzzy on how burn-down rates work, and how to track it. You'll start creating a chart of your own in the next chapter, tracking your project's progress.

Software Development Planning Cross

Let's put what you've learned to use and stretch out your left brain a bit! All of the words below are somewhere in this chapter: Good luck!

Across

3. At the end of an iteration you should get .... from the customer.
5. Velocity does not account for .... events.
6. Ideally you apply velocity .... you break your Version 1.0 into iterations.
11. You should have one .... per calendar month.
13. Every 3 iterations you should have a complete and running and releasable .... of your software.
14. Velocity is a measuer of your ....'s work rate.
15. 0.7 is your first pass .... for a new team.
16. At the end of an iteration your software should be ....
17. When priotitizing, the highest priority (the most important to the customer) is set to a value of ....
18. Any more than .... people in a team and you run the risk of slowing your team down.

Down

1. Your customer can remove some less important user stories when .... them.
2. Every 90 days you should .... a complete version of your software.
4. The .... sets the priority of each user stor.
7. The rate that you complete user stories across your entire project.
8. You should always try be .... with the customer.
9. The set of features that must be present to have any working software at all is called the .... functionality.
10. At the end of an iteration your software should be ....
12. You should assume .... working days in a calendar month.

CHAPTER 3

Tools for your Software Development Toolbox

Software Development is all about developing and delivering great software. In this chapter, you added several new techniques to your toolbox... For a complete list of tools in the book, see Appendix ii.

Development Techniques

Iterations should ideally be no longer than a month. That means you have 20 working calendar days per iteration

Applying velocity to your plan lets you feel more confident in your ability to keep your development promises to your customer

Use (literally) a big board on your wall to plan and monitor your current iteration's work

Get your customer's buy-in when choosing what user stories can be completed for Milestone 1.0, and when choosing what iteration a user story will be built in.

Development Principles

Keep iterations short and manageable

Ultimately, the customer decides what is in and what is out for Milestone 1.0

Promise, and deliver

ALWAYS be honest with the customer

BULLET POINTS

- Your **customer prioritizes** what is in and what is out for Milestone 1.0.
- Build **short iterations** of about 1 calendar month, **20 calendar days** of work.
- Throughout an iteration your software should be **buildable** and **runnable**.
- Apply your team's **velocity** to your estimates to figure out exactly how much work you can **realistically manage** in your first iteration.
- Keep your customers happy by coming up with a Milestone 1.0 that **you can achieve** so that you can be confident of delivering and getting paid. Then if you deliver more, they'll be even happier.

Software Development Planning Cross Solution

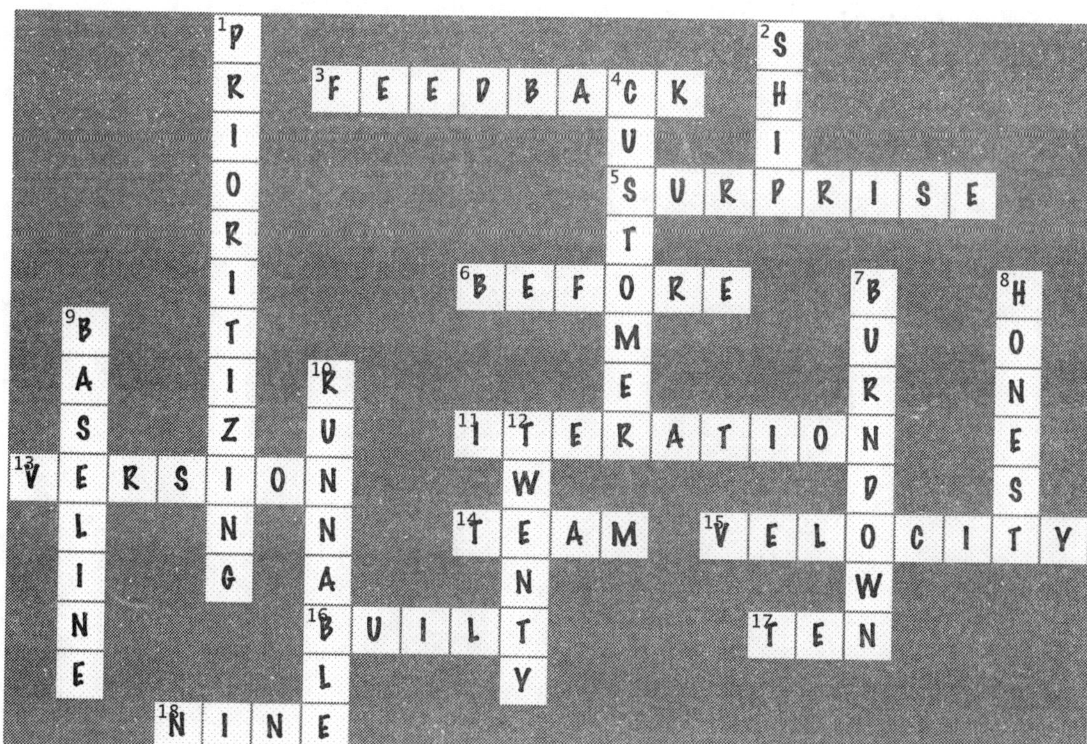

4 user stories and tasks

Getting to the real work

It's time to go to work. User stories capture what you need to develop, but now it's time to knuckle down and **dish out the work that needs to be done** so that you can bring those user stories to life. In this chapter you'll learn how to **break your user stories into tasks,** and how **task estimates** help you track your project from inception to completion. You'll learn how to update your board, moving tasks from in progress to complete, to finally **completing an entire user story**. Along the way, you'll handle and prioritize the inevitable **unexpected work** your customer will add to your plate.

Introducing iSwoon

Welcome to iSwoon, soon to be the world's finest desktop date planner! Here's the big board, already loaded with user stories broken down into 20-work-day iterations:

Date Rights Management (DRM) included

Part of the big board on your wall from Chapter 3

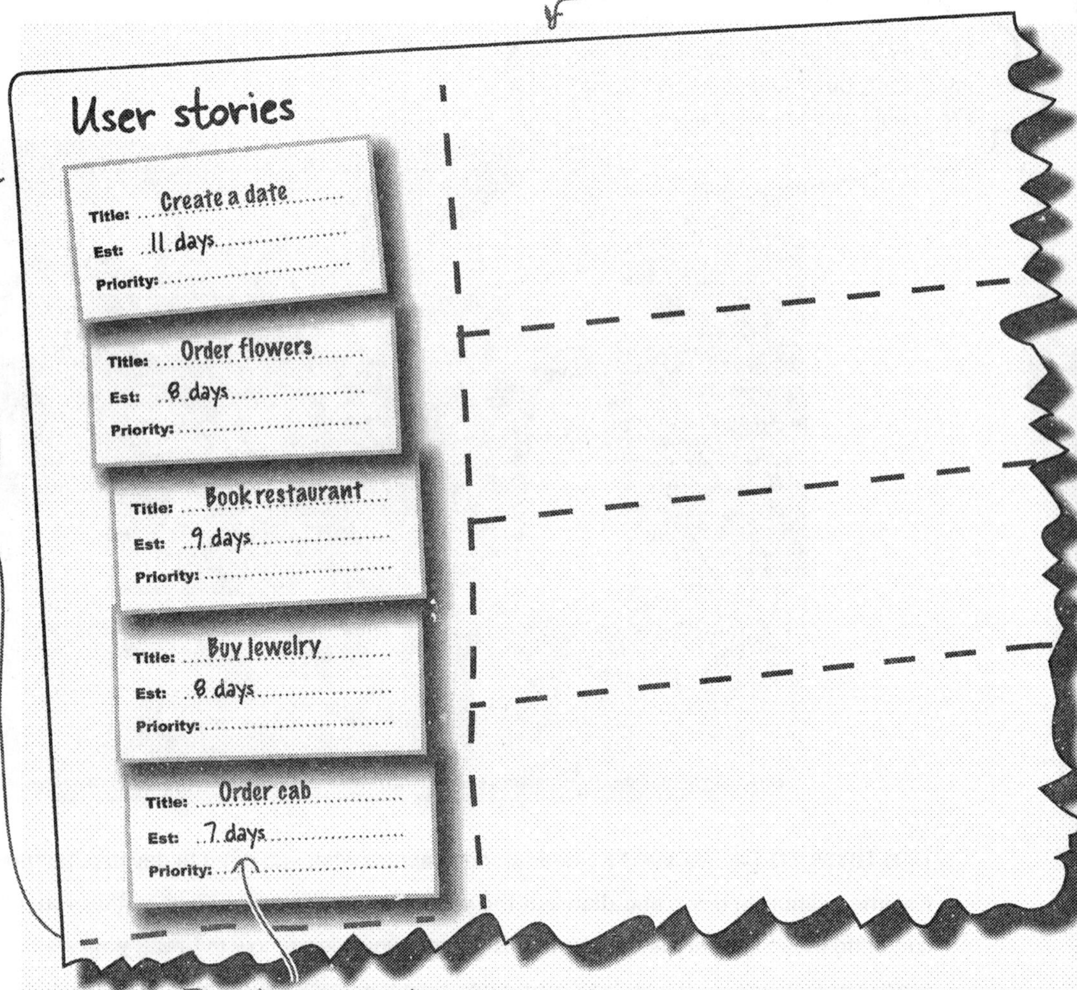

User stories for Iteration 1

The initial estimates for how long each user story will take to develop

Exercise

It's time to get you and your team of developers working. Take each of the iSwoon user stories for Iteration 1 and assign each to a developer by drawing a line from the user story to the developer of your choice...

Title: Order flowers
Est: 8 days
Priority:

Title: Book restaurant
Est: 9 days
Priority:

Title: Create a date
Est: 11 days
Priority:

Title: Buy Jewelry
Est: 8 days
Priority:

Title: Order cab
Est: 7 days
Priority:

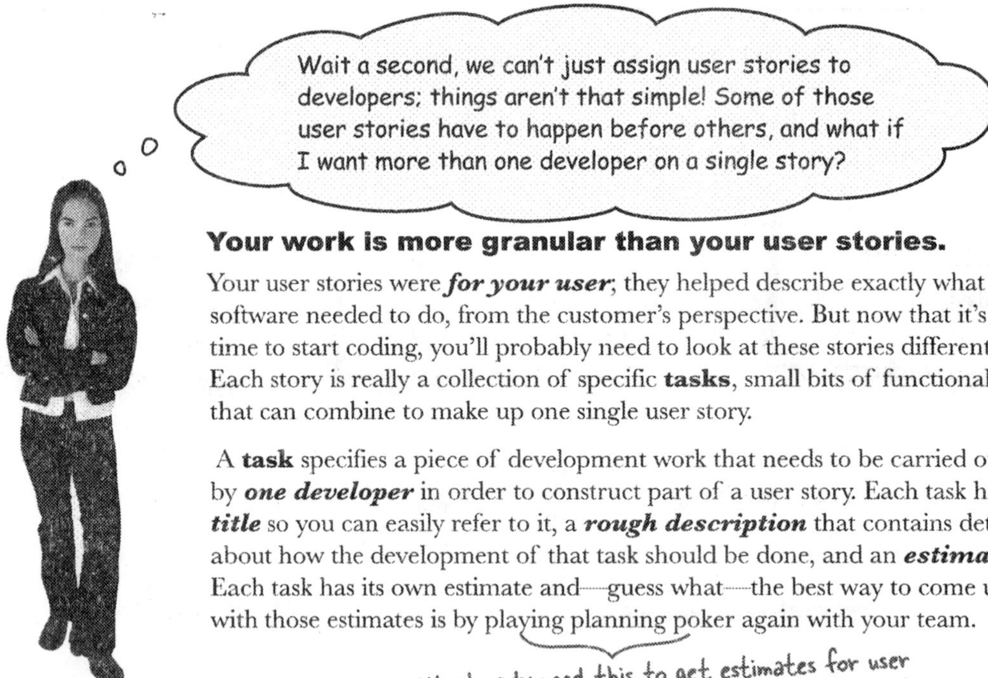

Your work is more granular than your user stories.

Your user stories were ***for your user***; they helped describe exactly what you software needed to do, from the customer's perspective. But now that it's time to start coding, you'll probably need to look at these stories differently. Each story is really a collection of specific **tasks**, small bits of functionality that can combine to make up one single user story.

A **task** specifies a piece of development work that needs to be carried out by ***one developer*** in order to construct part of a user story. Each task has a ***title*** so you can easily refer to it, a ***rough description*** that contains details about how the development of that task should be done, and an ***estimate***. Each task has its own estimate and—guess what—the best way to come up with those estimates is by playing planning poker again with your team.

We already used this to get estimates for user stories in Chapter 2, and it works for tasks, too.

Sharpen your pencil

Now it's your turn. Take the user story of creating a date and break it into tasks you think you and your team need to execute. Write one task down on each of the sticky notes, and don't forget to add an estimate to each task.

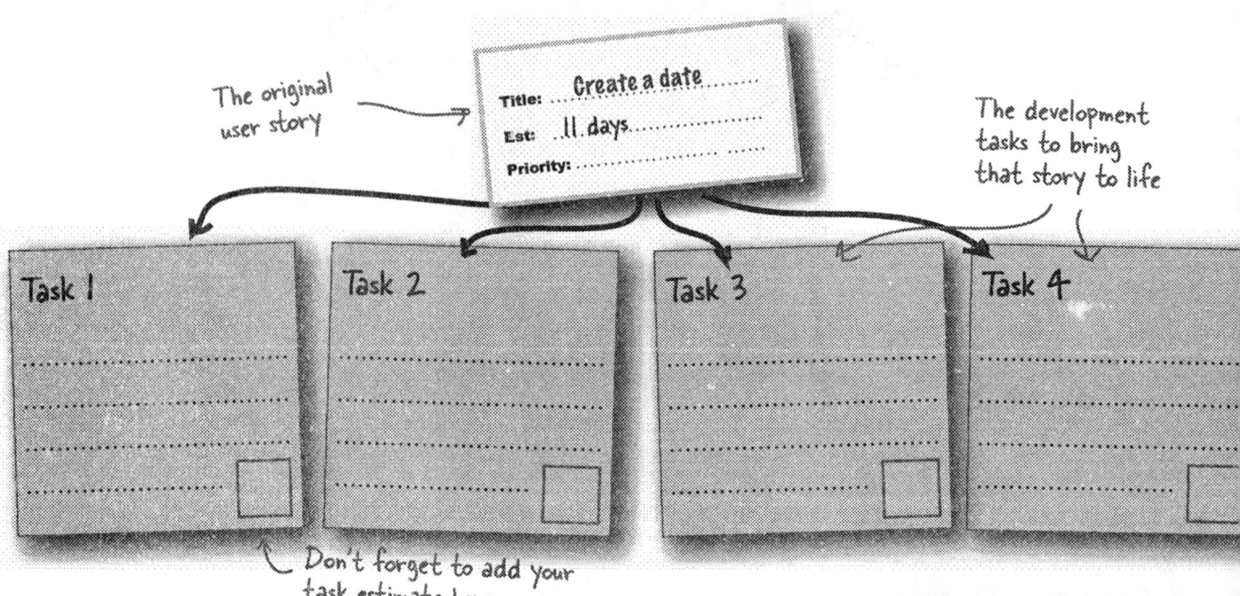

Answers on page 114.

'o your tasks add up?

'id you notice a possible problem with your estimates? We've got a user :ory with an estimate, but now we're adding *new* estimates to our tasks. /hat happens when the two sets of estimates don't agree?

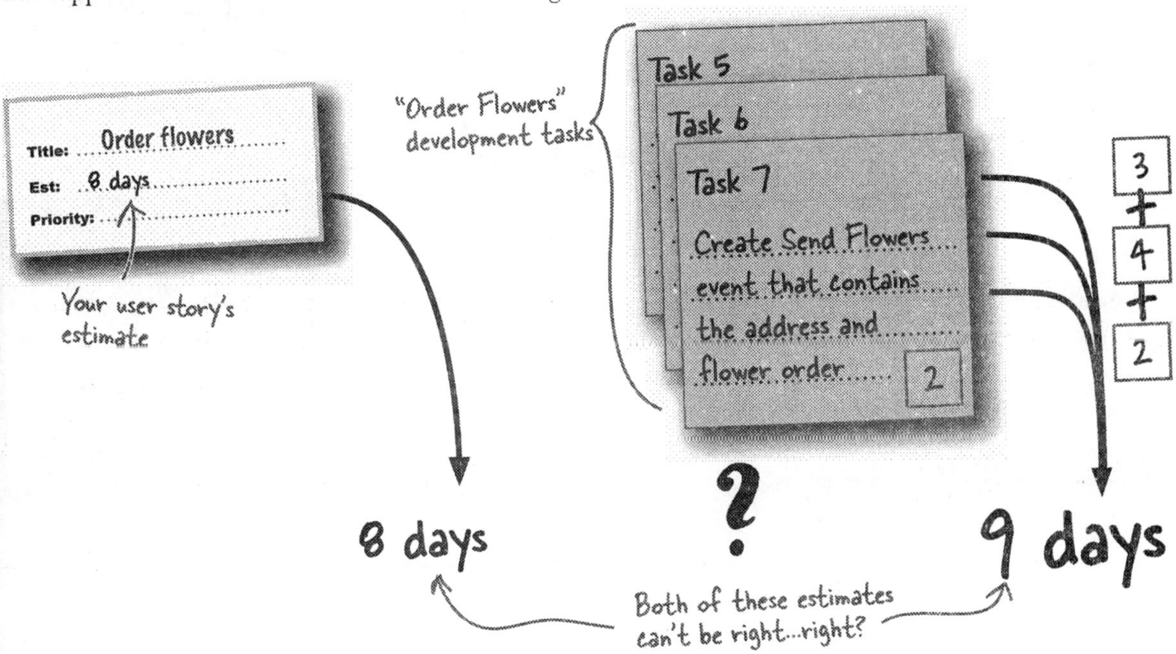

ask estimates add confidence to user tory estimates

›ur user story estimates kept you in the right ballpark 'hen you were planning your iterations, but tasks really add nother level of detail specific to the actual coding you'll do ›r a user story.

ı fact, it's often best to break out tasks from your user ories right ***at the beginning*** of the estimation process, if ›u have time. This way you'll add even more confidence › the plan that you give your customer. ***It's always best › rely on the task estimates.*** Tasks describe the actual ›ftware development work that needs to be done and are ır less of a guesstimate than a coarse-grained user story stimate.

Break user stories into tasks to add CONFIDENCE to your estimates and your plan.

And the earlier you can do this, the better.

Sharpen your pencil Solution

You were asked to take the user story of creating a date and break out the tasks that you think you and your team will need to execute to develop this user story, not forgetting to add task estimates...

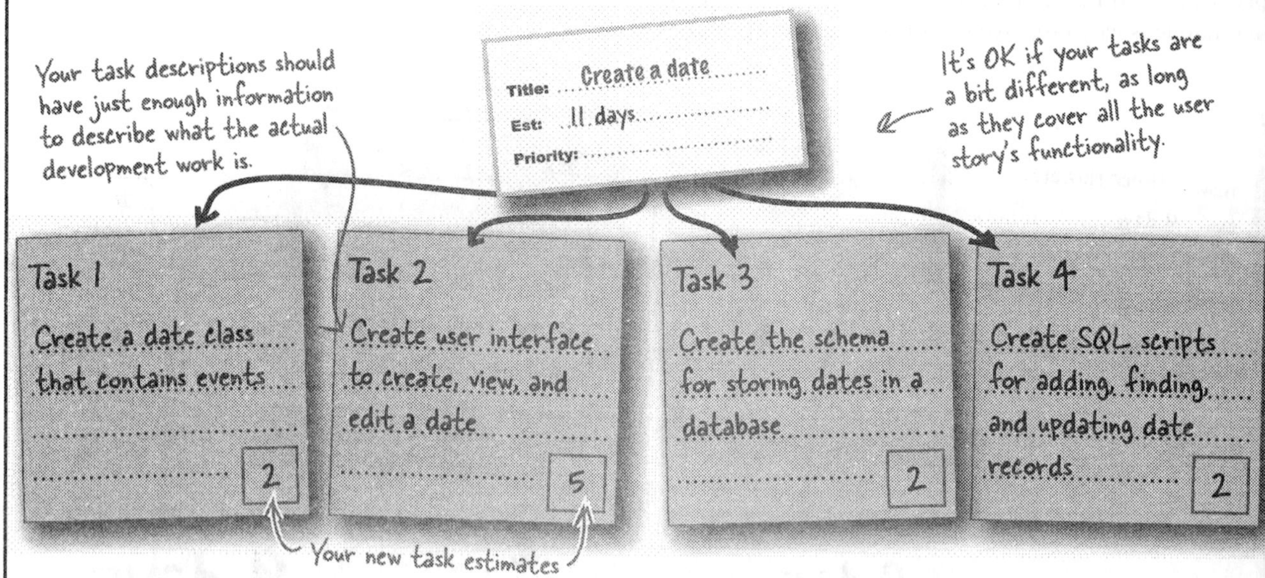

there are no Dumb Questions

Q: My tasks add up to a new estimate for my user story, so were my original user story estimates wrong?

A: Well, yes and no. Your user story estimate was accurate enough in the beginning to let you organize your iterations. Now, with task estimates, you have a set of **more accurate data** that either backs up your user story estimates or conflicts with them.

You always want to rely on data that you trust, the estimates that you feel are most accurate. In this case, those are your task estimates.

Q: How big should a task estimate be?

A: Your task estimates should ideally be between 1/2 and 5 days in length. A shorter task, measured in hours, is too small a task. A task that is longer than five days spreads across more than one working week, and that gives the developer working on the task too much time to lose focus.

Q: What happens when I discover a big missing task?

A: Sometimes—hopefully not too often—you'll come across a task that just breaks your user story estimate completely. You might have forgotten something important when first coming up with the user story estimates, and suddenly the devil in the details rears its ugly head, and you have a more accurate, task-based estimate that completely blows your user story estimate out of the water.

When this happens you can really only do one thing, and that's adju[st] your iteration. To keep your iteration within 20 working days, you can postpone that large task (and user story) until the next iteration, reshuffling the rest of your iterations accordingly.

To avoid these problem, you could break your user stories into tasks earlier. For instance, you might break up your user stories into tasks when you initially plan your iterations, always relying on your task estimates over your original user story estimates as you balance ou[t] your iterations to 20 working days each.

Plot just the work you have left

Remember that burn-down rate chart from Chapter 3? Here's where it starts to help us track what's going on in our project. Every time we do any work or review an estimate, we update our new estimates, and the time we have left, on our burn-down chart:

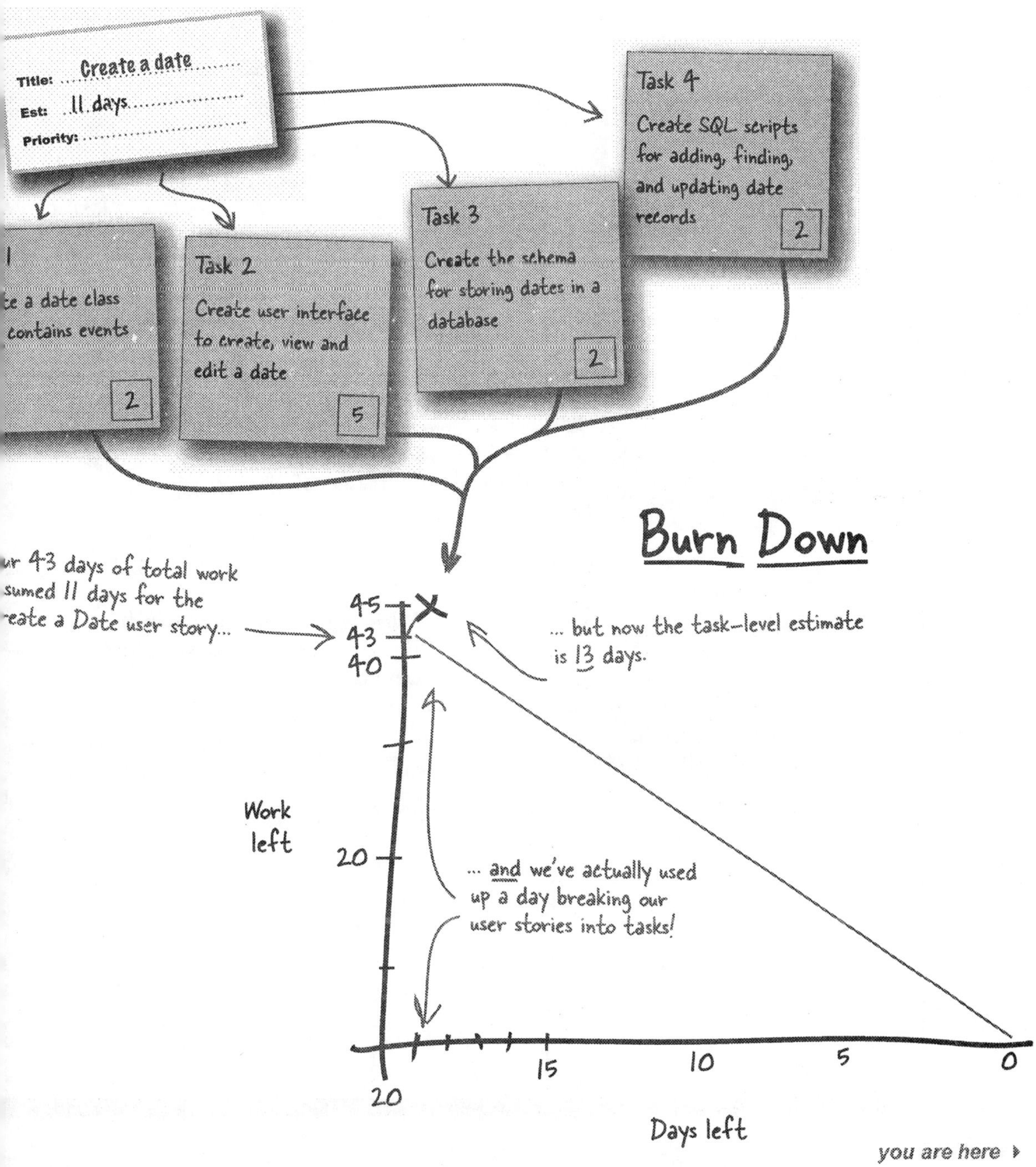

Add your tasks to your board

You and your team are now almost ready to start working on your ... st you need to update the big board on your wall. Add your task sticky notes to yo... es. and also add an In Progress and Complete section for tracking tasks and user stor...

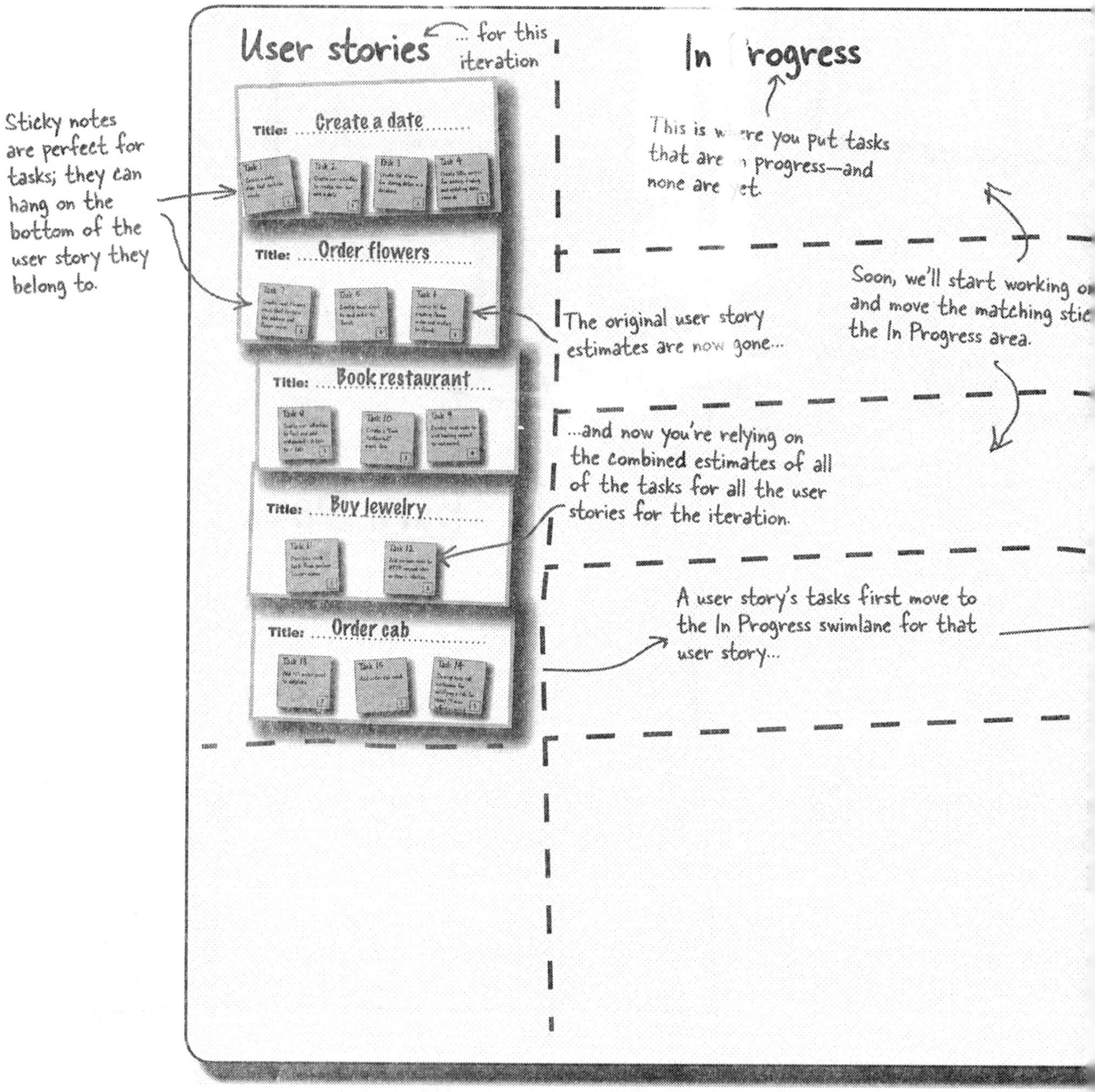

This isn't a virtual board—it should be a <u>real</u> bulletin or whiteboard hanging somewhere, like a common area or maybe the office where you and your team meet each morning.

Yes, you should meet each morning! More on that in just a minute...

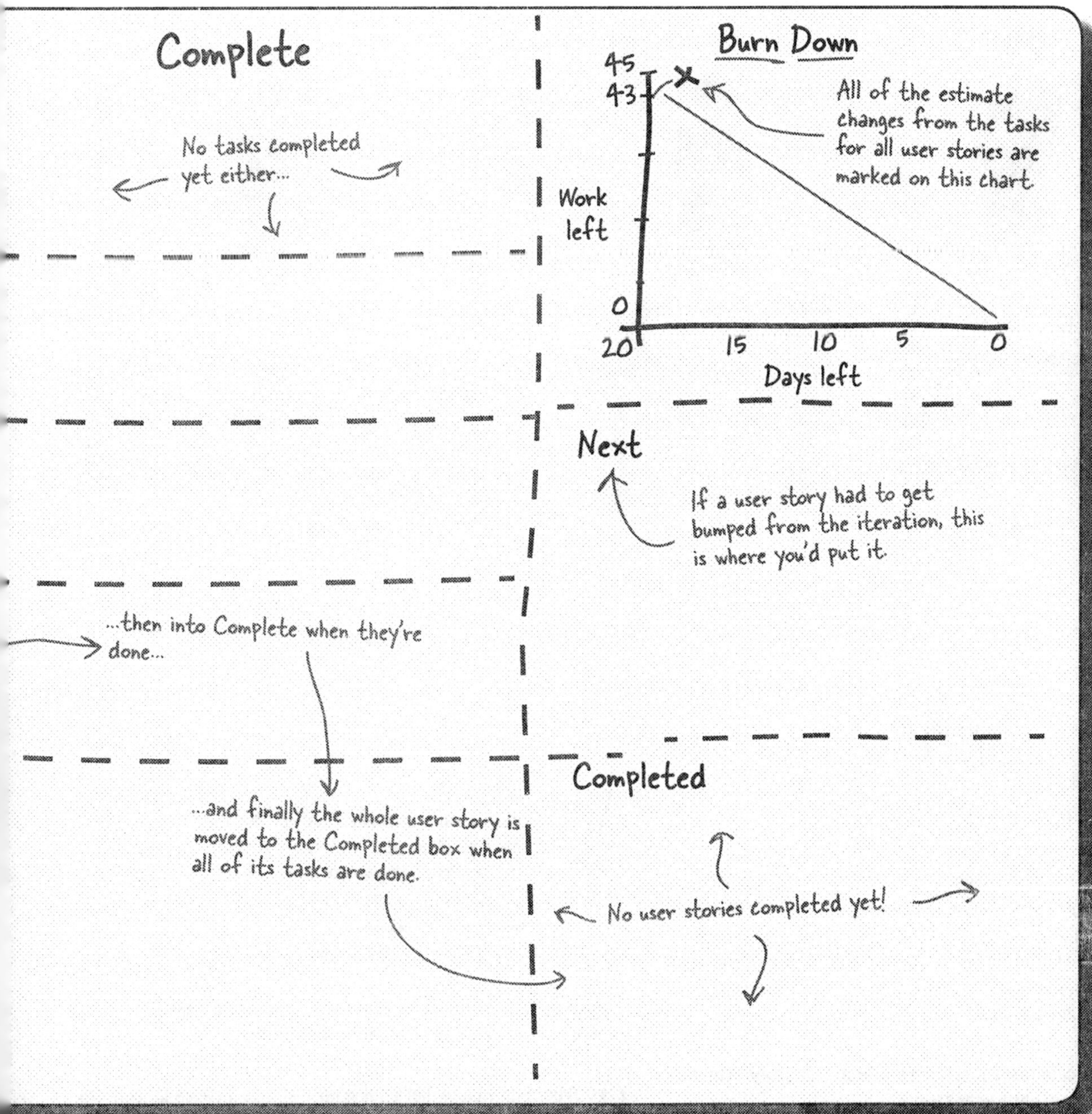

Start working on your tasks

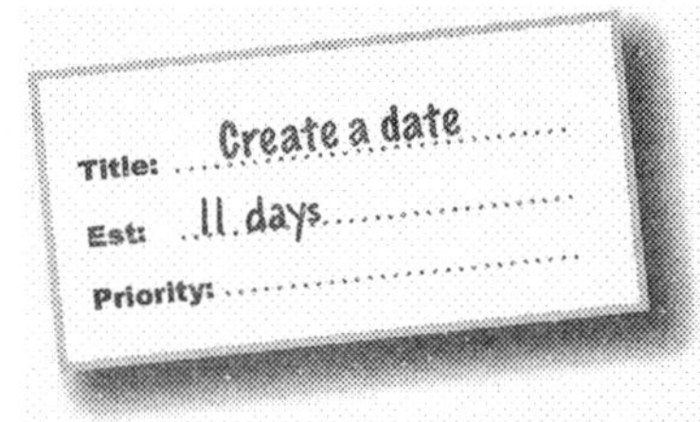

It's time to bring that burn-down rate back under control by getting started developing on your first user story. And, with small tasks, you can assign your team work in a sensible, trackable way:

there are no Dumb Questions

Q: How do I figure out who to assign a task to?

A: There are no hard-and-fast rules about who to give a task to, but it's best to just apply some common sense. Figure out who would be most productive or—if you have the time, will learn most from a particular task by looking at their own expertise—and then allocate the task to the best-suited developer, or the one who will gain the most, that's not already busy.

Q: Why allocate tasks just from the first user story. Why not take one task from each user story?

A: One good reason is so that so that you don't wind up with five stories in a half-done state, and instead can wrap up a user story and move on to the next. If you've got one story your other stories depend on, you may want to get all that first story's tasks done at once. However, if your stories are independent of each other, you may work on tasks from multiple stories all at the same time.

Q: I'm still worried about that burn-down rate being way up, is there anything I can do right now to fix that?

A: A burn-down rate that's going up is always a cause for concern, but since you're early on, let's wait a bit and see if we catch up.

A task is only in progress when it's IN PROGRESS

Now that everyone's got some work to do, it's time to move those task stickies off of user story cards, and onto the In Progress area of your big board. But you only put tasks that are **actually being worked on** in the In Progress column—even if you already know who'll be working on tasks yet to be tackled.

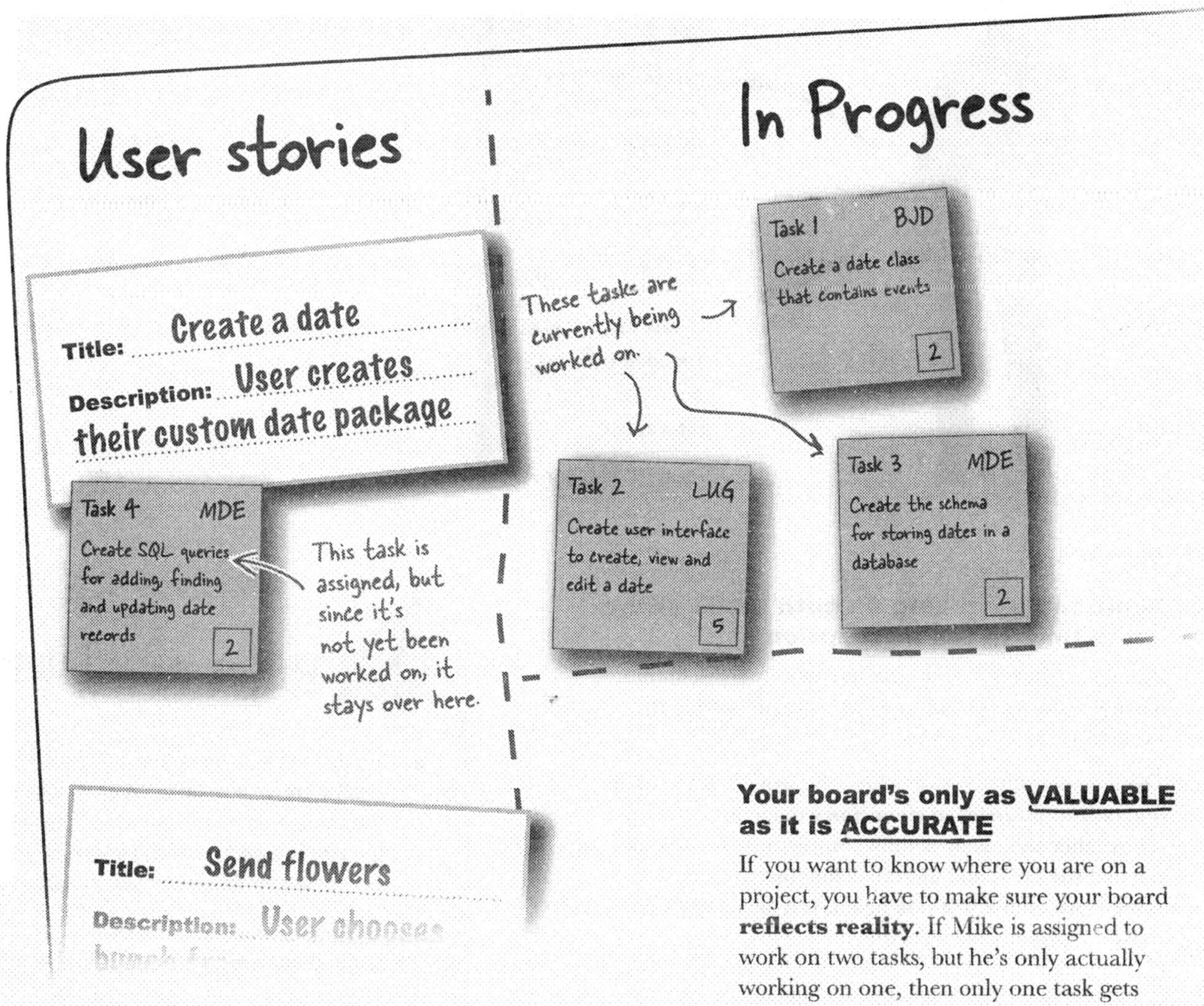

Your board's only as VALUABLE as it is ACCURATE

If you want to know where you are on a project, you have to make sure your board **reflects reality**. If Mike is assigned to work on two tasks, but he's only actually working on one, then only one task gets put up in the In Progress area. Otherwise, it looks like more is being worked on than really is.

What if I'm working on two things at once?

Not all tasks are best executed in isolation. Sometimes two tasks are related, and, because there is so much overlap, it's actually more work to tackle one, and then the other separately. In these cases the most productive thing to do is work on those tasks ***at the same time***...

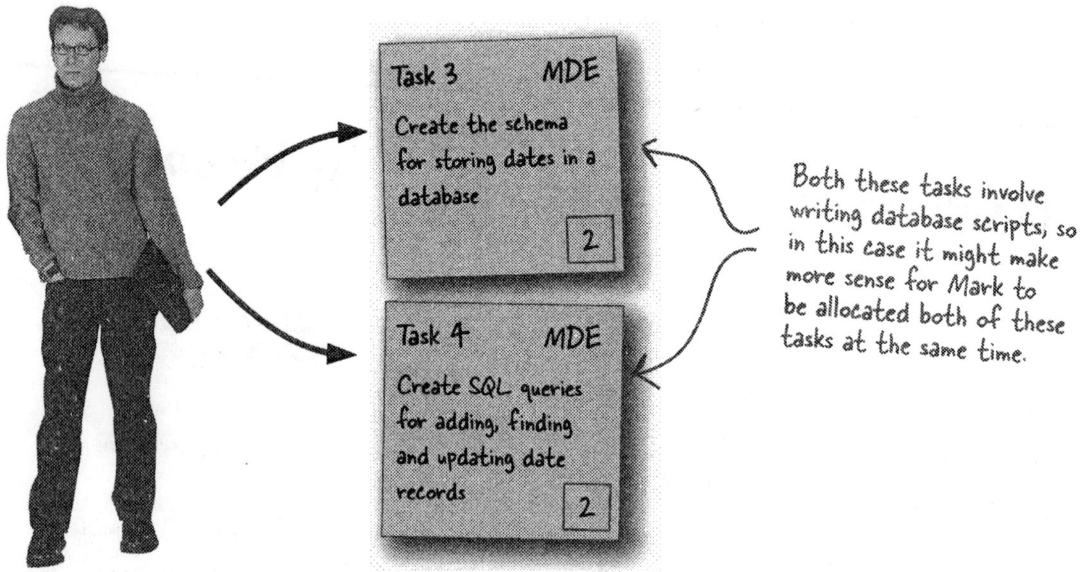

Sometimes working on both tasks at the same time IS the best option

When you have two tasks that are closely related. then it's not really a problem to work on them both at the same time.

This is especially the case where the work completed in one task could ***inform decisions*** made in the work for another task. Rather than completing one task and starting the next, and then realizing that you need to do some work on the first task again, it is far more efficient to work both tasks at the same time.

Rules of Thumb

- Try to double-up tasks that are related to each other, or at least focus on roughly the same area of your software. The less thought involved in moving from one task to another, the faster that switch will be.
- Try not to double-up on tasks that have large estimates. It's not only difficult to stay focused on a long task, but you will be more confident estimating the work involved the shorter the task is.

Exercise

Someone's been tampering with the board and things are a real mess. Take a look at the project below and annotate all of the problems you can spot.

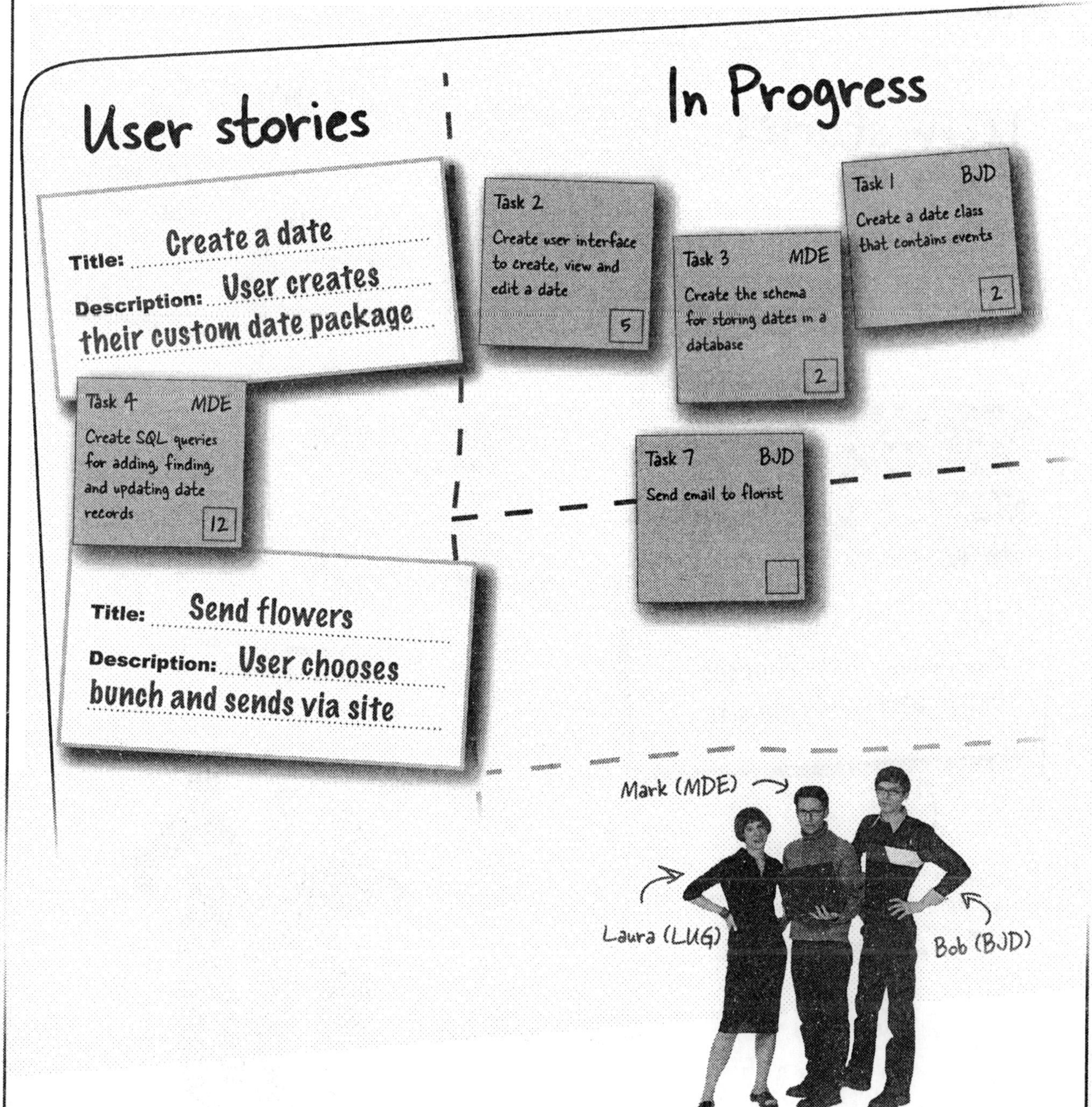

Exercise Solution

Your job was to to take a look at the project below and annotate all of the problems you could spot...

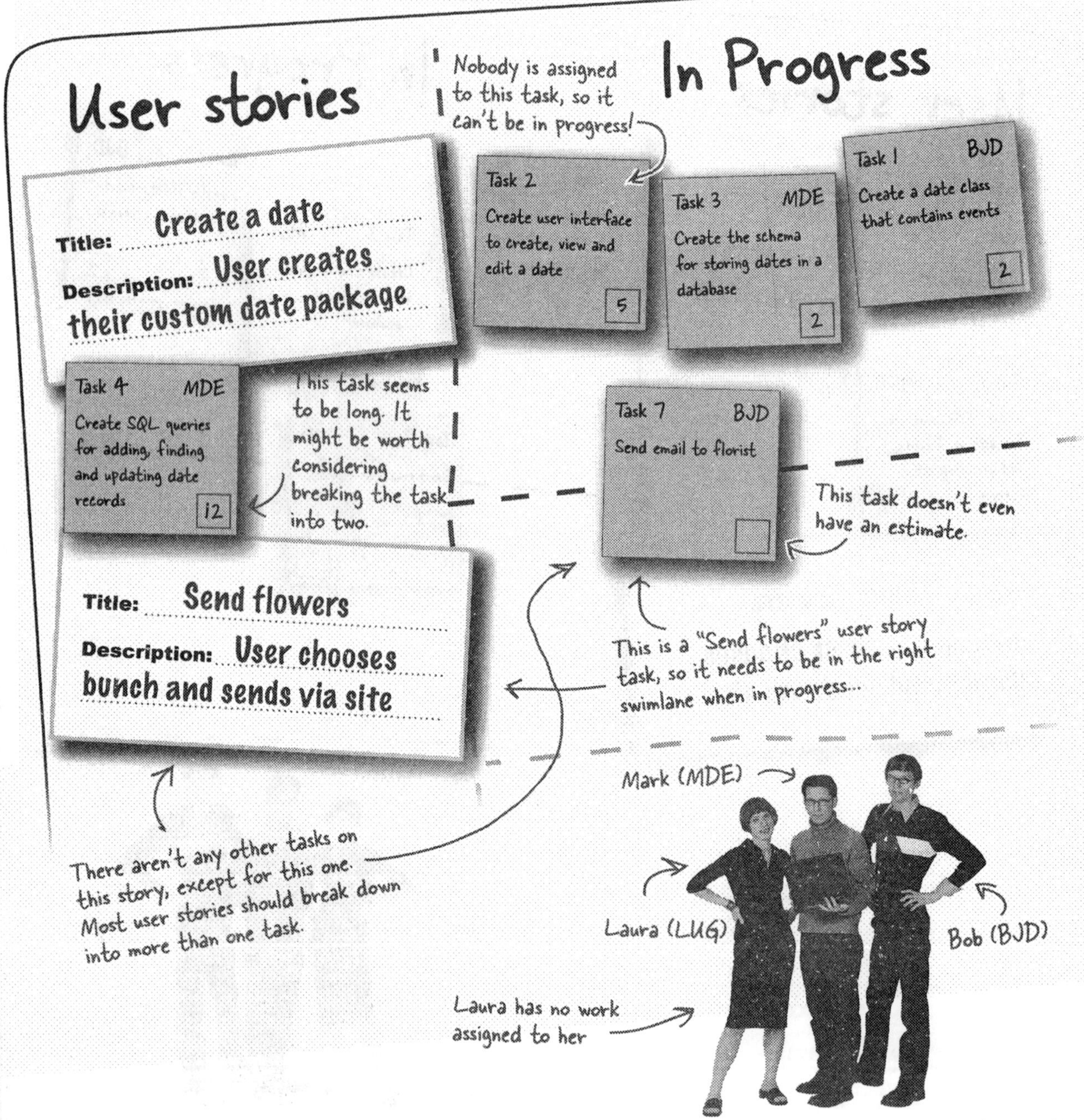

Your first standup meeting...

A meeting so quick you don't even have time to sit down.

You've now got some tasks in progress, and so to keep everyone in the loop, while not taking up too much of their time, you conduct a quick standup meeting every day.

Mark: So, we've all had our tasks for one day now. How are we doing?

Bob: Well, I haven't hit any big problems yet, so nothing new really to report.

Mark: That's great. I've had a bit of success and finished up on the scripts to create tables in the database...

Laura: Things are still in progress on my user interface task.

Mark: OK, that all sounds good, I'll update the board and move my task into Completed. We can update the burn rate, too; maybe we're making up for some of that time we lost earlier. Any other successes or issues to report?

Bob: Well, I guess I should probably mention that I'm finding creating the right Date class a little tricky...

Mark: That's fine. I'm really glad you brought it up, though. That's a two-day task and we need it done tomorrow, so I'll get you some help on that as soon as possible. OK, it's been about seven minutes, I think we're done here...

Your daily standup meetings should:

- **Track your progress.** Get everyone's input about how things are going.
- **Update your burn-down rate.** It's a new day so you need to update your burndown rate to see how things are going.
- **Update tasks.** If a task is completed then it's time to move it over into the Completed area and check those days off of your burn-down rate.
- **Talk about what happened yesterday and what's going to happen today.** Bring up any successes that happened since yesterday's standup meeting and make sure everyone knows what they're doing today.
- **Bring up any issues.** The standup meeting is not a place to be shy, so encourage everyone to bring up any problems they've encountered so that you all as a team can start to fix those problems.
- **Last between 5 and 15 minutes.** Keep things brief and focused on the short-term tasks at hand.

A daily standup meeting should keep everyone motivated, keep your board up-to-date, and highlight any problems early.

Task 1: Create the Date class

Bob's been busy creating the classes that bring the "Create a Date" user story to life, but he needs a hand. Here's a UML class diagram that describes the design he's come up with so far.

A UML class diagram shows the classes in your software and how they relate to each other.

The Date class is split into three classes, one class for each type of date...

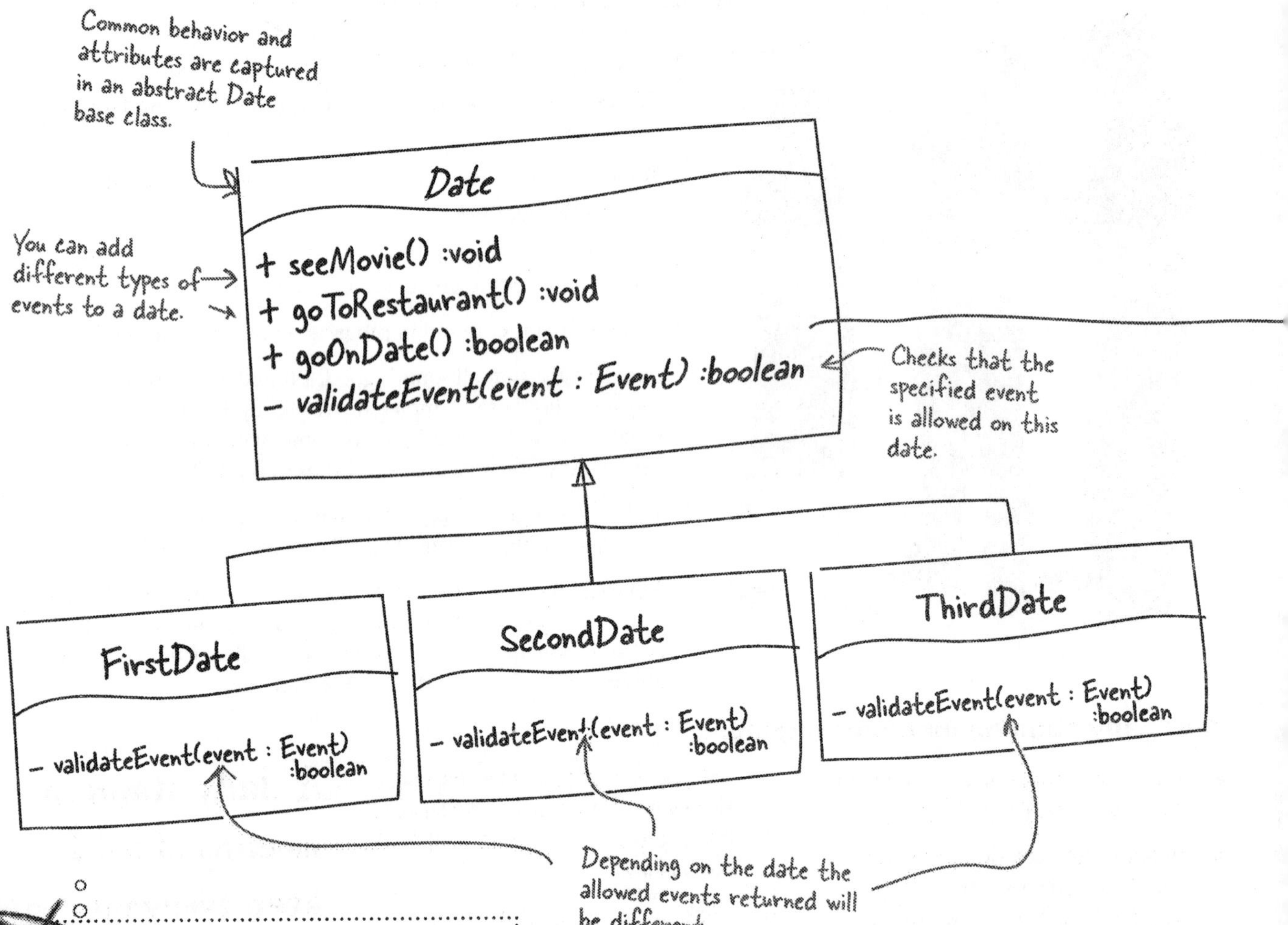

> **Relax**
>
> **It's okay if you've never seen UML before!**
>
> Don't worry if you don't know your UML class diagrams from your sequences; there's a short overview in Appendix i to help you get comfortable with UML notation as quickly as possible.

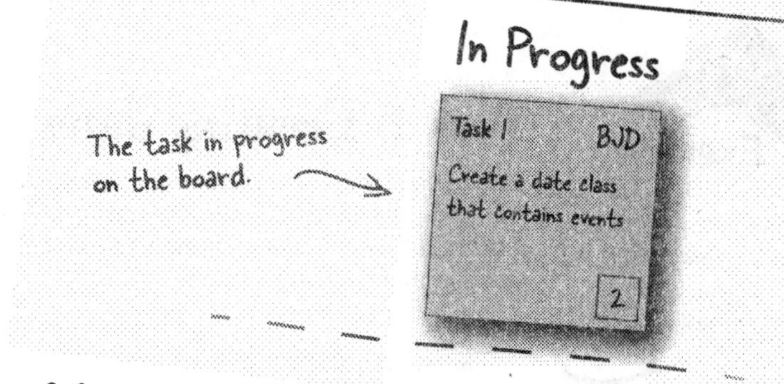

Each Date can then have a number of Events added to it...

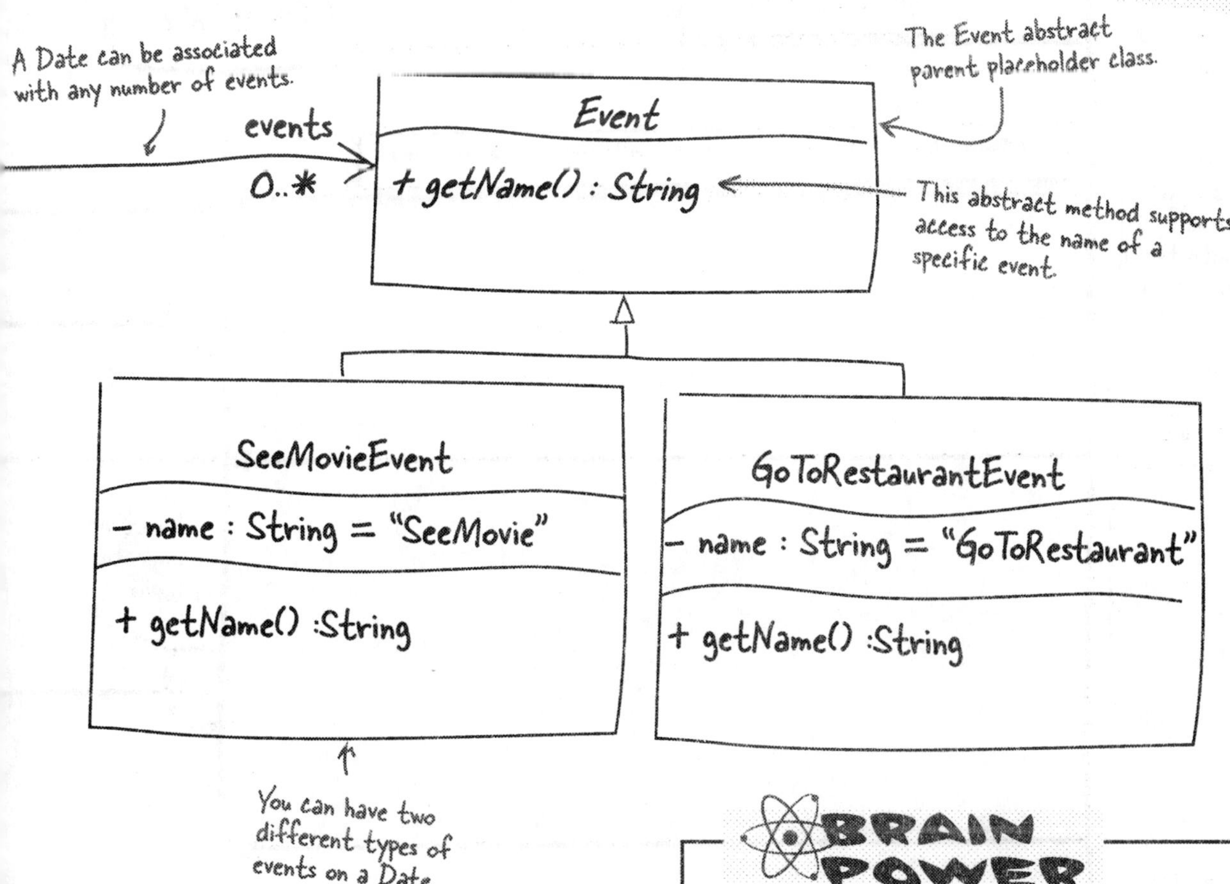

BRAIN POWER

What do you think of this design?

Exercise

Task 1: Creating dates

Let's test out the Date and Event classes by bringing them to life on a sequence diagram. Finish the sequence diagram by adding the right method names to each interaction between objects so that you are creating and validating that a first date that has two events, going to a restaurant and seeing a movie.

A diagram that brings objects to life, showing how they work together to make an interaction happen

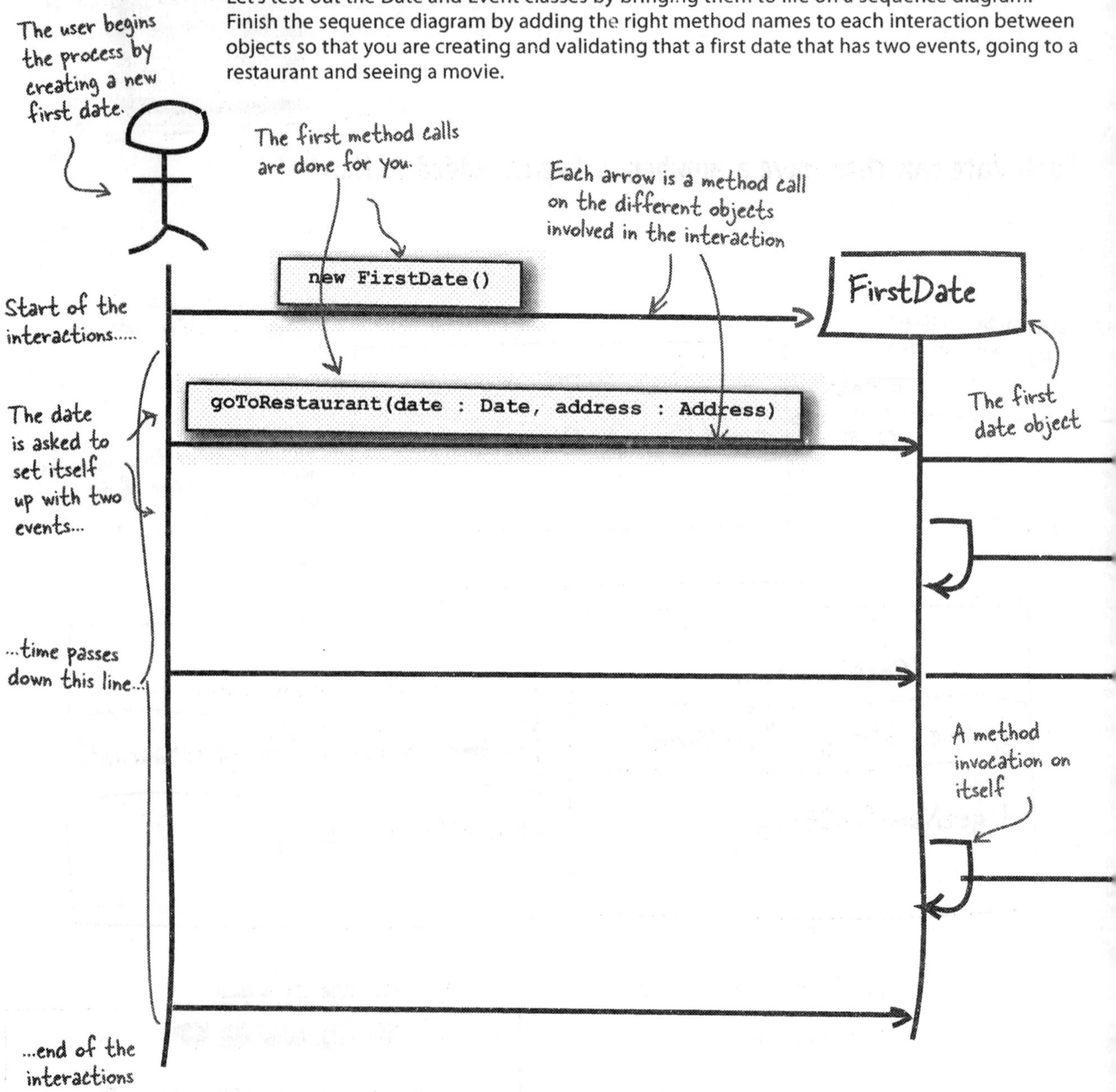

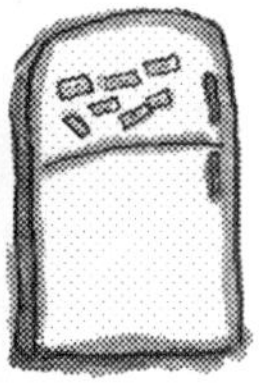

In Progress

Task 1 BJD
Create a date class that contains events
2

The magnets to place on the method calls

`new GoToRestaurantEvent()`

`getName() :String`

`validateEvent(event : Event) :boolean`

`goOnDate()`

`seeMovie(date : Date, address : Address)`

`new SeeMovieEvent()`

Each magnet is a method name.

`validateEvent(event : Event) :boolean`

`getName() :String`

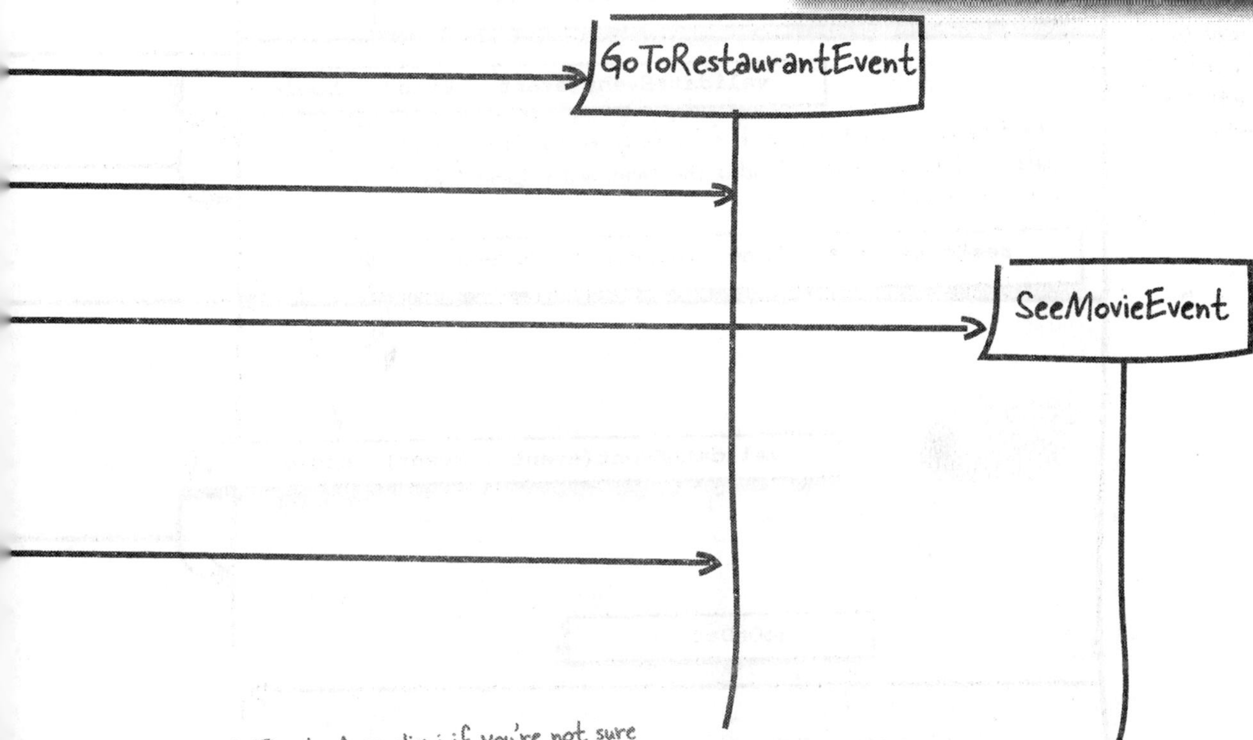

* Flip to Appendix i if you're not sure what this stuff means; you'll find more on UML class diagrams and sequence diagrams there.

Exercise Solution

Your job was to test out the Date and Event classes by bringing them to life on a sequence diagram. You should have finished the sequence diagram so that you plan and go on a first date with two events, going to a restaurant and seeing a movie.

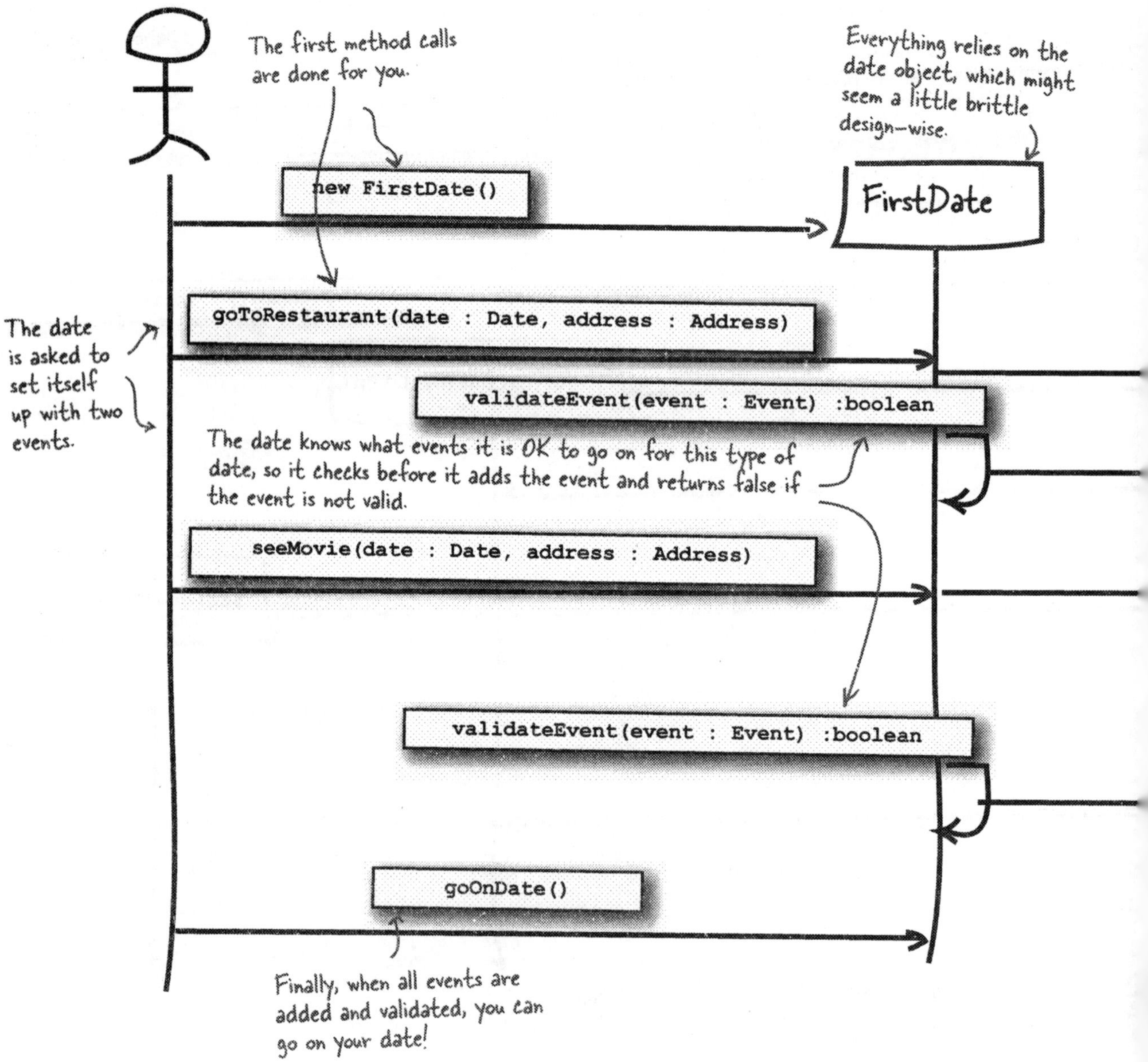

In Progress
Task 1
BJD
Create a date class that contains events
2

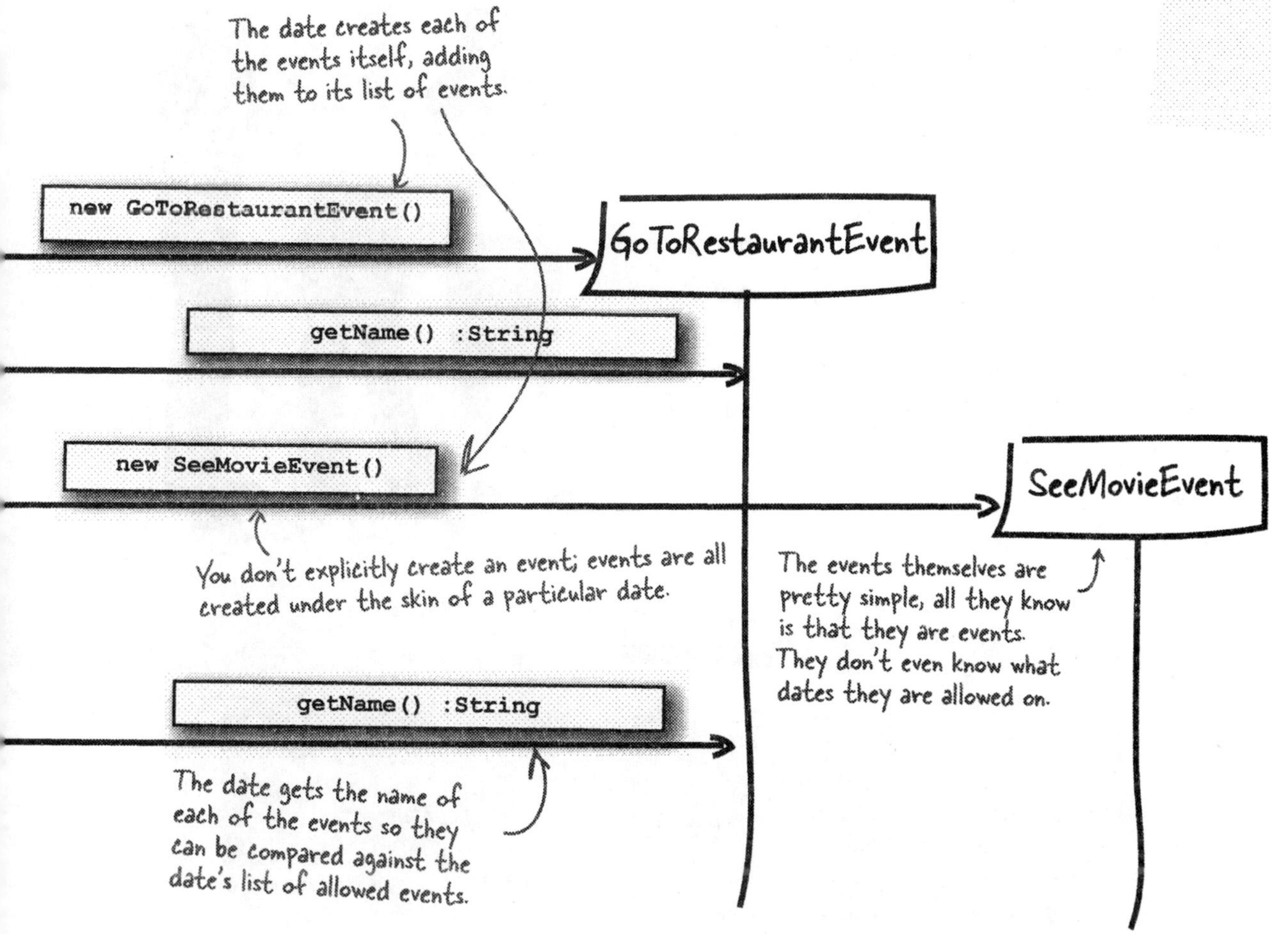
The date creates each of the events itself, adding them to its list of events.
new GoToRestaurantEvent()
GoToRestaurantEvent
getName() :String
new SeeMovieEvent()
SeeMovieEvent
You don't explicitly create an event; events are all created under the skin of a particular date.
The events themselves are pretty simple, all they know is that they are events. They don't even know what dates they are allowed on.
getName() :String
The date gets the name of each of the events so they can be compared against the date's list of allowed events.

Standup meeting: Day 5, end of Week 1...

Bob: Well, I finally got the date class finished with a little help, ran late by a day though...

Laura: That's OK, this time around. We can hopefully make some of that time up later.

Mark: All work on the database is now done; I'm all set for the next set of tasks.

Laura: Great, and I got my work done on the user interface pieces, so we've actually got something running.

Bob: Always a good week when you head out of the office with something working...

Laura: Absolutely. OK, it's time to update the board and our burn-down rate to get things set up for next week.

there are no Dumb Questions

Q: Do I REALLY have to get everyone to stand up during a tandup meeting?

A: No, not really. A standup meeting is called "standup" because is meant to be a fast meeting that lasts a **maximum** of 15 minutes; ou should ideally be aiming for 5 minutes.

Ve've all been stuck in endless meetings where nothing gets done, o the idea with a standup meeting is to keep things so short you on't even have time to find chairs. This keeps the focus and the nomentum on only two agenda items:

- Are there any issues?
- Have we finished anything?

Vith these issues addressed, you can update your project board and et on with the actual development work.

Q: An issue has come up in my standup meeting that is oing to take some discussion to resolve. Is it OK to lengthen ne standup meeting to an hour to solve these bigger problems?

A: Always try to keep a standup meeting to less than 15 minutes. an issue turns out to be something that requires further discussion, hen schedule another meeting ***specifically for that issue***. The tandup meeting has highlighted the issue, and so it's done its job.

Q: Do standup meetings have to be daily?

A: It certainly helps to make your standup meetings daily. With the pace of modern software development, issues arise on almost a daily basis, so a quick 15 minutes with your team is essential to keeping your finger on the pulse of the project.

Q: Is it best to do a standup meeting in the morning or the afternoon?

A: Ideally, standup meetings should be first thing in the morning. The meeting sets everyone up for the day's tasks and gives you time to hit issues straight away.

Still, there may be situations when you can't all meet in the morning, especially if you have remote employees. In those cases, standup meetings should be conducted when the majority of your team begin their working day. This isn't ideal for everyone, but at least most people get the full benefit of early feedback from the meeting.

On rare occasions, you can split the standup meeting in two. You might do this if part of your team works in a completely different time zone. If you go with this approach, keeping your board updated is even more critical, as this is the place where everyone's status from the standup meeting is captured for all to see.

Standup meetings keep your peers, employees, and managers up to date, and keep your finger on the pulse of how your development work is going.

BULLET POINTS

- Organize **daily standup meetings** to make sure you catch issues early.
- Keep standup meetings **less than 15 minutes**.
- A standup meeting is all about **progress**, **problematic issues**, and **updating your board**.
- Try to schedule your standup meetings for the **morning** so that everyone knows where they are at the **beginning of the working day**.

Long Exercise

It's the end of Week 1, and you and the team have just finished your standup meeting. It's time to update the project board. Take a look at the board below and write down what you think needs to be changed and updated on the board to get it ready for Week 2.

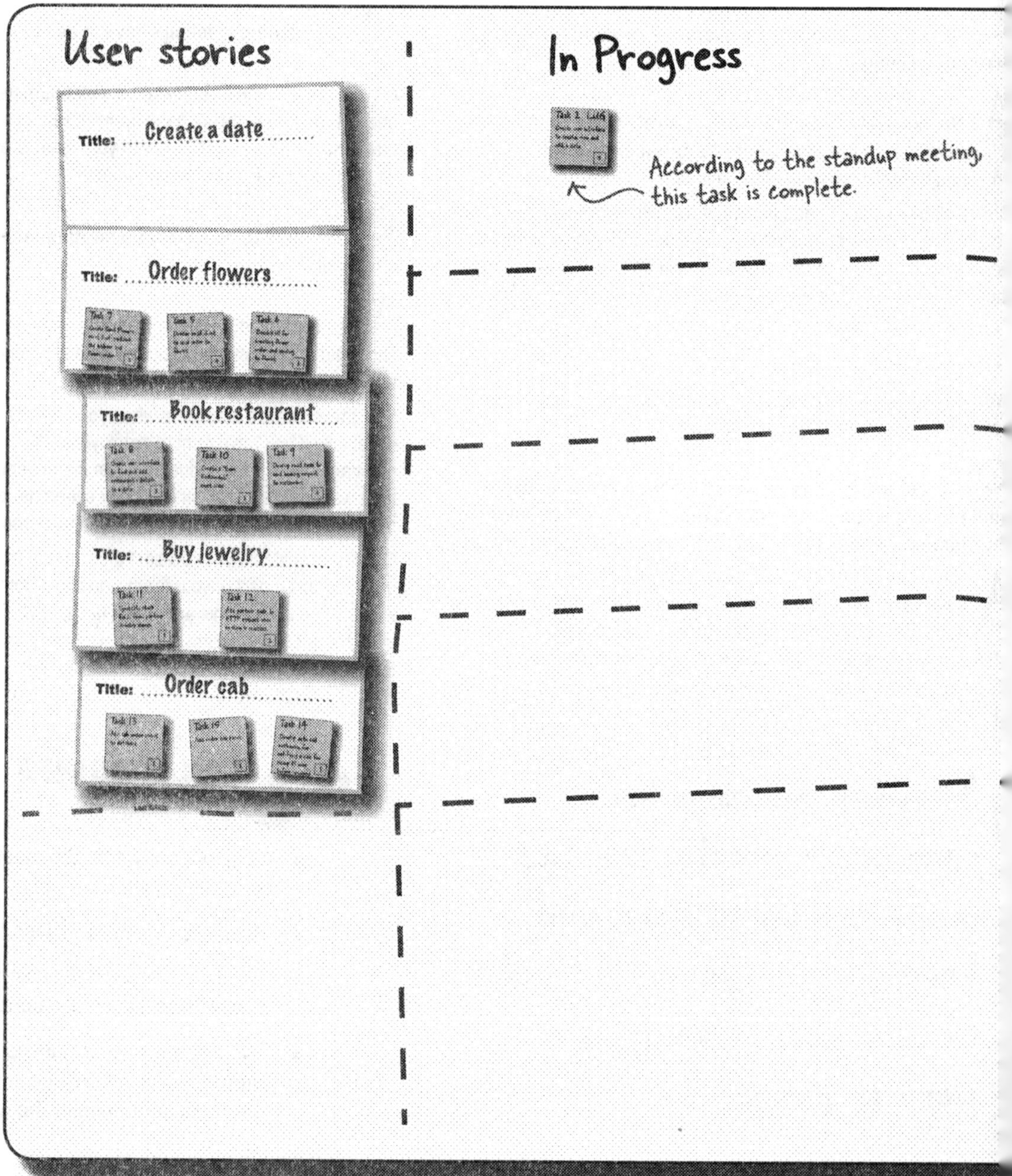

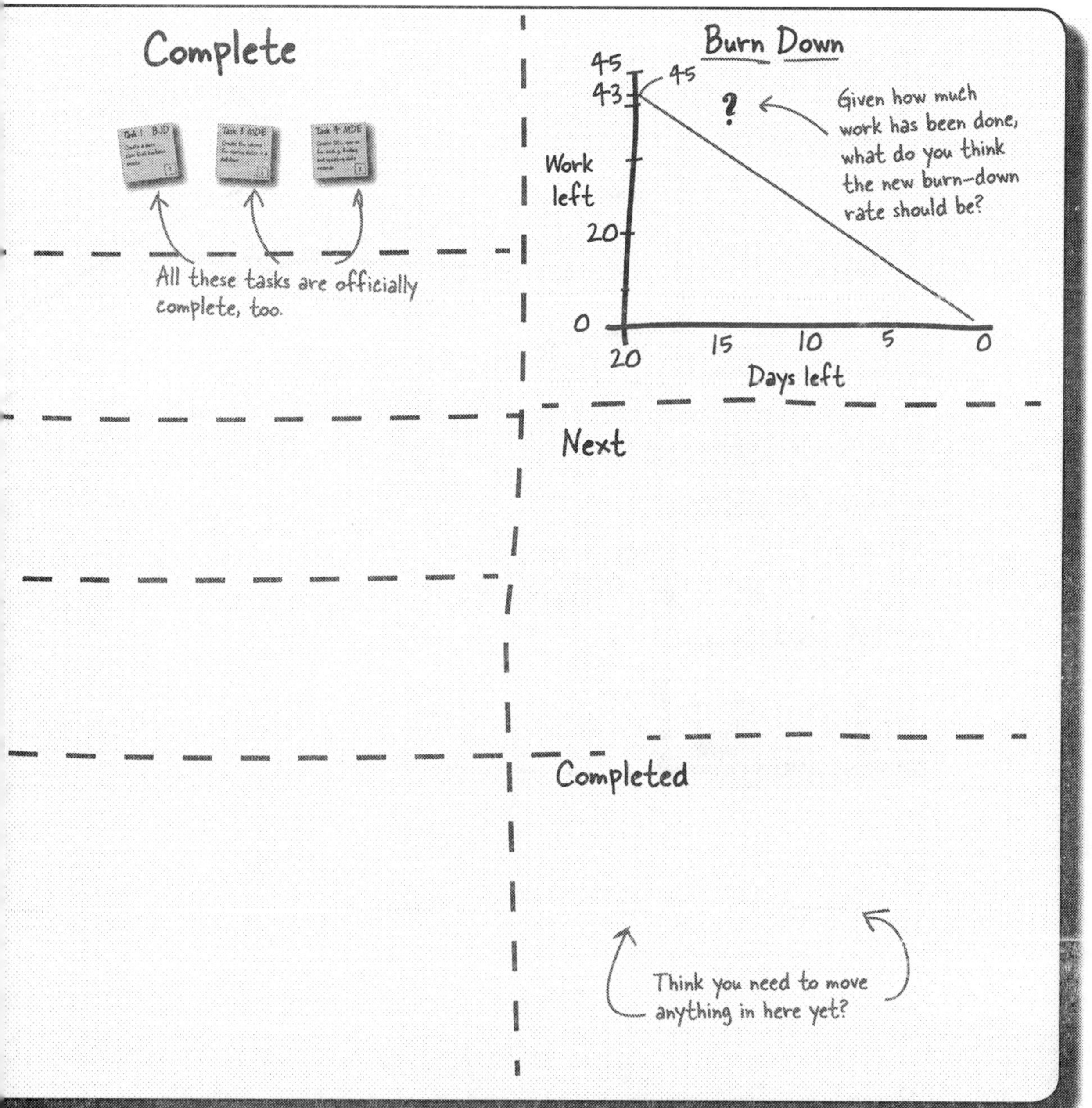
Complete
All these tasks are officially complete, too.
Burn Down
45
43
45
Work left
20
0
20
15
10
5
0
Days left
?
Given how much work has been done, what do you think the new burn-down rate should be?
Next
Completed
Think you need to move anything in here yet?

Long Exercise Solution

You were asked to update the board and write down what you think needs to be changed to get it ready for Week 2.

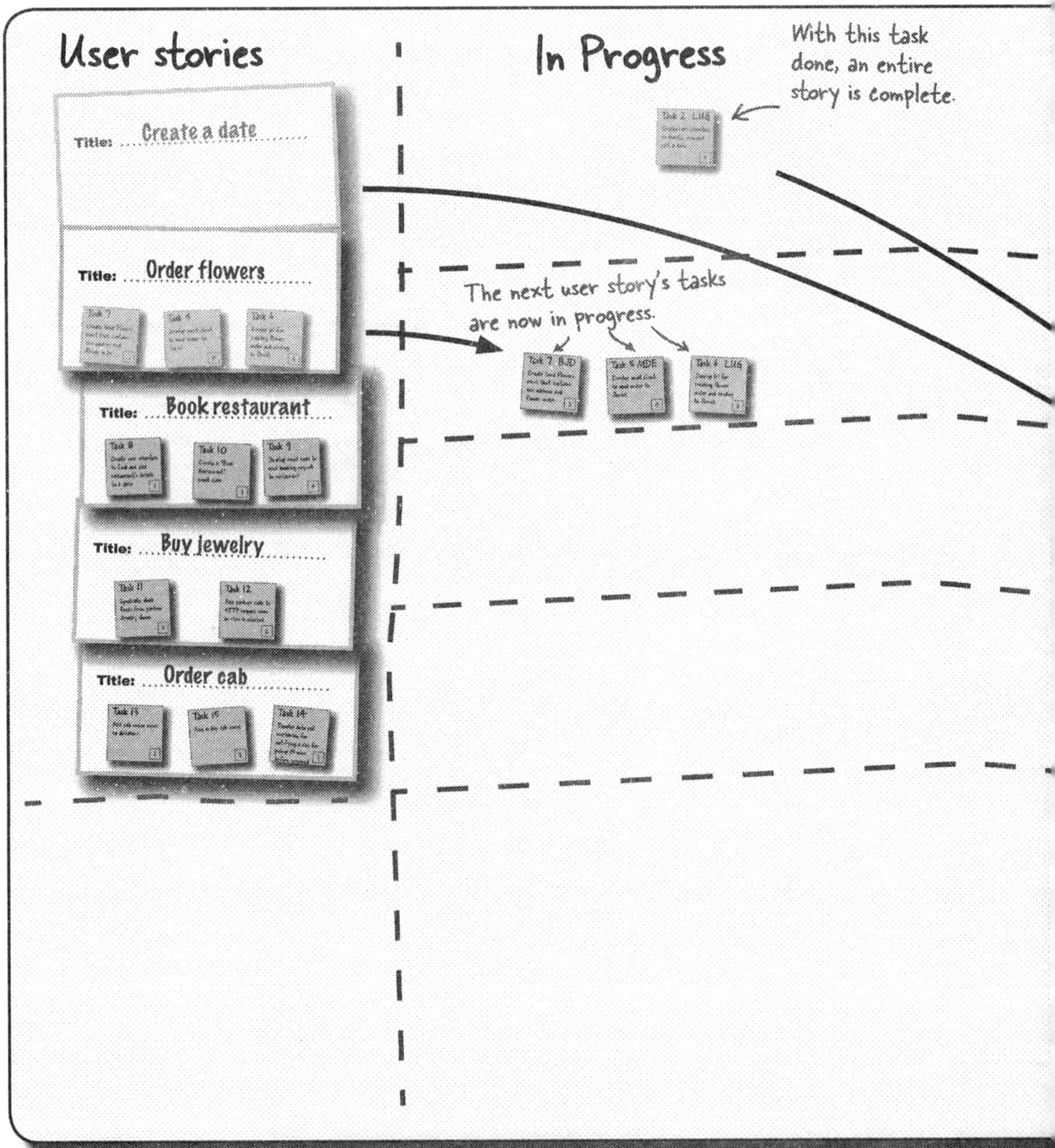

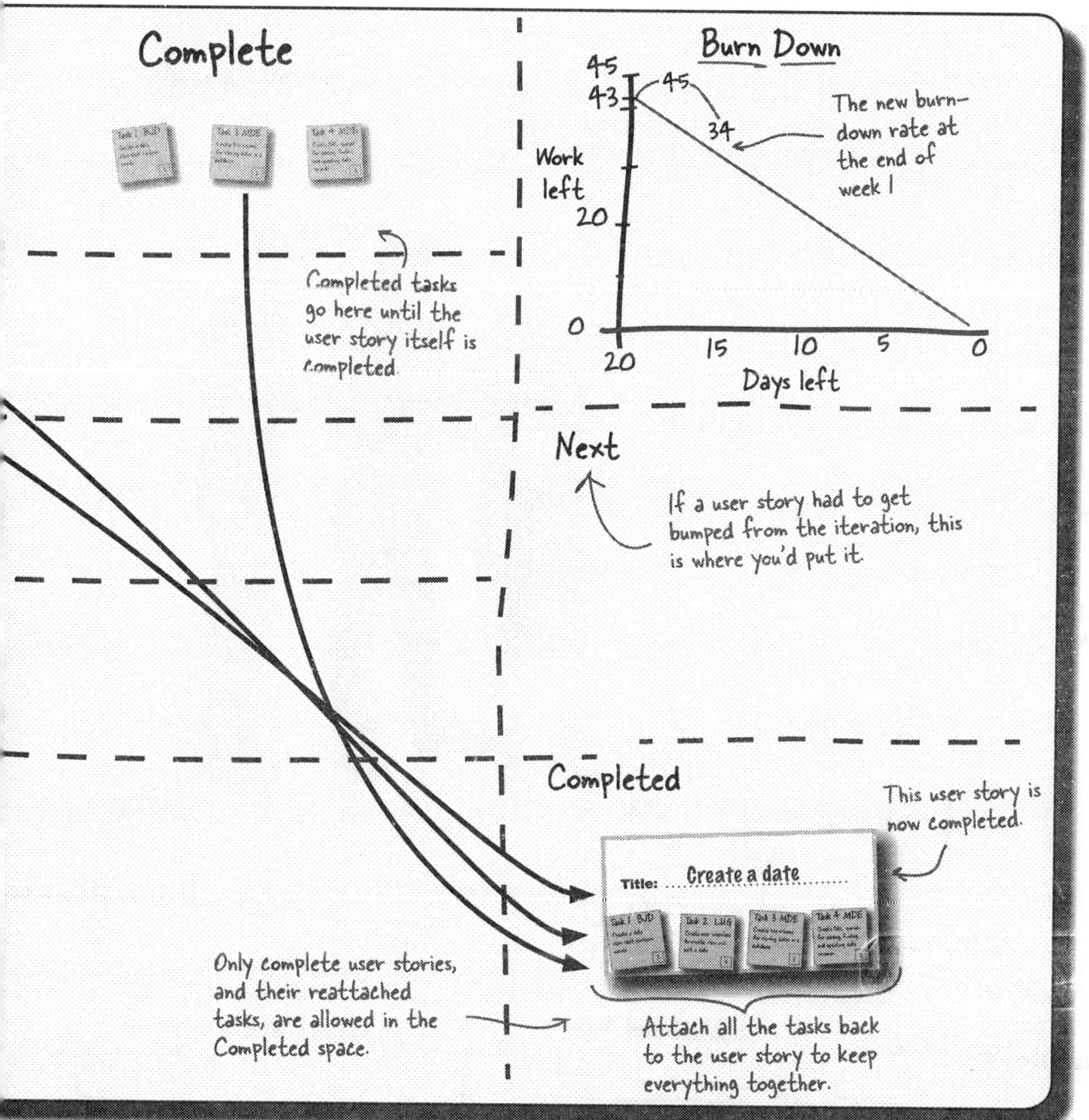
Complete
Burn Down
45
43
45
34
Work left
20
0
20
15
10
5
0
Days left
The new burn-down rate at the end of week 1
Completed tasks go here until the user story itself is completed.
Next
If a user story had to get bumped from the iteration, this is where you'd put it.
Completed
This user story is now completed.
Title: Create a date
Only complete user stories, and their reattached tasks, are allowed in the Completed space.
Attach all the tasks back to the user story to keep everything together.

Standup meeting: Day 2, Week 2...

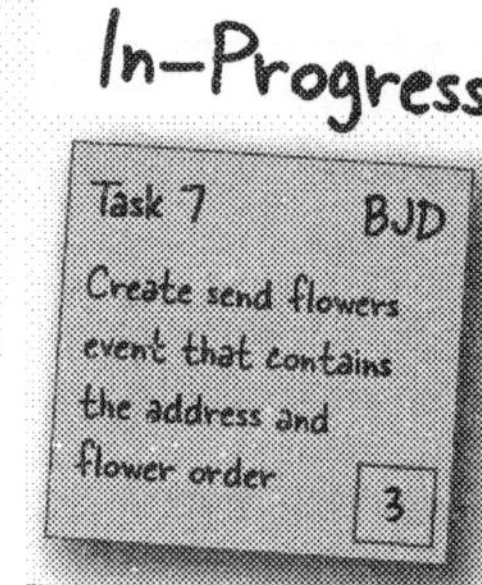

Laura's acting as the team lead, at least on this iteration.

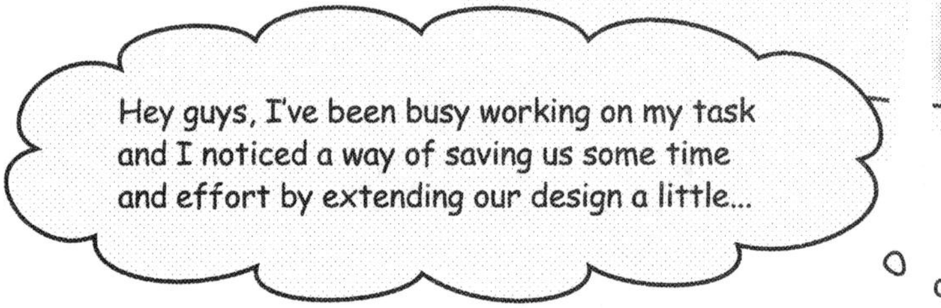

Laura: How are you going to do that?

Bob: Well, if you treat someone ordering flowers as just another type of event, then we can add it straight into our current class tree, and that should save us some time in the long run.

Laura: That's sounds good. What do you think, Mark?

Mark: I don't see any problems right now...

Bob: Apart from it might take an extra day right now to make the changes, but in the long run this should save us some time.

Laura: Mmm. We're still a little behind, but we can probably lose a day on the burn-down rate now if it saves us time later on in the iteration. OK, I'm sold, let's go for it...

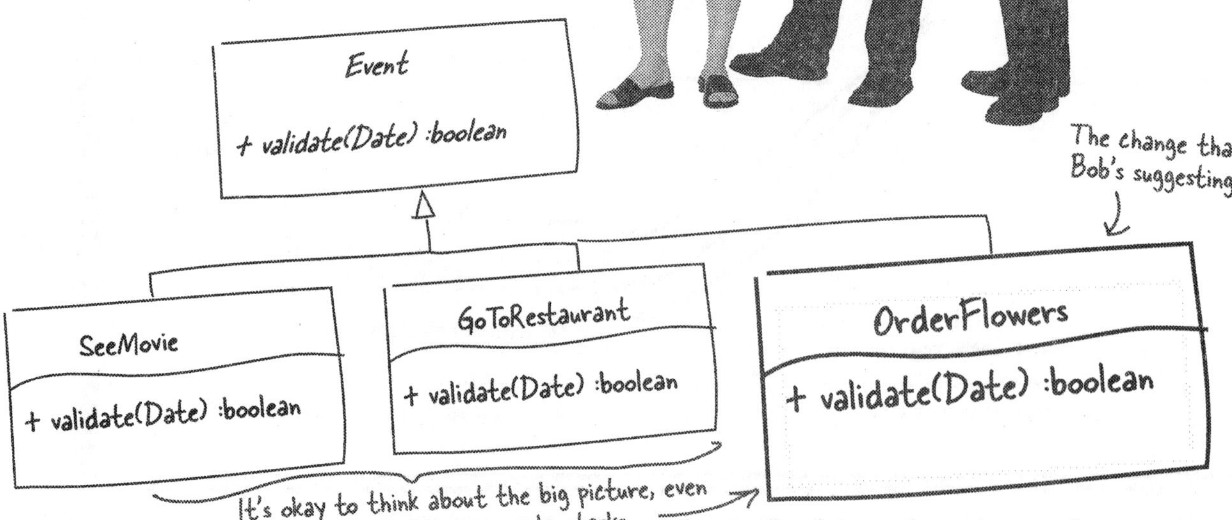

Exercise

What refactoring do you think Bob is talking about? Take the class hierarchy below and circle all the things that you think will need to change to accommodate a new OrderFlowers event.

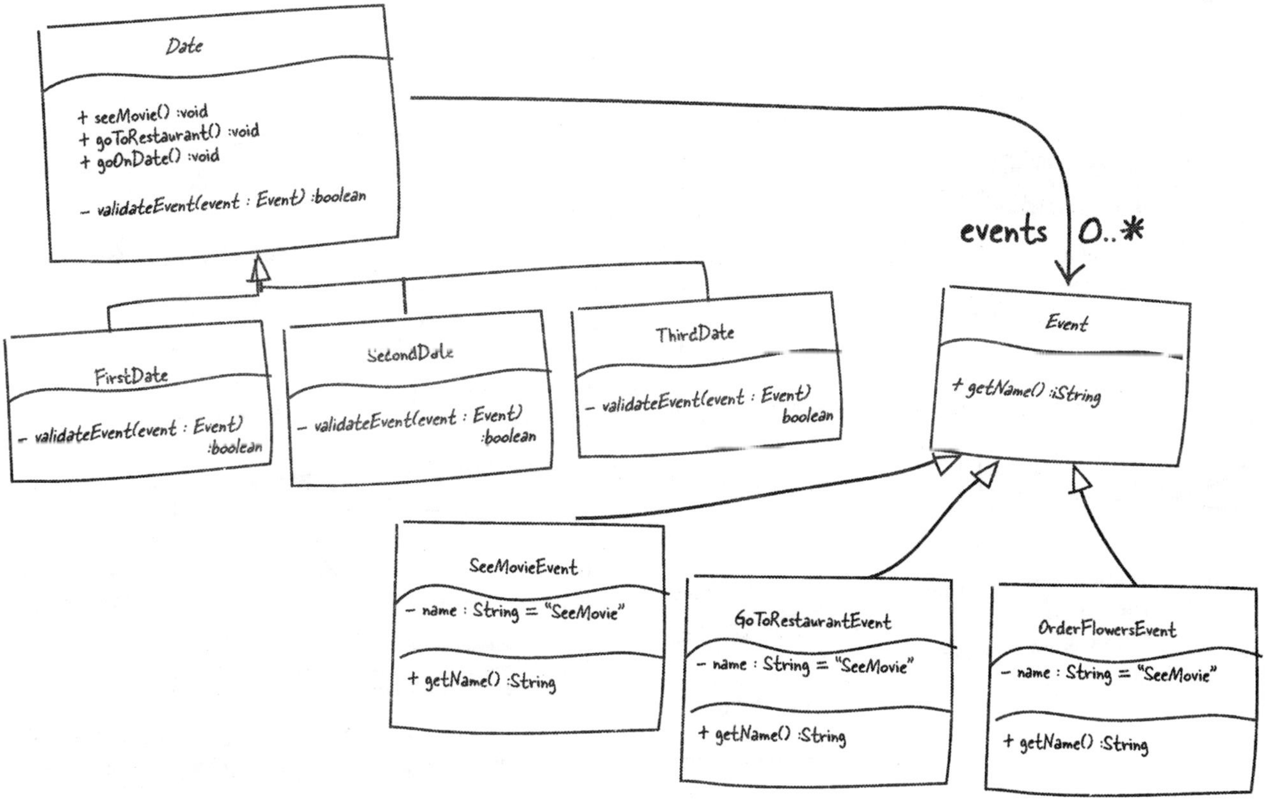

How many classes did you have to touch to make Bob's changes? ....

....

....

....

Are you happy with this design? Why or why not?

....

....

....

Exercise Solution

You were asked to take the class hierarchy below and circle all the places that you think will need to change to accommodate a new OrderFlowersEvent...

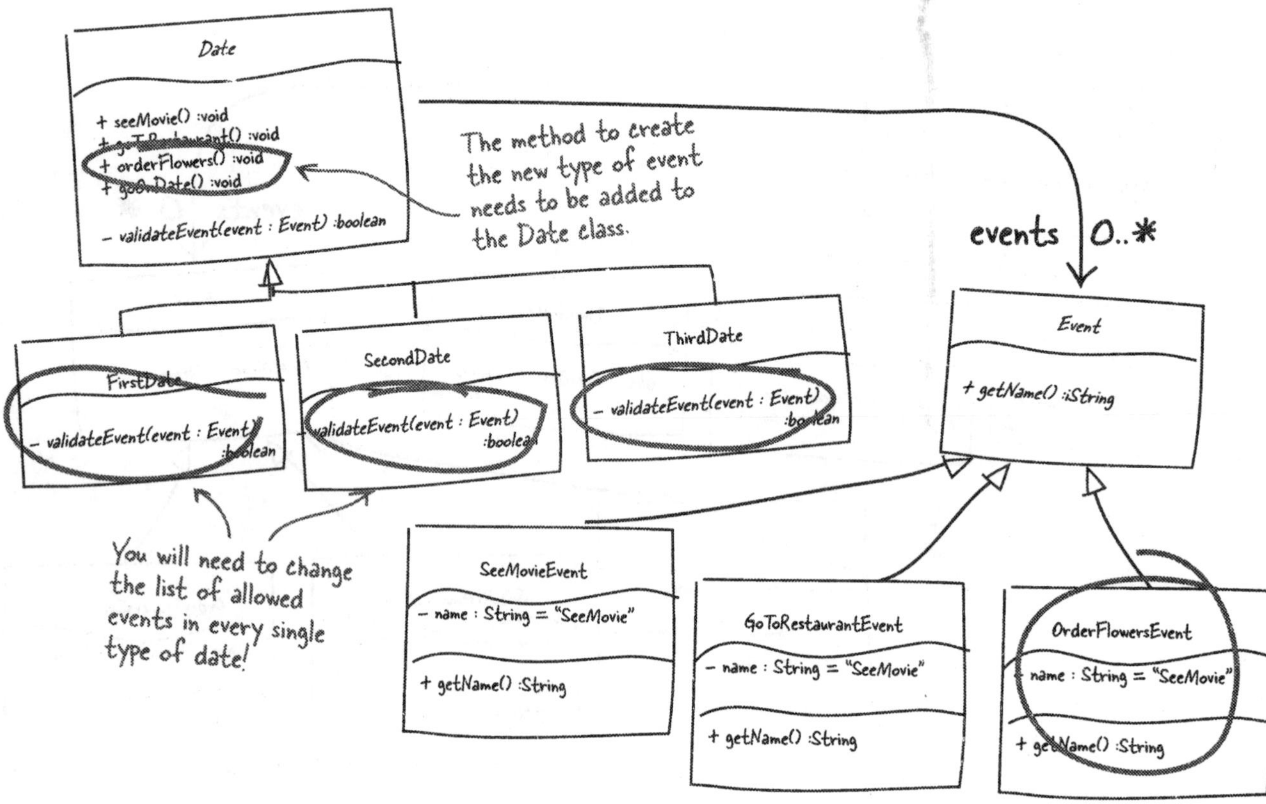

How many classes did you have to touch to make Bob's changes?

Five classes were changed or added to add just this one new type of event. First the "OrderFlowersEvent" class needed to be added, and then the method to order flowers on a date needed to be added to the Date class. Finally I had to update each of the different types of date to allow, or reject, the new type of event depending on whether it's allowed on that date or not

Are you happy with this design? Why or why not?

Five classes being changed seems like a LOT when all I'm adding is ONE new event. What happens when I have to add, say, a dozen new types of event; is it always going to involve this much work?

Laura: Hey, isn't "Buy jewelry" coming down the line? That works as just another event, too, right?

Bob: Yeah, but we'll need to add some time to make those changes to all the classes again.

Mark: Can't we come up with a more flexible design, so we can avoid this pain and effort each time we add a new event?

Bob: That's exactly what I was thinking.

Laura: But that will take even more time, right? I guess we're invested, though, huh? This will save us time later, I hope...

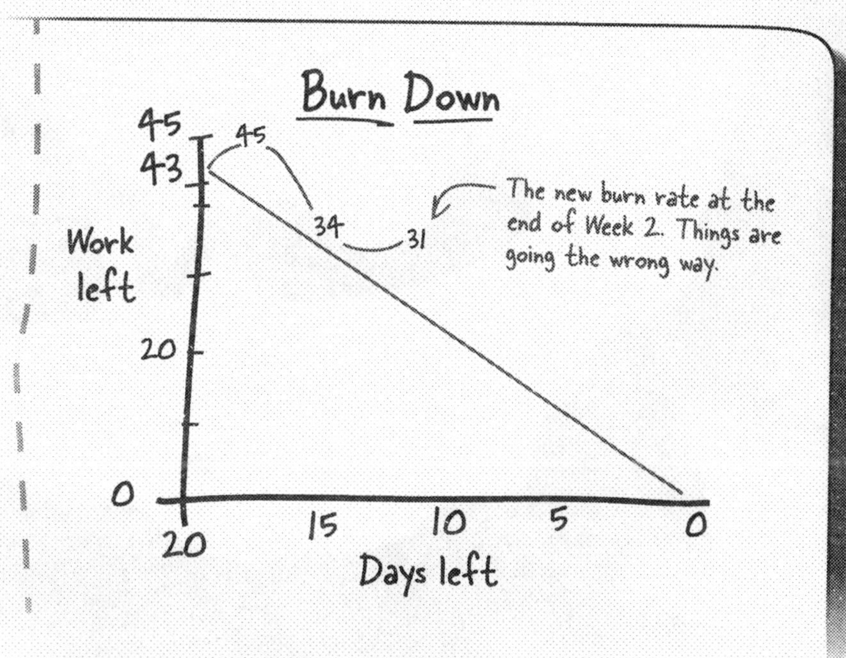

We interrupt this chapter...

You're already getting behind on your burn-down rate and then the inevitable happens: the customer calls with a last-minute request...

You have to track unplanned tasks

So far, your board has kept track of everything going on in your project. But what happens when somthing unplanned comes up? You have to track it, just like anything else. It affects your burn-down rate, the work you're doing on user stories, and more...

Let's take a look at a part of the board we haven't used yet:

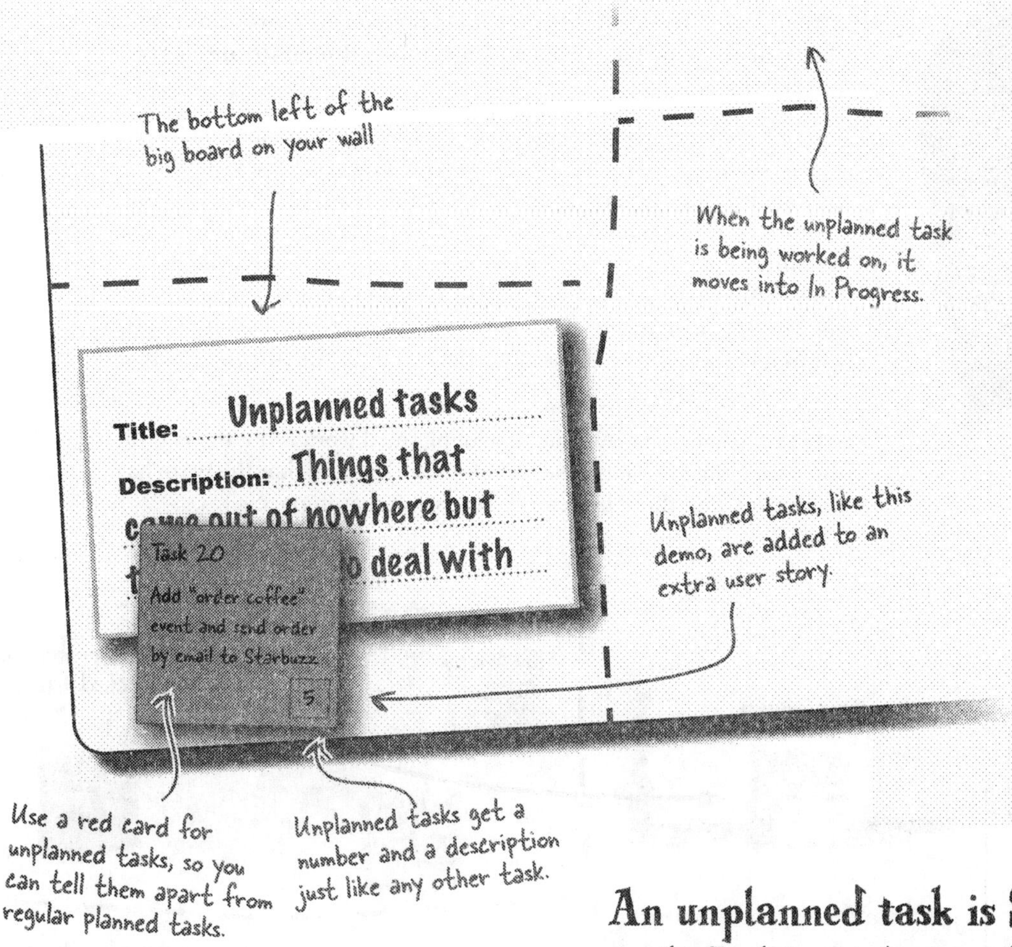

An unplanned task is STILL a task. It has to be tracked, put in progress, completed, and included in the burn-down rate just like EVERY OTHER TASK you have.

Wait a sec! You're saying we have to do the demo? What if it blows our deadlines?

Yes, you've heard it before, but talking to the customer is the answer to most scheduling- and deadline-related probl

Talk to the customer

You've been hit by the unexpected, but that's part of software development. You can't do everything, but you also can't make the choice about what takes priority. Remember, **the customer sets priorities**, not you.

You need to deal with new tasks like customer demos, and the best way to do this is to ask the customer what takes priority. Give the customer a chance to make a considered decision by estimating the amount of work that the new task requires and explaining how that will affect the current schedule. Ultimately, the customer rules, so as long as they have all the information needed to make a choice, then you need to be prepared to go with their decision by reshuffling your existing tasks and user stories to make room for the surprise work.

Ultimately you need to keep your customer in the picture as to what is in and what is out. Adding new unplanned work is not the end of the world, but your customer needs to understand that the work has an impact, and then they can choose what that impact is.

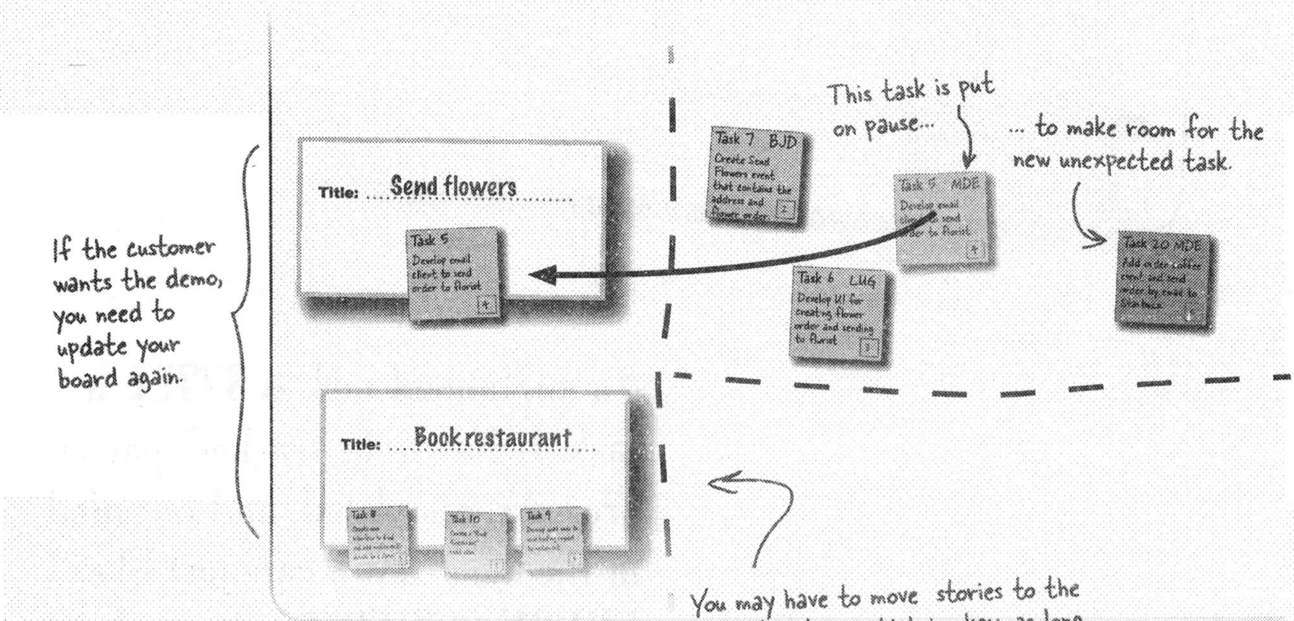

Unexpected tasks raise your burn-down rate

Unexpected task mean extra work. If the unexpected tasks can't be pushed into another iteration, then they need to be factored into your board. All of this means that your burn-down rate is affected, and not in a good way...

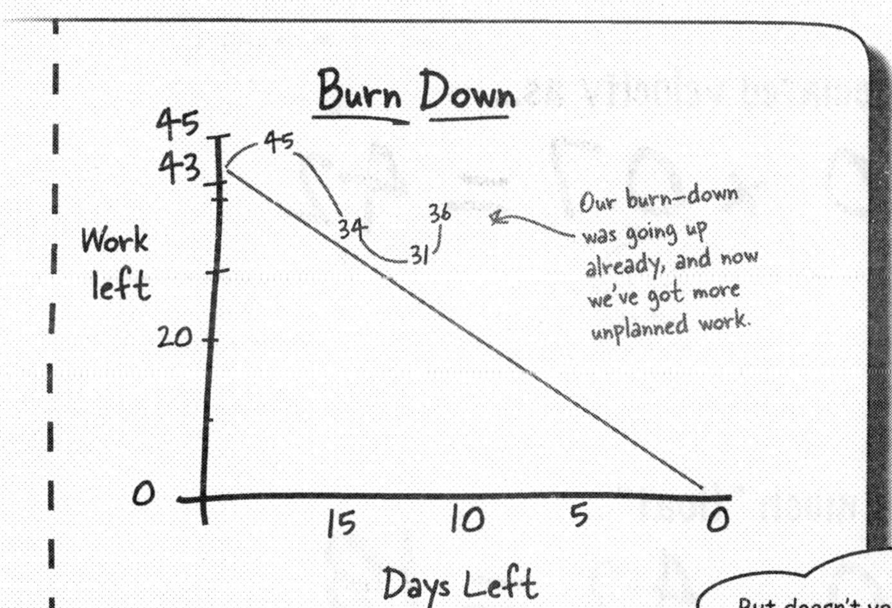

But doesn't velocity take some of this into account? We assumed 30% overhead when calculating our team's velocity, right?

We calculated velocity when planning our iteration in Chapter 3.

Velocity helps, but...

You've got more work thanks to some unexpected requirements from your customer, but didn't you factor this in when you calculated your team's velocity? Unfortunately, velocity is there to help you gauge how fast your team performs, but it's not there to handle unplanned tasks.

Remember this equation from Chapter 3?

We originally calculated velocity as...

$$3 \times 20 \times 0.7 = 42$$

3: The number of people in your team

0.7: Your team's first pass velocity, which is actually a guess at this point

42: The amount of work in days that your team can handle in one iteration

So we have this much "float"...

$$3 \times 20 - 42 = 18$$

18: These are the possible days we could have, if everyone worked at 100% velocity...

... but it may not be enough!

Float—the "extra" days in your schedule—disappear quickly.

An employee's car breaks down, someone has to go to the dentist, your daily standup meetings...those "extra" days disappear quickly. And remember, ***float is in work time, not actual time***. So if your company gives an extra Friday off for great work, that's *three* days of float lost because you are losing *three* developers for the whole day.

So when unplanned tasks come up, you may be able to absorb some of the extra time, but velocity won't take care of all of it.

So what do we do? This is major panic time, right? We're going to miss our deadlines...

there are no Dumb Questions

Q: You said to add unplanned tasks as red sticky notes. Do I have to use colored sticky notes? And why red?

A: We picked red because regular tasks are usually on regular yellow sticky notes, and because red stands out as a warning color. The idea is to quickly see what's part of your planned stories (the normal stickies), and what's unplanned (red). And red is a good "alert" color, since most unplanned tasks are high-priority (like that customer demo that came out of nowhere).

It's also important to know at the end of an iteration what you worked on.The red tasks make it easy to see what you dealt with that wasn't planned, so when you're recalculating velocity and seeing how good your estimates were, you know what was planned and what wasn't.

Q: So later on we're going to recalculate velocity?

A: Absolutely. Your team's velocity will be recalculated at the beginning of every single iteration. That way, you can get a realistic estimate of *your* team's productivity. 0.7 is just a good conservative place to start when you don't have any previous iterations to work from.

Q: So velocity is all about how me and my team performed in the last iteration?

A: Bingo. Velocity is a measure of how fast ***you*** and ***your team*** are working. The only way you can *reliably* come up with a figure for that is by looking at how well you performed in previous iterations.

Q: I really don't think 0.7 captures my team's velocity. Would it be OK to pick a faster or slower figure to start out with? Say 0.65, or 0.8?

A: You can pick a different starting velocity, but you have to stand by what you pick. If you know your team already at the beginning of a project, then it's perfectly alright to pick a velocity that matches your team's performance on other projects, although you should still factor in a slightly slower velocity at the beginning of any project. It always takes a little extra time to get your heads around what needs to be developed on a new project.

Remember, velocity is about how fast you and your team can comfortably work, for real. So you're aiming for a velocity that you believe in, and it's better to be slightly on the conservative side at the beginning of a new project, and then to refine that figure with hard data before each subsequent iteration.

Velocity is NOT a substitute for good estimation; it's a way of factoring in the real-world performance of you and your team.

We have a lot to do...

You're in a tough spot. Doing some refactoring work is going to cost you time now, but the hope is that it will save you time in the long run. In addition you have the new demo that you need to prepare for the iSwoon CEO....

You've got more work to do...

The task that came out of Bob's refactoring suggestion

The "surprise" work that's needed for the demo that the CEO of iSwoon is giving to the CEO of Starbuzz. Talk about pressure!

...and your burn-down rate is going in the wrong direction.

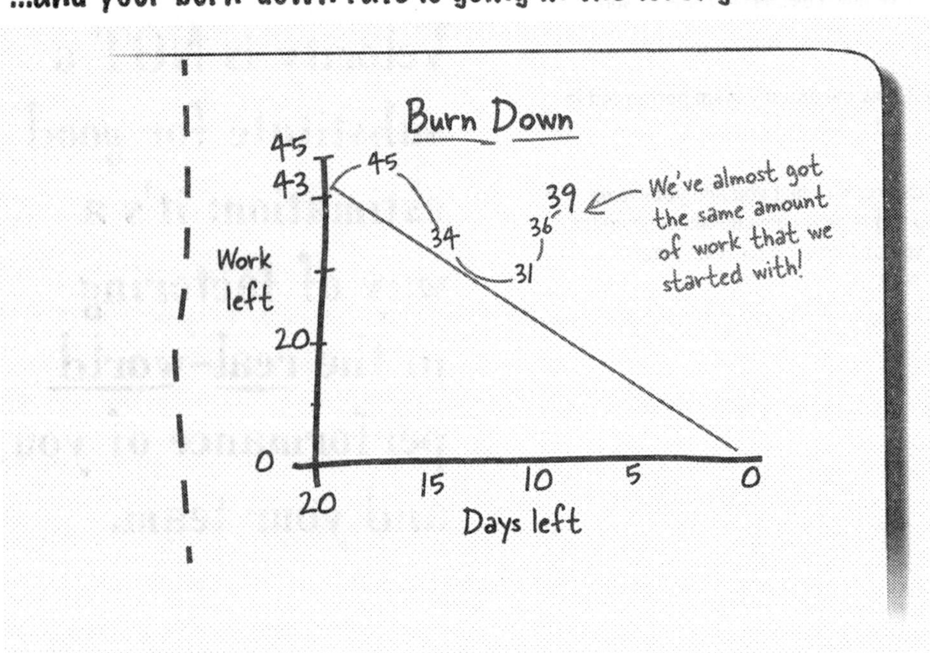

...but we know EXACTLY where we stand

The customer knows where you are

At every step you've kept the customer involved so they know exactly what work they've added, and you can show them exactly what the changes will impact.

YOU know where you are

You and your development team are also on exactly the same page thanks to your board and the burn-down rate. This means that although things look a bit bleak, at least no one is burying their heads in the sand. The challenges are right there on your wall.

Successful software development is about knowing where you are.

With an understanding of your progress and challenges, you can keep your customer in the loop, and deliver software when it's needed.

You know there are challenges, NOW.

Because you're monitoring your project using your board you know right now that there are challenges ahead if you're going to keep things on track. Compare this with the Big Bang "See you later, I'll deliver something in 3 months" approach from Chapter 1.

With the Big Bang approach, you didn't know you were in trouble until day 30, or even day 90! With your board and your burn-down rate you know immediately what you're facing, and that gives you the edge to make the calls to keep your development heading towards success.

Sometimes you'll hear this referred to as the waterfall approach

All is far from lost! We'll tackle all these problems in Chapter 5, when we dig deeper into good class and application design, and handle the customer demo.

Velocity Exposed

This week's interview: Keeping pace with Velocity

Head First: Welcome, Velocity, glad you could make time in your busy day to come talk with us.

Velocity: My pleasure, it's nice to be here.

Head First: So some would say that you have the potential to save a project that's in crisis, due perhaps to surprise changes or any of the other pieces of extra work that can hit a plan. What would you say to those people?

Velocity: Well, I'm really no superhero to be honest. I'm more of a safety net and confidence kinda guy.

Head First: What do you mean by "confidence"?

Velocity: I'm most useful when you're trying to come up with realistic plans, but not for dealing with the unexpected.

Head First: So you're really only useful at the beginning of a project?

Velocity: Well, I'm useful then, but at that point I'm usually just set to my default value of 0.7. My role gets much more interesting as you move from Iiteration 1 to Iteration 2 and onwards.

Head First: And what do you offer for each iteration, confidence?

Velocity: Absolutely. As you move from one iteration to the next you can recalculate me to make sure that you can successfully complete the work you need to.

Head First: So you're more like a retrospective player?

Velocity: Exactly! I tell you how fast you were performing in the last iteration. You can then take that value and come up with a chunk of work in the next iteration that you can be much more confident that you can accomplish.

Head First: But when the unexpected comes along...

Velocity: Well, I can't really help too much with that, except that if you can increase your team's velocity, you might be able to fit in some more work. But that's a risky approach...

Head First: Risky because you really represent how fast your team works?

Velocity: That's exactly my point! I represent how fast your team works. If I say that you and your team, that's 3 developers total, can get 40 days of work done in an iteration, that's 20 work days long, that doesn't mean that there's 20 days there that you could possibly use if you just worked harder. Your team is always working as hard as they can, and I'm a measure of that. The danger is when people start using me as a pool of possible extra days of work...

Head First: So, if you could sum yourself up in one sentence, what would it be?

Velocity: I'm the guy that tells you how fast your team worked in the last iteration. I'm a measure of how you perform in reality, based on how you performed in the past, and I'm here to help you plan your iterations realistically.

Head First: Well, that's actually two sentences, but we'll let you get away with that. Thanks for making the time to come here today, Velocity.

Velocity: It's been a pleasure, nice to get some of these things off of my chest.

5 good-enough design

Getting it done with great design

Good design helps you deliver. In the last chapter things were looking pretty dire. A bad design was making life **hard for everyone**, and, to make matters worse, an unplanned task cropped up. In this chapter you'll see how to **refactor** your design so that you and your team can be **more productive**. You'll apply **principles of good design**, while at the same time be wary of striving for the promise of the ***"perfect design."*** Finally you'll **handle unplanned tasks** in exactly the same way you handle all the other work on your project using the big project board on your wall.

iSwoon is in serious trouble...

In the last chapter things were in pretty bad shape at iSwoon. You had some refactoring work to do to improve your design that was going to impact your deadlines, and the customer had piped in with a surprise task to develop a demonstration for the CEO of Starbuzz. All is not lost, however. First let's get the refactoring work done so that you can turn what looks like a slip into a way of speeding up your development work. The current design called for lots of changes just to add a new event:

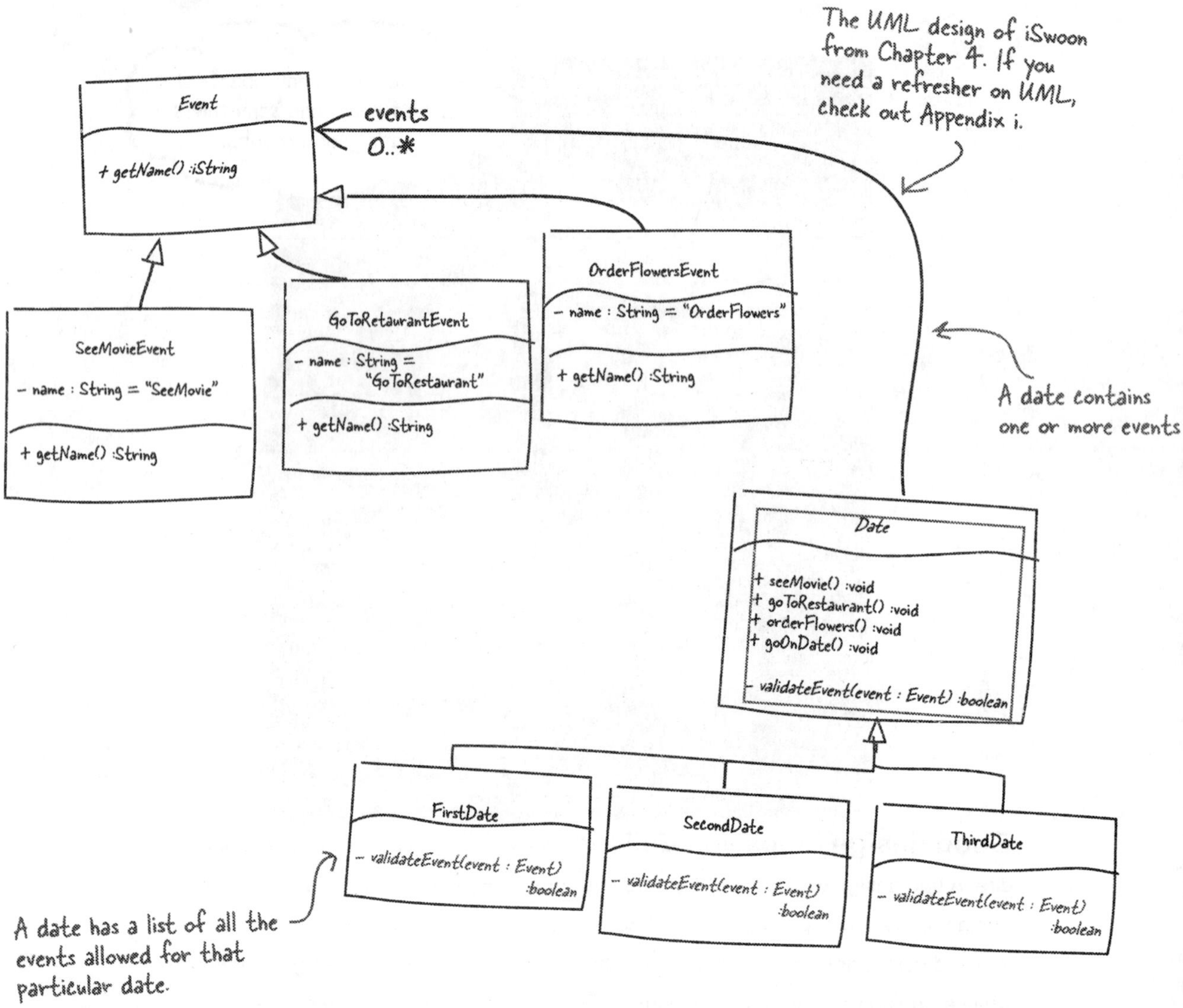

Sharpen your pencil

Write down the changes you think would be needed if...

What would you have to do to the software to implement these changes?

...you needed to add three new event types?

...you needed to add a new event type called "Sleeping over," but that event was only allowed on the third date?

The validateEvent( ) method will certainly come in handy here.

...you changed the value of the name attribute in the OrderFlowersEvent class to "SendFlowers"?

Sharpen your pencil Solution

You were asked to write down the changes you think would be needed if...

...you needed to add three new event types?

We'd need a new event class for each of the new types. Three new methods, one for each type of event, would need to be added to the abstract parent Date class. Then, each of the date classes, however many there are, will need to be updated to allow (or disallow) the three new types of event, depending on if the event is allowed for that date.

...you needed to add a new event type called "Sleeping over," but that event was only allowed on the third date?

A new event class would be added, called something like "SleepingOverEvent." Then a new method called "sleepOver" needs to be added to the Date class so the new event can be added to a date. Finally, all three of the existing date classes would need to be updated in order to specify that only the third date allows a SleepingOverEvent to be specified.

...you changed the value of the name attribute in the OrderFlowersEvent class to "SendFlowers"?

All three of the different concrete classes of Date would need to be updated so that the logic that decides if a particular event is allowed now uses the new name in regards to the OrderFlowersEvent class's name attribute value change. Also, the value of OrderFlowerEvent's name will need to change from "OrderFlowers" to "SendFlowers," then finally the class name will need to be changed to SendFlowersEvent so it follows the naming convention we're currently using for date events.

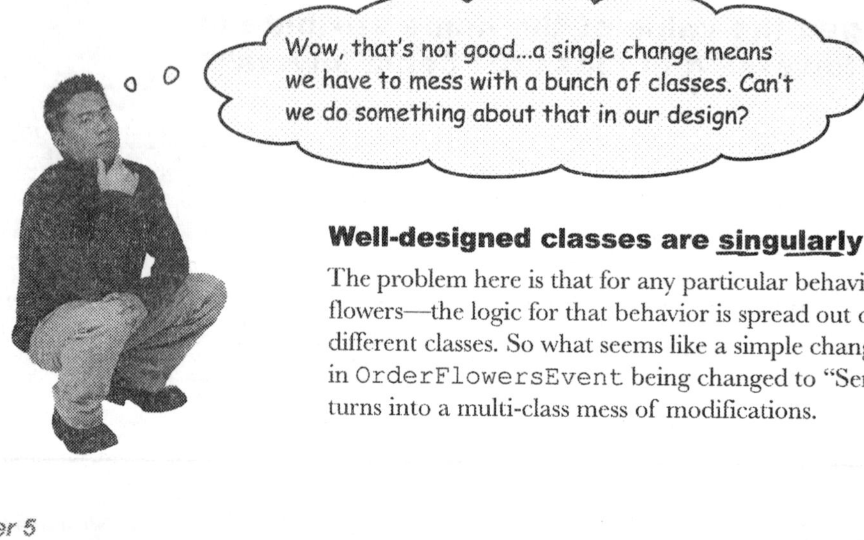

Well-designed classes are singularly focused.

The problem here is that for any particular behavior—like sending flowers—the logic for that behavior is spread out over a lot of different classes. So what seems like a simple change, like the name in `OrderFlowersEvent` being changed to "SendFlowers," turns into a multi-class mess of modifications.

This design breaks the single responsibility principle

iSwoon is such a headache to update because it breaks one of the fundamental principles of good object oriented design, the **single responsibility principle** (or **SRP** for short).

> **SRP**
>
> ***Single responsibility principle***
>
> *Every object in your system should have a **single responsibility**, and all the object's services should be focused on carrying out that single responsibility.*

Both the Date and Event class break the single responsibility principle

When a new type of event is added, the single responsibility principle states that all you should really need to do is add the new event class, and then you're done. However, with the current design, adding a new event also requires changes in the `Date` class ***and*** all of its subclasses.

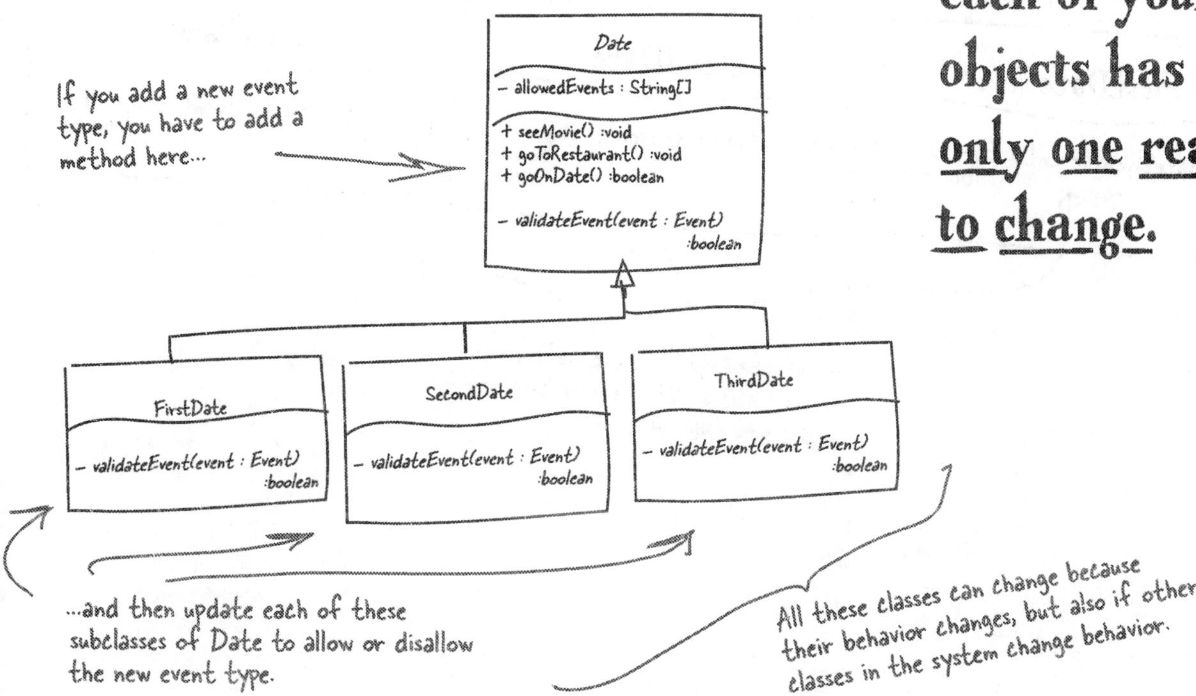

You've implemented the single responsibility principle correctly when each of your objects has only one reason to change.

Long Exercise

Your design at the moment makes it hard work to add events, change event names, and even deal with additional dates. Take a look at the current design and mark up what changes you'd make to apply the single responsibility principle to the iSwoon design (and in the process, make it easier to add new events and dates).

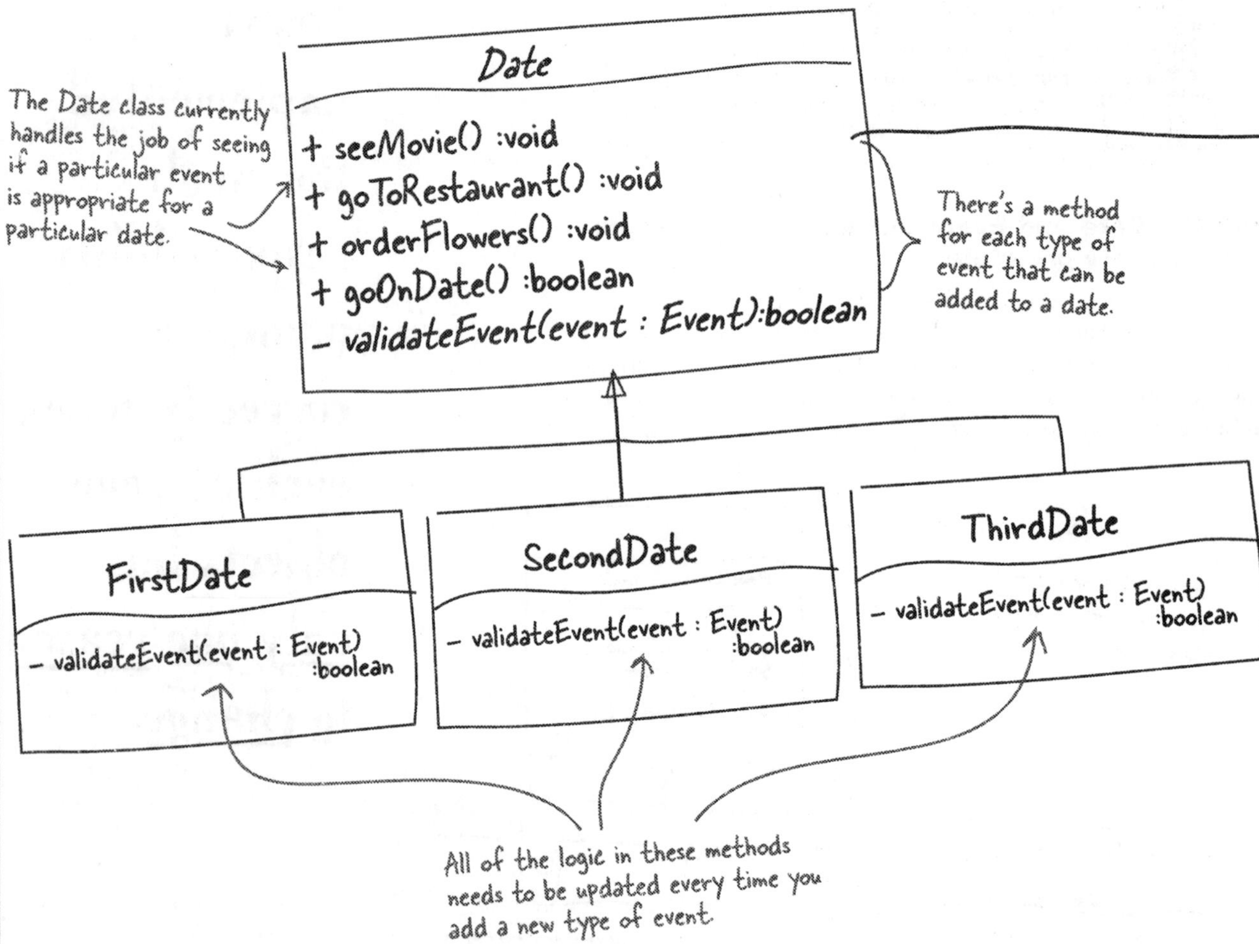

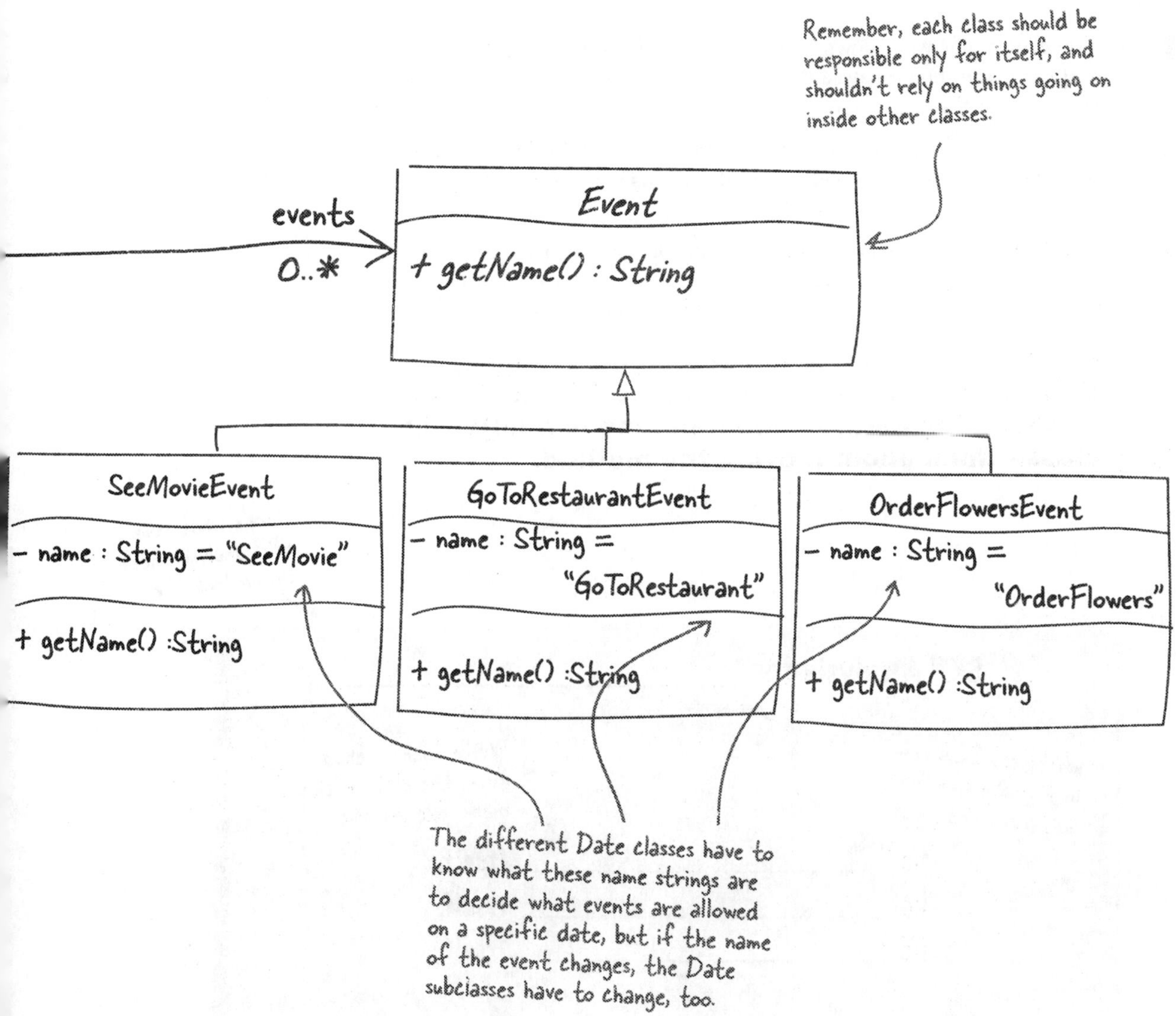

Answers on page 162.

If you're feeling stuck, turn the page for more on the single responsibility principle...

Spotting multiple responsibilies in your design

Most of the time, you can spot classes that aren't using the SRP with a simple test:

1. On a sheet of paper, write down a bunch of lines like this: The [blank] [blanks] itself. You should have a line like this for every method in the class you're testing for the SRP.
2. In the first blank of each line, write down the class name. In the second blank, write down one of the methods in the class. Do this for each method in the class.
3. Read each line out loud (you may have to add a letter or word to get it to read normally). Does what you just said make any sense? Does your class really have the responsibility that the method indicates it does?

If what you've just said doesn't make sense, then you're probably violating the SRP with that method. The method might belong in a different class—think about moving the method.

Here's what your SRP analysis sheet should look like.

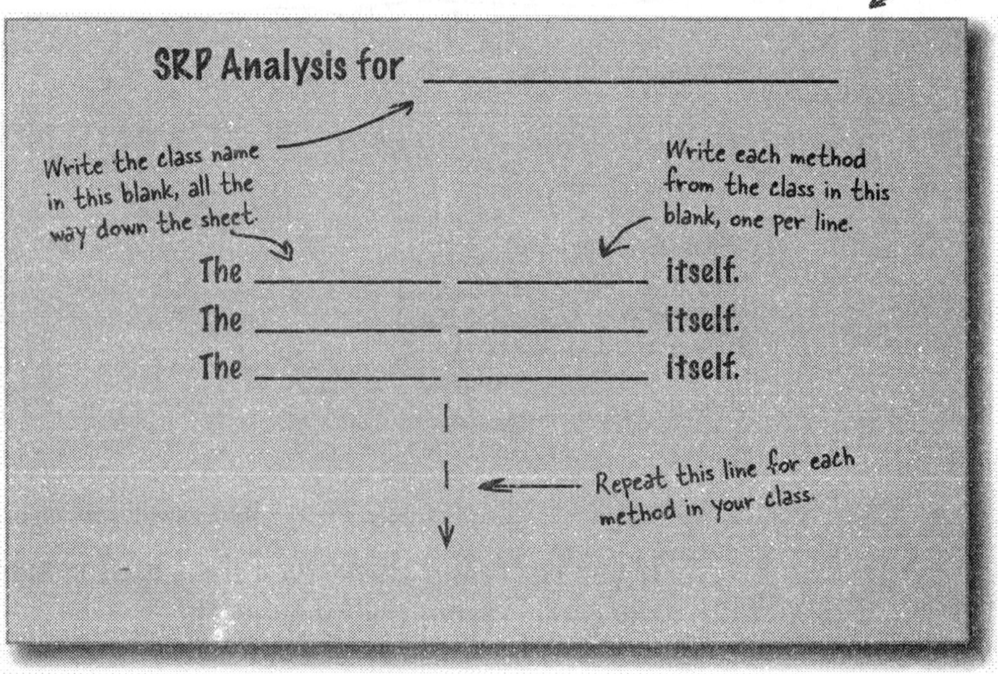

Sharpen your pencil

Apply the SRP to the Automobile class.

Do an SRP analysis on the Automobile class shown below. Fill out the sheet with the class name methods in Automobile, like we've described on the last page. Then, decide if you think it makes sense for the Automobile class to have each method, and check the right box.

```
Automobile
-----------------------------------
+ start() :void
+ stop() :void
+ changeTires(tires : Tire[]) :void
+ drive() :void
+ wash() :void
+ checkOil() :void
+ getOil() :int
```

SRP Analysis for Automobile

	Follows SRP	Violates SRP
The ____________ ____________ itself.	☐	☐
The ____________ ____________ itself.	☐	☐
The ____________ ____________ itself.	☐	☐
The ____________ ____________ itself.	☐	☐
The ____________ ____________ itself.	☐	☐
The ____________ ____________ itself.	☐	☐
The ____________ ____________ itself.	☐	☐

If what you read doesn't make sense, then the method on that line is probably violating the SRP.

Sharpen your pencil Solution

Apply the SRP to the Automobile class.

Your job was to do an SRP analysis on the Automobile class shown below. You should have filled out the sheet with the class name methods in Automobile, and decided if you think it makes sense for the Automobile class to have each method.

SRP Analysis for Automobile

				Follows SRP	Violate SRP
The	Automobile	start[s]	itself.	☑	☐
The	Automobile	stop[s]	itself.	☑	☐
The	Automobile	changesTires	itself.	☐	☑
The	Automobile	drive[s]	itself.	☐	☑
The	Automobile	wash[es]	itself.	☐	☑
The	Automobile	check[s] oil	itself.	☐	☑
The	Automobile	get[s] oil	itself.	☑	☐

It makes sense that the automobile is responsible for starting and stopping. That's a function of the automobile.

An automobile is NOT responsible for changing its own tires, washing itself, or checking its own oil.

You may have to add an "s" or a word or two to make the sentence readable.

This one was a little tricky—we thought that while an automobile might start and stop itself, it's really the responsibilty of a driver to drive the car.

You should have thought carefully about this one, and what "get" means. This is a method that just returns the amount of oil in the automobile—and that is something that the automobile should do.

Cases like this are why SRP analysis is just a guideline. You still are going to have to make some judgment calls using common sense and your own experience.

Going from multiple responsibilies to a single responsibility

Once you've done an analysis, you can take all the methods that don't make sense on a class, and move those methods to classes that do make sense for that particular responsibility.

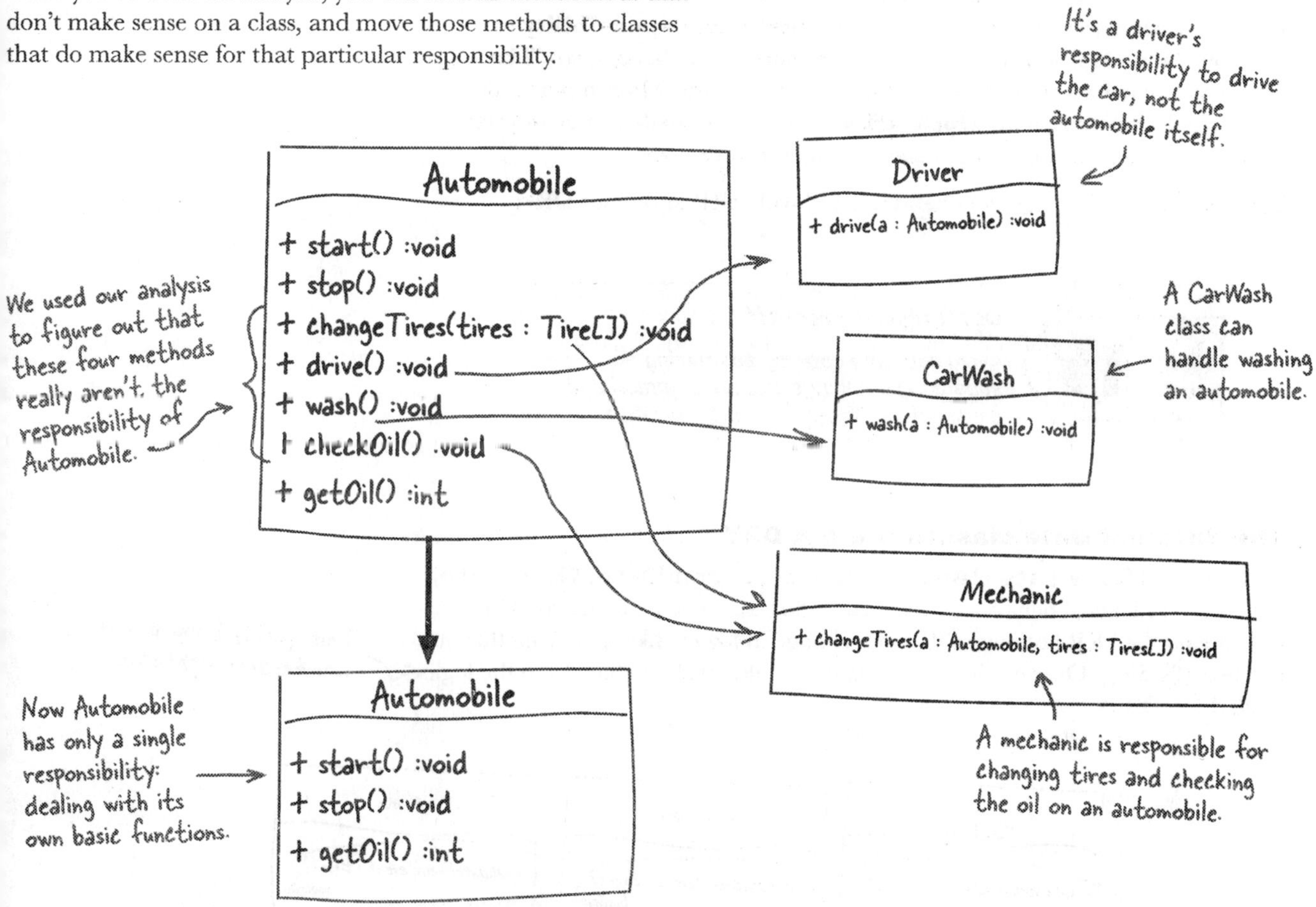

there are no Dumb Questions

Q: How does SRP analysis work when a method takes parameters, like wash(Automobile) on the CarWash class?

A: Good question! For your SRP analysis to make any sense, you need to include the parameter of the method in the method blank. So you would write "The CarWash washes [an] automobile itself." That method makes sense (with the `Automobile` parameter), so it would stay on the `CarWash` class.

Q: But what if CarWash took in an Automobile parameter as part of its constructor, and the method was just wash()? Wouldn't SRP analysis give you a wrong result?

A: It would. If a parameter that might cause a method to make sense, like an `Automobile` for the `wash()` method on `CarWash`, is passed into a class's constructor, your SRP analysis might be misleading. But that's why you always need to apply a good amount of your own common sense and knowledge of the system in addition to what you learn from the SRP analysis.

Your design should obey the SRP, but also be DRY...

The SRP is all about responsibility, and which objects in your system do what. You want each object that you design to have **just one responsibility** to focus on—and when something about that responsibility changes, you'll know exactly where to look to make those changes in your code. Most importantly you'll avoid what's called the **ripple effect**, where one small change to your software can cause a ripple of changes throughout your code.

But there's a principle that goes hand in hand with SRP, and that's DRY:

> **D1RY**
>
> ***Don't repeat yourself***
>
> *Avoid duplicate code by abstracting or separating out things that are common and placing those things in a single location.*

The different Date classes are not DRY

Each of the different `Date` classes (`FirstDate`, `SecondDate`, `ThirdDate`) have almost identical behavior in their `validateEvent()` methods. This not only breaks the SRP, but means that one change in logic—like specifying that you can actually Sleep Over on the second date—would result in changes to the logic in all three classes.

This quickly turns into a maintenance nightmare.

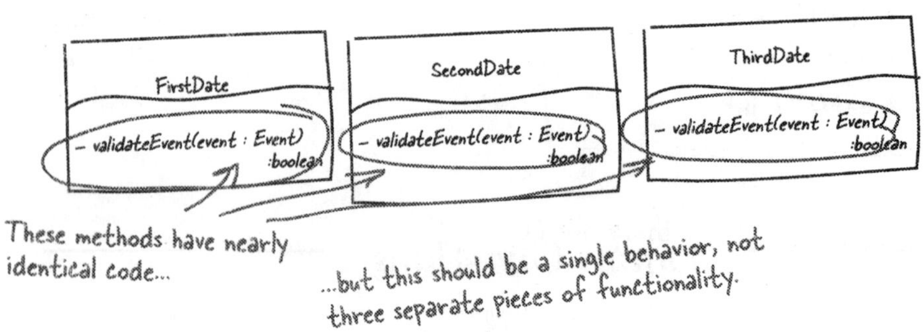

DRY is about having each piece of information and behavior in your system in a single, sensible place.

there are no Dumb Questions

Q: SRP sounded a lot like DRY to me. Aren't both about a single class doing the one thing it's supposed to do?

A: They are related, and often appear together. DRY is about putting a piece of functionality in a single place, such as a class; SRP is about making sure that a class does only one thing, and that it does that one thing well. In well-designed applications, one class does one thing, and does it well, and no other classes share that behavior.

Q: Isn't having each class do only one thing kind of limiting?

A: It's not, when you realize that the one thing a class does can be a pretty ***big*** thing. For example, the `Event` class in iSwoon and its subclasses only store and manage one thing, the details of the specific event. Currently those details are only the name of the event, but those classes could store any of a host of details about an event, such as times, dates, notifications and alarms, even addresses. However all this extra information is still only about ***one thing***, describing an event. The different `Event` classes do that one thing, and that's all they do, so they are great examples of the SRP.

Q: And using SRP will help my classes stay smaller, since they're only doing one thing, right?

A: Actually, the SRP will often make your classes bigger. Since you're not spreading out functionality over a lot of classes—which is what many programmers not familiar with the SRP will do—you're often putting more things into a class.

But using the SRP will usually result in fewer classes, and that generally makes your overall application a lot simpler to manage and maintain.

Q: I've heard of something called cohesion that sounds a lot like this. Are cohesion and the SRP the same thing?

A: Cohesion is actually just another name for the SRP. If you're writing **highly cohesive software**, then you're correctly applying the SRP. In the current iSwoon design, a `Date` does two things: it creates events *and* it stores the events that are happening on that specific date. When a class is cohesive, it has **one** main job. So in the case of the `Date` class, it makes more sense for the class to focus on storing events, and give up the responsibility for actually creating the events.

Want to know more about design principles? Check out Head First Object-Oriented Analysis and Design.

You've been loaded up with hints on how to make the iSwoon design, now make sure you've worked through and solved the exercise on pages 154 and 155 before turning the page...

For extra points, try to apply DRY as well as SRP to come up with a really great design.

Long Exercise Solution

You were asked to take a look at the current design and mark up what changes you'd make to apply the single responsibility principle to the iSwoon design to make it a breeze to update your software.

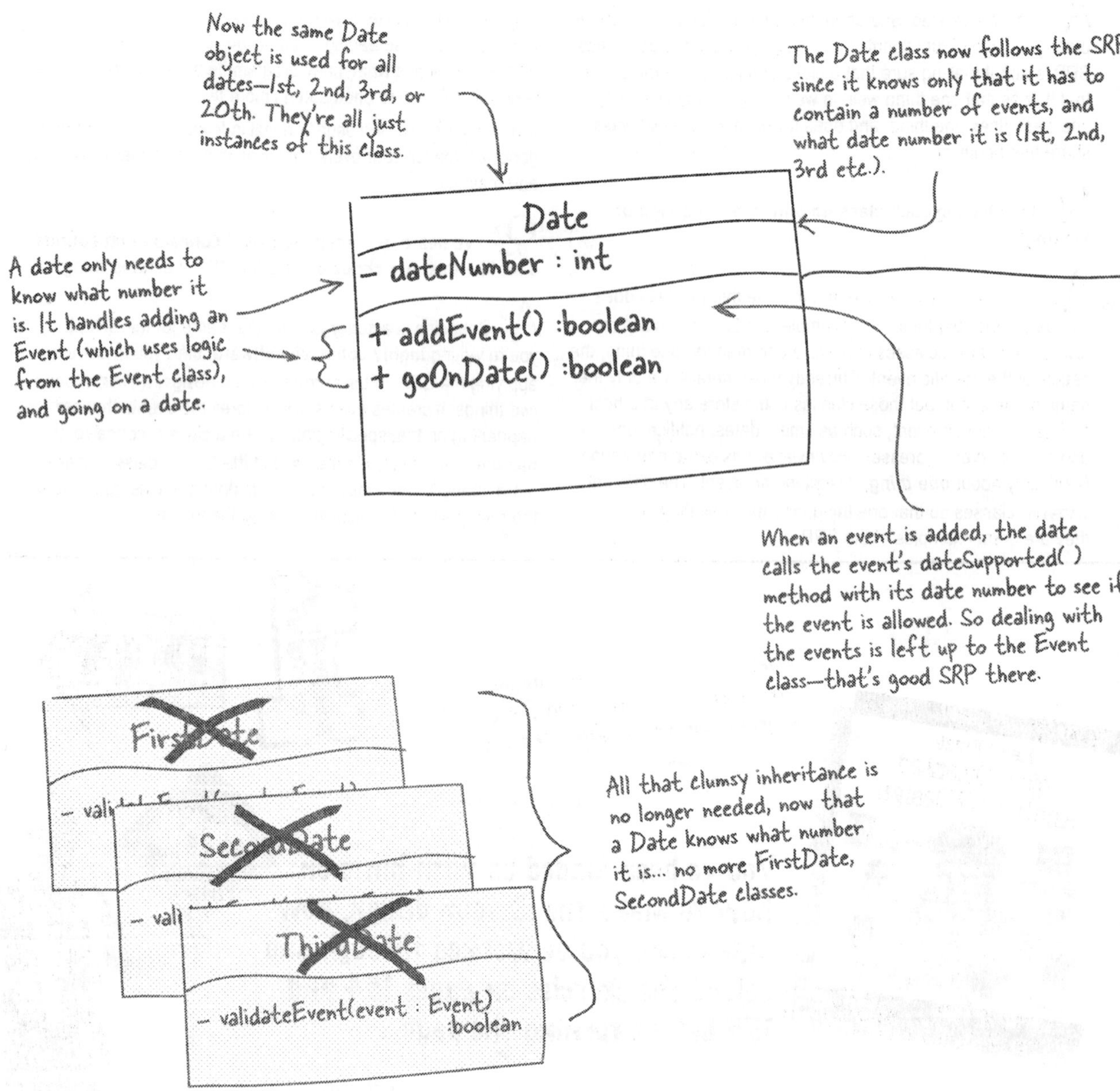

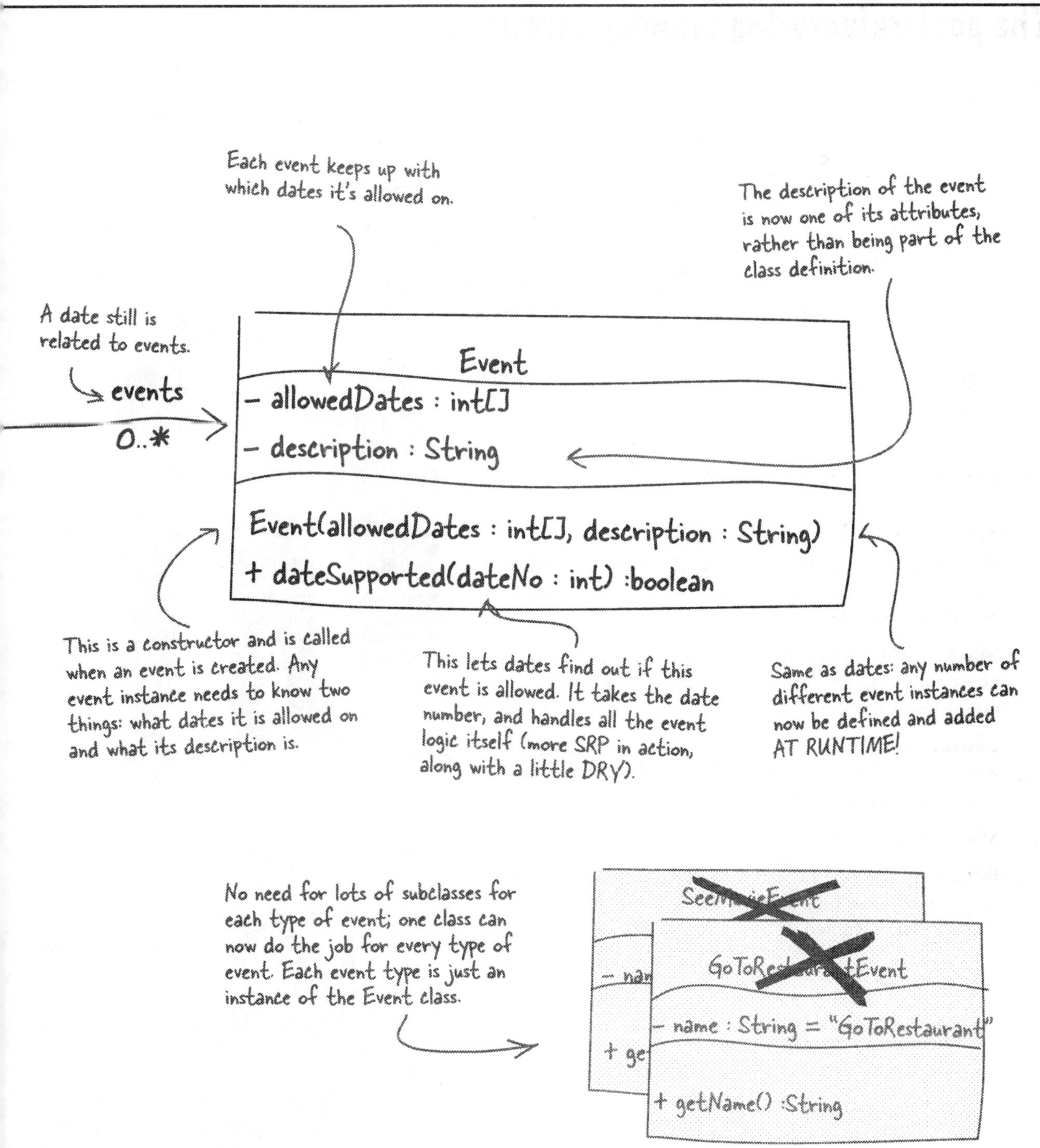
Each event keeps up with which dates it's allowed on.
The description of the event is now one of its attributes, rather than being part of the class definition.
A date still is related to events.
events
0..*
Event
- allowedDates : int[]
- description : String
Event(allowedDates : int[], description : String)
+ dateSupported(dateNo : int) :boolean
This is a constructor and is called when an event is created. Any event instance needs to know two things: what dates it is allowed on and what its description is.
This lets dates find out if this event is allowed. It takes the date number, and handles all the event logic itself (more SRP in action, along with a little DRY).
Same as dates: any number of different event instances can now be defined and added AT RUNTIME!
No need for lots of subclasses for each type of event; one class can now do the job for every type of event. Each event type is just an instance of the Event class.
- name : String = "GoToRestaurant"
+ getName() :String

The post-refactoring standup meeting...

Bob: Got it all done, we now have a really flexible piece of software that can support any number of different types of dates and events.

Laura: That's great! Sounds like the extra work might pay off for us; we've got a ton of new events to add...

Bob: Oh, it will. Now we can just write one or two lines of code, and, boom, the new event is in the system. We allowed between two and five days for each event, and now it only takes a day, at most.

Mark: You're not kidding. I've already added all the new events. And I'm sure we could make some more improvements as well...

Laura: Wait, just hang on a sec. For now the software is *more* than good enough, actually. Let's not starting making more changes just because we can.

Mark: So what's next?

Bob: Well, now that I've got the refactoring done, it looks like we have some time to focus on the demo that the Starbuzz CEO wanted...

there are no Dumb Questions

Q: When Laura says that the code is good enough, what does she mean?

A: Good question! We'll talk a lot more about testing in Chapters 7 and 8 and how you can be confident, and prove that your code does what it should.

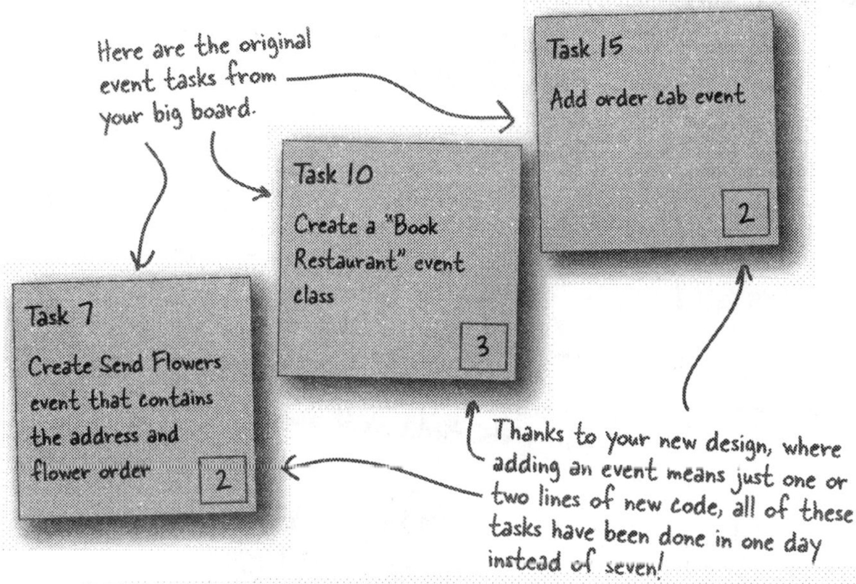

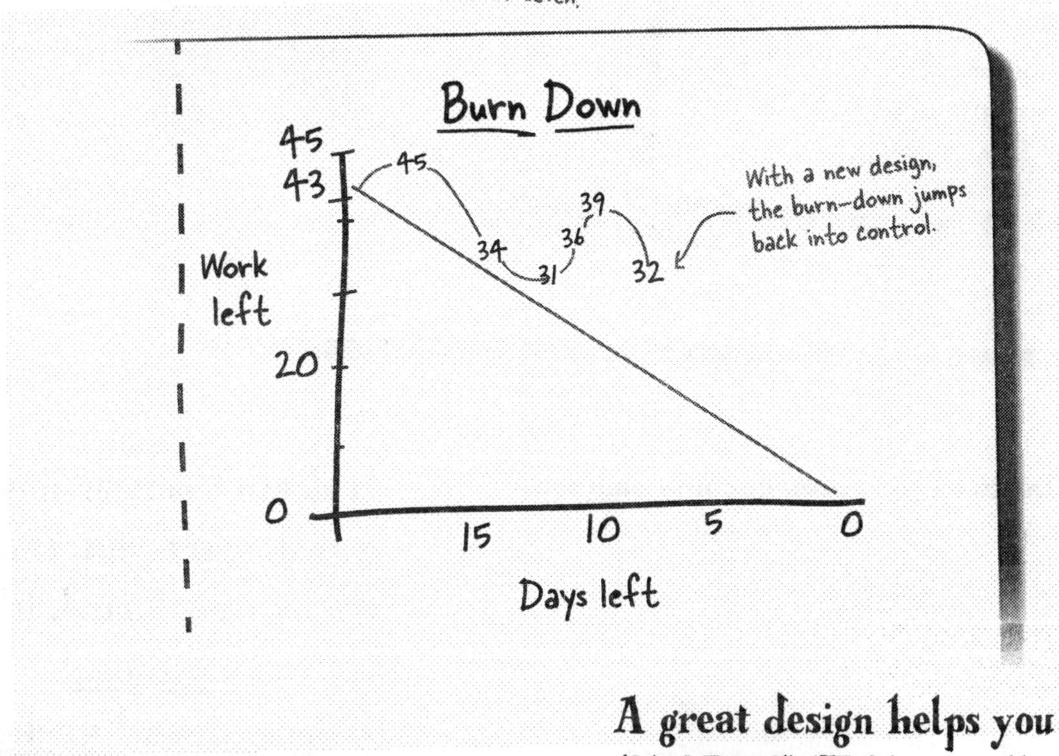

A great design helps you be more PRODUCTIVE as well as making your software more FLEXIBLE.

Unplanned tasks are still just tasks

The Starbuzz CEO's demo is an unplanned task, but you deal with it just like all the other tasks on your board. You estimate it, move it to the In Progress section of your board, and then go to work.

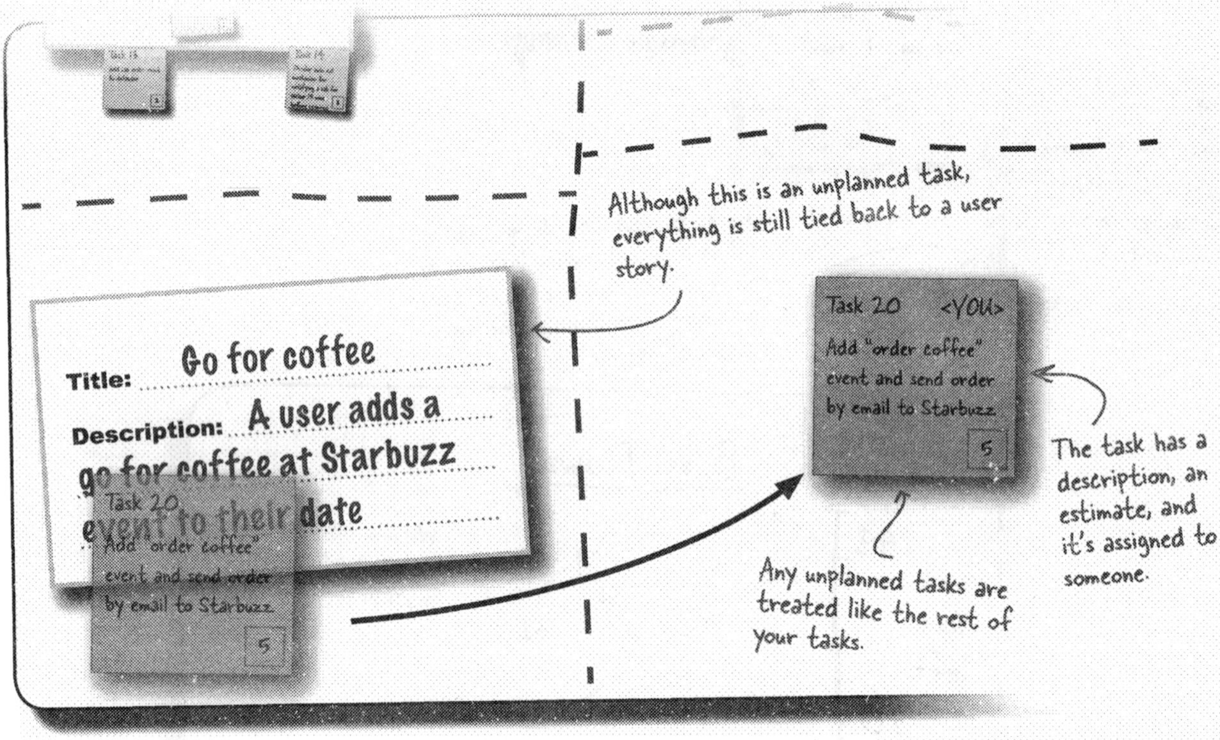

Unplanned tasks *on the board* become planned.

An unplanned task may start out differently, but once it goes on your board, it's treated just like all your planned tasks. In fact, as soon as you assign the task and give it an estimate, it really isn't unplanned anymore. It's just another task that has to be handled, along with everything else in your project.

And that's how you handle a task that starts out unplanned from its inception to completion: just like any other task. You estimate it, move it to the In Progress section of your board, and work it until it's done. Then you move it into the Completed section and move on.

It doesn't matter how a task starts out. Once it's on your board, it's got to be assigned, estimated, and worked on until it's complete.

Part of your task is the demo itself

In addition to the time you'd spend working on the demo, you've got to think about time spent actually ***doing*** the demo. If you and your lead web programmer both spend a day traveling to Starbuzz and showing off iSwoon, that's got to be part of your task estimate.

Your estimates should be complete

When you're estimating your tasks, you should come up with the time it takes to complete the task—and sometimes that involves more than just code. If you've got to demo the code or meet with a stakeholder, include time for those activities, too.

Four days to do the development, and another day for the actual demo and to field follow-up questions

Nice...can you email me the minimum system requirements? And does it work on Safari and Firefox, too? I want to start spreading the word to our customers right away.

Look! More unplanned tasks.

The Starbuzz CEO, now a happy iSwoon partner

Fireside Chats

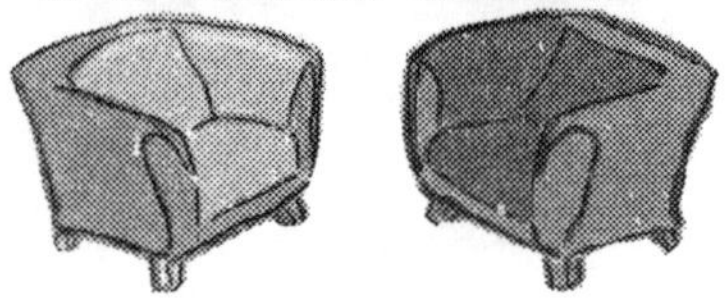

Tonight's talk: **A sit-down discussion between Perfect Design and "Good Enough" Design.**

"Good Enough" Design: Hi! So you're a Perfect Design? Man, I've always dreamed about meeting you!

Perfect Design: Thanks. Designs like me are pretty rare. In fact I may be the only one you'll ever meet.

"Good Enough" Design: Why's that?

Perfect Design: Well, the problem is that it's really hard to come up with a design that everyone thinks is perfect. There's always somebody out to get me with their criticisms. And with refactoring, I keep getting changed. But you're pretty valuable yourself, you know...

"Good Enough" Design: Yeah, I suppose so. As long as I help everyone be productive and meet their deadlines, and the customer is getting the software they need, then I'm doing my job.

Perfect Design: You see, that's the thing. People spend so much time on me that they never meet their deadlines, they never deliver software, and they never get paid. That can make me pretty unpopular. It kind of sucks, really.

"Good Enough" Design: Huh, I never thought of it like that. I thought when you came along everyone would be all hugs and kisses...

Perfect Design: Not at all. Usually by the time I show up, the team is running late and I can't help out anywhere near as much as as they thought. And then there's always the danger that I'm not completely perfect...

"Good Enough" Design: What do you mean? After all that hard work your team might still be able to make you even more, err...perfect?

Perfect Design: Unfortunately, yes. You see, perfection is a bit of a moving target. Sometimes, I just wish I could be like you and actually deliver. Maybe not great, but—

"Good Enough" Design:

Hey, wait a second. That sounded pretty condescending.

Perfect Design:

Well, sure. Everyone ships you out because you draw a line in the sand and say you're finished when the customer gets what they want. So even though you're not perfect you deliver. And a developer who delivers great software, whether it's designed perfectly or not, is a happy developer.

"Good Enough" Design:

Yeah, I suppose everyone is pretty stoked when I help them get great software out of the door. But I always figured that I was second class somehow and that they loved you...

Perfect Design:

If by love, you mean "never have time for," then you're right.

"Good Enough" Design:

So really what you're saying is that you'd like to be a design for software that actually got delivered?

Perfect Design:

Exactly! I aspire to be you, in many respects. People *want* to meet their deadlines and to ship software that the customer will sign off on. That's not settling; that's just being good developers and getting paid. You know developers, right, those guys that get paid for delivering? Well, I'm not in their good graces when they've come up with me and no software to actually ship...

"Good Enough" Design:

So, I guess I'm good enough to get the job done, to meet the customer's needs, and to be easy enough to work with that my developers can develop code on time. That's what really matters.

Perfect Design:

Yep, don't ever put yourself down. In this world it's nice to be perfect, but it's better to be ready and shipping.

When everything's complete, the iteration's done

Once you finish all your tasks, including any unplanned demos for forward-looking coffee addicts, you should end up with all your user stories, and the tasks that make them up, in your completed area of the board. And when you've got that, you're finished! There's nothing magical about it: when the work is done, so is your iteration.

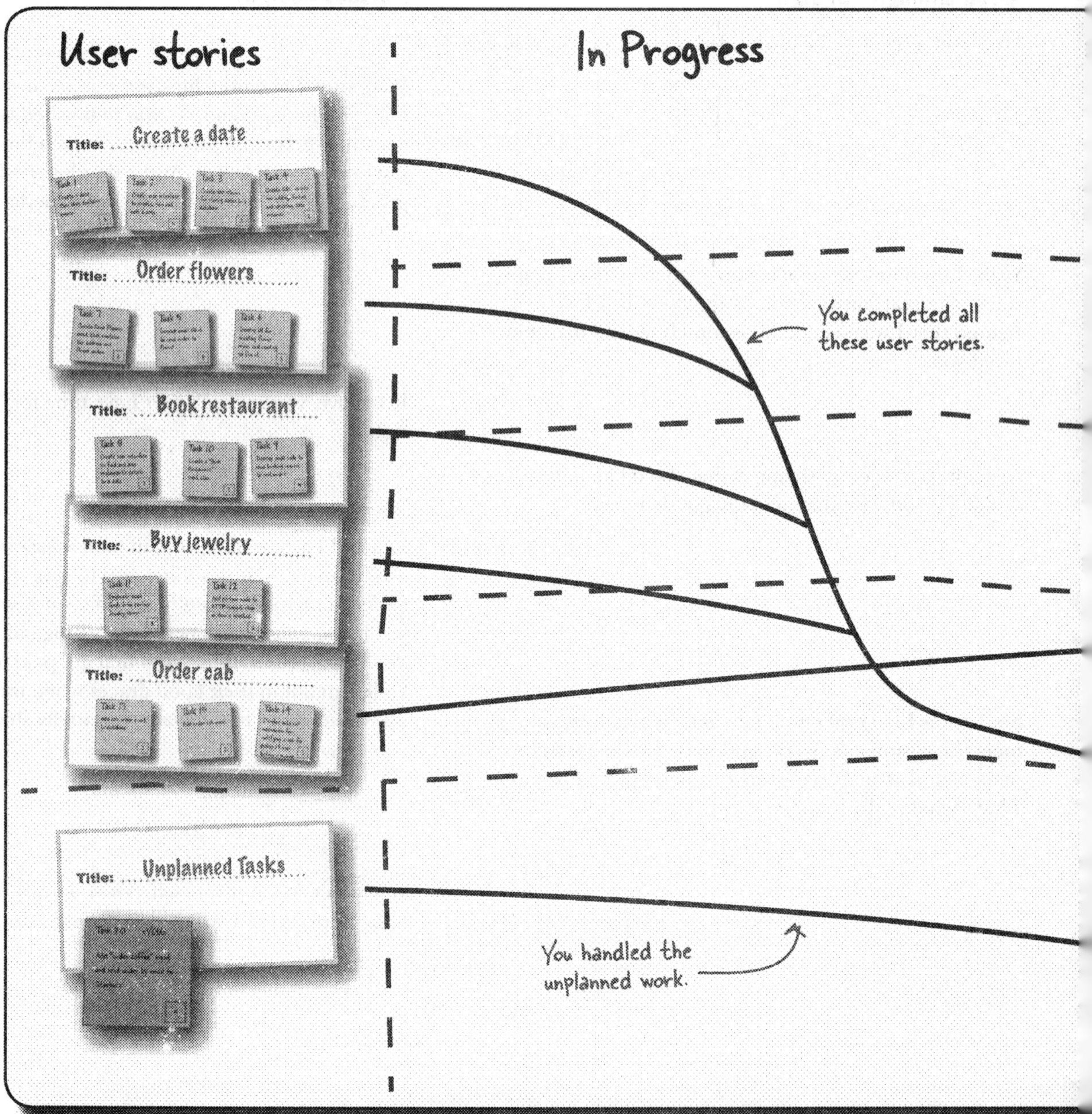

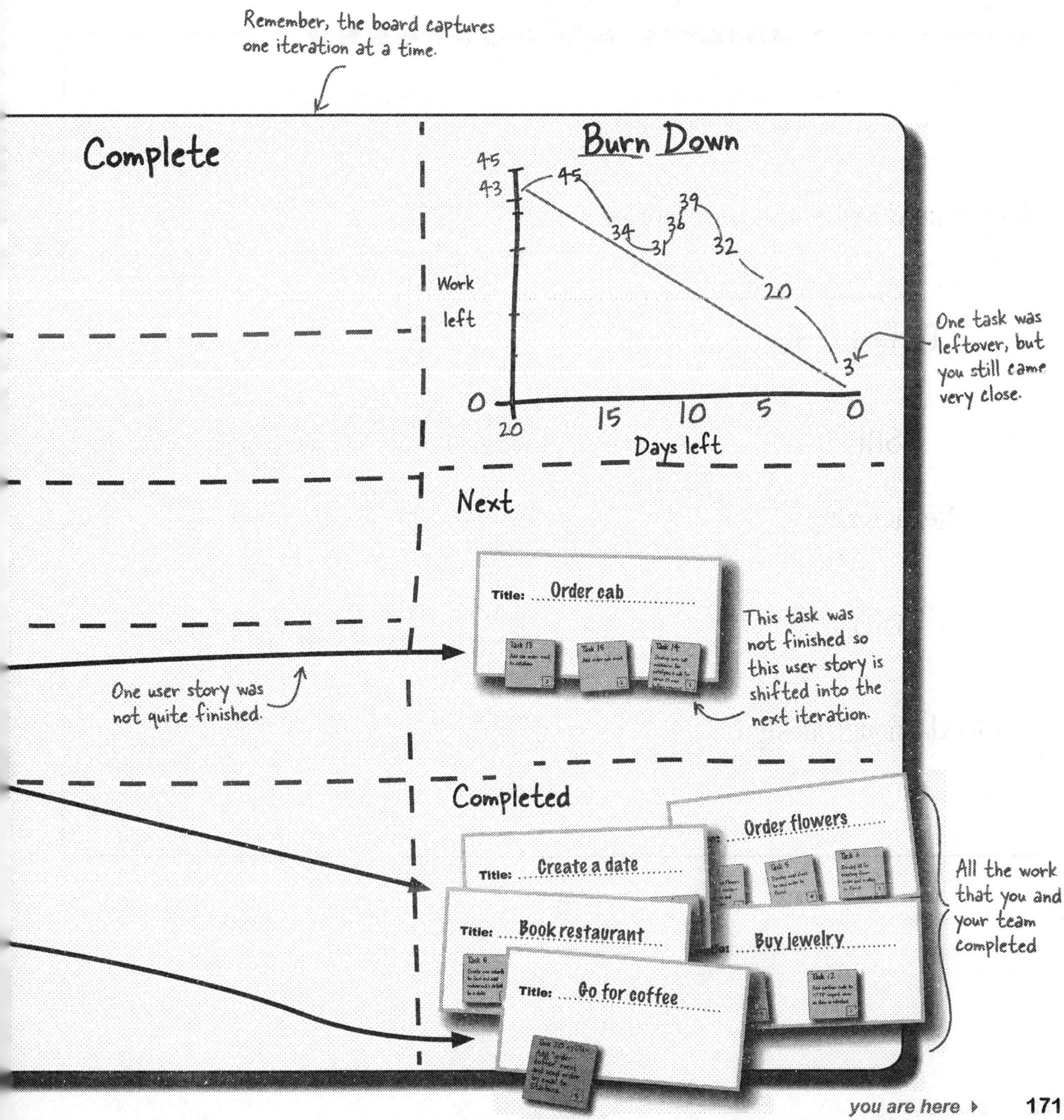
Remember, the board captures one iteration at a time.
Complete
Burn Down
45
43
45
34
31
36
39
32
20
3
Work left
0
20
15
10
5
0
Days left
One task was leftover, but you still came very close.
Next
Title: Order cab
This task was not finished so this user story is shifted into the next iteration.
One user story was not quite finished.
Completed
Order flowers
Title: Create a date
Title: Book restaurant
Buy jewelry
Title: Go for coffee
All the work that you and your team completed

WHAT'S MY PURPOSE?

Take each of the following techniques and artifacts from this chapter and match it to what it does.

Unplanned tasks and user stories	I help you make sure that everything has its place, and that place is only **one** place.
Perfect design	With me, the design gets better with small improvements throughout your code.
SRP	I make sure that the unexpected becomes the expected and managed.
Refactoring	My mantra is, "Perfect is great, but I deliver."
DRY	I make sure that all the parts of your software have one well-defined job.
Good-enough design	I'm what you strive for, but ultimately you might not deliver.

Software Development Design Cross

Let's put what you've learned to use and stretch out your left brain a bit! All of the words below are somewhere in this chapter. Good luck!

Across

1. Great developers ....
3. When an unplanned task is finished it is moved into the .... column.
4. Your burn down rate should show .... the work on your board, including any new unplanned tasks.
6. When a task is finished it goes in the .... column.
7. An unplanned user story and its tasks are moved into the .... bin on your project board when they are all finished.
9. If you find you are cutting and pasting large blocks of your design and code then there's a good chance that you're breaking the .... principle.
12. .... is the only constant in software development.
13. When a design helps you meet your deadlines, it is said to be a .... design.
14. If a user story is not quite finished at the end of an iteration, it is moved to the .... bin on your project board.
15. A good enough design helps you ....

Down

1. Unplanned tasks are treated the .... as unplanned tasks once they are on your board.
2. When you improve a design to make it more flexible and easier to maintain you are .... the design.
5. You should always be .... with your customer.
6. When all the tasks in a user story are finished, the user story is transferred to the .... bin
8. Striving for a .... design can mean that you never actually cut any code.
10. When a class does one job and it's the only class that does that job it is said to obey the .... responsibility principle.
11. An unplanned task is going to happen in your current iteration once you have added it to your ....

What's My Purpose? Solution

Take each of the following techniques and artifacts from this chapter and match it to what it does.

Unplanned tasks and user stories

Perfect design

SRP

Refactoring

DRY

Good-enough design

I help you make sure that everything has its place, and that place is only **one** place.

With me, the design gets better with small improvements throughout your code.

I make sure that the unexpected becomes the expected and managed.

My mantra is, "Perfect is great, but I deliver."

I make sure that all the parts of your software have one well-defined job.

I'm what you strive for, but ultimately you might not deliver.

Software Development Design Cross Solution

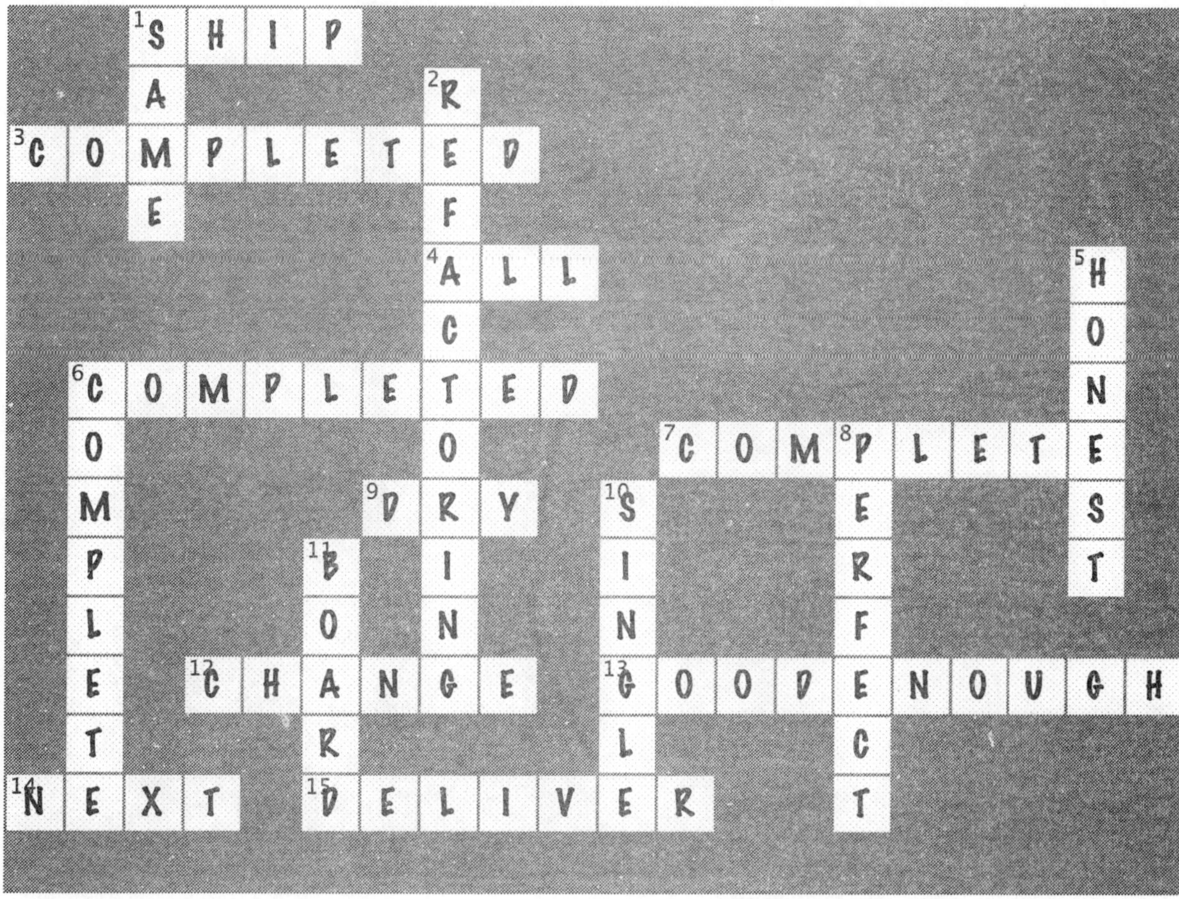

6 version control

Defensive development

When it comes to writing great software, *Safety First!*

Writing great software isn't easy...especially when you've got to make sure your code works, and **make sure it keeps working**. All it takes is one typo, one bad decision from a co-worker, one crashed hard drive, and suddenly all your work goes down the drain. But with **version control**, you can make sure your **code is always safe** in a code repository, you can **undo mistakes**, and you can make **bug fixes**—to new and old versions of your software.

You've got a new contract—BeatBox Pro

Congratulations—you've been getting rave reviews from iSwoon, and you've landed a new contract. You've been hired to add two new features to the legendary *Head First Java* BeatBox project. BeatBox is a multi-player drum machine that lets you send messages and drum loops to other users over the network.

Like every other software development project out there, the customer wants things done as soon as possible. They even let you bring along Bob, one of your junior developers, to help out. Since the stories aren't big enough to have more than one person work on them at a time, you'll work on one and Bob will work on the other. Here are the user stories for the new features you've got to add:

Title: Send a Poke to other users

Description: Click on the "Send a Poke" button to send an audible and visual alert to the other members in the chat. The alert should be short and not too annoying—you're just trying to get their attention.

Priority: 20 **Estimate:** 3

You'll take tasks associated with this story.

Title: Send a picture to other users

Description: Click on the "Send a Picture" button to send a picture (only JPEG needs to be supported) to another user. The other user should have the option to not accept the file. There are no size limits on the file being sent.

Priority: 20 **Estimate:** 4

Bob will pull tasks from this story.

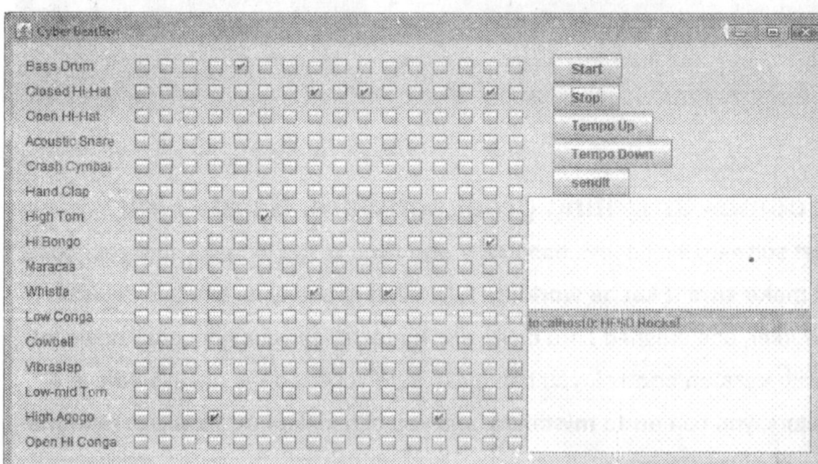

The BeatBox program from Head First Java, our starting point.

*You can download the code that we're starting with from http://www.headfirstlabs.com/books/hfsd/

Task ~~Magnets~~ Stickies

Let's get right to the new features. Here's a snippet from the BeatBox client code. Your job is to map the task stickies to the code that implements each part of the "Send a Poke..." story. We'll get to the GUI work in a minute.

```
// ... more BeatBox.java code above this

public class RemoteReader implements Runnable {
  boolean[] checkboxState = null;
  String nameToShow = null;
  Object obj = null;

  public void run() {
    try {
      while((obj=in.readObject()) != null) {
        System.out.println("got an object from server");
        System.out.println(obj.getClass());
        String nameToShow = (String) obj;
        checkboxState = (boolean[]) in.readObject();

        if (nameToShow.equals(POKE_START_SEQUENCE)) {
          playPoke();
          nameToShow = "Hey! Pay attention.";
        }

        otherSeqsMap.put(nameToShow, checkboxState);
        listVector.add(nameToShow);
        incomingList.setListData(listVector);
      } // close while
    } catch (Exception ex) { ex.printStackTrace(); }
  } // close run

  private void playPoke() {
    Toolkit.getDefaultToolkit().beep();
  }
} // close inner class
```

Task 1 MDE
Sound an audible alert when receiving a poke message (can't be annoying!)
.5

Task 2 LUG
Add support for checking for the Poke command and creating a message.
.5

Task 4 BJD
Merge Poke visual alert into message display system.
.5

Task 3 MDE
Implement receiver code to read the data off of the network.
1

Task ~~Magnets~~ Stickies Solution

We're not in *Head First Java* anymore; let's get right to the new features. Here's a snippet from the BeatBox client code. Your job was to map the task magnets to the code that implements each part of the "Send a Poke..." story.

All of this code goes into BeatBox.java.

```
// ... more BeatBox.java code above this

public class RemoteReader implements Runnable {
  boolean[] checkboxState = null;
  String nameToShow = null;
  Object obj = null;

  public void run() {
    try {
      while((obj=in.readObject()) != null) {
        System.out.println("got an object from server");
        System.out.println(obj.getClass());
        String nameToShow = (String) obj;
        checkboxState = (boolean[]) in.readObject();

        if (nameToShow.equals(POKE_START_SEQUENCE)) {
          playPoke();
          nameToShow = "Hey! Pay attention.";
        }

        otherSeqsMap.put(nameToShow, checkboxState);
        listVector.add(nameToShow);
        incomingList.setListData(listVector);
      } // close while
    } catch (Exception ex) { ex.printStackTrace(); }
  } // close run

  private void playPoke() {
    Toolkit.getDefaultToolkit().beep();
  }
} // close inner class
```

This is the inner class that receives data from the server.

Here's the code that will run in the new thread context for BeatBox.

This is original code—it reads messages sent from the server.

If we get the POKE_START_SEQUENCE, we play the poke sound and replace the message with our alert text.

Here's our new playPoke() method that just beeps for now. If you want a real challenge, add MP3 poke-sound support.

Task 3 — MDE: Implement receiver code to read the data off of the network. **1**

Task 2 — LUG: Add support for checking for the Poke command and creating a message. **.5**

Task 4 — BJD: Merge Poke visual alert into message display system. **.5**

Task 1 — MDE: Sound an audible alert when receiving a poke message (can't be annoying!) **.5**

there are no Dumb Questions

Q: This isn't a Java programming book. Why are we wasting time looking through all this code?

A: Software development techniques cover everything related to a project, from organization and estimation down through code. Earlier, we talked about the planning and execution parts of a project, and then we got a little closer to code and talked about design. Now, we need to dive all the way down and talk about some tools and techniques you can use ***on your code itself***. Software development isn't just about prioritization and estimation; you've still got to write good, working, reliable code.

Q: I don't develop in Java. I'm not sure what some of the code in there does. What do I do?

A: That's OK. Do your best to understand what the code is doing, and don't worry about all the Java-specific details. The main thing is to get an idea of how to handle and think about code in a solid software development process. The tools and techniques we'll talk about should make sense whether you know what a Java thread is or not.

Q: I think I must have...misplaced... my copy of *Head First Java*. What's this whole BeatBox thing about?

A: BeatBox is a program first discussed in Head First Java. It has a backend `MusicServer` and a Java Swing–based client piece (that's Java's graphical toolkit API). The client piece uses the Java Sound API to generate sound sequences that you can control with the checkboxes on the form's main page. When you enter a message and click "sendit," your message and your BeatBox settings are sent to any other copies of BeatBox connected to your `MusicServer`. If you click on the received message, then you can hear the new sequence that was just sent.

Q: So what's the deal with that POKE_START_SEQUENCE thing?

A: Our story requires us to send a poke message to the other BeatBoxes connected to the `MusicServer`. Normally when a message gets sent it's just a string that is displayed to the user. We added the Poke functionality on top of the original BeatBox by coming up with a unique string of characters that no one should ever type on purpose. We can use that to notify the other BeatBoxes that a "poke" was sent. This sequence is stored in the `POKE_START_SEQUENCE` constant (the actual string value is in the `BeatBox.java` file in the code you can download from *http://www.headfirstlabs.com/books/hfsd/*).

When other BeatBox instances see the `POKE_START_SEQUENCE` come through, they replace it with our visual alert message, and the receiving user never actually sees that code sequence.

Q: What's all this threading and Runnable stuff about?

A: BeatBox is always trying to grab data from the network so it can display incoming messages. However, if there's nothing available on the network, it could get stuck waiting for data. This means the screen wouldn't redraw and users couldn't type in a new message to send. In order to split those two things apart, BeatBox uses threads. It creates a thread to handle the network access, and then uses the main thread to handle the GUI work. The `Runnable` interface is Java's way of wrapping up some code that should be run in another thread. The code you just looked at, in the last exercise, is the network code.

BRAIN POWER

Bob's making good progress on his end, too. Can you think of anything else you should be worrying about at this point?

And now the GUI work...

We need one more piece of code to get this story together. We need to add a button to the GUI that lets the user actually send the Poke. Here's the code to take care of that task:

Task 5 <YOU>

Add button to GUI to send Poke sequence to other BeatBox instances.

.5

```
// The code below goes in BeatBox.java,
//   in the buildGUI() method
  JButton sendIt = new JButton("sendIt");
  sendIt.addActionListener(new MySendListener());
  buttonBox.add(sendIt);

  JButton sendPoke = new JButton("Send Poke");
  sendPoke.addActionListener(new MyPokeListener());
  buttonBox.add(sendPoke);

  userMessage = new JTextField();
  buttonBox.add(userMessage);
```

First we need to create a new button for our Poke feature.

Then we set up a listener so we can react when it's clicked.

Finally, add the button to the box holding the other buttons.

```
// Below is new code we need to add, also to BeatBox.java
public class MyPokeListener implements ActionListener {

  public void actionPerformed(ActionEvent a) {
    // We'll create an empty state array here
    boolean[] checkboxState = new boolean[255];

    try {
      out.writeObject(POKE_START_SEQUENCE);
      out.writeObject(checkboxState);
    } catch (Exception ex) {
      System.out.println("Failed to poke!");
    }
  }
}
```

Here we create an array of booleans for our state. We can leave them all false because the receiving side ignores them when it gets the POKE command.

Here's the magic: to send a poke we send the magic POKE_START_SEQUENCE and our array of booleans to the server. The server will relay our magic sequence to the other clients, and they'll beep at the user because of the earlier code we wrote (back on page 180).

And a quick test...

Now that both the client and server are implemented it's time to make sure things work. No software can go out without testing so...

1. First compile and start up the MusicServer.

```
File Edit Window Help Buildin'
hfsd> mkdir bin
hfsd> javac -d bin src\headfirst\sd\chapter6\*.java
hfsd> java -cp bin headfirst.sd.chapter6.MusicServer
```

e "-d" tells the compiler to the classes in bin directory.

The MusicServer will listen for connections and print out a line each time it gets one.

2. Then start the new BeatBox—we'll need two instances running so we can test the Poke.

We use different names here so we know which is which.

```
File Edit Window Help Ouch
hfsd> java -cp bin headfirst.sd.chapter6.BeatBox PokeReceiver
```

```
File Edit Window Help Hah
hfsd> java -cp bin headfirst.sd.chapter6.BeatBox PokeSender
```

3. Now send off a Poke by clicking the "Send Poke" button on the instance we named PokeSender.

Here's our new Poke button.

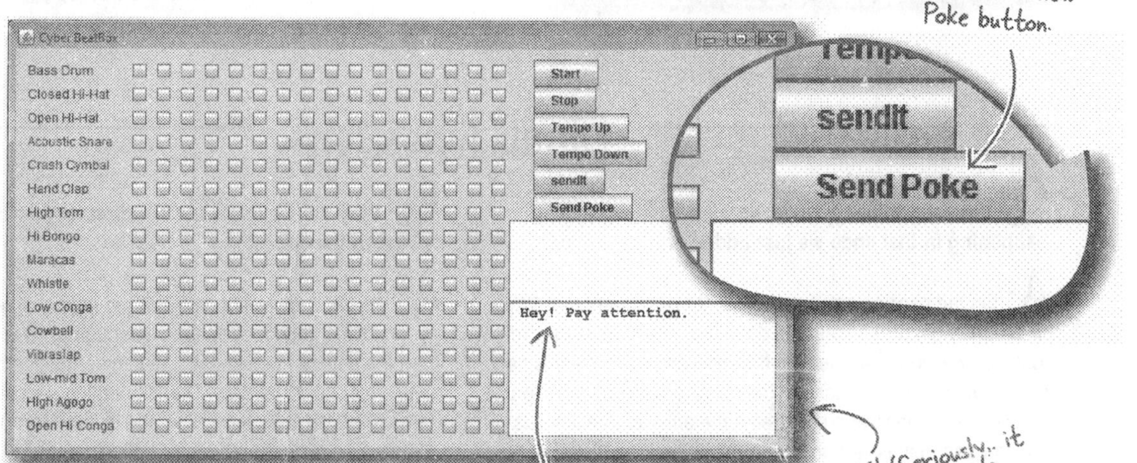

Here's our PokeReceiver instance.

Here's our alert message.

DING! (Seriously, it sounds like that.)

Excellent! Your changes work as advertised. We'll copy the code up to the demo server, and all that's left is for Bob to merge his stuff in. Time to call it a night.

And Bob does the same...

Bob finished up the tasks related to his story and ran a quick test on his end. His task is working, so he copies his code up to the server. In order to do the final build he merges his code in with ours, gets everything to compile, and retests sending a picture. Everything looks good. Tomorrow's demo is going to rock...

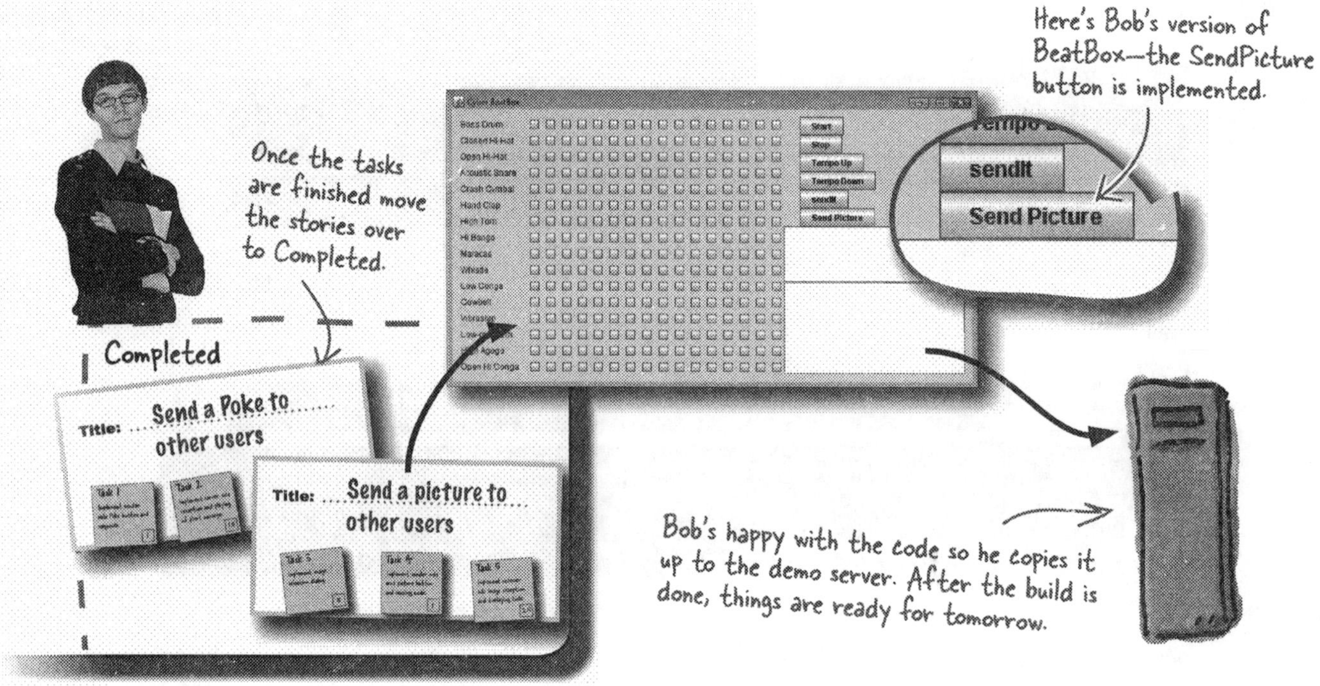

there are no Dumb Questions

Q: I'm not familiar with networking code. What's happening in that code we just added?

A: On the sending side we represent the sequence settings as an array of checkboxes. We don't really care what they're set to, since we won't use them on the receiving side. We still need to send something, though, so the existing code works. We use Java's object serialization to stream the array of checkboxes and our secret message that triggers the alert on the other side.

On the receiving side we pull off the secret sequence and the array of checkboxes. All of the serialization and deserialization is handled by Java.

Q: Why did we make the bin directory before we compiled the code?

A: We'll talk more about this in the next chapter, but in general it's a good idea to keep your compiled code separate from the source. It makes it a lot simpler to clean up and rebuild when you make changes. There's nothing special about the name "bin"; it's just convention and is short for "binaries"—i.e., compiled code.

Q: Wait, did Bob just merge code on the demo server?

A: Yup...

Demo the new BeatBox for the customer

We're all set to go. Your code is written, tested, and copied up to the demo server. Bob did the final build, so we call the customer and prepare to amaze the crowds.

So what went wrong?

Our code worked just a few pages ago. So what went wrong? More importantly, what would you do differently in the future to make sure nothing like this ever happens again?

Think beyond, "Do more testing." How can you prevent this problem from occurring in the first place?

Exercise

Something's clearly gone wrong. Below is some code we compiled on our machine and the same section of code from the demo machine. See if you can figure out what happened.

```
public class RemoteReader implements Runnable {
  boolean[] checkboxState = null;
  String nameToShow = null;
  Object obj = null;

  public void run() {
    try {
      while((obj=in.readObject()) != null) {
        System.out.println("got an object from server");
        System.out.println(obj.getClass());
        String nameToShow = (String) obj;
        checkboxState = (boolean[]) in.readObject();
        if (nameToShow.equals(POKE_START_SEQUENCE)) {
          playPoke();
          nameToShow = "Hey! Pay attention.";
        }
        otherSeqsMap.put(nameToShow, c
        listVector.add(nameToShow);
        incomingList.setListData(listV
      } // close while
    } catch (Exception ex) { ex.print
  } // close run
```

Here's the code from our machine—it worked fine when we ran it.

And here's the code on the demo server—the code that tanked.

```
public class RemoteReader implements Runnable {
  boolean[] checkboxState = null;
  String nameToShow = null;
  Object obj = null;

  public void run() {
  try {
    while ((obj = in.readObject()) != null) {
     System.out.println("got an object from server");
     System.out.println(obj.getClass());
     String nameToShow = (String) obj;
     checkboxState = (boolean[]) in.readObject();
     if (nameToShow.equals(PICTURE_START_SEQUENCE)) {
       receiveJPEG();
     }
     else {
       otherSeqsMap.put(nameToShow, checkboxState);
       listVector.add(nameToShow);
       incomingList.setListData(listVector);
     }
    } // close while
  } catch (Exception ex) {
    ex.printStackTrace();
  }
} // close run
```

What went wrong? ....

....

....

How did this happen? ....

....

....

What would you do? ....

....

....

Standup meeting

Your team, after the big flop at the customer demo

Mark: Wow. Bob really blew it with that demo.

Bob: What are you talking about? My code worked!

Laura: But you broke the other story we were trying to demo! It worked fine before you got to it.

Bob: Wait a minute—why am I getting blamed for this? You asked me to copy my code up to the demo server so we could build it. When I did that, I saw you guys had changed a lot of the same stuff. It was a mess.

Mark: So you just overwrote it??

Bob: No way—I spent a bunch of time comparing the files trying to figure out what you had changed and what I had changed. To make things worse, you guys had some variables renamed in your code so I had to sort that out, too. I got the button stuff right, but I guess I missed something in the receiver code.

Laura: So do we still have the working Poke code on there?

Bob: I doubt it. I copied my stuff up with a new name and merged them into the files you had up there. I didn't think to snag a copy of your stuff.

Mark: Not good. I probably have a copy on my machine, but I don't know if it's the latest. Laura, do you have it?

Laura: I might, but I've started working on new stuff, so I'll have to try and back all my changes out. We really need to find a better way to handle this stuff. This is costing us a ton of time to sort out and we're probably adding bugs left and right...

Not to mention we're going the <u>wrong</u> <u>way</u> on our burn-down rate again.

Let's start with VERSION CONTROL

You'll also see this referred to as configuration management, which is a little more formal term for the same thing.

Keeping track of source code (or any kind of files for that matter) across a project is tricky. You have lots of people working on files—sometimes the same ones, sometimes different. Any serious software project needs **version control**, which is also often called **configuration management**, or **CM** for short.

Version control is a tool (usually a piece of software) that will keep track of changes to your files and help you coordinate different developers working on different parts of your system at the same time. Here's the rundown on how version control works:

1 Bob **checks out** BeatBox.java from the server.

1.5 The rest of your team can **check out** Version 1 of BeatBox.java while Bob works on his version.

2 Bob **makes some changes** to the code and tests them.

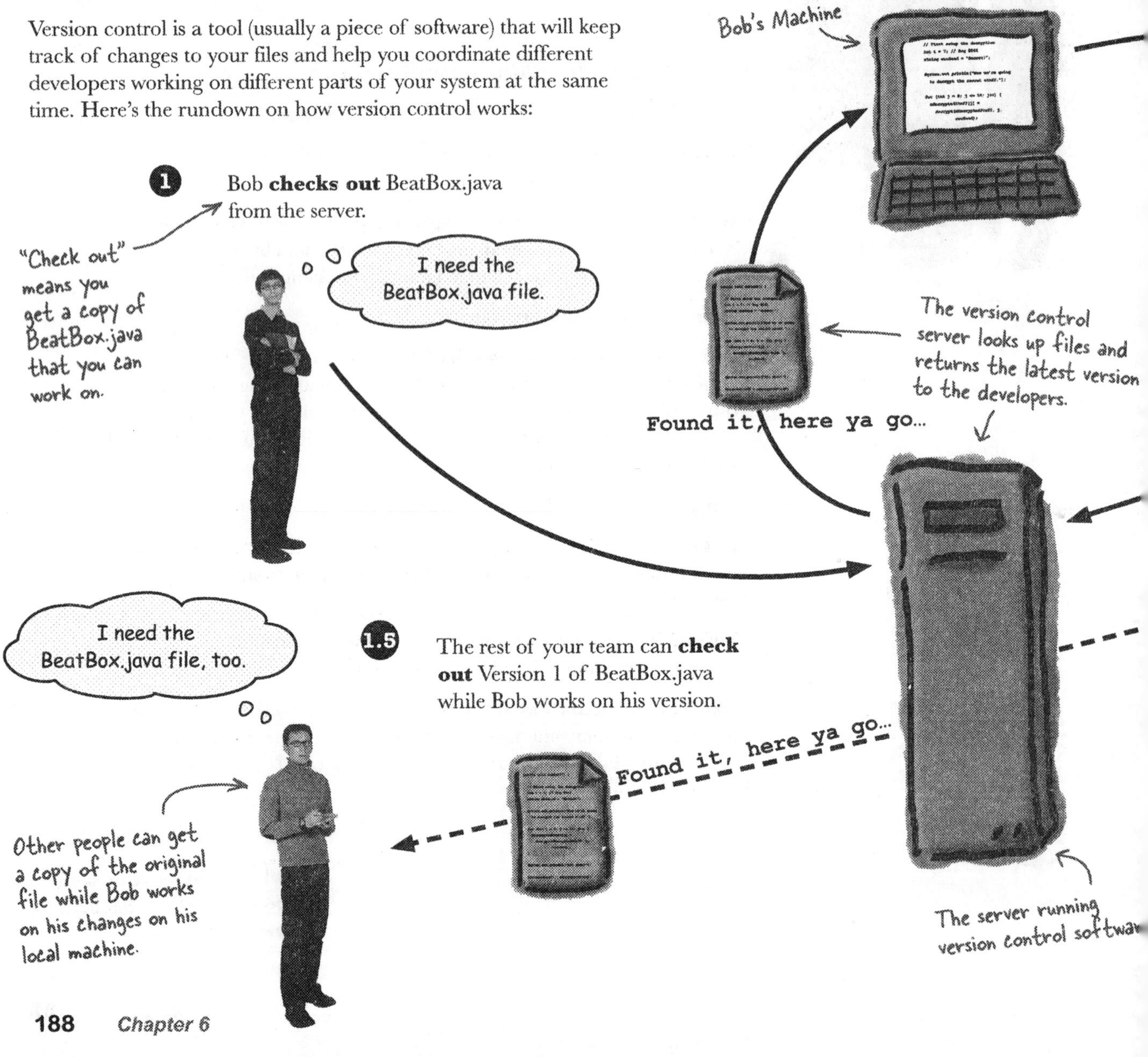

3 Bob **checks in** his changes.

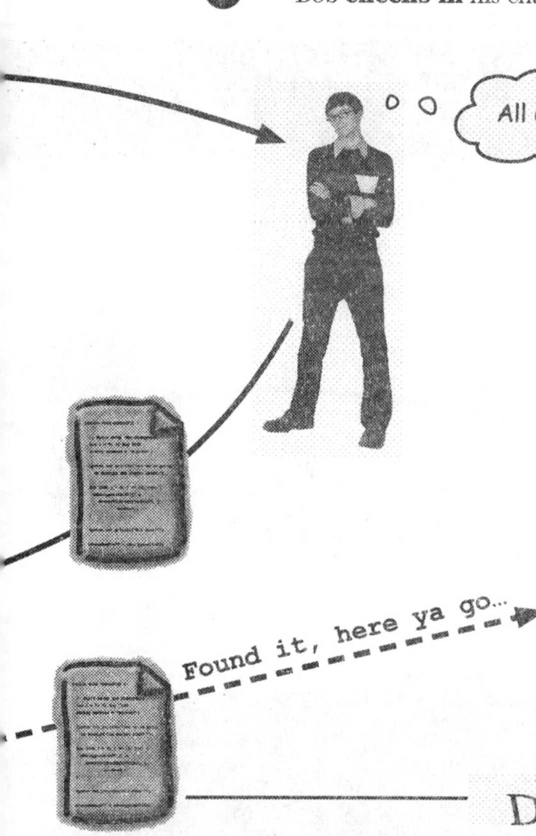

3.5 After Bob checks in his changes, the team can **get an update** from the server with the new code.

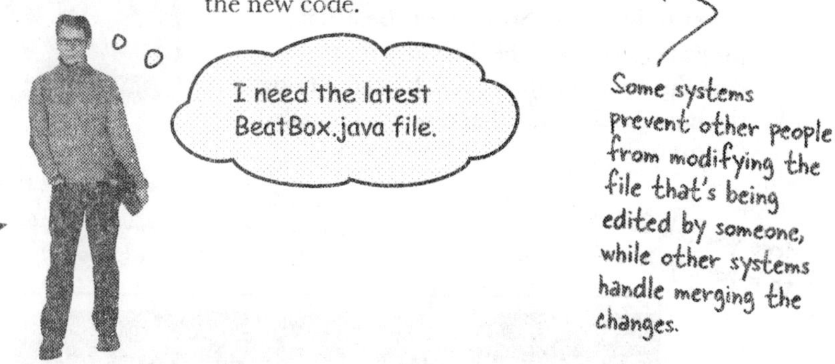

there are no Dumb Questions

Q: So if version control is a piece of software, which version control product should I use?

A: There are lots of choices out there for version control tools, both commercial and open source. One of the most popular open source ones is called Subversion, and that's the one we'll use in this chapter. Microsoft tools such as Visual Studio like to work with Microsoft's version control tool, called Visual SourceSafe, or Microsoft's new Team Foundation product.

Version control tools all do pretty much the same thing, but some offer different ways to do it. For example, some commercial systems have strict access control on where you can commit code so that your organization can control what goes into what build. Other tools show you the different versions of files as virtual directories.

Q: You're only showing one file and two developers. I'm guessing it can do more than that, right?

A: You bet. In fact, a good version control tool is really the only way you can ***scale a team***. We'll need some of those more sophisticated features (like merging changes, tagging versions, etc.) in just a minute...

First set up your project...

We're assuming you've got your version control software installed. If not, you can download it from the Subversion web site.

The first step in using a version control tool is to put your code in the **repository**; that's where your code is stored. There's nothing tricky about putting your code in the repository, just get the original files organized on your machine and create the project in the repository:

1. First create the repository—you only need to do this once for each version control install. After that you just add projects to the same repository.

```
File Edit Window Help TakeBacks
hfsd> svnadmin create c:\Users\Developer\Desktop\SVNRepo
hfsd>
```

This tells Subversion to create a new repository... ...in this directory.

After that runs, we have our repository.

2. Next you need to import your code into the repository. Just go to the directory above your code and tell your version control server to import it. So, for your BeatBox project, you'd go to the directory that contains your beat box code. If you're using the downloaded files, that directory is called `Chapter6`:

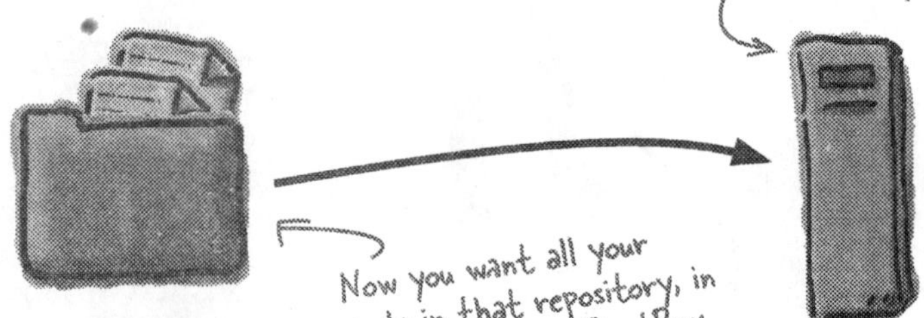

Now you want all your code in that repository, in a project called BeatBox.

Here you tell Subversion to import your code.

This is the repository you created in step 1. On Windows you'll need to use forward slash notation.

```
File Edit Window Help Tariffs
hfsd> svn import Chapter6 file:///c:/Users/Developer/Desktop/
SVNRepo/BeatBox/trunk -m "Initial Import"
Adding         Chapter6\src
Adding         Chapter6\src\headfirst
Adding         Chapter6\src\headfirst\sd
Adding         Chapter6\src\headfirst\sd\chapter6
Adding         Chapter6\src\headfirst\sd\chapter6\BeatBox.java
Adding         Chapter6\src\headfirst\sd\chapter6\MusicServer.java

Committed revision 1.

hfsd>
```

Here's what we want our project to be called—ignore the "trunk" thing for right now.

This is just a comment describing what we're doing; we'll talk more about this later, too.

Subversion adds each file it finds into your repository for the BeatBox project.

* You can get the full Subversion documentation here: http://svnbook.red-bean.com/

...then you can check code in and out.

Now that your code is in the repository, you can check it out, make your changes, and check your updated code back in. A version control system will keep track of your original code, all of the changes you make, and also handle sharing your changes with the rest of your team. First, check out your code (normally your repository wouldn't be on your local machine):

1. To check out your code, you just tell your version control software what project you want to check out, and where to put the files you requested.

This tells Subversion to check out a copy of the code.

This pulls code from the BeatBox Project in the repository and puts it in a local directory called BeatBox.

```
File Edit Window Help Gimme
hfsd> svn checkout file:///c:/Users/Developer/Desktop/SVNRepo/
BeatBox/trunk BeatBox

A    BeatBox\src
A    BeatBox\src\headfirst
A    BeatBox\src\headfirst\sd
A    BeatBox\src\headfirst\sd\chapter6
A    BeatBox\src\headfirst\sd\chapter6\BeatBox.java
A    BeatBox\src\headfirst\sd\chapter6\MusicServer.java

Checked out revision 1.

hfsd>
```

Subversion pulls your files back out of the repository and copies them into a new BeatBox directory (or an existing one if you've already got a BeatBox directory).

2. Now you can make changes to the code just like you normally would. You just work directly on the files you checked out from your version control system, compile, and save.

You can re-implement the Poke story, since Bob broke that feature when he wrote code for the Send Picture story.

This is a normal .java file. Subversion doesn't change it in any way...it's still just code.

3. Then you commit your changes back into the repository with a message describing what changes you've made.

This tells Subversion to commit your changes; it will figure out what files you've changed.

This is a log message, indicating what you did.

```
File Look What IDid
hfsd> svn commit -m "Added POKE support."

Sending        src\headfirst\sd\chapter6\BeatBox.java
Transmitting file data .
Committed revision 2.

hfsd>
```

Since you only changed one file, that's all that subversion sent to the repository—and notice that now you have a new revision number.

Most version control tools will try and solve problems for you

Suppose you had a version control system in place before the great BeatBox debacle of '08. You'd check in your code (with `commit`) to implement Send Poke, and then Bob would change his code, and try to commit his work on Send Picture:

Bob tries to check in his code...

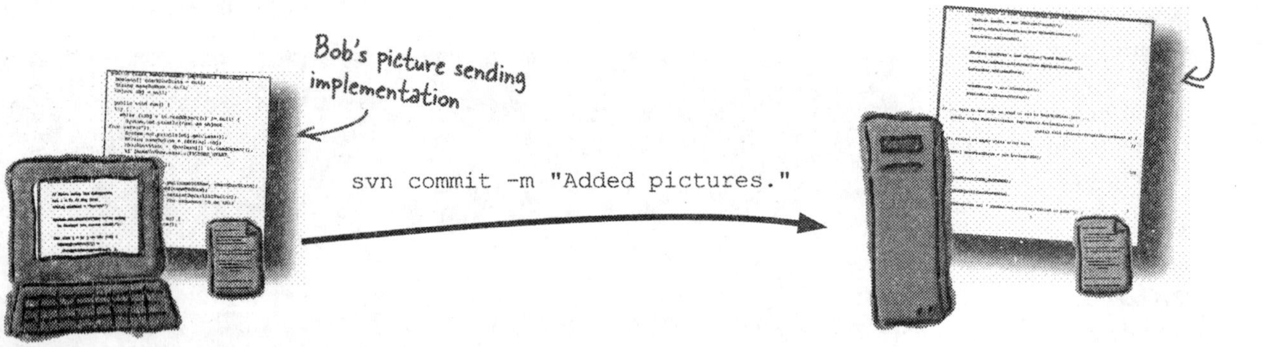

...but quickly runs into a problem.

You and Bob both made changes to the same file; you just got yours into the repository first.

Bob's code

```
public class RemoteReader implements Runnable {
  boolean[] checkboxState = null;
  String nameToShow = null;
  Object obj = null;

  public void run() {
  try {
    while ((obj = in.readObject()) != null) {
      System.out.println("got an object from server");
      System.out.println(obj.getClass());
      String nameToShow = (String) obj;
      checkboxState = (boolean[]) in.readObject();
      if (nameToShow.equals(PICTURE_START_SEQUENCE)) {
        receiveJPEG();
      }
      else {
        otherSeqsMap.put(nameToShow, checkboxState);
        listVector.add(nameToShow);
        incomingList.setListData(listVector);
        // now reset the sequence to be this
      }
    } // close while
  } catch (Exception ex) {
    ex.printStackTrace();
  }
} // close run
} // close inner class
```

Bob's BeatBox.java

The code on the server, with your changes

```
public class RemoteReader implements Runnable {
  boolean[] checkboxState = null;
  String nameToShow = null;
  Object obj = null;

  public void run() {
   try {
     while((obj=in.readObject()) != null) {
       System.out.println("got an object from server");
       System.out.println(obj.getClass());
       String nameToShow = (String) obj;
       checkboxState = (boolean[]) in.readObject();
       if (nameToShow.equals(POKE_START_SEQUENCE)) {
         playPoke();
         nameToShow = "Hey! Pay attention.";
       }
       otherSeqsMap.put(nameToShow, checkboxState);
       listVector.add(nameToShow);
       incomingList.setListData(listVector);
     } // close while
   } catch(Exception ex) {ex.printStackTrace();}
  } // close run

  private void playPoke() {
    Toolkit.getDefaultToolkit().beep();
  }
} // close inner class
```

BeatBox.java

The server tries to MERGE your changes

If two people make changes to the same file but in different places, most version control systems try to merge the changes together. This isn't *always* what you want, but most of the time it works great.

Nonconflicting code and methods are easy

In `BeatBox.java`, you added a `playPoke()` method, so the code on the version control server has that method. But Bob's code has no `playPoke()` method, so there's a potential problem.

Nothing here... Bob has no code for playPoke() at all.

Bob's BeatBox.java

The version on the server has a playPoke() method.

```
private void playPoke() {
  Toolkit.getDefaultToolkit().beep();
}
```

BeatBox.java

Your version control software will combine files

In a case like this, your version control server can simply combine the two files. In other words, the `playPoke()` method gets combined with nothing in Bob's file, and you end up with a `BeatBox.java` on the server that still retains the `playPoke()` method. So no problems yet...

But conflicting code IS a problem

But what if you have code in the same method that is different? That's exactly the case with Bob's version of `BeatBox.java`, and the version on the server, in the `run()` method:

These two bits of code are in the same place, but it's not clear how to merge them.

```
if (nameToShow.equals(PICTURE_START_SEQUENCE)) {
  receiveJPEG();
} else {
  otherSeqsMap.put(nameToShow, checkboxSt
  listVector.add(nameToShow);
  incomingList.setListData(listVector);
}
```

Bob's BeatBox.java

```
if (nameToShow.equals(POKE_START_SEQUENCE)) {
  playPoke();
  nameToShow = "Hey! Pay attention.";
}
otherSeqsMap.put(nameToShow, checkboxState)
listVector.add(nameToShow);
incomingList.setListData(listVector);
```

BeatBox.java

If your software can't merge the changes, it issues a conflict

If two people made changes to the same set of lines, there's no way for a version control system to know what to put in the final server copy. When this happens, most systems just punt. They'll kick the file back to the person trying to commit the code and ask them to sort out the problems.

Subversion rejects your commit. You can use the update command to pull the changes into your code, and Subversion will mark the lines where there are conflicts in your files... after you sort out the conflicts, you can recommit.

```
public class RemoteReader implements Runnable {
  boolean[] checkboxState = null;
  String nameToShow = null;
  Object obj = null;

  public void run() {
  try {
    while ((obj = in.readObject()) != null) {
      System.out.println("got an object from server");
      System.out.println(obj.getClass());
      String nameToShow = (String) obj;
      checkboxState = (boolean[]) in.readObject();
      if (nameToShow.equals(PICTURE_START_SEQUENCE)) {
        receiveJPEG();
      }
      else {
        otherSeqsMap.put(nameToShow, checkboxState);
        listVector.add(nameToShow);
        incomingList.setListData(listVector);
        // now reset the sequence to be this
      }
    } // close while
  } catch (Exception ex) {
    ex.printStackTrace();
  }
} // close run
} // close inner class
```

Bob's BeatBox.java

Your version control software doesn't know what to do with this conflicting code, so to protect everyone, it refuses to commit the new code, and marks up where problems might be.

```
public class RemoteReader implements Runnable {
  boolean[] checkboxState = null;
  String nameToShow = null;
  Object obj = null;

  public void run() {
   try {
     while((obj=in.readObject()) != null) {
       System.out.println("got an object from server");
       System.out.println(obj.getClass());
       String nameToShow = (String) obj;
       checkboxState = (boolean[]) in.readObject();
       if (nameToShow.equals(POKE_START_SEQUENCE)) {
         playPoke();
         nameToShow = "Hey! Pay attention.";
       }
       otherSeqsMap.put(nameToShow, checkboxState);
       listVector.add(nameToShow);
       incomingList.setListData(listVector);
   } // close while
  } catch(Exception ex) {ex.printStackTrace();}
  } // close run

  private void playPoke() {
    Toolkit.getDefaultToolkit().beep();
  }
} // close inner class
```

BeatBox.java

Exercise

Conflict Resolution: Here's the file the version control software kicked back to Bob, with all the conflicts marked. What should the final code look like that Bob commits back in?

```
public class RemoteReader implements Runnable {
  // variable declarations
  public void run() {
  try {
    // code without problems

<<<<<<< .mine
      if (nameToShow.equals(
                  PICTURE_START_SEQUENCE)) {
        receiveJPEG();
      } else {
        otherSeqsMap.put(
                  nameToShow, checkboxState);
        listVector.add(nameToShow);
        incomingList.setListData(listVector);
        // now reset the sequence to be this
      }
=======
      if (nameToShow.equals(
                  POKE_START_SEQUENCE)) {
        playPoke();
        nameToShow = "Hey! Pay attention.";
      }
      otherSeqsMap.put(
                 nameToShow, checkboxState);
      listVector.add(nameToShow);
      incomingList.setListData(listVector);
>>>>>>> .r2
    } // close while
  // more code without problems
} // close run
} // close inner class
```

Files with conflicts get both the local changes (Bob's changes) and the changes from the server. The ones between "<<<<<<< .mine" and the ===='s are Bob's—the ones after that up to the ">>>>>>> .r2" are the ones from the server.

```
public class RemoteReader implements
Runnable {
  // variable declarations
  public void run() {
  try {
    // code without problems

  ..........................................................
  ..........................................................
  ..........................................................
  ..........................................................
  ..........................................................
  ..........................................................
  ..........................................................
  ..........................................................
  ..........................................................
  ..........................................................
  ..........................................................
  ..........................................................
  ..........................................................
  ..........................................................
  ..........................................................
  ..........................................................
  ..........................................................
    } // close while
  // more code without problems
} // close run
} // close inner class
```

Exercise Solution

Conflict Resolution: Here's the file version control kicked back to Bob with both changes in it. What should the final section look like that Bob commits back in?

```
public class Remote
  // variable decla
  public void run()
  try {
    // code without
<<<<<<< .mine
      if (nameToSho

        receiveJPEG
      } else {
        otherSeqsMa
                  na
        listVector.
        incomingLis
        // now rese
      }
=======
      if (nameToSh

        playPoke()
        nameToShow
      }
      otherSeqsMap
                 nam
      listVector.a
      incomingList
>>>>>>> .r2
    } // close whil
  // more code with
} // close run
} // close inner cl
```

```
public class RemoteReader implements Runnable {
  // variable declarations
  public void run() {
  try {
    while ((obj = in.readObject()) != null) {
      System.out.println("got an object from server");
      System.out.println(obj.getClass());
      String nameToShow = (String) obj;
      checkboxState = (boolean[]) in.readObject();
      if (nameToShow.equals(PICTURE_START_SEQUENCE)) {
        receiveJPEG();
      }
      else {
       if (nameToShow.equals(POKE_START_SEQUENCE)) {
         playPoke();
         nameToShow = "Hey! Pay attention.";
       }

        otherSeqsMap.put(nameToShow, checkboxState);
        listVector.add(nameToShow);
        incomingList.setListData(listVector);
        // now reset the sequence to be this
      }
   } // close while
  } catch (Exception ex) {
    ex.printStackTrace();
  }
} // close run
} // close inner class
```

We need to support both the picture sequence and the poke sequence so we need to merge the conditional.

Make sure you delete the conflict characters (<<<<<<, =======, and >>>>>>>).

Make these changes to your own copy of BeatBox.java, and commit them to your code repository:

First, tell Subversion you resolved the conflict in the file using the "resolved" command and the path to the file.

```
File Edit Window Help Tranquility
hfsd> svn resolved src/headfirst/sd/chapter6/BeatBox.java
Resolved conflicted state of 'BeatBox.java'

hfsd> svn commit -m "Merged picture support with Poke stuff."
Sending        src\headfirst\sd\chapter6\BeatBox.java
Transmitting file data .
Committed revision 3.

hfsd>
```

You can skip this step if you didn't really get a conflict from Subversion.

Now, commit the file to your server, adding a comment indicating what you did.

Now show the customer...

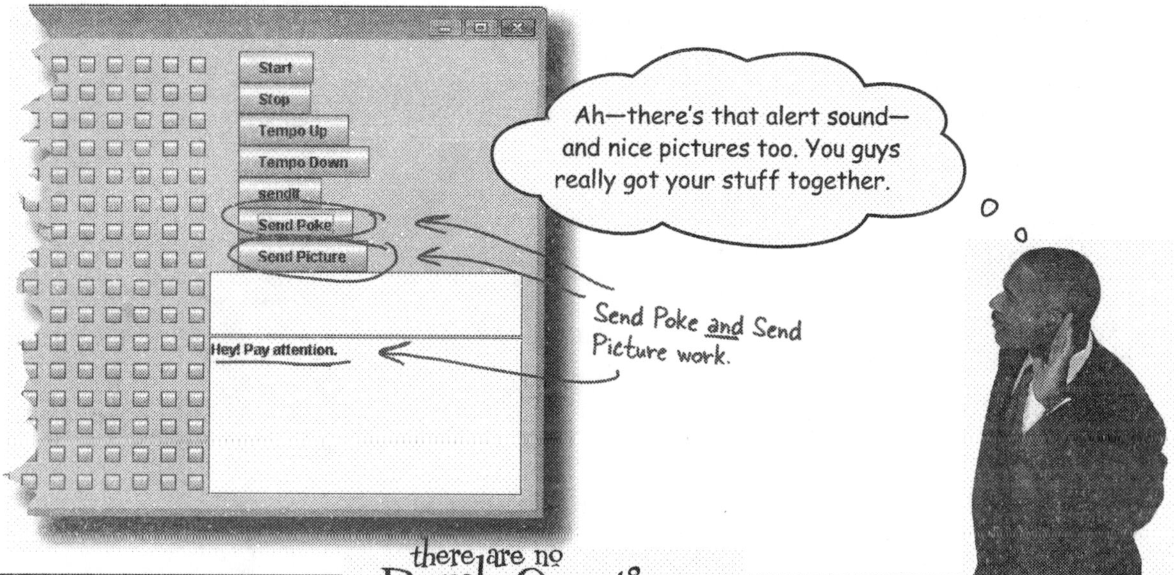

there are no Dumb Questions

Q: I see how checking out and committing works, but how do other people on the team get my changes?

A: Once you've got your project checked out, you can run `svn update`. That tells the version control server to give you the latest versions of all files in the project. Lots of teams run an update every morning, to make sure they're current with everyone else's work.

Q: This whole conflict thing seems pretty hairy. Can't my version control software do anything besides erroring out?

A: Some can. Certain version control tools work in a ***file locking mode***, which means when you check out files, the system locks those files so no one else can check them out. Once you make your changes and check the files back in, the system unlocks the files. This prevents conflicts, since only one person can edit a file at a time. But, it also means you might not be able to make changes to a file when you want to; you might need to wait for someone else to finish up first. To get around that, some locking version control systems allow you to check out a file in read-only mode while it's locked. But that's a bit heavy-handed, so other tools like Subversion allow multiple people to work on the same file at once. Good design, good division of labor, frequent commits, and good communication help reduce the number of manual merges you actually have to do.

Q: What is all this trunk business you keep saying to ignore?

A: The Subversion authors recommend putting your code into a directory called `trunk`. Then, other versions would go into a directory called `branches`. Once you've imported your code, the trunk thing doesn't really show up again, except during an initial checkout. We'll talk more about branches later in the chapter, but for now, stick with the `trunk`.

Q: Where are all of my messages going when I do a commit?

A: Subversion keeps track of each time you commit changes into the repository and associates your message with those changes. This lets you look at why people made a certain change—for instance, if you need to go back and figure out why something was done. That's why you should always use a sensible, explanatory message when you do a commit. The first time you go back through old commits and find "I changed stuff" as the log message, you'll be pretty cranky.

Q: Do I have to commit all of my changes at the same time?

A: Nope! Just put the path to the filename on the `commit` command like you did for the `resolved` command. Subversion will commit just the file(s) you specify.

More iterations, more stories...

Things are going well. The customer was happy with our Poke and Picture support, and after one more iteration, felt we had enough for Version 1.0. A few iterations later and everyone's looking forward to Version 2.0. Just a few more stories to implement...

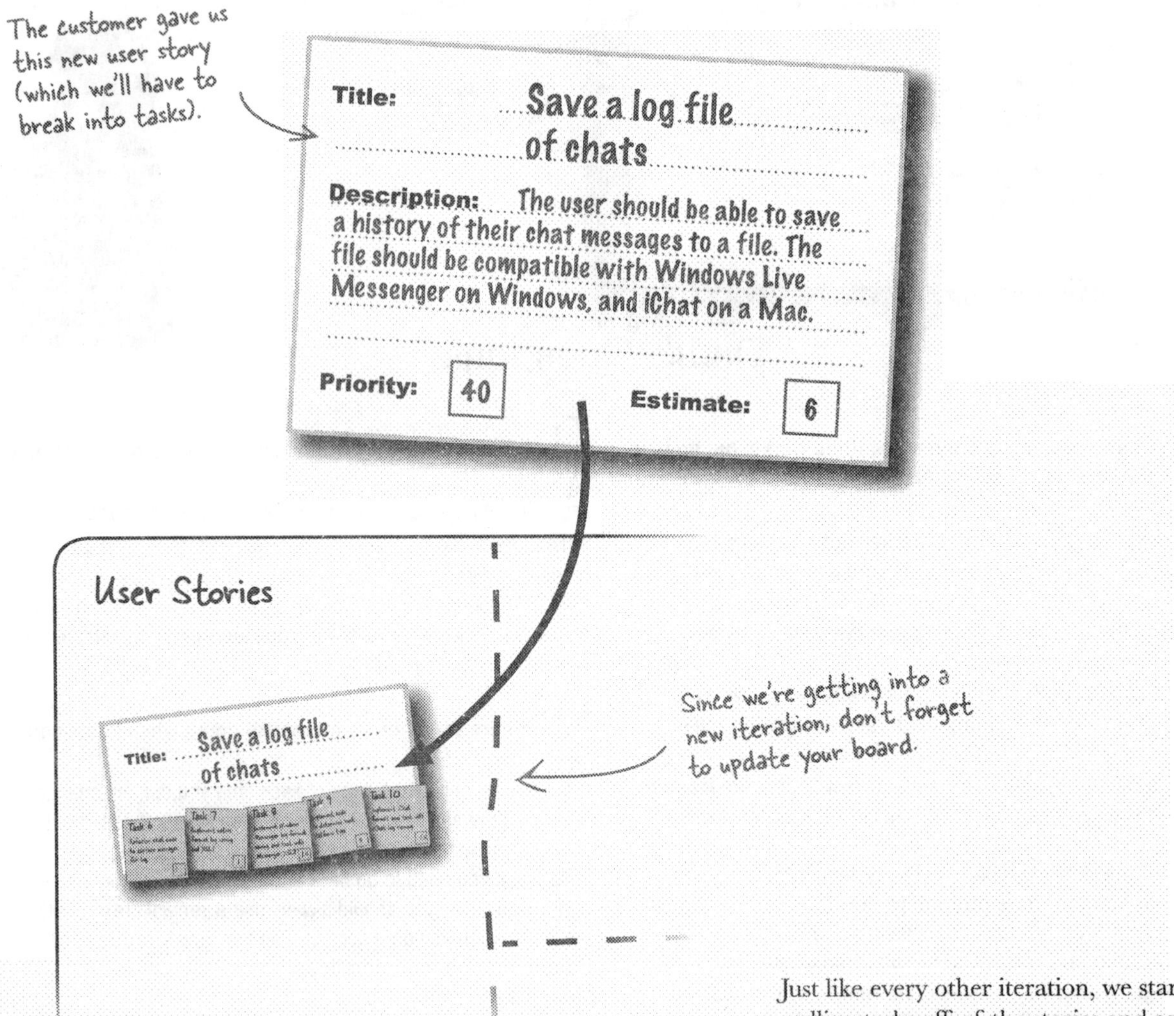

Just like every other iteration, we start pulling tasks off of the stories and assigning them to people. Things are moving along nicely until...

Standup meeting

Bob: Hey guys. Good news: I'm just about done with the Windows Messenger version, and it's working well. But there's bad news, too. I just found a bug in the way images are handled in our Send Picture feature from way back in the first iteration.

Laura: That's not good. Can we wait on fixing it?

Bob: I don't think so—it's a potential security hole if people figure out how to send a malicious picture. The users will be pretty annoyed over this.

Mark: Which means the customer is going to be *really* annoyed over this. Can you fix it?

Bob: I can fix it—but I've got a ton of code changes in there for the new story, the log files, that aren't ready to go out yet.

Laura: So we're going to have to roll your changes back and send out a patched 1.0 version.

Mark: What do we roll it back to? We have lots of little changes to lots of files. How do we know where version 1.0 was?

Bob: Forget version 1.0, what about all of my work?? If you roll back, you're going to drop everything I did.

BRAIN POWER

The team's in a tough spot—there's a pretty serious bug in the released version, but there's a lot effort invested in the new version. The new version isn't ready to go out the way it is. What would you do?

We have more than one version of our software...

The real problem here is that we have more than one version of our software—or more accurately, more than one version of our source code—that we need to make changes to. We have version 1.0 of the code built and out there, but Bob found a pretty serious bug. On top of that, we've got version 2.0 in the works, but it's full of untested, unworking features.

We need to separate them somehow...

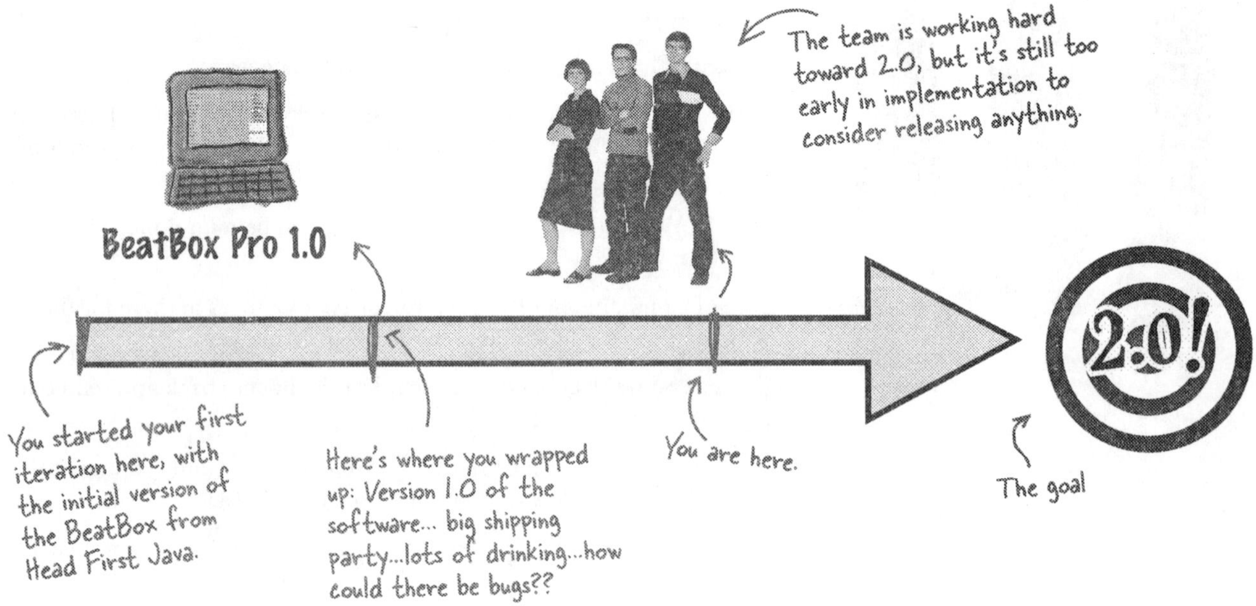

BULLET POINTS

- Bugs to released versions are usually a higher priority to the customer than implementing new features.
- Your bug fixes should affect released software and still be implemented in in-progress versions of your software.
- Effective bug fixing depends on being able to locate specific versions of your software and make changes to those versions without affecting current development.

You'll always have tension between bugs cropping up in released versions, and new features in upcoming versions. It's up to you to work with the customer to BALANCE those tensions.

You keep saying "Version 1.0," but what does that mean? We've committed tons of changes since then into the repository....

By default, your version control software gives you code from the trunk.

Some systems call this the HEAD or the main line.

You're right. When you check out the code from your version control system, you're checking it out from the **trunk**. That's the latest code by default and (assuming people are committing their changes on a regular basis) has all of the latest ~~bugs~~ features.

```
File Edit Window Help
hfsd> svn checkout file:///c:/Users/Developer/Desktop/SVNRepo/
BeatBox/trunk BeatBox
A    BeatBox\src
A    BeatBox\src\headfirst
A    BeatBox\src\headfirst\sd
A    BeatBox\src\headfirst\sd\chapter6
A    BeatBox\src\headfirst\sd\chapter6\BeatBox.java
A    BeatBox\src\headfirst\sd\chapter6\MusicServer.java

Checked out revision 1.

hfsd>
```

Remember the trunk thing that keeps coming up? That's the place where all the latest and greatest code is stored.

But we **do** have the 1.0 code **somewhere**, even if it's not labeled, right? We just have to find it on our server somehow...

Version control software stores ALL your code.

Every time you commit code into your version control system, a revision number was attached to the software at that point. So, if you can figure out which revision of your software was released as Version 1.0, you're good to go.

```
File Edit Window Help
hfsd> svn commit -m "Added POKE support."

Sending        src\headfirst\sd\chapter6\BeatBox.java
Transmitting file data .
Committed revision 18.

hfsd>
```

Here's the revision number for this set of changes; it increases with each commit.

Good commit messages make finding older software easier

You've been putting nice descriptive messages each time you committed code into your version control system, right? Here's where they matter. Just as each commit gets a revision number, your version control software also keeps your commit messages associated with that revision number, and you can view them in the log:

To get the log we use the "log" command...

...and specify which file to get the log for.

```
File Edit Window Help HeDidWhat?
hfsd> svn log src/headfirst/sd/chapter6/BeatBox.java
------------------------------------------------------------------------
r5 | Bob  | 2007-09-03 11:45:28 -0400 (Mon, 03 Sep 2007) | 52 lines
Tests and initial implementation of saving message log for Windows.
------------------------------------------------------------------------
r4 | Bob  | 2007-08-27 11:45:28 -0400 (Mon, 27 Aug 2007) | 3 lines
Quick bugfix for 1.0 release to handle cancelling the send picture dialog.
------------------------------------------------------------------------
r3 | Bob  | 2007-08-24 11:45:28 -0400 (Fri, 24 Aug 2007) | 23 lines
Merged picture support with Poke stuff.
------------------------------------------------------------------------
r2 | Mark | 2007-08-21 11:45:28 -0400 (Tues, 21 Aug 2007) | 37 lines
Added POKE support.
------------------------------------------------------------------------
r1 | Mark | 2007-08-20 20:08:14 -0400 (Mon, 20 Aug 2007) | 1 line
Initial Import
------------------------------------------------------------------------

hfsd>
```

Subversion responds by giving us all of the log entries for that file.

Here's the revision number...

And here's the log message to go with it.

Subversion keeps track of who made the changes and when.

Play "Find the features" with the log messages

You've got to figure out which features were in the software—in this case, for Version 1.0. Then, figure out which revision that matches up with.

Using the log messages above, which revision do you think matches up with Version 1.0 of BeatBox Pro?

.... ← *Write down the revision number you want to check out to get Version 1.0.*

Now you can check out Version 1.0

In Subversion, -r indicates you want a specific revision of code. We're grabbing revision 4.

1. Once you know which revision to check out, your version control server can give you the code you need:

This puts the code in a new directory, for Version 1.0.

```
File Edit Window Help ThatOne
hfsd> svn checkout -r 4 file:///c:/Users/Developer/Desktop/
SVNRepo/BeatBox/trunk BeatBoxV1.0
A    BeatBoxV1.0\src
A    BeatBoxV1.0\src\headfirst
A    BeatBoxV1.0\src\headfirst\sd
A    BeatBoxV1.0\src\headfirst\sd\chapter6
A    BeatBoxV1.0\src\headfirst\sd\chapter6\BeatBox.java
A    BeatBoxV1.0\src\headfirst\sd\chapter6\MusicServer.java

Checked out revision 4.

hfsd>
```

2. Now you can fix the bug Bob found...

BeatBox.java

Once again, the version control server gives you normal Java code you can work on.

3. With the changes in place, commit the code back to your server...

Uh oh, looks like the server isn't happy with your updated code.

```
File Edit Window Help Trouble
hfsd> svn commit src/headfirst/sd/chapter6/BeatBox.java -m
"Fixed the critical security bug in 1.0 release."

Sending        src\headfirst\sd\chapter6\BeatBox.java
svn: Commit failed (details follow):

svn: Out of date: '/BeatBox/trunk/src/headfirst/sd/chapter6/
BeatBox.java' in transaction '6-1'

hfsd>
```

Sharpen your pencil

What happened? ....

....

Why? ....

....

So now what do we do? ....

....

(Emergency) standup meeting

If you're having a problem, don't wait for the next day. Just grab everyone and have an impromptu standup meeting.

Laura: We could check out the version 1.0 code just fine, but now the version control server won't let us commit our changes back in. It says our file is out of date.

Mark: Oh—ya know, that's probably a good thing. If we could commit it, wouldn't that become revision 6, meaning the latest version of the code wouldn't have Bob's changes?

Bob: Hey that's right—you'd leapfrog my code with old version 1.0 code. I don't want to lose all of my work!

Laura: You still have your work saved locally, right? Just merge it in with the new changes and recommit it. You'll be fine.

Bob: Uggh, all that merging stuff sucks; it's a pain. And what about the next time we find a bug we need to patch in Version 1.0?

Mark: We'll have to remember what the new 1.0 revision is. Once we figure out how to commit this code, we'll write down the revision number and use that as our base for any other 1.0 changes.

Laura: New 1.0 changes? Wouldn't we be at Version 1.1 now?

Bob: Yeah, that's right. But this is still a mess...

Sharpen your pencil

Write down three problems with the approach outlined above for handling future changes to Version 1.0 (or is it 1.1?).

1. ....

2. ....

3. ....

→ Answers on page 217.

Tag your versions

The revision system worked great to let us get back to the version of the code we were looking for, and we got lucky that the log messages were enough for us to figure out what revision we needed. Most version control tools provide a better way of tracking which version corresponds to a meaningful event like a release or the end of an iteration. They're called **tags**.

Let's tag the code for BeatBox Pro we just located as Version 1.0:

1. First you need to create a directory in the repository for the tags. You only need to do this once for the project (and this is specific to Subversion; most version control tools support tags without this kind of directory).

Instead of trunk, specify the tags directory here.

You can use the mkdir command to create the tags directory.

```
File Edit Window Help Storage
hfsd> svn mkdir file:///c:/Users/Developer/Desktop/SVNRepo/BeatBox/tags
-m "Created tags directory"
Committed revision 6.
hfsd>
```

Here's the log message – and notice it creates a revision. This is a change to the project, so Subversion tracks it.

2. Now tag the initial 1.0 release, which is revision 4 from the repository.

We want revision 4 of the trunk...

ith Subversion, u create a tag by pying the revision u want into the gs directory. ubversion actually st relates that rsion tag to the elease.

```
File Edit Window Help YouIt
hfsd> svn copy -r 4 file:///c:/Users/Developer/Desktop/SVNRepo/BeatBox/
trunk file:///c:/Users/Developer/Desktop/SVNRepo/BeatBox/tags/version-1.0
-m "Tagging the 1.0 release of BeatBox Pro."
Committed revision 6.
hfsd>
```

And we want to put that code into a tag called version-1.0

So what?

So what did that get us? Well, instead of needing to know the revision number for version 1.0 and saying `svn checkout -r 4 ...`, you can check out Version 1.0 of the code like this:

```
svn checkout file:///c:/Users/Developer/Desktop/SVNRepo/BeatBox/tags/version-1.0
```

And let Subversion remember which revision of the repository that tag relates to.

So now I know where Version 1.0 is, great. But we still only have the 1.0 code, and need to commit those changes. Do we just commit our updated code into the Version 1.0 tag?

No! The tag is just that; it's a snapshot of the code at the point you made the tag. You don't want to commit any changes into that tag, or else the whole "version-1.0" thing becomes meaningless. Some version control tools treat tags so differently that it's impossible to commit changes into tags at all (Subversion doesn't. It's possible to commit into a tag, but it's a very, very bad idea).

BUT we can use the same idea and make a copy of revision 4 that we will commit changes into; this is called a branch. So a **tag** is a snapshot of your code at a certain time, and a **branch** is a place where you're working on code that isn't in the main development tree of the code.

1. Just like with tags, we need to create a directory for branches in our project.

Instead of trunk, we specify the branches directory here.

Use the mkdir command again to create the branches directory.

```
File Edit Window Help Expanding
hfsd> svn mkdir file:///c:/Users/Developer/Desktop/SVNRepo/BeatBox/branches
-m "Created branches directory"
Committed revision 8.
hfsd>
```

2. Now create a `version-1` branch from revision 4 in our repository.

We want revision 4 of the trunk...

```
File Edit Window Help Duplicating
hfsd> svn copy -r 4 file:///c:/Users/Developer/Desktop/SVNRepo/BeatBox/trunk
file:///c:/Users/Developer/Desktop/SVNRepo/BeatBox/branches/version-1
-m "Branched the 1.0 release of BeatBox Pro."
Committed revision 9.
hfsd>
```

With Subversion you create a branch just like a tag; you copy the revision you want into the branches directory. It won't actually copy anything; it just stores the revision number you supplied.

And we want to put it into a branch called version-1 (not Version 1.0, because we'll use this for Version 1.1, 1.2, etc.).

Tags, branches, and trunks, oh my!

Your version control system has got a lot going on now, but most of the complexity is managed by the server and isn't something you have to worry about. We've tagged the 1.0 code, made fixes in a new branch, and still have current development happening in the trunk. Here's what the repository looks like now:

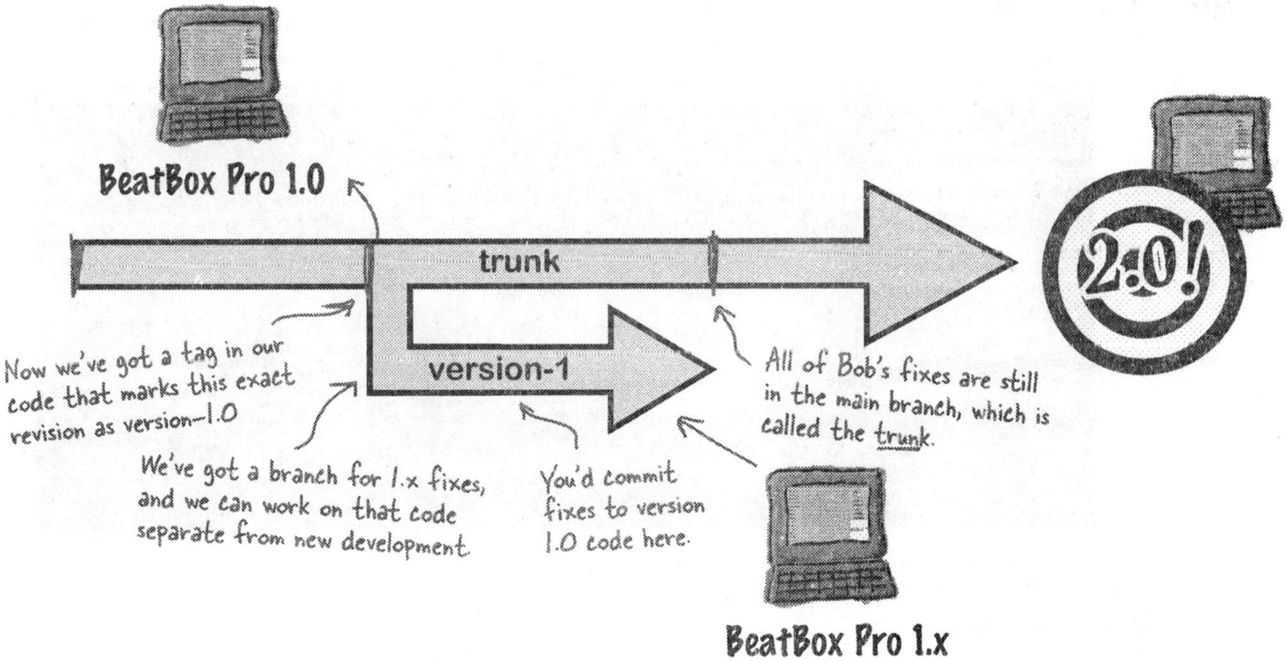

Tags are snapshots of your code. You should always commit to a branch, and never to a tag.

BULLET POINTS

- The **trunk** is where your active development should go; it should always represent the latest version of your software.
- A **tag** is a name attached to a specific revision of the items in your repository so that you can easily retrieve that revision later.
- Sometimes you might need to **commit the same changes to a branch and the trunk** if the change applies to both.
- **Branches** are copies of your code that you can make changes to without affecting code in the trunk. Branches often start from a tagged version of the code.
- **Tags are static**—you don't commit changes into them. **Branches** are for **changes that you don't want in the trunk** (or to keep code away from changes being made in the trunk).

Fixing Version 1.0...for real this time.

When we had everything in the trunk, we got an error trying to commit old patched code on top of our new code. Now, though, we've got a tag for version 1.0 and a branch to work in. Let's fix Version 1.0 in that branch:

1. First, check out the `version-1` branch of the BeatBox code:

Notice we didn't need to specify a revision here. The branch is a copy of the version 1.0 code.

We'll put this in the BeatBoxV1 directory this time.

```
File Edit Window Help History
hfsd> svn checkout file:///c:/Users/Developer/Desktop/SVNRepo/BeatBox/
branches/version-1 BeatBoxV1

A    BeatBoxV1\src
A    BeatBoxV1\src\headfirst
A    BeatBoxV1\src\headfirst\sd
A    BeatBoxV1\src\headfirst\sd\chapter6
A    BeatBoxV1\src\headfirst\sd\chapter6\BeatBox.java
A    BeatBoxV1\src\headfirst\sd\chapter6\MusicServer.java

Checked out revision 9.

hfsd>
```

These revisions numbers stop meaning as much, because we're using tags to reference revisions instead of revision numbers.

2. Now you can fix the bug Bob found...

This time, we're working on code from the version-1 branch.

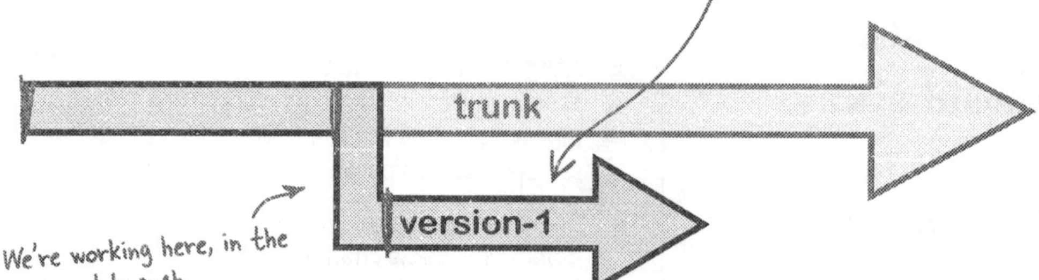

We're working here, in the version-1 branch.

3 ...and commit our changes back in. This time, though, no conflicts:

```
File Edit Window Help Sweet
hfsd> svn commit src/headfirst/sd/chapter6/BeatBox.java -m "Fixed the
critical security bug in 1.0 release."

Sending        src\headfirst\sd\chapter6\BeatBox.java

Committed revision 10.

hfsd>
```

The fix is in the branch.

We have TWO code bases now

With all these changes, we've actually got two different sets of code: the 1.x branch, where fixes are made to Version 1.0, and the trunk, which has all the new development.

- ☑ Our `trunk` directory in the repository has the latest and greatest code that's still in development (and Bob applied the security fix there, too).
- ☑ We have a `version-1.0` tag in our `tags` directory so we can pull out Version 1.0 whenever we want.
- ☑ We have a `version-1` branch in our `branches` directory that has all of our critical patches that have to go out as a 1.x version without any of the new development work.

Don't forget: when you actually do release v1.1 with these patches, create a version-1.1 tag in the tags directory so you can get back to that version later if you have to.

there are no Dumb Questions

Q: I've heard branches are a bad idea and should be avoided. Why are we talking about them?

A: Branches aren't always a bad thing; they have an important place in software development. But, they do come with a price. We'll talk about that over the next few pages.

Q: What else can tags be used for?

A: Tags are great for tracking released versions of software, but you can also use them for keeping track of versions as software goes through testing or QA—think `alpha1`, `alpha2`, `beta1`, `ReleaseCandidate1`, `ReleaseCandidate2`, `ExternalTesting`, etc. It's also a good practice to tag the project at the end of each iteration.

Q: Earlier, you said not to commit changes to a tag. What's that supposed to mean? And how can you prevent people from doing it?

A: The issue with commiting changes to a tag is really a Subversion peculiarity; other tools explicitly prohibit commiting to a tag. Since Subversion uses the copy command to create a tag, exactly like it does a branch, you technically can commit into a tag just like any other place in the repository. However, this is almost always a bad idea. The reason you tagged something was to be able to get back to the code ***just as it was when you tagged it***. If you commit changes into the tag, it's not the same code you originally tagged.

Subversion does have ways of putting permission controls on the tags directory so that you can prevent people from committing into it. However, once people get used to Subversion, it's usually not a major problem, and you can always revert changes to a tag in the odd case where it happens.

Q: We've been using file:///c:/... for our repository. How is that supposed to work with multiple developers?

A: Great question—there are a couple things you can do here. First, Subversion has full support for integration with a web server, which lets you specify your repository location as http:// or https://. That's when things get really interesting. For example, with https you get encrypted connections to your repository. With either web approach, you can share your repository over a much larger network without worrying about mapping shared drives. It's a little more work to configure, but it's great from the developer perspective. If you can't use http access for your repository, Subversion also supports tunneling repository access through SSH. Check out the Subversion documentation (*http://svnbook.red-bean.com/*) for more information on how to set these up.

Q: When I run the log command, I see the same revision number all over the place. What's that about?

A: Different tools do versioning (or revisioning) differently. What you're seeing is how Subversion does its revision tracking. Whenever you commit a file, Subversion applies a revision number ***across the whole project***. Basically, that revision says that "The entire project looked like this at revision 9." This means that if you want to grab the project at a certain point you only need to know *one* revision number. Other tools version each file separately (most notably the version control tool called CVS which was a predecessor to Subversion). That means that to get a copy of a project at a certain state, you need to know the version numbers *of each file*. This really isn't practical, so tags become even more critical.

Q: Why did we branch the Version 1.0 code instead of leaving Version 1.0 in the trunk, and branch the new work?

A: That would work, but the problem with that approach is you end up buried in branches as development goes on. The trunk ends up being ancient code, and all the new work happens several branches deep. So you'd have a branch for the next version, and another branch for the next...

With branches for older software, you'll eventually stop working with some of those branches. (Do you think Microsoft is still making fixes to Word 95?)

Q: To create tags and branches with Subversion, we used the copy command. Is that normal?

A: Well, it's normal for Subversion. That's because Subversion was designed for very "cheap" copies, which just means a copy doesn't create lots of overhead. When you create a copy, Subversion actually just marks the revision you copied from, and then stores changes relative to that. Other version control tools do things differently. For example, CVS has an explicit tag command, and branches result in "real" copies of files, meaning they take a lot of time and resources.

Sharpen your pencil

With the security fix to Version 1.0 taken care of, we're back to our original user story. Bob needs to implement two different saving mechanisms for the BeatBox application: one for when the user is on a Mac, and one for when a user is on a Windows PC. Since these are two completely different platforms, what should Bob do here?

What should Bob do? ....

....

....

....

Why? ....

....

....

....

When NOT to branch...

Did you say that Bob should branch his code to support the two different features? Modern version control tools do make branching cheap from a **technical perspective.** The problem is there's a lot of hidden cost from the **people perspective**. Each branch is a separate code base that needs to be maintained, tested, documented, etc.

For example, remember that critical security fix we made to Version 1.0 of BeatBox? Did that fix get applied to the trunk so that it stays fixed in Version 2.0 of the software? Has the trunk code changed enough that the fix isn't a straightforward copy, and we need to so something differently to fix it?

The same would apply with branching to support two different platforms. New features would have to be implemented to **both** branches. And then, when you get to a new version, what do you do? Tag both branches? Branch both branches? It gets confusing, fast. Here are some rules of thumb for helping you know when ***not*** to branch:

Branch when...

☐ You have released a **version of the software** that you need to maintain **outside of the main development cycle**.

☐ You want to try some **radical changes to code** that you might need to throw away, and you **don't want to impact the rest of the team** while you work on it.

Do not branch when...

☐ You can accomplish your goal by **splitting code into different files** or libraries that can be built as appropriate on different platforms.

☐ You have a bunch of developers that can't keep their code compiling in the trunk so you try to **give them their own sandbox** to work in.

There are other ways to keep people from breaking other people's builds. We'll talk about those in a later chapter.

The Zen of good branching

Branch only when you absolutely have to. Each branch is a potentially large piece of software you have to maintain, test, release, and keep up with. If you view branching as a major decision that doesn't happen often, you're ahead of the game.

We fixed Version 1...

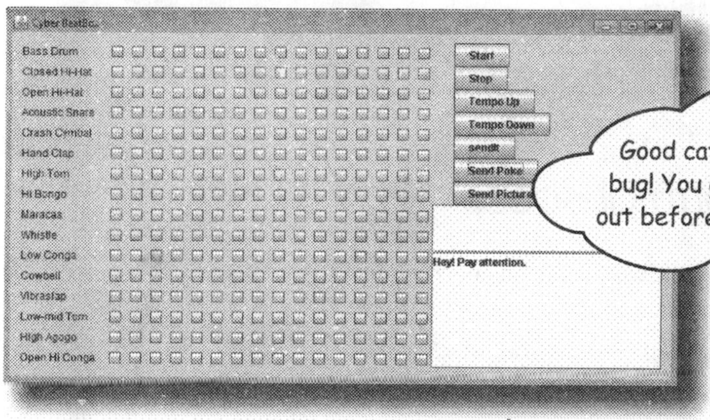

... and Bob finished Version 2.0 (so he says)

We've come a long way in this chapter, but there are ~~people~~ things that version control alone just can't fix...Can you list some troubles that Bob can still get into, even if he uses version control to manage his code?

....

....

....

....

What version control does...

- [x] Lets you **create a repository** to keep your code in a single place to ease backup and recovery.
- [x] Lets multiple people **check out copies of the code** and work efficiently as a team.
- [x] Lets multiple people **check changes back into the repository** and distribute them to the rest of the team.
- [x] Keeps track of **who changes what**, when, and why.
- [x] **Branches** and **tags code** so you can find and change versions of code from way back when.
- [x] **Rolls back changes** that never should have happened in the first place.

...and what version control doesn't do

- [ ] Makes sure your code compiles.
- [ ] Tests code.
- [ ] Thinks for you.
- [ ] Makes sure your code is readable and well-written.

These are pretty important...looks like our tool set is nowhere near complete.

Version control can't make sure your code actually works...

CHAPTER 6

Tools for your Software Development Toolbox

Software Development is all about developing and delivering great software. In this chapter, you learned about several techniques to keep you on track. For a complete list of tools in the book, see Appendix ii.

Development Techniques

Use a version control tool to track and distribute changes in your software to your team

Use tags to keep track of major milestones in your project (ends of iterations, releases, bug fixes, etc.)

Use branches to maintain a separate copy of your code, but only branch if absolutely necessary

Here are some of the key techniques you learned in this chapter...

... and some of the principles behind those techniques.

Development Principles

Always know where changes should (and shouldn't) go

Know what code went into a given release – and be able to get to it again

Control code change and distribution

BULLET POINTS

- **Back up** your version control repository! It should have all of your code and a history of changes in it.
- Always use a **good commit message** when you commit your code—you and your team will appreciate it later.
- **Use tags liberally**. If there's any question about needing to know what the code looked like before a change, tag that version of your code.
- **Commit frequently** into the repository, but be careful about breaking other people's code. The longer you go between commits, the harder merges will be.
- There are lots of **GUI tools** for version control systems. They help a lot with merges and dealing with conflicts.

Sharpen your pencil Solution

Write down three problems with the approach outlined above for handling future changes to version 1.0 (or is it 1.1?).

1. You need to keep track of what revisions go with what version of the software.
2. It's going to be very difficult to keep 2.0 code changes from slipping into v1.x patches.
3. Changes for Version 2.0 could mean you need to delete a file or change a class so much that it would be very difficult to keep a v1.x patch without conflicting.

6 ½ building your code

Insert tab a into slot b...

It pays to follow the instructions...

...especially when you write them yourself.

It's not enough to use version control to ensure your code stays safe. You've also got to worry about **compiling your code** and packaging it into a deployable unit. On top of all that, which class should be the main class of your application? How should that class be run? In this chapter, you'll learn how a **build tool** allows you to **write your own instructions** for dealing with your source code.

Developers aren't mind readers

Suppose you've got a new developer on your team. He can check out code from your version control server, and you're protected from his overwriting your code, too. But how does your new team member know which dependencies he's got to worry about? Or which class he should run to test things out?

There are lots of things you could do with source code: compile it all at once, run a particular class (or a set of classes); package classes up into a single JAR or DLL file, or multiple library files; include a bunch of dependencies... and these details change for every project you'll work on.

Good code is easy to USE, as well as easy to GET.

Software must be usable

It doesn't do you much good to put in a version control server if you can't also be sure your code is used properly once it's checked out. And that's where build scripts come in.

Building your project in one step

When someone wants to run your project, they need to do more than just compile source code—they need to **build** the project. Compiling source code into binary files is important, but building a project usually involves ***finding dependencies***, ***packaging up your project*** into a usable form, and more.

And since tasks like these are the same each time they're run, building a project is a perfect candidate for **automation**: using a tool to handle the repetitive work for you. If you're using an IDE to write your code, a lot of this is handled for you when you click "Build." But there's a lot of work going on when you press that "Build" button:

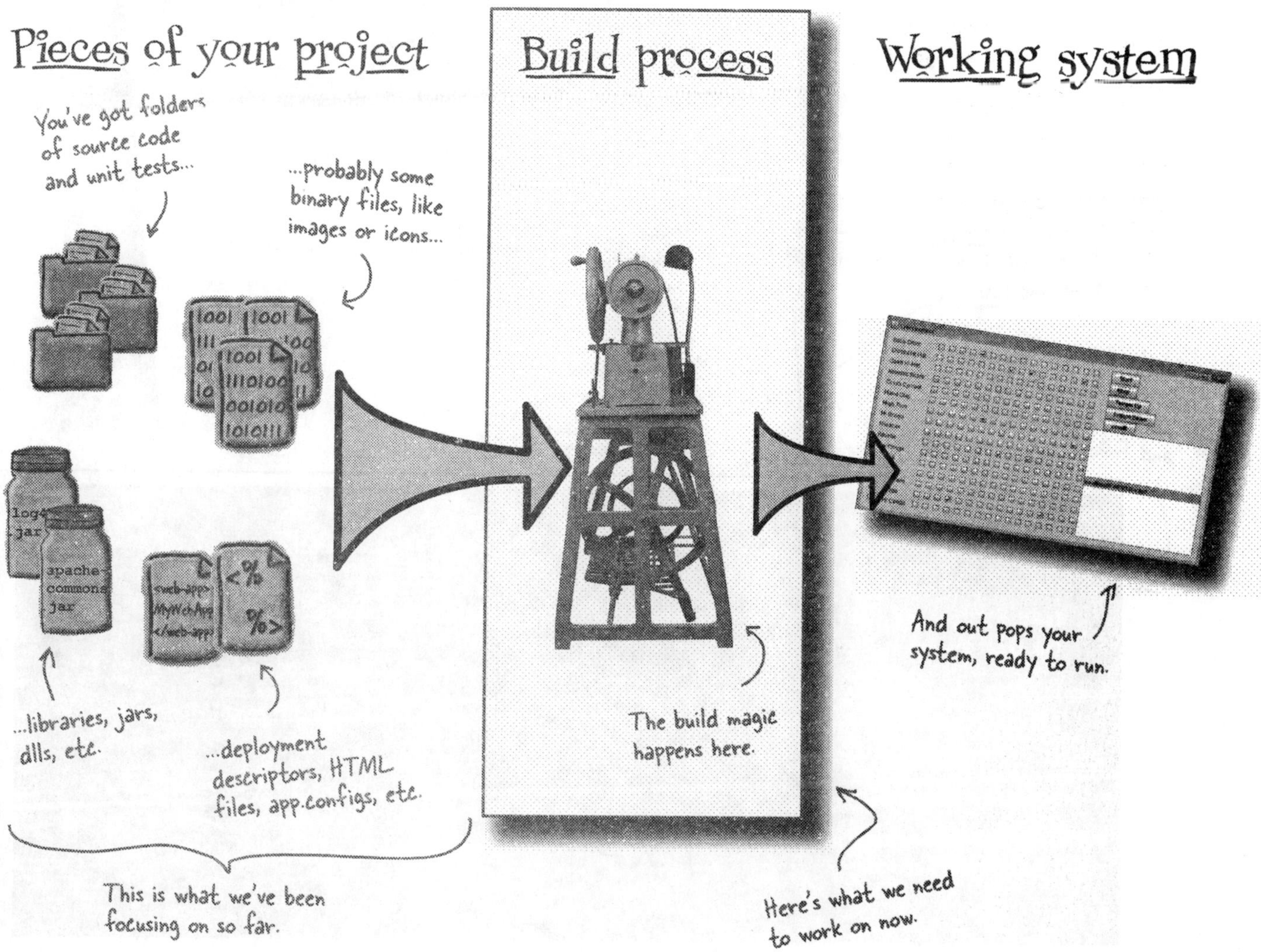

Ant: a build tool for Java projects

Ant is a build tool for Java that can compile code, create and delete directories, and even package up files for you. It all centers around a **build script**. That's a file you write, in XML for Ant, that tells the tool what to do when you need to build your program.

You can download Ant from http://ant.apache.org/

The steps to build your project are stored in an XML file, usually named build.xml.

This whole file is called a build script.

Each build file represents a single project.

What's needed to build your project is broken up into steps called targets. Each target can have more than one task.

```
<project name="HFSDCoverage" default="dist" basedir=".">

  <property name="src" location="src"/>
  <property name="bin" location="bin"/>
  <property name="bin-instrumented" location="bin-
instrumented"/>
  <property name="reportdir" location="reportdir"/>

<target name="clean">
        <delete dir="${bin}"/>
        <delete dir="${reportdir}"/>
        <delete dir="${bin-instrumented}"/>
        <delete file="cobertura.ser"/>
</target>

<target name="init">
      <mkdir dir="${bin}"/>
      <mkdir dir="${reportdir}"/>
      <mkdir dir="${bin-instrumented}"/>
</target>
```

You just kick off a build with a single command. Ant runs the default target in build.xml, and follows your instructions.

```
File Edit Window Help DoIt
hfsd> ant
Buildfile: build.xml

init:
    [mkdir] Created dir: C:\Users\Developer\workspaces\HFSD\BeatBox\bin
    [mkdir] Created dir: C:\Users\Developer\workspaces\HFSD\BeatBox\dist

compile:
    [javac] Compiling 4 source files to C:\Users\Developer\workspaces\HFSD\BeatBox\bin

dist:
      [jar] Building jar: C:\Users\Developer\workspaces\HFSD\BeatBox\dist\BeatBox.jar

BUILD SUCCESSFUL
Total time: 16 seconds

hfsd>
```

In this case, Ant creates a directory structure...

...compiles code into that structure...

...and builds a JAR file.

Projects, properties, targets, tasks

An Ant build file is broken into four basic chunks:

1 Projects

Everything in your build file is part of a single project:

Everything in Ant is represented by an XML element tag.

```
<project name="BeatBox" default="dist">
```

In this case, Ant will run the dist target when the script is run.

Everything else in the build file is nested inside the project tag.

Your project should have a name and a default target to run when the script is run.

2 Properties

Ant properties are a lot like constants. They let you refer to values in the script, but you can change those values in a single place:

A property has a name and a value.

```
<property name="version" value="1.1" />
<property name="src" location="src" />
<property name="xerces-src" location="${src}/xerces" />
```

You can use properties with ${property-name}, like this.

You can use location instead of value if you're dealing with paths.

3 Targets

You can group different actions into a target, which is just a set of work. For example, you might have a `compile` target for compilation, and an `init` target for setting up your project's directory structure.

A target has a bunch of tasks nested within it.

```
<target name="compile" depends="init">
```

A target has a name, and optionally a list of targets that must be run before it.

4 Tasks

Tasks are the work horses of your build script. A task in Ant usually maps to a specific command, like `javac`, `mkdir`, or even `javadoc`:

This makes a new directory, using the value of the src property.

```
<mkdir dir="${src}">
<javac srcdir="${src}" destdir="${bin}" />
```

Each Ant task has different parameters, depending on what the task does and is used for.

> **Relax**
>
> **The syntax here is particular to Ant, but the principles work with all build tools, in any language.**
>
> Ant is great for Java, but not everyone uses Java. For now, though, focus on what a good build tool gives you: a way to manage projects, constants, and specific tasks. In a few pages, we'll talk about build tools that work with other languages, like PHP, Ruby, and C#.

No... you're supposed to learn a new tool so *someone (or something) ELSE* can *build* your project.

It's easy to see a build tool as just one more thing to learn and keep up with. But most build tools, like Ant, are really easy to learn. In fact, you're just about to put together your first build script, and you already know more than you think!

On top of that, your build tool is just that: ***a tool***. It helps you get things done faster, especially over a lot of projects. You'll learn a little bit of syntax for your build tool, and hardly need to learn anything else about it.

Oh, and remember: ***the build tool is for your team, not just you***. While you may know how to compile your project, and keep up with its dependencies, everyone else might not. A build tool and build script lets everyone on your team use the same process to turn source code into a running application. With a good build script all it takes is one command to build the software; it's impossible for a developer to accidentally leave a step out—even after working on two other projects for six months.

Ant Build Magnets

Ant files are easier to use—and write—than you think. Below is part of a build script, but lots of pieces are missing. It's up to you to use the build magnets at the bottom of the page to complete the build script.

Put the magnets between the target elements to complete the build.xml file.

```
<project name="BeatBox" default="dist">
  <target name="init"
          description="Creates the needed directories.">
     ________________________________________
     ________________________________________
  </target>

  <target name="clean"
          description="Cleans up the build and dist directories.">
     ________________________________________
     ________________________________________
  </target>

  <target name="compile" depends="init"
          description="____________________________________________">
     ________________________________________
     ________________________________________
  </target>

  <target name="dist" depends="________"
          description="Packages up BeatBox into BeatBox.jar">
     ________________________________________
  ________________________________________

</project>
```

s like there are ple of extra ts, so be careful.

```
destfile="dist/BeatBox.jar"
Compiles the source files to the bin directory.
debug="true"
Compiles the binary files to the src directory.
<mkdir dir="bin"/>
/>
>
compile
<jarc
<javac
srcdir="src"
<delete dir="bin"/>
init
dist
<jar
clean
clean
<java
destdir="bin"
<delete dir="dist"/>
init
compile
<target>
<mkdir dir="dist"/>
/>
>
dist
basedir="bin"
</target>
</target>
</target>
>
```

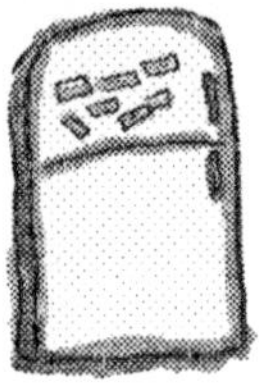

Ant Build Magnet Solutions

Your task was to reassemble a working build file for building the BeatBox application.

```
<project name="BeatBox" default="dist">
  <target name="init"
        description="Creates the needed directories.">
    <mkdir dir="bin"/>
    <mkdir dir="dist"/>
  </target>

  <target name="clean"
        description="Cleans up the build and dist directories.">
    <delete dir="bin"/>
    <delete dir="dist"/>
  </target>

  <target name="compile" depends="init"
        description="Compiles the source files to the bin directory.">
    <javac srcdir="src" destdir="bin" />
  </target>

  <target name="dist" depends="compile"
        description="Packages up BeatBox into BeatBox.jar">
    <jar destfile="dist/BeatBox.jar" basedir="bin" />
  </target>
</project>
```

You specify the default target to call (in this case, dist) if the person running Ant doesn't specify one. In general this should do everything it needs to do to get your project from zero to running.

The mkdir task creates the directory specified by the "dir" attribute.

The delete task can delete directories or files by specifying a dir or file attribute.

The javac task compiles java code in the srcdir and puts classes in the destdir.

The dist target depends on compile, which in turn depends on the init target.

Each target can have a description that is printed if you ask Ant to display project information.

Here's the default target.

The jar task creates a JAR from the files it finds in the basedir. You can also specify manifest information, files to exclude, etc.

Be sure to close these elements with "/>", which is like a closing tag.

there are no Dumb Questions

Q: My project isn't in Java—do I still need a build tool?

A: Probably, and depending on what environment you're working in, you might already be using one. If you're developing in Microsoft Visual Studio, you're almost certainly ***already*** using their build system, called MSBuild (open your csproj file in Notepad...seriously). It uses an XML description of the build process similar to the way Ant does. Visual Studio started that file for you, but there's a whole lot more MSBuild can do for you that the IDE doesn't expose. If you're not in Visual Studio but are doing .NET development, you might want to check out NAnt. It's basically a port of Ant for the .NET world. Ruby uses a tool called rake to kick off tests, package up the application, clean up after itself, etc.

But there are some technologies, like Perl or PHP, where build scripts aren't quite as valuable, because those languages don't compile or package code. However, you can still use a build tool to package, test, and deploy your applications, even if you don't need everything a build tool brings to the table.

Q: I'm using an IDE that builds everything for me. Isn't that enough?

A: It might be enough for *you*, but what about everyone else on your team? Does everyone on your team have to use that IDE? This can be a problem on larger projects where there's an entirely separate group responsible for building and packaging your project for other teams like testers or QA.

Then there are tasks that your IDE *doesn't* do... (If you can't think of anything like that, we'll talk about some great ones in the next few chapters). In general, if your project is more than a one-person show (or you want to use any of the best practices we're going to talk about in the next few chapters) you need to think about a build tool.

Q: Where did you come up with those bin, dist, and src directory names?

A: Those directories are an unofficial standard for Java projects. A few others you're likely to see are `docs` for generated documenation, `generated` for things like web-service-generated clients and stubs, and `lib` for library dependencies you might need.

There's nothing about these directory names that's set in stone, and you can adjust your build file to deal with whatever you use on your project. However, if you stick with common conventions, it makes it easier for new team members to get their heads around your project.

Q: Why are you even talking about Ant? Don't you know about Maven?

A: Maven is a Java-oriented "software project management and comprehension tool." Basically, it goes beyond the smaller-scale Ant tasks we've been talking about and adds support for automatically fetching library dependencies, publishing libraries you build to well-known places, test automation, etc. It's a great tool, but it masks a lot of what's going on behind the scenes. To get the most out of Maven you need to structure your project in a particular way.

For most small- to medium-sized projects, Ant can do everything you'll need. That's not to discourage you from checking out Maven, but it's important to understand the underlying concepts that Maven does such a great job of hiding. You can find out more about Maven at *http://maven.apache.org/*.

Q: What should my default target be? Should it compile my code, package it, generate documentation, all of the above?

A: That really depends on your project. If someone new was to check out your code, what are they most likely looking to do with it? Would they want to be able to check out your project and expect to be able to run it in one step? If so, you probably want your default target to do everything. But if "everything" means signing things with encryption keys and generating an installer with InstallShield and so on, you probably don't want that by default. A lot of projects actually set up the default target to output the project help information so that new people can see what their options are and pick appropriately.

Q: The build.xml file has directory names repeated all over the place. Is that a good idea?

A: Great catch! For a build script the size of the one we're using here, it's OK. But if you're writing a more complex build file, it's generally a good idea to use properties to let you define the directories once, and refer to them by aliases throughout the rest of the file. In Ant, you'd use the `property` tag for this, like on page 223.

Q: Couldn't I just do all of this with a batch file or shell script?

A: Technically, yes. But a build system comes with lots of software-development-oriented tasks that you'd either have to write yourself or lean on external tools to handle. Build tools also integrate into continuous integration systems, which we'll talk about in the next chapter.

Good build scripts...

A build script captures the details that developers probably don't need to know right from the start about how to compile and package an application, like BeatBox. The information isn't trapped in one person's head; it's captured in a version-controlled, repeatable process. But what exactly should a standard build script do?

You'll probably add tasks to your own build scripts, but all build scripts should do a few common things...

...generate documentation

Remember those description tags in the build file? Just type `ant -projecthelp` and you'll get a nice printout of what targets are available, a description of each, and what the default target is (which is usually what you want to use).

```
File Edit Window Help Huh?
hfsd> ant -projecthelp
Buildfile: build.xml

Main targets:

 clean     Cleans up the build and dist directories.
 compile   Compiles the source files to the bin directory.
 dist      Packages up BeatBox into BeatBox.jar
 init      Creates the needed directories.
Default target: dist

hfsd>
```

Your build tool probably has a way to generate documentation about itself and your project, even if you're not using Ant and Java.

...compile your project

Most importantly, your build scripts compile the code in your project. And in most scripts, you want a single command that you can run to handle everything, from setup to compilation to packaging.

Here you can see the target dependencies in action: our build script tells Ant to run the dist target by default, but in order to do that, it has to run compile, and in order to do that, it has to run init.

```
File Edit Window Help Build
hfsd> ant
Buildfile: build.xml

init:
    [mkdir] Created dir: C:\Users\Developer\workspaces\HFSD\BeatBox\bin
    [mkdir] Created dir: C:\Users\Developer\workspaces\HFSD\BeatBox\dist

compile:
    [javac] Compiling 4 source files to C:\Users\Developer\workspaces\HFSD\BeatBox\bin

dist:
      [jar] Building jar: C:\Users\Developer\workspaces\HFSD\BeatBox\dist\BeatBox.jar

BUILD SUCCESSFUL
Total time: 16 seconds

hfsd>
```

Good catch—a clean target is there to clean up the scraps of things that compiling leaves laying around. It's important to have a target that will get the project back to what it would look like if you checked the project out from the repository. That way, you can test things from a new developer's perspective.

Your tool may call this something else, but the idea is the same—clean up the mess made by building your project.

...clean up the mess they make

The final target we'll discuss in the BeatBox build script deletes the directories created during the build process: the `bin` directory for compiled classes and the `dist` directory for the final JAR file.

Since dist is the default target, you have to explicitly tell Ant to run the clean target.

```
hfsd> ant clean
Buildfile: build.xml

clean:
   [delete] Deleting directory C:\Users\Developer\workspaces\HFSD\BeatBox\bin
   [delete] Deleting directory C:\Users\Developer\workspaces\HFSD\BeatBox\dist

BUILD SUCCESSFUL
Total time: 3 seconds

hfsd>
```

Ant runs the delete tasks to clean up the bin and dist directories and remove all of their contents.

Good build scripts go BEYOND the basics

Even though there are some standard things your scripts should do, you'll find plenty of places a good build tool will let your script go beyond the basics:

1. **Reference libraries your project needs**

   You can add libraries to your build path in Ant by using the `classpath` element in the `javac` task:

```
<javac srcdir="src" destdir="bin">
  <classpath>
    <pathelement location="libs/junit.jar"/>
    <pathelement location="libs/log4j.jar"/>
  </classpath>
</javac>
```

Each pathelement points to a single JAR to add to the classpath. You can also point to a directory if you need to.

   If your project depends on libraries you don't want to include in your `libs` directory, you can also have Ant download libraries using FTP, HTTP, SCP, etc., using additional Ant tasks (check out the Ant task documentation for details).

2. **Run your application**

   Sometimes it's not just compiling your application that requires some background knowledge; running it can be tricky, too. Suppose your app requires the setting of a complex library path or a long string of command-line options. You can wrap all of that up in your build script using the `exec` task:

```
<exec executable="cmd">
  <arg value="/c"/>
  <arg value="iexplorer.exe"/>
  <arg value="http://www.headfirstlabs.com/"/>
</exec>
```

Executing something on the system directly is obviously going to be platform-dependent. Don't try to run iexplorer.exe on Linux.

(but do go to Head First Labs)

   or the `java` task:

```
<java classname="headfirst.sd.chapter6.BeatBox">
  <arg value="HFBuildWizard"/>
  <classpath>
    <pathelement location="dist/BeatBox.jar"/>
  </classpath>
</java>
```

If you wrap this in a target then you won't ever have to type "java -cp blahblah..." again to launch BeatBox.

3 Generate documentation

You've already seen how Ant can display documentation for the build file, but it can also generate JavaDoc from your source code:

```
<javadoc packagenames="headfirst.sd.*"
  sourcepath="src"
  destdir="docs"
  windowtitle="BeatBox Documentation"/>
```

Note that Ant can generate your HTML files for you—but it can't write the documentation you've been putting off.

There are other elements you can include in the JavaDoc task to generate headers and footers for each page if you need to.

4 Check out code, run tests, copy builds to archival directories, encrypt files, email you when the build finishes, execute SQL...

There are lots more tasks you can use depending on what you need your build file to do. Now that you know the basics, all of the other tasks look pretty much the same. To get a look at the tasks Ant offers go to: `http://ant.apache.org/manual/index.html`.

Automation lets you focus on code, not repetitive tasks.

With a good build script, you can automate a pretty sophisticated build process. It's not uncommon to see multiple build files on a single project, one for each library or component. In cases like that, you might want to think about a master build file (sometimes called a **bootstrap** script) that ties everything together.

Your build script is code, too

You've put a lot of work into your build script. In fact, ***it's really code***, just like your source files and deployment descriptors. When you look at your build script as code, you'll realize there are lots of clever things you can do with it, like deal with platform differences between Windows and Unix, use timestamps to track builds or figure out what needs to be recompiled—all completely hidden from the person trying to do the build. But, like all other code, it belongs in a repository...

You should always check your build script into your code repository:

Since we're adding a new file to our checked-out code, we use the subversion add command and tell it which file we want added.

When you add a file to the repository, you're telling Subversion that it should care about that file. But you still need to commit that file, even after it's been added.

```
File Edit Window Help Safe
hfsd> svn add build.xml

A         build2.xml

hfsd> svn commit -m "Added Ant build.xml file."

Sending        build.xml
Transmitting file data .

Committed revision 11.

hfsd>
```

Don't forget your check in comments.

With your build script in the repository, it's available to everyone else when they do an update. Your version control software will track any changes to the script, and the script gets tagged with everything else whenever you do a release. This means that you won't have to remember all the magic commands you needed to build the nostalgic Version 1.0 in a few years at your IPO party!

Your build script is code...ACT LIKE IT! Code belongs in a version control system, where it's versioned, tagged, and saved for later use.

New developer, take two

We haven't written any new classes, talked to the customer, broken tasks up into stories, or demoed software for the customer...but things are still looking a lot better. With a build tool in place, let's see what bringing on the new developer looks like:

BULLET POINTS

- A build tool is simply a **tool**. It should make building your project **easier**, not harder.
- Most build tools use a **build script**, where you can specify what to build, several different instruction sets, and locations of external files and resources.
- Be sure you create a way to **clean up** any files your script creates.
- Your build script is **code** and should be versioned and checked into your code repository.
- **Build tools are for your team**, not just you. Choose a build tool that works for everyone on your team.

Tools for your Software Development Toolbox

Software Development is all about developing and delivering great software. In this chapter, you learned about several techniques to keep you on track. For a complete list of tools in the book, see Appendix ii.

Development Techniques

Use a build tool to script building, packaging, testing, and deploying your system

Most IDEs are already using a build tool underneath. Get familiar with that tool, and you can build on what the IDE already does

Treat your build script like code and check it into version control

Here are some of the key techniques you learned in this chapter...

... and some of the principles behind those techniques.

Development Principles

Building a project should be repeatable and automated

Build scripts set the stage for other automation tools

Build scripts go beyond just step-by-step automation and can capture compilation and deployment logic decisions

BULLET POINTS

- All but the smallest projects have a **nontrivial build process**.
- You want to **capture** and **automate** the knowledge of **how to build your system**—ideally in a single command.
- **Ant** is a build tool for **Java projects** and captures build information in an XML file named build.xml.
- The more you take advantage of **common conventions**, the more **familiar** your project will look to someone else, and the easier the project will be to integrate with external tools.
- Your **build script** is just as much a part of your project as **any other piece of code**. It should be checked into version control with everything else.

7 testing and continuous integration

Things fall apart

Sometimes even the best developer breaks the build.

Everyone's done it at least once. You're sure **your code compiles**; you've tested it over and over again on your machine and committed it into the repository. But somewhere between your machine and that black box they call a server, *someone* must have changed your code. The unlucky soul who does the next checkout is about to have a bad morning sorting out **what used to be working code**. In this chapter we'll talk about how to put together a **safety net** to keep the build in working order and you **productive**.

Things will ALWAYS go wrong...

Everyone who's ever done development knows what it's like. It's late, you're on you're eleventh can of Rock Star energy drink, and you still leave out that one ++ operator somewhere. Suddenly, your elegant code goes to pieces...bad news is, you don't ***realize*** you've got a problem.

At least, not until you're demoing the software for your boss. Remember the issues we had with Bob's code in Chapter 6?

Bob's code seemed to work in some places...

...but not in others.

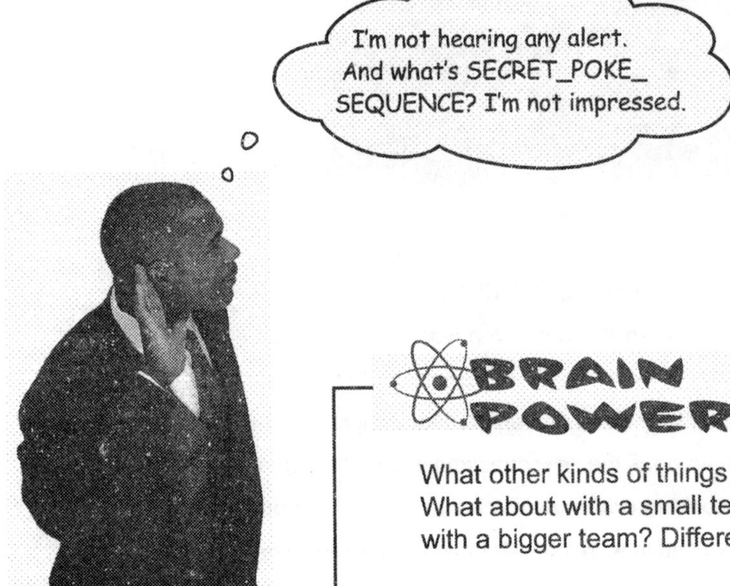

The real problem was that we were as surprised as the customer was when things went wrong.

BRAIN POWER

What other kinds of things can go wrong on a development project? What about with a small team? Do you have the same problems with a bigger team? Different problems?

Standup meeting

Bob: I did get it compiling! It took me forever to integrate the changes and get everything building again. It's not my fault.

Mark: Yeah, the code compiled; it just didn't work. So he didn't screw up as badly as it looks, really.

Laura: Didn't you test things?

Bob: Well, the code worked fine on my machine. I ran it and everything seemed fine...

Mark: OK, but running your code and doing a quick checkover is not really putting your code to the test.

Laura: Exactly. The functionality of your software is part of your responsibility, not just that the code "seems to work"; that's never going to wash with the customer...

Bob: Well, now that we have a version control server and build tool in place, this shouldn't be a problem anymore. So enough beating up on me, alright?

Mark: Hardly! Our build tool makes sure the code compiles, and we can back out changes with version control, but that doesn't help making sure things work right. Your code compiled; that was never the problem. It's the functionality of the system that got screwed up, and our build tool does nothing for that.

Laura: Yeah, you didn't even realize anything had gone wrong...

There are three ways to look at your system...

Good testing is essential on any software project. If your software doesn't work, it won't get used—and there's a good chance you won't get paid. So before getting into the nitty-gritty of software testing, it's important to step back and remember that different people look at your system from totally different perspectives, or views.

For more on these different types of testing, see Appendix i.

Your users see the system from the outside

Your users don't see your code, they don't look at the database tables, they don't evaluate your algorithms...and generally *they don't want to*. Your system is a ***black box*** to them; it either does what they asked it to do, or it doesn't. Your users are all about **functionality**.

Testers peek under the covers a little

Testers are a different breed. They're looking for functionality, but they're usually poking underneath to make sure things are really happening the way you said they would. Your system is more of a ***grey box*** to them. Testers are probably looking at the data in your database to make sure things are being cleaned up correctly; they might be checking that ports are closed, network connections dropped, and that memory usage is staying steady.

Developers let it all hang out

Developers are in the weeds. They see good (and sometimes bad) class design, patterns, duplicated code, inconsistencies in how things are represented. The system is wide open to them. If users see a system as a closed black box, developers see it as an open ***white box***. But sometimes because developers see so much detail, it's possible for them to miss broken functionality or make an assumption that a tester or end user might not.

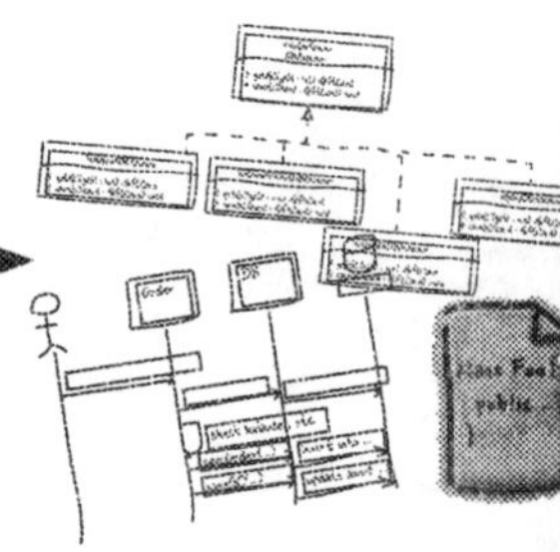

...and you need to consider each of these views

Each view of your system is valid, and you have to test from each of those three perspectives.

Black-box testing focuses on INPUT and OUTPUT

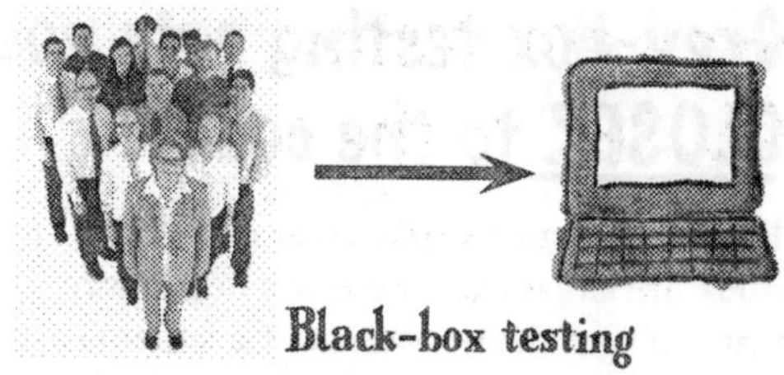

Your users are outside your system. They only see what they put into the system and what comes back out. When you do black-box testing you should look for:

- [ ] **Functionality**. Hands down, this is the most important black box testing. Does the system do what the user story says it is supposed to do? With black box testing, you don't care if your data is being stored in a text file or a massively parallel clustered database. You just care that the data gets in there like the story says and you get back the results the story says you should.

This isn't "the OrderProcessor class can handle GiftCard objects" functionality; it's about if a customer can buy a drink with their gift card.

- [ ] **User input validation**. Feed your system 3.995 for a dollar amount or -1 for your birthday. If you're writing a web application, put some HTML in your name field or try some SQL. The system better reject those values, and do it in a way that a typical end user can understand.

Error conditions are usually the last thing most developers think about, but it's the first thing most customers notice.

- [ ] **Output results**. Hand-check numerical values that your system returns. Make sure all of the functional paths have been tested ("if the user enters an invalid ending location, and then clicks "Get Directions"...") It's often helpful to put together a table showing the various inputs you could give the system, and what you'd expect the results to be for each input.

- [ ] **State transitions**. Some systems need to move from one state to another according to very specific rules. This is similar to output results, but it's about making sure your system handles moving from state to state like it's supposed to. This is particularly critical if you're implementing some kind of protocol like SMTP, a satellite communications link, or GPS receiver. Again, having a map of the states and what it takes to move the system from one to the other is very useful here.

- [ ] **Boundary cases and off-by-one errors**. You should test your system with a value that's just a little too small or just outside the maximum allowable value. For example, checking month 12 (if your months go from 0–11) or month 13 will let you know if you've got things just right, or if someone slipped up and forgot about zero-based arrays.

Customers don't usually make huge mistakes—they make little typos, and those are the things you're testing for here.

Grey-box testing gets you CLOSER to the code

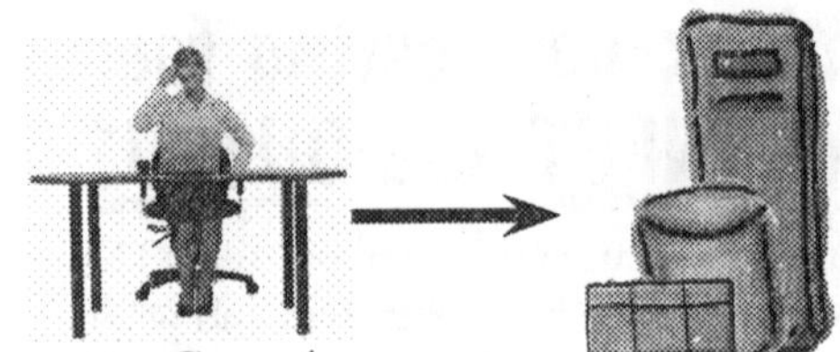

Black-box testing works great for a lot of applications, but there are situations where you need more. Sometimes you just can't get the results out of a system easily without looking inside, at least a little. This is particularly true with a lot of web applications, where the web interface just moves data around in a database. You've got to deal with the database code ***as well as*** the web interface itself.

Grey-box testing is like black-box testing...but you can peek

When doing grey box testing, you're generally looking for the same things as black box testing, but you can dig around a little to make sure the system works as it's supposed to below the surface. Use grey box testing for things like:

- [ ] **Verifying auditing and logging**. When important data (or money) is on the line, there's usually a lot of auditing and logging going on inside a system. This information isn't usually available through the normal user interface, either. You might need to use a log viewing tool or auditing report, or maybe just query some database tables directly.

But be careful of logging confidential information to unsecured places, you won't make the right sorts of friends that way...

- [ ] **Data destined for other systems**. If you're building a system that sends information to another system at a later time (say an order for 50 copies of *Head First Software Development*), you should check the output format and data you're sending to the other systems...and that means looking underneath what's exposed by the system.

- [ ] **System-added information**. It's common for applications to create checksums or hashes of data to make sure things are stored correctly (or securely). You should hand-check these. Make sure system-generated timestamps are being created in the right time zone and stored with the right data.

- [ ] **Scraps left laying around**. It's so easy as a developer to miss doing cleanup after a system is done with data. This can be a security risk as well as a resource leak. Make sure data is really deleted if it's supposed to be, and make sure it isn't deleted if it's not. Check that the system isn't leaking memory while it's running. Look for things that might leave scraps of files or registry entries after they should have been cleaned up. Verify that uninstalling your application leaves the system clean.

Exercise

Below is a user story from BeatBox Pro. Your job is to write up three ideas for black or grey box tests, and descriptions of what you'd do to implement those tests.

Title: Send a picture to other users

Description: Click on the "Send a Picture" button to send a picture (only JPEG needs to be supported) to the other users. They should have the option to not accept the file. There are no size limits on the file right now.

Priority: 20 **Estimate:** 4

Here's one to get you started.

1. Test for... sending a small JPEG to another user

How would you test this? Describe the test case in plain English.

2. Test for...

Think about the different ways the fuctionality in the user story could be tested, like testing when it handles things going wrong...

3. Test for...

Exercise Solution

Below is a user story from BeatBox Pro. Your job was to write up three ideas for black or grey box tests, and descriptions of what you'd do to implement those tests.

Title: Send a picture to other users

Description: Click on the "Send a Picture" button to send a picture (only JPEG needs to be supported) to the other users. They should have the option to not accept the file. There are no size limits on the file right now.

Priority: 20 **Estimate:** 4

* Here are the three tests we came up with. It's okay if you have three different ones... you'll just have more ideas for actual tests.

1. Test for... sending a small JPEG to another user.

Get two instances of BeatBox Pro running. On the first instance, click the Send Picture button. When the image selection dialog pops up, select SmallImage.jpg and click OK.

Then check and make sure that the second BeatBox displays a Receive Image dialog box. Click OK to accept the image. Check that the image displays correctly.

This is a black-box test. Also notice that we needed some JPEG resources to support the test. That's OK; using sample input is fine. You should version-control those resources, though, for later reuse.

2. Test for... sending an invalid JPEG to another user.

Get two instances of BeatBox Pro running. On the first instance, click the Send Picture button. When the image selection dialog pops up, select InvalidImage.jpg and click OK.

Check that BeatBox shows a dialog telling you that the image is invalid and can't be sent. Confirm that the second BeatBox did not display a Receive Image dialog. Also make sure no exceptions were thrown from either instance.

These tests are a little more on the grey side. You need to know how BeatBox Pro should handle these conditions, and where exceptions would be sent if an error occurred.

3. Test for... losing connectivity while transferring an image.

Start two instances of BeatBox Pro. On the first instance, click the Send Picture button. When the image selection dialog pops up, select GiantImage.jpg and click OK.

Check that the second BeatBox shows a Receive Image dialog box and click OK. While this image is transferring (make the image several MB so it will take a while), kill the second BeatBox instance. Check that the first BeatBox displays a dialog saying the transfer failed and that no exceptions were thrown.

White-box testing uses inside knowledge

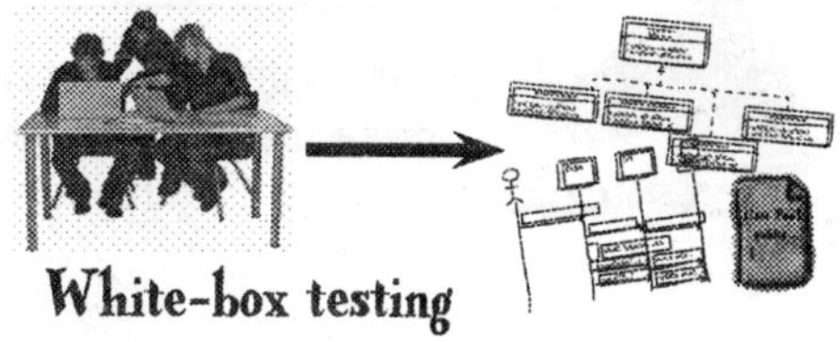

At the deepest levels of testing, you'll find white box tests. This is where you know exactly what's going on inside the code, and you do your best to make that code break. If you put aside the fact that you have to fix the code when it does break, white-box testing can actually be fun: it becomes a challenge to dig into code and generate problem situations that will cause errors and crashes.

When doing white-box testing you should be familiar with the code you're about to test. You still care about functionality, but you should also be thinking about the fact that method X is going to divide by one of the numbers you're sending in... is that number being checked properly? With white-box testing you're generally looking for:

- ☐ **Testing all the different branches of code.** With white-box testing you should be looking at ***all*** of your code. You can see all of the `if/elses` and all the case and switch statements. What data do you need to send in to get the class you're looking at to run each of those branches?

Most code works great when things are going as expected—the so-called "happy path"—but what about when things go off-track?

- ☐ **Proper error handling.** If you do feed invalid data into a method, are you getting the right error back? Is your code cleaning up after itself nicely by releasing resources like file handles, mutexes, or allocated memory?

Black-box testing looked at error messages, but what about what the code left around when things go wrong? That's for white-box testing to examine.

- ☐ **Working as documented.** If the method claims it's thread-safe, test the method from multiple threads If the documentation says you can pass null in as an argument to a method and you'll then get back a certain set of values, is that what's really going on? If a method claims you need a certain security role to call it, try the method with and without that role.

- ☐ **Proper handling of resource constraints.** If a method tries to grab resources—like memory, disk space, or a network connection—what does the code do if it can't get the resource it needs? Are these problems handled gracefully? Can you write a test to force the code into one of those problematic conditions?

White-box tests tend to be code-on-code

Since white-box tests tend to get up close and personal with the code they're trying to test, it's common to see them written in code and run on a machine rather than exercised by a human. Let's write some code-on-code tests now...

Exercise

Below is the block of code that Bob built for the BeatBox Pro demo (the one that failed spectacularly), and the two user stories that version of the software was focused on. On the next page are three tests that need to pass. How would you test these in code?

Title: Send a poke to other users

Description: Click on the "Send a Poke" button to send an audible and visual alert to the other members in the chat. The alert should be short and not too annoying—you're just trying to get their attention.

Priority: 20 **Estimate:** 3

Title: Send a picture to other users

Description: Click on the "Send a Picture" button to send a picture (only JPEG needs to be supported) to the other users. They should have the option to not accept the file. There are no size limits on the file right now.

Priority: 20 **Estimate:** 4

These stories have to work in the demo—you have to test for this functionality.

```
public class RemoteReader implements Runnable {
  boolean[] checkboxState = null;
  String nameToShow = null;
  Object obj = null;

  public void run() {
  try {
    while ((obj = in.readObject()) != null) {
      System.out.println("got an object from server");
      System.out.println(obj.getClass());
      String nameToShow = (String) obj;
      checkboxState = (boolean[]) in.readObject();
      if (nameToShow.equals(PICTURE_START_SEQUENCE)) {
        receiveJPEG();
      }
      else {
        otherSeqsMap.put(nameToShow, checkboxState);
        listVector.add(nameToShow);
        incomingList.setListData(listVector);
        // now reset the sequence to be this
      }
    } // close while
  } catch (Exception ex) {
    ex.printStackTrace();
  }
 } // close run
}
```

Remember that Bob overwrote the code to handle the POKE_START_SEQUENCE command.

How could you test this code to make sure it works, even if *another* problem comes up?

Definitely pseudocode...if you need a resource, assume you can get it. This is just the basic code-level steps you'd need.

1. Test for... a picture start sequence to test picture functionality.

Here's what you need to test.

establish a new network connection
send the PICTURE_START_SEQUENCE
send over an empty array of check boxes (no audio)
send the picture data
verify picture data received and displayed properly

This one is done for you to give you an idea of the pseudocode to use to describe a test.

2. Test for... a poke start sequence to test for poke functionality.

establish a new network connection

What would this test do? This should be pseudocode. What code are you going to have to write to implement this test?

3. Test for... a normal text message that's sent to all clients.

establish a new network connection

Exercise Solution

Below is the block of code that Bob built for the demo (the one that failed spectacularly), and the two user stories this version of the software was focused on. Your job was to figure out how to white-box-test for at least three problem situations.

test for a picture start sequence to test picture functionality.

This is to test the basic picture functionality, since it was one of our new stories, but digs into the code involved.

establish a new network connection
send the PICTURE_START_SEQUENCE
send over an empty array of checkboxes (no audio)
send the picture data
verify picture data received and displayed properly

This is more in-depth than just using the GUI: you're really testing specific methods, with specific inputs, to make sure the result is what's expected.

test for a poke start sequence to test for poke functionality.

establish a new network connection
send the POKE_START_SEQUENCE
send over an empty array of check boxes (no audio)
verify alert sound is heard and the alert message is shown.

You'll probably need to verify this works by watching a running chat client—that's okay, use whatever you need to test properly.

This one is based on the other story, and is a lot like the picture test.

With a test to check the POKE_START_SEQUENCE, you can see if it fails before showing it the customer, and avoid any surprises.

test for a normal text message is sent to all clients.

establish a new network connection
send the message, "Test message"
send an array of valid checkbox options
verify the test message was received by all clients and the checkboxes are updated to match the array values.

Don't forget to test stuff that should still be working! This is just as important as testing new functionality.

There are lots more tests you could have come up with—things like testing that clicking on one of the messages retrieves the checkboxes correctly, and testing for failure conditions. What happens if too many checkbox values are sent in an array? Or too few? See how many ways you can break BeatBox Pro.

Coming up with tests is <u>YOUR</u> job.

There are lots of good frameworks out there, but they ***run*** your tests; they don't write them for you.* A testing frameworks is really just a collection of tools that help you express your tests. Even though that makes them really useful, there are a few things you still need to keep in mind:

First, **you still need to figure out what you have to test**. Figuring out what to test and how you express that test are usually two different things. Regardless of your framework, you need to think about functional testing, performance testing, boundary or edge cases, race conditions, security risks, valid data, invalid data, etc.

Next, **your choice of testing frameworks is almost certainly going to impact how you test**. That's not always a bad thing, but don't forget about it. This might mean you need more than one way to test your software. For example, if you decide to use a code-level testing framework for your desktop application, you're still leaving yourself open for bugs in your GUI, so you'll probably want something to test that, too. Another great example: say you're writing a 3-D game. Testing the backend code isn't too hard, but making sure that the game renders correctly and people can't walk through walls or fall through small cracks in your world...well, that's a mess, and no framework can generate those tests for you.

* Actually, some frameworks can generate tests for you, but they have very specific goals in mind. Security frameworks are a common example: the framework can throw tons of common security errors at your software and see what happens. But this doesn't replace real application testing to make sure the system does what you think it does (and what the customer actually wants it to do).

Hanging your tests on a framework

We're talking about frameworks, but what does that really mean? The obvious way to test is to have someone **use your application**. But, if we can automate our tests we can ~~get paid while the computer tests our stuff~~ be more effective and know that our tests are run exactly the same way each time. That's important, because consistency in how a test is run isn't something humans are very good at.

Testing EVERYTHING with one step ← Well, one command actually

There are lots more advantages to automating your tests. As well as not requiring you to sit there and manually run the tests yourself, you also build up a **library of tests** that are all run at the same time to test your software completely every time you run the **test suite**:

1. **Build up a suite of tests**

   As your software grows so will the tests that need to be applied to it. At first, this might seem a little scary, especially if you're running tests by hand. Large software systems can have literally thousands of tests that take days of developer time to run. If you automate your tests you can collect all the tests for your software into one library and then run those tests at will, without having to rely on having somebody, probably a poor test engineer who looked at you wrong, running those tests manually for a day or so.

2. **Run all your tests with one command**

   Once you have a suite of tests that can be run automatically in a framework, the next step is to build that set of tests such that they can all be run with just one command. The easier a test suite is to run, the more often it will actually be used and that can only mean that your software quality will improve. Any new tests are simply added to the test suite, and bang, everyone gets the benefit of the test you have written.

3. **Get regression testing for free**

   The big advantage of creating a one-command suite of tests that you continually add to as you add more code to your software is that you get **regression testing** for free. Detecting when a new change that you've made to your software has actually introduced bugs in the older code, called **software regression**, is a danger for any developer working with old or inherited code. The best way to deal with the threat of regression problems is to not only run your own tests for your newly added code, but to run all the older tests as well.

   Now, because you'll be adding your new tests into your test suite, you'll get this for free. All you have to do is add your new tests to the existing test suite and kick things off with one command—you'll have regression tested your changes.

Of course, this relies on the existing code base having a suite of tests available for you to extend. Check out Chapter 10 for what to do when that isn't the case.

Tailor your test suites to suit the occasion

It's unfortunately true that large unit test suites become ungainly and, therefore, tend to get used less. One technique is to break out fast and slow tests so that a developer can run all the fast tests often while they are changing and adding code, but only run the full suite when they think they need to.

What tests fall into the fast or slow categories is really up to your particular project, and which category specific tests fall into can change depending on the development work that you are doing. For example, if you have barely-ever-changes code that takes a long time to test, then that would be a good candidate for the slow test suite. However if you were working on code that might well impact the barely-ever-changes code, then you might consider moving its tests into the fast test suite while you are working those changes.

Let's try it out with a popular free testing framework for Java, called JUnit.

To download the JUnit framework, go to http://www.junit.org

You can also speed up slow tests using mocks; see Chapter 8 for more on those.

there are no Dumb Questions

Q: So how often should we run our entire test suite?

A: This is really up to you and your team. If you're happy with running your full test suite once a day, and know that any regression bugs will only be caught once a day, then that's fine. However, we'd still recommend you have a set of tests that can be run much more frequently.

Keep the time it takes to run your tests as short as possible. The longer a test suite takes to run, the less often it is likely to be run!

Automate your tests with a testing framework

Let's take a simple test case and automate it using JUnit. JUnit provides common resources and behaviors you need for your tests, and then invokes each of your tests, one at a time. JUnit gives you a nice GUI to see your tests run, as well, but that's really a small thing compared to the power of automating your tests.

JUnit also has a text-based test runner and plug-ins for most popular IDEs.

You've got to import the JUnit classes.

These are objects used in several of the test cases.

Here's a static final of empty checkboxes that can be used in several different tests.

JUnit calls setUp() before each test is run, so here's where to initialize variables used in the test methods.

tearDown() is for cleaning up. JUnit calls this method when each test is finished.

Since these are annotated with @Before and @After, they'll get called by JUnit before and after each test.

Here's an actual test. You annotate it with @Test so JUnit knows it's a test and can run it. The method just sends a test message and a checkboxState.

```
package headfirst.sd.chapter7;
import java.io.*;
import java.net.Socket;
import org.junit.*;

public class TestRemoteReader {
    private Socket mTestSocket;
    private ObjectOutputStream mOutStream;
    private ObjectInputStream mInStream;

    public static final boolean[] EMPTY_CHECKBOXES = new boolean[256];

    @Before
    public void setUp() throws IOException {
            mTestSocket = new Socket("127.0.0.1", 4242);
            mOutStream =
              new ObjectOutputStream(mTestSocket.getOutputStream());
            mInStream =
              new ObjectInputStream(mTestSocket.getInputStream());
    }

    @After
    public void tearDown() throws IOException {
            mTestSocket.close();
            mOutStream = null;
            mInStream = null;
            mTestSocket = null;
    }

      @Test
      public void testNormalMessage()throws IOException {
            boolean[] checkboxState = new boolean[256];
            checkboxState[0] = true;
            checkboxState[5] = true;
            checkboxState[19] = true;
            mOutStream.writeObject("This is a test message!");
            mOutStream.writeObject(checkboxState);
      }
}
```

You can use mOutStream because it was set up in the setup() method that JUnit will already have called.

Use your framework to run your tests

Invoke the JUnit test runner, `org.junit.runner.JUnitCore`. The only information you need to give the runner is which test class to run: `headfirst.sd.chapter7.TestRemoteReader`. The framework handles running each test in that class::

Don't forget to start the MusicServer and a copy of the BeatBox Pro. JUnit won't take care of that for you, unless you add code for that into setUp().

Don't forget to put junit.jar in your classpath.

```
File Edit Window Help
hfsd> java -cp junit.jar;. org.junit.runner.JUnitCore
          headfirst.sd.chapter7.TestRemoteReader
JUnit version 4.3.1
.
Time: 0.321

OK (1 test)

hfsd>
```

JUnit will print a dot for each test it ran. Since this class has only one test, you get a single dot.

"OK" is JUnit's understated way of saying all the tests ran.

And here's what BeatBox Pro looks like after the test has run. Checkmarks are where they're supposed to be and the test message is in the log.

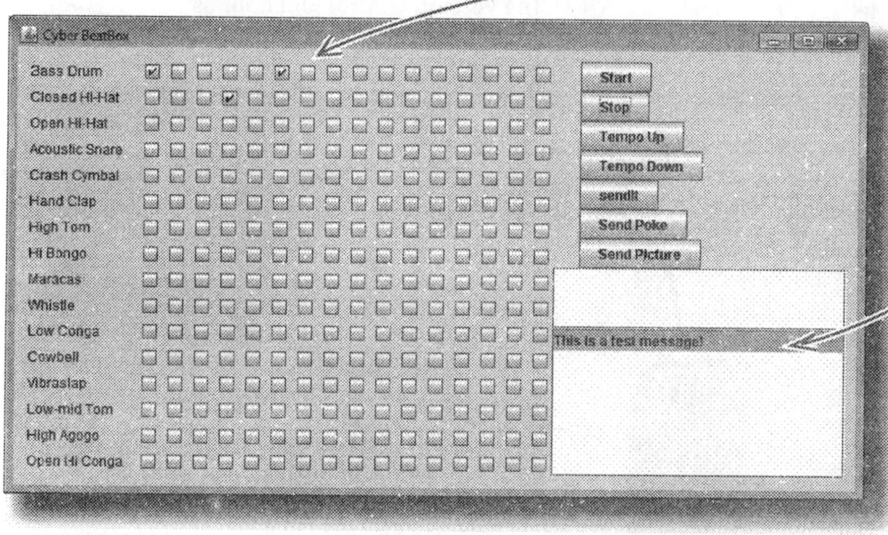

With a framework in place, you can easily add the other tests from page 246. Just add more test methods and annotate them with `@Test`. You can then run your test classes and watch the results.

Wouldn't it be dreamy if there was a tool that ran all my tests for me, every time I checked in code, so I wouldn't be embarrassed in front of my team?

Continuous integration tools run your tests when you check in your code

We've already got a version control tool that keeps track of our code, and now we've got a set of automated tests. We just need a way to tie these two systems together. There are version control tools (or applications that integrate with version control tools) that will compile your code, run your automated tests, and even display and mail out reports—as soon as you (or Bob) commit code into your repository.

This is all part of **continuous integration** (CI), and it looks like this:

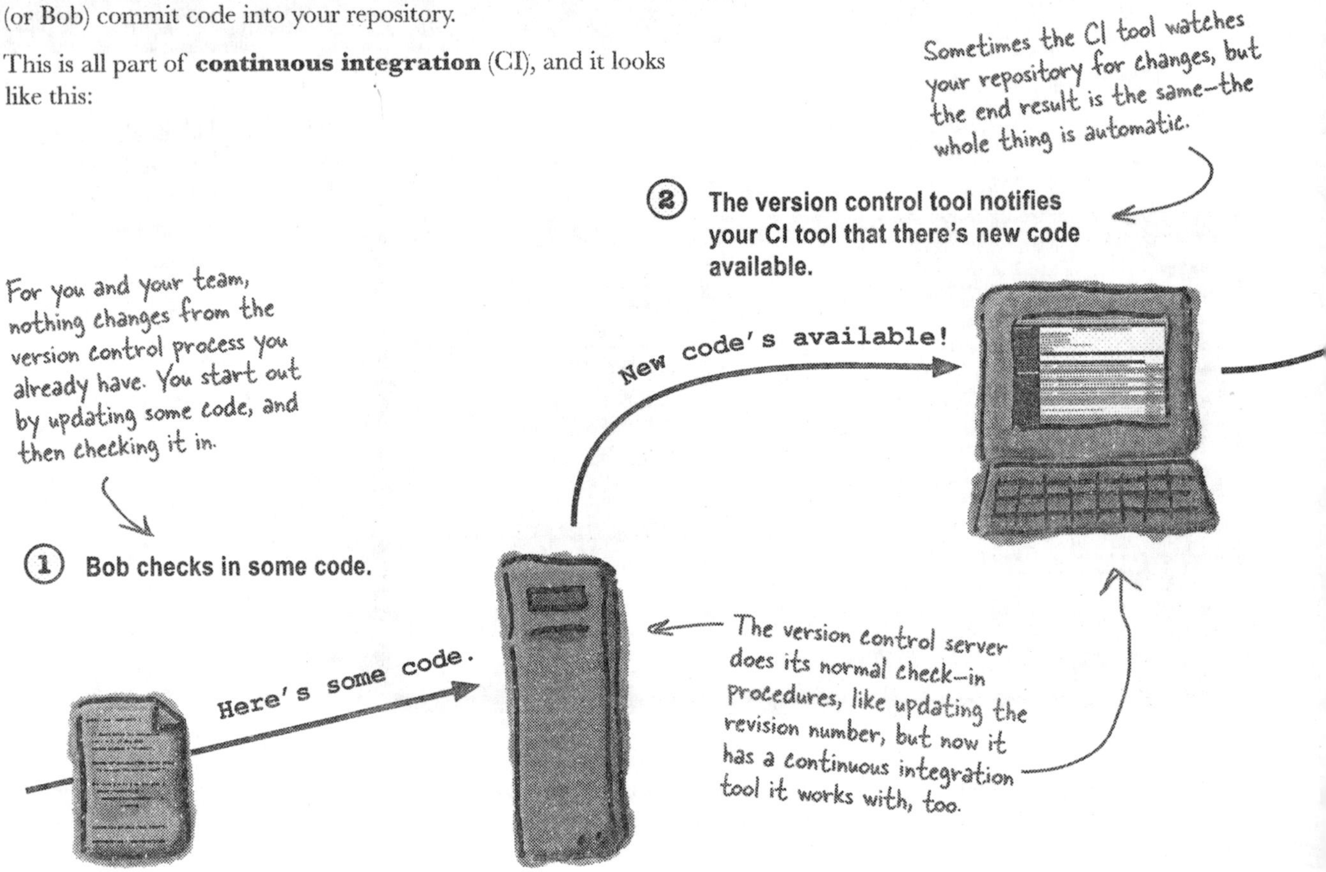

The great thing about version control and CI is that they happen without you having to do anything—it's all going on "under the hood."

Continuous integration and build tools are two more processes that improves communication amongst your team.

(3) The CI tool checks out the new code, compiles it, and runs all your tests. Most build tools create web pages and emails to let everyone know how the builds are going.

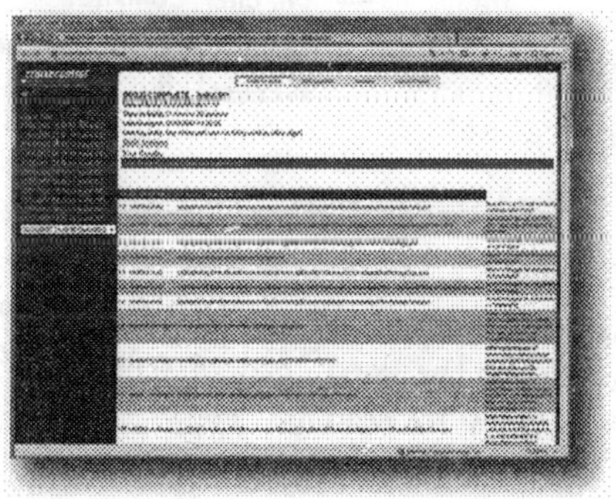

This particular build tool is called CruiseControl, but there are lots of similar products out there.

there are no Dumb Questions

Q: Does CI have to build and test my code every time I check it in? My project is so large that could really slow things down.

A: No, defnitely not. Although building and running your tests every time you commit changes to version control is a good practice, sometimes it's not entirely practical. If you have a really large set of tests that use significant computing resources, you might want to schedule things a bit differently.

Continuous integration wraps version control, compilation, and testing into a <u>single</u> repeatable process.

At the wheel of CI with CruiseControl

The three main jobs of a CI tool are to get a version of the code from your repository, build that code, and then run a suite of tests against it. To give you a flavor of how CI is set up, let's take a look at how that works in CruiseControl:

1. **Add your JUnit test suite to your Ant build**
   Before you build your CruiseControl project, you need to add your JUnit tests into your Ant build file.

You last saw Ant in Chapter 6.5.

```
<target name="test" depends="compile">
  <junit>
    <classpath refid="classpath.test" />
    <formatter type="brief" usefile="false" />
    <batchtest>
      <fileset dir="${tst-dir}" includes="**/Test*.class" />
    </batchtest>
  </junit>
</target>

<target name="all" depends="test" />
```

A new target called "test" that depends on the "compile" target having finished successfully

Here's where the magic happens. All of the classes in your project that begin with the word "Test" are automatically executed as JUnit tests. No need for you to specify each one individually.

The "all" target is just a nicer way of saying "compile, build, and test everything."

2. **Create your CruiseControl project**
   The next step is to create a CruiseControl project and begin to define your build and test process.

```
<cruisecontrol>
  <project name="BeatBox" buildafterfailed="true">
    <!-- This is where the rest of your project configuration will go -->
  </project>
</cruisecontrol>
```

The project tag bounds all of your project's configuration.

In CruiseControl, your project is described using an XML document, much the same as in Ant, except this script describes what is going be done, and when.

3 Check to see if there have been any changes in the repository

Inside your CruiseControl project you can describe where to get your code from and then what to do with it. In this case, code changes are grabbed from your subversion repository. If the code has changed, then a full build is run; otherwise the scheduled build is skipped.

The "modificationset" tells the repository to check against the local copy to see if it actually needs to build changes in or not

```
<modificationset quietperiod="10">
  <svn LocalWorkingCopy="hfsd/chapter7/cc"
   RepositoryLocation="file:///c:/Users/Developer/Desktop/SVNRepo/BeatBox/trunk"/>
</modificationset>
```

Here you declare what local copy and remote repository to check against for changes

4 Schedule the build

Finally, you describe how often you want your continuous integration build to take place. In CruiseControl this is done with the `schedule` tag, inside of which you describe the type of build that you want to perform.

```
<schedule interval="60">
  <ant antworkingdir="hfsd/chapter7/cc"
       buildfile="build.xml"
       uselogger="true"
       usedebug="true"
       target="all"/>
</schedule>
```

Schedules the build to occur every 60 minutes.

Here, you plug in your Ant build script

Building the "all" target

Testing guarantees things will work... right?

Version control, CI, test frameworks, build tools...you've come a long way since it was you and your college buddies hacking away on laptops in your garage. With all your testing, you should be confident showing the customer what you've built:

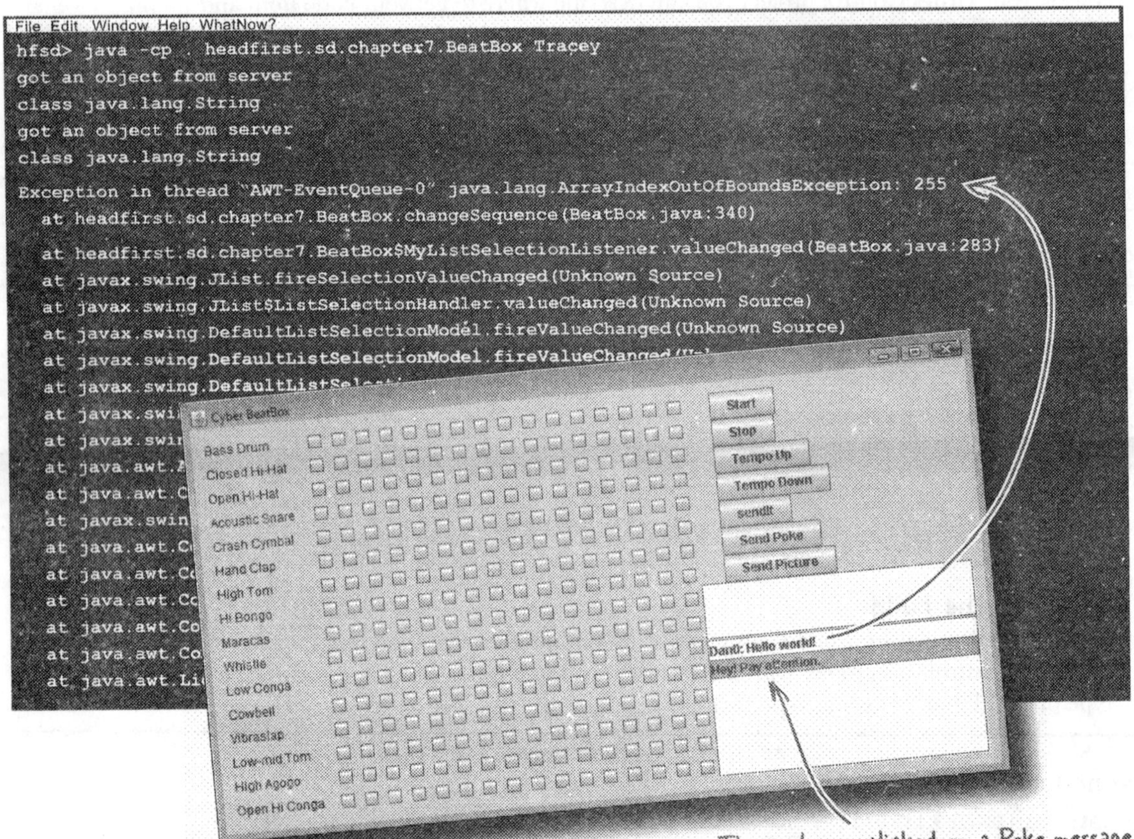

Exercise

Here's the code we changed in Chapter 6. The bug has to be related to this stuff somewhere. Find the bug that bit us this time.

```
public void buildGUI() {
  // code from buildGUI
  JButton sendIt = new JButton("sendIt");
  sendIt.addActionListener(new MySendListener());
  buttonBox.add(sendIt);
  JButton sendPoke = new JButton("Send Poke");
  sendPoke.addActionListener(new MyPokeListener());
  buttonBox.add(sendPoke);
  userMessage = new JTextField();
  buttonBox.add(userMessage);
  // more code in buildGUI()
}

public class MyPokeListener implements ActionListener {
  public void actionPerformed(ActionEvent a) {
    // We'll create an empty state array here
    boolean[] checkboxState = new boolean[255];
    try {
      out.writeObject(POKE_START_SEQUENCE);
      out.writeObject(checkboxState);
    } catch (Exception ex) {
        System.out.println("Failed to poke!"); }
    }
  }
  // other code in BeatBoxFinal.java
}
```

Here's the code we modified from BeatBox.java's buildGUI() method.

This inner class is from BeatBox.java, too.

What went wrong in this code? ....

....

Why didn't our tests catch this? ....

....

What would you do differently? ....

....

Exercise Solution

Here's the code we changed in Chapter 6. The bug has to be related to this stuff somewhere. Find the bug that bit us this time.

```
public void buildGUI() {
  // code from buildGUI
  JButton sendIt = new JButton("sendIt");
  sendIt.addActionListener(new MySendListener());
  buttonBox.add(sendIt);
  JButton sendPoke = new JButton("Send Poke");
  sendPoke.addActionListener(new MyPokeListener());
  buttonBox.add(sendPoke);
  userMessage = new JTextField();
  buttonBox.add(userMessage);
  // more code in buildGUI()
}

public class MyPokeListener implements ActionListener {
  public void actionPerformed(ActionEvent a) {
    // We'll create an empty state array here
    boolean[] checkboxState = new boolean[255];
    try {
      out.writeObject(POKE_START_SEQUENCE);
      out.writeObject(checkboxState);
  } catch (Exception ex) {
        System.out.println("Failed to poke!"); }
  }
}
// other code in BeatBoxFinal.java
}
```

Here's the bug. We create an array of 255 booleans instead of 256.

What went wrong in this code? *When we send the dummy array of checkboxes, we're off by one—we only send 255 checkboxes, and it should be 256 (16x16).*

Why didn't our tests catch this? *Our tests sent valid arrays to our receiver code, but we didn't really test the GUI side of the application.*

What would you do differently? *We need a way to test more of our code. We should add a test that will catch this. (But what else are we missing?)*

Code that doesn't work isn't complete!

Complete code is ***working*** code. Not many people will pay you to write code that doesn't do what it's supposed to. Writing tests is very much a part of getting your work done. In fact, tests let you know when you've written the code you meant to write, and when it does what it's supposed to do.

But how many tests do you need? Well, it becomes a trade-off between how much of the code you test versus how likely are you to find a bug in the part you *haven't* tested. A hundred tests that all test the same 50-line method in a 100,000-line system isn't going to give you much confidence—that leaves a whopping 99,950 lines of untested code, no matter how many tests you've written.

Instead of talking about number of tests, it's better to think about **code coverage**: what percentage of your code are your tests actually testing?

Your code's not finished until it passes its tests.

You should be writing your tests to make sure your code does what it's supposed to. If you don't have a test for a certain piece of functionality, how do you know your code really implements that functionality? And if you do have a test and it's not passing, your code doesn't work.

Tools are your friends.

Tools and frameworks can't do your work for you, but they can make it easier for you to get to your work—and figure out what you should be working on. Code coverage is no different.

Sharpen your pencil

Below is some code from the BeatBox Pro application. Your job is to come up with tests to get 100% coverage on this code... or as close to it as you can get.

This is the code that handles the picture and poke sequences, as well as normal messages.

```
public class RemoteReader implements Runnable {
  boolean[] checkboxState = null;
  String nameToShow = null;
  Object obj = null;

  public void run() {
    try {
      while ((obj = in.readObject()) != null) {
        System.out.println("got an object from server");
        System.out.println(obj.getClass());
        String nameToShow = (String) obj;
        checkboxState = (boolean[]) in.readObject();
        if (nameToShow.equals(PICTURE_START_SEQUENCE)) {
          receiveJPEG();
        } else {
         if (nameToShow.equals(POKE_START_SEQUENCE)) {
          playPoke();
          nameToShow = "Hey! Pay attention.";
         }

         otherSeqsMap.put(nameToShow, checkboxState);
         listVector.add(nameToShow);
         incomingList.setListData(listVector);
         // now reset the sequence to be this
        }
      } // close while
    } catch (Exception ex) {
      ex.printStackTrace();
    }
  } // close run
} // close inner class
```

Circle any code that your tests don't cover.

1. Write a test to exercise this section of the code (pseudocode is fine).

....

....

....

....

....

Some of these tests may test more than just the section of code bracketed—write notes indicating what else your tests exercise.

2. Write a test to exercise this section of the code.

....

....

....

....

....

3. Write a test to exercise this section of the code.

....

....

....

....

....

4. Did we get 100% coverage? What else would you test? How?

....

....

....

....

Sharpen your pencil Solution

Below is some code from the BeatBox Pro application. Your job was to come up with tests to get 100% coverage on this code...or as close to it as you can get.

```
public class RemoteReader implem
  boolean[] checkboxState = null
  String nameToShow = null;
  Object obj = null;

  public void run() {
    try {
      while ((obj = in.readObject()
        System.out.println("got an object from server");
        System.out.println(obj.getClass());
        String nameToShow = (String)
        checkboxState = (boolean[]) i
        if (nameToShow.equals(PICTURE
          receiveJPEG();
        } else {
         if (nameToShow.equals(POKE_ST
           playPoke();
           nameToShow = "Hey! Pay attent
         }

          otherSeqsMap.put(nameToShow, c
          listVector.add(nameToShow);
          incomingList.setListData(listVector);
          // now reset the sequence to be this
        }
      } // close while
    } catch (Exception ex) {
      ex.printStackTrace();
    }
  } // close run
} // close inner class
```

1

```
@Test
public void testNormalMessage()throws IOException {
  boolean[] checkboxState = new boolean[256];
  checkboxState[0] = true;
  checkboxState[5] = true;
  checkboxState[19] = true;
  mOutStream.writeObject("This is a test message!");
  mOutStream.writeObject(checkboxState);
}
```

2

```
@Test
public void testPictureMessage()throws IOException {
  mOutStream.writeObject(PICTURE_START_SEQUENCE);
  mOutStream.writeObject(EMPTY_CHECKBOXES);
  sendJPEG(TEST_JPEG_FILENAME);
}
```

3

```
@Test
public void testPoke()throws IOException {
  mOutStream.writeObject(POKE_START_SEQUENCE);
  mOutStream.writeObject(EMPTY_CHECKBOXES);
}
```

All three of these tests cover the code before the if statement.

This test exercises multiple chunks of code. In fact, most tests aren't isolated to just a few lines, even though it might be the only test that covers those few lines.

4 Did we get 100% coverage? What else would you test? How?

We didn't test the exception-handling code, so we'd need to create exceptional situations. We also didn't test the GUI at all—that would take someone playing with the interface.

Standup meeting

Mark: No, I don't think so; running every method doesn't mean every ***line*** of each method will run. We need to have different kinds of tests to get to all the different error conditions and branches.

Laura: Wow...so I guess every variation of every method should have a separate test?

Bob: But how are we going to do all that? We'll have to make up all kinds of bogus data to get every weird error condition. That could take forever...

Mark: And that's not all. We've got to try things like pulling the network plug at some point to test what happens if the network goes down and I/O problems crop up.

Bob: You don't think that's going a little too far?

Mark: Well, if we want to catch all of the corner cases and every bit of exception handling...

Laura: But a lot of that stuff never really happens...

Bob: Then why did I bother to write all that exception-handling code? I've got all kinds of logging and reconnection code in my methods. Now you're saying I didn't need to write that?

Mark: You did, but—

Laura: This is impossible!

Testing all your code means testing EVERY BRANCH

Some of the easiest areas to miss are methods or code that have lots of branches. Suppose you've got login code like this:

```
public class ComplexCode {
  public class UserCredentials {
    private String mToken;

    UserCredentials(String token) {
      mToken = token;
    }
    public String getUserToken() { return mToken; }
  }

  public UserCredentials login(String userId, String password) {
    if (userId == null) {
      throw new IllegalArgumentException("userId cannot be null");
    }
    if (password == null) {
      throw new IllegalArgumentException("password cannot be null");
    }
    User user = findUserByIdAndPassword(userId, password);
    if (user != null) {
      return new UserCredentials(generateToken(userId, password,
                 Calendar.getInstance().getTimeInMillis()));
    }
    throw new RuntimeException("Can't find user: " + userId);
  }

  private User findUserByIdAndPassword(String userId, String password) {
    // code here only used by class internals
  }

  private String generateToken(String userId, String password,
                               long nonce) {
    // utility method used only by this class
  }
}
```

You'd probably only need one test case for all of the UserCredential code, since there's no behavior, just data to access and set.

You'll need lots of tests for this method. One with a valid username and password...

...one where the userId is null...

...another where the password is null...

...and one where the username is valid but the password is wrong.

...one where the userId isn't null but isn't a valid ID...

And then there are these private methods...We can't get to these directly.

Use a coverage report to see what's covered

Most coverage tools—especially ones like CruiseControl that integrate with other CI and version control tools—can generate a report telling you how much of your code is covered.

Here's a report for testing the `ComplexCode` class on the last page, and providing a valid username and password:

Code complexity basically tells us how many different paths there are through a given class's code. If there are lots of conditionals (more complicated code), this number will be high.

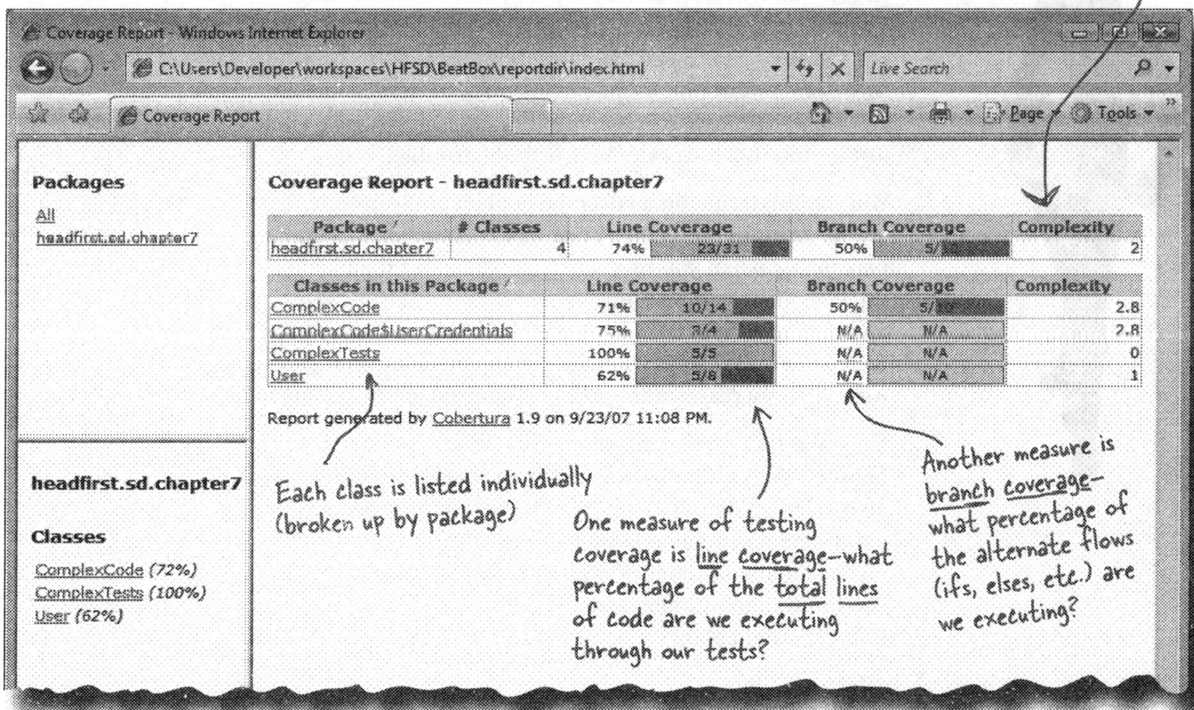

So the above test manages to test 62% of the `User` class, 71% of the `ComplexCode` class, and 75% of `UserCredentials`. Things get a lot better if you add in all the failure cases described on page 264.

Add in the failure cases and we're in much better shape with the ComplexCode class. Still need work on the User class though...

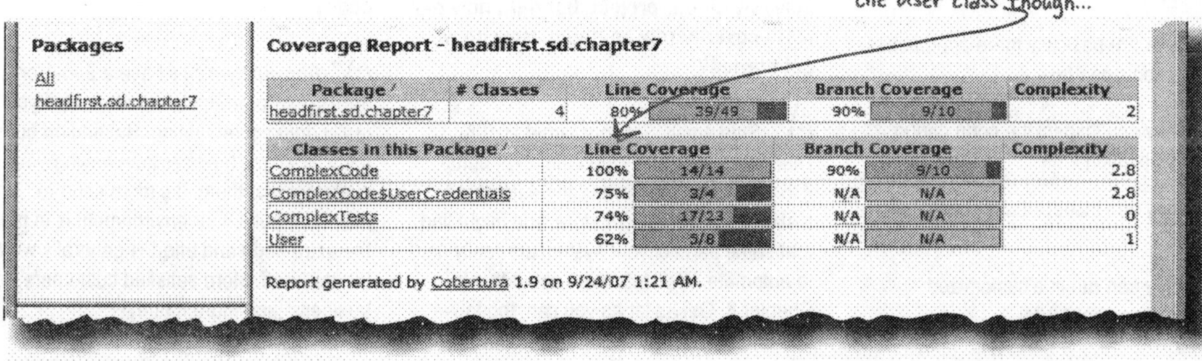

Are you kidding me? All that testing, and we're still not at 100%? How could you ever do this on a real project?

Good testing takes lots of time.

In general, it's not practical to always hit 100% coverage. You'll get diminishing returns on your testing after a certain point. For most projects, aim for about 85%–90% coverage. More often than not, it's just not possible to tease out that last 10%–15% of coverage. In other cases, it's possible but just far too much work to be worth the trouble.

You should decide on a coverage goal on a per-project, and sometimes even a per-class, basis. Shoot for a certain percentage when you first start, say 80%, and then keep track of the number of bugs found, first using your tests, and then after you release your code. If you get more bugs back after you release your code than you're comfortable with, then increase your coverage requirement by 5% or so.

Keep track of your numbers again. What's the ratio between bugs found by your testing versus bugs found after release? At some point you'll see that increasing your coverage percentage is taking a long time, but not really increasing the number of bugs you find internally. When you hit that point, then back off a little and know you've found a good balance.

there are no Dumb Questions

Q: How do coverage tools work?

A: There are basically three approaches coverage tools can take:

1. They can inspect the code during compilation time
2. They can inspect it after compilation, or
3. They can run in a customized environment (JVM)

Q: We want to try doing coverage analysis on our project, but right now our tests cover hardly anything. How do we get started?

A: Start small. Set your target at 10%. Then when you hit it, celebrate, then bump it to 15%. If you've never done automated testing on your project before, you might find that some parts of your system are really hard to automate. We'll talk more about that in Chapter 8. Get as far as you can, though—some testing is way better than no testing.

Q: Don't you end up with a lot of test code?

A: Absolutely. You'll have a 2-to-1 or 3-to-1 test-to-production code ratio if you're really doing good testing. But finding bugs early is so much easier than having your customer find them. It's more code to maintain, but if your environment is in place, the extra code and effort is generally worth the trade-off. More satisfied customers, more business, and more money!

Getting good coverage isn't always easy...

Now that we've gotten our heads around coverage, let's look back at BeatBox Pro. Now that we know what to look for, there are all kinds of things not being tested:

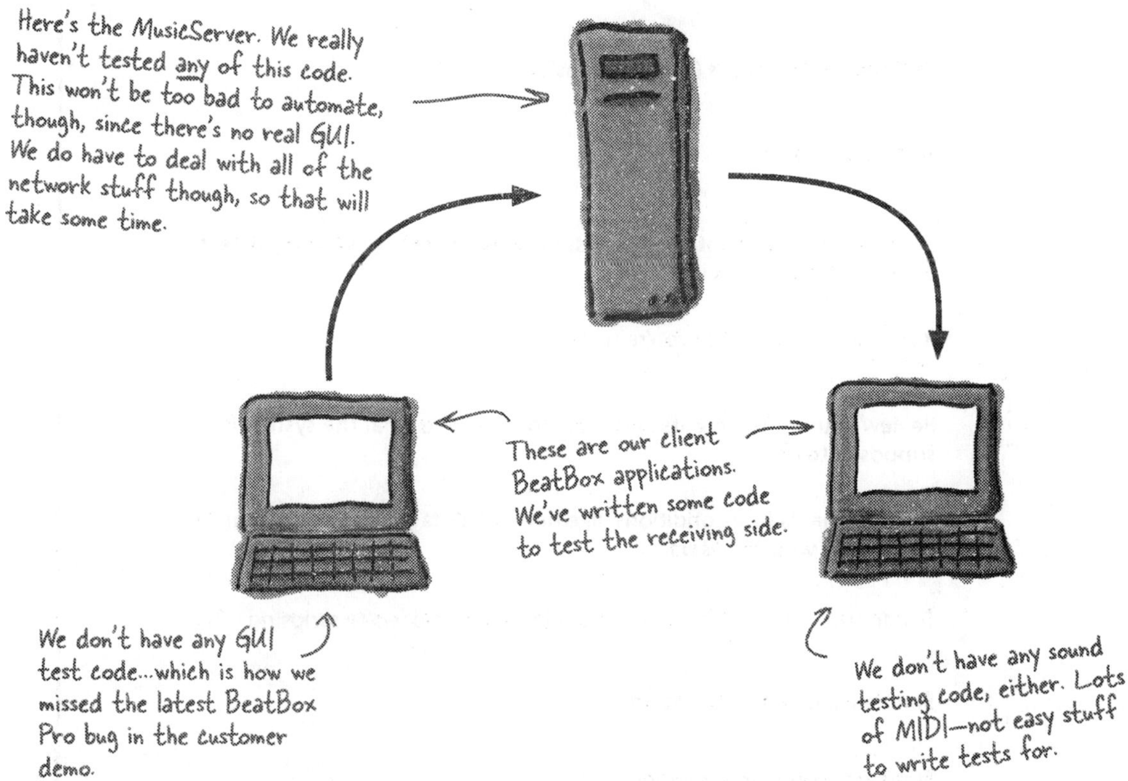

There are some things that are just inherently hard to test. GUIs actually aren't impossible; there are tools available that can simulate button clicks and keyboard input. Things like audio or 3-D graphics, though, those are tough. The answer? **Get a real person to try things out.** Software tests can't cover all the different variations of an animated game or audio in a music program.

So what about code you just can't seem to reach? Private methods, third-party libraries, or maybe your own code that's abstracted away from the inputs and outputs of your main interface modules? Well, we'll get to that in just a few more pages, in Chapter 8.

And then...enter **test-driven development**.

Sharpen your pencil

Check off all of the things you should do to get good coverage when testing.

- [ ] Test the success cases ("happy paths").
- [ ] Test failure cases.
- [ ] Stage known input data if your system uses a database so you can test various backend problems.
- [ ] Read through the code you're testing.
- [ ] Review your requirements and user stories to see what the system is supposed to do.
- [ ] Test external failure conditions, like network outages or people shutting down their web browsers.
- [ ] Test for security problems like SQL injection or cross-site scripting (XSS).
- [ ] Simulate a disk-full condition.
- [ ] Simulate high-load scenarios.
- [ ] Use different operating systems, platforms, and browsers.

→ Answers on page 272.

Standup meeting

Laura: I really wish we knew all this going in...before we started doing demos with the customer.

Bob: Yeah, I could have run tests on my code, and known I'd screwed up the other user story when I got mine to work. Anything to get us to full coverage...

Mark: Whoa, I'm not sure full coverage is reasonable. You ever heard of the 80/20 rule? Why spend all our time on a tiny bit of the code that probably ***won't*** ever get run?

Bob: Well, I'm going for 100%. I figure with another few days of writing tests, I can get there.

Mark: A few ***days***? We don't have time for that; don't you have a lot of GUI code to work on?

Laura: I agree. But I'm not sure we can even get to 80% coverage: there's a lot of complex code buried pretty deep in the GUI, and I'm not sure how to write tests to get to all of that stuff.

Mark: Hmmm...what about 50%? We could start there, and then add tests for things we think are missing. The coverage report will tell us what we're missing, right?

Bob: Yeah, we can look at which methods we're not calling. If we could hit every method, and then test the edge cases on code that's used a lot, that's pretty good...

Laura: Sounds like a plan...You just committed some stuff, right? I'll check the coverage report as soon as CruiseControl finishes its build.

What ~~version control~~ your environment does...

- [x] Lets you **create a repository** to keep your code in a secure place.
- [x] Lets multiple people **check out copies of the code** and work efficiently as a team.
- [x] Lets multiple people **check changes back into the repository** and distribute them to the rest of the team.
- [x] Keeps track of **who changes what**, when, and why.
- [x] **Branches** and **tags code** so you can find and change versions of code from way back when.
- [x] **Rolls back changes** that never should have happened in the first place.
- [x] Makes sure **your code compiles**.
- [x] **Tests** your code.
- [x] Tells us **how well we're testing.**

You've gotten a couple of these things into your environment now with a continuous integration tool.

... and what version control doesn't do

- [ ] ~~Makes sure your code compiles~~
- [ ] ~~Tests code.~~
- [ ] Thinks for you.
- [ ] Makes sure your code is readable and well-written.

Testcross

Take some time to sit back and test the right side of your brain (get it?).

Across

5. The practice of automatically building and testing your code on each commit.
7. This should fail if a test doesn't pass.
8. Instead of running your tests by hand, use ....
10. Coverage tells you how much .... you're actually testing.
11. When white box testing you want to exercise each of these.
12. Ability to be climbed - or support a lot of users.
13. 3 lines of this to 1 line of production isn't crazy.

Down

1. Just slightly outside the valid range, this case can be bad news.
2. All of your functional testing ties back to these.
3. Peeking under the covers a little, you might check out some DB tables when you use this kind of testing.
4. 85% of this and you're doing ok.
6. Continuous integration watches this to know when things change.
7. Test the system like a user and forget how it works inside.
9. You're done when all your ....

Sharpen your pencil Solution

Check off all of the things you should do to get good coverage when testing.

- [x] Test the success cases ("happy paths").
- [x] Test failure cases.
- [x] Stage known input data if your system uses a database so you can test various backend problems.
- [x] Read through the code you're testing.
- [x] Review your requirements and user stories to see what the system is supposed to do.
- [x] Test external failure conditions, like network outages or people shutting down their web browsers.
- [x] Test for security problems like SQL injection or cross-site scripting (XSS).
- [x] Simulate a disk-full condition.
- [x] Simulate high-load scenarios.
- [x] Use different operating systems, platforms, and browsers.

* Depending on your app, all of these are critical to getting good tests. But, if you're using a coverage tool, you can figure out where you might be missing tests on part of your system.

Testcross Solution

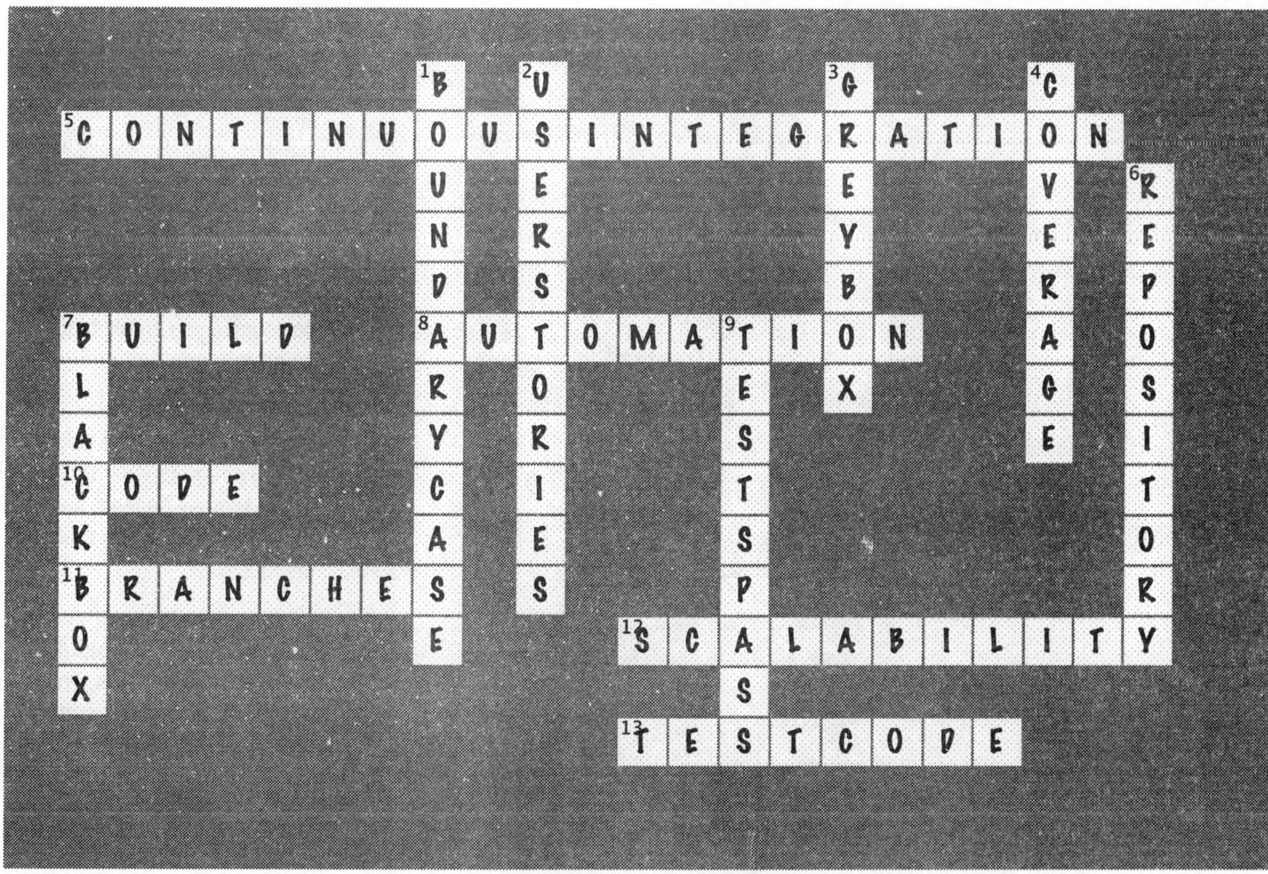

Tools for your Software Development Toolbox

Software Development is all about developing and delivering great software. In this chapter, you learned about several techniques to keep you on track. For a complete list of tools in the book, see Appendix ii.

Development Techniques

There are different views of your system, and you need to test them all

Testing has to account for success cases as well as failure cases

Automate testing whenever possible

Use a continuous integration tool to automate building and testing your code on each commit

Here are some of the key techniques you learned in this chapter...

... and some of the principles behind those techniques.

Development Principles

Testing is a tool to let you know where your project is at all times

Continuous integration gives you confidence that the code in your repository is correct and builds properly

Code coverage is a much better metric of testing effectiveness than test count

BULLET POINTS

- Using **Continuous Integration** tools means something is always watching over the quality of the code in the repository.
- **Automated testing** can be addictive. You still get to write code, so it's fun. And sometimes you break things. Also fun.
- Make the results of your continuous integration builds and coverage reports **public to the team**—the team owns the project and should feel responsible.
- Have your continuous integration tool **fail a build** if an automated test fails. Then have it **email the committer** until they fix it.
- Testing for **overall functionality** is critical to declaring a project as working.

8 test-driven development

Holding your code accountable

Sometimes it's all about setting expectations. Good code needs to work, everyone knows that. But how do **you know your code works**? Even with unit testing, there are still parts of most code that go untested. But what if testing was a **fundamental part of software development**? What if you did ***everything*** with testing in mind? In this chapter, you'll take what you know about version control, CI, and automated testing and tie it all together into an environment where you can feel **confident** about **fixing bugs**, **refactoring**, and even **reimplementing** parts of your system.

Test FIRST, not last

Instead of trying to retrofit testing onto an existing project, let's look at a project from the ground up using a new technique, **test-driven development**, and write your code with testing in mind right from the start.

Starbuzz Coffee has been selling gift cards for several months, but now they need a way to accept those gift cards as payment for their drinks. Starbuzz already knows how their page should look, so your job is to focus on the design and implementation of the gift card ordering system itself.

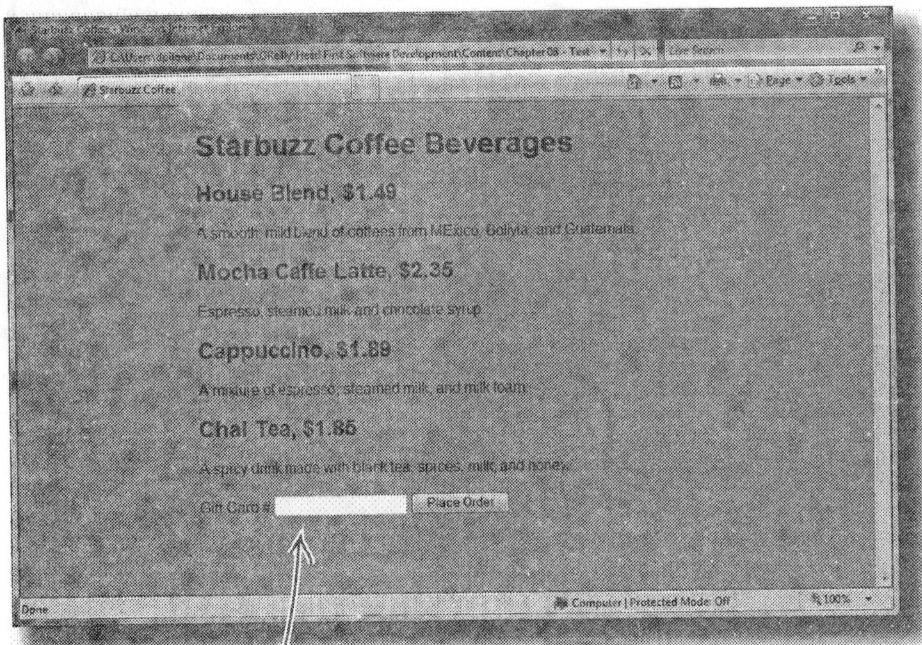

Customers can use a gift card to purchase drinks at the new web kiosks in Starbuzz stores.

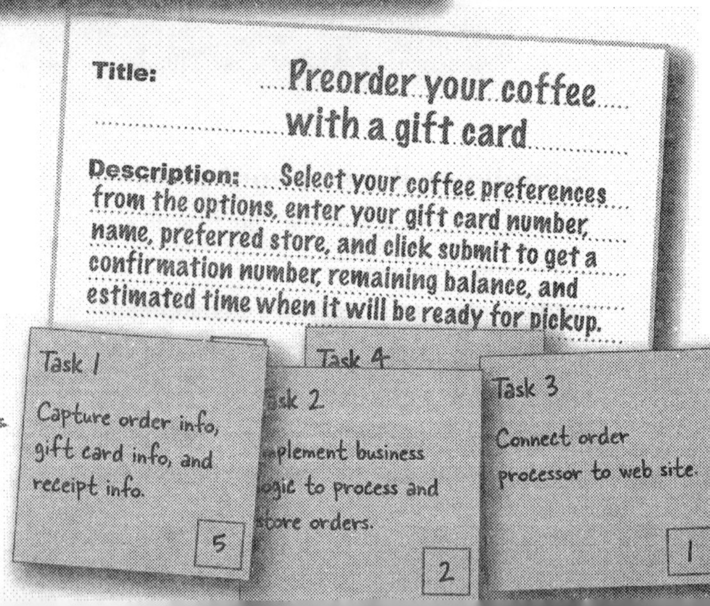

Let's start with this task...

So we're going to test FIRST...

The Starbuzz Gift Cards story is broken down into tasks, so if we're going to test first, we need to begin by looking at our first task, which is capturing information about orders, gift cards, and receipts. Remember, if we jump right into code, we'll end up right back where we did in the last few chapters...

Analyze the task

First break down the task. For this task you'll need to...

Lingo alert: "customer" in these cases refers to shoppers at Starbuzz—in fact, your customer's customer. That's typical language for user stories.

- ☐ **Represent the order information.** You need to capture the customer's name, the drink description, the store number the customer wants to pick up the drink from, and a gift card number.
- ☐ **Represent gift card information.** You need to capture the activation date, the expiration date, and the remaining balance.
- ☐ **Represent receipt information.** You need to capture the confirmation number and the pickup time, as well as the remaining balance on a gift card.

Usually, tasks are just one thing, but the three items in this task are so small, they're easier to treat as a single unit of work.

Write the test BEFORE any other code

We're testing first, remember? That means you have to actually write a test... ***first***. Start with the order information part of the task. Now, using your test framework, you need to write a test for that functionality.

Just like in Chapter 7, you can use any testing framework you want—although an automated framework is easiest to integrate into your version control and CI processes.

Welcome to test-driven development

When you're writing tests before any code, and then letting those tests drive your code, you're using **test-driven development**, or **TDD**. That's just a formal term to describe the process of testing from the outset of development—and writing every line of code specifically as a response to your tests. Turn the page for a lot more on TDD.

Your first test...

The first step in writing a test is to figure out what ***exactly*** it is you should be testing. Since this is testing at a really fine-grained level—**unit testing**—you should start small. What's the ***smallest test you could write*** that uses the order information you've got to store as part of the first task? Well, that's just creating the object itself, right? Here's how to test creating a new `OrderInformation` object:

This is a JUnit test... a single method that tests object creation.

```
package headfirst.sd.chapter8;

import org.junit.*;

public class TestOrderInformation {
  @Test
  public void testCreateOrderInformation() {
    OrderInformation orderInfo = new OrderInformation();
  }
}
```

Keep it as simple as possible: just create a new OrderInformation object.

You're exactly right! We're writing tests ***first***, remember? We have **no code**. There's no way this test could (or should) pass the first time through. In fact, this test won't even compile, and that's OK, too. We'll fix it in a minute. The point here is that at first, your test...

...fails miserably.

Unlike pretty much everything else in life, in TDD **you want your tests to fail when you first write them.** The point of a test is to establish a measurable success—and in this case, that measure is a compiling `OrderInformation` object that you can instantiate. And, because you've got a failing test, now it's clear what you have to do to make sure that test passes.

The first rule of effective test-driven development

Rule #1: Your test should always FAIL before you implement any code.

NOW write code to get the test to pass.

You've got a failing test...but that's OK. Before going any further, either writing more tests or working on the task, ***write the simplest code possible to get just this test to pass***. And right now, the test won't even compile!

```
File Edit Window Help
hfsd> javac -cp junit.jar
          headfirst.sd.chapter8.TestOrderInformation.java
TestOrderInformation.java:8: cannot find symbol
symbol  : class OrderInformation
location: class headfirst.sd.chapter8.TestOrderInformation
    OrderInformation orderInfo = new OrderInformation();
    ^
TestOrderInformation.java:8: cannot find symbol
symbol  : class OrderInformation
location: class headfirst.sd.chapter8.TestOrderInformation
    OrderInformation orderInfo = new OrderInformation();
                                     ^
2 errors

hfsd>
```

Running our first test isn't even possible yet; it fails when you try to compile.

Sharpen your pencil

We have a failing test that we need to get to pass. What's the simplest thing you can do to get this test passing?

....

....

....

Get your tests to GREEN

The only goal you should have at this point is to get your test to pass. So write *just the code you have to* in order for your test to pass; that's called ***getting your tests to green***.

Green refers to the green bar that JUnit's GUI displays when all tests pass. If any test failed, it displays a red bar.

```
public class OrderInformation {


}
```

Here's the UML for the new class. No attributes, no methods—just an empty class.

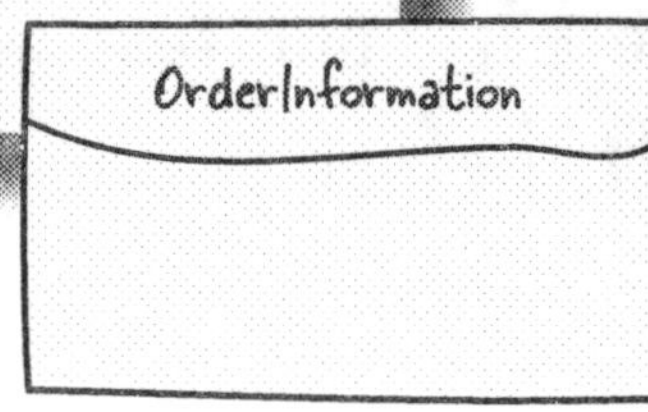

Yes, that's it. An empty class. Now try running your test again:

```
File Edit Window Help Classy
hfsd> javac -d bin -cp junit.jar *.java

hfsd> java -cp junit.jar;.\bin org.junit.runner.
JUnitCore headfirst.sd.chapter8.TestOrderInformation
JUnit version 4.4
.
Time: 0.018

OK (1 test)

hfsd>
```

SUCCESS!

The test compiles now, as does the OrderInformation class.

With this test passing, you're ready to write the next test, still focusing on your first task. That's it—you've just made it through your first round of test-driven development. Remember, the goal was to write just the code you needed to get that test to pass.

Rule #2: Implement the SIMPLEST CODE POSSIBLE to make your tests pass.

Seriously? You made an empty class to get a test to pass and you call that SUCCESS?

Test-driven development is about doing the simplest thing you can to get your test to pass.

Resist the urge to add anything you *might need in the future*. If you need that something later, you'll write a test then and the code to pass that test. In the meantime, leave it alone. Obviously you can't stop here—you need to move on to the next test—but **focusing on small bits of code** is the heart and soul of test-driven development.

This is the YAGNI principle... You Ain't Gonna Need It.

Red, green, refactor...

Test-driven development works on a very simple cycle:

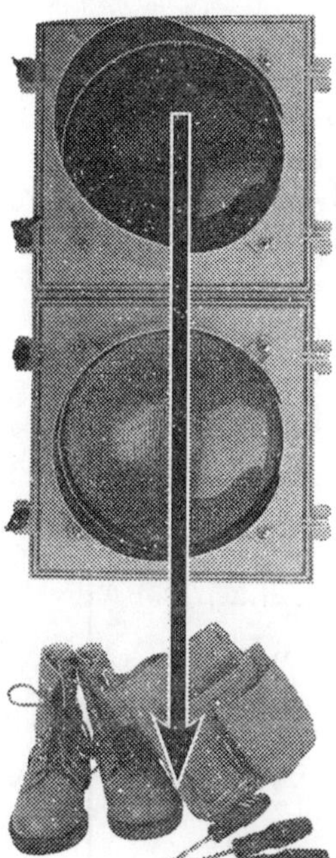

1. **Red: Your test fails.**
   First you write a test that checks whatever functionality you're about to write. Obviously it fails, since you haven't implemented the functionality yet. This is the **red stage**, since your test GUI probably shows the test in red (failing).

2. **Green: Your test passes.**
   Next, implement the functionality to get that test to pass. That's it. No more. Nothing fancy. Write the ***simplest code*** you can to get your test to pass. This is the **green stage**.

3. **Refactor: Clean up any duplication, ugliness, old code, etc.**
   Finally, after your test passes, you can go back in and clean up some things that you may have noticed while implementing your code. This is the **refactor stage**. In the example for Starbuzz, you don't have any other code to refactor, so you can go right on to the next test.

When you're done refactoring, move on to the next test and go through the cycle again.

Exercise

Below is the task we're working on and the user story it came from. Your job is to add the next test to the `TestOrderInformation` class to make progress on this task.

Title: Preorder your coffee with a gift card

Description: Select your coffee preferences from the options, enter your gift card number, name, preferred store, and click submit to get a confirmation number, remaining balance, and estimated time when it will be ready for pickup.

Priority: 20

Task 1

Capture order info, gift card info, and receipt info.

5

You should always look to the story to figure out what you should be testing at a higher, functional level.

For this test you should be focusing on the OrderInformation class. We'll get to the gift card and receipt later.

```
import org.junit.*;

public class TestOrderInformation {
  @Test
  public void testCreateOrderInformationInstance() {
    OrderInformation orderInfo = new OrderInformation();
  }

  @Test
  public void testOrderInformation() {
    ......................................................
    ......................................................
    ......................................................
    ......................................................
    ......................................................
  }
}
```

** If you're not a Java programmer, try and write out the test in the framework you're using, or type it into your IDE.*

Now implement the code to make your test pass. Remember, you just want the simplest code possible to get the test passing.

Here's the OrderInformation class created to pass the first test. You need to fill it out to pass the test you just wrote.

```
public class OrderInformation {

    ............................................................
    ............................................................
    ............................................................
    ............................................................
    ............................................................
    ............................................................
    ............................................................
    ............................................................
    ............................................................
    ............................................................
    ............................................................
    ............................................................
    ............................................................

}
```

OrderInformation

Update the OrderInformation class diagram, too.

Exercise Solution

Below is the task we're working on and the user story it came from. Your job is to add the next test to the `TestOrderInformation` class to make progress on this task.

Title: Preorder your coffee with a gift card

Description: Select your coffee preferences from the options, enter your gift card number, name, preferred store, and click submit to get a confirmation number, remaining balance, and estimated time when it will be ready for pickup.

Priority: 20

Task 1

Capture order info, gift card info, and receipt info.

5

To get the rest of the OrderInformation class together, you need to add coffee preference, gift card number, customer name, and preferred store to the order information.

```
import org.junit.*;

public class TestOrderInformation {
  @Test
  public void testCreateOrderInformationInstance() { // existing test }

  @Test
  public void testOrderInformation() {
   OrderInformation orderInfo = new OrderInfomation();
   orderInfo.setCustomerName("Dan");
   orderInfo.setDrinkDescription("Mocha cappa-latte-with-half-whip-skim-fracino");
   orderInfo.setGiftCardNumber(123456);
   orderInfo.setPreferredStoreNumber(8675309);
   assertEqual(orderInfo.getCustomerName(), "Dan");
   assertEqual(orderInfo.getDrinkDescription(),
     "Mocha cappa-latte-with-half-whip-skim-fracino");
   assertEqual(orderInfo.getGiftCardNumber(), 123456);
   assertEqual(orderInfo.getPreferredStoreNumber(), 8675309);
  }
}
```

Our test simply creates the OrderInformation, sets each value we need to track, and then checks to make sure we get the same values out.

You might want to use constants in your own code, so you don't have any typos beween setting values and checking against the returned values (especially in those long coffee-drink names).

Now implement the code to make your test pass. Remember, you just want the simplest code possible to get the test passing.

```
public class OrderInformation {

  private String customerName;
  private String drinkDescription;
  private int giftCardNumber;
  private int preferredStoreNumber;

  public void setCustomerName(String name) {
    customerName = name;
  }
  public void setDrinkDescription(String desc) {
    drinkDescription = desc;
  }
  public void setGiftCardNumber(int gcNum) {
    giftCardNumber = gcNum;
  }
  public void setPreferredStoreNumber(int num) {
    preferredStoreNumber = num;
  }
  public String getCustomerName() {
    return customerName;
  }
  public String getDrinkDescription() {
    return drinkDescription;
  }
  public int getGiftCardNumber() {
    return giftCardNumber;
  }
  public int getPreferredStoreNumber() {
    return preferredStoreNumber;
  }
}
```

This class is really just a few member variables, and then methods to get and set those variables.

Is there anything less you could do here and still pass the test case?

```
OrderInformation
- customerName : String
- drinkDescription : String
- giftCardNumber : int
- preferredStoreNumber : int
------------------------------------------
+ setCustomerName(name : String)
+ setDrinkDescription(desc : String)
+ setGiftCardNumber(gcNum : int)
+ setPreferredStoreNumber(num : int)
+ getCustomerName() : String
+ getDrinkDescription() : String
+ getGiftCardNumber() : int
+ getPreferredStoreNumber() : int
```

In TDD, tests DRIVE your implementation

Now you've got a working and tested `OrderInformation` class. And, because of the latest test, you've got getters and setters that all work, too. In fact, the things you put in the class were completely driven by your tests.

Test-driven development is different from just *test-first development* in that it drives your implementation ***all the way through development***. By writing your tests before your code, you have to focus on the functionality right away. What exactly is the code you're about to write actually supposed to do?

To help keep your tests manageable and effective, there are some good habits to get into:

1. **Each test should verify ONLY ONE THING**
   To keep your tests straightforward and focused on what you need to implement, try to make each test only test one thing. In the Starbuzz system, each test is a method on our test class. So `testCreateOrderInformation()` is an example of a test that only checks one thing: all it does is test creating a new order object. The next test, which tests multiple methods, still tests only one piece of functionality: that the order stores the right information within it.

2. **AVOID DUPLICATE test code**
   You should try to avoid duplicated test code just like you'd try to avoid duplicated production code. Some testing frameworks have setup and teardown methods that let you consolidate code common to all your tests, and you should use those liberally. You also may need to mock up test objects—we'll talk more about how to do that later in this chapter.

Suppose you need a database connection: you could set that up in your setup() method, and release the connection in your teardown() method of your test framework

3. **Keep your tests in a MIRROR DIRECTORY of your source code**
   Once you start using TDD on your project, you'll write tons of tests. To help keep things organized, keep the tests in a separate directory (usually called `test/`) at the same level as your source directory, and with the same directory structure. This helps avoid problems with languages that assume that directories map to package names (like Java) while keeping your tests cases out of the way of your production code. This also makes things easier on your build files, too; all tests are in one place.

there are no Dumb Questions

Q: If TDD drives my implementation, when do we do design?

A: TDD is usually used with what's called **evolutionary design**. Note that this **doesn't** mean code all you want, and magically you'll end up with a nicely designed system. The critical part of getting to a good design is the refactoring step in TDD. Basically TDD works hard to prevent overdesigning something. As you add functionality to your system, you'll be increasing the code base. After a while you'll see things getting naturally disorganized, so after you get your test to pass, refactor it. Redesign it, apply the appropriate design patterns, whatever it takes. And all along your tests should keep passing and let you know that you haven't broken anything.

Q: What if I need more than one class to implement a piece of functionality?

A: That's fine functionally, but you should really consider adding tests for each class you need to realize the functionality. If you add tests for each class, you'll add a test, implement the code, add a test, etc., and build up your functionality with the red, green, refactor cycle.

Q: The test example we just did had us writing tests for getter and setter methods. I thought we weren't supposed to test those.

A: There's nothing wrong with testing setters and getters; you just don't get much bang for the buck. The setter and getter example was just the beginning. The next few pages really dig into a challenging TDD problem.

Q: So when I implement code to make a particular test pass, I know what the next test I have to write is. Can't I just add the code I'm going to need for that test too?

A: No. There's a couple problems with that approach. First, it's a really slippery slope once you start adding things that are outside of the scope of the test you're trying to get to pass. You might think you need it, but until a test says you do, don't tempt yourself.

The second, and possibly more severe problem is that if you add code now for the next test you're going to write, that second test probably won't fail. Which means you don't know that it's actually testing what you think it is. You can't be sure that it will let you know if the underlying code breaks. Write the test—then implement code for that test.

Test-driven development is all about creating tests for specific functionality, and then writing code to satisfy that functionality.

Anything beyond that functionality is NOT IMPORTANT to your software (right now).

Exercise

Finish up the remaining work on the current Starbuzz task by writing tests and then the implementation for the gift card and receipt objects.

We've left the answers out on this one...it's up to you to write these tests on your own.

Completing a task means you've got all the tests you need, and they all pass

To finish up the first task, you'll need to be able to test that order, gift card, and receipt information can be captured and accessed. You should have created objects for all three of these items. Here's how we implemented each object...

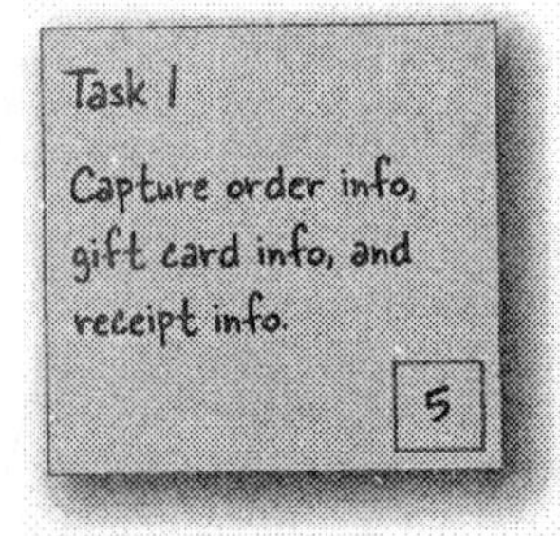

When your tests pass, move on!

The first task is complete and we have `Receipt`, `GiftCard`, and `OrderInformation` classes written and tested. Now it's time to try our TDD approach on a tougher task: implementing the business logic to process and store orders.

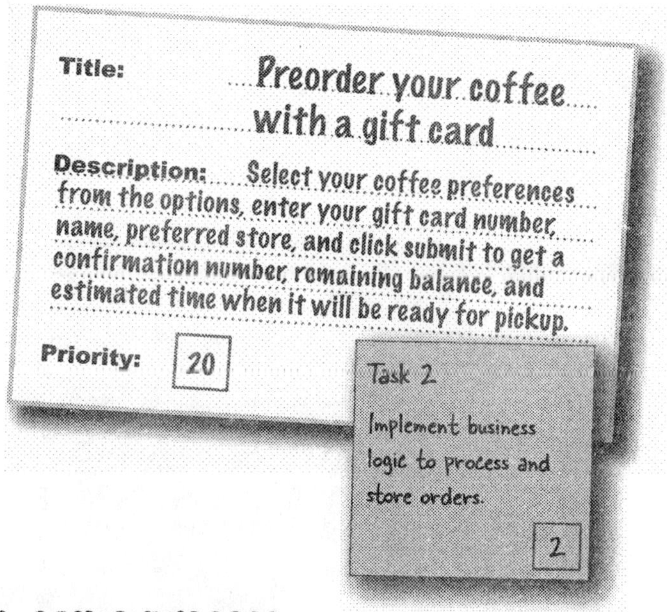

Different task, same process

This task is no different than the last one. We'll just follow the same approach. Write a test that fails, implement the code to get the test passing, perform any cleanup, and then repeat.

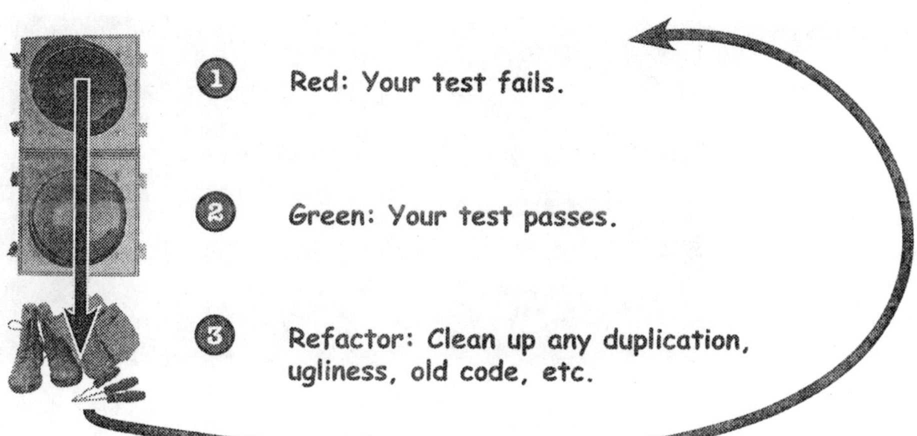

Red: write (failing) tests

The first step is to write a test. The user story says we need to process and store order information, so let's assume we'll need a new class for that, called `OrderProcessor`:

```
import org.junit.*;

public class TestOrderProcessor {
  @Test
  public void testCreateOrderProcessor() {
    OrderProcessor orderProcessor = new OrderProcessor();
  }
}
```

There's nothing special about the name OrderProcessor. It's just a place to put business logic, since the only other classes in the app are for storing data.

```
File Edit Window Help Failure
hfsd> javac -cp junit.jar
      headfirst.sd.chapter8.TestOrderProcessor.java

TestOrderProcessor.java:8: cannot find symbol
symbol  : class OrderProcessor
location: class headfirst.sd.chapter8.TestOrderProcessor
    OrderProcessor orderProcessor = new OrderProcessor();
    ^
TestOrderProcessor.java:8: cannot find symbol
symbol  : class OrderProcessor
location: class headfirst.sd.chapter8.TestOrderProcessor
    OrderProcessor orderProcessor = new OrderProcessor();
                                        ^

2 errors

hfsd>
```

As you would expect, this test will fail—you don't have an `OrderProcessor` yet. So now you can fix that pretty easily.

This test doesn't even compile, let alone pass.

Green: write code to pass tests

To get your first test to pass, just add an empty `OrderProcessor` class:

```
public class OrderProcessor {
}
```

Green: test compiles and passes.

```
File Edit Window Help Success
hfsd> javac -d bin -cp junit.jar *.java


hfsd> java -cp junit.jar;.\bin org.junit.runner.
JUnitCore headfirst.sd.chapter8.TestOrderProcessor
JUnit version 4.4

Time: 0.018
OK (1 test)

hfsd>
```

That's it. Recompile, retest, and you're back to green. The user story says you need to process and store order information. You've already got classes that represent order information (and a receipt), so use those now along with the `OrderProcessor` class that you just created.

Red

Below is a new test method. Implement a test that will verify your software can process a simple order.

You'll need to put the pieces together to describe the order...

...and then pass it on to the order processor and make sure it worked.

```
// other tests

@Test
public void testSimpleOrder() {
  OrderProcessor orderProcessor = new OrderProcessor();
  ..........................................................
  ..........................................................
  ..........................................................
  ..........................................................
  ..........................................................
  ..........................................................
  ..........................................................
  ..........................................................
  ..........................................................
  ..........................................................
  ..........................................................
  ..........................................................
  ..........................................................
  ..........................................................
  ..........................................................
}
```

Don't forget about your classes from the last task.

OrderInformation

- customerName : String
- drinkDescription : String
- giftCardNumber : int
- preferredStoreNumber : int

+ setCustomerName(name : String)
+ setDrinkDescription(desc : String)
+ setGiftCardNumber(gcNum : int)
+ setPreferredStoreNumber(num : int)
+ getCustomerName() : String
+ getDrinkDescription() : String
+ getGiftCardNumber() : int
+ getPreferredStoreNumber() : int

Receipt

- confirmationNumber : int
- pickupTime : Date
- gcBalance : BigDecimal

+ setConfirmationNumber(no : int)
+ setPickupTime(date : Date)
+ setGCBalance(bal : BigDecimal)
+ getConfirmationNumber() : int
+ getPickupTime() : Date
+ getGCBalance() : BigDecimal

GiftCard

- activationDate : Date
- expirationDate : Date
- balance : BigDecimal

+ getActivationDate() : Date
+ getExpirationDate() : Date
+ getBalance() : BigDecimal
+ setBalance(BigDecimal) : void
+ equals(object : Object) : boolean

Exercise Solution

Red

Your job was to implement a test that will verify your software can process a simple order.

```
// existing tests

@Test
public void testSimpleOrder() {

    // First create the order processor
    OrderProcessor orderProcessor = new OrderProcessor();

    // Then you need to describe the order that should be placed
    OrderInformation orderInfo = new OrderInformation();
    orderInfo.setCustomerName("Dan");
    orderInfo.setDrinkDescription("Bold with room");
    orderInfo.setGiftCardNumber(12345);
    orderInfo.setPreferredStoreNumber(123);

    // Hand the order off to the order processor and check the receipt
    Receipt receipt = orderProcessor.processOrder(orderInfo);
    assertNotNull(receipt.getPickupTime());
    assertTrue(receipt.getConfirmationNumber() > 0);
    assertTrue(receipt.getGCBalance().equals(0));

}
```

You can just make up a gift card number here...

The simplest thing here is to not worry about the balance on the card... this is just testing the simplest version of order processing.

there are no Dumb Questions

Q: How can you just assume that the gift card has the right amount on it? Isn't that an assumption? Aren't those bad?

A: We're writing our first test, and then we need to make it pass. So, we're sort of assuming that the gift card has enough on it, but since we're about to implement the backend code, we can make sure it does then. What we are setting ourselves up for is some refactoring. Once we get this test passing we'll obviously need to add a test for a gift card that doesn't have enough money on it. When we do that, we'll certainly have to revisit the code we wrote to get this test going and rework it to support different gift cards and different values. But, this is going to take some thought. Read on...

Q: There are a bunch of values in that test that aren't constants—should I care?

A: Yes, you should. To keep the code sample short we didn't pull those values into constants, but you should treat your test code just like production code you write and apply the same style and discipline. Remember, this isn't throwaway code; it lives in the repository with the rest of your system, and you rely on it to let you know if things aren't working right. Treat it with respect.

Simplicity means avoiding dependencies

Let's add a `processOrder()` method to `OrderProcessor`, since that's what our latest test needs to pass. The method should return a `Receipt` object, like this:

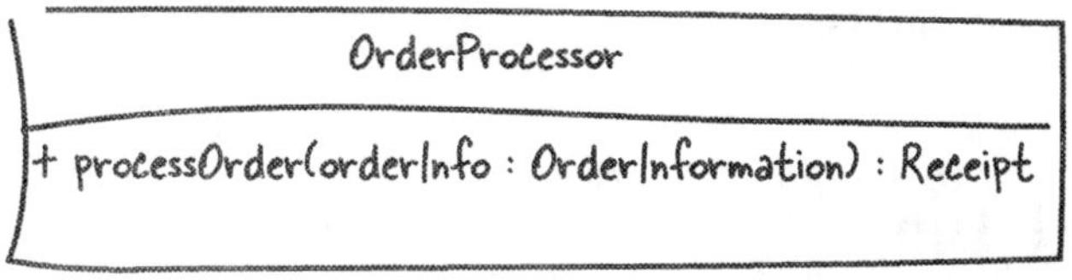

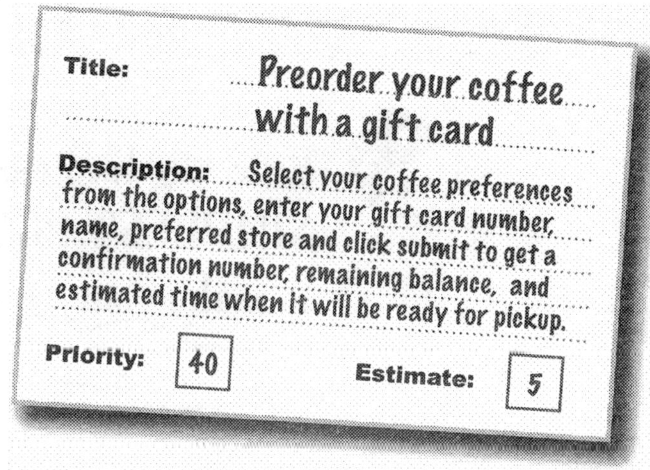

But here's where things get tricky: `processOrder()` needs to connect to the Starbuzz database. Here's the task that involves that piece of the system's functionality:

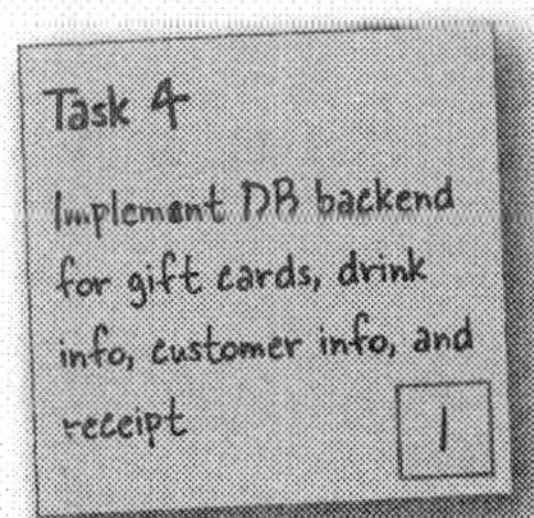

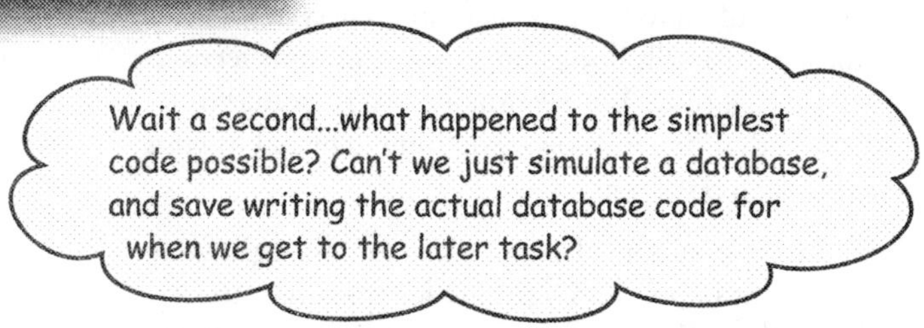

Dependencies make your code more complex, but the point of TDD is to keep things as simple as possible.

You've got to have `processOrder()` talk to a database, but the database access code is part of another task you haven't dealt with yet.

On top of that, is the simplest code possible to get this test to pass really to write database-access code?

What would you do in this situation?

Always write testable code

When you first start practicing TDD, you will often find yourself in situations where the code you want to test seems to depend on everything else in your project. This can often be a maintenance problem later on, but it's a huge problem ***right now*** when it comes to TDD. Remember our rules? We really don't want that "simplest thing" to be "an order processor with a database connection, four tables, and a full-time DBA."

Rule #2: Implement the SIMPLEST CODE POSSIBLE to make your tests pass.

And our problem is that the code for this task is all tied up with other tasks, and with database code, right?

All real-world code has dependencies

When you only have basic classes in your system, it's not too hard to split things up so you can test pieces one thing at a time. But eventually, you're going to have code that depends on something external to your system, like a database.

This can show up lots of other ways too, though: your system might depend on a network connection to send or receive data, or you might need to read data from files that are created by another application, or you might need to use a sound API to generate annoying thumps and beeps. In all of these cases, the dependencies make it hard to test one thing at a time.

Hmmm...like a Java-based chat client with BeatBox capabilities?

But that doesn't mean you don't have to test. It just means you have to figure out a way to test things ***independent*** of all those dependencies.

When things get hard to test, examine your design

One of the first things you can do to remove dependencies is to see if you can remove the dependencies. Take a look at your design, and see if you really need everything to be as ***tightly coupled***—or interdependent—as your current design calls for. In the case of Starbuzz, here's what we've assumed so far:

What we have...

The order processor has to fetch gift cards from the database, check the order, save it, and update the gift card (again in the database). So `processOrder()` is hardwired to connect to the database...and that's what makes testing the method tricky.

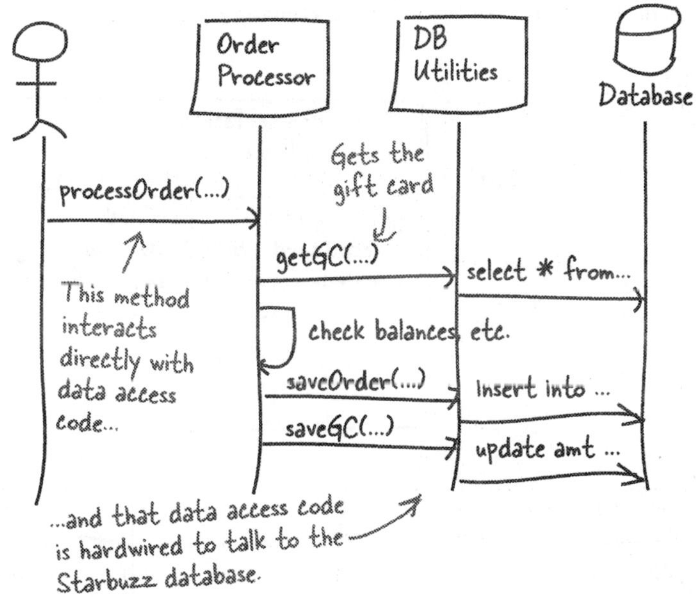

What we need...

How can we have `processOrder()` make the same calls, but avoid database access code? We need a way to get data ***without*** requiring a database—it's almost like we need a fake data access layer.

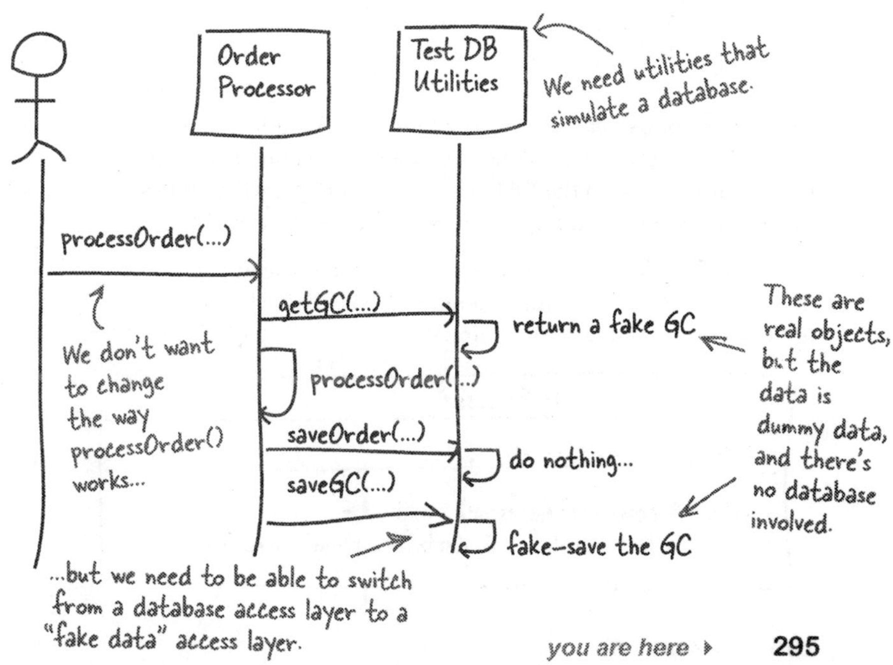

The strategy pattern provides for multiple implementations of a single interface

We want to hide how the system gets gift cards, and vary it depending on whether we're testing the code or we're running the system in production. Flip to Chapter 1 of *Head First Design Patterns* and you'll find there's a ready made pattern to help us deal with just this problem: the **strategy pattern**.

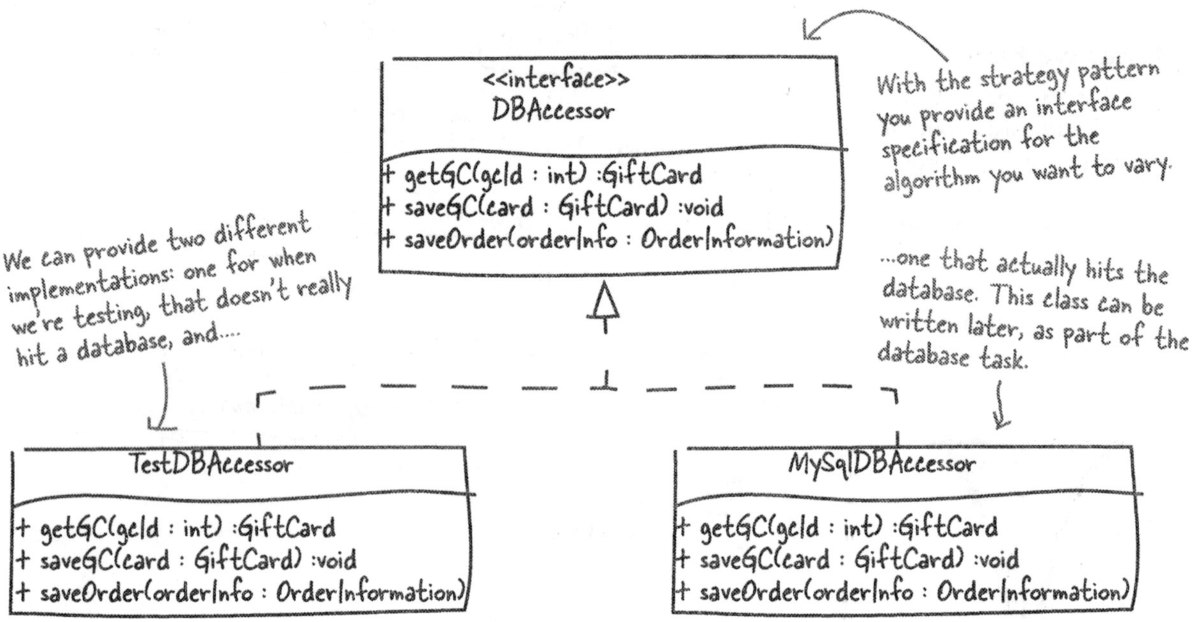

* If your customer was unsure about what database they might use in production, this same approach would make it easy to swap out database vendors and implementations.

Now we've got two *different* ways of hitting the database, and `OrderProcessor` doesn't need to know which one it's using. Instead, it just talks to the `DBAccessor` interface, which hides the details about which implementation is actually used.

All we need to do now is add a way to give the OrderProcessor the correct DBAccessor implementation, based on whether the test code or the system is providing it.

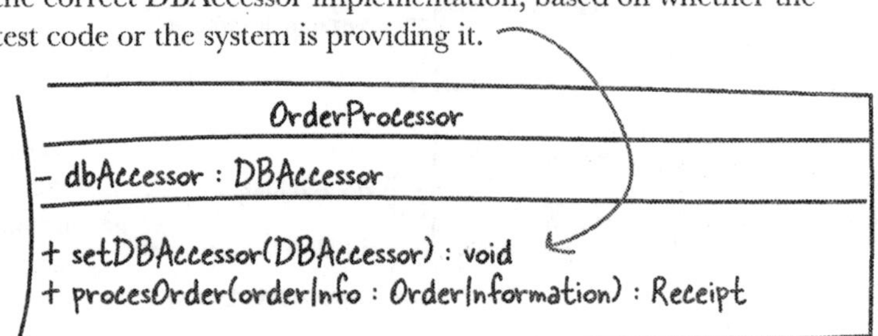

The strategy pattern encapsulates a family of algorithms and makes them interchangeable.

Exercise

Getting to Green... again

Now you've got a way to isolate the OrderProcessor class from the database. Implement the processOrder() method using the right database strategy.

```
// existing code

private DBAccessor mDBAccessor;
public void setDBAccessor(DBAccessor accessor) {
  dbAccessor = accessor;
}
public Receipt processOrder(OrderInformation orderInfo) {
  .................................................................
  .................................................................
  .................................................................
  .................................................................
  .................................................................
  .................................................................
  .................................................................
  .................................................................
  .................................................................
  .................................................................
  .................................................................
  .................................................................
  .................................................................

 } ................................................................
}
```

This allows the right database accessor to be set for order processing.

You'll need to pull the gift card from the database

...save the order...

...then save the updated gift card back out.

OrderInformation
- − customerName: : String
- − drinkDescription : String
- − giftCardNumber : int
- − preferredStoreNumber : int

- + setCustomerName(name : String)
- + setDrinkDescription(desc : String)
- + setGiftCardNumber(gcNum : int)
- + setPreferredStoreNumber(num : int)
- + getCustomerName() : String
- + getDrinkDescription() : String
- + getGiftCardNumber() : int
- + getPreferredStoreNumber() : int

Receipt
- − confirmationNumber : int
- − pickupTime : Date
- − gcBalance : BigDecimal

- + setConfirmationNumber(no : int)
- + setPickupTime(date : Date)
- + setGCBalance(bal : BigDecimal)
- + getConfirmationNumber() : int
- + getPickupTime() : Date
- + getGCBalance() : BigDecimal

GiftCard
- − activationDate : Date
- − expirationDate : Date
- − balance : BigDecimal

- + getActivationDate() : Date
- + getExpirationDate() : Date
- + getBalance() : BigDecimal
- + setBalance(BigDecimal) : void
- + equals(object : Object) :boolean

Getting to Green...again.

Now you've got a way to isolate the OrderProcessor class from the database. Implement the processOrder() method using the right database strategy.

```
// existing code

private DBAccessor dbAccessor;
public void setDBAccessor(DBAccessor accessor) {
  mDBAccessor = accessor;
}
public Receipt processOrder(OrderInformation orderInfo) {

  GiftCard gc = dbAccessor.getGC(orderInfo.getGiftCardNumber());
  dbAccessor.saveOrder(orderInfo);

  // This is what our test is expecting
  gc.setBalance(new BigDecimal(0));

  dbAccessor.saveGC(gc);

  Receipt receipt = new Receipt();
  receipt.setConfirmationNumber(12345);
  receipt.setPickupTime(new Date());
  receipt.setGCBalance(gc.getBalance());

  return receipt;

 }
}
```

Remember, as long as you're using the test DBAccessor this is just a placeholder.

The test wants a zero-balance gift card at the end. So we simulate that.

Remember, this is just the code needed to get our test passing; it's OK that we're going to have to revisit this code for the next test.

Hmm, this isn't good; this is what the test wants but we're obviously going to have to revisit this. We'll need another test.

there are no Dumb Questions

Q: I just don't buy it. We just wrote a bunch of code that we know is wrong. How is this helping me?

A: The test we wrote is valid—we need that test to work. The code we wrote makes that test work so we can move on to the next one. That's the principle behind TDD—just like we broke stories into tasks to get small pieces, we're breaking our functionality into small code pieces. It didn't take long to write the code to get the first test to pass and it won't take long to refactor it to get the second one to pass, or the third. When you're finished you'll have a set of tests that makes sure the system does what it needs to, and you won't have any more code than necessary to do it.

Keep your test code with your tests

All that's left is to write up an implementation of `DBAccessor` for the `processOrder()` method to use, and finish the `testSimpleOrder()` test method. But the test implementation of `DBAccessor` is really only used for tests, so it belongs with your testing classes, ***not*** in your production code:

```
public class TestOrderProcessing {
  // other tests

  public class TestAccessor implements DBAccessor {
    public GiftCard getGC(int gcId) {
      GiftCard gc = new GiftCard();
      gc.setActivationDate(new Date());
      gc.setExpirationDate(new Date());
      gc.setBalance(new BigDecimal(100));
    }
    // ... the other DBAccessor methods go here...
  }

  @Test
  public void testSimpleOrder() {
    // First create the order processor
    OrderProcessor orderProcessor = new OrderProcessor();
    orderProcessor.setDBAccessor(new TestAccessor());

    // Then we need to describe the order we're about to place
    OrderInformation orderInfo = new OrderInformation();
    orderInfo.setCustomerName("Dan");
    orderInfo.setDrinkDescription("Bold with room");
    orderInfo.setGiftCardNumber(12345);
    orderInfo.setPreferredStoreNumber(123);


    // Hand it off to the order processor and check the receipt
    Receipt receipt = orderProcessor.processOrder(orderInfo);
    assertNotNull(receipt.getPickupTime());
    assertTrue(receipt.getConfirmationNumber() > 0);
    assertTrue(receipt.getGCBalance().equals(0));
  }
}
```

All this code is in our test class, which is in a separate directory from production code.

Here's a simple DBAccessor implementation that returns the values we want.

Since this is only used for testing, it's defined <u>inside</u> our test class.

Set the OrderProcessor object to use the test implementation for database access—which means no real database access at all.

With the testing database accessor, we can test this method, even without hitting a live database.

Remember, this was all about the simplest code possible to return the expected values here.

Testing produces better code

We've been working on testing, but writing tests first has done more than just test our system. It's caused us to organize code better, keeping production code in one place, and everything else in another. We've also written simpler code—and although not everything in the system works yet, the parts that do are streamlined, without anything that's not absolutely required.

And, because of the tight coupling between our system's business logic and database code, we implemented a design pattern, the strategy pattern. Not only does this make testing easier, it decouples our code, and even makes it easy to work with different types of databases.

So testing first has gotten us a lot of things:

- ☑ **Well-organized code.** Production code is in one place; testing code is in another. Even implementations of our database access code used for testing are separate from production code.
- ☑ **Code that always does the same thing.** Lots of approaches to testing result in code that does one thing in testing, but another in production (ever seen an `if (debug)` statement?). TDD means writing production code, all the time.
- ☑ **Loosely coupled code.** Tightly coupled systems are brittle and difficult to maintain, not to mention really, really hard to test. Because we wanted to test our code, we ended up breaking our design into a loosely coupled, more flexible system.

Our test uses a testing-specific implementation of DBAccessor, but the order processor runs the same code, because of our strategy pattern, in testing or in production.

Ever heard your computer science professor or lead architect talking about low coupling and high cohesion? This is what they were talking about. We have low coupling because of our use of interfaces and the strategy pattern, and we've got high cohesion by having our database and business logic code concentrated into separate but well defined classes.

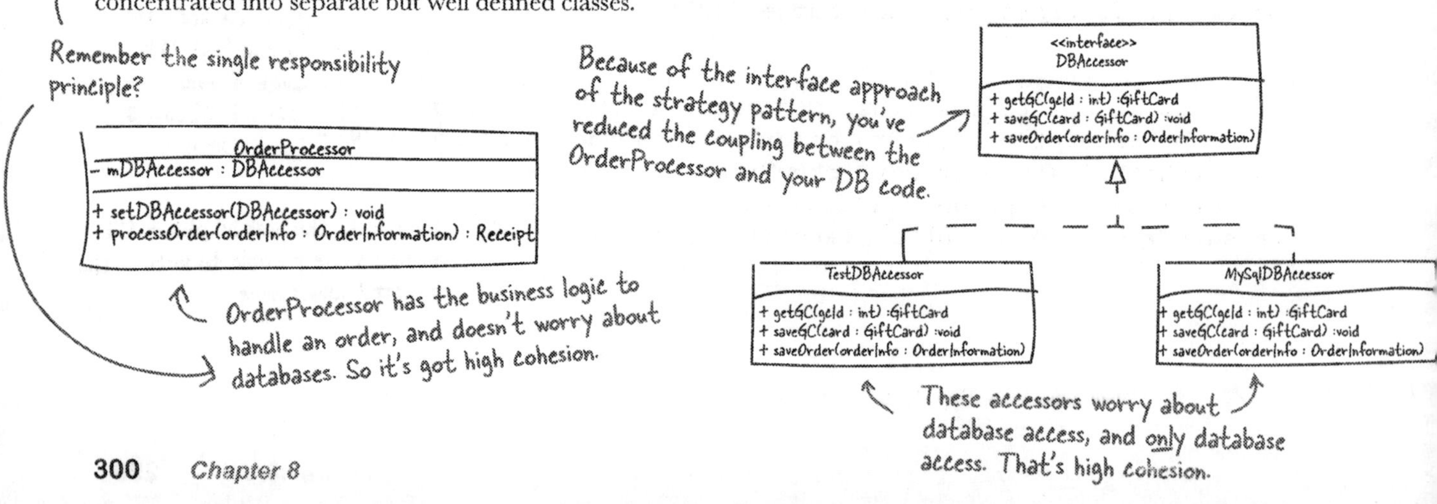

Are you kidding me? Did you look at that code we just wrote? We never once look at the expiration date on a gift card, and we always set the balance to 0. How can you call this ***better code***?

Your code may be incomplete, but it's still in better shape.

Remember the second rule of test-driven development?

Rule #2: Implement the SIMPLEST CODE POSSIBLE to make your tests pass.

Even though not everything works, the code that we do have works, is testable, and is slim and uncluttered. However, it's pretty clear that we still have lots of work left. The goal is getting everything else working and keeping any additional code just as high-quality as what you've got so far.

So once you get your basic tests, start thinking about what else you need to test...which will motivate the next piece of functionality to write code for. Sometimes it's obvious what to test next, like adding a test to deal with gift card balances. Other times, the user story might detail additional functionality to work on. And once all that's done, think about things like testing for boundary conditions, passing in invalid values, scalability tests, etc.

All of this...testing for functionality, edge cases, and hokey implementations, adds up to a complete testing approach.

BRAIN POWER

We've implemented the basic success-case test for processing an order, but there are clearly problems with our implementation. Write another test that finds one of those problems, and then write code to get the test to pass.

More tests always means lots more code

The gift card class for Starbuzz has four attributes, so we're going to need several tests to exercise those attributes. We could test for:

- ☐ A gift card with more than enough to cover the cost of the order
- ☐ A gift card without enough to cover the cost of the order
- ☐ An invalid gift card number
- ☐ A gift card with exactly the right amount
- ☐ A gift card that hasn't been activated
- ☐ A gift card that's expired

In each case, we need a gift card object with a slightly different set of values, so we can test each variation in our order processing class.

And that's just for the gift cards. You'll need tests for variations on the `OrderInformation` class, too...and we still haven't tested for the bigger failure cases, like what happens if the database fails to save an order.

Automated test-driven development means a LOT of test code.

The more functionality you have, the more tests you'll need. And more tests means more code... lots and lots of code. But all that code also means a lot more stability. You'll know your system is working, at every step of the way.

And sometimes, you may not need quite as much code as you first thought...

Strategy patterns, loose couplings, object stand ins...

Suppose we used the strategy pattern again for all the different variations on the types of gift card a database could return, like this:

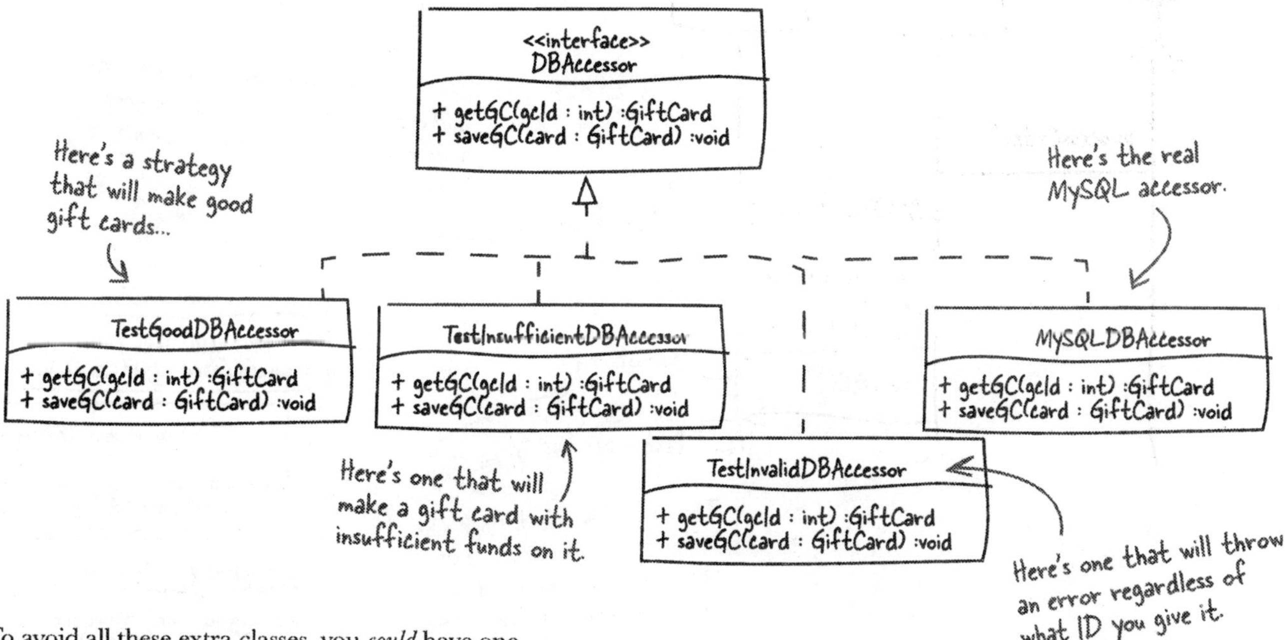

To avoid all these extra classes, you *could* have one `TestDBAccessor` implementation that returned different cards based on the ID you gave it, but that's screwing up loose coupling. `TestDBAccessor` would have to be in sync with your test code to make sure they agree on what each ID means.

We need lots of different, but similar, objects

The problem right now is that we have a sequence like this:

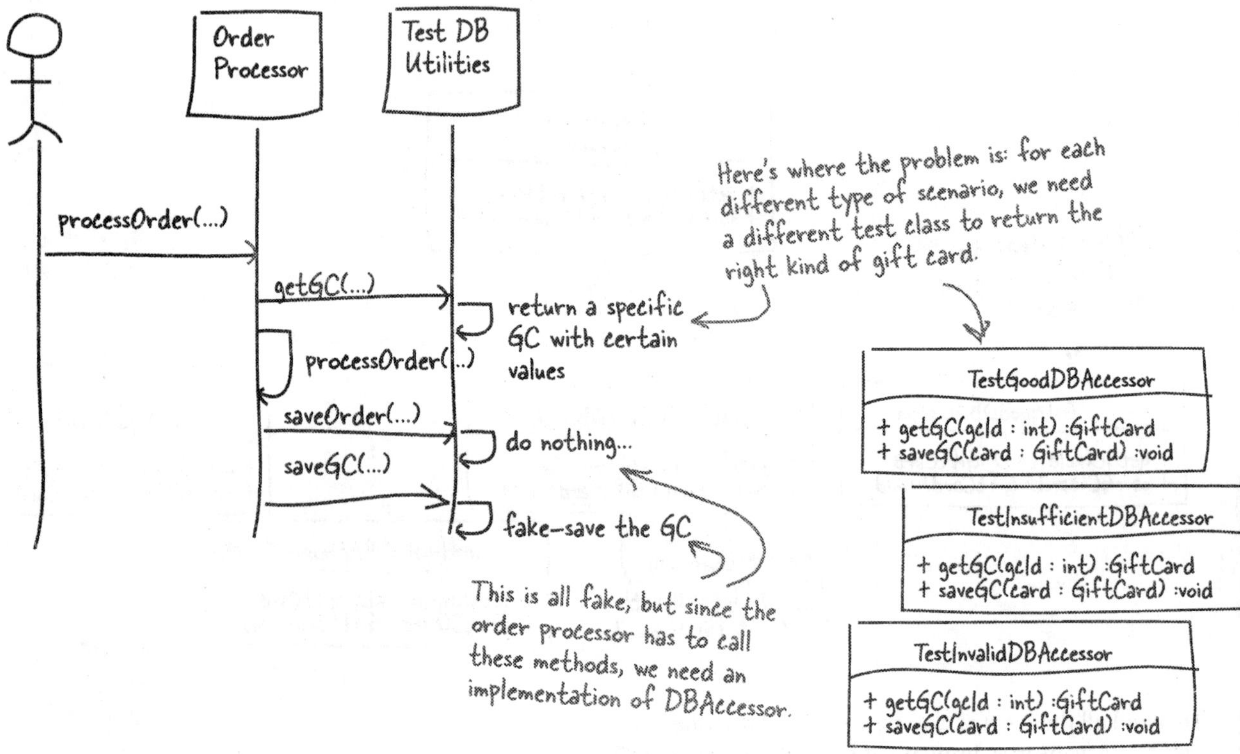

What if we generated objects?

Instead of writing all these `DBAccessor` implementations, what if we had a tool—or a framework—that we could tell to create a new object, conforming to a certain interface (like `DBAccessor`), and that would behave in a certain way, like returning a gift card with a zero balance provided a certain input was passed in?

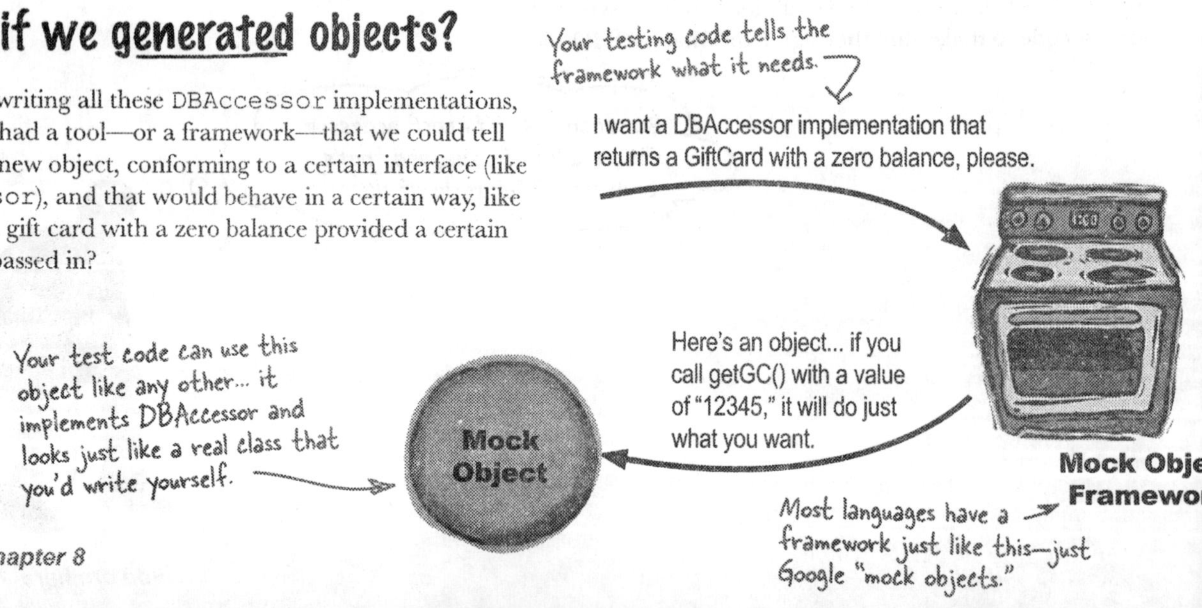

A mock object stands in for real objects

There's really no need for three different accessors, all of which create a new `GiftCard` object and populate it with different data. That's a lot of extra code to instantiate a `GiftCard` and call some setter methods.

Since we have an interface that describes what each of these implementations should look like, we can take advantage of a **mock object framework** to do the heavy lifting. Instead of implementing all of the classes ourselves, we can give the framework the interface we want implemented and then tell it what we expect to happen.

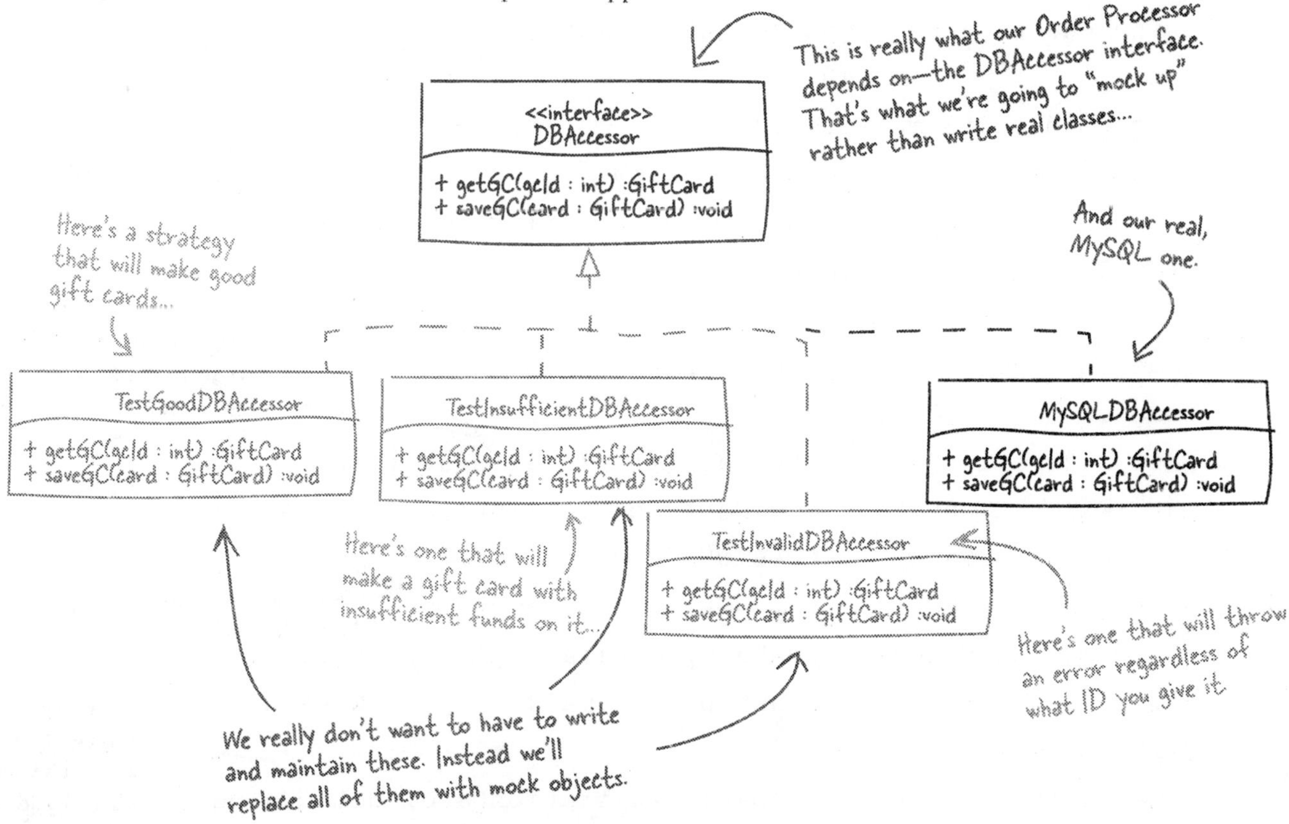

The mock framework will handle creating implementations of the interface and keeping track of what methods we say should be called, what they should return when they are called, what shouldn't be called, etc. The mock framework's implementation of our interface will track all of this and throw an error if something doesn't go according to the plan we gave it.

* We're going to use the EasyMock framework here but a mock object framework exists for most languages and they all work similarly.

Mock objects are working object stand-ins

Let's look at a mock object framework in action. Below is a test that uses the EasyMock framework, a mock object framework for Java. A good mock object framework allows you to **simulate an object's behavior**, without writing code for that object.

```
import org.easymock.*;
// This test will test placing an order with a valid gift card
// with exactly the right amount of money on it.
@Test
public void testSimpleOrder() {
  // Set everything up and get ready
  OrderInformation orderInfo = new OrderInformation();
  orderInfo.setCustomerName("Dan");
  orderInfo.setDrinkDescription("Bold with room");
  orderInfo.setGiftCardNumber(12345);
  orderInfo.setPreferredStoreNumber(123);
  Date activationDate = new Date(); // Valid starting today
  Date exipirationDate = new Date(activationDate.getTime() + 3600);
  BigDecimal gcValue = new BigDecimal("2.75"); // Exactly enough
  GiftCard startGC =
    new GiftCard(activationDate, expirationDate, gcValue);
  BigDecimal gcEndValue = new BigDecimal("0"); // Nothing left
  GiftCard endGC =
    new GiftCard(activationDate, expirationDate, gcEndValue);

  // Here's where the mock object creation happens
  DBAccessor mockAccessor = EasyMock.createMock(DBAccessor.class);
```

Whatever framework you use, you'll need to import the right classes.

This is all part of the test orderInfo object we want to use.

This sets up test values that we'll use in the GiftCard we're testing.

This is all "normal" test code... no mock objects involved yet.

We need a gift card representing the starting values we're testing...

...and then an "ending" gift card. This has what should be returned from testing order processing.

We want an object that implements this interface...

...so we tell our framework to create a mock object that implements the right interface.

At this point, the mock object framework doesn't know much—just that it has to create a stand-in for the DBAccessor class. So it knows the methods it "mocks", but nothing more than that—no behavior yet at all.

Once you create a mock object, it's in "record mode." That means you tell it what to expect and what to do...so when you put it in replay mode, and your tests use it, you've set up exactly what the mock object should do.

Remember, you haven't had to write your own class... that's the big win here.

```
  // Tell our test framework what to call, and what to expect
  EasyMock.expect(mockAccessor.getGC(12345)).andReturn(startGC);
```

First, expect a call to getGC() with the value 12345... that matches up with the orderInfo object we created over here.

When getGC() is called with that value, return the startGC object... this simulates getting a card from the database, and we've supplied the exact values we want for this test scenario.

```
  // Simulate processing an order
  mockAccessor.saveOrder(orderInfo);
```

This doesn't do anything...but it tells the mock object that you should have saveOrder() called, with orderInfo as the parameter. Otherwise, something's gone wrong, and it should throw an exception.

```
  // Then the processor should call saveGC(...) with an empty GC
  mockAccessor.saveGC(endGC);
```

Then, the mock object should have saveGC() called on it, with the endGC gift card simulating the right amount of money being spent. If this isn't called, with these values, then the test should fail.

```
  // And nothing else should get called on our mock.
  EasyMock.replay(mockAccessor);
```

Calling replay() tells the mock object framework "OK, something is going to replay these activities, so get ready."

This is like activating the object; it's ready to be used now.

```
  // Create an OrderProcessor...
  OrderProcessor processor = new OrderProcessor();
  processor.setDBAccessor(mockAccessor);
  Receipt rpt = processor.processOrder(orderInfo);

  // Validate receipt...
}
```

And here's where we use the mock object as a stand-in for a DBAccessor implementation: we test order processing, never having to write a custom implementation for this particular test case (or for any of the other specific test cases we need to check out).

This might seem like a good bit of work here, but we've saved one class. Add in all the other variations of testing for specific gift card things, and you'll save lots of classes...and that's a big deal.

there are no Dumb Questions

Q: These mock objects don't seem to be doing anything I couldn't do myself. What are they buying me again?

A: Mock objects give you a way to create custom implementations of interfaces without needing to actually write the code. Just look at page 303. We needed three different variations of gift cards (if you count the testInvalidGiftCard one). Two of them had different behavior, not just different values. Without the mock objects we'd have to implement that code ourselves. You could do it, but why?

Q: Why didn't we use mock objects for the gift cards themselves?

A: Well, two reasons. First, we'd have to introduce an interface for the gift cards. Since we don't have any behavioral variations it really doesn't make a lot of sense to put an interface here. Second, all we're really changing are the values it returns since it's pretty much a simple data object anyway. We can get that same result by just instantiating a couple different gift cards at the beginning of our test and set them to have the values we want. Mock objects (and the required interface) would be overkill here.

Q: Speaking of interfaces, doesn't this mean I'll need an interface at any point I'd want a mock object in my tests?

A: Yes—and truthfully sometimes you end up putting interfaces in places that you really don't ever intend on having more than one implementation. It's not ideal, but as long as you're aware that you're adding the interface strictly for testing it's not usually a big deal. Generally the value you get from being able to unit-test effectively with less test code makes it worth the trade-off.

Q: What's that replay(...) method all about?

A: That's how you tell the mock object that you're done telling it what's about to happen. Once you call replay on the mock object it will verify any method calls it gets after that. If it gets calls it wasn't expecting, in a different order, or with different arguments, it will throw an exception (and thereby fail your test).

Q: What about arguments...you say they're compared with Java's equals( ) method?

A: Right—EasyMock tests the arguments the mock object gets during execution against the ones you said it should get by using the `equals()` method. This means you need to provide an `equals()` method on classes you use for arguments to methods. There are other comparison operators to help you deal with things like arrays where the reference value is actually compared. Check out the EasyMock docs (*www.easymock.org/Documentation*) for more details.

Q: So we changed our design a pretty good bit to get all this testing stuff going. The design feels.. upside-down. We're telling the OrderProcessor how to talk to the database now...

A: Yes, we are. This pattern is called **dependency injection**, and it shows up in a lot of frameworks. Specifically the Spring Framework is built on the concepts of dependency injection and inversion of control. In general, dependency injection really supports testing—particularly in cases where you need to hide something ugly like a database or the network. It's all about dependency management and limiting how much of the system you need to be concerned about for any given test.

Q: So do you need dependency injection to do good testing or mock objects?

A: No. You could do a lot of what we did with the `DBAccessor` by using a factory pattern that can create different kinds of `DBAccessors`. However, some people feel that dependency injection just feels cleaner. It does have an impact on your design, and it does often mean adding an interface where you might not have put one before, but those typically aren't the parts of your design that cause problems; it's usually that part of the code that no one bothered to look at because time was getting tight and the project had to ship.

Good software is testable...

There are lots of things to think about when designing software: reusability, clean APIs, design patterns, etc. Equally important is to think about your code's testability. We've talked about a few measures of testability like well-factored code and code coverage. However, don't forget that just because you have JUnit running on every commit that your code isn't guaranteed to be good.

There are a few testing bad habits you need to watch out for:

A whole-lotta-nuthin'

If you're new to test driven development it's very easy to write a whole lot of test code but not really test anything. For example, you could write a test that places a Starbuzz order but never checks the gift card value or receipt after the order is placed "Didn't throw an exception? Good to go." That's a lot like saying "it compiles—ship it."

It's still me...

In an overeager attempt to validate data it's easy to go crazy testing fake data you fed into the system initially and miss the actual code you need to test. For example, suppose you write a test that checks that the gift card value and expiration date are correct when you call `getGC()` ... on our `TestDBAccessor`. This is a simplistic example but if you're traversing a few layers of code with your test, it's not too hard to forget that you put the value you're about to test in there in the first place.

Ghosts from the past

You need to be extremely careful that your system is in a known state every time your automated tests kick off. If you don't have an established pattern for how to write your tests (like rolling back database transactions at the end of each test) it's very easy to leave scraps of test results laying around in the system. Even worse is writing other tests that **rely** on these scraps being there. For example, imagine if our end-to-end testing placed an order, and then a subsequent test used the same gift card to test the "insufficient funds" test. What happens the second time this pair of tests execute? What if someone just reruns the second test? Each test should execute from a known, restorable state.

There are a lot of ways to write bad tests—these are just a few of them. Pick your search engine of choice and do a search for "TDD antipatterns" to find a whole lot more. Don't let the possibility of bad tests scare you off, though—just like everything else, the more tests you write the better you'll get at it!

It's not easy bein' green...

You did it—through the help of the strategy pattern, dependency injection (see the previous No Dumb Questions), and mock objects, you have a really powerful, but not too bulky, suite of unit tests. You now have piles of tests that make sure your system does what it's supposed to be doing at all times. So to keep your system in line:

1. Always write a test before you write the real production code.
2. Make sure your test fails, and then implement the simplest thing that will make that test pass.
3. Each test should really only test one thing; that might mean more than one assertion, but one real concept.
4. Once your're back to green (your test passes) you can refactor some surrounding code if you saw something you didn't like. No new functionality—just cleanup and reorganization.
5. Start over with the next test. When you're out of tests to write, you're done!

When all of your tests pass, you're done

Before we never really had a way of knowing when we were finished. You wrote a bunch of code, probably ran it a few times to make sure it seemed to be working, and then moved on. Unless someone said something bad happened, most developers won't look back. With test-driven development we know exactly when we're done—and exactly what works.

Which do you think is better?

Bob again...

vs

```
File Edit Window Help Bliss
hfsd> java -cp junit.jar;. org.junit.runner.JUnitCore
                    headfirst.sd.chapter8.TestOrderProcessor
JUnit version 4.4
.........................................
.....
Time: 0.321
OK (86 test)

hfsd>
```

Our test suite in action

* If you said Bob, please donate this book to your library.

TDDcross

The crossword tests are below; fill in the answers to make each one pass.

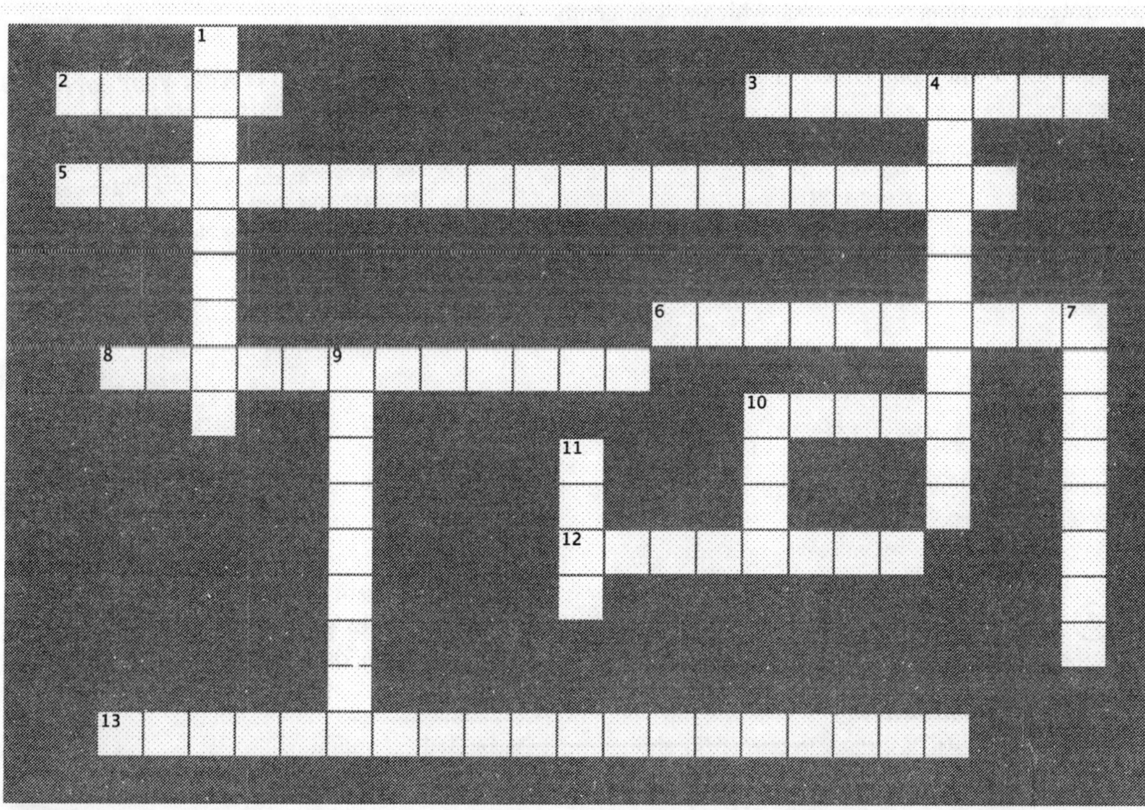

Across

2. You ain't gonna need it.
3. Red, Green, ...
5. TDD.
6. Mock objects realize ....
8. Bad approaches to TDD are called ....
10. TDD means writing tests ....
12. To do effective TDD you need to have low ....
13. To help reduce dependencies to real classes you can use ....

Down

1. Fine grained tests.
4. When you should test.
7. Write the .... code that will get the test to pass.
9. .... testing is essential to TDD.
10. Your tests should .... at first.
11. To help reduce test code you can use .... objects.

Answers on page 315.

A day in the life of a test-driven developer...

Once you have your tests passing, you know you built what you set out to. You're done. Check the code in, knowing that your version control tool will ping your CI tool, which will diligently check out your new code, build it, and run your tests. All night. All the next day. Even when Bob checks in some code that breaks yours...*

Then the automated mail starts....

1 **Start with the task you're going to work on.**

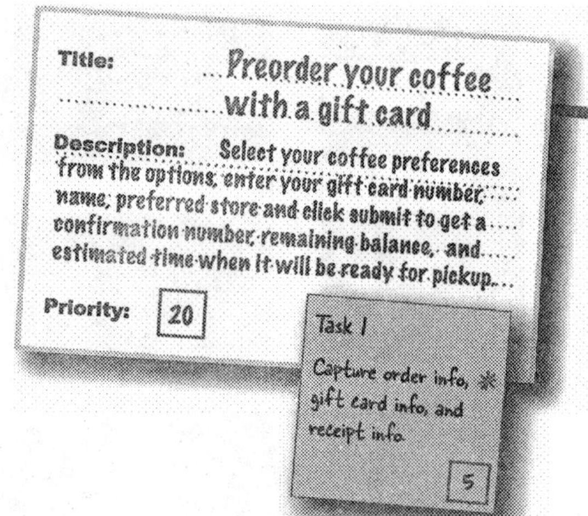

5 **Write code to get your test to pass, refactor, add another test, and get it to pass. Repeat until you run out of tests to add.**

Once your code is passing, it's time to check it into your repository and move onto the next task.

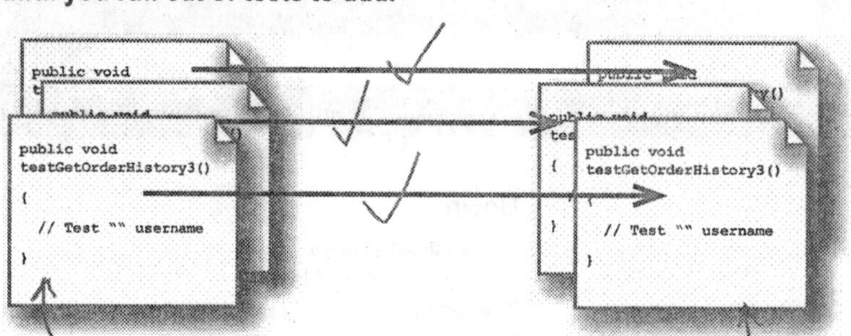

All your tests should be passing (and your CI tool should make sure they stay passing).

Real implementation code

* but in fact, with TDD, Bob will know instantly because the tests will fail and he will know exactly what code he broke.

② Work up the first test for the very first piece of functionality you need to implement. You're now Red.

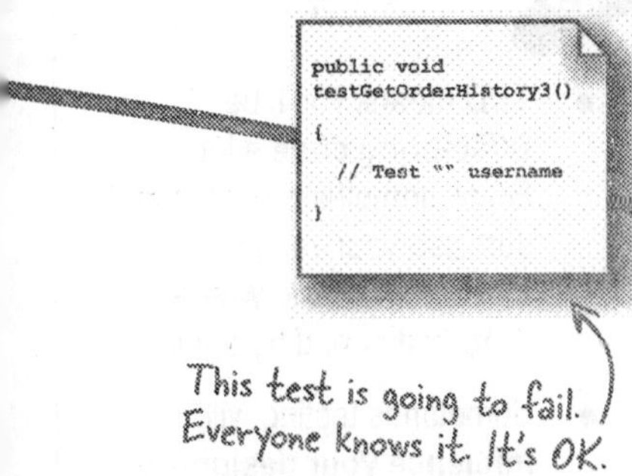

③ Write the simplest implementation code you can to get the test to pass. You're now Green.

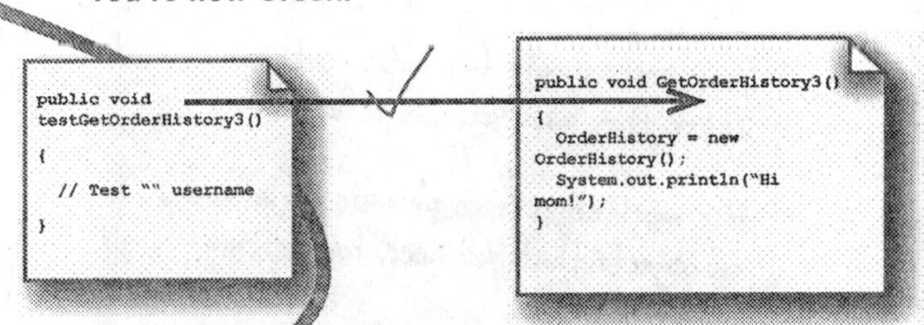

④ Refactor any code you want cleaned up, then write the next test...Red again.

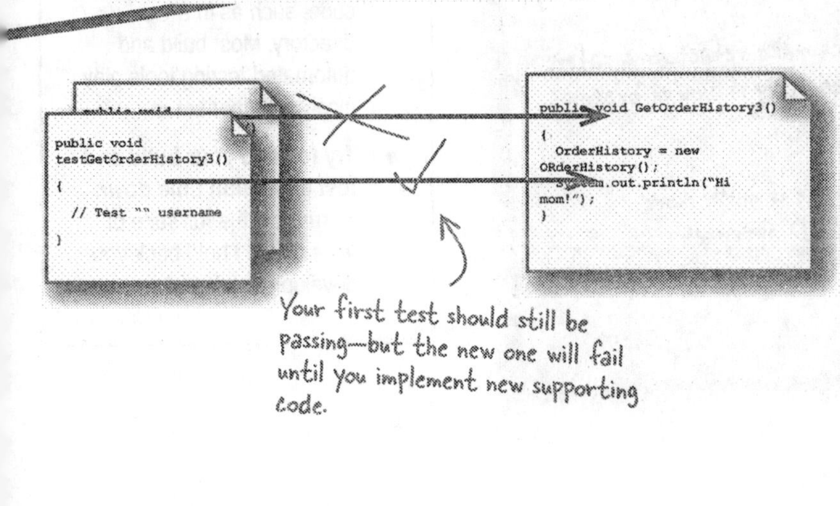

CHAPTER 8

Tools for your Software Development Toolbox

Software Development is all about developing and delivering great software. In this chapter, you learned about several techniques to keep you on track. For a complete list of tools in the book, see Appendix ii.

Development Techniques

Write tests first, then code to make those tests pass

Your tests should fail initially; then after they pass you can refactor

Use mock objects to provide variations on objects that you need for testing

Here are some of the key techniques you learned in this chapter...

... and some of the principles behind those techniques.

Development Principles

TDD forces you to focus on functionality

Automated tests make refactoring safer; you'll know immediately if you've broken something

Good code coverage is much more achievable in a TDD approach

BULLET POINTS

- TDD means you'll be **refactoring code** a lot. Break something pretty bad? Just use your version control tool to roll back to where you were earlier and try again.
- Sometimes testing will **influence your design**—be aware of the trade-offs and deliberately make the choice as to whether it's worth the **increased testability**.
- Use the **strategy pattern** with **dependency injection** to help **decouple classes**.
- Keep your tests in a **parallel structure** to your source code, such as in a `tests/` directory. Most build and automated testing tools play nicely with that setup.
- **Try to keep your build and test execution time down** so running the full suite of tests doesn't hold back your development speed.

TDDcross Solution

The crossword tests are below—fill in the answers to make each one pass.

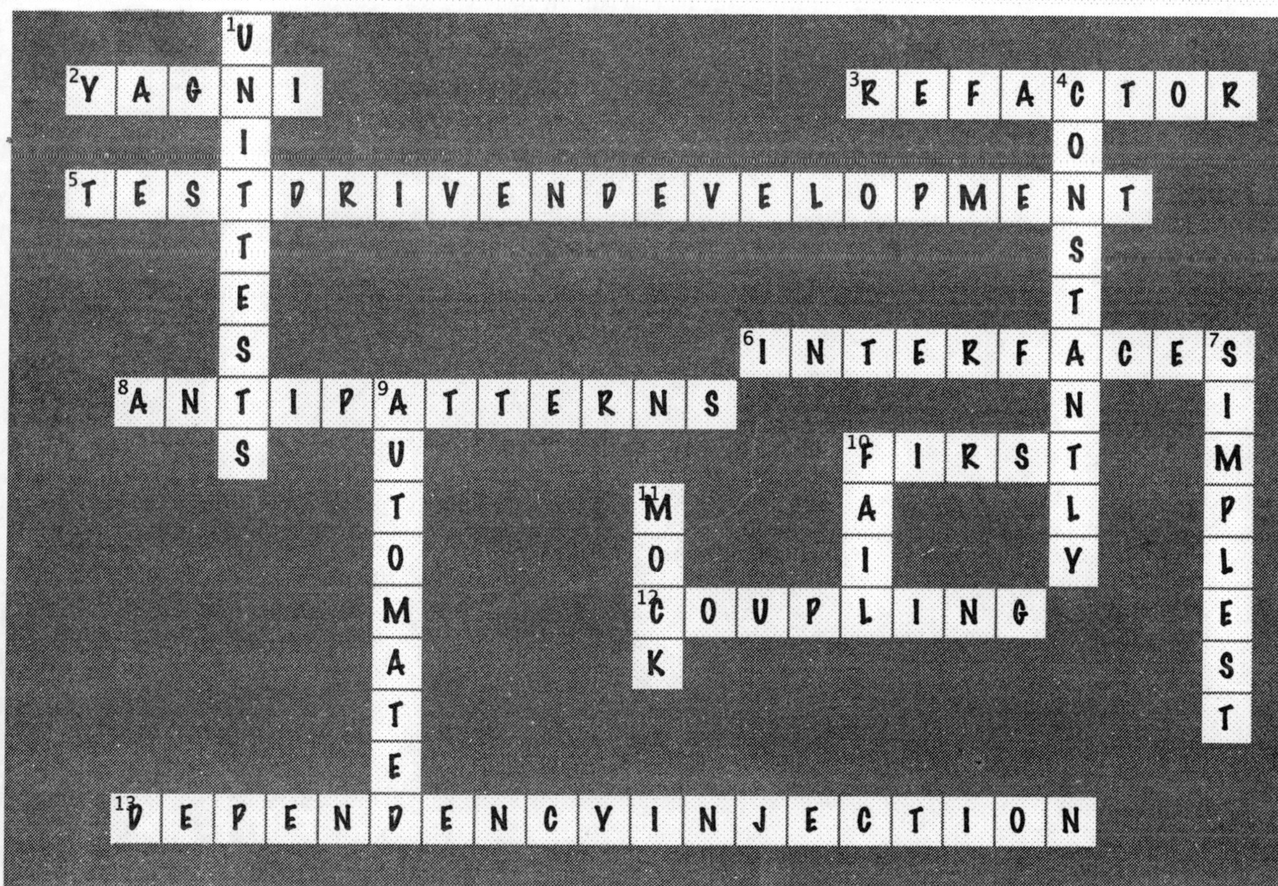

9 ending an iteration

It's all coming together...

You're almost finished! The team's been working hard, and things are wrapping up. Your tasks and user stories are **complete**, but what's the best way to spend that extra day you ended up with? Where does **user testing** fit in? Can you squeeze in one more round of **refactoring** and **redesign**? And there sure are a lot of lingering **bugs**...when do those get fixed? It's all part of **the end of an iteration**... so let's get started on getting finished.

Your iteration is just about complete...

You've made it! You've successfully put your process in place: the stories have piled up in the Completed section of your board, and everyone's ready for a little breather. Before people head out for the weekend, though, let's do a quick status check:

What we've got

- [x] Customer-driven functionality
- [x] Compiling code
- [x] Monitored builds
- [x] Continuously tested code
- [x] Solid test coverage
- [x] Reliable progress tracking
- [x] Pacing that adapts to the team

User stories and frequent customer interaction ensure your software does what the customer wants it to do.

You know if someone tries to check in code that won't build—and because of continuous integration, you know your code is always buildable.

With test-driven development and automated testing, your code works... and you'll always know if it stops working.

The burn-down graph and velocity turn idealistic schedules into real, quantifiable dates and deliverables.

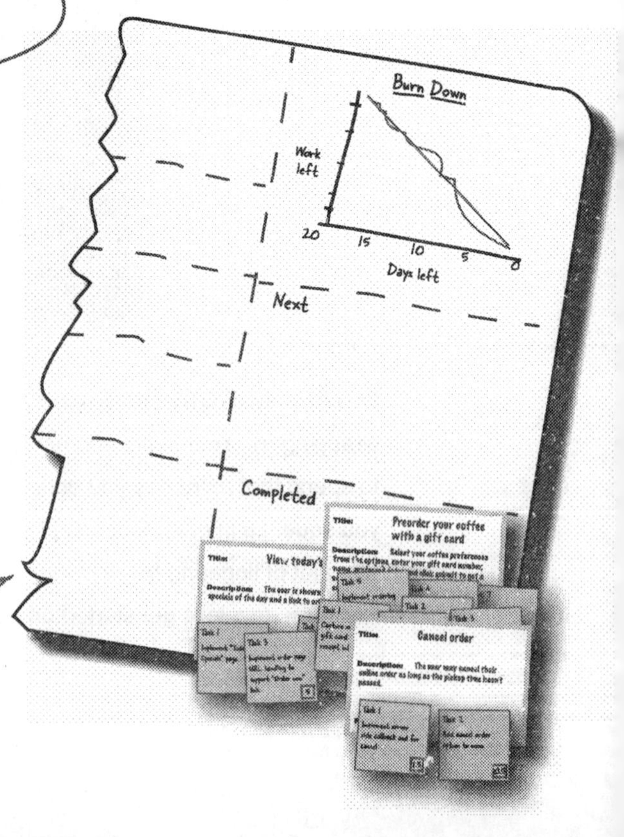

That's an impressive list—but don't turn the lights out in the office just yet. Suppose all your hard work has resulted in a day or two to spare at the end of your iteration. What else could you do if you had more time?

Skeptical you could have time left? A good velocity calculation, staying on task, and accurate estimates will get you there faster than you think.

...but there's lots left you could do

There are always more things you can do on a project. One benefit of iterative development is that you get a chance to step back and think about what you've just built every month or so. But lots of the time, you'll end up wishing you'd done a few things differently. Or, maybe you'll think of a few things you wish you could ***still*** do...

What we don't have

- [ ] Process improvements
- [ ] System testing
- [ ] Refactoring of code using lessons you've learned
- [ ] Code cleanup and documentation updates
- [ ] More design patterns?
- [ ] Development environment updates
- [ ] R&D on a new technology you're considering
- [ ] Personal development time to let people explore new tools or read

You've worked hard putting this process together, but the whole point of iterative development is to learn from each iteration... how can you improve your processes on the next iteration?

You've got unit tests, but users haven't tried the system out yet. And users always find things the best testers miss...

Everyone documented their code, right? No typos, misspelliins, or incomplete ?

No matter how slick your design seemed early on, you'll always come up with just a little something that will make it so much sweeter. Do you do that now?

Sometimes a design pattern doesn't really show itself until you've implemented something more than once. Maybe you didn't need a factory in the first iteration... or the second. But by the time you add more code in the third iteration, things are screaming for a helpful pattern.

There's always some new tool out there that will "revolutionize" your build environment—or maybe you just need to reorganize dependencies. Either way, when do you update your environment?

You may be cutting-edge now, but when do you have time to learn about even newer technologies and work them into your projects?

BRAIN POWER

Which of these things would you feel like you **have** to do? Which ones do you think you **should** do? Are there things that can be put off indefinitely? Are there other things you'd like to do that are not on this list?

Standup Meeting

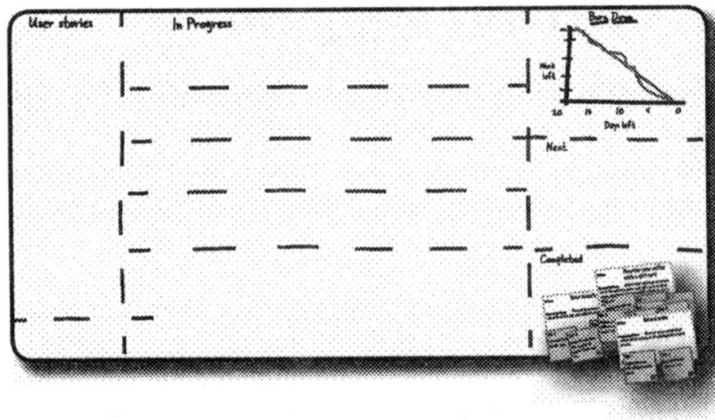

Laura: OK, my code's all checked in. But I need another couple days to refactor it. A way better design came to me last night at the gym!

Mark: No way. Have you seen some of the documentation Bob put in there? I mean, it's English, I guess, but it needs some work. So no time for more code changes; we've got to work on the documentation.

Bob: Hey—back off. It says what the code does, right? Besides, we really need to test more. Everybody's tests pass, but I'm just not convinced the user isn't going to get confused navigating through some of the site's pages. And I'd like to run the app for at least a day straight, make sure we're not chewing up resources somewhere.

Laura: But we're going to have to add more complex ordering in the next iteration; the current framework just isn't going to hold up. I need to get in there and sort this out before we build more on top of it.

Mark: Are you listening? The documentation's ***awful***; that's got to be the priority with the time we've got left.

Bob: We need to focus on the project—how did our burn-down rate look this iteration? Where did we spend our time?

Standup Meeting Tips for Pros

- Keep them to 10 people or less.
- Literally stand up to help keep them short—ideally 15 minutes or less, 30 if you absolutely have to, but then kick everyone out.
- Meet at the same time, same place, every day, ideally in the morning, and make them mandatory.
- Only people with direct, immediate impact on the progress of the iteration should participate; this is typically the development team and possibly a tester, marketing, etc.
- Everyone must feel comfortable talking honestly: standups are about communication and bringing the whole team to bear on immediate problems.
- Always report on *what you did yesterday, what you're going to do today*, and *what is holding you up*. Focus on the outstanding tasks!
- Take things offline to solve bigger issues—remember, 15 minutes.
- Standups should build the sense of team: be supportive, solve hard issues offline, and communicate!

Exercise

Do you think the tasks you'd do at the end of an iteration should be changed based on how the iteration progressed? Below are three different burn-down graphs. Can you figure out how the iteration went in each case? Describe what you think happened in the provided blanks.

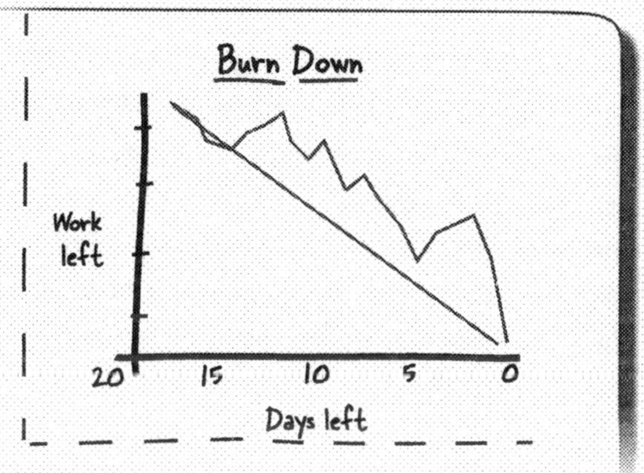

....

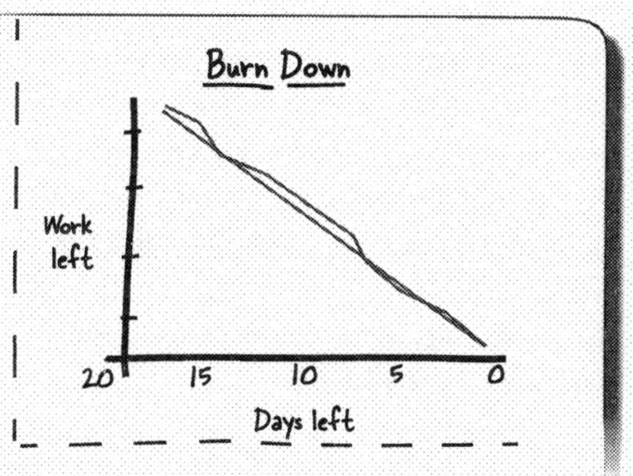

....

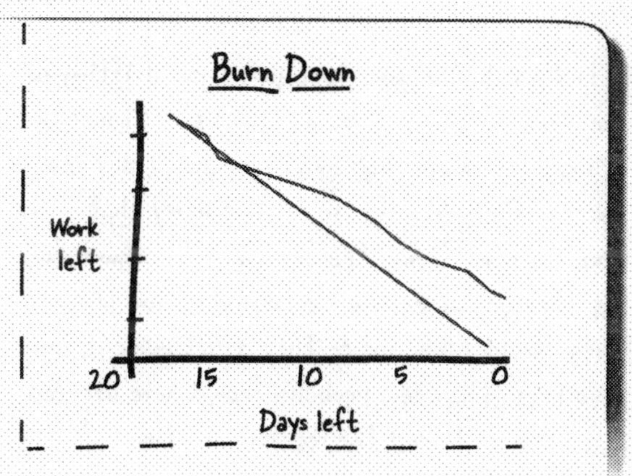

....

Exercise Solution

Before we go on let's take a look at some burn rates. Your job was to take a look at each graph and figure out what probably went on during that iteration.

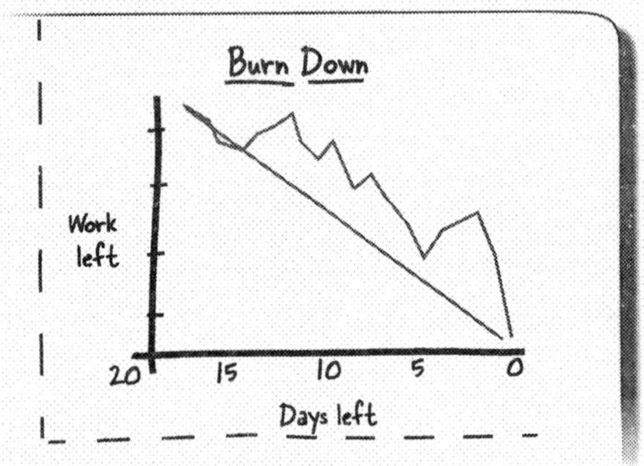

In this graph, the work remaining kept increasing as the iteration progressed. The team probably missed some things in their user stories: maybe lots of unplanned tasks—remember, red stickies are great for those—or bad estimates that got uncovered when user stories were broken down into tasks. Note the steep drop at the end—odds are that the team had to cut out things, or drop stories altogether, as deadlines started creeping up.

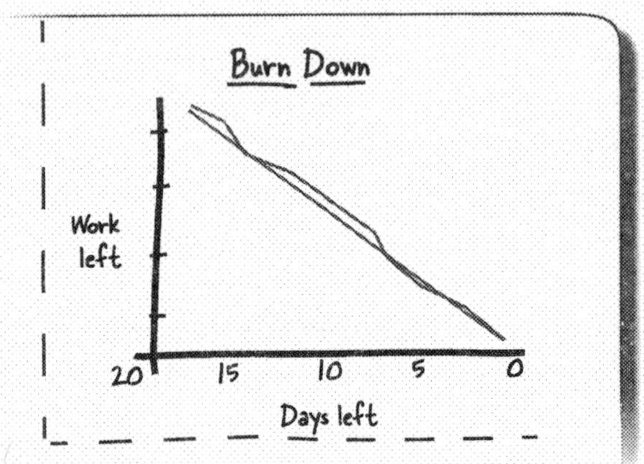

This is a perfect graph—what every team wants. The team probably had a good idea what they were getting into, their estimates were pretty close at both the user story and task level, and they moved through tasks and stories at a nice predictable pace. Remember, a good iteration doesn't have lots of time at the end—it ends right when it's scheduled to.

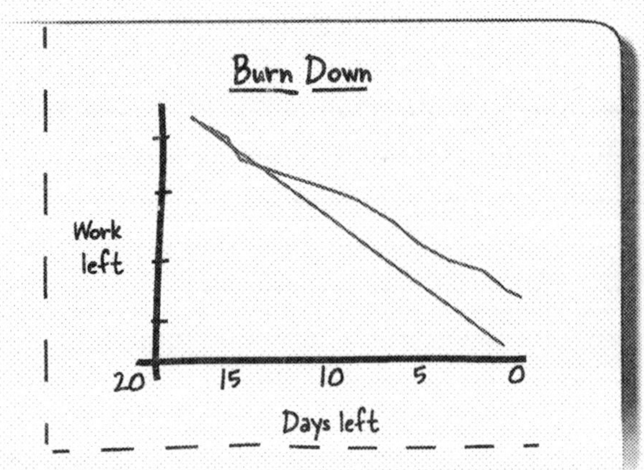

In this graph, the work left just keeps drifting to the right of the ideal burn-down rate. Chances are this is an estimate problem. There aren't any real spikes in the work left, so it's not likely that there were too many things the team didn't account for, but they just severely underestimated how long things would take. Notice they didn't make it to zero here... The team probably should have dropped a few stories to end the iteration on time.

there are no Dumb Questions

Q: How do you know the first graph is things the team missed? Couldn't it be things they didn't expect, like extra demos or presentations?

A: Absolutely. The burn-down graph isn't enough to go on to determine where all those extra work items came from. You need to look at the completed tasks and figure out whether the extra work came from outside forces that you couldn't control or if they were a result of not really understanding what the team was getting into. Either way, it's important to make progress in addressing the extra work before the next iteration. If the work came from outside sources, can you do something to limit that from happening again, or at least incorporate it into your work for the estimate? For example, if the marketing team keeps asking you for demos, can you pick one day a week where they could get a demo if needed? You can block that time off and count it toward the total work left. You can use the same approach if things like recruiting or interviewing candidate team members is taking time away from development. Remember—your job is to do ***what the customer wants***. However, it's also your responsibility to know where your time is going and prioritize appropriately.

If the extra work came from not understanding what you were getting into, do you have a better sense now, after working on the project for another iteration? Would spending more time during task breakdowns help the team get a better sense of what has to be done? Maybe some more up-front design, or possibly quick-and-dirty code (called spike implementations) to help shake out the details?

Q: So spending more time doing up-front design usually helps create better burn-down rates, right?

A: Maybe...but not necessarily. First, remember that by the time you start doing design, you're *already* into your iteration. Ideally you'd find those issues earlier.

It's also important to think about ***when*** is the right time to do the design for an iteration. Some teams do most of the detailed design work at the beginning of the iteration to get a good grasp of everything that needs to be done. That's not necessarily a bad approach, but keep an eye on how efficient you are with your designs. If you had driven a couple stories to completion before you worked up designs for some of the remaining ones, would you have known more about the rest of the iteration? Would the design work have gone faster, or would you realize things you'd need to go back and fix in the first few stories? It's a trade off between how much up-front design you do before you start coding.

Having said all of that, sometimes doing some rough whiteboard design sketches and spending a little extra time estimating poorly understood stories can help a lot with identifying any problem issues.

Q: For that third graph, couldn't the velocity be a big part of the problem?

A: That's a possibility, for sure. It could either be that the team's estimates were wrong and things just took a lot longer than they thought the would, or their estimates were reasonable but they just couldn't implement as fast as they thought. At the end of the day it doesn't make too much difference. As long as a team is consistent with their estimates, then velocity can be tweaked to compensate for over- or underestimating. What you ***don't*** want to do is keep shifting your estimates around. Keep trying to estimate for that ***ideal workday for your average developer***—if that person was locked in a room with a computer and a case of Jolt, how long would it take? Then, use velocity to adjust for the reality of your work environment and mixed skill level on your team.

Q: So should the team with the third graph just add time to the end of their iteration to get the extra work done?

A: In general that's not a great idea. Typically, when the burn-down graph looks like that, people are already working hard and feeling stressed. Remember one of the benefits of that graph on the board is communication—everyone sees it at each standup, and they know things are running behind. Adding a day or two is usually OK in a crisis, but not something you want to do on a regular basis. Adding a week or two... well, unless it's your last iteration, that's probably not a good idea. It's generally better to punt on a user story or two and move them to the next iteration. Clean up the stories you finished, get the tests passing, and let everyone take a breather. You can adjust your velocity and get a handle on what went wrong before you start the next iteration, and go into it with a refreshed team and a more realistic pace.

Q: We have one guy who just constantly underestimates how long something is going to take and wrecks our burn-down. How do we handle that?

A: First, try to handle the bad estimates during estimation, and remember, you should be estimating as a team. Try reminding the person that they aren't estimating for themselves, but for the average person on your team. If that still doesn't work, try keeping track of the date a task gets moved to In Progress, and then the date it gets moved to Done. At the end of your iteration, use that information to calibrate your estimations. Remember, this isn't about making anyone feel bad because they took longer than originally expected; it's to calibrate your estimates from the beginning.

System testing MUST be done...

Your system has to work, and that means **using the system**. So you've got to either have a dedicated end-to-end system testing period, or you actually let the real users work on the system (even if it's on a beta release). No matter which route you go, you've got to test the system in a situation that's as close to real-world as you can manage. That's called **system testing**, and it's all about reality, and the system as a whole, rather than all its individual parts.

So far, we've been **unit testing**. Our tests focus on small pieces of code, one at a time, and deliberately try to isolate components from each other to minimize dependencies. This works great for automated test suites, but can potentially miss bugs that only show up when components interact, or when real, live users start banging on your system.

And that's where **system testing** comes in: hooking everything together and treating the system like a black box. You're not thinking about how to avoid garbage collection, or creating a new instance of your `RouteFinder` object. Instead, you're focusing on the functionality the customer asked for... and making sure your system handles that functionality.

System testing exercises the FUNCTIONALITY of the system from front to back in real-world, black-box scenarios.

...but WHO does system testing?

You should try your best to have a **different set of people** doing your system testing. It's not that developers aren't really bright people; it's just that dedicated testers bring a testing mentality to your project.

Developer testing

Developers come preloaded with lots of knowledge about the system and how things work underneath. No matter how hard they try, it's really tough for developers to ***put themselves in the shoes of end users*** when they use the system. Once you've seen the guts, you just can't go back.

Tester testing

Testers can often bring a fresh perspective to the project. They approach the system with a fundamentally different view. They're *trying* to find bugs. They don't care how slick your multithreaded, templated, massively parallel configuration file parser is. ***They just want the system to work.***

there are no Dumb Questions

Q: So developers can't be testers? We can't afford a separate test team!

A: Ideally, you'd have developers doing your unit testing with an automated approach, and a different group of people doing the full, black-box system testing. But, if that's not doable, then ***at a minimum***, don't let a developer black-box-test their own code. They just know too much about the code, and it's way too easy to steer clear of that sketchy part of the code that just might fail.

Never system-test your own code! You know it too well to be unbiased.

System testing depends on a complete system to test

If you're velocity is pretty accurate and your estimates are on, you should have a reasonably full iteration. It also means you don't have a stack of empty days for system testing...and on top of that, you won't have a system to test until the end of your iteration.

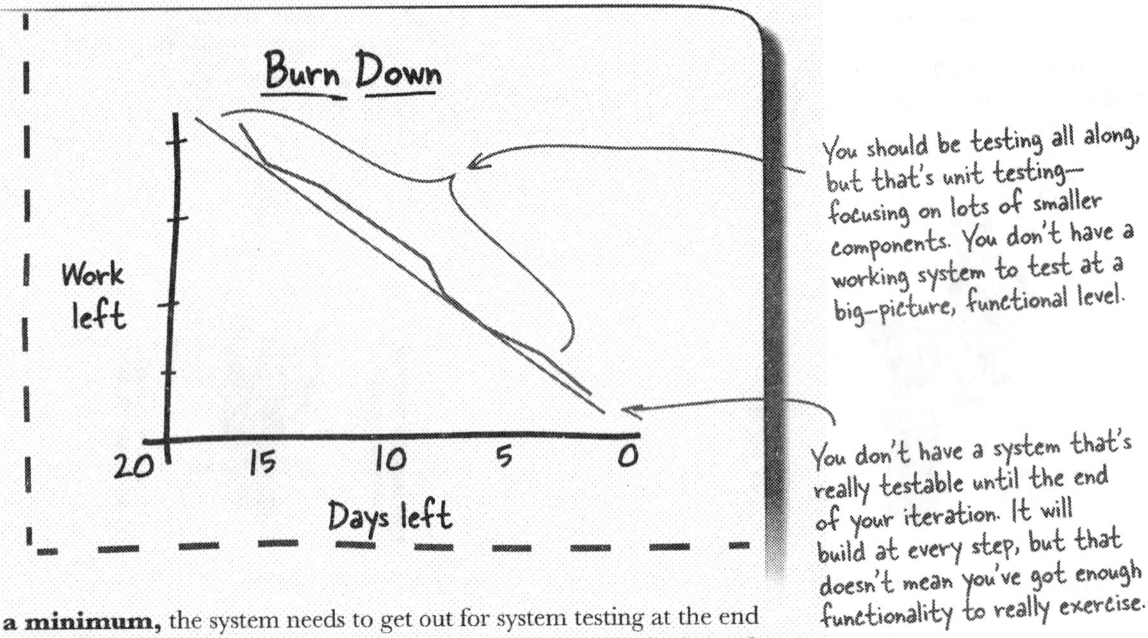

At a minimum, the system needs to get out for system testing at the end of each iteration. The system won't have all of its functionality in the early iterations, but there should always be some completed stories that can be tested for functionality.

there are no Dumb Questions

Q: Can't we start system testing earlier?

A: Technically, you can start system testing earlier in an iteration, but you really have to think about whether that makes much sense. Within an iteration, developers often need to refactor, break, fix, clean up, and implement code. Having to deliver a build to another group in the middle of an iteration is extremely distracting and likely to including half-baked features. You also want to try to avoid doing bug fix builds in the middle of an iteration—an iteration is a fixed amount of time the team has to make changes to the system. They need to have the freedom to get work done without worrying about what code goes in which build during the iteration. Builds get distributed at the end of an iteration—protect your team in between!

Q: So what about the people doing testing? Where do they fit in?

A: It's definitely best to have a separate group doing system testing, but as for what they should do while your main team is writing code, that's a good question. And even if you have other developers do system testing, the question still applies...

Good system testing requires TWO iteration cycles

Iterations help your team stay focused, deal with just a manageable amount of user stories, and keep you from getting too far ahead without built-in checkpoints with your customer.

But you need all the same things for good system testing. So what if you had ***two*** cycles of iterations going on?

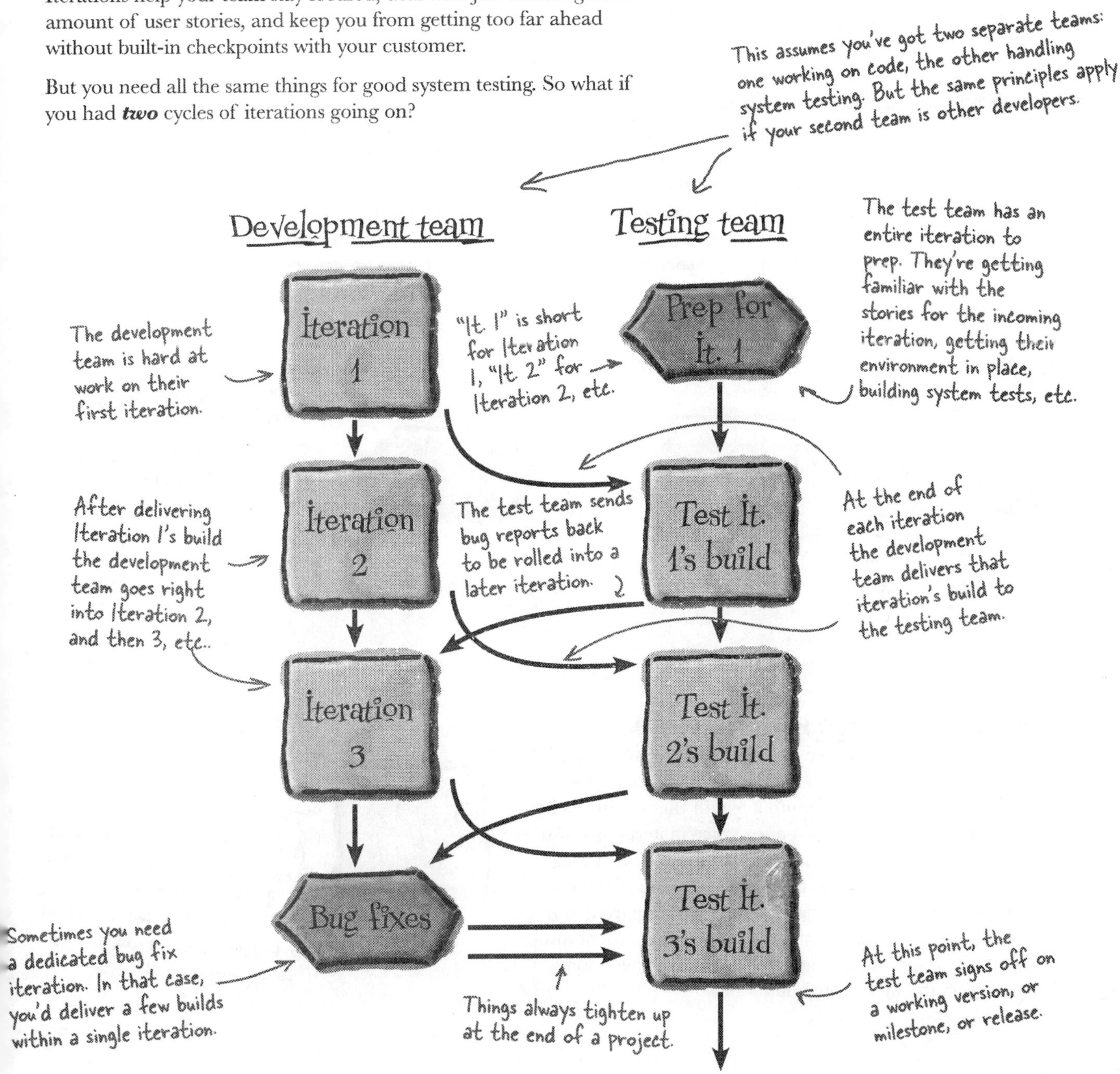

More iterations means more problems

System testing works best with two separate teams, working two separate iteration cycles. But with more iterations comes more trouble—problems that aren't easy to solve.

Running two cycles of iterations means you've got to deal with:

LOTS more communication

Now, not only do you have inter-team communication issues, but you've got two teams trying to work together. The testing team will have questions on an iteration, especially about error conditions, and the development team wants to get on to the next story, not field queries. One way to help this is to bring a representative from the test team into your standup meetings as an observer. He'll get a chance to hear what's going on each day and get to see the any notes or red stickies on the board as the iteration progresses. Remember that your standup meeting is ***your*** meeting, though—it's not a time to prioritize bugs or ask questions about how to run things.

The test team (reasonably) needs to know some details that the development team probably doesn't have yet. Error codes, invalid values, API information, how to set things up, etc.

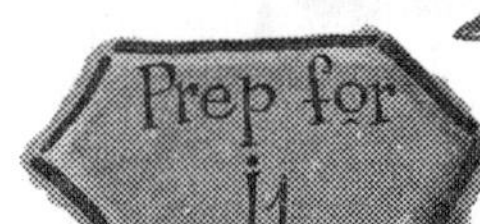

The testing team is looking ahead to what's coming at the end of Iteration 1, even while your developers are still coding.

Testing in a FIXED iteration length

If you're keeping your two iteration cycles in sync—and that's the best way to keep the testing team caught up—you're forcing testing to fit into a length that might not be ideal. To help give the test team a voice in iterations, you can have them provide you a testing estimate for stories you're planning on including in your iteration. Even if you don't use that to adjust what's in your iteration (remember, you're priority-driven) it might give you some insight into where the testing team might get hung up or need some help to get through a tough iteration.

A fixed iteration length forces testing into the same time box as development. But if you've got different teams and different schedules, this may be tricky, if even possible at all.

Fixing bugs while you keep working

The development team will start getting bug reports on their first iteration about the time they're getting into the ***third*** iteration! And then you have to figure out if the bug's important enough to fix right away, roll into the current iteration, or put off for later. We'll talk more about this in a minute, but the straightforward approach is to treat a bug like any other story. Prioritize it against everything else and bump lower-priority stories if you need to in order to get it done sooner.

Another approach is to carve off a portion of time every week that you'll dedicate to bug fixes. Take this off of the available hours when you do your iteration planning, so you don't need to worry about it affecting your velocity. For example, you could have everyone spend one day a week on bug fixes—about 20% of their time.

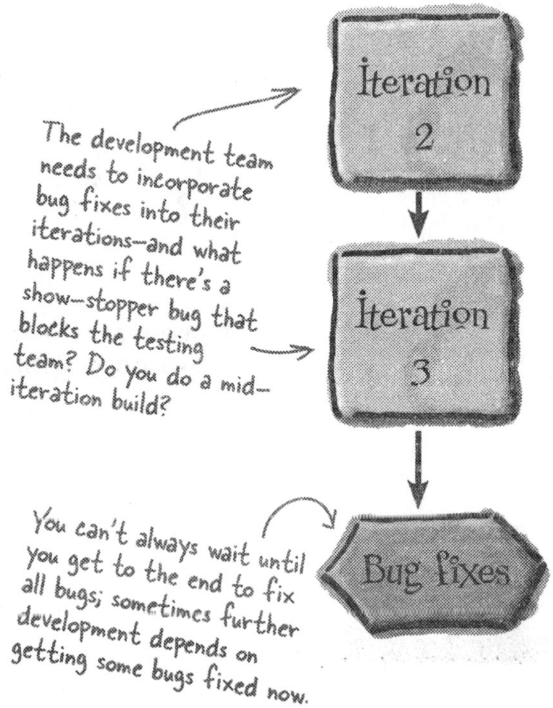

Writing tests for a moving target

Functionality in user stories—even if it's agreed upon by the customer—can change. So lots of times, tests and effort are being put into something that changes 30 days later. That's a source of a lot of irritation and frustration for people working on tests. There's not much you can do here except **communicate**. Communicate as soon as you think something might change. Make sure testing is aware of ongoing discussions or areas most likely to be revisited. Have formal turnover meetings that describe new features and bug fixes as well as known issues. One subtle trick that people often miss is to *communicate how the process works*. Make sure the testing team understands to expect change. It's a lot easier to deal with change if it's just part of your job rather than something that's keeping you from completing your job.

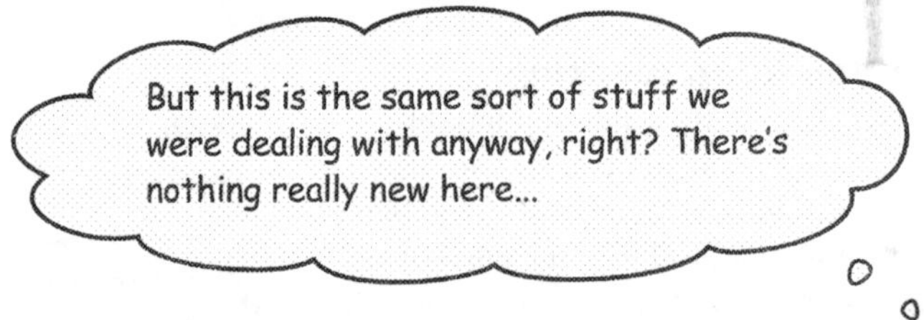

More iterations really just means more communication.

During an iteration there are some messy things to deal with: multiple team members, your customer changing requirements and user stories, priorities of different pieces of functionality, and sometimes having to guess at what you're going to build before your requirements are complete.

Adding another cycle of iterations might mean more of the same issues, but you won't have any new ones. That means you can rely on the same things you've already been doing: standup meetings, tracking everything you do on your big board, using velocity to account for real life, and lots and lots of communication—with your team, with the testing team, and, of course, with your customer.

The key to most problems you'll run into in software development is COMMUNICATION.

When in doubt, TALK to your team, other teams, and your customer.

Sharpen your pencil

Below are some different approaches to testing, all of which involve just one cycle of iterations. What are some **good things** about these approaches? What are some **bad things**?

This approach has one big testing iteration at the end.

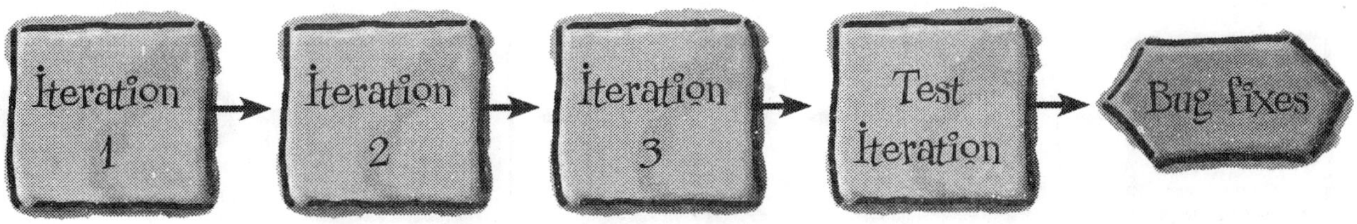

This approach adds a testing iteration after every coding iteration.

Sharpen your pencil Solution

Below are some different approaches to testing, all of which involve just one cycle of iterations. What are some **good things** about these approaches? What are some **bad things**?

If you only have one team to work with, this approach isn't too bad. One big drawback is that serious system testing starts very late in the process. If you take this approach, it's critical that the results of each iteration get out to at least a set of beta users and the customer. You can't wait until the end of the third iteration to start any testing and collecting feedback.

This approach also works pretty well if you need to do formal testing with the customer before they sign off on your work. Since you've been doing automated testing during each iteration and releasing your software to users at the end of each iteration you have a pretty good sense that you're building the right software and it's more or less working as expected. The test iteration at the end is where the formal "check-off" happens before you start looking at Version 2.0.

This is usually called acceptance testing.

This approach requires a lot of iterations, and 50% of your time is spent in testing. It really would only work in situations where your customer is willing to expend a lot of time on testing and debugging. Let's say that your customer is thrilled with the idea of monthly releases to the public; it keeps the site fresh and dynamic in their users' eyes. However, the customer insists on a formal validation process before the code goes anywhere. If you don't have a separate acceptance- and system-testing team, you're going to be looking at a situation a lot like this.

Top 10 Traits of Effective System Testing

10 **Good, frequent communication** between the customer, development team, and testing team.

9 **Know the starting and ending state of the system.** Make sure you start with a known set of test data, and that the data ends up exactly like you'd expect it at the end of your tests.

8 **Document your tests.** Don't rely on that one awesome tester who knows the system inside and out to always be around to answer questions. Capture what each tester is doing, and do those same things at each round of system testing (along with adding new tests).

7 **Establish clear success criteria.** When is the system good enough to go live? Testers can test forever—know before you start what it means to be finished. A **zero-bug-bounce** (when you get to zero outstanding bugs, even if you bounce back up after that) is a good sign you're getting close.

6 **Good, frequent communication** between the customer, development team, and testing team.

5 **Automate your testing wherever possible.** People just aren't great at performing repetitive tasks carefully, but computers are. Let the testers exercise their brains on new tests, not on repeating the same five over and over and over again.

4 **A cooperative dynamic between the development team and testing team.** Everyone should want solid, working software that they can be proud of. Remember, testers help developers look good.

3 **A good view of the big picture by the testing team.** Make sure that all your testers understand the overall system and how the pieces fit together.

2 **Accurate system documentation** (stories, use cases, requirements documents, manuals, whatever). In addition to testing docs, you should capture all of the subtle changes that happen during an iteration, and especially *between* iterations.

1 **Good, frequent communication** between the customer, development team, and testing team.

The life (and death) of a bug

Eventually, your testers are going to find a bug. In fact, they'll probably find a lot of them. So what happens then? Do you just fix the bug, and not worry about it? Do you write it down? What really happens to bugs?

Just like with version control and building, there are great tools for tracking and storing bugs.

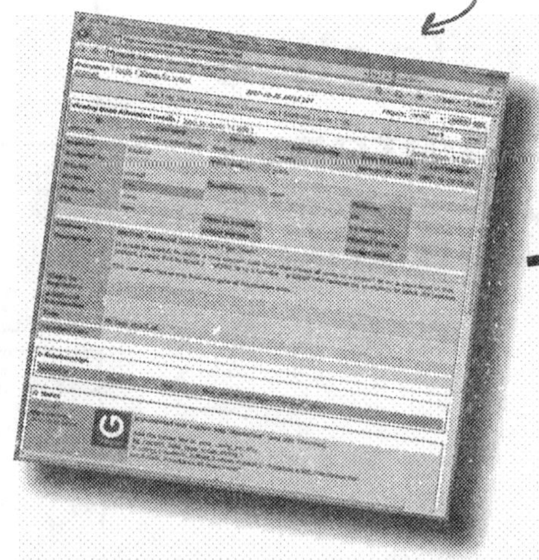

At the system-testing level, bugs aren't always code; sometimes they're confusing or malfunctioning user interfaces.

❷ **The tester <u>FILES A BUG REPORT</u>**

This is one of the most critical steps: ***you have to track bugs!*** It doesn't matter who reports a bug, but level of detail is crucial. Always record what you were trying to do, and if possible, the steps to re-create the bug, any error messages, what you did immediately before the bug occurred, and what you would have expected to happen.

❶ **A tester <u>FINDS A BUG</u>**

A bug doesn't have to be something that's clearly failing. It could be ambiguity in the documentation, a missing feature, or a break from the style guide for a web site.

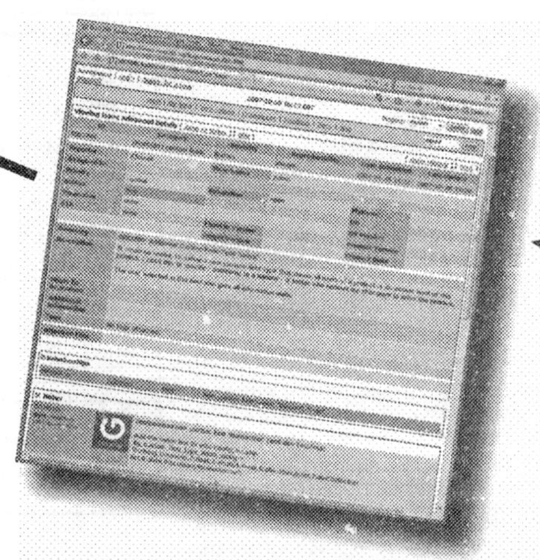

❻ **<u>UPDATE</u> the bug report**

Once the tester (and original reporter) are happy with the fix, close the bug report. The updated report can be used as a script to retest. Don't delete it...you never know when you might want to refer back to it.

Some teams work with their customer to prioritize which bugs get fixed using the bug tracker, and don't create stories or tasks for ones that aren't going to get fixed in the current iteration. Other teams create the stories and tasks right away and let the customer prioritize the bugs like any other story. Either way works great as long as things are being prioritized by the customer.

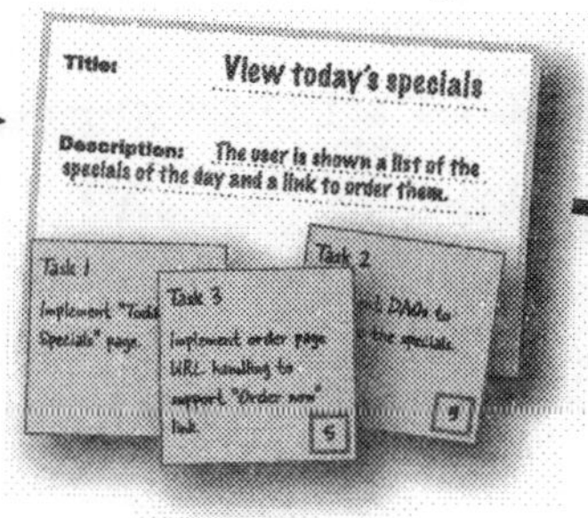

3 **CREATE A STORY (or task) to fix the bug**

Bugs are just work that has to be done in your system—sometimes in the current iteration, sometimes in a later one. You'll need to capture them and prioritize each bug with the customer. These are tricky to estimate, though, because it's not always clear what's wrong. Some teams have a "Bug Fix" story that they just keep around, and they add tasks to it as needed.

A bug is just like an unplanned task. Once it's on the board, it's handled like any other story and task.

4 **FIX THE BUG**

The development team works on the bug as part of an iteration. Start by writing a test that exposes the bug (the test should fail before you change any code). Once the team's fixed the bug (and the test lets you know when that is), they should mark it as "Fixed" in the bug tracker. But don't mark it as tested, closed, or verified—that's for the original reporter to take care of. This also helps you get a list of what's ready for turnover to the test team.

A build usually has more than just one bug fix in it, but it can depend on how critical the bug was.

5 **CHECK THE FIX and verify it works**

The tester (or original reporter) verifies the new build and makes sure they're happy with the resolution. *Now* the bug can be marked as closed (or verified).

So you found a bug....

No matter how hard you work at coding carefully, some bugs are going to slip through. Sometimes they're programming errors; sometimes they're just functional issues that no one picked up on when writing the user stories. Either way, a bug is an issue that you ***have*** to address.

Bugs belong in a bug tracker

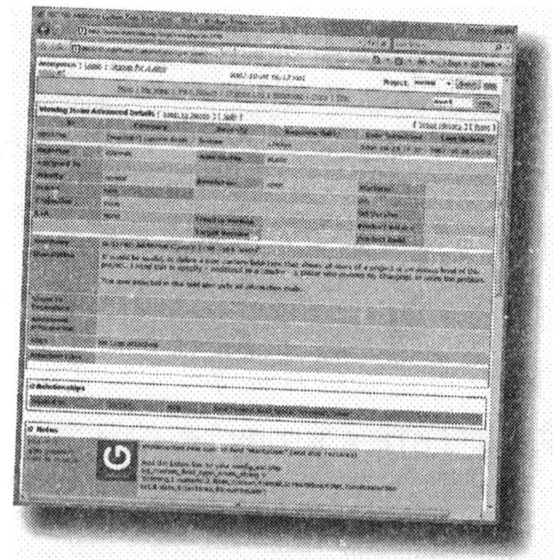

The most important thing about dealing with bugs on a software project is making sure they get recorded and tracked. For the most part it doesn't matter which bug tracking software you use; there are free ones like Bugzilla and Mantis or commercial ones like TestTrackPro and ClearQuest. The main thing is to make sure the whole team knows how to use whatever piece of software you choose.

You should also use your tracker for more than just writing down the bug, too. Make sure you:

1. **Record and communicate priorities**
   Bug trackers can record priority and severity information for bugs. One way to work this in with your board is to pick a priority level—say priority 1, for example—and all bugs of that priority level get turned into stories and prioritized with everything else for the next iteration. Any bugs below priority 1 stay where they are until you're out of priority 1 bugs.

Bug trackers usually work off priorities like 1, 2, and 3, even though your user stories have priorities more like 10, 20, and 30.

2. **Keep track of everything**
   Bug trackers can record a history of discussion, tests, code changes, verification, and decisions about a bug. By tracking everything, your entire team knows what's going on with a bug, how to test it, or what the original developer thought they did to fix it.

3. **Generate metrics**
   Bug trackers can give you a great insight into what's really going on with your project. What's your new-bug submission rate? And is it going up or down? Do a significant number of bugs seem to come from the same area in the code? How many bugs are left to be fixed? What's their priority? Some teams look for a **zero-bug-bounce** before even discussing a production release; that means all of the outstanding bugs are fixed (bug count at zero) before a release.

We'll talk more about delivering software in Chapter 12.

Anatomy of a bug report

Different bug tracking systems give you different templates for submitting a bug, but the basic elements are the same. As a general rule of thumb, the more information you can provide in a bug report, the better. Even if you work on a bug and don't fix it, you should record what you've done, and any ideas about what else might need to be done. You—or another developer—might save hours by referring to that information when you come back to that bug later.

A good bug report should have:

- [ ] **Summary:** Describe your bug in a sentence or so. This should be a detailed action phrase like "Clicking on received message throws ArrayOutOfBoundsException," not something like "Exception thrown." You should be able to read the summary and have a clear understanding of what the problem is.

- [ ] **Steps to reproduce:** Describe how you got this bug to happen. You might not always know the exact steps to reproduce it, but list everything you think might have contributed. If you can reproduce the bug, then explain the steps in detail:
  1. Type "test message" into message box.
  2. Click "sendIt."
  3. Click on the received message in the second application.

- [ ] **What you expected to happen and what really did happen:** Explain what you thought was going to happen, and then what actually *did* happen. This is particularly helpful in finding story or requirement problems where a user expected something that the developers didn't know about.

- [ ] **Version, platform, and location information:** What version of the software were you using? If your application is web-based, what URL were you hitting? If the app's installed on your machine, what kind of installation was it? A test build? A build you compiled yourself from the source code?

- [ ] **Severity and priority:** How bad is the impact of this bug? Does it crash the system? Is there data corruption? Or is it just annoying? How important is it that the bug gets fixed? Severity and priority are often two different things. It's possible that something is severe (kills a user's session or crashes the application) but happens in such a contrived situation (like the user has to have a particular antivirus program installed, be running as a non-Administrator user, and have their network die while downloading a file) that it's a low-priority fix.

BRAIN POWER

What else would you want to see in a bug report? What kind of information would you want to see from the user? How about any kind of output from the system?

But there's still plenty left you COULD do...

So you've handled system testing and dealt with the major bugs you wanted to tackle this iteration. Now what?

What we don't have

- [ ] Process improvements
- [x] System testing
- [ ] Review the iteration for what worked and what didn't
- [ ] Refactor code using lessons you've learned
- [ ] Code cleanup and documentation updates
- [ ] More design patterns?
- [ ] Development environment updates
- [ ] R&D on a new technology you're considering
- [ ] Personal development time to let people explore new tools or read

System testing is taken care of, and you've knocked out your bug reports (or you're waiting on some to get filed).

The right thing to do at any time on your project is the right thing to do AT THAT TIME on YOUR project.

There are no hard-and-fast rules—you've got to make this decision yourself.

A good software process is all about **prioritization**. You want to make sure you're doing the right thing on the project at all times.

Producing working software is critical, but what about quality code? Could you be writing even better code if your process was improved? Or if you dropped a couple thousand lines by incorporating that new persistence framework?

Exercise

Below are three burn-down graphs. It's up to you to decide what to do next.

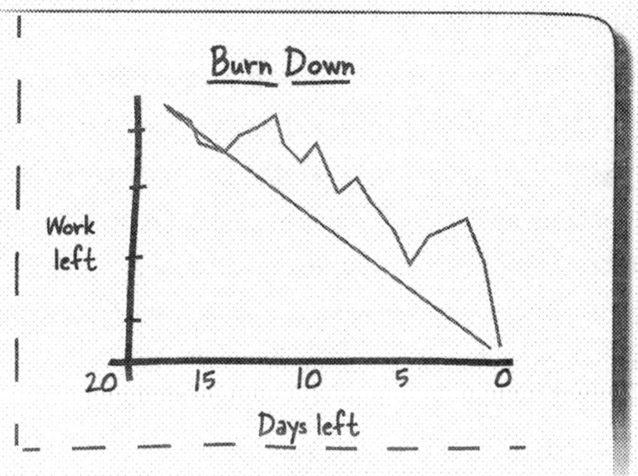

What would you do next?

....

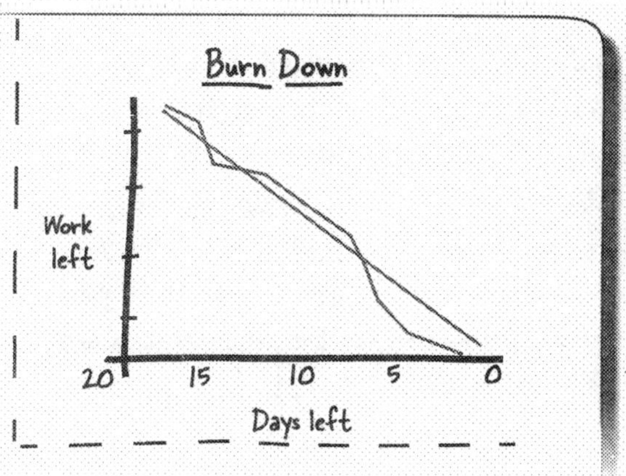

What would you do next?

....

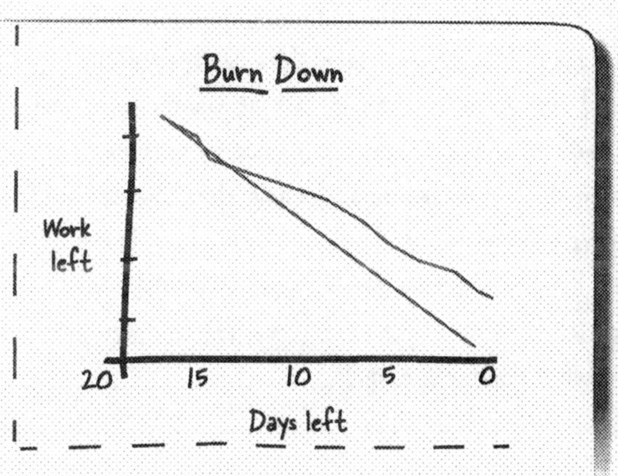

What would you do next?

....

Exercise Solution

Below are three burn-down graphs. It's up to you to decide what to do next.

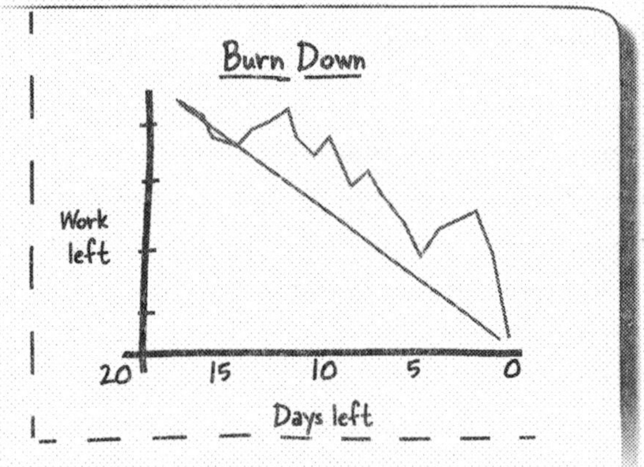

What would you do next?

Here, the team just got finished at the end of the iteration, so there's likely nothing you can squeeze in. However, that steep drop at the end probably means something was skipped. Testing is going to be vital after this iteration, and you should probably expect to schedule some time next iteration for refactoring and cleanup, to recover from the rush. You could probably revisit your task breakdown approach, too, as well as take a look at adjusting velocity.

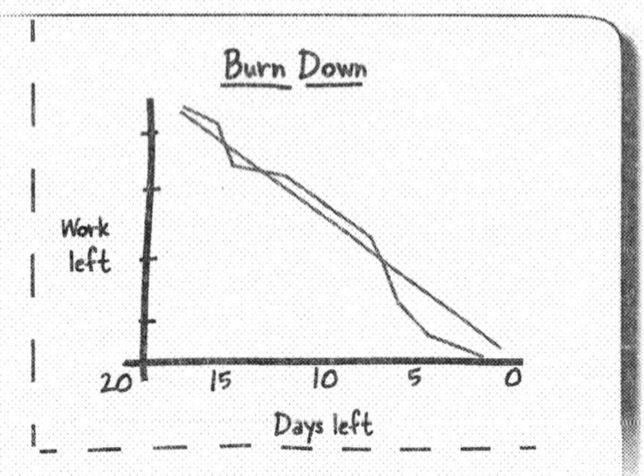

What would you do next?

In this iteration, things wrapped up early; the team may have a couple of days at the end of the iteration. If the project has been ticking along for a little bit, you may have a backlog of bugs you can start to tick off. Or, depending on how big your stories are, you might be able to grab the highest priority story waiting for the next iteration and get started on that.

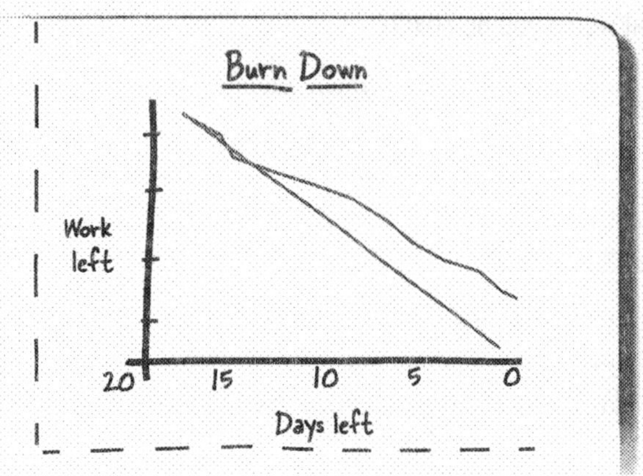

What would you do next?

Nothing! This team is late already. Before the next iteration, you should look at what caused the slowdown and whether it's a velocity problem, an estimation problem, or something else. Chances are there's unfinished code, too, which means there are going to be bugs coming your way. Make sure you leave room in the next iteration to cover any problems that come up.

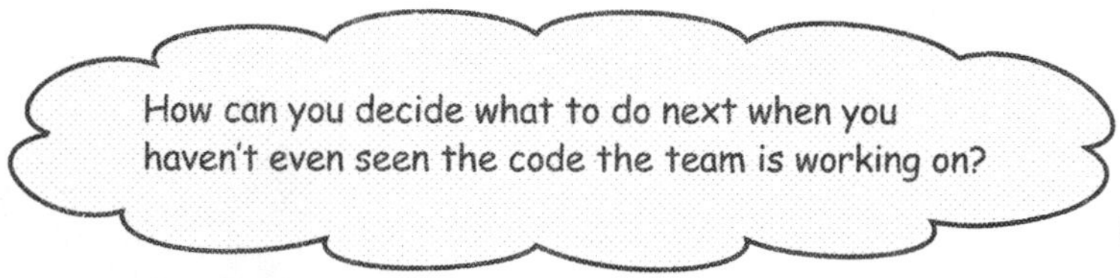

Each project *is* different...sort of.

Remember, software development isn't about just code. It's about good habits and approaches to deliver working software, on time and on budget. Besides, we already have:

- [x] Compiling code
- [x] Automated unit testing
- [x] User stories and tasks that capture what needs to happen
- [x] A process for prioritizing what gets done next
- [x] A working build of the software we can deliver to the customer

So this is about how to prioritize additional, nice-to-have tasks, if you've got extra time. And that's all about ***where you are in your project.*** Early on you'll likely need more refactoring to refine your design. Later, when the project is a little more stable, you'll probably spend more time on documentation or looking at alternatives to that aging technology the team started with six months ago.

Time for the iteration review

It's here: the end of your iteration. You're remaining work is at zero, you've hit the last day of the iteration, and it's time to start getting ready for the next iteration.

But, before you prioritize your next stories, remember: it's not just software we're developing iteratively. You should develop and define your process iteratively, too. At the end of each iteration, take some time to do an iteration review with your team. Everyone has to live with this process so make sure you incorporate their opinions.

Elements of an iteration review

1. **Prepare ahead of time**
   An iteration review is a chance for the team to give you their input on how the iteration went, not a time for you to lecture. However, it's important to keep the review focused, too. Bring a list of things you want to make sure get discussed and introduce them when things start wandering off.

2. **Be forward-looking**
   It's OK if the last iteration was tragic or if one if the developers consistently introduced bugs, as long as the team has a way to address it in the next iteration. People need to vent sometimes, but don't let iteration reviews turn into whining sessions; it demoralizes everyone in the end.

3. **Calculate your metrics**
   Know what your velocity and coverage were for the iteration that just completed. In general, it's best to add up all of the task estimates and divide by the theoretical person-days in your iteration to get your velocity. Whether or not you reveal the actual number during the review is up to you (sometimes it helps to not give the actual number just yet so as not to bias any upcoming estimates), but you should convey whether the team's velocity went up or down.

   The actual time spent on a task versus the estimated time isn't too important since your velocity calculation should account for any mismatch. We'll talk about velocity again in the next chapter.

4. **Have a standard set of questions to review**
   Have a set of questions you go through at the end of each iteration. The set of questions can change if someone would like to add something or a question really doesn't make sense for your team. Having recurring discussion topics means people will expect the questions and prepare (even unconsciously during an iteration) for the review.

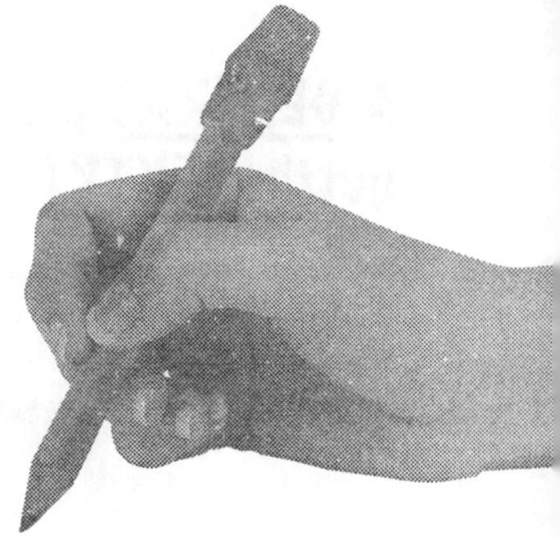

Some iteration review questions

Here is a set of review questions you can use to put together your first iteration review. Add or remove questions as appropriate for your team, but try to touch on each of the general areas.

Iteration Review Questions

- [ ] Is everyone happy with the quality of work? Documentation? Testing?
- [ ] How did everyone feel about the pace of the iteration? Was it frantic? Reasonable? Boring?
- [ ] Is everyone comfortable with the area of the system they were working in?
- [ ] Are there any tools particularly helping or hurting productivity? Are there any new tools the team should consider incorporating?
- [ ] Was the process effective? Were any reviews conducted? Were they effective? Are there any process changes to consider? ← See Chapter 12 for more on this.
- [ ] Was there any code identified that should be revisited, refactored, or rewritten?
- [ ] Were any performance problems identified?
- [ ] Were any bugs identified that must be discussed before prioritization?
- [ ] Was testing effective? Is our test coverage high enough for everyone to have confidence in the system?
- [ ] Is deployment of the system under control? Is it repeatable?

Any of these questions could turn into things you'd like to get done next iteration. Remember, you should be story-driven, so make sure any changes you want to introduce support some customer need (either directly or indirectly) and get prioritized along with everything else. It might mean you need to make a case for a technology or process change to the customer, but it's important to remember why you're writing the software in the first place.

A GENERAL priority list for getting EXTRA things done...

You've got to figure out what's best for your project, but here are some general things you can look at if you've got extra time in your iteration.

Fix bugs

Obviously this depends on what your bug backlog looks like. Remember to prioritize bugs with the customer, too. There might be some bugs that are vital to the customer, and others they just don't care that much about.

Pull in stories that are on deck for next iteration

Since the customer has prioritized more stories than typically fit in an iteration, you can try pulling in a story from the next iteration and get working on it now. Be careful doing this, though, as the customer's priorities or ideas for the story may have changed during your iteration. It's also good to make sure you know whether or not the test team has time to test any extra stories you pull in.

Prototype solutions for the next iteration

If you have an idea about what's likely coming in the next iteration, you might want to take advantage of an extra day or two to start looking ahead. You could try writing some prototype code or testing technologies or libraries you might want to include. You probably won't commit this code into the repository, but you can get some early experience with things you plan on rolling into the next iteration. It will almost certainly help your estimates when you get back to planning poker.

Training or learning time

This could be for your team or for your users. Maybe the team goes to a local users group's session during work hours. Get a speaker or technology demo setup. Run a team-building exercise like sailing or paintball. **Care and feeding of your team** is an important part of a successful project.

there are no Dumb Questions

Q: Seriously, do people ever really have time at the end of the iteration?

A: Yes, absolutely! It usually goes something like this: The first iteration or two are bad news. People always underestimate how long something is going to take early on. At the end of each iteration, you adjust your velocity, so you end up fitting less into subsequent iterations. As the team gets more experienced, their estimates get better, and they get more familiar with the project. That means that the velocity from previous iterations is actually *too low*. This ends up leaving room at the end of an iteration—at least until you recalculate the team's velocity. And believe it or not, sometimes, well, things just go right and you have extra time.

Q: Wait, you said the first two iterations will be bad?

A: You don't want them to be, but realize that people almost always underestimate how long things will take—or how much time they're spending on little things that no one is thinking about, like setting up a co-worker's environment or answering questions on the user's mailing list.

Those are all important things, but need to be accounted for in your work estimates. That's part of why a velocity of 0.7 for your first iteration is a good idea. It gives you some breathing room until you really know how things are going. You'll be surprised how fast you can fill an iteration with user stories, too. Strike a balance between getting a lot squeezed in and being realistic about what you can hope to get done.

Q: We seem to always have extra time at the end of our iterations—and lots of it. What's going on?

A: One idea is that your velocity might be way off. Are you updating it at the end of each iteration? (We'll talk more about that in the next chapter) Another idea is that your estimates are off—on the high side. If you've recently had an iteration where things got really tight at the end, people will naturally be more conservative in their estimates in the next iteration. That's OK, though. If you have lots of time, pull in another story or two at the end of the iteration, and when you update your velocity it will all balance back out.

Q: We tried pulling a story into our iteration, but now it's not finished and we're just about out of time.

A: Punt on the story. Remember, you're working ahead of the curve anyway. It's better to punt on the story and put it back into the next iteration than it is to commit half-written, untested code and just "wrap that up" next iteration. Remember, you're going to send your iteration's build out into the wild. You want it as stable and clean as possible.

If there is extra time at the end of an iteration some teams will tag their code before they pull anything else into the repository. That way, if things go south, they have no problems releasing a stable build by using the tag.

Q: You keep saying to prioritize bugs... but we're in the middle of an iteration. So how do bugs fit in?

A: Some projects have regularly scheduled bug reviews with the customer once a week or so to prioritize outstanding bugs. In those cases, there's always a pool of work to pull from if there's time available. If you don't meet with your customer to talk about bugs regularly, you might want to think about that...although be sure to factor in the time you'll spend on your burn rate and big board. Remember, if the bug is sufficiently important to fix, it should get scheduled into an iteration like anything else.

It's important to note we're talking about bugs found outside of developing a story. If you find a bug in a story you're working on, you should almost always fix it (after adding a test!). Nothing is "done" until it works according to the story—and the tests are proving it.

You shouldn't have LOTS of time left over. So choose SMALL TASKS to take on with any extra time you have... and get ready for the NEXT iteration.

CHAPTER 9

Tools for your Software Development Toolbox

Software Development is all about developing and delivering great software. In this chapter, you learned how to end an iteration effectively. For a complete list of tools in the book, see Appendix ii.

Development Techniques

Pay attention to your burn-down rate—especially after the iteration ends

Iteration pacing is important—drop stories if you need to keep it going

Don't punish people for getting done early—if their stuff works, let them use the extra time to get ahead or learn something new

Here are some of the key techniques you learned in this chapter...

... and some of the principles behind those techniques.

Development Principles

Iterations are a way to impose intermediate deadlines—stick to them

Always estimate for the ideal day for the average team member

Keep the big picture in mind when planning iterations—and that might include external testing of the system

Improve your process iteratively through iteration reviews

BULLET POINTS

- If you have some room at the end of an iteration, that's a good time to **brainstorm for new stories** that might have come up. They'll need to be prioritized with everything else, but it's great to capture them.
- **Resist the temptation** to forget about all of your good habits in the last day or two of an iteration. Don't just "sneak in" that one quick feature that has a low priority because you have a day or make that little refactoring that you're "sure won't break anything." You worked really hard to get done a day or so early, **don't blow it**.
- Work hard to keep a **healthy relationship** with your **testing team**. The two teams can make each other miserable if communication goes bad.
- Recording actual time spent on a task versus estimated time on a task isn't necessary since your velocity will account for estimation errors. But, if you know something went really wrong, **it's worth discussing in the iteration review**.

Iterationcross

You've reached the end of your iteration. Take a breather and enjoy a nice crossword puzzle.

Across

4. Estimate for the .... day and the .... team member.
5. Pay attention to your .... rate to help understand how your team is doing.
6. Make sure your testing team understands the ....
9. Standup meetings are about ....
11. Try really hard to end an iteration ....
12. A quick and dirty test implementation is a .... solution.
13. System testing is usually .... testing, but sometimes .... testing.

Down

1. Since testing can usually go on forever, make sure you have this defined and agreed to by everyone.
2. When your bug fixing rate exceeds your bug finding rate for a while.
3. You should estimate consistently because random disruptions are included in your ....
7. A good way to work through a bug backlog is to treat them as ....
8. .... system testing whenever possible.
10. System testing should really be done by a .... team.

Iterationcross Solution

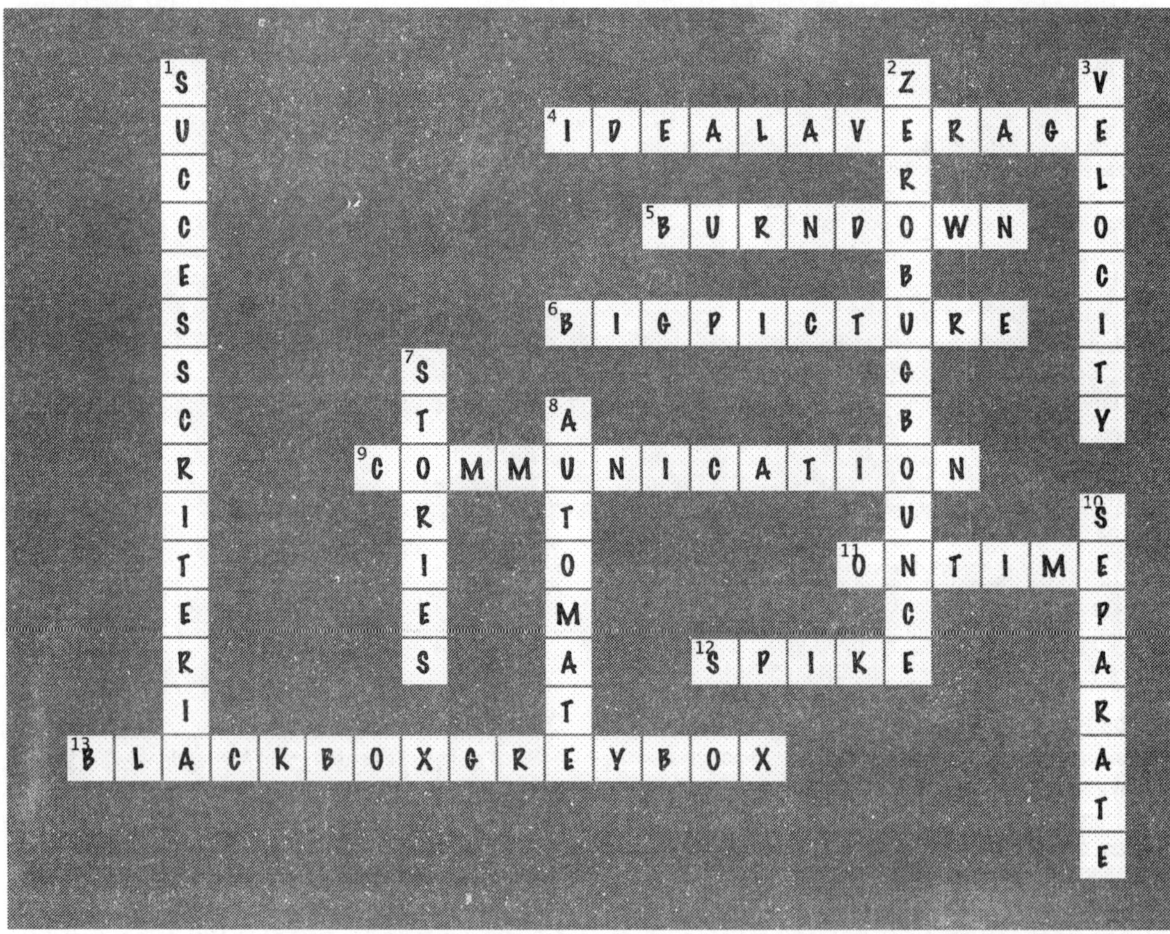

10 the next iteration

If it ain't broke... you still better fix it

Think things are going well? Hold on, that just might change...

Your iteration went great, and you're delivering working software on time. Time for the next iteration? No problem, right? Unfortunately, not right at all. Software development is all about **change,** and **moving to your next iteration** is no exception. In this chapter you'll learn how to prepare for the ***next*** iteration. You've got to **rebuild your board** and **adjust your stories** and expecations based on what the customer wants ***NOW,*** not a month ago.

What is working software?

When you come to the end of an iteration, you should have a buildable piece of software. But complete software is more than just code. It's also...

...completing your iteration's work

You're getting paid to get a certain amount of work done. No matter how clever your code, you've got to complete tasks to be successful.

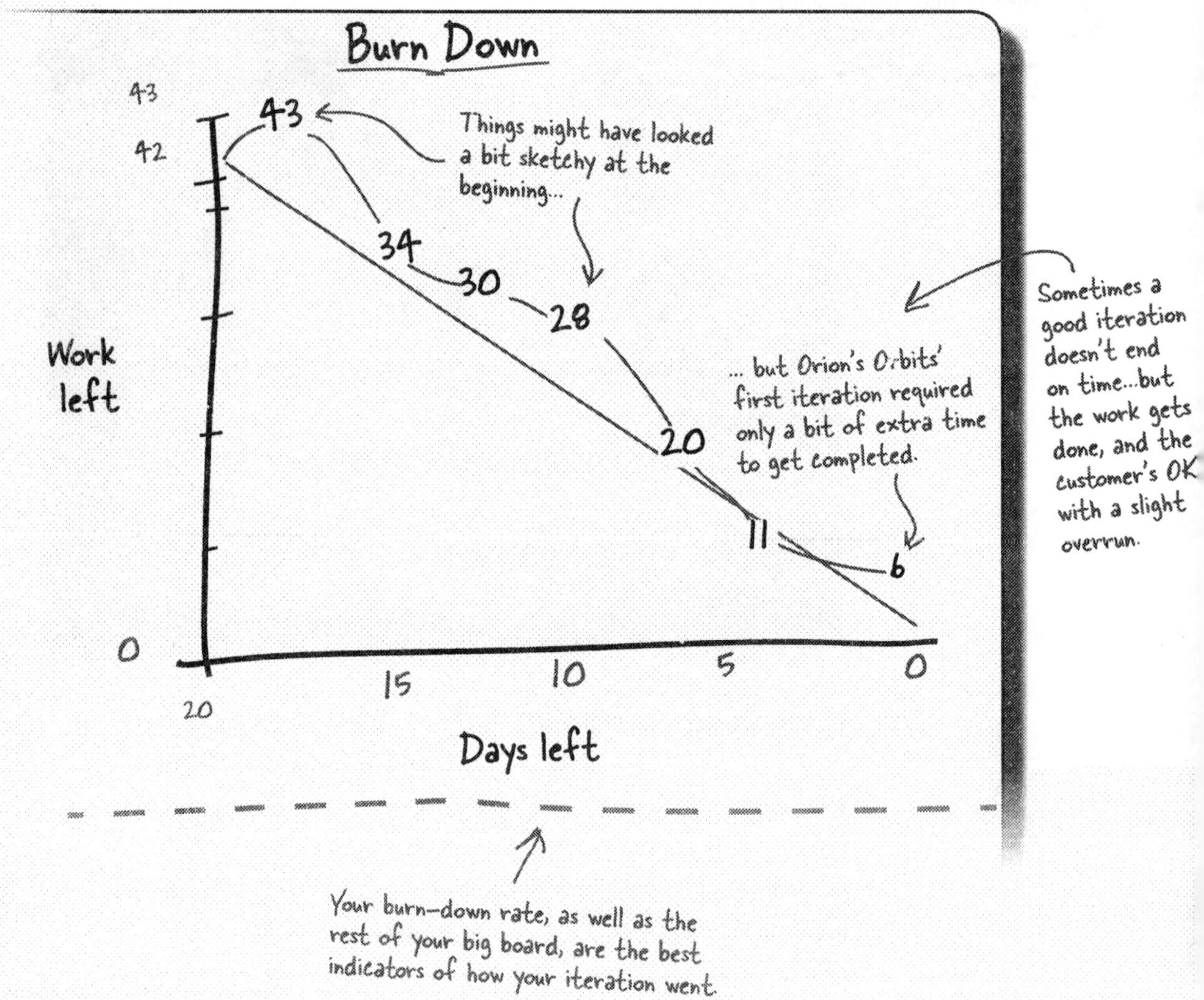

...passing all your tests

Unit tests, system tests, black- and white-box tests...if your system doesn't pass your tests, it's not working.

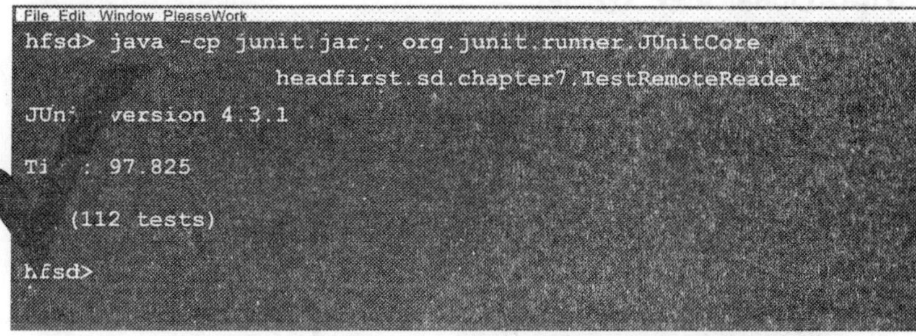

...satisfying your customer

Software that does what it's supposed to do, in the time you promised it, usually makes customers pretty excited. And in lots of cases, it means you've got another iteration's worth of work.

BRAIN POWER

What would you do to get going on the next iteration?

You need to plan for the next iteration

Before diving into the next iteration, there are several things that all play a crucial part in getting ready. Here are the key things to pay attention to:

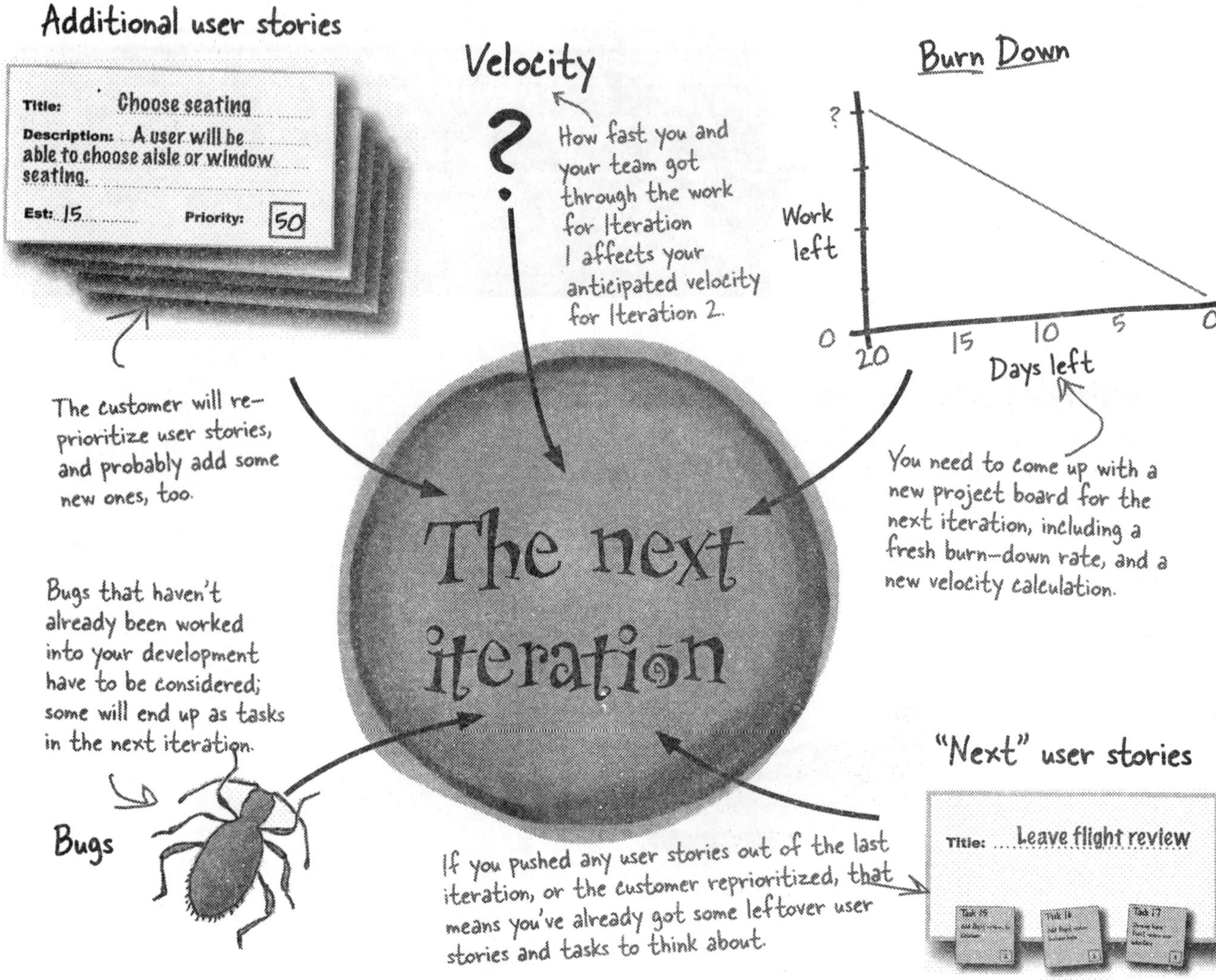

there are no Dumb Questions

Q: So what happend to the board from Iteration 1?

A: Once the iteration is finished, you can archive everything on the old Iteration 1 board. You might want to take a photo of it for archival purposes, but the important thing is to capture how much work you managed to get through in the iteration, how much work was planned, and, of course, to also take any user stories that ended up in the "Next" section back into the pack of candidate user stories for Iteration 2.

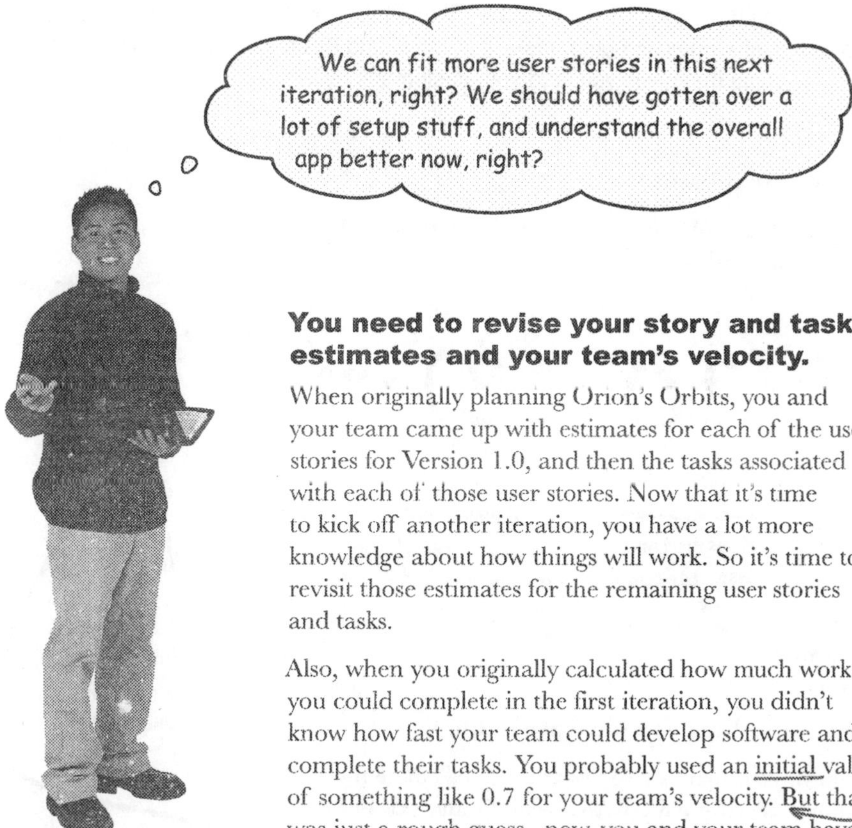

You need to revise your story and task estimates and your team's velocity.

When originally planning Orion's Orbits, you and your team came up with estimates for each of the user stories for Version 1.0, and then the tasks associated with each of those user stories. Now that it's time to kick off another iteration, you have a lot more knowledge about how things will work. So it's time to revisit those estimates for the remaining user stories and tasks.

Also, when you originally calculated how much work you could complete in the first iteration, you didn't know how fast your team could develop software and complete their tasks. You probably used an initial value of something like 0.7 for your team's velocity. But that was just a rough guess...now, you and your team have completed an iteration. That means you've got hard data you can use for recalculating velocity, and getting a more accurate figure.

Velocity accounts for overhead in your estimates. A value of 0.7 says that you expect 30% of your team's time to be spent on other things than the actual development work. Flip back to Chapter 3 for more on velocity.

Remember, your estimates and your velocity are about providing confident statements to your customer about what can be done, and when it will be done. You should revise both your estimates and your velocity at every iteration.

Recalculate your estimates and velocity at each iteration, applying the things you learned from the previous iteration.

Long Exercise

It's time to plan out the work for another iteration at Orion's. First, calculate your team's new velocity according to how well everyone performed in the last iteration. Then, calculate the maximum amount of days of work you can fit into this next iteration. Finally, fill out your project board with user stories and other tasks that will fit into this next iteration using your new velocity, the time that gives you, and your customer's estimates.

1 Calculate your new velocity

Take your team's performance from the previous iteration and calculate a new value for this iteration's velocity.

$$38 \,/\, (20 \times 3) = \boxed{}$$

- 38: This is the total days of work you accomplished, based on what you actually completed.
- 20: Number of actual working days in the last iteration.
- 3: The number of developers on your team during the last iteration.
- Box: Enter your team's new velocity.

Remember, we used calendar days here.

This number helps you figure out how many days of work you can handle for stories and tasks.

2 Calculate the work days you have available

Now that you have your team's velocity, you can calculate the maximum number of work days that you can fit into this iteration.

$$3 \times 20 \times \boxed{} = \boxed{}$$

- 3: The number of people on your team
- 20: The next iteration is a month long again, so that's 20 calendary days
- First box: The new velocity you just calculated
- Second box: The amount of work, in days, that your team can handle in this next iteration

3 Fill up the board with new work

You know how many work days you've got, so all that's left is to take the candidate user stories and bugs, as well as stories left over the last iteration, and add them to your board—make sure you have a manageable workload.

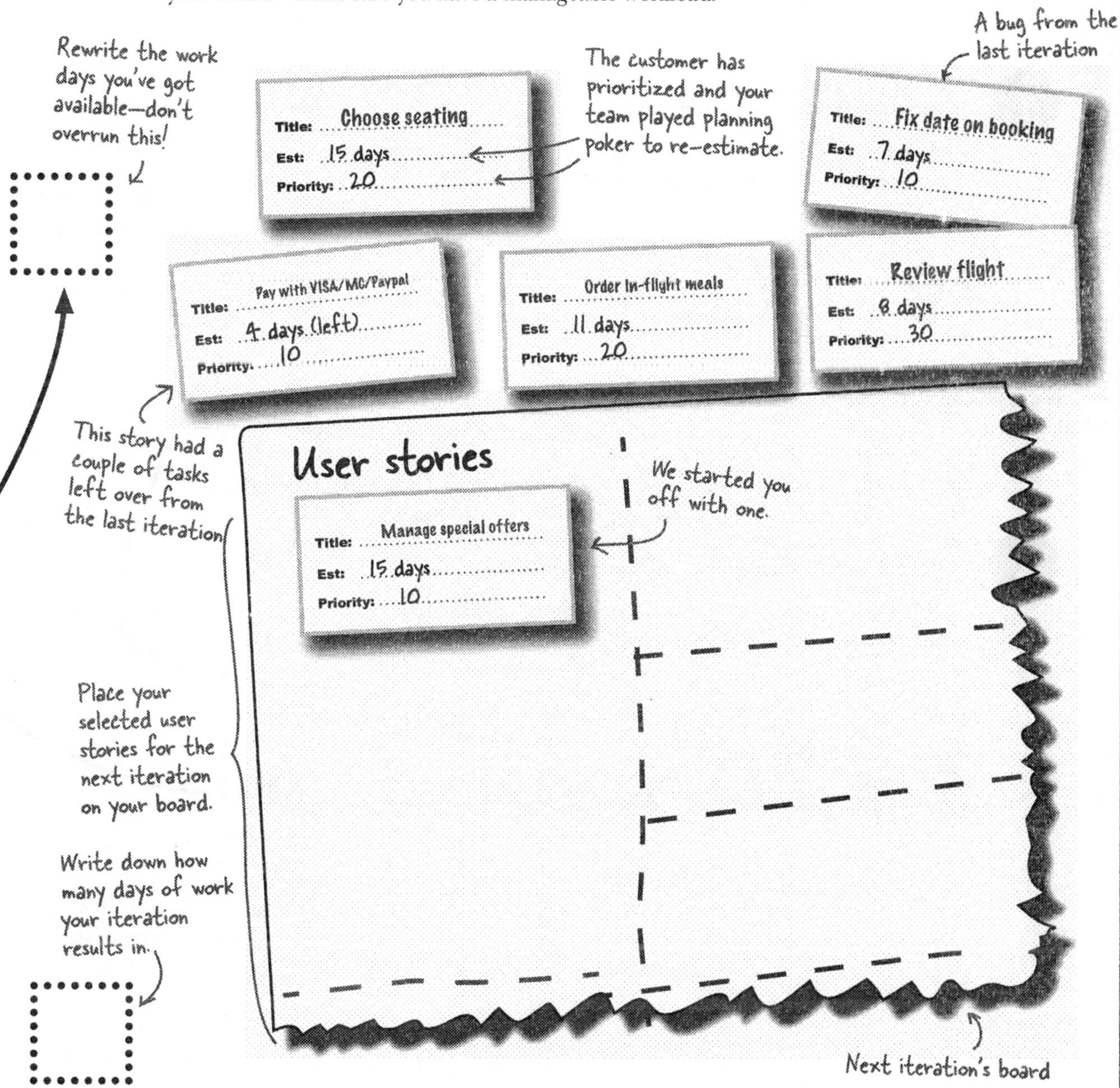

Long Exercise Solution

Your job was to calculate your team's new velocity, the maximum amount of days of work you can fit into the next iteration, and then to fill out your project board with user stories and other tasks that will fit into this next iteration.

1 **Calculate your new velocity**

Take your team's performance from the previous iteration and calculate a new value for this iteration's velocity.

$$38 \,/\, (20 \times 3) = \boxed{0.6}$$

You got 38 days of work done, including unplanned tasks that hit the board.

Your team's velocity has actually dropped...

Remember, velocity is a measure of how fast you and your team can get through work on your board. Regardless of whether that work is unplanned or not, it all counts.

2 **Calculate the work days you have available**

Now that you have your team's velocity, you can calculate the maximum number of work days that you can fit into this iteration.

$$3 \times 20 \times \boxed{0.6} = \boxed{36}$$

.. as has the total amount of work that your team can execute in the next iteration.

3 Fill up the board with new work

You know how many work days you've got, so all that's left is to take the candidate user stories and bugs, as well as stories left over the last iteration, and add them to your board—make sure you have a manageable work load.

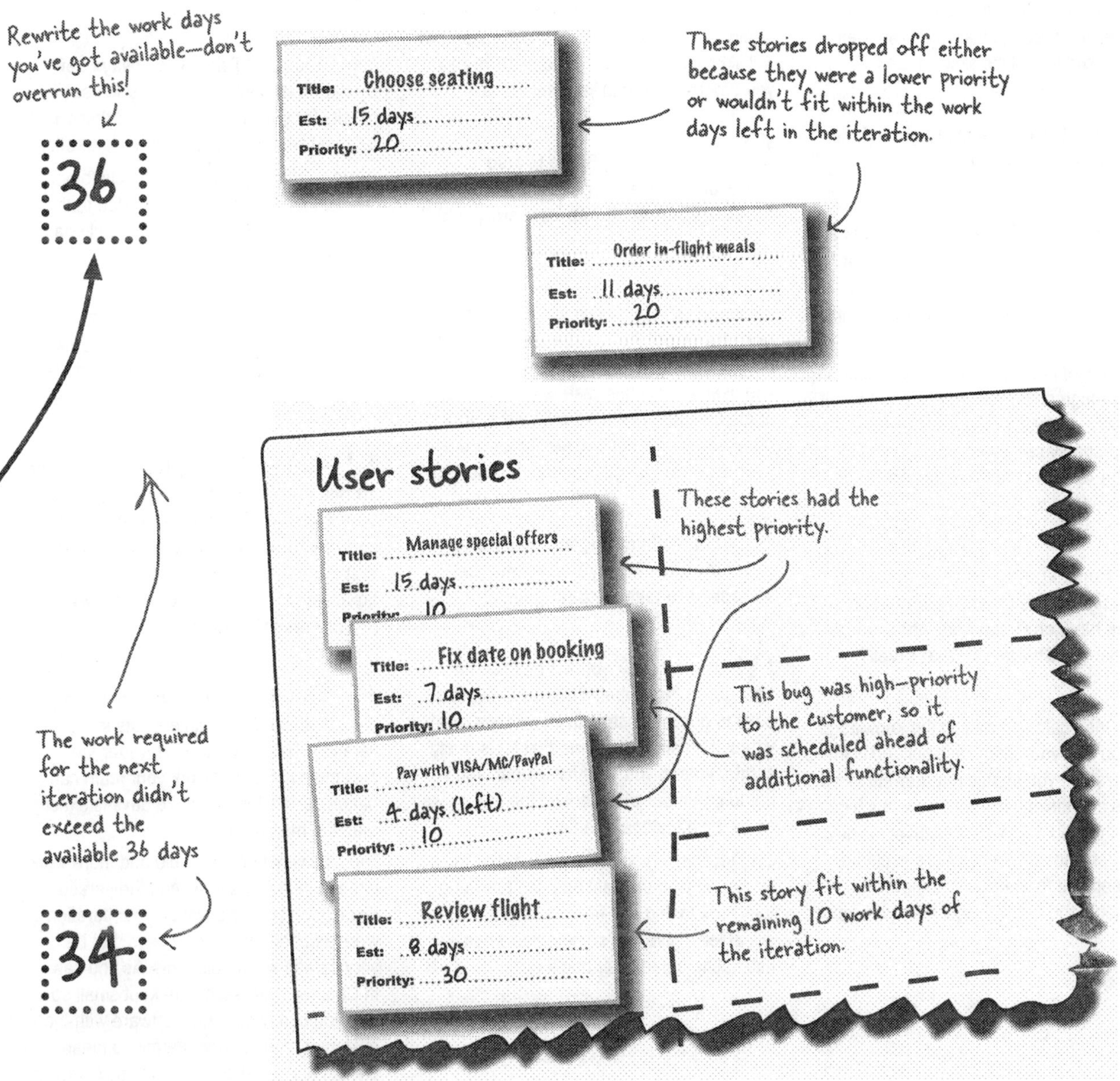

there are no Dumb Questions

Q: A team velocity of 0.6!? That's even slower than before. What happened?

A: Based on the work done in the last iteration, it turned out that your team was actually working a little *slower* than 0.7.

Q: Shouldn't my velocity get quicker as my iterations progress?

A: Not always. Remember, velocity is a measure of how fast *your* team can burn through their tasks, and 0.7 was just an original rough guess when you had nothing else to go by.

It's not uncommon for you and your team to have a tough first iteration, which will result in a lower velocity for the next iteration. But you'll probably see your velocity get better over the *next* several iterations, so you've got something to look forward to.

Q: Hmm, I noticed that some of the estimates for the Orion's Orbits user stories have changed from when we last saw them in Chapter 3. What gives?

A: Good catch! Based on the knowledge that you and your team have built up in the last iteration, you should **re-estimate** all your stories and tasks. Now you know much more about the work that will be involved so new estimates should be even more accurate, and keep you from missing something important, and taking longer than you expect.

Q: So the estimates for our user stories and their tasks will get smaller?

A: Not necessarily. They could get smaller, or bigger, but the important thing is that they will likely get more and more ***accurate*** as you progress through your iterations.

Q: I see that bug fixing is also represented as a user story. Doesn't that break the definition of a user story a bit?

A: A little, but a user story really ends up being—when it is broken into tasks—nothing more than work that you have to do. And a bug fix is certainly work for you to take on. The user story in this case is a description of the bug, and the tasks will be the work necessary to fix that bug (as far as you and your team can gauge from the description).

Q: I'm really struggling coming up with estimates for my bugs. Am I just supposed to take my best guess?

A: Unfortunately, you will be taking a best guess. And when it comes to bugs, it pays to guess conservatively. Always give yourself an amount of time that feels really comfortable to you. And remember, you've got to figure out what caused the bug as well as fix it; both steps take time.

One technique you can use is to look for similar bugs in the past and see how long they took to find and fix. That information will at least give you some guide when estimating a particular bug's work.

Q: If I have a collection of bugs, how do I decide what ones should make it into the board and be fixed in the next iteration?

A: " You don't! **Priority is always set by the customer.** So the customer sets a priority for each of the bugs, and that's what tells you what to deal with in each iteration

Besides, this approach lets the customer see that for each bug that is added to the iteration, other work—like new functionality—has to be sacrificed.

The decision is functionality versus bug fixes, and it's the customer who has to make that call... because it's the customer who decides ultimately what they want delivered at the end of the ***next*** iteration.

Q: I understand why the high-priority stories made it onto the next iteration's board, but wouldn't it be a better idea to add in another high-priority user story that slightly breaks the maximum work limit, rather than schedule in a lower priority task that fits?

A: **Never** break the maximum working days that your team can execute in an iteration. That value of 36 days for the maximum amount of work your team can handle for an iteration of 20 days is exactly that: the **maximum**.

The only way that you could add more work into the iteration is to extend the iteration. You could fit in more work if your iteration were extended to, say, 22 days, but be very careful when doing this. As you saw in Chapter 1, iterations are kept small so that you can check your software with the customer often. Longer iterations mean less checks and more chance that you'll deviate further from what your customer needs.

Velocity accounts for... the REAL WORLD

Velocity is a key part of planning out your next iteration. You're looking for a value that corresponds to how fast your team **actually works**, in reality, based on how they've worked in the past.

This is why you only factor in the work that has been completed in your last iteration. Any work that got put off doesn't matter; you want to know what was done, and how long it took to get done. That's the key information that tells you what to expect in the next iteration.

Velocity tells you what your team can expect to get done in the NEXT iteration

> **Be confident in your estimates**
>
> Velocity gives you an accurate way to forecast your productivity. Use it to make sure you have the right amount of work in your next iteration, and that you can successfully deliver on your promises to the customer.

By calculating velocity, you take into account the REALITY of how you and your team develop, so that you can plan your next iteration for SUCCESS.

And it's STILL about the customer

Let's say you've calculated your new velocity. You collected bugs and put them all in a bug tracker. You waded through all the piles of unfinished and delayed tasks and stories, and had the customer reprioritize those along with stories planned for the next iteration. You've got your board ready to go.

You still have to go back and get your customer's approval on your overall plan. And that's when things can go really wrong...

All your estimates from planning poker, your stories, your nice organized big board...they all have to get trashed (well, not the board itself) if the customer makes a big change.

You've suddenly got a ton of new code that you know nothing about, and it replaces a lot of what you had planned for the next iteration.

Software is still about CHANGE

Sometimes the customer is going to come up with a big change at the last minute. Or your best plans break down when your star programmer takes a new job. Or the company you're working for lays off an entire department...

But even though what you're working on has changed, the mechanics of planning haven't. You have a new velocity, and you know how many days of work your team has available. So you simply need to build new user stories, reprioritize, and replan.

You already know how to...

- [ ] Calculate your team's velocity
- [ ] Estimate your team's user stories and tasks
- [ ] Calculate your iteration size in days of work that your team can handle

BRAIN POWER

You've got a ton of new code that you've never seen or used before. What would be the first thing you do to try and estimate the time it will take to integrate that code into the Orion's system?

Someone else's software is STILL just software

Even though the Mercury Meals library is not code you have written, you still treat the work necessary to integrate the code into Orion's Orbits as you would any other software development activities. You'll need to tackle all the same basic activities:

Sometimes you'll have one story just for integrating new code; other times you might roll that into different stories that involve the code.

User stories

Every change to the software is motivated by and written down as a user story. In this case, your story card will be a description of how the Mercury Meals code is used by the Orion's Orbit system to achieve some particular piece of functionality.

The Mercury Meals code

Estimates

Every user story needs an estimate. So each of the user stories that the Mercury Meals code library plays a part in has to be estimated. How much time will it take to build that functionality, including time spent integrating the Mercury Meals code?

Priorities

The final piece of the puzzle is, of course, priorities. Each of the user stories associated with the Mercury Meals code needs to have an associated priority from your customer so that you can plan out the work for the next iteration, in the order that your customer wants it done.

Exercise

You've got new stories related to Mercury Meals, as well as the stories you thought you'd be doing in this next iteration. Your job is to re-create the board using your velocity and the customer's priorities. (We've left out the stories that didn't make the first-pass plan.)

The new Mercury Meals user stories

Title	Est	Priority
Order Regular Meal	12 days	10
Order vegetarian or vegan meal	6 days	20
View all the orders for a flight	4 days	10

These were the user stories that made it onto your board the first planning pass.

Title	Est	Priority
Edit Special Deals	15 days	10
Fix date on booking	7 days	10
Leave flight review	8 days	30
Pay with Visa/MC/PayPal	4 days (left)	10

36

The number of people in your team and their velocity hasn't changed since your first attempt at a project board for this iteration, so neither has the number of work days you've got.

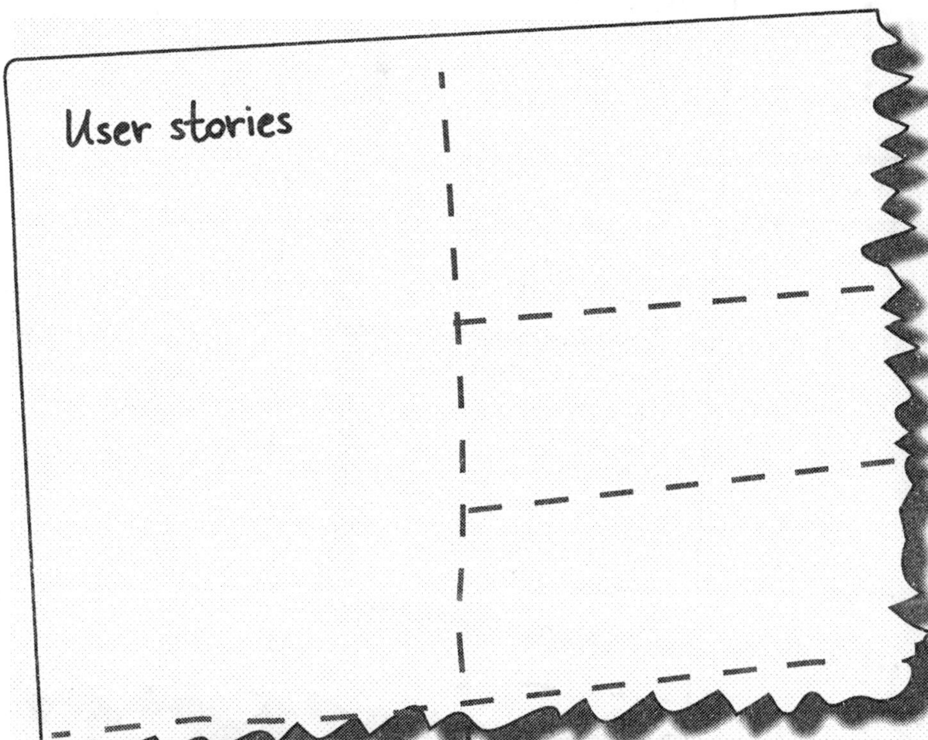

Add up your new total work for the next iteration.

Exercise Solution

Your job was to re-create the board using your velocity and the customer's priorities.

Title: Order vegetarian or vegan meal
Est: 6 days
Priority: 20

This Mercury Meals user story was a lower priority and so will have to wait until the following iteration.

Title: Leave flight review
Est: 8 days
Priority: 30

Title: Fix date on booking
Est: 7 days
Priority: 10

Even though it's a high priority, we couldn't fit in this bug fix so it'll be first up for the following iteration, assuming that's what the customer still wants then.

36

Your budget was 36 days of work for your team, factoring in velocity...

User stories

Title: Order Regular Meal
Est: 12 days
Priority: 10

Title: View all the orders for a flight
Est: 4 days
Priority: 10

These were the top priority in terms of the Mercury Meals user stories.

Title: Edit Special Deals
Est: 15 days
Priority: 10

Title: Pay with Visa/MC/PayPal
Est: 4 days (left)
Priority: 10

Going on priority, these two features also made it into this iteration.

... and you've planned out 35.

35

Customer approval? Check!

Once again, you've got to get customer approval once everything's planned out. And this time, there aren't any surprises...

there are no Dumb Questions

Q: Can you tell me again why we've got user stories for working with third-party code? And why did you estimate 12 days for ordering a meal? Isn't the whole point of getting third-party code that it saves us time?

A: A user story isn't as much about writing code as it is about what a user needs your system to do. So no matter who wrote the code, if you're responsible for functionality, capture it as a user story.

As for why the estimates are pretty large, reuse is great, but you're still going to have to write some code that interacts with the third-party software. But just think how long it would take if you had to write all the Mercury Meals code yourself.

Q: Are there any times when I shouldn't consider reusing someone else's code library or API?

A: Reuse can really give your development work a shot in the arm, but third-party code has to be used with care. When you use someone else's software, you're **relying** on that software, placing your success in the hands of the people that developed the code that *your* code now uses.

So if you're using someone else's work, you better be sure you can trust that work.

Exercise

It's time to write the code for the two Mercury Meals user stories, "Order Regular Meals" and "View all the orders for a flight." On the left you have the Mercury Meals code's interface, which is a collection of methods that you can call from your own code. On the right, you need to wire up your code so that it uses the Mercury Meals API to bring both of the user stories below to life.

The two stories you have to implement

Title:	Order Regular Meal
Est:	12 days
Priority:	10

Title:	View all the orders for a flight
Est:	4 days
Priority:	10

Reality check: assume your tea[m] spent several days getting class diagrams together for the Mercury Meals API.

The main interface to the Mercury Meals code

MercuryMeals

- + getInstance() :MercuryMeals — How you get access to the MercuryMeals object
- + createOrder() :Order — Creates a blank order
- + submitOrder(order : Order) :boolean — Submits a completed order to Mercury Meals
- + getMealOption(name : String) :MealOption — Returns a meal option, like "Roast Beef"
- + getOrdersThatMatchKeywords(keywords : String[]) :Order[] — Returns a list of orders that match a specific set of keywords

Methods on the interface that can be called from your code

Interface that represents an order for a mea[l]

Order

- + addMealOption(mealOption : MealOption) :void — You can add options to an order...
- + addKeyword(keyword : String) :void — ...and add keywords that you can then search on later to retrieve a set of orders.

You can download the Mercury Meals code from http://www.headfirstlabs.com/books/hfsd

```
//...
// Adds a meal order to a flight
public void orderMeal(String[] options, String flightNo)
                         throws MealOptionNotFoundException,
                                OrderNotAcceptedException {
    MercuryMeals mercuryMeals = MercuryMeals.getInstance();

    for (int x = 0; x < options.length;x++) {

    }

}

// Finds all the orders for a specific flight
public String[] getAllOrdersForFlight(String flightNo) {

}
// ...
```

The first line of code has already been added for you.

Add these code magnets into the main program.

```
return mercuryMeals.getOrdersThatMatchKeyword({flightNo});
```

```
Order order = mercuryMeals.createOrder();
```

```
order.addKeyword(flightNo);
```

```
MercuryMeals mercuryMeals = MercuryMeals.getInstance();
```

```
if (!mercuryMeals.submitOrder(order)) {
   throw new OrderNotAcceptedException(order);
}
```

```
MealOption mealOption = mercuryMeals.getMealOption(options[x]);
```

```
if (mealOption != null) {
   order.addMealOption(mealOption);
} else {
   throw new MealOptionNotFoundException(mealOption);
}
```

Exercise Solution

Your job was to complete the code so that it uses the Mercury Meals API to bring both of the user stories to life.

```
//...
// Adds a meal order to a flight
public void orderMeal(String[] options, String flightNo)
                            throws MealOptionNotFoundException,
                                   OrderNotAcceptedException {
   MercuryMeals mercuryMeals = MercuryMeals.getInstance();
   Order order = mercuryMeals.createOrder();
   for (int x = 0; x < options.length;x++) {
      MealOption mealOption = mercuryMeals.getMealOption(options[x]);
      if (mealOption != null) {
         order.addMealOption(mealOption);
      } else {
         throw new MealOptionNotFoundException(mealOption);
      }
   }
   order.addKeyword(flightNo);
   if (!mercuryMeals.submitOrder(order)) {
      throw new OrderNotAcceptedException(order);
   }
}

// Finds all the orders for a specific flight
public Order[] getAllOrdersForFlight(String flightNo) {
   MercuryMeals mercuryMeals = MercuryMeals.getInstance();
   return mercuryMeals.getOrdersThatMatchKeyword({flightNo});
}
// ...
```

This gets a Mercury Meals object for this code to use.

Creates a new blank order

For each of the options selected, a new option is added to the order.

If an option isn't found, then an exception is raised.

The flight number is added to the order as a keyword so that the orders for a particular flight can be retrieved.

Attempt to submit the new complete order to Mercury Meals.

Searches for and returns all orders that have the specified flight number as a keyword

there are no Dumb Questions

Q: That was easy. Why did we estimate 16 days for integrating the Mercury Meals code?

A: There's more going on here than just integrating code. First you and your team will have to come to grips with the Mercury Meals documentation. There'll be sequence diagrams to understand and class diagrams to pick through, all of which takes time. Factor in your own updates to your design and thinking about how best to integrate the code in the first place, and you've got a meaty task on your hands. In fact, it's often the thinking time up front that takes longer than the actual implementation.

Q: Does it matter if the third-party code is compiled or not?

A: If the library works then it doesn't matter if it's in source code or compiled form. You have to add in extra time to compile the code if it comes as source, but often that's an easy comand-line job and you'll have a compiled library anyway.

However, if the library doesn't work for any reason, then it really does matter if you can get at the source or not. If you are reusing a compiled library of code then you are limited to simply using that code, according to its accompanying documentation. You might be able to decompile the code, but if you're not careful, that can mean you are breaking the license of the third-party software. With compiled libraries you usually can't actually delve into the code in the library itself to fix any problems. If there's an issue, you have to try and get back in touch with the person who originally wrote the code.

However, if you are actually given the source code to the library—if it's open source or something that you've purchased—then you can get into the library itself to fix any problems. This sounds great, but bear in mind that in both cases you're trusting the third-party library to work. Otherwise you're either signing up for a barrage of questions being sent to the original developers, or for extra work to develop fixes in the code itself.

Q: What if the third-party code doesn't work?

A: Then your trust in that library quickly disappears, and you have two choices: You can continue to persevere with the library, particularly if you have the source code and can perform some serious debugging to see what is going wrong. Or you can discard the library for another, if one's available, or try to write the code yourself, if you know how.

With any of these options you are taking on extra work. That's why when you consider using third-party code, you have to think very carefully. Sometimes that code is forced upon you, like with Mercury Meals, but often you have a choice. You need to be aware of just how much trust you are putting in that library working.

Be careful when deciding to reuse something. When you reuse code, you are assuming that code WORKS.

Exercise

This is a good time to go grab the code!

The code for Mercury Meals is available from the Head First Labs site. Just go to *http://www.headfirstlabs.com/books/hfsd/*, and follow the links to download the code for Chapter 10.

Testing your code

Make sure you've downloaded the Mercury Meals and Orion's Orbits code from Head First Labs. Make the additions shown on page 368, compile everything, and give things a whirl...

You should have a build tool that makes this a piece of cake.

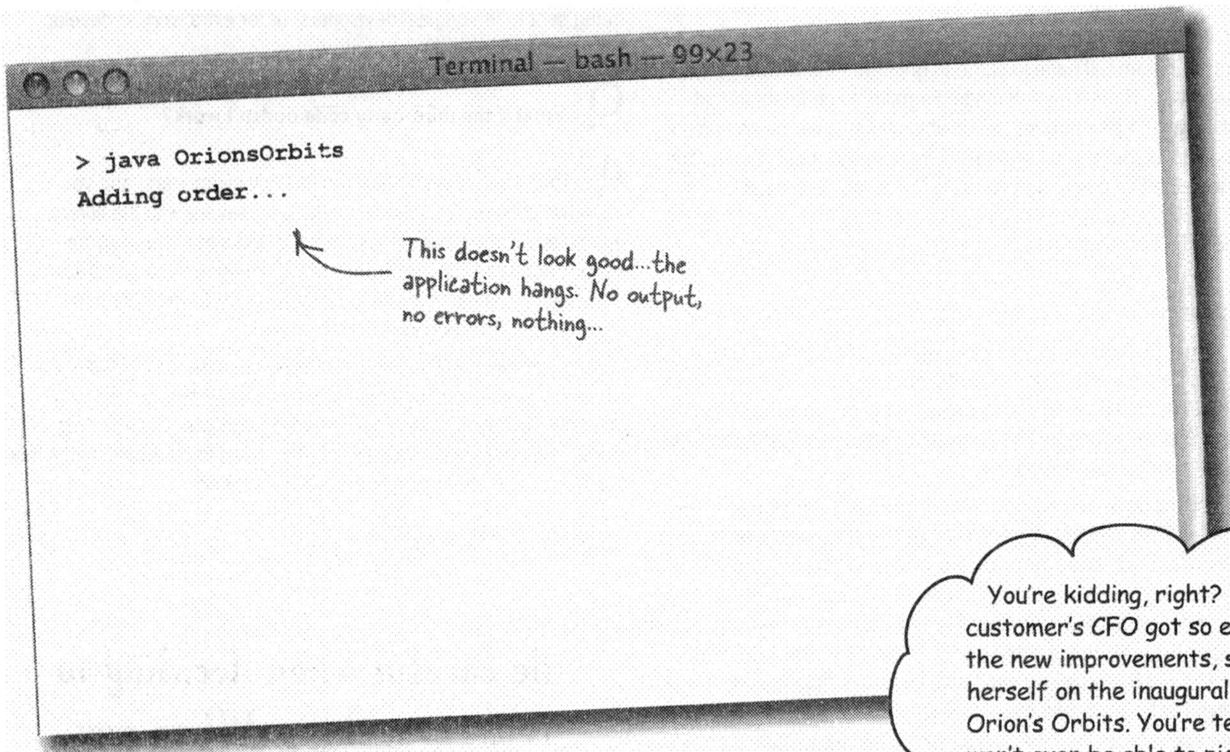

Houston, we really do have a problem...

All that hard work has resulted in a big fat nothing. Your code...or the Mercury Meals code...***some*** code isn't working. Somewhere. And your customer, and your customer's *boss*, is about to really be upset...

Sharpen your pencil

You've just integrated a huge amount of third-party code, and something's not working. Time's short, and the pressure's on.

What would you do? ....

....

....

....

....

....

....

Standup meeting

Laura: We assumed that the Mercury Meals code would work, and it clearly doesn't, or at least doesn't in the way we expect. What a mess.

Bob: Well, that sounds like a reasonable assumption to me. ***We*** would never release code that doesn't work...

Mark: Yeah, but that's us. Who knows what the developers at Mercury Meals were doing?

Laura: We just took the code and assumed it would work, maybe we should have tested it out first...

Bob: So you think the developers at Mercury Meals just kicked out a dud piece of code?

Laura: It certainly looks like it. Who knows if it was ever even run, it could have been only half a project.

Mark: But it's our code and our problem now...

Bob: And it's way too late to start from scratch...

Mark: ...and we don't know how the Mercury Meals system works anyhow...

Laura: And worse than all of that, what are we going to tell the CFO? Our butts are seriously on the line here...

Trust NO ONE

When it comes to code that someone else has written, it's all about trust, and the real lesson here is to ***trust no one*** when it comes to code. Unless you've *seen* a piece of code running, or run your own tests against it, someone else's code could be a ticking time bomb that's just waiting to explode—right when you need it the most.

When you take on code from a third party, you are relying on that code to work. It's no good complaining that it doesn't work if you never tried to use it, and until you have seen it running, it's best to assume that third-party code doesn't really work at all.

Your software...your responsibility

You're responsible for how your software works. It doesn't matter if the buggy code in the software wasn't code you wrote. A bug is a bug, and as a pro software developer, you're responsible for ***all*** the software you deliver.

A third party is not you. That might sound a little obvious, but it's really important when you're tempted to assume that just because you use a great testing and development process, everyone else does, too.

Never assume that other people are following your process

Treat every line of code developed elsewhere with suspicion until you've tested it, because not everyone is as professional in their approach to software development as you are.

It doesn't matter who wrote the code. If it's in YOUR software, it's YOUR responsibility.

Exercise

The Mercury Meals classes are now **your** code...but they're a mess. Circle and annotate all the problems you can see in the code below. You're looking for everything from readability of the code right through to problems with functionality.

```
// Follows the Singleton design pattern
public class MercuryMeals
{
   public MercuryMeals meallythang;
   private Order cO;
   private String qk = "select * from order-table where keywords like %1;";

public MercuryMeals() {
}

public MercuryMeals getInstance()
{
   this.meallythang = new MercuryMeals();
   return this.instance;
}
   // TODO Really should document this at some point... TBD
   public Order createOrder {
      return new Order();}

public MealOption getMealOption(String option)
throws MercuryMealsConnectionException {
   if (MM.establish().isAnyOptionsForKey(option))
   { return MM.establish.getMealOption(option).[0] };
   return null;
}
```

```
// Mercury Meals class continued...

    public boolean submitOrder(Order cO)
{
    try {
      MM mm = MM.establish();
      mm.su(this.cO);
    catch (Exception e)
    { // write out an error message } return false; }

    public Order[] getOrdersThatMatchKeyword(String qk)
                                        throws MercuryMealsConnectionException {
      Order o = new Order[];
      try {
          o = MM.establish().find(qk, qk);
       } catch (Exception e) {
          return null;
       }
       return o;
    }}
```

Exercise Solution

Your job was to to circle and annotate all the problems you can see in this Mercury Meals code.

```
// Follows the Singleton design pattern
public class MercuryMeals

{

   public MercuryMeals meallythang;

   private Order cO;

   private String qk = "select * from order-table where keywords like %1;";

   private MercuryMeals instance;

   public MercuryMeals() {

   }


   public MercuryMeals getInstance()

   {

      this.instance = new MercuryMeals();

      return this.instance;

   }

   // TODO Really should document this at some point... TBD

   public Order createOrder {

      return new Order();}

   public MealOption getMealOption(String option)

   throws MercuryMealsConnectionException {

      if (MM.establish().isAnyOptionsForKey(option))

      { return MM.establish().getMealOption(option).[0] };

      return null;

   }
```

No real documentation on the class, other than the fact that it tries to implement the Singleton pattern...

Not the most descriptive of attribute names.

This attribute is public! That's a major object-oriented no-no.

Why is there an Order attribute? Even a few comments would help...

Surely this should be a constant? And does qk make any sense as an attribute name?

Why have an explicit constructor declared that does nothing?

Hang on! This class is supposed to be implementing the singleton pattern but this looks like it creates a new instance of MercuryMeals every time this method is called...

Looks like the original developer just didn't ever finish this bit off.

This method seems to not do anything of any real value at the moment. You could just as easily create an order without the Mercury Meals class—and as for the indentation, it's all over the place.

Why not establish the connection just once?

Returning null is a bad practice. It's a better idea to raise an exception that gives the caller more info to work with.

```
// Mercury Meals class continued...

   public boolean submitOrder(Order cO)
{
   try {
     MM mm = MM.establish();
     mm.su(this.cO);
   catch (Exception e)
   { // write out an error message } return false; }

   public Order[] getOrdersThatMatchKeyword(String qk)
                                  throws MercuryMealsConnectionException {
     Order o = new Order[];
     try {
         o = MM.establish().find(qk, qk);
       } catch (Exception e) {
         return null;
       }
      return o;
}}
```

No documentation on any of this class's methods. Something that described what the methods are supposed to do would make life a LOT easier.

No wonder the software gave no indication whether it was working or not (except by just hanging...) This method swallows all exceptions that are raised. This is a classic exception anti-pattern. If an exception gets raised, and you can't deal with it locally, then pass the exception up to the caller so they can at least know what went wrong.

The code indentation is still all over the place. This makes things very hard to read.

Which qk is being used here? This doesn't make sense, and might be a bug.

Hiding exceptions again! The caller of this method will never have to handle a MercuryMealsConnectionException or any other exception because this method is hiding anything that goes wrong and just returning null.

Believe it or not, this bracket here closes the class, but from the poor use of indentation, you'd be hard-pressed to be sure of that from looking.

You without your process

Right now things are looking pretty bleak, and without your process you would really be in trouble...

You with your process

It's not a perfect world. When your code—or someone else's code you depend on—isn't working, and your customer is breathing down your neck, it's easy to panic or catch the next flight to a non-extradition country. But that's when a good process can be your best friend.

BULLET POINTS

- When you're gearing up for the next iteration, always **check back with the customer** to make sure that the work you are planning is the work that they want done.
- You and your team's **velocity is recalculated** at the end of every iteration.
- Let your customer **reprioritize your user stories** for a new iteration, based on the working days you've got available for that iteration.
- Whether you're writing new code or reusing someone else's **it's all still just software** and your **process remains the same**.
- Every piece of code in your software, whether it be your own code or a third party's like Mercury Meals, should be represented by at least one user story.
- **Never assume anything** about code you are reusing.
- A great interface to a library of code is no guarantee that the code works. **Trust nothing** until you've seen it work for yourself.
- **Code is written once but read (by others) many times.** Treat your code as you would any other piece of work that you present to other people. It should be readable, reliable, and easy to understand.

there are no Dumb Questions

Q: Things seem to be in a really bad shape right now. What good is our process if we still end up in crappy situations like this?

A: The problem here is that when you reused Mercury Meals' software, you and your team brought in code that was developed under a different process than yours, with an entirely different result—broken code.

Not everyone developing software is going to test first, use version control and continuous integration, and track bugs. Sometimes, it's up to you to take software you didn't develop and deal with it.

Q: So how common is this situation? Couldn't I just always use my own code?

A: Most software developed today is created on really tight timelines. You have to be productive and deliver great software quicker and quicker, and often with success, so the tempo rises as your customers demand even more.

One of the best ways to save time in those situations is to reuse code—often code that your team didn't write. So the better you get at development, the more reuse will be part of your normal routine.

And when you start to reuse code, there's always that crucial time when you encounter code that simply does not work, and it's easier to fix that code than to start over. But hold on...Chapter 11 is all about just how to do that, without abandoning your process.

Dealing with code that doesn't work is part of software development!

In Chapter 11, you'll see how your process can handle the heat.

Software Development Cross

Let's put what you've learned to use and stretch out your left brain a bit! Good luck!

Across

2. If your software doesn't work, it's your .... to get it fixed.
6. If you .... that a piece of code works you are heading for a world of pain.
8. The .... decides what is in or out for iteration 2.
11. Your velocity helps you calculate how many .... days you can handle in iteration 2.
12. .... deals with the real world when you're planning your next iteration.
13. Mercury Meals, other frameworks, code libraries and even code samples are all cases where you will want to consider .... code.
14. .... are also included in the candidate work for the next iteration.

Down

1. Code .... is one very useful technique to get you developing quickly and productively.
3. Any work for the next iteration should appear on the .... for the iteration.
4. Trust .... when it comes to reusing software.
5. Never .... any code you haven't written or run in some way.
7. You should let your customer .... your user stories, bug reports and other pieces of work before you begin planning iteration 2.
9. You treat third party code the .... as your own code.
10. You may be following a great ...., but don't assume that anyone else is.

Software Development Cross Solution

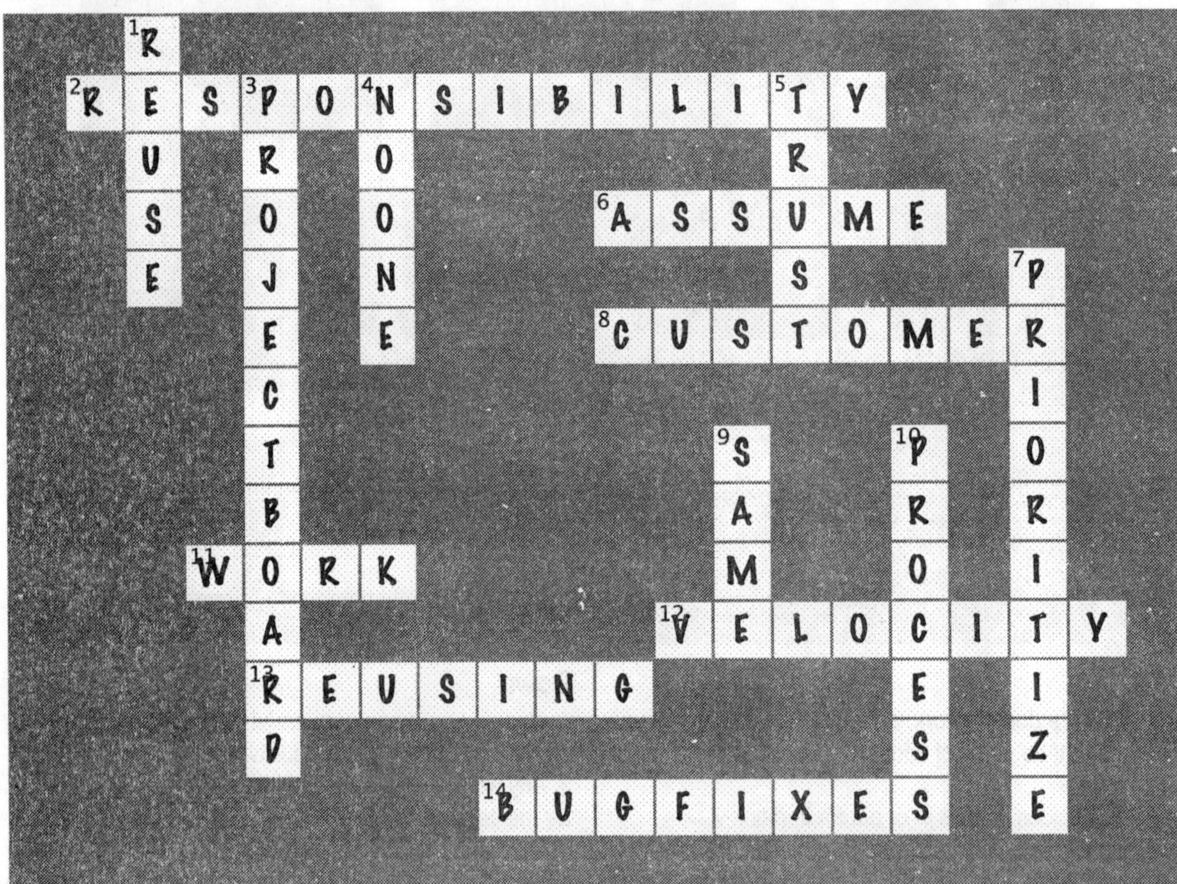

11 bugs

Squashing bugs like a pro

Your code, your responsibility...your bug, your reputation!

When things get tough, it's **up to you** to bring them back from the brink. **Bugs**, whether they're in your code or just in code that your software uses, are a **fact of life** in software development. And, like everything else, the way you handle bugs should fit into the rest of your process. You'll need to **prepare your board**, **keep your customer in the loop**, **confidently estimate** the work it will take to fix your bugs, and apply **refactoring** and **prefactoring** to fix and avoid bugs in the future.

At the end of the last chapter, things were in a pretty bad way. You'd added Mercury Meals' code into Orion's Orbits and were all set to demo things to the CFO when you hit a problem. Well, actually ***three*** problems—and that adds up to ***one big mess***...

Orion's Orbits is NOT working.

Your customer added three new user stories that relied on some new code from Mercury Meals. Everything looked good, the board was balanced and you completed the integration work when, BOOM!, you ran your code and absolutely nothing happened. The application just froze...

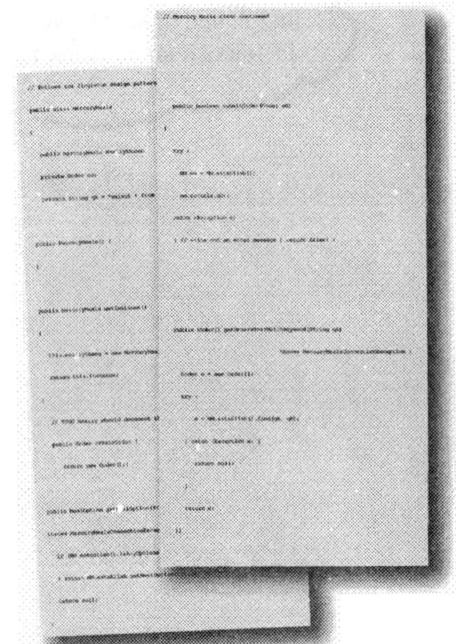

You have a LOT of ugly new code

When you dug into the Mercury Meals code, you found a ton of problems. What's causing the problems in Orion's Orbits, and where should you start looking?

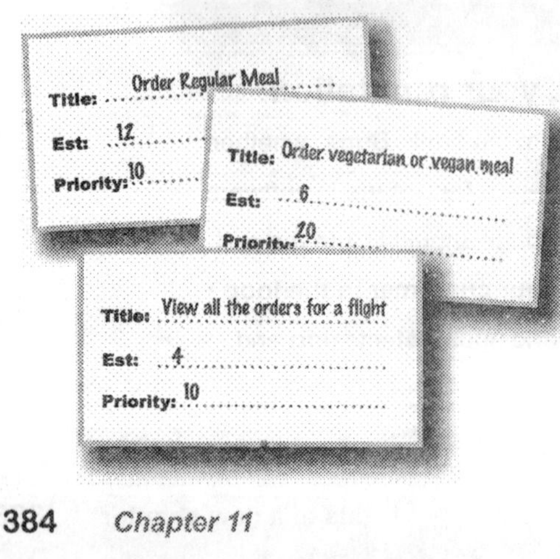

You have THREE user stories that rely on your code working.

All of this would be bad enough, but there are three user stories that rely on the Mercury Meals code working, not just one.

To make matters even worse, the CEO of Orion's Orbits has talked you up to the CFO, and both are looking forward to seeing everything working, and soon...

Sharpen your pencil

Your software isn't working, you've got code to fix, and the CEO of Orion's Orbits is breathing down your neck, because the CFO is soon to be breathing down his. But how does any of this fit into your process?

What would you do next?

Wait! Think through what you would do next and fill in the blanks above before turning the page...

You, too, impatient developer... come up with a good answer, and <u>then</u> go on to the next section.

First, you've got to talk to the customer

Whenever something changes, talk it over with your team. If the impact is significant, in terms of functionality or schedule, then you've got to go back to the customer. And this is a big issue, so that means making a tough phone call...

The customer's right. You need to get things to a point where you can make a confident estimate as to how long this mess will take to fix...and get that estimate FAST.

Standup meeting

Laura: Well, that's why they were fired after the merger. It doesn't really matter that they screwed up, though, it's our code now...

Bob: I know, I know. But poorly written code just burns me up. It makes us look like idiots.

Mark: Look, can we move on? What do we do next?

Laura: Well, we're stuck with this code. So better start treating it like it's ours.

Mark: I think you might be on to something there...

Laura: We already know how to deal with our own new code. if we treat Mercury Meals the same way, that should at least give us a good starting point.

Bob: Ugh...you mean we have to manage its configuration, build it, and test it, don't you? Build scripts and CI all around?

Mark: Yep, we're going to have to maintain this stuff so the best first step would be to get all the Mercury Meals code into our code repository and building correctly before we can even start to fix the problem.

It's <u>your</u> <u>code</u>, so the first step is to get it building...

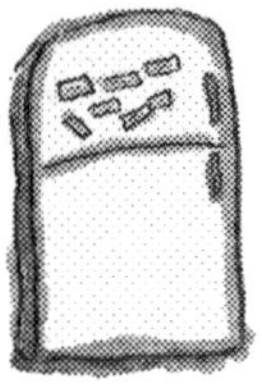

Broken Code Magnets

Here are a bunch of things you could do to work your way through the Mercury Meals code. Put them in the order you think you should do them. Be careful, though, there might be some you don't think will be worth doing at all.

- Figure out what dependencies this code has and if it has any impact on Orion's Orbits' code.
- Figure out how to package the compiled version to include in Orion's Orbits.
- Organize the source code into your standard src, test, docs, etc., directories.
- Put the code in your repository.
- Create a place in your bug tracker for issues.
- Write tests simulating how you need to use the software.
- Integrate the code into your CI configuration.
- Document the code.
- Write a build script.
- File bugs for issues you find.
- Run a coverage report to see how much code you need to fix.
- Get a line count of the code and estimate how long it will take to fix.
- Do a security audit on the code.
- Use a UML tool to reverse-engineer the code and create class diagrams.

Hint: some things may need to be done more than once.

Put your magnets on here in the order you would do them.

To-Do List

Broken Code Magnets

Here are a bunch of things you could do to work your way through the Mercury Meals code. Put them in the order you think you should do them. Be careful, though, there might be some you don't think will be worth doing at all.

To-Do List

This is a tricky one. It's going to pop up all over the place, so we put it vertically. Keep track of things as soon as you find them. You might decide it's not important later, but for now, just record everything you think could be an issue.

`File bugs for issues you find.`

`Create a place in your bug tracker for issues.`

You need to get the code building, but you'll be finding things you didn't know as you go. Set up a place to capture these right away so you don't lose this information. You'll need it to fix things later.

`Organize the source code into your standard src, test, docs, etc., directories.`

`Write a build script.`

Keeping with the information theme, you want to capture how to build the software. In order to do that, you need a build script. It's best to get the code organized before you write your script, though, so you don't have to write it, organize the code, and then change your script.

`Put the code in your repository.`

Next you need to get this code version controlled. By organizing it into directories before this step, you won't have to deal with shuffling around code you've already committed.

You could also make a strong case for putting this in your repository <u>before</u> you shuffle stuff around, so you can roll things back if you mess it up.

`Integrate the code into your CI configuration.`

Once it's in the repository, turn you CI tool loose on it. This gets your safety net set up.

`Write tests simulating how you need to use the software.`

And now we can start thinking about getting it to work. We'll talk more about this in a few pages.

So what about all the magnets we didn't use? They're not necessarily bad ideas, but here's why we didn't put them on our short list.

Figure out what dependencies this code has and if it has any impact on Orion's Orbits' code.

This is important, but we don't know what changes we're going to have to make to the code yet. We're just not ready to focus on library versions.

Figure out how to package the compiled version to include in Orion's Orbits.

This is going to be important once this code is stable, but until we get things tested and working, it's not much use worrying about how to package anything up beyond the library we already have.

Document the code.

Another important one, and it almost got a vertical spot next to "File bugs...". But since we're not making changes to the code yet, and don't even know what parts we'll need, we decided to leave this one off of our short list...although we might come back to it later.

Run a coverage report to see how much code you need to fix.

This one just can't happen yet. We don't have tests, we don't know what code we actually need, and we know some of the code isn't working. Test coverage at this point won't tell us much of value.

Get a line count of the code and estimate how long it will take to fix.

This is oh-so-tempting. It provides a solid metric to latch onto, which seems like a good thing. The problem with this is that we don't know how much of the code we'll need, and we have absolutely no idea how much is missing. What if there is a stubbed-out class where a whole section of the library is supposed to be? Concerns like this make a metric here useless.

Do a security audit on the code.

At some point this will be a great idea, but like some of the other tasks, we don't know what code we need yet, and we're about to go changing things anyway, so let's hold off on this for now.

Use a UML tool to reverse-engineer the code and create class diagrams.

Of all the tasks we didn't choose to do, this is the most likely candidate to get added back in. But right now, we don't know how much of the library we need. Let's get a handle on what we have to use; then we'll try and figure out how it's supposed to work.

Priority one: get things buildable

The code is in version control, you've written build scripts, and you've added continuous integration with CruiseControl. Mercury Meals is still a junky piece of nonworking code, but at least you should have a little bit of control over the code...and that's your first priority.

An email generated by your continuous integration tool when the Mercury Meals build is run.

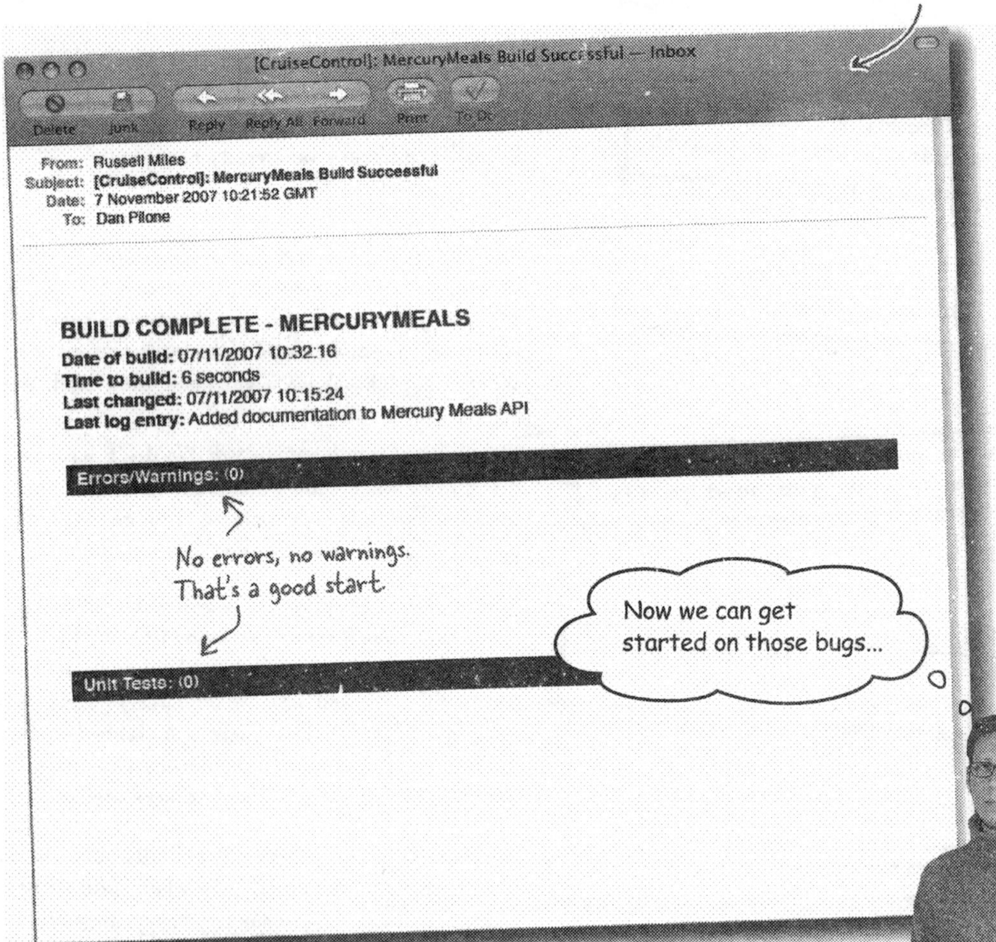

[CruiseControl]: MercuryMeals Build Successful — Inbox

Delete Junk Reply Reply All Forward Print To Do

From: Russell Miles
Subject: [CruiseControl]: MercuryMeals Build Successful
Date: 7 November 2007 10:21:52 GMT
To: Dan Pilone

BUILD COMPLETE - MERCURYMEALS

Date of build: 07/11/2007 10:32:16
Time to build: 6 seconds
Last changed: 07/11/2007 10:15:24
Last log entry: Added documentation to Mercury Meals API

Errors/Warnings: (0)

Unit Tests: (0)

No errors, no warnings. That's a good start.

This assumes that you fixed anything that kept all the Mercury classes from at least compiling—but resist the urge to start fixing other things right now.

A little time now can save a LOT of time later.

None of the original bugs are fixed just yet, but that's OK. You've got a development environment set up, your code's under version control, and you can easily write tests and run them automatically. In other words, you've just prevented all the problems you've seen over the last several hundred pages from sneaking up and biting you in the ass.

You know that the code doesn't work, but now that everything is dialed into your process, you're ready to attack bugs in a sensible way. You've taken ownership of the Mercury Meals code, and anything you fix from here on out will stay fixed... saving you wasted time on the back end.

Get the code under source control and building successfully before you change anything... including fixing bugs.

We could fix code...

Now it's time to figure out what needs to be fixed. At the end of Chapter 10 you took a look at the Mercury Meals code, and the prognosis was not good...

All of these problems were found, and this was only when you peeked into the first layer of the Mercury Meals code.

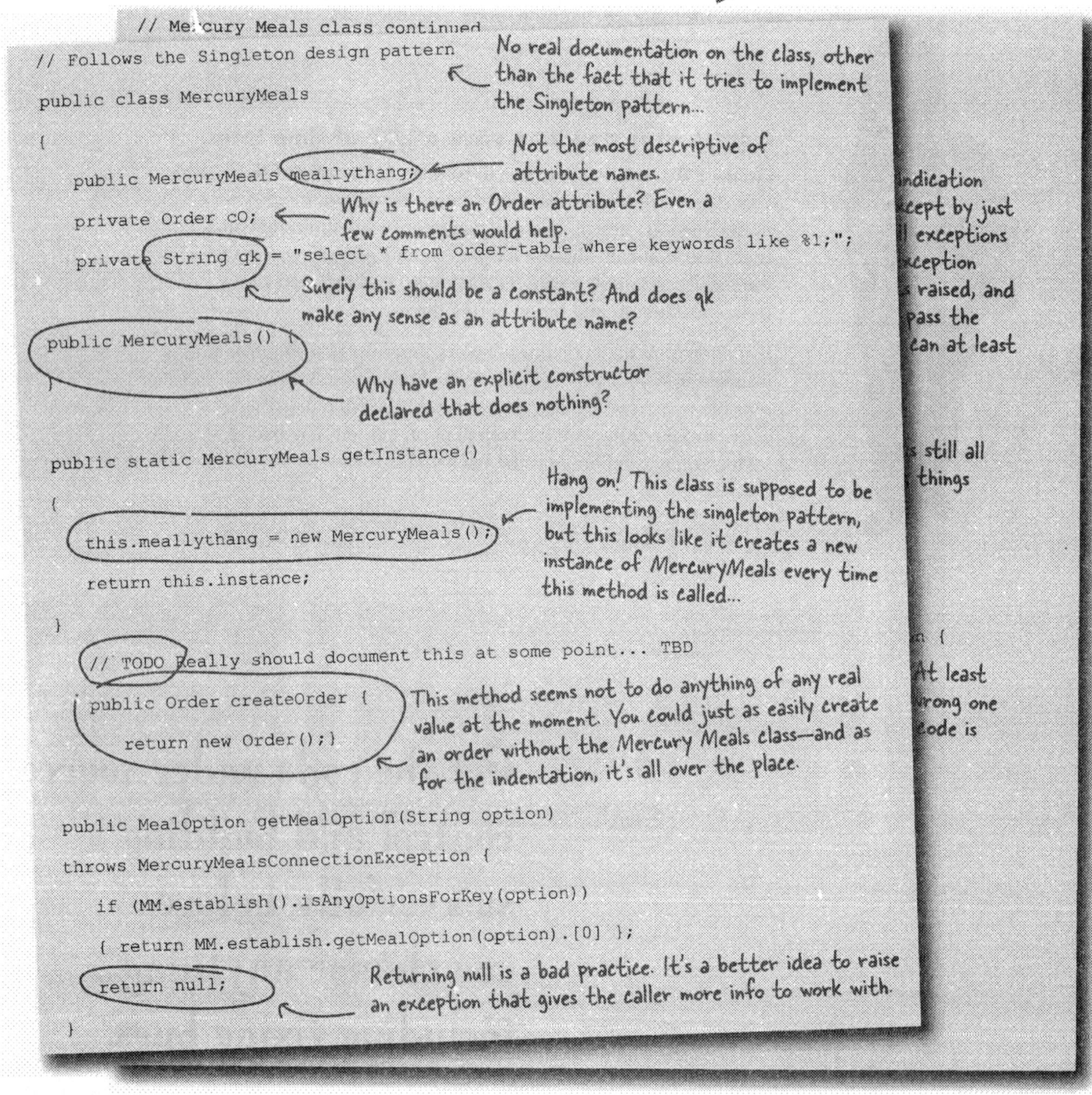

```
// Mercury Meals class continued
// Follows the Singleton design pattern
public class MercuryMeals
{
   public MercuryMeals meallythang;
   private Order cO;
   private String qk = "select * from order-table where keywords like %1;";

public MercuryMeals() {
}

public static MercuryMeals getInstance()
{
   this.meallythang = new MercuryMeals();
   return this.instance;
}

  // TODO Really should document this at some point... TBD
  public Order createOrder {
     return new Order();}

public MealOption getMealOption(String option)
throws MercuryMealsConnectionException {
   if (MM.establish().isAnyOptionsForKey(option))
   { return MM.establish.getMealOption(option).[0] };
  return null;
}
```

...but we need to fix functionality

But things might not be quite as bad as they look. You don't have to fix ***all*** the bugs in Mercury Meals; ***you just have to fix the bugs that affect the functionality that you need.*** Don't worry about the rest of the code—focus just on the functionality in your user stories.

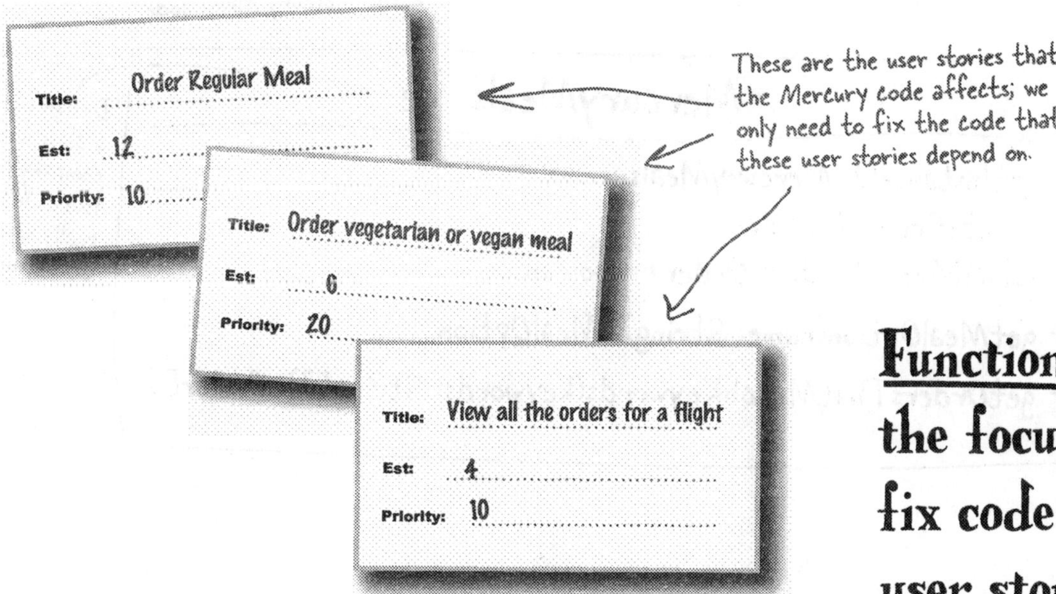

Functionality is the focus. Only fix code to fix user stories.

BULLET POINTS

- Everything revolves around **customer-oriented functionality**.
- You write and fix code to **satisfy user stories**.
- You **only fix what is broken**, and you know what is broken because you have **tests that fail**.
- **Tests are your safety net.** You use tests to make sure you didn't break anything and to know when you've fixed something.
- If there's **no test** for a piece of functionality, then it's the same as saying that functionality is broken.
- While beautiful code is great, ***functional code trumps beautiful code every single time***. This doesn't mean to let things stay sloppy, but always keep in mind why you're working on this code in the first place: **for the customer**.

Figure out what functionality works

You know that Orion's Orbits was working fine until you integrated the Mercury Meals library, so let's focus on that code. The first step is to find out what's actually working, and that means tests. Remember, if it's not testable, assume it's broken.

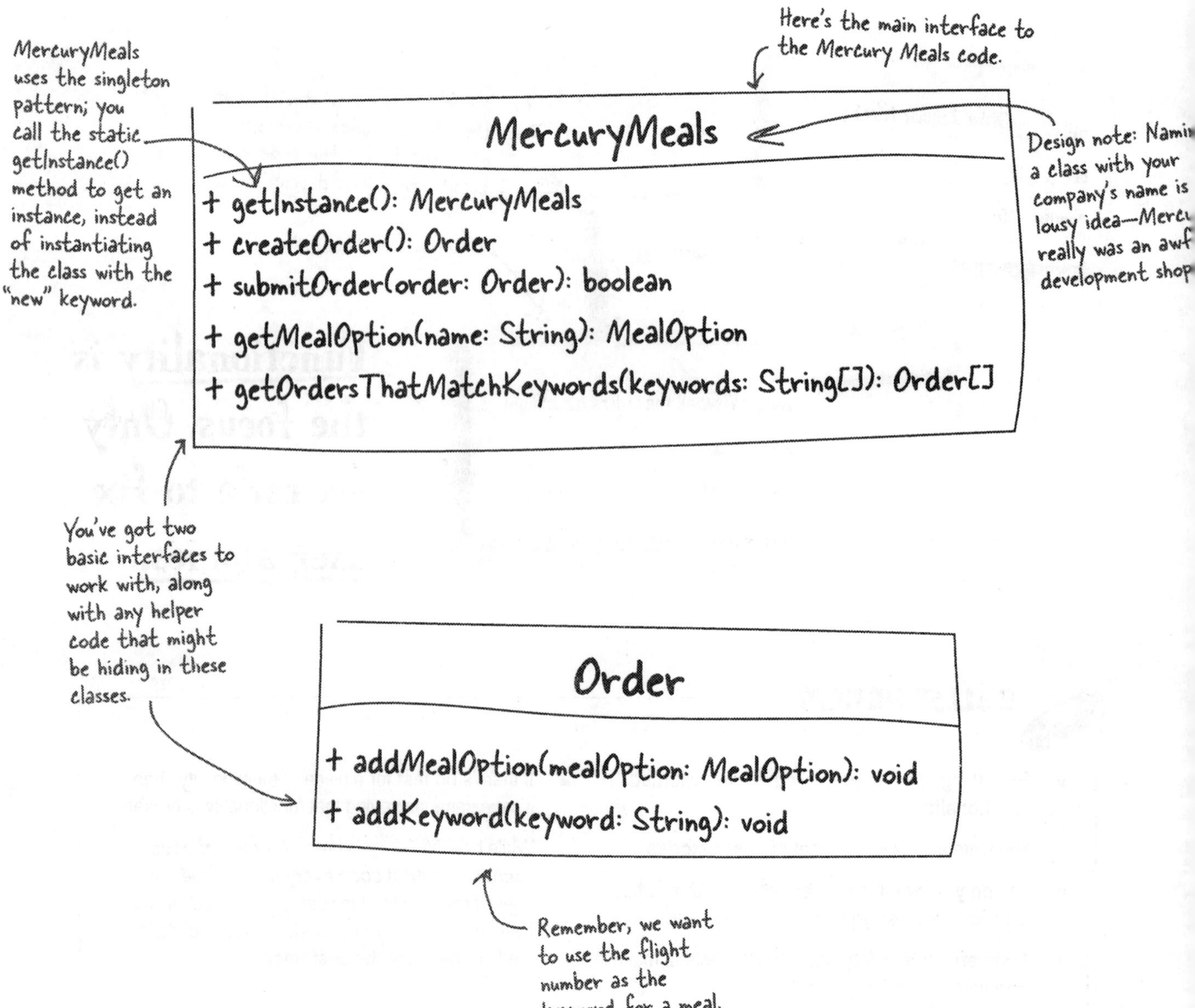

Exercise

Your job is to create a unit test that exercises all of the functionality your user stories need. The "Order Regular Meal" test creates an order, adds a regular meal option to it (in this case, "Fish and chips"), and then submits the order to Mercury Meals. Using the class diagrams on the lefthand page, write the code for this test of the "Order Regular Meal" user story in the spaces provided below.

Title: Order Regular Meal
Est: 12 days
Priority: 10

The user story this test focuses on.

```
package test.com.orionsorbits.mercurymeals;
import com.orionsorbits.mercurymeals.*;
import org.junit.*;

public class TestMercuryMeals {
  String[] options;
  String flightNo;

  @Before
  public void setUp() {
    options = {"Fish and chips");
    flightNo = "VS01";
  }

  @After
  public void tearDown() {
    options = null;
    flightNo = null;
  }

  @Test
  public void testOrderRegularMeal()
    throws MealOptionNotFoundException, OrderNotAcceptedException {

    MercuryMeals mercuryMeals = MercuryMeals.getInstance();
    ...........................................................
    ...........................................................
    ...........................................................
    ...........................................................
    ...........................................................
    ...........................................................
    ...........................................................
    ...........................................................
    ...........................................................
    ...........................................................
    ...........................................................

  }
}
```

This should be a valid meal option.

The code for setUp() and tearDown() are already in place.

Throw a MealOptionNotFoundException if the meal isn't found, and an OrderNotAcceptedException if the order can't be submitted.

You may need more—or fewer—lines to implement your solution... this is what it took to get our test written.

Exercise Solution

Your job was to create a unit test that exercises all of the functionality your user stories need. The "Order Regular Meal" test creates an order, adds a regular meal option to it (in this case, "Fish and chips"), and then submits the order to Mercury Meals.

```
package test.com.orionsorbits.mercurymeals;
import com.orionsorbits.mercurymeals.*;
import org.junit.*;

public class TestMercuryMeals {
  String[] options;
  String flightNo;

  @Before
  public void setUp() {
    options = {"Fish and chips"};
    flightNo = "VS01";
  }

  @After
  public void tearDown() {
    options = null;
    flightNo = null;
  }

  @Test
  public void testOrderRegularMeal()
    throws MealOptionNotFoundException, OrderNotAcceptedException {

    MercuryMeals mercuryMeals = MercuryMeals.getInstance();
    Order order = mercuryMeals.createOrder();
    MealOption mealOption = mercuryMeals.getMealOption(options[0]);
    if (mealOption != null) {
     order.addMealOption(mealOption);
    } else {
     throw new MealOptionNotFoundException(mealOption);
    }
    order.addKeyword(flightNo);
    if (!mercuryMeals.submitOrder(order)) {
     throw new OrderNotAcceptedException(order);
    }
  }
}
```

Title: Order Regular Meal
Est: 12 days
Priority: 10

Here's the user story you're testing Mercury Meals functionality for.

Even though you don't know exactly how this code works, it should be clear what it should do.

Create an order and get the single meal option that was set up prior to the test being run.

Add the "Fish and chips" meal option to the order, tie the order to the flight number, and then submit the order to Mercury Meals.

These exceptions are just ways to cause the test to fail, and say something in the Mercury Meals API didn't work.

NOW you know what's ^not^ working

Here's the build and test report email from your automated testing tool.

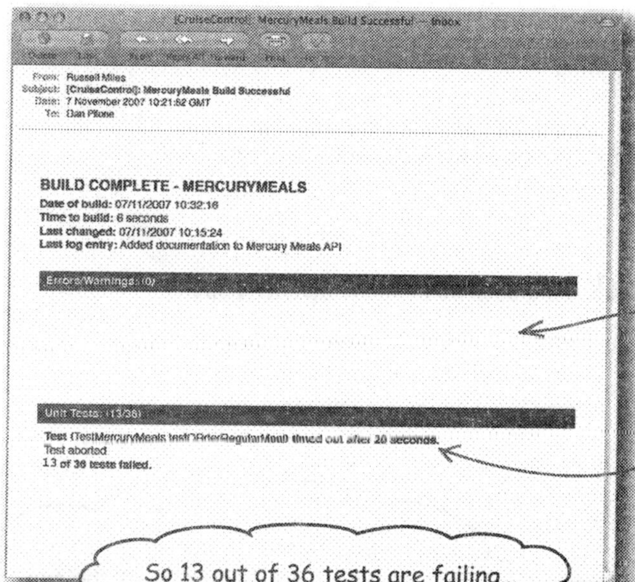

No errors or warnings were triggered...

...but a lot of the tests are failing.

So 13 out of 36 tests are failing...

Laura: Right, about 30% of the code we need to use is failing our tests.

Mark: But that doesn't tell us anything about how much work it will take to fix thing. And it's 30% of the code that's written...how much of that do we need?

Bob: And there could be whole chunks of code completely missing, too. I don't know how much new code we're going to have to write.

Mark: How do we estimate this?

Bob: There has to be a better way to come up with an estimate besides just guessing, right?

What would you do?

Spike test to estimate

30% of the tests you wrote are failing, but you really have no idea if a single line of code would fix most of that, or if even passing one more test could take new classes and hundreds of lines of code. There's no way to know how big a problem those 13 test failures really represent. So what if we take a little time to work on the code, see what we can get done, and then extrapolate out from that?

This is called **spike testing**: you're doing one burst of activity, seeing what you get done, and using that to estimate how much time it will take to get everything else done.

1 Take a week to conduct your spike test

Get the customer to give you five working days to work on your problem. That's not a ton of time, and at the end, you should be able to supply a reasonable estimate.

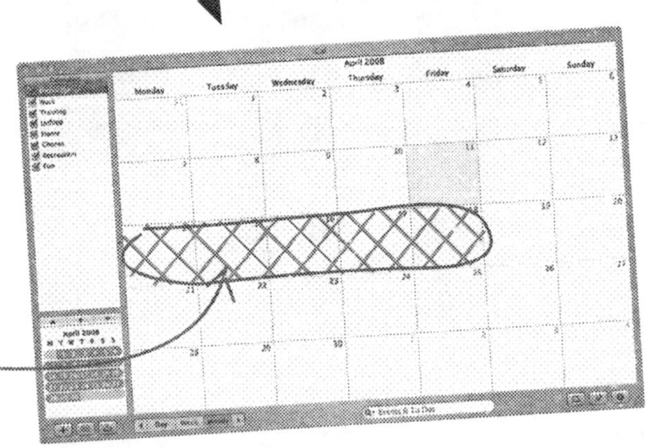

2 Pick a random sampling from the tests that are failing

Take a random sample of the tests that are failing, and try to fix just those tests. But be sure it's random—don't pick just the easy tests to fix, or the really hard ones. You want to get a real idea of the work to get things going again.

Write code the right way... don't rush. You're getting an estimate, not running a race, so make sure you're following your process, even in spike testing.

Use your bug tracker. Note what you're working on, what happened, and how you made the fix. Remember, spike testing should fit into your normal development process.

3 At the end of the week, calculate your bug fix rate

Look at how fast you and your team are knocking off bugs, and come up with a more confident estimate for how long you think it will take to fix all the bugs, based on your current fix rate.

Bugs fixed / 5 = Your daily bug fix rate

Bugs fixed: Total bugs your entire team fixed

5: Number of days in the spike test

Your daily bug fix rate: Bugs likely to be fixed per day, assuming this rate stays steady

What do the spike test results tell you?

Your tests gave you an idea as to how much of your code was failing. With the results of your spike test, you should have an idea about how long it will take to fix the remaining bugs.

The number of bugs fixed during the week-long spike test

$$4 \,/\, 5 = 0.8 \text{ bugs per day}$$

The number of work days in the spike test

Your team's bug fix rate for the spike test

You can then figure out how long it will take for your team to fix all the bugs

The bugs left, after you fixed some on the spike test.

$$0.8 \times (13 - 4) = 7 \text{ days}$$

Your bug fix rate.

How long it would take your whole team to fix all the remaining bugs

So we fixed some bugs AND we now know how long it will take for the entire team to fix all the problems. But I'm still not feeling very confident...

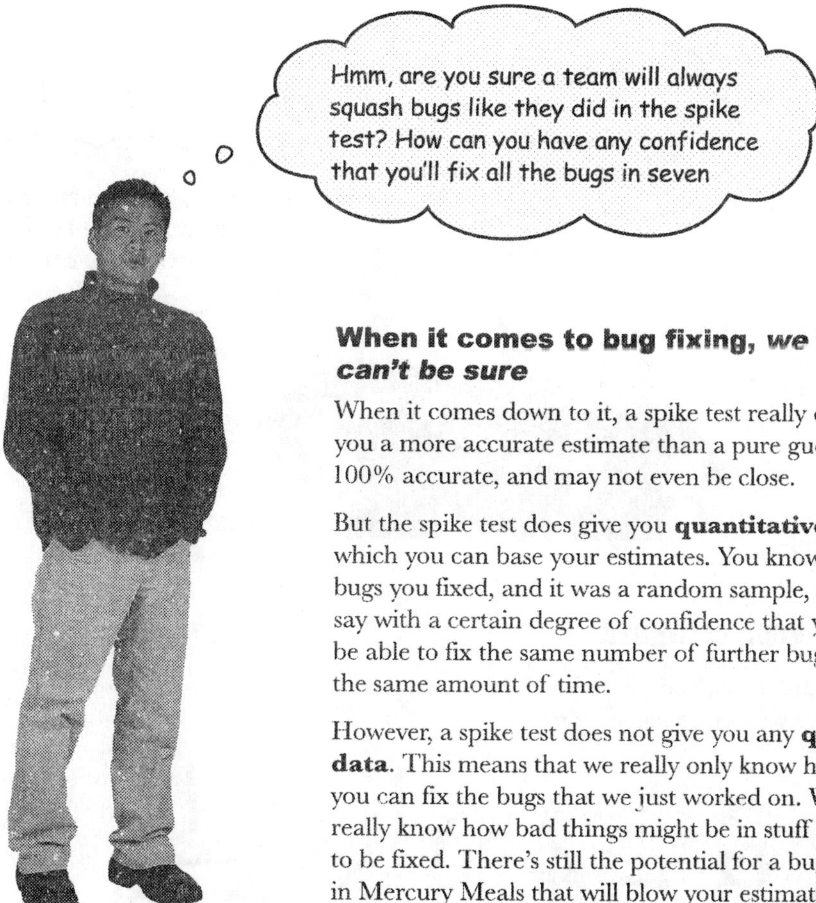

When it comes to bug fixing, *we really can't be sure*

When it comes down to it, a spike test really only gives you a more accurate estimate than a pure guess. It's not 100% accurate, and may not even be close.

But the spike test does give you **quantitative data** upon which you can base your estimates. You know how many bugs you fixed, and it was a random sample, so you can say with a certain degree of confidence that you should be able to fix the same number of further bugs in roughly the same amount of time.

However, a spike test does not give you any **qualitative data**. This means that we really only know how fast you can fix the bugs that we just worked on. We *don't* really know how bad things might be in stuff waiting to be fixed. There's still the potential for a bug to be in Mercury Meals that will blow your estimate out of the water, and unfortunately, that's a fact of life when it comes to bug fixing, especially on third-party software.

Your team's gut feeling matters

One quick way that you can add some qualitative feedback into your bug fix estimate is by factoring in the confidence of your team. During the spike test week, you've all have seen the Mercury Meals code, probably in some depth, so now's the time to run your fix rate past your team to factor in their confidence in that number.

Feed confidence into your estimate

$\frac{(80\% + 60\% + 70\%)}{3}$

Take the average of your team's confidence, in this case 70%, and factor that into your estimate to give you some wiggle room:

$$\left(0.8 \times (13 - 4)\right) \times \frac{1}{70\%}$$

The estimate for your customer

$$= 10 \text{ days}$$

to fix the remaining bugs

there are no Dumb Questions

Q: How many people should be involved in a spike test?

A: Ideally you'd get everyone that you think will be involved in the actual bug fixing involved in the spike test. This means that you not only get a more accurate estimate, because the actual people who will finish off the bug fixing will be involved in the future estimated fixing task, but those individuals also have a week to get familiar with the code.

This especially helps when you ask those members of your team to assess their confidence in the estimate that comes out of your spike test. They'll have seen the code base and have a feel for how big all the problems might have been, so their gut feeling is worth that much more.

Q: How do I pick the right tests to be part of the spike testing when I have *thousands* of tests failing?!

A: Try to pick a random sampling, but with an eye towards getting a selection of bugs that vary in difficulty. So what you're looking for first is a random sample, but then you want to make sure that you have a cross-section of bugs that, at a glance, at least appear to be challenging and not just the easiest things to fix.

Q: I thought in test-driven development, we fixed each test as we came across it. Are we not using TDD anymore?

A: This is still TDD, for sure. But this is about existing code, not writing tests for new code. You don't want to stop and try to fix each test just yet. We need a big picture view of the code right now.

However, this does cause a problem if you're using CI, and your build fails when a test fails. In that case, after you get a count of failing tests it might make sense to cheat a little and comment out the failing tests. Then add them back in one at a time. This is risky, and might get you on the TDD Most Wanted list in no time flat, but practically speaking you might want to consider it. The most important thing is you get all of those tests passing, and nothing's left commented out.

Q: Why did we add in that confidence factor again?

A: Factoring in confidence gives you that qualitative input into your estimates where your team gets a chance to say how difficult they feel the rest of the bugs may be to fix. You can take this pretty far, by playing planning poker with your bugs, but remember that the longer you spend assessing confidence, the less time you have to actually fix the bugs.

It's always a compromise between getting an absolute estimate for how long it will take to fix the bugs (and this can really only be obtained by actually fixing them all) and getting a good enough feel for how fast you can squash bugs and getting that estimate to your customer.

Q: Why five days for a spike test?

A: Good question. Five days is a good length because it focuses your team on just the spike test for a week (rather than attempting to multitask during that week), and it gives everyone enough time to do some serious bug fixing.

Q: Can I use a shorter length?

A: You can, but this will affect how many bugs your team can work through, and that affects your confidence in your final estimate. In the worst case scenario, no bugs at all are fixed in your spike test, and you're left confused and without a real end in sight.

Five days is enough time for some serious bugs to be fixed and for you to be able to come out of the spike test with some confidence in your estimate for fixing the remainder of the bugs. And in the best case scenario, you come out of the spike test week with no bugs at all!

Q: So should I do this on code we've developed, too?

A: You really shouldn't need to. First of all, you shouldn't have a massive stack of failing tests. If a test is failing, the build should be failing, and you should fix things immediately. And with bugs, they should be prioritized in with your other work, so it's unlikely you'll suddenly get a giant stack of bugs you need to sort through. And finally, you and your team should know your code base pretty well. Your coverage reports provide value, and you know there can't be too much code involved in any given bug.

Q: How can I be absolutely sure that, even when I've factored in my team's confidence, that 10 days is definitely enough to fix all these bugs?

A: You can't. Ten days is still just an estimate, and so it's how long you think it will take, based on your spike test and your team's gut feelings. You've done everything you can to be confident in your estimate, but it is still ***just an estimate***. When it comes to bugs, you need to be aware that there is a risk that your estimates will be wrong, and that's a message that you need to convey to your customer too...

Give your customer the bug fix estimate

You've got an estimate you can be reasonably confident in, so head back to the customer. Tell him how long it will take to fix the bugs in the Mercury Meals code, and see if you can get fixing.

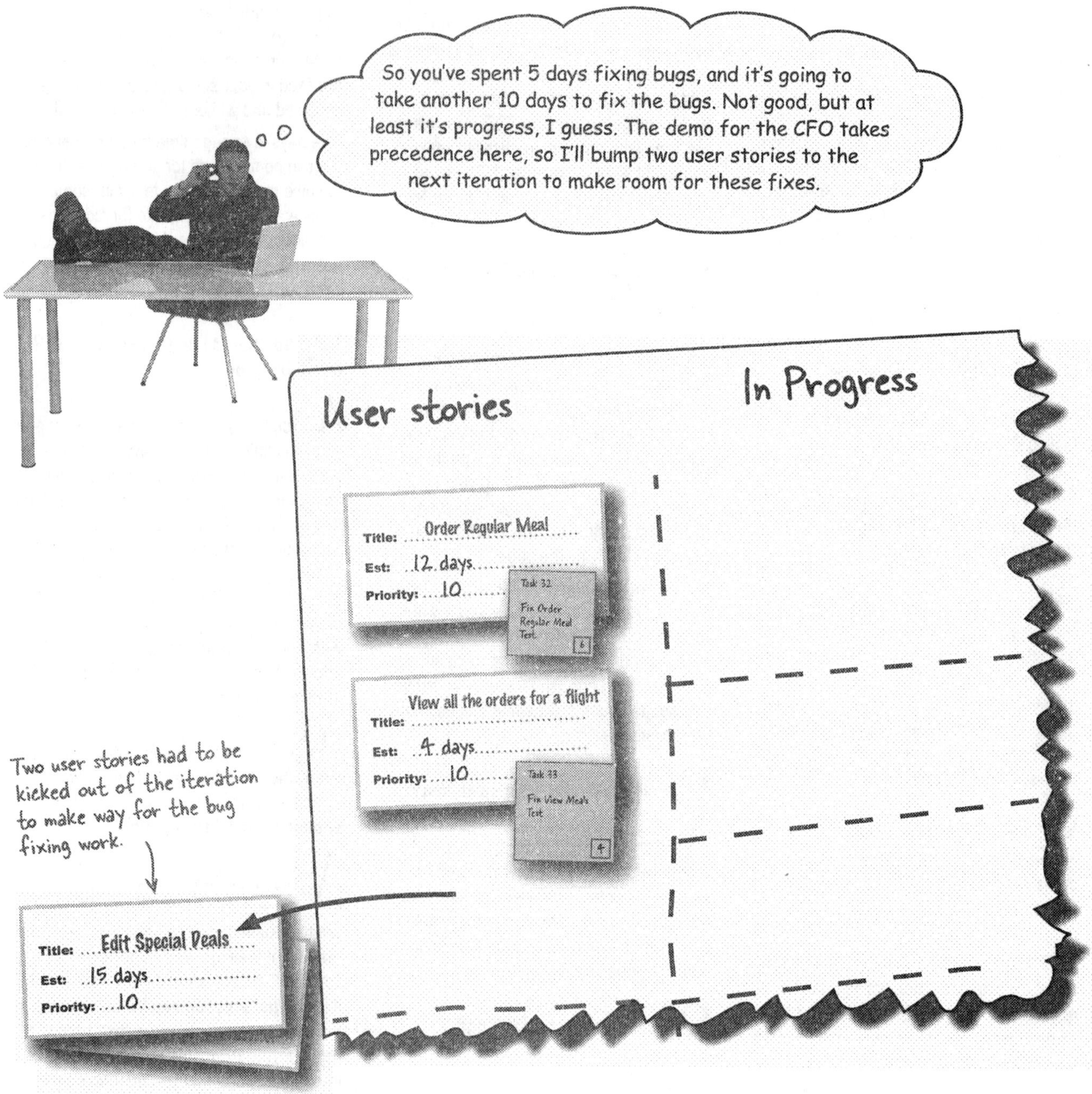

Exercise

Back to the magnets we didn't use on page 391. Would you do any of these activities now? Why? Any others you might add that aren't on this list?

Figure out what dependencies this code has and if it has any impact on Orion's Orbits' code.

Would you do this now? Why? ....

Figure out how to package the compiled version to include in Orion's Orbits.

Would you do this now? Why? ....

Document the code.

Would you do this now? Why? ....

Run a coverage report to see how much code you need to fix.

Would you do this now? Why? ....

Get a line count of the code and estimate how long it will take to fix.

Would you do this now? Why? ....

Do a security audit on the code.

Would you do this now? Why? ....

Use a UML tool to reverse-engineer the code and create class diagrams.

Would you do this now? Why? ....

Exercise Solution

Back to the magnets we didn't use on page 391. Would you do any of these activities now? Why? Any others you might add that aren't on this list?

> Figure out what dependencies this code has and if it has any impact on Orion's Orbits' code.

Would you do this now? Why? Maybe. It's possible that some kind of library conflict is behind one of our bugs. You're going to need to figure this out to get everything working by the end of the iteration anyway.

> Figure out how to package the compiled version to include in Orion's Orbits.

Would you do this now? Why? Only if the current packaging approach isn't going to cut it. This is basically refactoring at the packaging level. If things are working and it's maintainable, you should probably skip this.

> Document the code.

Would you do this now? Why? Absolutely! Every file you touch should come out of your cleanup with clear documentation. At a minimum, explain the code you've touched while fixing a bug.

> Run a coverage report to see how much code you need to fix.

Would you do this now? Why? Probably. You now have a set of tests that scope how much of the system you need. This will give you an idea of how much of the overall code base you actually use, which is a useful metric.

> Get a line count of the code and estimate how long it will take to fix.

Would you do this now? Why? Nope. Still not a terribly useful measure. Who cares how big a code base is, except as to how it relates to the functionality you need to get working?

> Do a security audit on the code.

Would you do this now? Why? Yes. Any code that gets touched with your tests should be checked for security issues. If you can fix any problems as part of getting your test to pass, go for it. If not, capture it and prioritize it in a later iteration.

> Use a UML tool to reverse-engineer the code and create class diagrams.

Would you do this now? Why? Maybe—it depends on how complicated the code is. If you're having trouble figuring out what a block of code is trying to do, this might help you get your head around it.

there are no Dumb Questions

Q: I noticed that the bug fixing tasks on page 406 both had estimates. Where did those estimates come from?

A: Good catch! Bug fixing tasks are just like any other type of task; they need an estimate, and there are a number of ways that you can come up with that.

You can derive the estimate, dividing the total amount of days you've calculated evenly by the number of bugs to fix, or you can play planning poker with your team. Whichever approach you take, your total planned tasks for bug fixes must never be greater than the number of days calculated from your spike test.

Q: When fixing bugs, how much time should I spend on cleaning up other problems I notice, or just generally cleaning up the code?

A: This is a tough call. It would be great to fix every bug or problem you see, but then you'll likely finish all your tasks late or, worse, end up refactoring your code indefinitely.

The best guideline is to get the code into a working, pretty decent state, within the time allotted for your bug fixing task, and then move on to the next task. First priority is to get the code working; second is to make it as easily readable and understandable as possible so that bugs are not accidentally introduced in the future. If there are problems you found but couldn't get to, file them as new bugs and prioritize them into a later iteration.

Q: What did that five-day spike test period do to our iteration length?

A: Right now, we're getting ready for the next iteration so we're between iterations. If there's a master schedule, the five days needs to be accounted for there, but in terms of iteration time, it's basically off the clock. After you get your board sorted out and everything approved by the customer, though, you should kick off a normal iteration. If you're forced to do a spike test in the middle of an iteration, that's a case where it's probably OK to slip the iteration end date by a week, assuming nearly everyone is participating.

If only a small number of developers are participating in the spike test and everyone else is continuing the iteration, you probably want to drop that five days' worth of other work from the iteration, but still end on time.

Remember, this is five days per person, not five days total.

Q: You said try and get code into a "pretty decent" state. What does that really mean?

A: This is really a judgment call, and in fact this is where you get into the aesthetics of code, which is a whole book on its own. However there are some rules of thumb that can help you decide when your code is good enough and you can move on.

First, **the code must work according to your tests**. Those tests must exercise your code thoroughly, and you should feel very confident that the code works as it should.

Secondly, **your code should be readable**. Do you have cryptic variable names? Do the lines of code read like Sanskrit? Are you using too much complicated syntax just because you can? These are all huge warning signs that your code needs to be improved in readability.

And finally, **you should be proud of your code**. When your code is correct and easily readable by another developer, then you've really done your job. It doesn't have to be perfect, but "pretty decent" starts with your code doing what it should and ends with it being readable.

Q: This sounds like the same approach as the perfect-versus-good-enough design stuff we talked about earlier, right?

A: Yes, it's based on exactly the same principle. Just as you can spend hours improving a design, trying to reach perfection, you can waste exactly the same time in your coding. Don't fall into the trap of perfection. If you achieve it, then that's great, but what you're aiming for is code that does what it should, and that can be read and understood by others. Do that, and you're coding like a pro.

Beautiful code is nice, but tested and readable code is delivered on time.

Things are looking good...

So you've picked off all the bugs from Orion's Orbits, and all functionality is working according to the results of your continuous integration build process...

Your CI tool is happy again; everything builds and passes its tests.

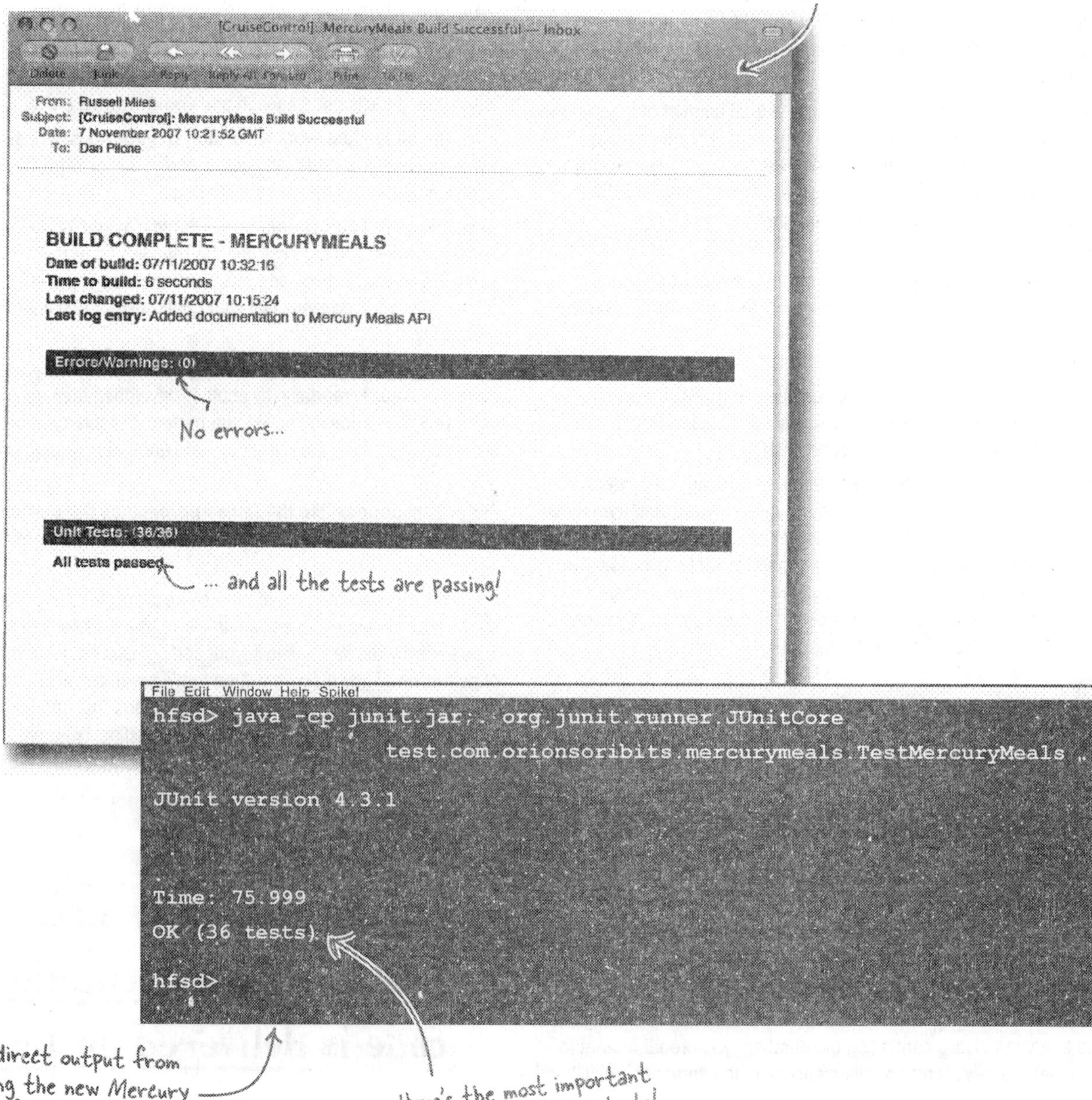

The direct output from testing the new Mercury Meals functionality

Here's the most important part...OK. No failing tests!

...and you finish the iteration successfully!

Remember, success changes as your iteration goes on. In this case, success turned out to mean dropping two stories, but getting the CFO demo done.

You've reached the end of this iteration and, by managing the work and keeping the customer involved, you've successfully overcome the Mercury Meals bug nightmare. Most importantly, you've developed what your customer needed.

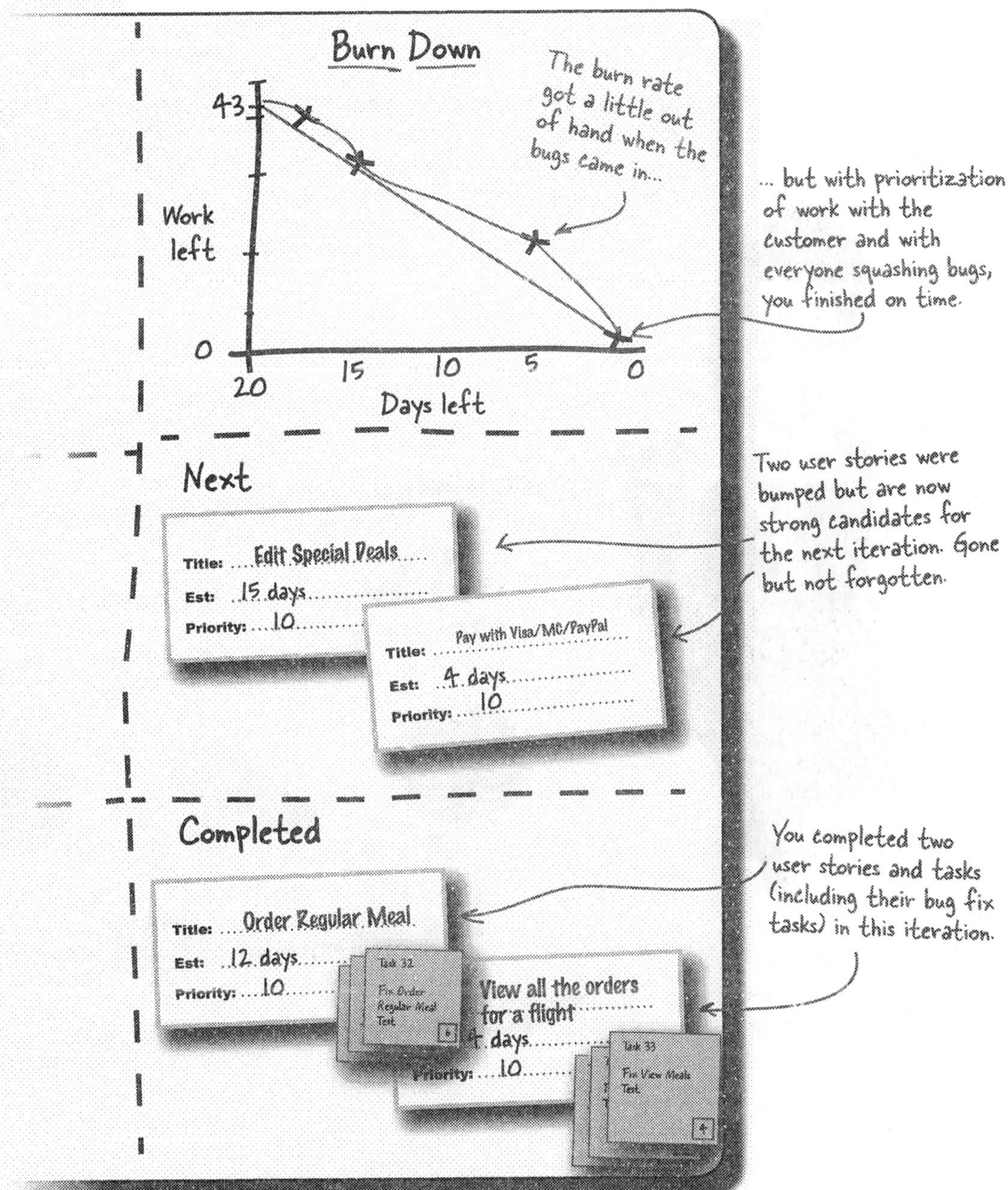

AND most importantly the customer is happy

You and your team of developers, by applying your best practices and professional process, have overcome the perils of integrating third-party code, fixed the bugs that arose from that integration, and have delivered the demo on time. The CFO, who just cares that things work, is pretty stoked.

You got the Mercury Meals integration working!? That's fantastic, guys; you really deliver! You'll all be featured in my review to the board—better start ordering those PlayStation 3's now!

The Orion's Orbits CFO...you know, the woman who signs your paychecks (and approves raises)

The all-new Orion's Orbits, with the Mercury Meals features

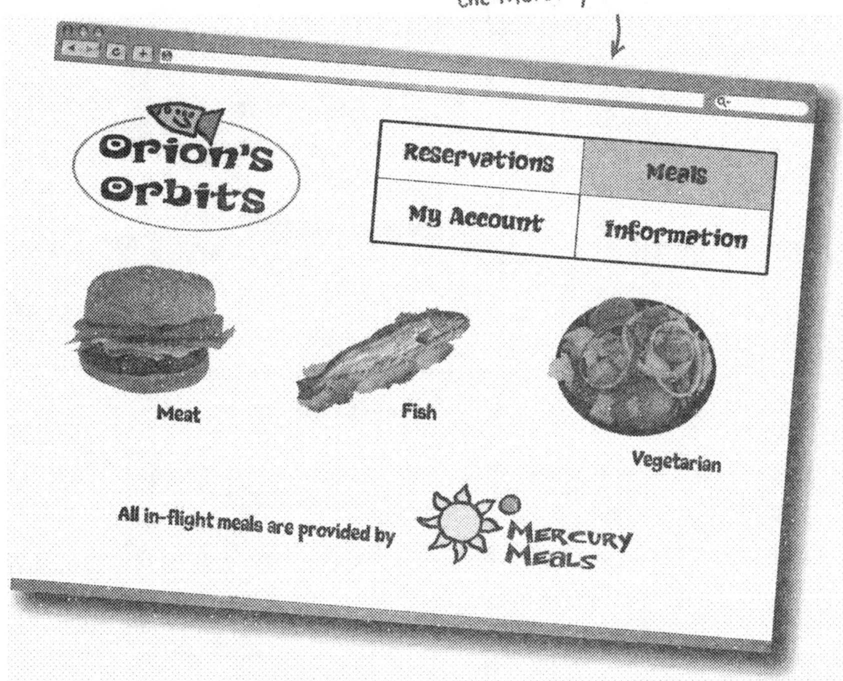

You've uncovered an unfortunate truth.

Yes, there may be bugs in the code, particularly in the Mercury Meals code that you inherited. ***But you delivered code that worked.***

Yes, there are potentially large pieces of that library that haven't yet been covered by tests. ***But you have tested all the code that you actually use to complete your user stories.***

The bottom line is that pretty much *all software has some bugs*. However, by applying your process you can avoid those bugs rearing their ugly head in your software's functionality.

Remember, your code doesn't have to be perfect, and often good enough is exactly that: good enough. But as long as any problems in the code don't result in bugs (or software bloat), and you deliver the functionality that your customer needs, then you'll be a success, and get paid, every time.

Security issues are the one exception. You need to be careful that code that isn't tested isn't available for people to use—either accidentally or deliberately. Your coverage report can help identify which code you're actually using.

Real success is about DELIVERING FUNCTIONALITY, period.

Tools for your Software Development Toolbox

Software Development is all about developing and delivering great software. In this chapter, you learned how to debug like a pro. For a complete list of tools in the book, see Appendix ii.

Development Techniques

Before you change a single line of code, make sure it is controlled and buildable

When bugs hit code you don't know, use a spike test to estimate how long it will take to fix them

Factor in your team's confidence when estimating the work remaining to fix bugs

Use tests to tell you when a bug is fixed

← Here are some of the key techniques you learned in this chapter...

...and some of the principles behind those techniques.

Development Principles

Be honest with your customer, especially when the news is bad

Working software is your top priority

Readable and understandable code comes a close second

If you haven't tested a piece of code, assume that it doesn't work

Fix functionality

Be proud of your code

All the code in your software, even the bits you didn't write, is your responsibility

BULLET POINTS

- Before you change a single line of code, **take ownership** of it by adding it into your build process and putting it under source code management.
- **Take responsibility** for all the code in your software. If you see a problem, then don't cry "it's someone else's code"; write a test, then **fix it**.
- **Don't assume** a single line of **code works** until there is a **test** that proves it.
- **Working software** comes first; **beautiful code** is second.
- Use the **pride test**. If you'd be happy for someone else to read your code and rely on your software, then it's probably in good shape.

CHAPTER 11

BugSquashingCross

Flex your brain with this crossword puzzle. All of the words below are somewhere in this chapter.

Across

2. At the end of a spike test you have a good idea what your team's .... is
4. When you apply your refactoring experience to avoid problems up front, that is called ....
9. When new bug fix tasks appear on your board, your customer might need to re-.... the work left in the current iteration.
10. When fixing bugs you are fixing ....
11. Fixing bugs becomes .... or sometimes full stories on your board.
12. A spike test should be around a .... in duration.
14. Close second priority is for your code to be .... and understandable by other developers
15. You should always be .... with your customer
16. The first step when dealing with a new chunk of unfamiliar code is to get it under source code ....
17. Before you change anything, get all your code ....

Down

1. Take .... for all the code in your software, not just the bits that you wrote
3. The best spike tests include attempting to fix a .... of the bugs.
5. You should be .... of your software.
6. When you change code to make it work or just to tidy it up, this is called ....
7. You can account for your team's gut feeling about a collection of bugs by factoring in their .... in your big fixing estimate.
8. To help you estimate how long it will take to fix a collection of bugs in software you are unfamiliar with, use a ....
13. Top priority is for your code to ....

BugSquashingCross Solution

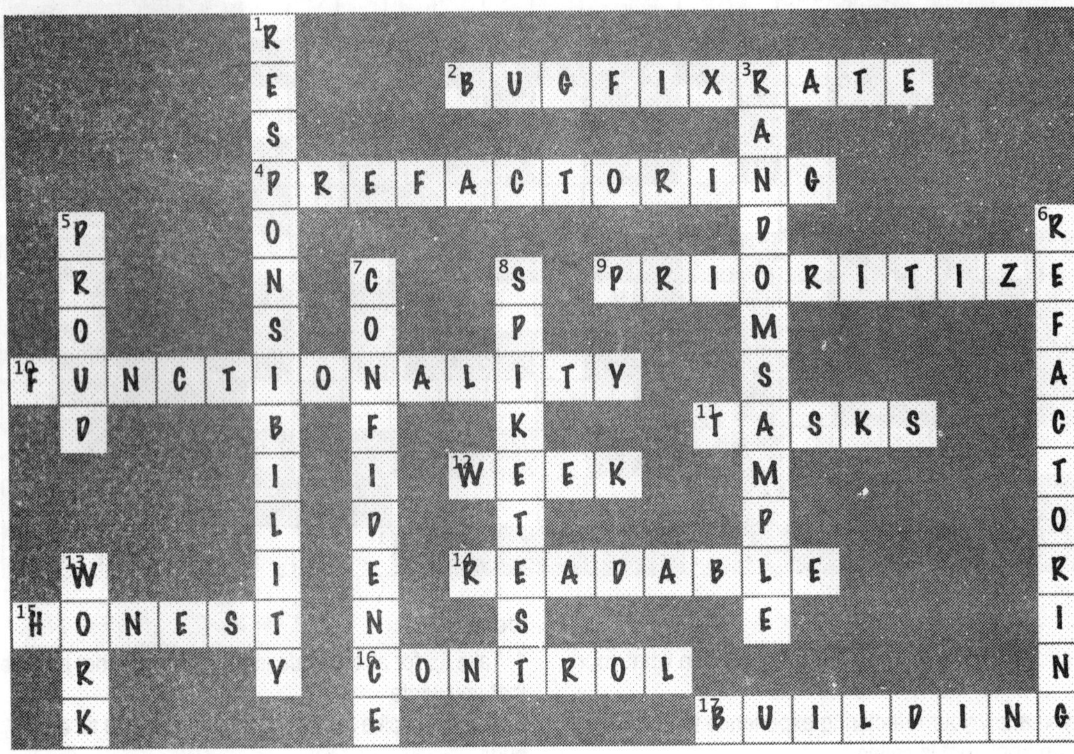

12 the real world

Having a process in life

You've learned a lot about software development. But before you go pinning burn-down graphs in everyone's office, there's just a little more you need to know about dealing with each project—on its own terms. There are a lot of **similarities** and **best practices** you should carry from project to project, but there are **unique** things everywhere you go, and you need to be ready for them. It's time to look at how to apply what you've learned to **your particular project**, and where to go next for **more learning**.

Pinning down a software development process

You've read a lot of pages about software development process, but we haven't pinned down exactly what that term really means.

> A **software development process** is a structure imposed on the development of a software product.

Wikipedia's definition of a software development process.

Notice that definition doesn't say "a software development process is four-week iterations with requirements written on index cards from a user-focused point of view..." ***A software development process is a framework that should enable you to make quality software.***

There is no silver-bullet process

There's no single process that magically makes software development succeed. A good software process is one that lets ***your*** development team be successful. However, there are some common traits among processes that work:

- [ ] **Develop iteratively**. Project after project and process after process have shown that big-bang deliveries and waterfall processes are extremely risky and prone to failure. Whatever process you settle on, make sure it involves developing in iterations.

- [ ] **Always evaluate and assess**. No process is going to be perfect from day one. Even if your process is really, really good, your project will change as you work on it. People will be promoted or quit, new developers will join the team, requirements will change. Be sure to incorporate some way of evaluating how well your process is working, and be willing to change parts of the process where it makes sense.

- [ ] **Incorporate best practices**. Don't do something just because it's trendy, but don't avoid something because it's trendy either. Most of the things that people takes for granted as good software development started out as a goofy idea at some point. Be critical—but fair—about other processes' approaches to problems, and incorporate those approaches when they might help your project. Some people call this ***process***

A great software process is a process that lets <u>YOUR</u> development team be successful.

A good process delivers good software

Let's say your team loves its process. But suppose your team has yet to deliver a project on time, or deliver software that's working correctly. If that's the case, you may have a **process problem**. The ultimate measure of a process is how good the software is that the process produces. So you and your team might need to change a few things around.

Before you go changing things, you need to be careful—there are lots of wrong ways to change things. Here are a few rules to think about if you're considering changing part (or even all) of your process:

1. **Unless someone is on fire, don't change things mid-iteration.**
Changes are usually disruptive to a project, no matter how well-planned they are. It's up to you to minimize disruptions to other developers. Iterations give you a very natural breaking point. And good iterations are short, so if you need to change your process, ***wait until the end of your current iteration***.

2. **Develop metrics to determine if your changes are helping.**
If you're going to change something, you'd better have a good reason. And you should also have a way to measure whether or not your change worked. This means every change is examined at least twice: first, to decide to make the change, and then again—at least an iteration later—to measure if the change was a good idea or not. Try to avoid touchy-feely measures of success, too. Look at things like test coverage, bug counts, velocity, standup meeting durations. If you're getting better numbers and better results, you've made a good change. If not, wait for the next iteration, and be willing to change again.

3. **Value the other members of your team.**
The single biggest determinant of success or failure on a project are the people on your team. No process can overcome bad people, but good people can sometimes overcome a bad process. Respect your fellow team members—and their opinions—when evaluating your process and any changes you might want to make. This doesn't necessarily mean you have to run everything by committee, but it does mean you should try and build consensus whenever possible.

BRAIN POWER

If you could change one thing about your current software process, what would it be? Why? How would you measure whether or not your change was effective?

Exercise

Below are some of the best practices you've learned about in earlier chapters. For each technique, write down what you think it offers to a software process, and then how you could measure whether or not that technique helped ***your*** project.

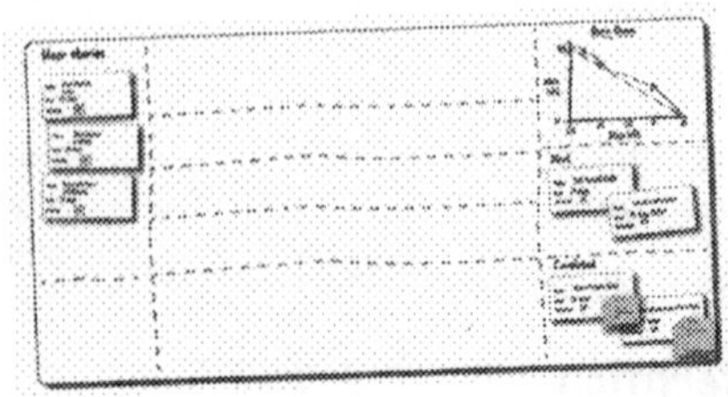

The big board

What does this technique offer? ....

How do you know if it worked? ....

User stories

What does this technique offer? ....

How do you know if it worked? ....

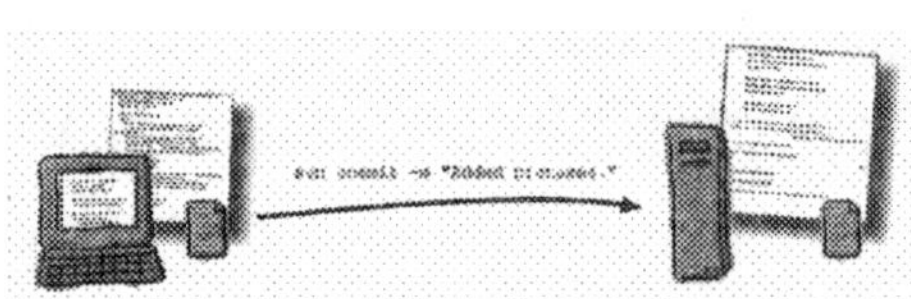

Version control

What does this technique offer? ....

How do you know if it worked? ....

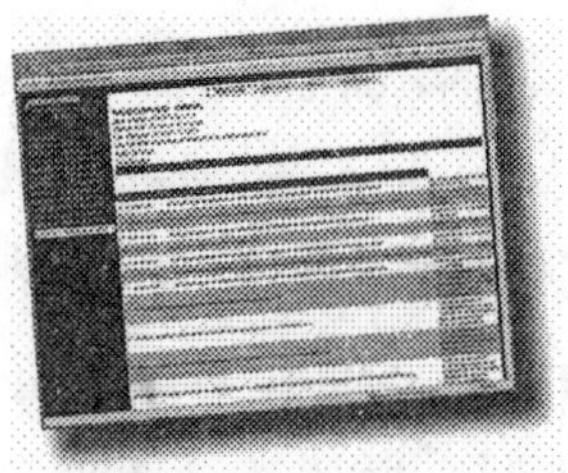

Continuous integration (CI)

What does this technique offer? ....

How do you know if it worked? ....

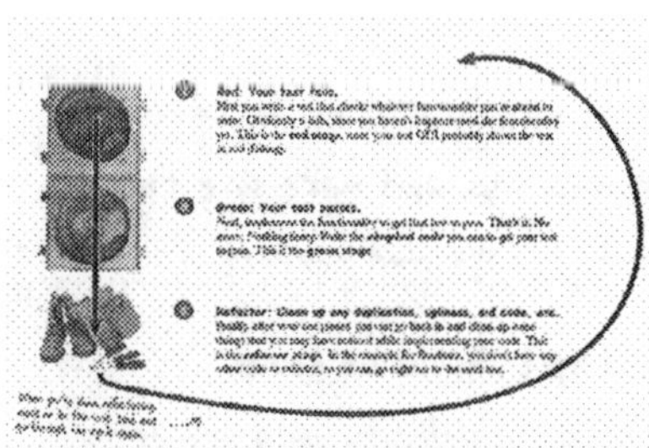

Test-driven development (TDD)

What does this technique offer? ....

How do you know if it worked? ....

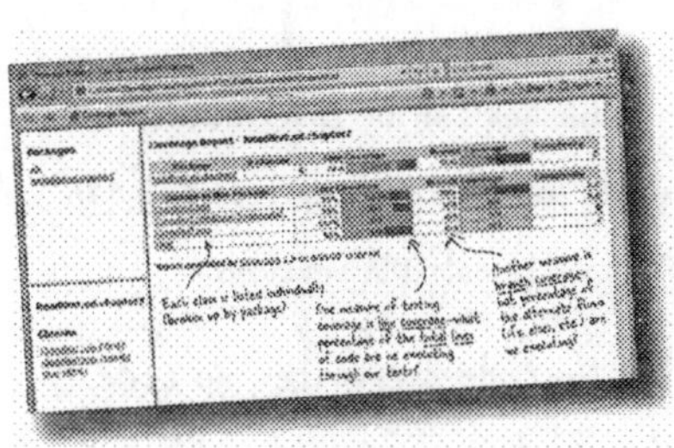

Test coverage

What does this technique offer? ....

How do you know if it worked? ....

Exercise Solution

Below are some of the best practices you've learned about in earlier chapters. For each technique, you were asked to write down what you think each technique offers, and then how you could measure whether or not that technique helped ***your*** project.

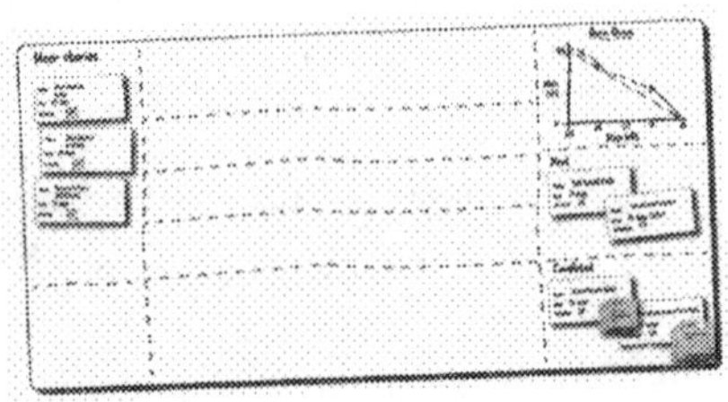

The big board

What does this technique offer? Everyone on the team knows where they are, what else needs to be done, and what has to happen in this iteration. You can also see if you're on schedule.

How do you know if it worked? There should be fewer bugs resulting from missed features, better handling of unplanned items, and an idea of exactly what's done during this iteration.

User stories

What does this technique offer? A way to split up software requirements, track those requirements, and make sure the functionality the customer wants is captured correctly.

How do you know if it worked? There should be fewer misunderstandings about functionality. Velocity on a project should also go up, since developers know what to build better.

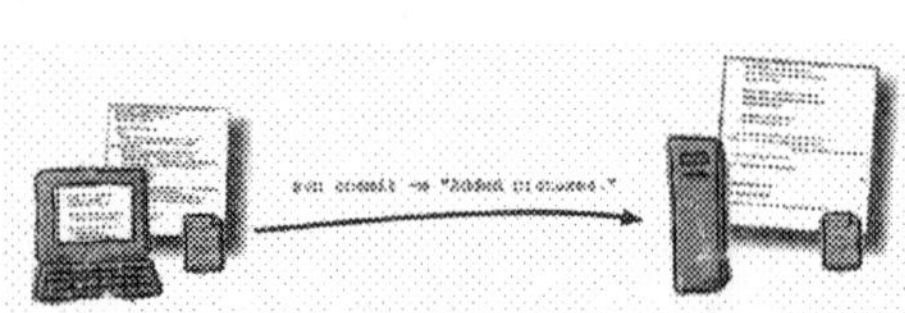

Version control

What does this technique offer? Changes can be distributed across a team without risking file loss and overwrites. You can also tag and branch and keep up with multiple versions.

How do you know if it worked? No code overwrites, no code lost from bad merges, and changes to one part of software shouldn't affect other pieces and cause them to break.

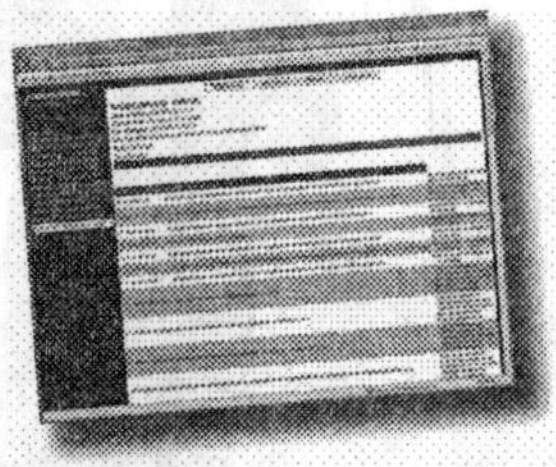

Continuous integration (CI)

What does this technique offer? The repository always builds because compilation and testing are part of check-in, and the code in the repository always works.

How do you know if it worked? Nobody checks out code and finds out it doesn't work, or doesn't compile. Bug reports should go down, since code must pass tests to be checked in.

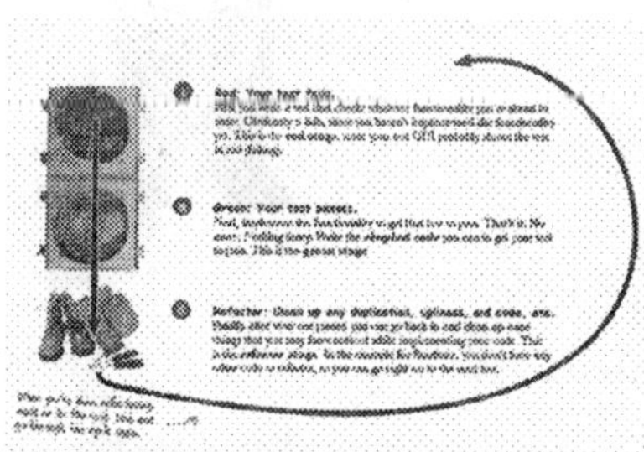

Test-driven development (TDD)

What does this technique offer? A way to ensure your code is testable from the very beginning of development. Also introduces test-friendly patterns into your code.

How do you know if it worked? Fewer bugs because testing starts earlier. Better coverage, and every line of code matters. Possibly better design, and less legacy code.

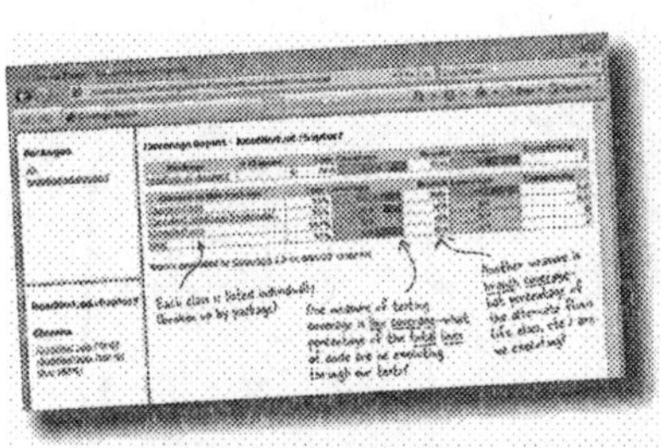

Test coverage

What does this technique offer? Better metrics on how much code is being tested and used. A way to find bugs because they usually exist in untested and uncovered code.

How do you know if it worked? Bugs becomes focused on edge cases because the main parts of code are well-tested. Less unused or "cruft" code that's uncovered and not useful.

Formal attire required...

There are projects where you may need more formality than index cards and sticky notes. Some customers and companies want documents that are a little more formal. It's OK, though; everything you've learned still applies, and you don't need to scrap a process that's working just to dress up your development a bit.

First, remember that unless you absolutely have to, wait until the end of your current iteration to make any changes to your process. Next, know why you're making a change and how you're going to measure its effectiveness. "The customer won't pay me unless we have design documentation" is a perfectly reasonable starting point for dressing up your process. However, it's still important to know how you're going to measure effectiveness. Most customers are (rightfully) concerned about their business and aren't just looking to give you extra work.

If you're going to put together more documentation, project plans, use cases, or anything else, make sure it helps your customer—and hopefully your team—be better at communication. That's a result that is good for your project.

Do what you're doing...just prettier

Most of the work you're doing can be captured and reported in a more formal fashion. With software and a little extra polish, everything from your big board to your user stories can be converted into something that meets your customer's needs.

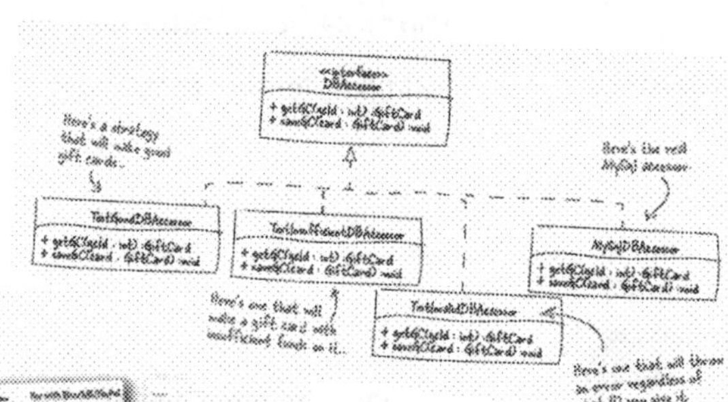

Your class diagrams might need to be translated into a tool like Rational Rose, or captured in design documents.

You may need to turn your user stories into use cases. Flip to Appendix i for some examples of use cases.

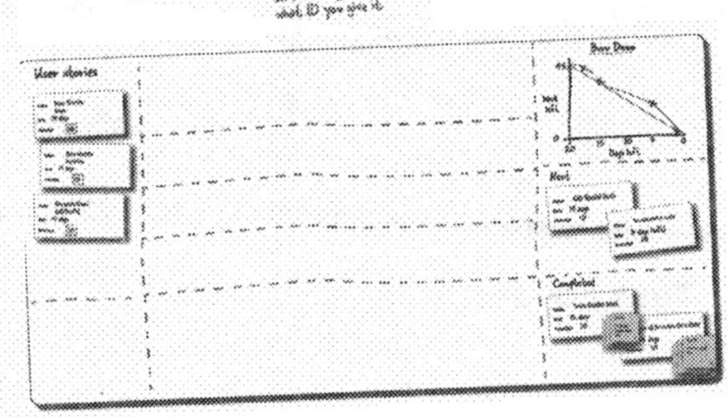

You can usually capture most of what's on your board in software like Microsoft Project if you need more formal project planning.

there are no Dumb Questions

Q: Isn't less formality better? Can't I convince my customer that index cards are all I need?

A: It's not about more formal versus less formal. It's about what works to get the right software written. The board with stories and tasks works well for lots of teams because it's simple, visual, and effective at communicating what needs to be done. It's not effective at lining up external teams that might be relying on your software or for when marketing should schedule the major release events and start shipping leaflets. Don't add formality for the sake of being formal, but there are times when you will need more than index cards.

Q: If we have to use a project planning tool, should I keep the board too?

A: Yes. There'll be some duplication of effort, but the board works so well with small teams that it's very hard to get anything more effective. The tangible tasks hanging on the board that team members physically move around just keeps the team in sync better than a screenshot or printout does.

Q: My customer wants design documentation and just doesn't get that my design just "evolves"...

A: Be careful with this one. Refactoring and evolutionary design work well with experienced teams who know their product, but it's very easy to get something wrong. On top of that, not giving your customer the design documentation they want is asking them to take a huge leap of faith in what you're doing—and that leap might not be justified yet. Most successful teams do at least some up-front design each iteration. You need to make sure the design documentation they're asking for is providing value, but design material is usually pretty useful for both you and the customer. Just make sure you account for the work in your estimates. Don't let TDD or "evolutionary design" be an excuse for "random code that I typed in late last night."

Q: My customer wants a requirements document, but user stories are working really well for my team. Now what?

A: If your customer has a history with more formal requirements documents, it may be very difficult to make the shift to user stories. In general, you don't want more than one requirement document directing how things should be implemented. It's very difficult to keep a document and user stories in sync, and someone always gets stuck resolving the conflicts.

Instead, try starting with a user story and at the end of the iteration break up the user story into "the user shall" statements that can fit into a formal requirements document. Or, if the customer wants nothing to do with user stories, you can try going the other direction: pull several "The user shall" type statements into a user story and work from the stories. But watch out—those "the user shall" type requirements often don't give you a lot of context about the application as a whole, and what it's doing.

Neither approach is ideal, but one may be a compromise that's workable. You need to be absolutely diligent about changes in both directions, though.

Choose a process that works for <u>YOUR</u> team and <u>YOUR</u> project...

...and then tailor the artifacts it produces to match what <u>YOUR</u> customer wants and needs.

Some additional resources...

Even with all of the new tools available to you, there's always more to learn. Here are some places to go for some more great information on software development, and the techniques and approaches you've been learning about.

Head First PMP

If you've managing your team, there's more to good software—and project management—than just the big board. PMP takes you beyond the basics into a tried-and-true project management process—and help you get certified along the way.

Even if you've never considered yourself a project manager, if you're leading or in charge of a team, this book could help.

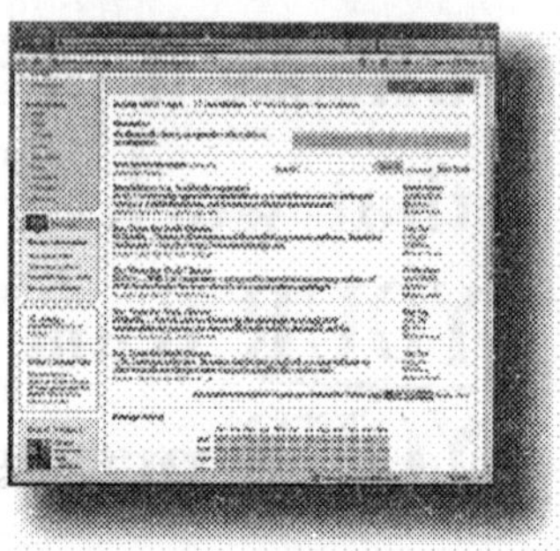

Test-driven development Yahoo! group

One of the all-time great resources for information on test-driven development is on the "Test-driven Development" group at Yahoo!. The group is pretty active, with current discussions and debates as well as some great historical information. You can find the group online at `http://tech.groups.yahoo.com/group/testdrivendevelopment/`.

Head First Object-Oriented Analysis and Design

Want to get deeper into code? To learn more about object-oriented principles of design and implementation? If you loved drawing class diagrams and implementing the strategy pattern, check out this book for a lot more on getting down deep with code.

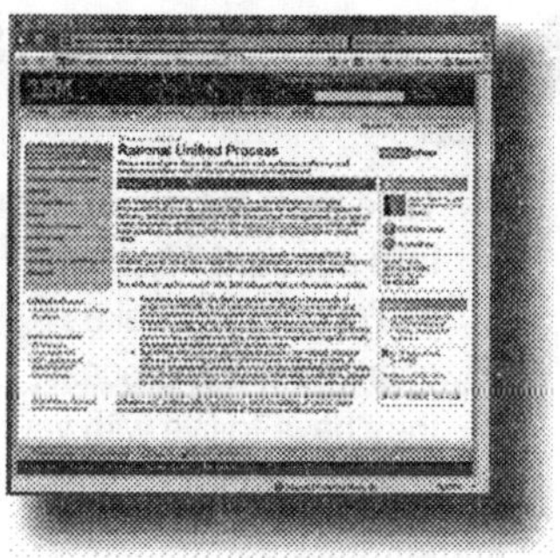

Rational Unified Process web site

One of the founding iterative processes is the Rational Unified Process (RUP). It's a pretty heavy process out-of-the-box, but it's designed to be tailored to your needs. It's also a common approach to large-scale enterprise development. Be sure and read this and some Agile- or XP-leaning sites, so you get a balanced picture. Check it out online at `http://www-306.ibm.com/software/awdtools/rup/`.

The Agile Alliance

The Agile Alliance is a great kickoff point for information on Agile processes like extreme programming, Scrum, or Crystal. Agile processes are very lightweight, and you'll see many of the things you learned about, albeit from a different perspective at times. Check it out at `http://www.agilealliance.org/`.

More knowledge == better process

There are tons more resources than just these. Part of good software development is keeping on top of what's going on. And that means reading, Googling, asking your buddies on other projects—anything you can do to find out what other people are doing, and what works for them.

And never be afraid to try something new, even for just an iteration. You never know what might work, or what you might pick up that's just perfect for **your** project.

Tools for your Software Development Toolbox

Software Development is all about developing and delivering great software. In this chapter, you got some additional resources to help you take your knowledge out into the real world. For a complete list of tools in the book, see Appendix ii.

Development Techniques

Critically evaluate any changes to your process with real metrics.

Formalize your deliverables if you need to, but always know how it's providing value.

Try hard to only change your process between iterations.

Here are some of the key techniques you learned in this chapter...

...and some of the principles behind those techniques.

Development Principles

Good developers develop—great developers ship.

Good developers can usually overcome a bad process.

A good process is one that lets <u>your</u> team be successful.

BULLET POINTS

- **Take your team's opinion into account** whenever you're going to make changes to the process; they have to live with your changes, too.
- Any process change should show up **twice**: once to **decide to do it** and once to **evaluate whether or not it worked**.
- Steer clear of **more than one place to store requirements**. It's always a maintenance nightmare.
- Be **skeptical** of magic, **out-of-the-box processes**. Each project has something **unique** to it, and your process should be flexible.

SoftwareDevelopmentcross

This is it, the last crossword. This time the solutions are from anywhere in the book.

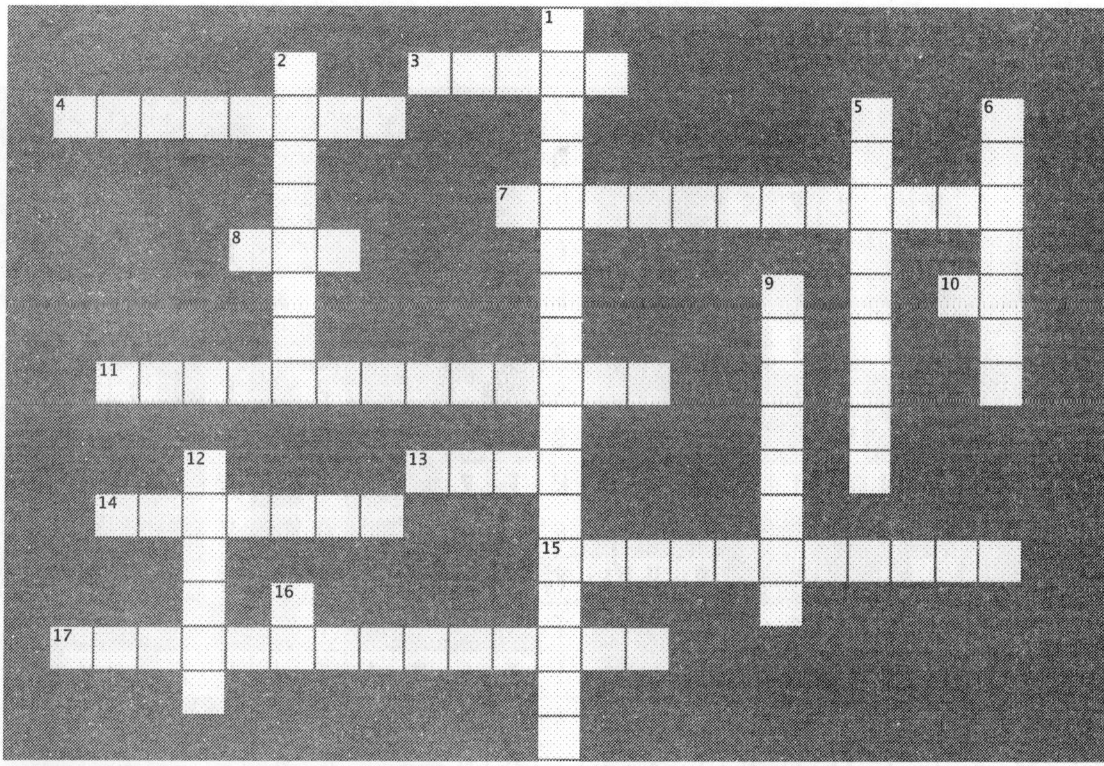

Across

3. Project planning tools can help with projections and presentation of schedule, but do them in parallel with your.........
4. No more than 15 minutes, these keep the team functioning as a team toward a common goal.
7. Every iteration involves ....
8. This is an approach where you write your tests first and refactor like mad.
10. This is a process that checks out your code, builds it, and probably runs tests.
11. High stakes game of estimation.
13. Good Developers develop, Great developers ....
14. The team member you should estimate for.
15. No matter what process you pick, develop ....
17. Every iteration involves ....

Down

1. This means to evaluate processes critically and demand results from each of the practices they promote.
2. Shows how you're progressing through an iteration.
5. What you should be estimating in.
6. Every iteration involves ....
9. How you rack and stack your user stories.
12. The greatest indicator of success or failure on a project.
16. This is a process that tracks changes to your code and distributes them among developers.

SoftwareDevelopmentcross

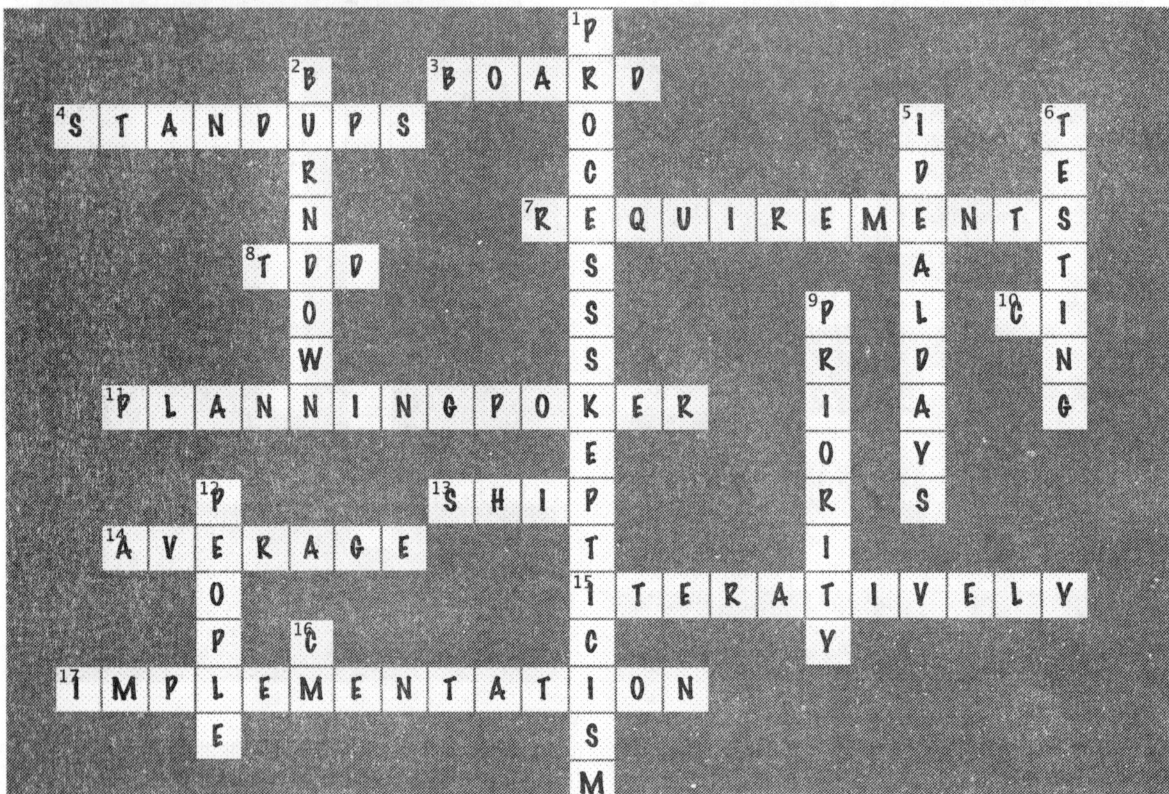

It's time to leave a mark on the ~~board~~ world!

There are exciting times ahead! Armed with all of your software development knowledge, it's time to put what you know to work...so get out there and change the world. Don't forget that the realm of software never stops changing, either. Keep reading, learning, and please, if you can schedule it in your iteration, swing by Head First Labs (*www.headfirstlabs.com*) and drop us a note on how these tools have helped you out.

And be sure and move your "Visit Head First Labs" task to Completed when you're through.

i leftovers

The top 5 topics (we didn't cover)

Ever feel like something's missing? We know what you mean...

Just when you thought you were done... there's more. We couldn't leave you without a few extra things, things we just couldn't fit into the rest of the book. At least, not if you want to be able to carry this book around without a metallic case and castor wheels on the bottom. So take a peek and see what you (still) might be missing out on.

#1. UML class diagrams

When you were developing the iSwoon application in Chapters 4 and 5, we described the design using UML, the ***Unified Modeling Language***, which is a language used to communicate just the **important details** about your **code** and **application's structure** that other developers and customers need, without getting into things that *aren't* necessary.

UML is a great way of working through your design for iSwoon without getting too bogged down in code. After all, it's pretty hard to look at 200 lines of code and focus on the big picture.

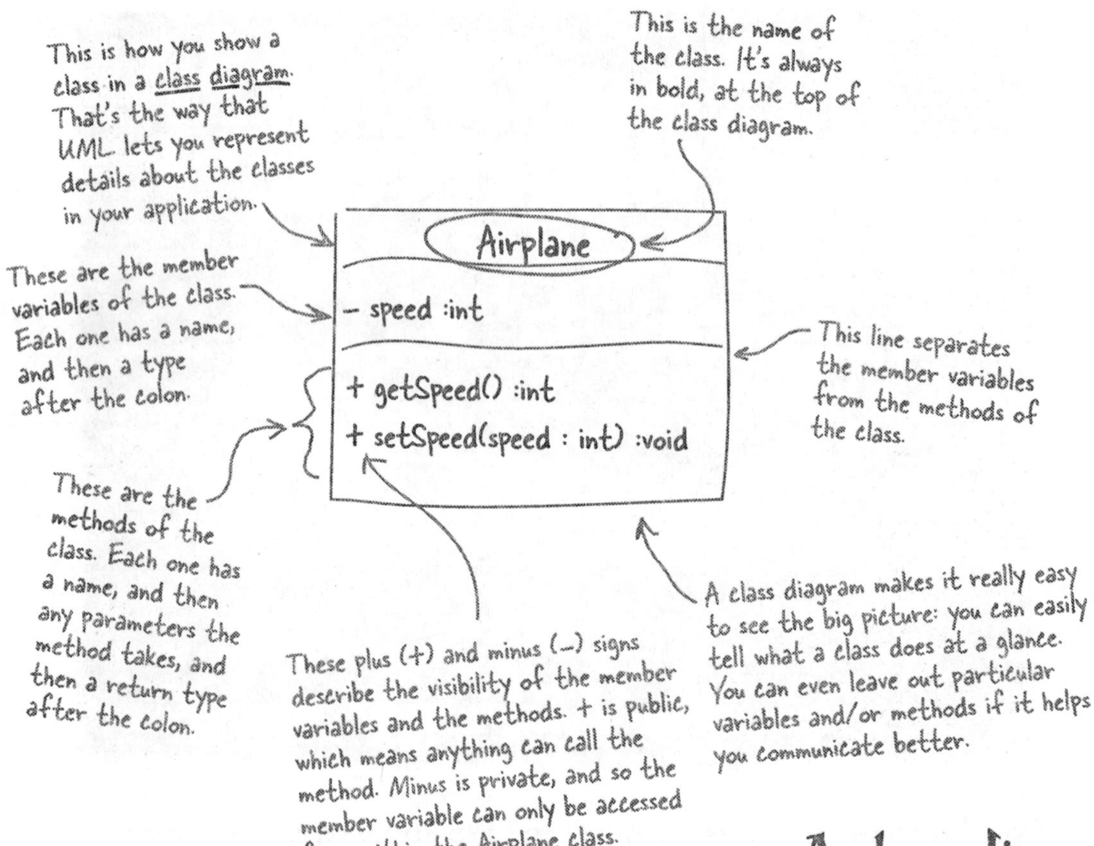

A class diagram describes the static structure of your classes.

Class diagrams show relationships

Classes in your software don't exist in a vacuum, they interact with each other at runtime and have relationships to each other. In this book you've seen two relationships, called association and inheritance.

Association

Association is where one class is made up of objects of another class. For example, you might say "A Date is associated with a collection of Events."

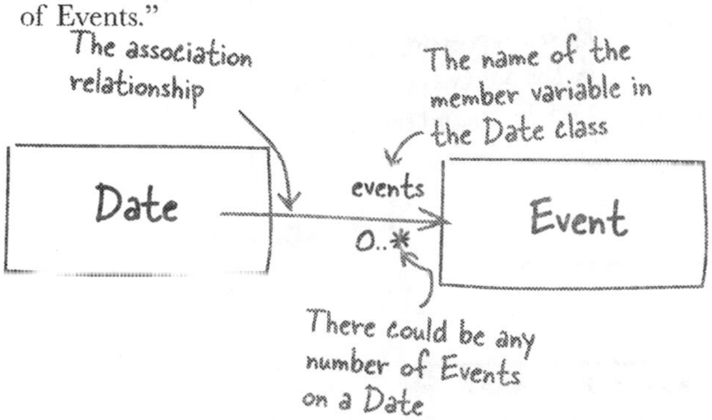

Inheritance

Inheritance is useful when a class inherits from another class. For example, you might "A Sword inherits from Weapon."

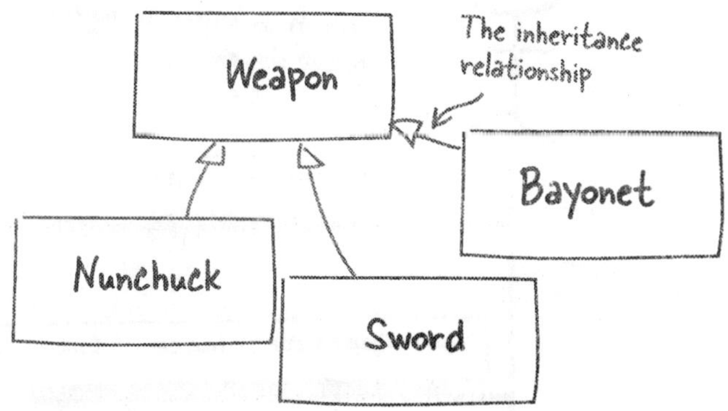

there are no Dumb Questions

Q: Don't I need a big expensive set of tools to create UML diagrams?

A: No, not al all. The UML language was originally designed such that you could jot down a reasonably complex design with just a pencil and some paper. So if you've got access to a heavyweight UML modeling tool then that's great, but you don't actually need it to use UML.

Q: So the class diagram isn't a very complete representation of a class, is it?

A: No, but it's not meant to be. Class diagrams are just a way to communicate the basic details of a class's variables and methods. It also makes it easy to talk about code without forcing you to wade through hundreds of lines of Java, or C, or Perl.

Q: I've got my own way of drawing classes; what's wrong with that?

A: There's nothing wrong with your own notation, but it can make things harder for other people to understand. By using a standard like UML, we can all speak the same language and be sure we're talking about the same thing in our diagrams

Q: So who came up with this UML deal, anyway?

A: The UML specification was developed by Rational Software, under the leadership of Grady Booch, Ivar Jacobson, and Jim Rumbaugh (three really smart guys). These days it's managed by the OMG, the Object Management Group.

Q: Sounds like a lot of fuss over that simple little class diagram thing.

A: UML is actually a lot more than that class diagram. UML has diagrams for the state of your objects, the sequence of events in your application, and it even has a way to represent customer requirements and interactions with your system. And there's a lot more to learn about class diagrams, too.

#2. Sequence diagrams

A static class diagram only goes so far. It shows you the classes that make up your software, but it doesn't show how those classes work together. For that, you need a UML **sequence diagram**. A sequence diagram is just what it sounds like: a visual way to show the order of events that happen, such as invoking methods on classes, between the different parts of your software.

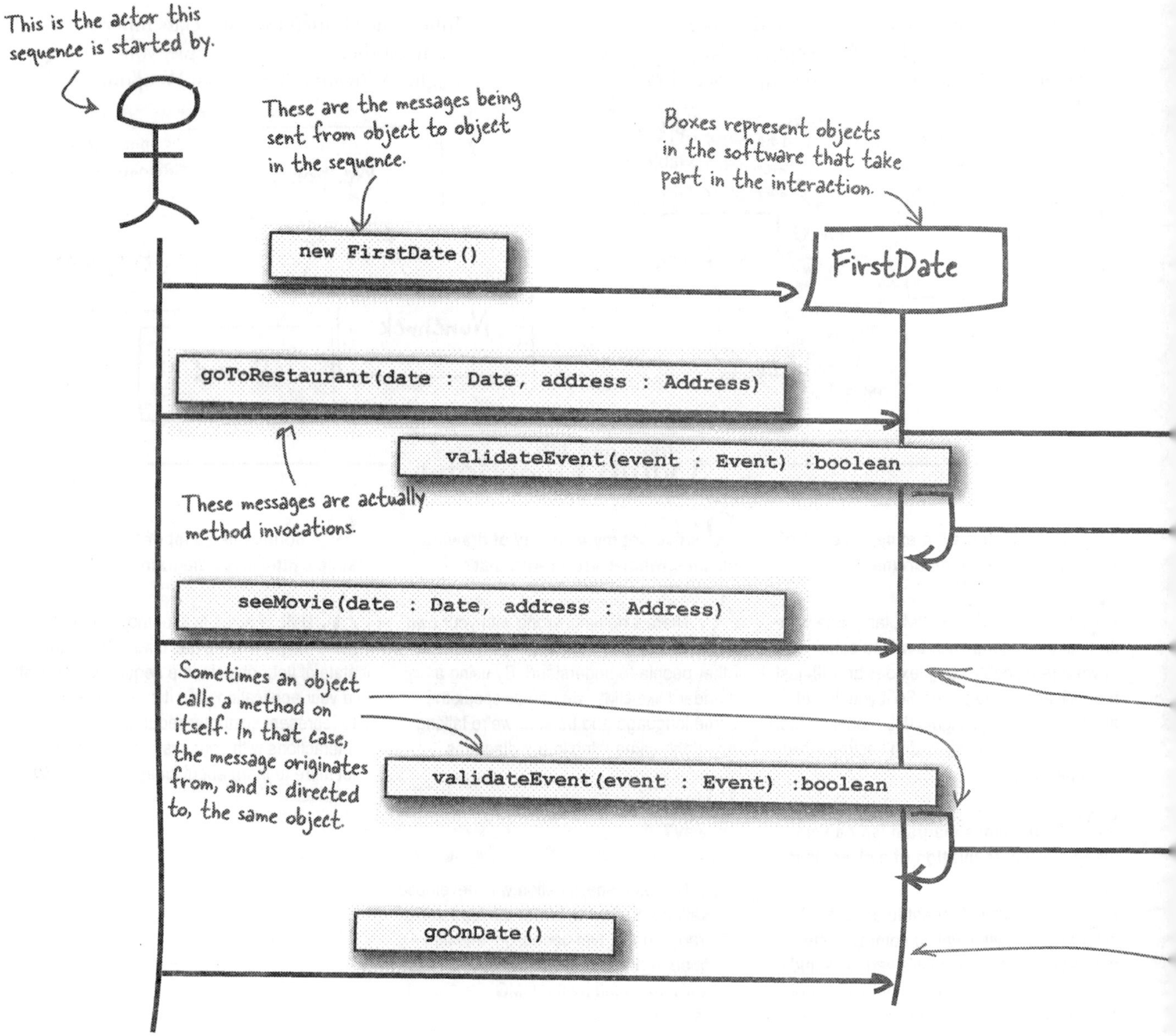

Sequence diagrams show how your objects <u>interact</u> <u>at</u> <u>runtime</u> to bring your software's functionality to life.

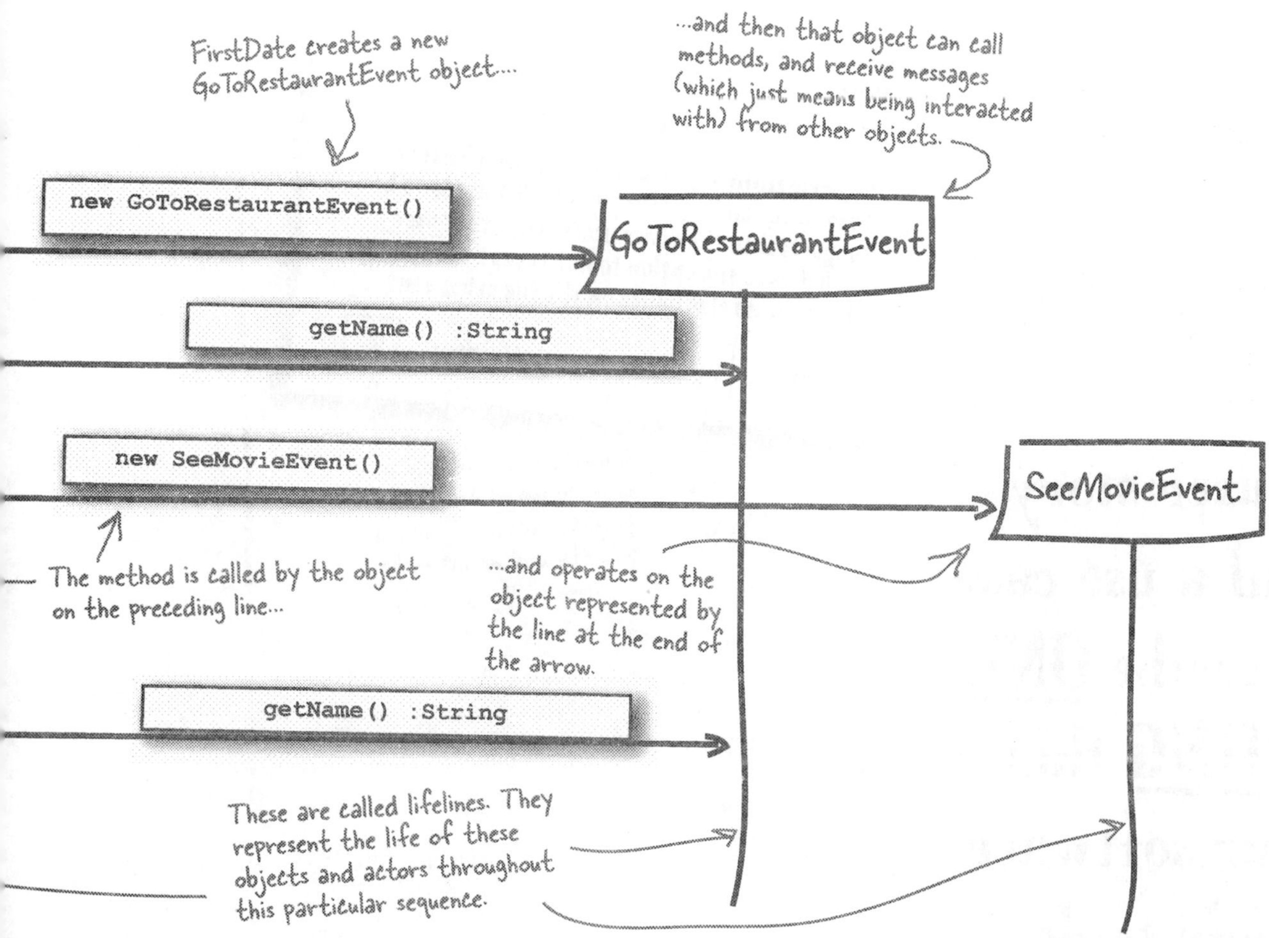

#3. User stories and use cases

You used user stories throughout this book to capture your requirements. User stories are really great at getting a neat description of exactly what the customer needs your software to do. But a lot of more formal processes recommend something called a **use case**.

Luckily, there's easily enough overlap between user stories and use cases for you to use either technique to capture your customer's requirements:

A user story that describes sending a picture using the Beatbox software from chapter 6.

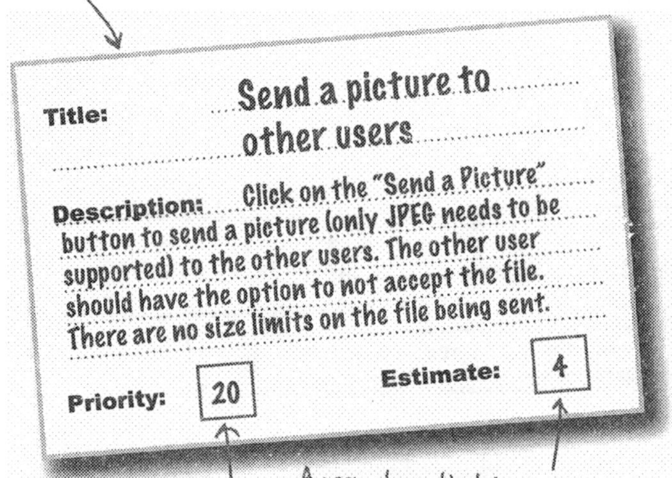

A user story that has been prepared for your project board contains a priority and an estimate

A user story and a use case describe <u>ONE THING</u> that your software needs to do.

...and only one thing.

An equivalent Use Case that describes the same "Send a picture to other users" requirement

You can add more detail to your user story, or modify your use case to have a little less detail... it's really up to you and your customer.

Send a picture to other users

1. Click on the "Send a Picture button"
2. Display users the picture can be sent to in the address book list box.
   2a. Enter the destination user's name in the search box
   2b. Click on search to find the user
3. Select the user to send the picture to
4. Click on send
5. The receiver is asked if they want to accept the photo
   5a.1. The receiver accepts the photo
   5a.2. The receiver views the photo
   5b.1. The recevier rejects the photo
   5b.2. The photo is trashed.

Observation is a key component in getting good use cases written.

A use case's sequence normally contains more steps and detail than a user story. This makes it easier to work to for developers, but means extra work with the customer to nail these details down.

There are a number of different ways that you can write down a use case. This one describes the interactions that a user has with the software, step by step.

So what's the big difference?

Well, actually not a lot, really. User stories are usually around three lines long, and are accompanied by an estimate and a priority, so the information is all in one bite-sized place. Use cases are usually reasonably more detailed descriptions of a user's interaction with the software. Use cases also aren't usually written along with a priority or an estimate—those details are often captured elsewhere, in more detailed design documentation.

User stories are ideally written by the customer, whereas traditionally use cases are not. Ultimately either approach does the same job, capturing what your customer needs your software to do. And one use case, with alternate paths (different ways to use the software in a specific situation) may capture more than one user story.

#4. System tests vs. unit tests

In chapters 7 and 8, you learned how to build testing and continuous integration into your development process. Testing is one of the key tools you have to prove that **your code works** and **meets the requirements** set by your customer. These two different goals are supported by two different types of tests.

Unit testing is at a very low level... source files and XML descriptors.

Unit tests test your CODE

Unit tests are used to test that your code ***does what it should***. These are the tests that you build right into your continuous build and integration cycle, to make sure that any changes that you make to code don't break these tests, on your code and the rest of the code base.

Ideally, every class in your software should have an associated unit test. In fact, with test-driven development, your tests are developed before any code is even written, so there is no code without a test. Unit tests have their limits, though. For example, maybe you make sure that calling `drive()` on the `Automobile` class works... but what happens when other instances of `Automobile` are also driving, and using the same `RaceTrack` object, too?

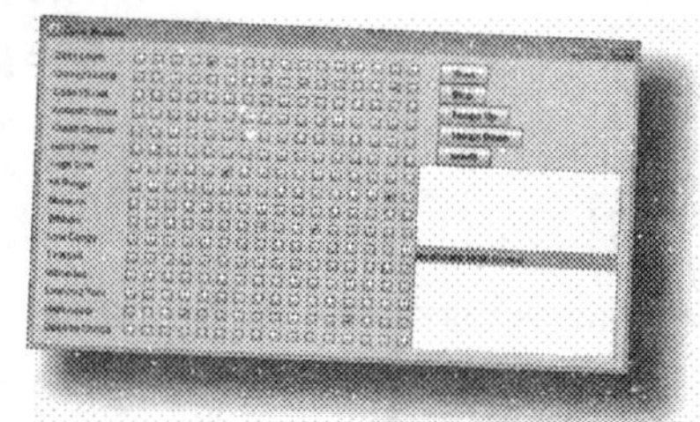

System testing looks at your application as a whole.

System tests test your SOFTWARE

System tests pick up where unit tests leave off. A system test tests your code when it is integrated into a **fully functional system**. System tests are sometimes automated, but often involve someone actually exercising your entire system in very much the same way as the end user will.

For example, you might fire up the GUI for monitoring a race, press the "Start Race" button, watch animated versions of cars spin around the track, and then initiate a wreck. Does everything work the way the customer expects? That's a system test.

there are no Dumb Questions

Q: In addition to unit and system tests, aren't there lots of other types of tests as well?

A: Yes. Testing is a BIG field of work. There are various names for testing, conducted at anything from the source code level to enterprise software integration level. For example, you may hear of **acceptance tests**. Acceptance tests are often conducted with the customer, where the customer either accepts or rejects your software as doing what they need..

Unit tests prove that your code WORKS. System tests prove that your software meets its REQUIREMENTS.

#5. Refactoring

Refactoring is the process of modifying the structure of your code, ***without*** modifying its behavior. Refactoring is done to increase the cleanness, flexibility, and extensibility of your code, and usually is related to a **specific improvement in your design**.

Most refactorings are fairly simple, and focus on one specific design aspect of your code. For example:

```
public double getDisabilityAmount() {
  // Check for eligibility
  if (seniority < 2)
    return 0;
  if (monthsDisabled > 12)
    return 0;
  if (isPartTime)
    return 0;
  // Calculate disability amount and return it
}
```

Refactoring changes the internal structure of your code WITHOUT affecting your code's behavior.

While there's nothing particularly wrong with this code, it's not as maintainable as it could be. The **getDisabilityAmount()** method is really doing two things: checking the eligibility for disability, and then calculating the amount.

By now, you should know that violates the Single Responsibility Principle. We really should separate the code that handles eligibility requirements from the code that does disability calculations. So we can *refactor* this code to look more like this:

```
public double getDisabilityAmount() {
  // Check for eligibility
  if (isEligibleForDisability()) {
    // Calculate disability amount and return it
  } else {
    return 0;
  }
}
```

We've taken two responsibilities, and placed them in two separate methods, adhering to the SRP.

Now, if the eligibility requirements for disability change, only the **isEligibleForDisability()** methods needs to change—and the method responsible for calculating the disability amount doesn't.

Think of refactoring as a checkup for your code. It should be an ongoing process, as code that is left alone tends to become harder and harder to reuse. Go back to old code, and refactor it to take advantage of new design techniques you've learned. The programmers who have to maintain and reuse your code will thank you for it.

ii techniques and principles

Tools for the experienced software developer

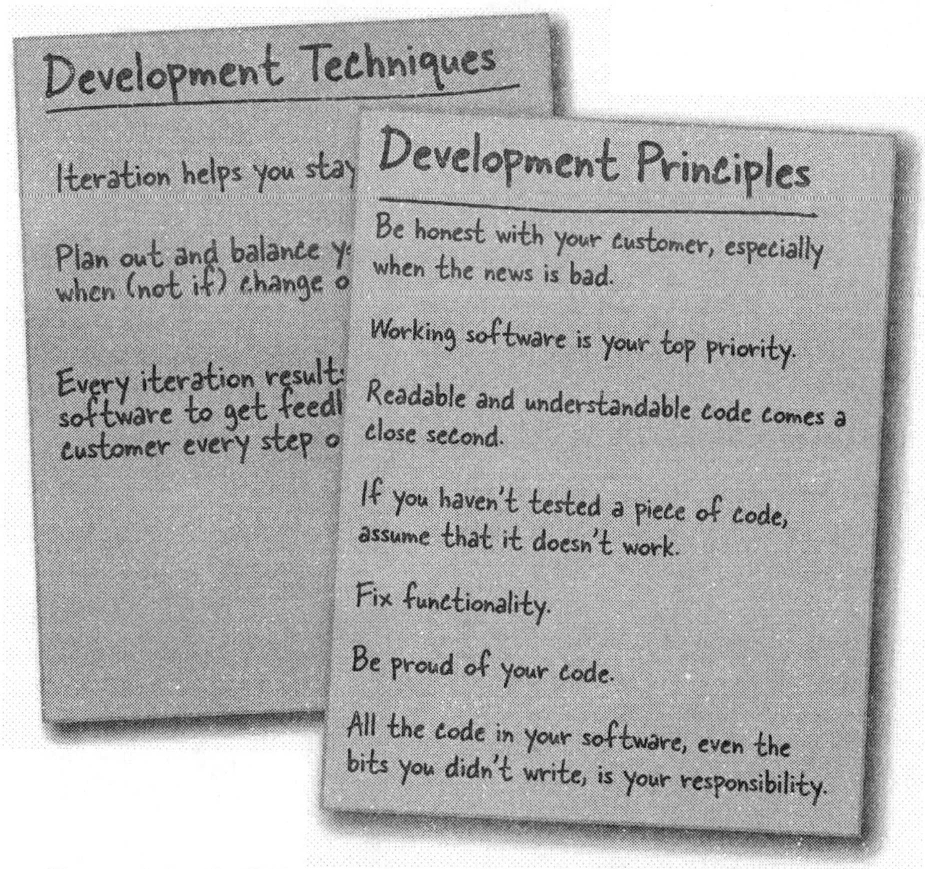

Ever wished all those great tools and techniques were in one place? This is a roundup of all the software development **techniques** and **principles** we've covered. Take a look over them all, and see if you can **remember what each one means**. You might even want to **cut these pages out** and tape them to the bottom of your **big board**, for everyone to see in your daily standup meetings.

Development Techniques

CHAPTER 1

Iteration helps you stay on course

Plan out and balance your iterations when (not if) change occurs

Every iteration results in working software and gathers feedback from your customer every step of the way

CHAPTER 2

Bluesky, Observation, and Roleplay to figure out how your system should behave

Use user stories to keep the focus on functionality

Play planning poker for estimation

CHAPTER 3

Iterations should ideally be no longer than a month. That means you have 20 working calendar days per iteration

Applying velocity to your plan lets you feel more confident in your ability to keep your development promises to your customer

Use (literally) a big board on your wall to plan and monitor your current iteration's work

Get your customer's buy-in when choosing what user stories can be completed for Milestone 1.0, and when choosing what iteration a user story will be built in

CHAPTER 4

You didn't think the exercises were over, did you? Write your own techniques for Chapters 4 and 5.

CHAPTER 5

CHAPTER 6

Use a version control tool to track and distribute changes in your software to your team

Use tags to keep track of major milestones in your project (ends of iterations, releases, bug fixes, etc.)

Use branches to maintain a separate copy of your code, but only branch if absolutely necessary

CHAPTER 6.5

- Use a build tool to script building, packaging, testing, and deploying your system
- Most IDEs are already using a build tool underneath. Get familiar with that tool, and you can build on what the IDE already does
- Treat your build script like code and check it into version control

CHAPTER 7

- There are different views of your system, and you need to test them all
- Testing has to account for success cases as well as failure cases
- Automate testing whenever possible
- Use a continuous integration tool to automate building and testing your code on each commit

CHAPTER 8

- Write tests first, then code to make those tests pass
- Your tests should fail initially; then after they pass you can refactor
- Use mock objects to provide variations on objects that you need for testing

CHAPTER 9

- Pay attention to your burn-down rate—especially after the iteration ends
- Iteration pacing is important—drop stories if you need to keep it going
- Don't punish people for getting done early—if their stuff works, let them use the extra time to get ahead or learn something new

CHAPTER 10

What did you learn in Chapter 10? Write it down here.

CHAPTER 11

- Before you change a single line of code, make sure it is controlled and buildable
- When bugs hit code you don't know, use a spike test to estimate how long it will take to fix them
- Factor in your team's confidence when estimating the work remaining to fix bugs
- Use tests to tell you when a bug is fixed

CHAPTER 12

- Critically evaluate any changes to your process with real metrics
- Formalize your deliverables if you need to, but always know how it's providing value
- Try hard to only change your process between iterations

Development Principles

CHAPTER 1

Deliver software that's needed

Deliver software on time

Deliver software on budget

CHAPTER 2

The customer knows what they want, but sometimes you need to help them nail it down

Keep requirements customer-oriented

Develop and refine your requirements iteratively with the customer

CHAPTER 3

Keep iterations short and manageable

Ultimately, the customer decides what is in and what is out for Milestone 1.0

Promise, and deliver

ALWAYS be honest with the customer

CHAPTER 4

We didn't add any techniques and principles to Chapter 4... can you come up with a few and write them here?

CHAPTER 5

Be the author... write your own principles based on what you learned in Chapter 5.

CHAPTER 6

Always know where changes should (and shouldn't) go

Know what code went into a given release—and be able to get to it again

Control code change and distribution

CHAPTER 6.5

Building a project should be repeatable and automated

Build scripts set the stage for other automation tools

Build scripts go beyond just step-by-step automation and can capture compilation and deployment logic decisions

CHAPTER 7

- Testing is a tool to let you know where your project is at all times
- Continuous integration gives you confidence that the code in your repository is correct and builds properly
- Code coverage is a much better metric of testing effectiveness than test count

CHAPTER 8

- TDD forces you to focus on functionality
- Automated tests make refactoring safer; you'll know immediately if you've broken something
- Good code coverage is much more achievable in a TDD approach

CHAPTER 9

- Iterations are a way to impose intermediate deadlines—stick to them
- Always estimate for the ideal day for the average team member
- Keep the big picture in mind when planning iterations—and that might include external testing of the system
- Improve your process iteratively through iteration reviews

CHAPTER 10

Chapter 10 was all about third-party code. What principles did you pick up?

CHAPTER 11

- Be honest with your customer, especially when the news is bad
- Working software is your top priority
- Readable and understandable code comes a close second
- If you haven't tested a piece of code, assume that it doesn't work
- Fix functionality
- Be proud of your code
- All the code in your software, even the bits you didn't write, is your responsibility

CHAPTER 12

- Good developers develop—great developers ship
- Good developers can usually overcome a bad process
- A good process is one that lets YOUR team be successful

Index

D

E

F

G

H

I

J

L

M

O

P

T

U

ISBN	Title	Author	Year	Price
[illegible]	A+, Network+, Security+ Exams in a Nutshell: [illegible] 220-601, 220-602, 220-603, 220-604, N10-003, SY0-101 [illegible]	[illegible]	2007	[illegible]
[illegible]	Access 2003 Personal Trainer (BRCD), (2 Color Book), [illegible] Pages	Custom Guide	2005	[illegible]
[illegible]	Access 2007: The Missing Manual, 776 Pages	MacDonald	2006	[illegible]
[illegible]	ActionScript for Flash MX: The Definitive Guide, 2nd Ed., [illegible] Pages	Moock	[illegible]	[illegible]
[illegible]	Active Directory Cookbook for Windows Server 2003 and Windows 2000, [illegible] Pages	Allen	[illegible]	[illegible]
[illegible]	Active Directory for Windows Server 2003, 2nd Ed., [illegible]	Allen	[illegible]	[illegible]
[illegible]	[illegible]	[illegible]	[illegible]	[illegible]
[illegible]	[illegible]	[illegible]	[illegible]	[illegible]
[illegible]	[illegible]	[illegible]	[illegible]	[illegible]
[illegible]	[illegible]	[illegible]	[illegible]	[illegible]
[illegible]	[illegible]	[illegible]	[illegible]	[illegible]
[illegible]	[illegible] 292 Pages	[illegible]	[illegible]	[illegible]
[illegible]	[illegible]	[illegible]	[illegible]	[illegible]
[illegible]	[illegible] Pages	[illegible]	[illegible]	[illegible]
[illegible]	[illegible]	[illegible]	[illegible]	[illegible]
[illegible]	[illegible] Applications, [illegible] Pages	[illegible]	[illegible]	[illegible]
[illegible]	[illegible] (BRCD) [illegible]	[illegible]	[illegible]	[illegible]
[illegible]	Building [illegible], 464 Pages	[illegible]	[illegible]	[illegible]
[illegible]	Building Wireless Community Networks, [illegible] Pages	[illegible]	[illegible]	[illegible]
[illegible]	[illegible]	[illegible]	[illegible]	[illegible]
[illegible]	[illegible] Pages	[illegible]	[illegible]	[illegible]
[illegible]	[illegible] with Visual Basic, [illegible] Pages	[illegible]	[illegible]	[illegible]
[illegible]	COM & .NET Component Services, 390 Pages	[illegible]	[illegible]	[illegible]
[illegible]	Computer Privacy Annoyances, 2?? Pages	[illegible]	2005	[illegible]
[illegible]	CSS Pocket Reference, 2nd Ed., [illegible] Pages	[illegible]	[illegible]	[illegible]
[illegible]	[illegible]	[illegible]	[illegible]	[illegible]
[illegible]	Databases in Depth: [illegible]	[illegible]	[illegible]	[illegible]
[illegible]	Designing [illegible], 1?? Pages	[illegible]	[illegible]	[illegible]
[illegible]	Developing [illegible]	[illegible]	[illegible]	[illegible]
[illegible]	DNS on Windows 2000, 2nd Ed., [illegible] Pages	[illegible]	[illegible]	[illegible]
[illegible]	Dreamweaver [illegible]: The Missing Manual, [illegible] Pages	[illegible]	[illegible]	[illegible]
[illegible]	Dynamic HTML: The Definitive Reference, 2nd Ed., [illegible]	[illegible]	[illegible]	[illegible]
[illegible]	Enterprise Service Architecture - O'Reilly [illegible] Series, [illegible] Pages	[illegible]	[illegible]	[illegible]

ISBN	Title	Author	Year	Price

Shroff / O'Reilly

Titles at Reduced Prices

ISBN	Title	Author	Year	Price
9788184043099	A+, Network+, Security+ Exams in a Nutshell (Cover Essentials 220-602,220-603,220-604 N10-00), 826 Pgs	Bhardwaj	2007	150.00
9788173661990	Access 2003 Personal Trainer **(B/CD)**, (2 Color book), 372 Pages	Custom Guide	2005	150.00
9788184042573	Access 2007: The Missing Manual, 776 Pages	MacDonald	2006	100.00
9788173665769	ActionScript for Flash MX: The Definitive Guide, 2/ed, 904 Pgs	Colin Moock	2003	150.00
9788173667350	Active Directory Cookbook for Windows Server 2003 and Windows 2000, 632 Pages	Allen	1993	150.00
9788173666568	Active Directory for Windows Server 2003, 2/ed, 692 Pages	Allen	2003	150.00
9788173668203	AI for Game Developers, 400 Pages	Bourg	2004	100.00
9788173667442	Apache Cookbook (Covers Apache 2.0 & 1.3), 264 Pages	Coar	2003	75.00
9788184041026	ASP .NET 2.0 Cookbook (Cover ASP .NET 2.0), 1,028 Pages	Kittel	2005	150.00
9788184040012	Asterisk: The Future of Telephony, 414 Pages	Meggelen	2005	50.00
9788173662348	AutoCAD 2000 In a Nutshell: A Command Reference Guide, 592 Pgs	Kent	1999	75.00
9788173668982	Better, Faster, Lighter Java, 270 Pages	Tate	2004	75.00
9788173666582	BGP, 292 Pages	van Beijnum	2002	100.00
9788184040548	Blackberry Hacks: Tips & Tools for Your Mobile Office, 350 Pages	Mabe	2005	75.00
9788173665127	BLAST, 372 Pages	Korf	2003	100.00
9788173668999	BSD Hacks:100 Industrial-Strength Tips & Tools, 458 Pages	Lavigne	2004	75.00
9788173662287	Building Java Enterprise Applications: Vol. 1 - Architecture, 324 Pages	McLaughlin	2002	75.00
9788173662881	Building Oracle XML Applications **(B/CD)**, 824 Pages	Muench	2000	100.00
9788173665622	Building Secure Servers with Linux, 454 Pages	Bauer	2003	100.00
9788173664250	Building Wireless Community Networks, 144 Pages	Flickenger	2002	50.00
9788184043846	C# 3.0 in a Nutshell: A Desktop Quick Reference, 3/ed, 874 Pgs	Albahari	2007	150.00
9788184040937	C# Cookbook, 2/ed 1,196 Pages	Hilyard	2006	150.00
9788173662263	CDO & MAPI Programming with Visual Basic, 388 Pages	Grundgeiger	2002	75.00
9788173663659	COM & .NET Component Services, 390 Pages	Lowy	2001	75.00
9788184040197	Computer Privacy Annoyances, 218 Pages	Tynan	2005	50.00
9788184042658	CSS Pocket Reference, 2/ed, 142 Pages	Meyer	2007	25.00
9788173669163	CSS Cookbook (Cover CSS 2.1), 280 Pages	Schmitt	2004	75.00
9788173667800	Database In Depth: The Relational Model for Practitioners, 250 Pgs	C.J.Date	2005	75.00
9788173663888	Designing Large Scale LANs, 408 Pages	Dooley	2002	75.00
9788173662874	Developing ASP Components 2/ed, 864 Pages	Powers	1998	100.00
9788173663789	DNS on Windows 2000, 2/ed, 376 Pages	Larson	2001	50.00
9788173662997	Dreamweaver MX: The Missing Manual, 750 Pages	McFarland	2003	150.00
9788173665288	Dynamic HTML: The Definitive Reference, 2/ed, 1,428 Pages	Goodman	2006	150.00
9788173668166	Enterprise Service Architecture - O'Reilly SAP Series, 236 Pages	Woods	2003	50.00

ISBN	Title	Author	Year	Price
9788173669439	Essentail SharePoint, 338 Pages	Webb	2005	50.00
9788184040920	Essential Microsoft Operation Manager, 400 Pages	Fox	2006	75.00
9788173663581	Essential SNMP, 338 Pages	Mauro	2001	75.00
9788173669613	Excel 2003 Personal Trainer **(B/CD)**, (2 Color book) 490 Pgs	CustomGuide	2004	200.00
9788173668296	Excel 2003 Programming: A Developer's Notebook, 330 Pages	Webb	2004	100.00
9788184042955	Excel 2007 for Starters: The Missing Manual, 408 Pages	MacDonald	2005	150.00
9788173669408	Excel Annoyances: How to Fix the Most Annoying Things about Your Favorite Spreadsheet , 266 Pages	Frye	2004	75.00
9788184040845	Excel Scientific and Engineering Cookbook, 442 Pages	Bourg	2006	100.00
9788173663598	Exim: The Mail Transport Agent, 638 Pages	Hazel	2001	75.00
9788173665257	Exploring the JDS Linux Desktop **(B/CD)**, 418 Pages	Adelstein	2004	100.00
9788184042177	Fedora Linux, 672 Pages	Tyler	2006	150.00
9788184043488	Flash CS3 the Missing Manual, 542 Pages	Veer	2007	100.00
9788184040500	FrontPage 2003: The Missing Manual, 446 Pages	Mantaro	2005	150.00
9788184040852	Google Advertising Tools, 366 Pages	Davis	2006	150.00
9788173669491	Google Hacks: Tips & Tools for Smarter Searching 2/ed, 496 Pgs	Calishain	2005	100.00
9788173663420	Hardening Cisco Routers, 196 Pages	Akin	2002	50.00
9788173668210	Hardware Hacking Projects for Geeks, 358 Pages	Fullam	2004	100.00
9788173663161	Home Hacking Projects for Geeks, 346 Pages	Faulkner	2004	75.00
9788173669446	Home Networking Annoyances: How to Fix the Most Annoying Things About Your Home Network, 234 Pages	Ivens	2005	50.00
9788184040203	Home Networking: The Missing Manual, 263 Pages	Lowe	2005	75.00
9788173669415	Internet Annoyances: How to Fix the Most Annoying Things about Going Online, 266 Pages	Gralla	2005	75.00
9788184040159	Internet Forensics, 250 Pages	Jones	2005	75.00
9788173664489	IPv6 Essentials, 362 Pages	Hagen	2002	75.00
9788173667480	IRC Hack: 100 Industrial-Strength Tips & Tools, 442 Pages	Mutton	2004	75.00
9788173664496	Java & XML Data Binding, 224 Pages	McLaughlin	2002	75.00
9788173666674	Java Data Objects, 568 Pages	Jordan	2003	100.00
9788173666681	Java Extreme Programming Cookbook, 296 Pages	Burke	2003	75.00
9788173664403	Java Management Extensions, 318 Pages	Perry	2002	75.00
9788173665783	Java Performance Tuning, 2/ed, 600 Pages	Shirazi	2003	150.00
9788173660573	Java Threads, 2/ed, 336 Pages	Oaks	1999	100.00
9788173661105	JavaScript Application Cookbook, 512 Pages	Bradenbaugh	1999	75.00
9788173664441	Learning the Korn Shell, 2/ed, 438 Pages	Rosenblett	2002	100.00
9788173665639	Learning Visual Basic .NET, 326 Pages	Liberty	2002	100.00
9788173669422	Learning Windows Server 2003, 682 Pages	Hassell	2006	150.00
9788173663178	Learning WML & WMLScript, 204 Pages	Frost	2002	50.00
9788184041439	Linux Annoyances for Geeks, 516 Pages	Jang	2006	100.00
9788173663604	Linux Device Drivers, 2/ed, 650 Pages	Rubini	2002	150.00
9788173669453	Linux in a Windows World, 504 Pages	Smith	2005	125.00
9788184040319	Linux Multimedia Hacks, 342 Pages	Rankin	2005	100.00
9788173666759	Linux Server Hacks: 100 Industrial - Strength Tips & Tools, 240 Pages	Flickenger	2003	75.00
9788184040517	Linux Server Hacks: Volume 2, 490 Pages	Hagen	2005	100.00

ISBN	Title	Author	Year	Price
9788173662560	Lotus Domino in a Nutshell, 374 Pages	Neilson	2000	50.00
9788184041781	LPI Linux Certification in a Nutshell, 2/ed, 996 Pages	Pritchard	2006	150.00
9788173663611	Managing NFS & NIS, 2/ed, 518 Pages	Stern	2001	100.00
9788173665233	Managing RAID on Linux, 268 Pages	Vadala	2002	100.00
9788173668654	Managing Security with Snort & IDS Tools, 296 Pages	Cox Ph.D.	2004	100.00
9788173662805	Managing the Windows 2000 Registry, 564 Pages	Robicheaux	2000	100.00
9788173664458	Mastering FreeBSD and OpenBSD Security, 472 Pages	Korff	2005	100.00
9788173665707	Mastering Visual Studio .NET 2003, 420 Pages	Flanders	2003	100.00
9788184040524	Monad, 218 Pages	Oakley	2005	75.00
9788173667497	Mono: A Developer's Notebook, 312 Pages	Dumbill	2004	100.00
9788173665646	MySQL Cookbook (Covers MySQL 4.0), 1,028 Pages	DuBois	2003	150.00
9788173666773	MySQL Pocket Reference, 94 Pages	Reese	2003	25.00
9788173663529	Network Security Hacks: 100 Industrial-Strength Tips & Tools, 328 Pages	Lockhart	2004	100.00
9788173665615	Object-Oriented Programming with Visual Basic .NET, 306 Pgs	Hamilton	2003	50.00
9788173667510	OpenOffice.org Writer **(B/CD)**, 234 Pages	Weber	2004	75.00
9788173660672	Oracle Database Administration: The Essential Reference, 552 Pages	Kreines	1999	50.00
9788173660689	Oracle Distributed Systems **(Book / DISK)**, 552 Pages	Dye	2000	75.00
9788173669354	Oracle Essentials: Oracle Database 10g, 3/ed, 368 Pages	Greenwald	2004	100.00
9788173664113	Oracle Essentials: Oracle9i, Oracle8i & Oracle8, 2/ed, 382 Pgs	Greenwald	2001	50.00
9788173663246	Oracle Net8 Configuration & Troubleshooting, 412 Pages	Toledo	1998	75.00
9788173663628	Oracle PL/SQL Best Practices, 208 Pages	Feuerstein	2001	50.00
9788184042542	Oracle PL/SQL Language Pocket Reference, 3/ed, 140 Pages	Feuerstein	2006	25.00
9788184040487	Oracle PL/SQL Programming, 4/ed, 1,210 Pages	Feuerstein	2005	200.00
9788173661198	Oracle PL/SQL Programming: Guide to Oracle8i Features **(Book / DISK)**, 264 Pages	Feuerstein	1999	50.00
9788173660290	Oracle Scripts **(B/CD)**, 208 Pages	Lomansky	1998	50.00
9788173660719	Oracle Security, 448 Pages	Theriault	1998	75.00
9788173662911	Oracle SQL: The Essential Reference, 424 Pages	Kreines	2000	75.00
9788173661211	Oracle Web Applications: PL/SQL Developer's Intro, 264 Pages	Odewahn	1999	75.00
9788173660283	Oracle8 Design Tips, 136 Pages	Ensor	1997	50.00
9788173668029	PC Annoyances: How to Fix the Most Annoying Things about your Personal Computer, 236 Pages	Bass	2003	75.00
9788173668272	PC Pest Control, 296 Pages	Gralla	2005	75.00
9788184041392	PC's: The Missing Manual, 612 Pages	Rathbone	2005	100.00
9788173661228	Perl 5 Pocket Reference, 2/ed, 96 Pages	Vromans	2002	25.00
9788173667190	Perl 6 Essentials, 208 Pages	Randal	2003	75.00
9788173668043	Perl Template Toolkit, 600 Pages	Chamberlain	2003	150.00
9788173661242	Perl/Tk Pocket Reference, 104 Pages	Lidie	1998	25.00
9788173662690	PHP Pocket Reference, 124 Pages	Lerdorf	2000	25.00
9788173669804	Powerpoint 2003 Personal Trainer **(B/CD), (2 Color Book)** 242 Pages	CustomGuide	2004	150.00
9788173661266	Practical Internet Groupware, 520 Pages	Udell	1999	75.00
9788173667114	Practical mod_perl, 932 Pages	Bekman	2003	150.00

ISBN	Title	Author	Year	Price
9788184040326	Practical Perforce, 370 Pages	Wingerd	2005	100.00
9788173666735	Practical RDF, 360 Pages	Powers	2003	100.00
9788184040098	Prefactoring, 248 Pages	Pugh	2005	100.00
9788184047226	**Programming Entity Framework, 844 Pages**	**Lerman**	**2009**	**150.00**
9788173661273	Programming Internet E-mail, 384 Pages	Wood	1999	50.00
9788184040791	Programming MapPoint in .NET **(B/CD)**, 400 Pages	Thota	2005	100.00
9788173667060	Programming Visual Basic .NET 2003, 2/ed, 564 Pages	Liberty	2003	100.00
9788184040371	Programming Visual Basic 2005, 580 Pages	Liberty	2005	100.00
9788173662072	Programming Web Services with XML-RPC, 240 Pages	St.Laurent	2001	50.00
9788173668173	Programming with QT (Covers Qt 3), 2/ed, 532 Pages	Dalheimer	2002	125.00
9788184041507	Project 2003 Personal Trainer, **(B/CD)**, 246 Pages	CustomGuide	2005	100.00
9788173660191	QuarkXPress in a Nutshell, 552 Pages	O'Quinn	1998	50.00
9788173669682	RT Essentials, 228 Pages	Vincent	2005	75.00
9788173664229	SAX2 (Simple API for XML), 248 Pages	Brownell	2002	50.00
9788173667282	Secure Programming Cookbook for C and C++, 800 Pages	Viega	2003	150.00
9788173663260	Securing Windows NT/2000 Servers for the Internet, 200 Pages	Norberg	1998	50.00
9788173669378	Securing Windows Server 2003, 456 Pages	Danseglio	2004	100.00
9788173662485	sed & awk Pocket Reference, 60 Pages	Robbins	1998	25.00
9788173661297	sendmail Desktop Reference, 74 Pages	Costales	1997	25.00
9788173665837	sendmail, 3/ed, 1,238 Pages	Costales	2002	150.00
9788184040678	Skype Hacks: Tips & Tools for Cheap, Fun, Innovative Phone Service, 354 Pages	Sheppard	2005	75.00
9788173663864	Solaris 8 Administrator's Guide, 308 Pages	Watters	2002	100.00
9788173669194	SpamAssassin (Covers 3.0), 232 Pages	Schwartz	2004	100.00
9788173668418	Squid: The Definitive Guide, 472 Pages	Wessels	2004	100.00
9788173662928	SSH: The Secure Shell: The Definitive Guide, 564 Pages	Barrett	2001	75.00
9788184042634	Statistics Hacks, 380 Pages	Frey	2006	100.00
9788184041798	SUSE Linux, 460 Pages	Brown	2006	100.00
9788173669514	SWT: A Developer's Notebook, 330 Pages	Hatton	2004	100.00
9788173663253	T1: A Survival Guide, 312 Pages	Gast	2001	50.00
9788184040531	Talk is Cheap: Switching to Internet Telephones, 278 Pages	Gaskin	2005	100.00
9788173662607	Tcl/Tk Pocket Reference, 100 Pages	Raines	1998	25.00
9788173666872	Tomcat: The Definitive Guide (Cover Tomcat 4), 336 Pages	Brittain	2004	100.00
9788184040210	Twisted Network Programming Essentials, 210 Pages	Fettig	2005	100.00
9788173663307	VBScript Pocket Reference, 118 Pages	Childs	2000	25.00
9788173661341	Virtual Private Networks, 2/ed, 228 Pages	Scott	1998	50.00
9788184042092	Visual Basic 2005 Cookbook, 754 Pages	Craig	2006	150.00
9788184040913	Visual Basic 2005 in a Nutshell 3/ed, 766 Pages	Patrick	2006	150.00
9788184040067	Visual Basic 2005 Jumpstart, 226 Pages	Lee	2005	75.00
9788173666162	Visual Basic 2005: A Developer's Notebook, 272 Pages	MacDonald	2005	100.00
9788173669743	Visual C# 2005: A Developer's Notebook, 250 Pages	Liberty	2005	100.00
9788173665011	Visual Studio Hacks: Tips & Tools for Turbo charging the IDE, 304 Pages	Avery	2005	75.00
9788173663475	Web Database Applications with PHP & MySQL, 600 Pages	Williams	2002	75.00
9788173664410	Web Performance Tuning, 2/ed, 488 Pages	Killelea	2002	75.00

ISBN	Title	Author	Year	Price
9788173665219	Web Privacy with P3P, 350 Pages	Cranor	2002	100.00
9788184046151	Web Security Testing Cookbook, 328 Pages	Hope	2008	100.00
9788173669675	Web Site Measurement Hacks: Tips & Tools to Help Optimize Your Online Business, 442 Pages	Peterson	2005	75.00
9788173665936	WebLogic Server 6.1 Workbook for Enterprise JavaBeans, 3/ed, 264 Pages	Nyberg	2001	50.00
9788173662638	Windows 2000 Active Directory, 624 Pages	Lowe-Norris	2002	75.00
9788173662782	Windows 2000 Administration in a Nutshell: A Desktop Quick Reference, 1,000 Pages	Tulloch	2001	50.00
9788173663314	Windows 2000 Commands Pocket Reference, 122 Pages	Frisch	2001	25.00
9788173663321	Windows 2000 Performance Guide, 650 Pages	Friedman	2002	75.00
9788173660740	Windows 2000 Quick Fixes, 304 Pages	Boyce	2001	50.00
9788184042603	Windows Developers Power Tools, 1,322 Pages	Avery	2006	250.00
9788173660887	Windows NT TCP/IP Network Administration, 512 Pages	Hunt	1999	100.00
9788184040777	Windows Server 2003 Security Cookbook, 522 Pages	Danseglio	2005	150.00
9788184042986	Windows Vista In A Nutshell, 766 Pages	Gralla	2006	100.00
9788184043075	Windows Vista Pocket Reference, 208 Pages	Gralla	2007	50.00
9788184042139	Windows Vista: The Definitive Guide, 958 Pages	Stanek	2007	150.00
9788184042580	Windows Vista: The Missing Manual, 860 Pages	Pogue	2006	150.00
9788173669644	Windows XP Personal Trainer **(B/CD)**, 480 Pages	Custom Guide	2004	150.00
9788173665912	Windows XP Unwired: A Guide for Home, Office, and the Road, 316 Pages	Lee	2003	75.00
9788173667466	Wireless Hacks: 100 Industrial-Strength Tips & Tools, 424 Pages	Flickenger	2003	100.00
9788184043020	Wireless Hacks, 2/ed: Tips & Tools For Building, Extending & Securing Your Network 2/ed, 480 Pages	Flickenger	2005	100.00
9788173666117	Word Annoyances, 218 Pages	Hart	2005	75.00
9788184041422	XAML in a Nutshell, 316 Pages	MacVittie	2006	100.00
9788184045574	XSLT, 2/ed (Now Covers XSLT 2.0), 1,002 Pages	Tidwell	2008	150.00
9788184040074	Yahoo! Hacks: Tips & Tools for Living on the Web Frontier, 504 Pgs	Bausch	2005	75.00
9788184040883	Zero Configuration Networking: The Definitive Guide, 252 Pages	Cheshire	2005	50.00

CURRENT TITLES

ISBN	Title	Author	Year	Price
9788184049510	**97 Things Every Programmer Should Know, 272 Pages**	**Henney**	**2010**	**300.00**
9788184048131	97 Things Every Project Manager Should Know, 268 Pages	Davis	2009	300.00
9788184046892	97 Things Every Software Architect Should Know, 236 Pages	Monson	2009	300.00
9788173666537	.NET and XML, 484 Pages	Bornstein	2004	425.00
9788173669200	.NET Compact Framework Pocket Guide, 122 Pages	Lee	2004	125.00
9788173665721	.NET Gotchas: 75 Ways to Improve Your C# and VB.NET Programs, 402 Pages	Subramaniam	2005	300.00
9788184041637	802.11 Wireless Networks: The Definitive Guide, 2nd Edition (Covers 802.11a, g, n & i), 668 Pages	Gast	2005	550.00
9789350230503	**Access 2010: The Missing Manual, 852 Pages**	**MacDonald**	**2010**	**700.00**
9788184042924	Access 2007 For Starters: The Missing Manual, 426 Pages	MacDonald	2007	400.00
9788184043334	Access Data Analysis Cookbook, 384 Pages	Bluttman	2007	375.00
9788173664281	Access Database Design & Programming, 3/ed, 454 Pages	Roman	2002	325.00

ISBN	Title	Author	Year	Price
9788173666377	Access Hacks: Tips & Tools for Wrangling Your Data, 362 Pages	Bluttman	2005	325.00
9788184042832	ActionScript 3.0 Cookbook, 600 Pages	Lott	2006	475.00
9788173667237	ActionScript Cookbook, 904 Pages	Lott	2003	675.00
9788184043747	ActionScript 3.0 Design Patterns: Object Oriented Programming Techniques (Adobe Developer Library), 552 Pages	Sanders	2007	500.00
9788184046120	ActionScript 3.0 Quick Reference Guide, The, 508 Pages	Stiller	2008	425.00
9788173666551	ActionScript for Flash MX Pocket Reference, 152 Pages	Moock	2003	125.00
8184046496496	Active Directory: Designing, Deploying, and Running Active Directory, 4/ed, 876 Pages	Desmond	2008	800.00
9788184047103	Active Directory Cookbook, 3/ed: Solutions for Administrators & Developers, 1104 Pages	Hunter	2009	750.00
9788184045390	Adobe AIR for JavaScript Developers Pocket Guide, 220 Pages	Chambers	2008	150.00
9788184043501	Adding Ajax, 418 Pages	Power	2007	400.00
9788184044980	ADO.NET 3.5 Cookbook, 2/ed (Updated for .NET 3.5, LINQ, and SQL Server 2008), 1,098 Pages	Hamilton	2008	750.00
8184046446441	Adobe AIR 1.5 Cookbook: Solutions and Examples for Rich Internet Application Developers, 460 Pages	Tucker	2008	500.00
9788184043563	Adobe Integrated Runtime(AIR) for JavaScript Developers Pocket Reference, 192 Pages	Dura	2007	150.00
9788173668302	Advanced Perl Programming, 2/ed, 308 Pages	Cozens	2005	325.00
9788184044409	Advanced Rails, 374 Pages	Ediger	2008	375.00
9788184046083	Algorithms in a Nutshell: A Desktop Quick Reference, 376 Pages	Heineman	2008	250.00
9788184041576	Ajax Design Patterns, 668 Pages	Mahemoff	2006	500.00
9788184041064	Ajax Hacks: Tips & Tools for Creating Responsive Web Sites, 304 Pages	Perry	2006	350.00
9788184043082	Ajax on Java, 176 Pages	Olson	2007	250.00
9788184042610	Ajax on Rails, 364 Pages	Raymond	2007	350.00
9788184044898	Ajax: The Definitive Guide, 996 Pages	Holdener	2008	750.00
9788173667299	Amazon Hacks: 100 Industrial Strength Tips & Tricks, 312 Pages	Bausch	2003	250.00
9788173667794	Analyzing Business Data with Excel, 276 Pages	Knight	2006	300.00
9788184047332	Android Application Development, 354 Pages	Rogers	2009	425.00
9788184040807	ANT: The Definitive Guide, 2/ed (Cover ANT 1.6), 346 Pages	Holzner	2005	375.00
9788184044416	Apache Cookbook, 2/ed, 322 Pages	Bowen	2008	375.00
9788184046007	Apache 2 Pocket Reference, 230 Pages	Ford	2008	150.00
9788173662270	Apache Security, 428 Pages	Ristic	2005	400.00
9788173665134	Apache: The Definitive Guide, 3/ed, 594 Pages	Laurie	2002	500.00
9788184043549	Apollo for Adobe Flex Developers Pocket Guide, 154 Pages	Dixon	2007	125.00
9788184040395	Applied Software Project Management, 304 Pages	Stellman	2005	350.00
9788184048452	Apprenticeship Patterns: Guidance for the Aspiring Sofware Craftsman, 184 pages	Hoover	2009	225.00
9789350231371	**App Savy: Turning Ideas Into ipad and iphone Apps Customers Really Want, 376 Pages**	**Yarmosh**	**2010**	**450.00**
9788184044232	The Art of Agile Development, 446 Pages	Shore	2007	450.00
9788184045963	The Art of Capacity Planning, 168 Pages	Allspaw	2008	200.00
9788184047370	The Art of Concurrency, 322 Pages	Breshears	2009	375.00

ISBN	Title	Author	Year	Price
9788173667831	The Art of Project Management, 512 Pages	Berkun	2005	350.00
9788184048513	The Art of SEO, 620 Pages	Enge	2009	575.00
9788184041415	The Art of SQL, 382 Pages	Faroult	2006	400.00
9788173664588	ASP.NET 2.0: Developer's Notebook, 358 Pages	Lee	2005	425.00
9788173669385	AspectJ Cookbook, 364 Pages	Miles	2004	350.00
9788184045468	Asterisk: The Future of Telephony, 2/ed, 618 Pages	Meggelen	2008	575.00
9788184042702	Astronomy Hacks, 420 Pages	Thompson	2005	450.00
9788184047318	Automating System Administration with Perl, 2/ed, 686 Pages	Edelman	2009	600.00
9788184042900	Backup & Recovery, 774 Pages	Preston	2007	600.00
9788184043471	Bash Cookbook, 640 Pages	Albing	2007	500.00
9789350230312	**bash Pocket Reference, 148 Pages**	**Robbins**	**2010**	**125.00**
9788184043556	Beautiful Code: Leading Programmers Explain How They Think, 634 Pages	Wilson	2007	500.00
9788184046908	Beautiful Architecture, 442 Pages	Gousios	2009	500.00
9788184047967	Beautiful Data, 404 Pages	Segaran	2009	500.00
9788184047110	Beautiful Security, 316 Pages	Oram	2009	350.00
9788184047035	Beautiful Teams, 524 Pages	Stellman	2009	475.00
9788184048650	Beautiful Testing, 358 Pages	Goucher	2009	400.00
9789350230510	**Beautiful Visualization, 404 Pages**	**Steele**	**2010**	**500.00**
9789350230657	**Being Geek: The Software Developer's Career Handbook, 360 Pages**	**Lopp**	**2010**	**400.00**
9789350231142	**Best iPhone Apps, 2/ed,**	**Biersdorfer**	**2010**	**325.00**
9788173663956	Beginning Perl for Bioinformatics, 390 Pages	Tisdall	2001	350.00
9788184040036	Beyond Java, 206 Pages	Tate	2005	200.00
9788184048988	**Bioinformatics Programming Using Python, 540 Pages**	**Model**	**2010**	**500.00**
9789350231173	**Building Android Apps with HTML, CSS, and JavaScript, 204 Pgs**	**Stark**	**2010**	**300.00**
9788184044393	Building a Web 2.0 Portal with ASP.NET 3.5, 324 Pages	Zabir	2008	325.00
9788184047127	Building Embedded Linux Systems, 2/ed: Concepts, techniques, tricks, and traps, 478 Pages	Gerum	2009	450.00
9789350230527	**Building the Realtime User Experience, 344 Pages**	**Roden**	**2010**	**425.00**
9788173661013	Building Internet Firewalls 2/ed, 904 Pages	Chapman	2000	650.00
9788184048428	**Building iPhone Apps with HTML, CSS, & JavaScript, 202 Pgs**	**Stark**	**2010**	**250.00**
9788173661396	Building Linux Clusters **(B/CD)**, 360 Pages	Spector	2002	350.00
9788184041545	Building Scalable Web Sites, 362 Pages	Henderson	2006	325.00
9788184048322	Building Social Web Applications, 452 Pages	Bell	2009	450.00
9788173664748	Building the Perfect PC, 360 Pages	Thompson	2004	350.00
9789350230415	**Buying a Home: The Missing Manual, 372 Pages**	**Conner**	**2010**	**425.00**
9788184040494	C in a Nutshell, 618 Pages	Prinz	2005	350.00
9788173666605	C Pocket Reference, 142 Pages	Prinz	2002	125.00
9788184044423	C# 3.0 Cookbook, 3/ed, 902 Pages	Hilyard	2008	650.00
9788184044379	C# 3.0 Design Patterns, 338 Pages	Bishop	2008	350.00
9788184049459	**C# 4.0 in a Nutshell, 1064 Pages**	**Albahari**	**2010**	**600.00**
9788184044911	C# 3.0 Pocket Reference, 2/ed, 258 Pages	Albahari	2008	175.00
9789350230831	**C# 4.0 Pocktet Reference, 3/ed, 232 Pages**	**Albahari**	**2010**	**175.00**
9788173664298	C# Essentials, 2/ed, 224 Pages	Albahari	2002	175.00

ISBN	Title	Author	Year	Price
9788173665196	C# Language Pocket Reference, 132 Pages	Drayton	2002	100.00
9788173664434	C# & VB .NET Conversion Pocket Reference, 156 Pages	Mojica	2002	75.00
9788184040364	C++ Cookbook, 604 Pages	Stephens	2005	400.00
9788173666629	C++ in a Nutshell, (Cover ISO/IEC 14882 STD) 816 Pages	Lischner	2003	500.00
9788173667107	C++ Pocket Reference, 148 Pages	Loudon	2003	100.00
9788173660450	CGI Programming with Perl 2/ed, 476 Pages	Gundavaram	2000	350.00
9788184042849	Cisco IOS Cookbook, 2/ed, 1,250 Pages	Dooley	2006	850.00
9788173669842	Cisco IOS in a Nutshell, 2/ed: A Desktop Quick Reference for IOS on IP Network, 808 Pages	Boney	2005	500.00
9788184047134	CJKV Information Processing, 2/ed, 916 Pages	Lunde	2009	700.00
9788173668463	Classic Shell Scripting, 568 Pages	Robbins	2005	425.00
9789350231111	**Closure: The Definitive Guide, 616**	**Bolin**	**2010**	**550.00**
9788184047141	Cloud Application Architectures: Building Applications and Infrastructure in the Cloud, 220 Pages	Reese	2009	300.00
9788184048155	Cloud Security and Privacy, 352 Pages	Mather	2009	375.00
9789350230152	**Cocoa and Objective-C: Up and Running, 436 Pages**	**Stevenson**	**2010**	**525.00**
9788184047455	Complete Web Monitoring, 682 Pages	Croll	2009	600.00
9788184041583	Computer Security Basics, 2/ed, 324 Pages	Lehtinen	2006	325.00
9788184048469	Confessions of a Public Speaker, 256 Pages	Berkun	2009	250.00
9788184049473	**CouchDB: The Definitive Guide, 288 Pages**	**Anderson**	**2010**	**350.00**
9788184047158	Creating a Web Site: The Missing Manual, 2/ed: 622 Pages	MacDonald	2009	550.00
9788184048971	CSS Cookbook, 3/ed, 746 Pages	Schmitt	2009	600.00
9788184047165	CSS Pocket Reference: Visual Presentation for the Web, 3/ed: 184 Pgs	Meyer	2009	150.00
9788184048124	CSS: The Missing Manual, 2/ed, 580 Pages	McFarland	2009	475.00
9788184042788	CSS: The Definitive Guide, 3/ed, 550 Pages	Meyer	2006	500.00
9788173662362	Database Nation: The Death of Privacy in the 21st Century, 336 Pages	Garfinkel	2000	235.00
9788173662898	Database Programming with JDBC & Java 2/ed, 348 Pages	Reese	2000	300.00
9788184046632	Data-Driven Services with Silverlight 2, 372 Pages	Papa	2009	400.00
9788184042597	Designing Embedded Hardware, 2/ed, 406 Pages	Catsoulis	2005	275.00
9788173662423	Developing Bio-informatics Computer Skills, 504 Pages	Gibas	2001	225.00
9788173669477	Developing Feeds with RSS and Atom, 280 Pages	Hammersley	2005	300.00
9788184049626	**Developing Large Web Applications, 306 Pages**	**Loudon**	**2010**	**325.00**
9788184040111	Digital Identity, 266 Pages	Windley	2005	275.00
9788173665677	DNS & BIND Cookbook, 248 Pages	Liu	2002	250.00
9788184041965	DNS & BIND (Covers BIND 9.3), 5/ed, 654 Pages	Albitz	2006	600.00
9789350230374	**DocBook 5: The Definitive Guide, 568 Pages**	**Walsh**	**2010**	**525.00**
9788184045567	Dojo: The Definitive Guide, 502 Pages	Russell	2008	400.00
9788184041200	Dreamweaver 8 Design and Construction, 330 Pages	Campbell	2006	375.00
9788184041033	Dreamweaver 8: The Missing Manual, 964 Pages	David	2005	600.00
8184046516519	Dreamweaver CS4: The Missing Manual, 1,104 Pages	McFarland	2008	850.00
9789350230534	**Dreamweaver CS5: The Missing Manual, 1116 Pages**	**McFarland**	**2010**	**750.00**
9788184042771	Dynamic HTML: The Definitive Reference, 3/ed, 1,336 Pages	Goodman	2006	800.00
9788184048308	Essential Blogging, 280 Pages	Doctorow	2009	325.00

ISBN	Title	Author	Year	Price
9788173669019	Eclipse (Coverage of 3.0), 344 Pages	Holzner	2004	325.00
9788173669309	Eclipse Cookbook (Cover 3.0), 372 Pages	Holzner	2004	350.00
9788173669941	Eclipse IDE Pocket Guide, 140 Pages	Burnette	2005	125.00
9788173663017	Effective awk Programming, 3/ed, 454 Pages	Robbins	2001	325.00
9788184049886	**Enterprise Development with Flex, 700 Pages**	**Fain**	**2010**	**650.00**
9788184041194	Enterprise JavaBeans 3.0, 5/ed, 774 Pages	Monson-Haefel	2006	500.00
9789350231135	**Enterprise JavaBeans 3.1, 6/ed, 788 Pages**	**Monson-Haefel**	**2010**	**525.00**
9788184046137	Enterprise Rails, 366 Pages	Chak	2008	350.00
9788173666780	Enterprise Service Bus, 284 Pages	Chappell	2004	300.00
9788184041446	Enterprise SOA, 468 Pages	Woods	2006	450.00
9788184047493	Erlang Programming, 514 Pages	Cesarini	2009	550.00
9788173669316	Essential ActionScript 2.0, 528 Pages	Moock	2004	475.00
9788184043662	Essential ActionScript 3.0, 962 Pages	Moock	2007	600.00
9788184040104	Essential Business Process Modeling, 362 Pages	Havey	2005	350.00
9788184042757	Essential CVS, 2/ed, 442 Pages	Vesperman	2006	425.00
9788184040241	Essentail PHP Security, 310 Pages	Shiflett	2005	125.00
9788184045437	Essentail SharePoint 2007, 2/ed, 462 Pages	Webb	2008	475.00
9788184042825	Essentail SNMP, 2/ed, 480 Pages	Mauro	2005	400.00
9788184045277	Essential SQLAlchemy, 242 Pages	Copeland	2008	275.00
9788173665295	Essential System Administration, 3/ed, 1,178 Pages	Frisch	2002	525.00
9788173666643	Essential System Administration Pocket Reference, 152 Pages	Frisch	2002	125.00
9788173660252	Essential Windows NT System Administration, 488 Pages	Frisch	1998	225.00
9788173662492	Ethernet: The Definitive Guide, 528 Pages	Spurgeon	2000	300.00
9788184047462	Even Faster Web Sites, 274 Pages	Souders	2009	325.00
9788184042955	Excel 2007 For Starters: The Missing Manual, 364 Pages	MacDonald	2007	350.00
9788184044058	Excel 2007 Pocket Guide, 2/ed, 180 Pages	Frye	2007	125.00
9788184042559	Excel 2007: The Missing Manual, 870 Pages	MacDonald	2006	550.00
9789350230541	**Excel 2010: The Missing Manual 928 Pages**	**MacDonald**	**2010**	**500.00**
9788184043518	Excel Hacks, 2/ed, Tips & Tools for Streamlining Your Spreadsheets, 428 Pages	David	2007	400.00
9788184041361	Flash 8 Cookbook, 548 Pages	Lott	2006	400.00
9788184041040	Flash 8 Project for Learning Animation and Interactivity **(B/CD)**, 372 Pages	Shupe	2006	400.00
9788184046502	Flash CS4: The Missing Manual, 768 Pages	Grover	2008	700.00
9789350230381	**Flash CS5: The Missing Manual, 796 Pages**	**Grover**	**2010**	**725.00**
9788173667473	Flash Hacks: 100 Industrial Strength Tips & Tools, 504 Pages	Bhangal	2004	400.00
9788173668593	Flash Out of the Box: A User-Centric Beginner's Guide to Flash **(B/CD)**, 264 Pages	Hoekman	2004	300.00
9788173667312	Flash Remoting MX: The Definitive Guide, 652 Pages	Muck	2003	550.00
9788184048162	flex & bison	Levine	2009	350.00
9788184045246	Flex 3 Cookbook, 798 Pages	Noble	2008	600.00
9789350230428	**Flex 4 Cookbook, 780 Pages**	**Noble**	**2010**	**550.00**
9788184048940	Flex 3 with Java, 309 Pages	Kore	2009	350.00

ISBN	Title	Author	Year	Price
9789350230664	**Gamestorming: A Plabook for Innovators, Rulebreakers, and Changemakers, 308 Pages**	**Gray**	**2010**	**400.00**
9788173668685	GDB Pocket Reference, 78 Pages	Robbins	2005	75.00
9788184045284	Getting Started with Flex 3: An Adobe Developer Library Pocket Guide, 162 Pages	Herrington	2008	125.00
9789350230596	**Getting Started with Processing, 232 Pages**	**Reas**	**2010**	**300.00**
9788184049503	**Google Advertising Tools, 2nd Edition, 452 Pages**	**Davis**	**2010**	**550.00**
9789350230923	**Google Analytics, 238 Pages**	**Cutroni**	**2010**	**300.00**
9788184045079	Google Apps Hacks, 396 Pages	Lenssen	2008	525.00
9788184044942	Google Hacks, 3/ed, Tips & Tools for Finding and Using the World's Information, 558 Pages	Dornfest	2008	400.00
9788184040876	Google Maps Hacks: Tips & Tools for Geographic Searching & Remixing, 366 Pages	Gibson	2006	350.00
9788173667138	Google Pocket Guide, 144 Pages	Calishain	2003	125.00
9788184042856	Google: The Missing Manual, 2/ed, 478 Pages	Milstein	2006	425.00
9788184048285	Google SketchUp, 616 Pages	Grover	2009	575.00
9788184046915	Grep Pocket Reference, 98 Pages	Bambenek	2009	125.00
9789350230398	**Hackers & Painters: Big Ideas from the Computer Age, 292 Pages**	**Graham**	**2010**	**275.00**
9789350230404	**Hackers: Heroes of the Computer Revolution, 540 Pages**	**Levy**	**2010**	**425.00**
9788184048148	Hacking: The Next Generation, 314 Pages	Dhanjani	2009	350.00
9788184048667	Hadoop: The Definitive Guide, 544 Pages	White	2009	550.00
9788173668258	Hardcore Java, 354 Pages	Simmons	2004	300.00
9788184045024	Harnessing Hibernate, 396 Pages	Elliott	2008	400.00
9788184048735	Head First 2D Geometry, 372 Pages	Fallow	2009	350.00
9788184045819	Head First Ajax: A Brain-Friendly Guide, 544 Pages	Riordan	2008	450.00
9788184046595	Head First Algebra: A Brain-Friendly Guide, 576 Pages	Pilone	2009	450.00
9788184044195	Head First C#: Brain-Friendly Guide, 794 Pages	Stellman	2007	550.00
9788184047998	Head First Data Analysis, 504 Pages	Milton	2009	500.00
9788173664663	Head First Design Patterns, 688 Pages	Sierra	2004	500.00
9788173665264	Head First EJB: Passing the Sun Certified Business Component Developer Exam, 744 Pages	Sierra	2003	450.00
9788184049893	**Head First Excel: A Brain-Friendly Guide, 458 Pages**	**Milton**	**2010**	**350.00**
9788184040821	Head First HTML with CSS & XHTML, 694 Pages	Freeman	2005	500.00
9788184048476	Head First iPhone Development, 567 Pages	Pilone	2009	500.00
9788173666025	Head First Java: Your Brain on Java - A Learner's Guide, 2nd Edition (Cover Java 5.0), 730 Pages	Sierra	2005	550.00
9788184044362	Head First JavaScript: A Brain-Friendly Guide, 666 Pages	Morrison	2008	500.00
9788184047301	Head First Networking: A Brain-Friendly Guide, 556 Pages	Anderson	2009	500.00
9788184042214	Head First Object - Oriented Analysis & Design, 648 Pages	McLaughlin	2006	425.00
9788184048001	Head First PMP, 2nd Edition 852 Pages	Greene	2009	600.00
9788184048766	Head First Programming, 460 Pages	Griffiths	2009	350.00
9788184046571	Head First Rails: A learner's companion to Ruby on Rails, 478 Pgs	Griffiths	2009	425.00
9788184046588	Head First PHP & MySQL : A Brain-Friendly Guide, 828 Pages	Beighley	2009	500.00

ISBN	Title	Author	Year	Price
9788184045994	Head First Physics: A Learner's Companion to Mechanics and Practical Physics, 956 Pages	Lang	2008	525.00
9788184044973	Head First Servlets & JSP, 2/ed (COVER J2EE 1.5): Passing the Sun Certified Web Component Developer Exam, 948 Pages	Basham	2008	650.00
9788184044508	Head First Software Development, 512 Pages	Pilone	2008	425.00
9788184043686	Head First SQL: Your Brain on SQL -- A Learner's Guide, 624 Pgs	Beighley	2007	500.00
9788184045826	Head First Statistics: A Brain-Friendly Guide, 732 Pages	Griffiths	2008	425.00
9788184046601	Head First Web Design: A Brain-Friendly Guide, 512 Pages	Watrall	2009	400.00
9789350230671	**Head First WordPress, 386 Pages**	**Siarto**	**2010**	**450.00**
9788184041057	Head Rush Ajax, 464 Pages	McLaughlin	2006	375.00
9788173669347	Hibernate: A Developer's Notebook, 190 Pages	Elliott	2004	225.00
9788184049909	**High Performance JavaScript, 252 Pages**	**Zakas**	**2010**	**275.00**
9788173669262	High Performance Linux Cluster with OSCAR, Rocks, OpenMosix, and MPI, 380 Pages	Sloan	2004	350.00
9788173669026	High Performance MySQL: Optimization, Backups, Replication & Load Balancing, 304 Pages	Zawodny	2004	300.00
9788184047189	High Performance MySQL: Optimization, Backups, Replication 2/ed, 724 Pages	Schwartz	2009	625.00
9788184043808	High Performance Web Sites: Essential Knowledge for Front-End Engineers, 184 Pages	Souders	2007	200.00
9789350230824	**HTML 5: Up and Running, 244 Pages**	**Pilgrim**	**2010**	**300.00**
9788184049527	**HTML & CSS: The Good Parts, 368 Pages**	**Henick**	**2010**	**400.00**
9788184042146	HTML & XHTML the Definitive Guide, 6/ed, 692 Pages	Musciano	2006	500.00
9788184042696	HTML & XHTML Pocket Reference, 3/ed, 118 Pages	Robbins	2006	125.00
9788184048995	**HTML & XHTML Pockte Reference, 4/ed, 206 Pages**	**Robbins**	**2010**	**125.00**
9788184049466	**HTTP: The Definitive Guide, 676 Pages**	**Gourley**	**2010**	**750.00**
9788184042917	Information Architecture for The World Wide Web, 3/ed, 540 Pgs	Morville	2006	500.00
9788184049039	**Inside Cyber Warfare, 252 Pages**	**Carr**	**2010**	**300.00**
9788184040388	Integrating Excel and Access, 232 Pages	Schmalz	2005	250.00
9788184043617	Intel Threading Building Blocks Out fitting C++ for Multi-Core Processor Parallelism, 348 Pages	Reinders	2007	350.00
9788184045635	Intellectual Property and Open Source: A Practical Guide to Protecting Code, 406 Pages	Lindberg	2008	450.00
9788184040999	Intermediate Perl, 290 Pages	Schwartz	2006	300.00
9788173661051	Internet Core Protocols: The Definitive Guide **(B/CD)**, 476 Pgs	Hall	2000	375.00
9788184041811	The Internet: The Missing Manual, 466 Pages	Biersdorfer	2006	350.00
9788173663376	IP Routing, 244 Pages	Malhotra	2002	250.00
9789350230336	**iPhone 3D Programming, 460 Pages**	**Rideout**	**2010**	**550.00**
9789350230329	**iPhone App Development: The Missing Manual, 360 Pgs**	**Hockenberry**	**2010**	**425.00**
9788184048728	iPhone Game Development, 276 Pages	Zirkle	2009	352.00
9788184046922	iPhone SDK Application Development, 408 Pages	Zdziarski	2009	500.00
9788184048742	iPhone The Missing Manual 3/ed, 428 Pages	Pogue	2009	500.00
9789350230848	**iPhone: The Missing Manual 4/ed, 472 Pages**	**Pogue**	**2010**	**550.00**
9788184042818	IPv6 Essentials, 2/ed, 450 Pages	Hagen	2006	450.00
9788173663024	IPv6 Network Administration, 316 Pages	Murphy	2005	325.00

ISBN	Title	Author	Year	Price
9788173667374	J2EE Design Patterns, 390 Pages	Crawford	2003	400.00
9788173663437	J2ME in a Nutshell, 474 Pages	Topley	2002	450.00
9788173669293	Jakarta Commons Cookbook, 412 Pages	O'Brien	2004	375.00
9788173669484	Jakarta Struts Cookbook, 536 Pages	Siggelkow	2005	400.00
9788173667145	Jakarta Struts Pocket Reference, 142 Pages	Cavaness	2003	125.00
9788173664472	Java & SOAP, 286 Pages	Englander	2002	275.00
9788184043068	Java & XML, 3/ed, 496 Pages	McLaughlin	2006	450.00
9788173663796	Java & XSLT, 534 Pages	Burke	2001	350.00
9788173668470	Java 1.5 Tiger: A Developer's Notebook, 210 Pages	McLaughlin	2004	175.00
9788173669361	Java Cookbook (Coverage of 1.5), 2/ed, 872 Pages	Darwin	2004	600.00
9788173666667	Java Database Best Practices, 304 Pages	Eckstein	2003	275.00
9788173665776	Java Enterprise Best Practices, 296 Pages	Eckstein	2002	275.00
9788184042870	Java Enterprise in a Nutshell, 3/ed, 906 Pages	Farley	2005	600.00
9788173668630	Java Examples in a Nutshell: A Tutorial Companion to Java in a Nutshell, 3/ed, 728 Pages	Flanagan	2004	400.00
9788184042160	Java Generics and Collections, 308 Pages	Naftalin	2006	350.00
9788184042665	Java in a Nutshell, 5/ed, 1,266 Pages	Flanagan	2005	650.00
9788184041187	Java I/O, 2/ed, 740 Pages	Harold	2006	650.00
9788184047349	Java Message Service, 2/ed, 348 Pages	Richards	2009	350.00
9788173663536	Java Network Programming, 3/ed, 770 Pages	Harold	2004	500.00
9788173665110	Java NIO, 308 Pages	Hitchens	2002	275.00
9788184044881	Java Pocket Guide, 208 Pages	Liguori	2008	150.00
9788184045031	Java Power Tools, 926 Pages	Smart	2008	775.00
9788173663901	Java Programming with Oracle JDBC, 504 Pages	Bales	2001	300.00
9788173663819	Java RMI, 578 Pages	Grosso	2001	450.00
9788173664120	Java Security, 2/ed, 624 Pages	Oaks	2001	500.00
9788173668227	Java Servlet & JSP Cookbook, 756 Pages	Perry	2004	600.00
9788173662850	Java Servlet Programming 2/ed, 786 Pages	Hunter	2001	500.00
9788173665684	Java Swing, 2/ed, 1,288 Pages	Loy	2002	750.00
9788173665929	Java Threads (Covers J2SE 5.0), 3/ed, 368 Pages	Oaks	2004	400.00
9788173663444	Java Web Services, 286 Pages	Chappell	2002	300.00
9788173666698	Java Web Services in a Nutshell: A Desktop Quick Reference (Covers J2EE 1.4 & JWSDP), 696 Pages	Topley	2003	500.00
9788184047196	Java Web Services: Up and Running, 332 Pages	Kalin	2009	325.00
9789350230138	**Java: The Good Parts, 212 Pages**	**Waldo**	**2010**	**250.00**
9789350230688	**JavaScript Cookbook, 576 Pages**	**Powers**	**2010**	**575.00**
9788184045451	JavaScript and DHTML Cookbook, 2/ed, 620 Pages	Goodman	2008	475.00
9788184045222	JavaScript: The Good Parts, 186 Pages	Crockford	2008	200.00
9788184041941	JavaScript: The Definitive Guide, 5/ed, 1,032 Pages	Flanagan	2006	750.00
9788184045659	JavaScript: The Missing Manual, 560 Pages	McFarland	2008	450.00
9788173669033	JavaServer Faces, 614 Pages	Bergsten	2004	450.00
9788173663833	JavaServer Pages Pocket Reference, 96 Pages	Bergsten	2001	65.00
9788173665301	JavaServer Pages (Covers JSP 2.0 & JSTL 1.1), 3/ed, 762 Pgs	Bergsten	2003	550.00
9789350231159	**JavaScript Patterns, 256 Pages**	**Stefanov**	**2010**	**300.00**
9788184047011	Java SOA Cookbook, 756 Pages	Hewitt	2009	600.00

ISBN	Title	Author	Year	Price
9788173669460	JBoss: A Developer's Notebook, 182 Pages	Richards	2005	225.00
9788184040173	JBoss at Work: A Practical Guide, 318 Pages	Marrs	2005	325.00
9788173666711	JDBC Pocket Reference, 160 Pages	Bales	2003	100.00
9788173668609	JUnit Pocket Guide, 100 Pages	Beck	2004	100.00
9788184041163	JUNOS Cookbook, 682 Pages	Garrett	2006	450.00
9788184044997	JUNOS Enterprise Routing, 828 Pages	Marschke	2008	800.00
9788184047974	JUNOS Enterprise Switching, 772 Pages	Marschke	2009	600.00
9788184048193	JUNOS High Availability, 704 Pages	Sonderegger	2009	650.00
9789350231104	**Junos Security, 872 Pages**	**Cameron**	**2010**	**800.00**
9788184048018	Just a Geek, 316 Pages	Wheaton	2009	350.00
9788184048759	jQuery Cookbook, 594 Pages	Experts	2009	550.00
9788184046427	JRuby Cookbook, 238 Pages	Edelson	2008	300.00
9788173665158	JXTA in a Nutshell: A Desktop Quick Reference, 422 Pages	Oaks	2002	225.00
9788173665608	Kerberos: The Definitive Guide, 280 Pages	Garman	2003	275.00
9788173669729	Killer Game Programming in Java, 986 Pages	Davison	2005	675.00
9788184040265	Knoppix Pocket Reference, 104 Pages	Rankin	2005	100.00
9788173666728	LDAP System Administration, 318 Pages	Carter	2003	400.00
9789350231364	**Learning ActionScript 3.0 2/ed, 480 Pages**	**Shupe**	**2010**	**500.00**
9788184040456	Learning ASP.NET 2.0 with AJAX, 536 Pgs	Liberty	2007	400.00
9788184045666	Learning ASP.NET 3.5, 2/ed, 624 Pages	Liberty	2008	400.00
9788184046465	Learning C# 3.0, 708 Pages	Liberty	2008	450.00
9788173669637	Learning GNU Emacs, 3/ed, 544 Pages	Cameron	2004	450.00
9788184049718	**Learning iPhone Programming, 396 Pages**	**Allan**	**2010**	**400.00**
9788184040333	Learning Java,3/ed **(B/CD)** (Cover J2SE 5.0), 986 Pages	Niemeyer	2005	650.00
9788184047202	Learning JavaScript 2/ed, 412 Pages	Powers	2009	400.00
9788184042672	Learning MySQL, 632 Pages	Tahaghoghi	2006	525.00
9788184045970	Learning OpenCV: Computer Vision with the OpenCV Library, 592 Pages	Dr. Bradski	2008	525.00
9788173663918	Learning Oracle PL/SQL (Covers Oracle9i), 452 Pages	Pribyl	2001	325.00
9788184044263	Learning Perl, 5/ed (Covers Perl 5.10), 364 Pages	Schwartz	2008	325.00
9788184043716	Learning PHP & MySQL, 2/ed: Step-by-Step Guide to Creating Database-Driven Web Sites, 444 Pages	Davis	2007	400.00
9788184047943	Learning PHP, MySQL, and JavaScript, 548 Pages	Nixon	2009	450.00
9788173667329	Learning PHP 5, 378 Pages	Sklar	2004	350.00
9788184048261	Learning Python, 4/ed, 1230 Pages	Lutz	2009	675.00
9788184046458	Learning Rails, 458 Pages	St. Laurent	2008	500.00
9788184043341	Learning Ruby, 272 Pages	Fitzgerald	2007	300.00
9788184047219	Learning SQL 2/ed, 352 Pages	Beaulieu	2009	325.00
9788184043044	Learning SQL on SQL Server 2005, 342 Pages	Bagui	2006	350.00
9788173668050	Learning the Bash Shell, 3/ed, 362 Pages	Newham	2005	375.00
9788173664236	Learning the UNIX Operating System, 5/ed, 174 Pages	Peek	2001	150.00
9788173660610	Learning the vi Editor 6/ed, 352 Pages	Lamb	1998	250.00
9788184045840	Learning the vi and Vim Editors, 7th Edition, 508 Pages	Robbins	2008	400.00
9788184042689	Learning UML 2.0, 300 Pages	Miles	2006	275.00
9788184048292	Learning VBScript, 636 Pages	Lomax	2009	600.00

ISBN	Title	Author	Year	Price
9788184040906	Learning Web Design, 2nd Edition, 484 Pages	Robbins	2003	425.00
9788184049381	**Learning Web Design, 3rd Edition, 500 Pages**	**Robbins**	**2010**	**450.00**
9788184043495	Learning WCF, 624 Pages	Bustamante	2007	500.00
9788184048964	Learning XML, 2nd Edition, 436 Pages	Ray	2009	400.00
8184046476472	Learning XNA 3.0: XNA 3.0 Game Development for the PC, Xbox 360, and Zune, 506 Pages	Reed	2008	500.00
9788173660627	lex & yacc 2/ed, 392 Pages	Levine	1992	225.00
9788184044904	LINQ Pocket Reference, 188 Pages	Albahari	2008	150.00
9788173668449	Linux Cookbook, 590 Pages	Schroder	2004	450.00
9788184040166	Linux Desktop Pocket Guide, 202 Pages	Brickner	2005	150.00
9788173668494	Linux Device Drivers, 3/ed, 646 Pgs	Rubini	2005	450.00
9788184048278	Linux in a Nutshell 6/ed, 960 Pages	Siever	2009	450.00
9788173668500	Linux iptables Pocket Reference, 106 Pages	Purdy	2004	100.00
9788184043525	Linux Kernel In A Nutshell, 216 Pages	Kroah	2006	225.00
9788173664540	Linux Network Administrator's Guide, 3/ed, 372 Pages	Kirch	2005	350.00
9788184044218	Linux Networking Cookbook, 654 Pages	Schroder	2007	525.00
9788173668647	Linux Pocket Guide, 212 Pages	Barrett	2004	150.00
9788173667183	Linux Security Cookbook, 340 Pages	Barrett	2003	325.00
9788184042887	Linux Server Security, 2/ed, 556 Pages	Bauer	2005	450.00
9788184043105	Linux System Administration, 310 Pages	Adelstein	2007	300.00
9788184043815	Linux System Programming: Talking Directly to the Kernel and C Library, 404 Pages	Love	2007	375.00
9788173668432	Linux Unwired, 322 Pages	Weeks	2004	300.00
9788184048216	Living Green: The Missing Manual, 332 Pages	Conner	2009	350.00
9789350230558	**LPI Linux Certification In a Nutshell 3/ed, 544 Pages**	**Haeder**	**2010**	**500.00**
9788184048483	Mac OS X Snow Leopard, 924 Pages	Pogue	2009	850.00
9788184048704	Mac OS X Snow Leopard: Pocket Guide, 252 Pages	Seibold	2009	175.00
9788173664656	Managing & Using MySQL, 2/ed, 448 Pages	Reese	2002	325.00
9788173660276	Managing IP Networks with Cisco Routers, 352 Pages	Ballew	1997	200.00
9788173669583	Managing Projects with GNU Make, 3/ed, 310 Pages	Mecklenburg	2004	325.00
9788184047028	Masterminds of Programming, 510 Pages	Biancuzzi	2009	450.00
9788173661167	Mastering Algorithms with C (B/DISK), 572 Pages	Loudon	1999	400.00
9788173664618	Mastering Oracle SQL, 2/ed, 504 Pages	Mishra	2004	400.00
9788184043648	Mastering Perl, 458 Pages	Foy	2007	400.00
9788173666766	Mastering Perl for Bioinformatics, 406 Pages	Tisdall	2003	300.00
9788184043013	Mastering Regular Expressions, 3/ed, 556 Pages	Friedl	2006	450.00
9789350230305	**Mathematica Cookbook, 848 Pages**	**Mangano**	**2010**	**750.00**
9788173667916	Maven: A Developer's Notebook, 232 Pages	Massol	2005	250.00
9788184045987	Maven: The Definitive Guide, 484 Pages	Sonatype	2008	450.00
9788184042184	MCSE Core Elective Exams in a Nutshell, 604 Pages	Bhardwaj	2006	500.00
9788184041552	MCSE Core Required Exams in a Nutshell, 3/ed, 750 Pages	Stanek	2006	450.00
9788184043730	Microsoft Project 2007: The Missing Manual, 720 Pages	Biafore	2007	625.00
9788184047479	Mercurial: The Definitive Guide, 300 Pages	O'Sullivan	2009	350.00
9789350230565	**Microsoft Project 2010: The Missing Manual, 788 Pages**	**Biafore**	**2010**	**600.00**
9788184048179	Mobile Design and Development, 352 Pages	Fling	2009	400.00

ISBN	Title	Author	Year	Price
9789350231128	**MongoDB: The Definitive Guide, 240 Pages**	**Chodorow**	**2010**	**300.00**
9788184042801	MySQL Cookbook, 2/ed, 990 Pages	DuBois	2006	900.00
9789350230695	**MySQL High Availability, 644 Pages**	**Bell**	**2010**	**650.00**
9788173668067	MySQL in a Nutshell, 358 Pages	Dyer	2005	325.00
9788184045444	MySQL Pocket Reference, 2/ed 148 Pages	Reese	2008	125.00
9788184041408	MySQL Stored Procedure Programming, 650 Pages	Harrison	2006	450.00
9788184047486	Natural Language Processing with Python, 522 Pages	Bird	2009	550.00
9788173665240	NetBeans: The Definitive Guide, 662 Pages	Boudreau	2002	500.00
9788184044256	Network Security Assessment: Know Your Network, 2/ed, 520 Pgs	McNab	2007	450.00
9788184042740	Network Security Hacks, 2/ed, 492 Pages	Lockhart	2006	425.00
9788173668395	Network Security Tools: Writing, Hacking, and Modifying Security Tools , 350 Pages	Dhanjani	2005	350.00
9788173663680	Network Troubleshooting Tools, 370 Pages	Sloan	2005	250.00
9788184043532	Network Warrior, 614 Pages	Donahue	2007	450.00
9788173667923	Nokia Smartphone Hacks: Tips & Tools for Your Smallest Computer, 418 Pages	Yuan	2005	400.00
9788173667848	NUnit Pocket Reference, 100 Pages	Hamilton	2004	100.00
9788173668265	Office 2003 XML, 596 Pages	Lenz	2004	450.00
9788184043303	Office 2007 the Missing Manual, 890 Pages	Grover	2007	550.00
9789350230701	**Office 2010 the Missing Manual, 976 Pages**	**Conner**	**2010**	**500.00**
9788184049534	**Open Government, 452 Pages**	**Lathrop**	**2010**	**500.00**
9788173667725	Open Source for the Enterprise, 246 Pages	Woods	2005	250.00
9788184040296	Open Sources 2.0, 488 Pages	DiBona	2005	425.00
9788173667404	Optimizing Oracle Performance, 426 Pages	Milsap	2003	375.00
9788173669286	Oracle Applications Server 10g Essentials, 292 Pages	Greenwald	2004	275.00
9788173661174	Oracle Built-in Packages (Book / DISK), 956 Pages	Feuerstein	1998	475.00
9788173667077	Oracle Data Dictionary Pocket Reference, 150 Pages	Kreines	2003	125.00
9788173664175	Oracle DBA Checklist Pocket Reference, 88 Pages	RevealNet	2001	65.00
9788184040005	Oracle DBA Pocket Guide, 164 Pages	Kreines	2005	125.00
9788184044201	Oracle Essentials: Oracle Database 11g, 4/ed,422 Pages	Greenwald	2007	400.00
9788173665806	Oracle in a Nutshell: A Desktop Quick Reference, 934 Pages	Greenwald	2002	600.00
9788173664564	Oracle Initialization Parameters Pocket Reference (Oracle Database 10g), 128 Pages	Kreines	2004	125.00
9788184045413	Oracle PL/SQL Best Practices, 2/ed, 308 Pages	Feuerstein	2008	325.00
9788173661181	Oracle PL/SQL Built-ins Pocket Reference, 78 Pages	Feuerstein	1998	60.00
9788184040357	Oracle PL/SQL for DBAs: Security, Scheduling, Performance & More Includes Oracle Database 10g, 466 Pages	Feuerstein	2005	425.00
9788184045420	Oracle PL/SQL Language Pocket Reference, 4/ed, 194 Pages	Feuerstein	2008	125.00
9788184049497	**Oracle PL/SQL Programming, 5/ed, 1,246 Pages**	**Feuerstein**	**2010**	**650.00**
9788173662409	Oracle PL/SQL Programming: A Developer's Workbook, 576 Pages	Feuerstein	2000	300.00
9788173668111	Oracle Regular Expression Pocket Reference, 74 Pages	Burcham	2003	75.00
9788173661204	Oracle SAP Administration, 208 Pages	Burleson	1999	175.00
9788173663635	Oracle SQL* Loader: The Definitive Guide, 278 Pages	Gennick	2001	175.00
9788173669330	Oracle SQL*Plus Pocket Reference, 3/ed, 160 Pages	Gennick	2004	125.00
9788173666063	Oracle SQL*Plus: The Definitive Guide, 2/ed, 592 Pages	Gennick	2004	400.00

ISBN	Title	Author	Year	Price
9788173661846	Oracle Utilities Pocket Reference, 136 Pages	Mishra	2003	100.00
9788184042528	PC Annoyances, 2/ed :How To Fix The Most Annoying Things About Your Personal Compter, Wind & More, 268 Pages	Bass	2005	300.00
9788173667152	PC Hacks: 100 Industrial-Strength Tips & Tools, 316 Pages	Aspinwall	2004	300.00
9788173669736	PC Hardware Annoyances: How to Fix the Most ANNOYING Things About Your Computer Hardware, 276 Pages	Bigelow	2004	275.00
9788173665325	PC Hardware in a Nutshell: A Desktop Quick Reference, 3/ed, 848 Pgs	Thompson	2003	325.00
9788173667121	PDF Hacks: 100 Industrial-Strength Tips & Tools, 308 Pages	Steward	2004	300.00
9789350230169	**Perl & LWP, 280 Pages**	**Burke**	**2010**	**350.00**
9788173664465	Perl & XML, 224 Pages	Ray	2002	175.00
9788173661075	Perl 5 Pocket Reference, 3/ed, 96 Pages	Vromans	2001	70.00
9788184042764	Perl 6 and Parrot Essentials, 2/ed, 304 Pages	Randal	2004	325.00
9788173668289	Perl Best Practices, 554 Pages	Conway	2005	425.00
9789350230183	**Perl Graphics Programming, 498 Pages**	**Wallace**	**2010**	**600.00**
9788173667336	Perl Cookbook, 2/ed, 976 Pages	Christiansen	2003	675.00
9788184041385	Perl Hacks, 310 Pages	Chromatic	2006	325.00
9788173668364	Perl Testing: A Developer's Notebook, 212 Pages	Langworth	2005	225.00
9789350230411	**Personal Investing: The Missing Manual, 268 Pages**	**Biafore**	**2010**	**250.00**
9788184046625	Photoshop CS4: The Missing Manual, 804 Pages	King	2008	725.00
9789350230343	**Photoshop CS5: The Missing Manual, 836 Pages**	**Snider**	**2010**	**750.00**
9788184043006	PHP Cookbook, 2/ed, 842 Pages	Sklar	2006	750.00
9788184040814	PHP Hacks: Tips & Tools for Creating Dynamic Web Sites, 468 Pages	Herrington	2005	400.00
9788184040234	PHP in a Nutshell, 370 Pages	Hudson	2005	325.00
9789350230176	**PHP: The Good Parts, 194 Pages**	**MacIntyre**	**2010**	**225.00**
9788184040258	PHPUnit Pocket Guide, 88 Pages	Bergmann	2005	100.00
9788173668715	Postfix: The Definitive Guide, 288 Pages	Dent	2003	275.00
9788184042948	PowerPoint 2007 For Starters: The Missing Manual, 325 Pages	Vander	2007	325.00
9788184042566	Powerpoint 2007: The Missing Manual, 502 Pages	Veer	2006	450.00
9788173660306	Practical C Programming 3/ed, 456 Pages	Oualline	1997	225.00
9788173666827	Practical C++ Programming, 2/ed, 582 Pages	Oualline	2002	225.00
9788184040050	Practical Development Environments, 340 Pages	Doar	2005	325.00
9788173663925	Practical PostgreSQL **(B/CD)**, 642 Pages	Command Prompt Inc.	2002	450.00
9788173666834	Practical Unix & Internet Security, 3/ed, 994 Pages	Garfinkel	2003	650.00
9788173664397	Practical VoIP Using VOCAL, 532 Pages	Dang	2002	450.00
9788184042108	Process Improvement Essentials, 364 Pages	Persse, PhD	2006	400.00
9788184040227	Producing Open Sources Software, 302 Pages	Fogel	2005	325.00
9788184045581	The Productive Programmer, 238 Pages	Ford	2008	275.00
9788184040340	Programming .NET Components, 2/ed (Covers .NET 2.0 & Visual Studio 2005), 656 Pages	Lowy	2005	425.00
9788184045673	Programming .NET 3.5, 492 Pgs	Liberty	2008	400.00
9788173667206	Programming .NET Security, 704 Pages	Freeman	2003	550.00
9788173664380	Programming .NET Web Services, 500 Pages	Ferrara	2002	375.00
9788173667411	Programming .NET Windows Applications (Covers .NET 1.1, & Visual Studio .NET 2003), 1,316 Pages	Liberty	2003	750.00

ISBN	Title	Author	Year	Price
9788184045055	Programming Amazon Web Services: S3, EC2, SQS, FPS, and SimpleDB, 624 Pages	Murty	2008	600.00
9788184043839	Programming ASP.NET AJAX: Build rich, Web 2.0-style UI with ASP.NET AJAX, 490 Pages	Wenz	2007	400.00
9788184046113	Programming ASP.NET 3.5, 4/ed, 1,178 Pages	Liberty	2008	750.00
9788184042085	Programming Atlas, 418 Pages	Wenz	2006	375.00
9788184044386	Programming C# 3.0, 5/ed, (Cover Visual Studio 2008, LINQ, .NET 3.5 & More), 624 Pages	Liberty	2008	525.00
9789350230855	**Programming C# 4.0 6/ed, 878 Pages**	**Liberty**	**2010**	**500.00**
9788184043709	Programming Collective Intelligence: Building Smart Web 2.0 Applications, 376 Pages	Segaran	2007	375.00
9788173660764	Programming Embedded Systems in C & C++, 198 Pages	Barr	1999	150.00
9788184042627	Programming Embedded Systems with C and GNU Development Tools, 2/ed, 340 Pages	Barr	2006	250.00
9788184041453	Programming Excel with VBA and .NET, 1,128 Pages	Webb	2006	750.00
9789350230862	**Programming Entity Framework, 936 Pages**	**Lerman**	**2010**	**650.00**
9788184048490	Programming F#, 424 Pages	Smith	2009	425.00
9788173669699	Programming Flash Communication Server, 842 Pages	Lesser	2005	600.00
9788184043358	Programming Flex 2, 520 Pages	Kazoun	2007	250.00
9788184047233	Programming Flex 3, 674 Pages	Kazoun	2009	600.00
9788184047981	Programming Interactivity, 756 Pages	Noble	2009	800.00
9788173668180	Programming Jakarta Struts 2/ed, 470 Pages	Cavaness	2004	400.00
9788173662652	Programming Perl 3/ed, 1,116 Pages	Wall	2000	750.00
9788184042719	Programming PHP, 2/ed, 425 Pages	Lerdorf	2006	425.00
9788184043792	Programming Python (Covers Python 2) (B/CD), 3/ed, 1,582 Pgs	Lutzf	2006	800.00
9788173667862	Programming SQL Server 2005, 600 Pages	Wildermuth	2006	400.00
9788184048247	Programming Scala, 464 Pages	Qampler	2009	500.00
9788184048186	Programming the iPhone User Experience, 208 Pages	Boudreaux	2009	250.00
9789350230718	**Programming the Mobile Web, 532 Pages**	**Firtman**	**2010**	**550.00**
9788173662379	Programming the Perl DBI, 372 Pages	Descartes	2000	200.00
9788184047950	Programming the Semantic Web, 320 Pages	Segaran	2009	400.00
9788184045253	Programming Visual Basic 2008, 798 Pages	Patrick	2008	550.00
9789350230947	**Programming WCF Services, 3/ed, 933 Pages**	**Löwy**	**2010**	**550.00**
9788173665738	Programming Web Services with Perl, 492 Pages	Ray	2002	400.00
9788173662041	Programming Web Services with SOAP, 268 Pages	Snell	2001	200.00
9789350230367	**Programming Windows Azure, 388 Pages**	**Krishnan**	**2010**	**350.00**
9788184043723	Programming WPF, 2/ed, 880 Pages	Sells	2007	675.00
9788173664793	Python Cookbook (Covers Python 2.3 & 2.4), 2/ed, 852 Pages	Martelli	2005	600.00
9788184045833	Python for Unix and Linux System Administration, 472 Pages	Gift	2008	450.00
9788184045406	Python in a Nutshell 2/ed, 726 Pages	Martelli	2008	500.00
9788173669705	Python Pocket Reference (Covers Python 2.4), 3/ed, 168 Pages	Lutz	2005	125.00
9788184048506	Python Pocket Reference, 4/ed, 226 Pages	Lutz	2009	150.00
9788173668487	qmail, 268 Pages	Levine	2004	275.00
9788184049015	**R IN A NUTSHELL, 652 Pages**	**Adler**	**2010**	**550.00**
9788184049435	**RADIUS, 224 Pages**	**Hassell**	**2010**	**300.00**

ISBN	Title	Author	Year	Price
9788184042962	Rail Cookbook, 600 Pages	Orsini	2007	500.00
9788184046090	Rails: Up and Running, 2/ed, 232 Pages	Tate	2008	300.00
9788184045956	Rails Pocket Reference, 212 Pages	Berry	2008	150.00
9788184046489	Real World Haskell: Code You Can Believe In, 710 Pages	O'Sullivan	2008	600.00
9788173666896	Real World Web Services, 230 Pages	Iverson	2004	225.00
9788184045857	Refactoring SQL Applications, 372 Pages	Faroult	2008	350.00
9788184043761	Regular Expression Pocket Reference, 2/ed, 126 Pages	Stubblebine	2007	150.00
9788184047172	Regular Expressions Cookbook, 530 Pages	Goyvaerts	2009	500.00
9788184041989	The Relational Database Dictionary, 126 Pages	Date	2006	150.00
9788184041378	Repairing and Upgrading Your PC, 462 Pages	Thompson	2006	450.00
9789350231166	**REST in Practice, 468 Pages**	**Webber**	**2010**	**500.00**
9788184048698	RESTful Java with JAX-RS, 328 Pages	Burke	2009	350.00
9788184043327	Restful Web Services, 462 Pages	Richardson	2007	425.00
9788184049558	**RESTful Web Services Cookbook, 332 Pages**	**Allamaraju**	**2010**	**400.00**
9788184040869	RFID Essentials, 276 Pages	Glover	2006	275.00
9788184047509	Ruby Best Practices, 347 Pages	Brown	2009	375.00
9788184041804	Ruby Cookbook, 920 Pages	Carlson	2006	650.00
9788184041996	Ruby on Rails: Up and Running, 196 Pages	Tate	2006	225.00
9788184043624	Ruby Pocket Reference, 182 Pages	Fitzgerald	2007	150.00
9788184044928	The Ruby Programming Language, 460 Pages	Flanagan	2008	425.00
9788184042726	Running Linux, 5/ed, 986 Pages	Welsh	2005	600.00
9788173667053	Samba Pocket Reference, 2/ed, 146 Pages	Eckstein	2003	125.00
9788184044935	ScreenOS Cookbook, 854 Pages	Brunner	2008	600.00
9788173667213	Secure Coding: Principles & Practices, 200 Pages	Graff	2003	225.00
9788184047240	Search Engine Optimization for Flash, 294 Pages	Perkins	2009	350.00
9788184043600	Securing Ajax Applications, 266 Pages	Wells	2007	275.00
9788184047257	Security Monitoring, 262 Pages	Fry	2009	300.00
9788184040081	Security and Usability, 748 Pages	Cranor	2005	550.00
9788184043754	Security Power Tools, 872 Pages	Burns	2007	650.00
9788173668401	Security Warrior, 562 Pages	Peikari	2004	500.00
9788173660788	sed and awk, 2/ed, 440 Pages	Dougherty	1997	350.00
9788184049572	**sed and awk Pocket Reference, 2/ed, 64 Pages**	**Robbins**	**2010**	**100.00**
9788173669187	SELINUX NSA's Open Source Security Enhanced Linux, 264 Pgs	McCarty	2004	275.00
9788173668234	sendmail Cookbook, 418 Pages	Hunt	2003	400.00
9788184044225	sendmail, 4/ed, 1,324 Pages	Costales	2007	850.00
9788184048674	SEO Warrior, 512 Pages	Jerkovic	2009	525.00
9788173666865	Sequence Analysis in a Nutshell: A Guide to Common Tools & Databases (Covers EMBOSS 2.5.0), 310 Pages	Markel	2003	275.00
9788184040449	SharePoint 2007: The Definitive Guide, 836 Pages	Pyles	2007	600.00
9788184046144	SharePoint for Project Management, 266 Pages	Raymond	2008	300.00
9788173669835	SharePoint Office Pocket Guide, 94 Pages	Webb	2005	100.00
9788173667398	SharePoint User's Guide, 158 Pages	IDC	2005	150.00
9788173669507	Snort Cookbook, 296 Pages	Orebaugh	2005	300.00
9788184043693	SOA in Practice: The Art of Distributed System Design, 358 Pgs	Josuttis	2007	375.00
9788173668197	Spidering Hacks: 100 Industrial - Strength Tips & Tools, 436 Pages	Hemenway	2003	350.00

ISBN	Title	Author	Year	Price
9788173668371	Spring: A Developer's Notebook, 202 Pages	Tate	2005	225.00
9788184046939	SQL and Relational Theory: How to Write Accurate SQL Code, 442 Pages	Date	2009	350.00
9788184040685	SQL Cookbook, 640 Pages	Molinaro	2005	475.00
9788184042207	SQL Hacks, 424 Pages	Cumming	2006	400.00
9788184047264	SQL IN A NUTSHELL 3/ed, 606 Pages	Kline	2009	500.00
9788173667435	SQL Pocket Guide (Cover Oracle. DB2, SQL Server & MySQL), 170 Pgs	Gennick	2006	125.00
9788173668241	SQL Tunning (Covers Oracle, DB2 & SQL Server), 356 Pages	Tow	2003	325.00
9788184042795	SSH The Secure Shell: The Definitive Guide, 2/ed, 680 Pages	Barrett	2005	525.00
9788184048520	Sustainable Network, The: The Accidental Answer for a Troubled Planet, 364 Pages	Sorensen	2009	375.00
9788184048315	SVG Essentials, 376 Pages	Eisenberg	2009	400.00
9788184045680	Statistics in a Nutshell: A Desktop Quick Reference, 492 Pages	Boslaugh	2008	250.00
9788173668579	STL Pocket Reference, 136 Pages	Lischner	2003	100.00
9788184045048	Subject To Change: Creating Great Products & Services for an Uncertain World: Adaptive Path on Design, 226 Pages	Merholz	2008	300.00
9788173664816	Swing Hacks, 554 Pages	Marinacci	2005	425.00
9788173665318	Switching to VoIP, 514 Pages	Wallingford	2005	450.00
9788173660931	Tcl/Tk in a Nutshell: A Desktop Quick Reference, 480 Pages	Raines	1999	240.00
9788173664670	TCP/IP Network Administration 3/ed, 756 Pages	Hunt	2002	500.00
9788173666513	Test Driving Linux: From Windows to Linux in 60 Seconds **(B/CD)**, 372 Pages	Brickner	2005	350.00
9788184040302	Time Management for System Administrators, 238 Pages	Limoncelli	2005	250.00
9788173666032	TOAD Pocket Reference for Oracle, 2/ed, 136 Pages	McGrath	2005	125.00
9788184044041	Tomcat: The Definitive Guide, 2/ed (Cover TOMCAT 6.0), 358 Pgs	Brittain	2007	400.00
9788184046946	The Art of Application Performance Testing, 174 Pages	Molyneaux	2009	200.00
9788184047370	The Art of Concurrency, 321 Pages	Breshears	2009	375.00
9788184048209	The Art of Community, 412, Page	Bacon	2009	425.00
9788184046953	The Art of Lean Software Development, 158 Pages	Hibbs	2009	200.00
9788184047516	The Myths of Security, 280 Pages	Viega	2009	325.00
9788184048711	The New Community Rules, 384 Pages	Weinberg	2009	400.00
9788184049053	**The New How: Creating Business Solutions Through Collaborative Strategy**	**Nilofer**	**2010**	**400.00**
9788184047271	Twitter API: Up and Running, 429 Pages	Makice	2009	450.00
9788184041590	Ubuntu Hacks, 462 Pages	Oxer	2006	350.00
9788184040029	UML 2.0 in a Nutshell, 246 Pages	Pilone	2005	200.00
9788184042993	UML 2.0 Pocket Reference, 150 Pages	Pilone	2006	125.00
9788184040760	Understanding Linux Network Internals, 1,074 Pages	Benvenuti	2005	600.00
9788184043198	Understanding MySQL Internals, 208 Pages	Pachey	2007	300.00
9788184040838	Understanding the Linux Kernel (Cover Version 2.6), 3/ed, 954 Pgs	Bovet	2005	550.00
9788184041606	Unicode Explained, 692 Pages	Korpela	2006	525.00
8184046436434	Universal Design for Web Applications: Web Applications That Reach Everyone, 214 Pages	Chisholm	2008	300.00
88173666278	Unit Test Frameworks **(B/CD)**, 222 Pages	Hamill	2004	225.00

ISBN	Title	Author	Year	Price
9788184040609	Unix in a Nutshell, 4/ed, 992 Pages	Robbins	2005	450.00
9788173665653	Unix Power Tools, 3/ed, 1,162 Pages	Powers	2002	750.00
9788173666209	Upgrading to PHP 5 (Covers MySQL 4.1), 358 Pages	Trachtenberg	2004	350.00
9788173660948	Using & Managing PPP, 464 Pages	Sun	1999	240.00
9788184046649	Using Drupal, 504 Pages	Byron	2009	525.00
9788184047363	Using Google App Engine, 282 Pages	Severance	2009	350.00
9788184049008	**Using Joomla, 428 Pages**	**Severdia**	**2010**	**425.00**
9788184043037	Using Samba, 3/ed, 464 Pages	Carter	2007	450.00
9788173665943	VB .NET Language Pocket Reference, 160 Pages	Roman	2002	125.00
9788173666889	VBScript in a Nutshell: A Desktop Quick Reference, 2/e, 528 Pages	Lomax	2003	400.00
9788184047325	Version Control with Git, 348 Pages	Loeliger	2009	400.00
9788184047288	Version Control with Subversion 2/ed, 446 Pages	Pilato	2009	475.00
9788173662621	vi Editor Pocket Reference, 76 Pages	Robbins	1999	60.00
9788173660962	Visual Basic Controls in a Nutshell, 512 Pages	Dictor	1999	310.00
9788184048681	VMware Cookbook, 316 Pages	Troy	2009	350.00
9788184040692	VOIP Hacks: Tips & Tools for Internet Telephony, 326 Pages	Wallingford	2006	325.00
9788184045062	Web 2.0: A Strategy Guide: Business thinking and strategies behind successful Web 2.0 implementations, 302 Pages	Shuen	2008	350.00
9788184047356	Web 2.0 Architectures: What entrepreneurs and information architects need to know, 292 Pages	Nickull	2009	325.00
9788173669057	Web Database Application with PHP & MySQL (Covers PEAR, PHP 5 & MySQL 4.1), 2/ed, 828 Pages	Willaims	2004	600.00
9788184040982	Web Design in a Nutshell: A Desktop Quick Reference, 3/ed, 826 Pages	Niederst	2006	450.00
9788184049046	Web Mapping Illustrated, 388 Pages	Mitchell	2005	475.00
9788173663949	Web Security, Privacy & Commerce, 2/ed, 768 Pages	Garfinkel	2001	500.00
9788173663390	Web Services Essentials, 320 Pages	Cerami	2002	300.00
9788173667626	Web Site Cookbook, 262 Pages	Addison	2006	300.00
9788184045628	Website Optimization, 408 Pages	King	2008	450.00
9788173663093	WebLogic 8.1: The Definitive Guide, 860 Pages	Mountjoy	2004	650.00
9788173661303	The Whole Internet: The Next Generation, 576 Pages	Conner/Krol	1999	425.00
9788173661365	Win32 API Programming with Visual Basic **(B/CD)**, 534 Pages	Roman	1999	400.00
9789350230299	**Windows 7 Annoyances, 740 Pages**	**Karp**	**2010**	**650.00**
9788184048339	Windows 7: Up and Running, 220 Pages	Wei-Meng Lee	2009	275.00
9788184048537	Windows 7: The Definitive Guide, 1008 Pages	Stanek	2009	650.00
9788184049916	**Windows 7: The Missing Manual, 924 Pages**	**Pogue**	**2010**	**450.00**
9789350230930	**Windows PowerShell Cookbook 2/ed, 904 Pages**	**Holmes**	**2010**	**600.00**
9788184044034	Windows PowerShell Cookbook: for Windows, Exchange 2007, and MOM V3, 600 Pages	Holmes	2007	500.00
9788184045239	Windows PowerShell Pocket Reference, 182 Pages	Holmes	2008	150.00
9788184045000	Windows Server 2008: The Definitive Guide, 508 Pages	Hassell	2008	475.00
9788173668838	Windows Server Hacks: 100 Industrial-Strength Tips & Tools , 328 Pages	Tulloch	2004	325.00
9788184042979	Windows Vista For Starters: The Missing Manual, 493 Pages	Pogue	2007	325.00
9788173669668	Windows XP Cookbook, 690 Pages	Allen	2005	500.00

ISBN	Title	Author	Year	Price
9788173667459	Windows XP Hacks: 100 Industrial-Strength Tips & Tools, 294 Pages	Gralla	2003	350.00
9788173666919	Windows XP Pocket Reference, 196 Pages	Karp	2002	125.00
9788184042931	Word 2007 For Starters: The Missing Manual, 372 Pages	Grover	2007	350.00
9788173666926	Word Pocket Guide, 160 Pages	Glenn	2003	125.00
9788173665356	Writing Excel Macros with VBA, 2/ed, 580 Pages	Roman	2002	500.00
9788184044430	X Power Tools, 286 Pages	Tyler	2008	325.00
9788173666155	XML Hacks: 100 Industrial-Strength Tips & Tools, 490 Pages	Fitzgerald	2004	425.00
9788173668456	XML in a Nutshell (Covers XML 1.1 & XInclude), 3/ed, 724 Pgs	Harold	2005	500.00
9788184042641	XML Pocket Reference, 3/ed, 198 Pages	Laurent	2005	125.00
9788184047295	XMPP: The Definitive Guide, 324 Pages	Saint	2009	375.00
9788184043181	XQuery, 528 Pages	Walmsley	2007	500.00
9788173664908	XSLT 1.0 Pocket Reference, 188 Pages	Lenz	2005	150.00
9788184040784	XSLT Cookbook (Cover XSLT 1.0 & 2.0, 2/ed, 786 Pages	Mangano	2005	500.00

US EDITION AVAILABLE AT SPECIAL PRICE:

ISBN	Title	Author	Year	Price
9780596102364	Adobe Creative Suite 2 Workflow, 634 Pages	Alspach	2005	1,625.00
9780596006006	Adobe Encore DVD: In the Studio, 336 Pages	Dixon	2004	1,225.00
9780596529765	Adobe InDesign CS3 One-On-One **(Book / DVD)**, 560 Pages	McClelland	2007	$ 44.00
9780596529758	Adobe Photoshop CS3 One-On-One **(Book / DVD)**, 544 Pages	McClelland	2007	$ 40.00
9780596101367	Building Extreme PCs, 192 Pages	Hardwidge	2006	1,200.00
9780596001087	The Cathedral & The Bazaar, 256 Pages	Raymond	2001	525.00
9780596008499	Commercial Photoshop Retouching: In The Studio, 410 Pages	Honiball	2005	1,425.00
9780596008581	Creating Photomontages with Photoshop: A Designer's Notebook, 96 Pages	Collandre	2005	800.00
9780596100476	The Creative Digital Darkroom, 429 Pages	Eismann	2008	$ 40.00
9780596008031	Designing Interfaces, 352 Pages	Tidwell	2005	$ 49.95
9780596528102	Designing Web Navigation: Optimizing the User Experience, 456 Pgs	Kalbach	2007	$ 40.00
9780596526801	Devices of the Soul Batting for Our Selves in an Age of Machines, 302 Pages	Talbott	2007	$ 18.00
9780596005474	Digital Photography: Expert Techniques, 496 Pages	Milburn	2003	1,375.00
9780596006662	Digital Photography Hacks: 100 Industrial - Strength Tips & Tools, 336 Pages	Story	2004	800.00
9780596100155	Digital Photography Pocket Guide, 3/ed, 160 Pages	Story	2005	450.00
9780596008413	Digital Photography: The Missing Manual, 432 Pages	Grover	2006	1,200.00
9780596009465	Digital Video Hacks: Tips & Tools for Shooting, Editing & Sharing, 426 Pages	Paul	2005	800.00
9780596005238	Digital Video Pocket Guide, 474 Pages	Story	2003	500.00
9780596510572	Dynamic Learning Dreamweaver CS3 **(Book / DVD)**, 416 Pgs	Gerantabee	2007	$ 36.00
9780596510589	Dynamic Learning Flash CS3 **(Book / DVD)**, 456 Pages	Gerantabee	2007	$ 36.00
9780596510619	Dynamic Learning: Photoshop CS3 **(Book / DVD)**, 360 Pages	Smith	2007	$ 36.00
9780596102425	Fonts & Encodings, 1,037 Pages	Haralambous	2007	$ 48.00
9780596002879	Free As In Freedom: Richard Stallman's Crusade for Free Software, 243 Pages	Williams	2002	750.00
9780596006624	Hackers & Painters: Big Ideas From the Computer Age, 276 Pgs	Graham	2004	700.00
9780596526856	Illustrated Guide to Astronomical Wonders: From Novice to Master Observer (DIY Science), 519 Pages	Thompson	2007	$ 24.00

ISBN	Title	Author	Year	Price
9780596008598	Illustrations with Photoshop: A Designer's Notebook, 96 Pages	Rodarmor	2004	775.00
9780596100483	InDesign Production Cookbook, 224 Pages	Dabbs	2005	1,200.00
9780596007683	Just A Geek, 296 Pages	Wheaton	2004	700.00
9780596527877	Learning ActionScript 3.0: A Beginner's Guide, 382 Pages	Shupe	2008	$ 32.00
9780596517328	Learning Flex 3: Getting up to Speed with Rich Internet Applications (Adobe Developer Library), 304 Pages	Cole	2008	$ 32.00
9780596527525	Learning Web Design: A Beginner's Guide to (X)HTML, StyleSheets, and Web Graphics, 3/ed, 479 Pages	Robbins	2007	$ 36.00
9780596517717	Making Things Happen: Mastering Project Management (Theory in Practice), 408 Pages	Berkun	2008	$ 32.00
9780596007034	Mapping Hacks: Tips & Tools for Electronic Cartography, 574 Pgs	Erle	2005	900.00
9780596527051	Myths of Innovation, 196 Pages	Berkun	2007	$ 20.00
9780596008604	Photo Retouching with Photoshop: A Designer's Notebook, 96 Pgs	CLEC'H	2004	775.00
9780596100209	Photoshop Blending Modes Cookbook for Digital Photographers, 176 Pages	Beardsworth	2005	1,025.00
9780596515041	Photoshop CS3 Photo Effects Cookbook: 53 Easy-to-Follow Recipes for Digital Photographers, Designers, & Artists, 176 Pgs	Shelbourne	2007	$ 24.00
9780596008512	Photoshop CS2 Raw: Using Adobe Camera Raw, Bridge, and Photoshop to Get the Most Out of Your Digital Camera, 206 Pgs	Aaland	2006	1,075.00
9780596510527	Photoshop CS3 Raw: Get the Most Out of the Raw Format with Adobe Photoshop, Camera Raw, and Bridge, 272 Pages	Aaland	2008	$ 28.00
9780596100216	Photoshop Filter Effects Encyclopedia, 176 Pages	Pring	2005	1,050.00
9780596100629	Photoshop Fine Art Effects Cookbook, 176 Pages	Beardsworth	2006	1,050.00
9780596100995	Photoshop Lightroom Adventure: Mastering Adobe's next-generation tool for digital photographers, 350 Pages	Aaland	2007	$ 32.00
9780596100223	Photoshop Photo Effects Cookbook, 176 Pages	Shelbourne	2005	1,025.00
9780596100308	Photoshop Retouching Cookbook for Digital Photographers, 176 Pages	Huggins	2005	1,025.00
9780596101138	Programming Windows Presentation Foundation, 430 Pages	Sells	2005	1,100.00
9780596007195	Revolution in the Valley, 324 Pages	Hertzfeld	2004	775.00
9780596523701	Stephen Johnson on Digital Photography, 320 Pages	Johnson	2006	1,500.00
9780596007331	We the Media: Grassroots Journalism by the People, for the People, 320 Pages	Gillmor	2004	775.00
9780596100834	Windows Seat, 152 Pages	Kost	2006	1,600.00

- Prices are subject to change without notice.
- All Prices are in Indian Rupees except where indicated in € (Euro Dollar) $ (US Dollar) and £ (Pound)
- **Titles Released after January 2010 are marked in Bold.**